HUMAN RIGHTS, JUSTICE, AND CONSTITUTIONAL EMPOWERMENT

'An impressively comprehensive treatment of the many ways in which human rights have shaped and been shaped by both government and civil society in the world's largest democracy. The authors do not shy away from critiquing the many shortcomings of over-inflated expectations about what 'human rights' on paper can actually achieve, as well as the limitations of civil and political rights along-side corruption and persistent poverty.'

ANNE-MARIE SLAUGHTER, *Princeton University, U.S.A.*

'…offers a broad array of perspectives on topics ranging from the traditional issues of constitutions and constitutionalism to globalization and human rights. The essays are a wonderful way to explore vital topics bearing on India's evolution and prospects.'

HENRY J. STEINER, *Harvard Law School, U.S.A.*

'This book makes a significant contribution towards understanding the consti-tutional foundations of human rights and justice in the Indian context. The collection underscores the challenges India faces in establishing a society based on the rule of law.'

SHASHI THAROOR, *Former Under-Secretary-General, United Nations*

'One of the many beauties of this text is that it connects top-notch senior scholars who are well-known both in India and abroad with some of the next generation's brightest minds on Indian law. This volume is a must-read for anyone inter-ested in human rights and the current status of rights-empowerment in India.'

JAYANTH K. KRISHNAN, *Indiana University, Maurer School of Law, U.S.A.*

'A worthy tribute to…Justice V.R. Krishna Iyer, this first-rate collection of essays focuses our attention on the Indian tradition of constitutional human rights protection, in which social justice, economic development, and women's empowerment have been front and center. The essays are rich, the contributors diverse—an intellectual and analytic tour de force.'

DAVID W. KENNEDY, *Harvard Law School, U.S.A.*

'This book is to be welcomed as a scholarly effort to bring India's story of human rights as outcomes of the justice system to the wider international audience.'

RAMESH THAKUR
Former Vice Rector, United Nations University

'This brilliant anthology...excels...in its chapters on human rights for victims of crime and communal riots. This is a must for every lawyer and student.'

IRVIN WALLER
Institute for the Prevention of Crime, University of Ottawa, Canada

'In this special book...leading scholars of Indian constitutional jurisprudence and human rights offer critical understanding of the challenges of implementing social justice in a global age. This volume is a must-read for students of comparative constitutionalism and human rights.'

MICHAEL C. DAVIS
The Chinese University of Hong Kong, Hong Kong, China

'A very impressive Indian contribution to the general discourse on the global level about human rights and their constitutional protection. It is at the same time a scholarly tribute to the outstanding achievements of Judge Krishna Iyer.'

PETER MALANCZUK
Formerly in City University of Hong Kong, Hong Kong, China

'This book is essential reading for everyone interested in international jurisprudence. It is especially well-written and is meritorious in its content and scholarly resources...issues of human rights, victim rights, and justice have never, in my experience, found greater inspiration or motivation in one volume.'

MARLENE A. YOUNG
President, International Organization for Victim Assistance (IOVA), U.S.A.

'...[a] well-conceived, well-written, and provocative book. For the reader, the journey provides insights not only into how one state handles the never-ending task of improving the lot of its people, but also into what lessons other states and the international community at large can learn.'

DAVID KINLEY
University of Sydney, Australia

'I cannot imagine a more significant way to honour Justice V.R. Krishna Iyer than to ask these esteemed Indian scholars, activists, and leaders to write about the very subject that personifies his life and his persona the most: human rights.'

JOHN P. J. DUSSICH
Tokiwa University, Japan, and President, World Society of Victimology (WSV)

HUMAN RIGHTS, JUSTICE, AND CONSTITUTIONAL EMPOWERMENT

Second Edition

Edited by

C. Raj Kumar
K. Chockalingam

OXFORD
UNIVERSITY PRESS

OXFORD
UNIVERSITY PRESS

YMCA Library Building, Jai Singh Road, New Delhi 110 001

Oxford University Press is a department of the University of Oxford.
It furthers the University's objective of excellence in research,
scholarship, and education by publishing worldwide in

Oxford New York

Auckland Cape Town Dar es Salaam Hong Kong Karachi Kuala Lumpur
Madrid Melbourne Mexico City Nairobi New Delhi Shanghai Taipei Toronto

With offices in
Argentina Austria Brazil Chile Czech Republic France Greece Guatemala
Hungary Italy Japan Poland Portugal Singapore South Korea Switzerland
Thailand Turkey Ukraine Vietnam

Oxford is a registered trademark of Oxford University Press
in the UK and in certain other countries

Published in India by Oxford University Press, New Delhi

ISBN 13: 978-019-806886-0
ISBN 10: 019-806886-7

Typeset in Aldine401 BT 10/12
by Excellent Laser Typesetters, Pitampura, Delhi 110 034
Printed at Artxel, New Delhi 110 020
Published by Oxford University Press
YMCA Library Building, Jai Singh Road, New Delhi 110 001

This book is dedicated to

Justice V.R. Krishna Iyer

*for his tireless efforts and
contribution as a judge and jurist
to numerous struggles upholding
human rights and justice in India
and the world at large*

Contents

Prolegomenon*

V.R. KRISHNA IYER

Greetings to you gracious dignitaries, great jurists, and good friends,

I am overwhelmingly grateful to Professor C. Raj Kumar and Professor K. Chockalingam, both scholarly jurists and creative humanists who are dear to my heart, for the pains they have taken to produce this festschrift. Professor Raj Kumar is a brilliant juridical intellectual and Professor Chockalingam is an international pioneer of victimology. They deserve to be described as talented literary jurisprudents in the field of social sciences in its larger connotation. Together, they have assembled valuable articles from outstanding contributors to the world of progressive law, including Professor Yash Ghai, Professor Granville Austin, Mr Soli Sorabjee, Professor N.R. Madhava Menon, Professor M.P. Singh, Professor B.B. Pande, Mr N. Ravi, Professor Parmanand Singh, and many other distinguished scholars and practitioners. The book has a dedication to me, although I, in a stage of dotage and anecdotage, hardly deserve this tribute at 92. Law has national and international dimensions; this book, which contains articles of eminent jurists, is indeed a lush treasure and rare pleasure to a geriatric like me. Humanist jurisprudence is never jejune and ever challenging, because our vicissitudinous world is in radical transformation and regressive negation—a curious contradiction! Our great principles and sublime values are cultural casualties under 'Westoxicated' syndrome.

* Speech delivered at the book release function of Human Rights, Justice, and Constitutional Empowerment, C. Raj Kumar and K. Chockalingam (eds), Oxford University Press, 2007, to be held on 7 March 2007 at the India International Centre Annexe, New Delhi, India. The book was released by Justice K.G. Balakrishnan, Chief Justice of India and first copy of the book was received by Mr H.R. Bharadwaj, Union Minister for Law and Justice, Government of India.

Great judges, through their imaginative ideas, meliorative responses, and innovative judgments, make legal learning developmentally dynamic, and holistically creative. The process of law triggers order and harmony in society. The finer artists of the educative pages in this erudite volume are remarkable thinkers who have made these charming essays a lovely bouquet of luminous legal literature. I am too humble to be the object of dedication of such a profound work. But Professor Chockalingam and Professor Raj Kumar have affection and admiration for me and that gracious sentiment accounts for this grand collection. Oxford University Press, one of the leading publishers of the English-speaking world, is responsible for the publication of this beautiful book. I am beholden to the authors and editors and express my appreciation of this bunch of excellent writings inscribed as a reverential token to me, who has retired long ago from active life as a judge and is unable to travel to Delhi where judicial celebrities, juristic greats, and old personal comrades—all of you—have assembled for the formal, ceremonial release. Law is a social science and operates as an engineering adventure geared to people's material well-being. Justice confronts new social, economic, political, and cultural problems and law weaves 'fresh woods and pastures new' to restore equity and justice. The rule of law runs close to the rule of life. And when life undergoes metamorphosis under the impact of serendipitous technology with its startling wonders, novel discoveries reshaping our way of life and methods of work, wealth and happiness also suffer mutation. Technology has no heart. The rich harvest huge profits while the weak and poor diminish or perish. Two worlds emerge. 'The Gandhian concept of development rejected the idea that it should aim primarily at the creation of material wealth or the satisfaction of insatiable, endlessly multiplied needs. In so far as we have made the modern materialistic craze our goal', Mahatma Gandhi wrote, 'so far are we going downhill in the path of progress.'[1]

The New World Order demands fruitful changes because science and technology force inventions and innovations never conceived of before. Greed vulgarizes the appetite of tycoons and we are going downhill in morality and acquisition gluttony. Cosmos and chaos clash and produce disaster and imperialist rivalries compete, victimizing the masses, unless everything from nuclear fission to catastrophic explosion comes under United Nations' (UN's) absolute humanist regulation.

[1] Brown, Judith M., *The Essential Writings by Mahatama Gandhi*, (2008), New York: Oxford University Press, p. 86.

Inevitably, the compulsions of survival drive to battle for positive forensic juridical thinking, people oriented, not balvic-empty, new paradigm discover new parameters, principles, methodologies, and theories to obviate terrorisms and carnages, and to revolutionize a just system: the World Order. International law, because big powers become a law unto themselves, is now a vanishing point of humanist jurisprudence. Today, the new axis powers hardly listen to the United Nations or the Great Charter or their functional operations. And yet, the WHO, UNESCO, UNICEF, and other global instrumentalities are unique in their universal source and wise use of nature's resource. It is a pity President George W. Bush ignores the UN and attacks any country by playing the role of global police, keeping other nations in timid silence. Taciturnity is traumatic humiliation and toxic delinquency when international crime is committed in the name of self-righteous invasion in violation of world law by aggressive big powers. The UN and other national instruments must insist on security, sovereignty, and tranquility which alone can facilitate a better deal for assuring a civilized destiny for every member of the comity of nations. Mankind has deep divinity and integrity so necessary for its superlative future and astral ascent. Bharat is Gandhian, halcyonian, and never barbaric. When any power defiles international law, breaches panchsheel among nations and intimidates the sovereignty of other peaceful countries, India must stand for peace and haven. Silence is guilt where there is a duty to speak. (Who first used the atom bomb on Hiroshima and still corners nuclear bomb monopoly?) We are no longer free nor a leader of NAM if any megalomanic superpower terrorizes and occupies, with all its invincible armoury, any non-belligerent country with weak armoury. Americans are a great people and a world wonder with the marvel of the Declaration of Independence. That noble nation, with Abraham Lincoln, Walter Emerson, and Thoreau commands my homage. Our friendly relations embrace the US, Russia, China, Asia, and Europe. The universe is divine and unitary. That is our Vedic vision!

Superannuation and senility enfeeble my physique and faculties; but defying both, I venture on a respectful salutation to this venerable gathering. More than twenty-five years ago, I left the Bench of the highest court, but did involve myself in public affairs from a pro-bono perspective, with no bias or boast, no ideological yen nor political hubris. My only objective passion has been to defend human rights, to promote social justice, and to make Indian humanity supportive of a world order where the weak have a voice and the foreign corporate giants do not browbeat or bully the common people so as to freeboot the wealth of the world. Today the proprietariat seeks to liquidate the proletariat by show of force or coercive moves. The dominant agenda of the US mega-MNCs and the ruling classes is global colonization. My burning conviction and compassionate duty is to lend my feeble voice to make the masses matter. An old small man like me can achieve little to resist massive injustice when political leaders and cadres in power-hungry parties frustrate our historic tryst with socio-economic justice.

Age notwithstanding, my young aspirations are alive but I am in deep distress to see a sinister, treacherous, globomanic, unipolar power dominating even our foreign policy, although we have statesmen like Dr Manmohan Singh, historic predecessors like Nehru and cosmic heritage like Gandhi. Why are we, with our universal cultural glory, still vastly prostrate, para-colonial, and victims of a dependencia syndrome? Billions remain backward, overawed and exploited by the barbarity of the exotic billionaire proprietariat, who hold the world as their own. We have 'miles to go' and 'promises to keep' if the new century is to redeem our justice, dignity, and the freedom of the downtrodden. These are poignant thoughts, pensive, negative cerebrations but even education, hospitals, and shelter are alien to a majority. This is a malignant reality and painful veracity. India is great and I am proud to be an Indian. Swaraj is every Indian's birthright. 'I am a human; I count nothing pertaining to humans alien to me!'[2]

Once again I thank Professor Chockalingam and Professor Raj Kumar and all those great writers and thinkers who have made the festschrift a remarkable event. True, I am 92 but I have promises to keep.

I know that the day will come when my sight of this earth shall be lost, and life will take its leave in silence, drawing the last curtain over my eyes.

Yet stars will watch at night, and morning rise as before, and hours heave like sea waves casting up pleasures and pains.

Rabindranath Tagore,
Gitanjali, no. 92

---

[2] These lines have been taken from the latin play *Heavton Timorvmenos* by the latin playwright P. Terenti Afri better known as Terrence. Latin original available at http://www.thelatinlibrary.com/ter.heauton.html (last accessed on 28 May 2010).

My last words with vast demands on my frail frame remind me:

The song that I came to sing remains unsung to this day.
I have spent my days in stringing and in unstringing my instrument.
The time has not come true, the world have not been rightly set; only there is the agony of
wishing in my heart.

Rabindranath Tagore,
Gitanjali, no. 13

JUSTICE V.R. KRISHNA IYER
Former Judge, Supreme Court of India

Foreword

YASH P. GHAI

There is no doubt how history will judge Justice V.R. Krishna Iyer, to whom this volume is dedicated. His place among the most progressive and innovative judges of the Indian Supreme Court is secure. With a handful of his colleagues, Krishna Iyer transformed the Court into a great instrument of justice, the conscience of the nation. Together they breathed new life into the Constitution, whose capacity to protect rights and promote liberty was increasingly being questioned, especially, but not only, due to the excesses of Indira Gandhi's emergency regime and the inability of the courts to resist the arbitrary exercise of state power. In the years following the restoration of democracy, the court produced a powerful jurisprudence drawing upon the springs of the constitution, using fundamental rights and directive principles as the inspiration—true to the spirit of its founders. Krishna Iyer was driven by a clear vision of human dignity, and a deep understanding of the imperatives and principles of social justice. He had the courage and skills to turn these into a jurisprudence which has been widely admired and borrowed.

The central concern of the authors of this book, as a tribute to Krishna Iyer, is to explore the way in which, through the agency of the Supreme Court, human rights and directive principles of the Constitution have defined and influenced approaches to social justice, governance, and criminal justice. Apart from the US, India was the first major common law jurisdiction to provide a central place for human rights in its constitutional system. In the early years of independence, the Supreme Court appeared not to appreciate the centrality of human rights or directive principles. But in the golden period of the court, when Justices Bhagwati and Iyer sat on its bench, the manifold implications of human rights and directive principles, in numerous areas of life, were amply explicated. It is no exaggeration to say that the Supreme Court of India opened up the path and developed the techniques under which human rights have become, throughout the world, the most critical part of a constitution. Through its decisions, the reach of human rights has expanded, been woven into the fabric of everyday life, and established the framework for legislation and decision making within the institutions of the state.

Human rights play a complex role in Indian society: values and practice of human rights run counter to centuries-old structures of hierarchy and social and economic oppression, and interrogate and challenge the institutions that hinder India's journey out of poverty. They provide the framework for difficult balancing between claims of equality and justice; they mediate in the interactions between ethnic and religious communities, and between individuals and groups. They promote Indian identity through an expansive definition of rights and duties of citizenship. The Supreme Court has been alert to these dimensions, and has emphasized—and deployed—the concept of human rights and its values and balances in coping with the extraordinarily complex society that is India. Through its innovations facilitating access to the court, the court made human rights a weapon of the oppressed. It opened a public, and worldwide, dialogue on rights that would scarcely have been possible without its own discourse on rights and the social and economic condition of India.

The Supreme Court's explorations of the dialectics between human rights and poverty—the pervasive reality of the Indian condition—have been central in its interpretations of rights. One of the most remarkable achievements of the court was to give juridical effect to directive principles. The constitution's designation of the directive principles (embodying prescriptions of policy to redress numerous unfortunate consequences of India's legacy) as 'non-justiciable' was at first misinterpreted as establishing their norms to be of a lower order than civil and property rights, and as disabling the courts from engaging with them. The reformative agenda of the constitution was thus stifled. After the Emergency, the Supreme Court, in a flurry of extraordinary decisions (analysed in several contributions in the book), placed directive principles at the apex of constitutional norms. The court did this primarily by reading them into the definition and scope of the judicially enforceable fundamental rights, and thus controlling or expanding these rights by reference to directive principles. In this way, it harmonized fundamental rights with directive principles, moving away from the earlier position which saw conflicts between them. The right to life, for example, became the source of many entitlements beyond mere physical existence. This required very creative approaches and norms of interpretation (and the fact that these have become standard in many jurisdictions attests to the success of the endeavours of the Supreme Court). Indeed, the very concepts of 'human development' and 'rights-based development' owe a great deal to this jurisprudence.

Two principal features of this Indian approach are worth noting, as they have made great contributions to the debate on the nature of rights. First, by harmonizing fundamental (civil and political) rights with directive principles (based on economic and social objectives), the Supreme Court has clarified that the relationship between civil and economic rights is one of interdependence, and established the holistic and integrated nature of all human rights. In western ideology, economic and social entitlements are either denied the status of 'human rights', or regarded as inferior to civil and political rights. Further, they are regarded as 'aspirations', a matter of policy not susceptible to clear definitions or benchmarks that render them fit for judicial enforcement. Second, the Court has clarified the juristic nature of economic and social rights, and shown how courts may directly enforce such rights or assist in their enforcement. The Indian approach has influenced international thinking on the nature and feasibility of economic and social rights and on the necessity to consider different kinds of entitlements as part of an integrated regime of human rights. There is now a greater understanding of the impact of human rights (or of their denial) on poverty and welfare as well as of the impossibility of the enjoyment of rights or human dignity amidst poverty. There is also now a greater willingness to constitutionalize economic and social rights.

These are great achievements of which the Supreme Court (and one of its principal architects, Krishna Iyer) can rightly be proud. But how well the court has handled cases arising out of directive principles regarding, for example, health, education, and environment, remains controversial. It has not always been consistent in its approach. Sometimes it has, quite sensibly, restricted itself to broad directions (and has been respectful of both the constitutional division of powers and parliament's primary responsibility for policy, and the complexity of decision making in these areas). At other times it has issued detailed instructions. Occasionally, on the basis that the other branches of the state have failed in their responsibilities, it has justified the scope and mode of its interventions that amount to issuing legislative and administrative rules to be observed by the government and other public authorities. One can see perils in this approach: weakening the will of parliament or the government as well as the system of accountability, jeopardizing the court's relationship with these branches of the state, making decisions without adequate information and knowledge, and without a right to be heard for interested parties (some of which may have to bear the financial, administrative and even the political burdens of its decisions), threatening the integrity of the budgetary process, and ultimately, rendering its decisions futile for want of enforcement. This last point is a matter of serious concern, and can cause a spiral effect when the very knowledge that its decision may not be enforced, leads to a degree of recklessness in fashioning the decision.

It has to be acknowledged, however, that the constitution does not provide guidelines for the exercise of the court's jurisdiction in economic and social rights (and there have been massive failures on the part both of the executive and the legislature in meeting their constitutional responsibilities). The International Covenant on Economic, Social, and Cultural Rights (which, of course, came into being well after the Indian directive principles) and the comments of the committee charged with the supervision of its implementation, provide a more structured (if not necessarily more principled) approach. The South African Constitution, inspired in some ways by the Indian constitution, seeks to provide a restrictive framework for adjudication by the courts, and its constitutional court has tried to balance more carefully than the Indian Supreme Court its own powers with that of the other branches of the state (but has still run into difficulties of enforcement). There are some intimations that the Supreme Court may be reining itself in a bit more of late, abandoning or moderating its earlier adventurous stance. Whether this is the result of introspection on the judicial role or genuflection to economic globalization is unclear.

What is clear is that the Supreme Court has placed human rights at the centre of the Indian polity and has tried to turn them into a tool of advocacy and instrument of social justice, of fairness between communities as well as individuals, of protection of the guarantees of the criminal justice process, and above all, of strengthening the identity of the Indian state and society. Although rhetoric may not always match reality, the Supreme Court has inculcated in India a culture of human rights and pluralism, greatly strengthening democracy and secular values.

Most of these themes are explored in this book by leading Indian scholars and practitioners, with celebration of the achievements, wisdom, scholarship, and courage—but not blind reverence—of Krishna Iyer. The authors would not be respectful of Krishna Iyer if they were afraid to point to their assessment of his occasional weaknesses or misjudgments. Nor would Krishna Iyer, a man of great integrity as well as humility, want it any other way. It was my privilege some years ago to chair a committee charged with the responsibility of drafting an Asian Charter of Human Rights under the auspices of the Asian Human Rights Commission; both Praful Bhagwati and Krishna Iyer being members. It was hard to imagine any other judges and statesmen of their stature and distinction working so diligently, engaging with lesser mortals like us without a hint of condescension or a trace of pomposity, in less than luxurious conditions. The warmth of their personalities, their deep commitment to human rights and justice, and their constant concern that the values of rights should not be obscured by legalism of the drafting style, were an inspiration to us all.

The editors and authors of this volume are to be congratulated for their keen analyses of the historiography and jurisprudence of the supreme court and in particular, the judicial approach of Krishna Iyer, insights into the judicial process, the politics of rights, and the impact of rights on institutions, processes, and contemporary social, economic, and political developments. For those not familiar with the Indian constitution or jurisprudence, this book is a splendid introduction to an exciting experiment in, and development of, the judicial function (and other legal developments). For the initiated, there is much that will stimulate, provoke, and call for reassessment. If there is one criticism, it is the lack of sufficient comparative perspectives, which would have brought out more clearly the distinctiveness of the mission and approach of the Indian Supreme Court and its influence internationally. Nevertheless, the authors should be thanked for placing so clearly in print the achievements of a great and profound jurist, and the court that he adorned. Unfortunately, we are still the victims of western and white hegemony and these achievements do not receive the full international recognition that they deserve, unlike even the lesser achievements of white jurists. It is my earnest hope that this book will in some measure redress the imbalance.

Acknowledgements

We would like to thank Justice V.R. Krishna Iyer for his encouragement and support in bringing out this book, which has been prepared in recognition of his significant contribution to the world of jurisprudence. One of the editors of this book has had an opportunity to interact with Justice Iyer for more than ten years and the other for more than thirty years. It has been a privilege for both of us to know Justice Iyer all these years, as his contribution to promote human rights and social justice both within and outside the judiciary is unparalleled. This work has brought together scholars and practitioners to write about various issues relating to human rights, constitutionalism, and justice in the context of India and from comparative and international perspectives.

We thank Yash P. Ghai, former Chair Professor in Public Law at the Faculty of Law, the University of Hong Kong, and former Chairperson of the Kenya Constitution Review Commission for his erudite Foreword for the book. We record our appreciation to Soli J. Sorabjee, former Attorney General of India for his well-written introductory note on the many contributions of Justice Iyer. We thank Professor Granville Austin for his excellent introduction to some of the key issues relating to many chapters in the book. All the contributors to the book deserve our thanks and appreciation for having raised the quality of the work in every possible manner.

We place on record our thanks for the support offered by Jindal Global Law School, O.P. Jindal Global University and the School of Law, City University of Hong Kong, and the Tokiwa International Victimology Institute (TIVI), Tokiwa University in preparation of this work. Such encouragement is much appreciated as this is the best form of support one can get from an academic institution.

Our thanks are due to the research assistants, Sharron Fast, Elliot Fung, Amit Bindal, and Vincent Sze, for their research and assistance in proofreading of this book.

Last, but not least, the anonymous reviewers of Oxford University Press deserve our thanks for their useful comments and suggestions. The staff editors of OUP and in particular, the Commissioning Editor, Law deserve deep appreciation for their help and assistance in preparing this work.

We have immense pleasure in thanking our family members, especially Vijayalakshmi Chockalingam, Pratibha Jain, C. Ravi Kumar, Abhimanyu J. Kumar, and Avantika J. Kumar for their continuous moral support and encouragement in the preparation of this work.

C. RAJ KUMAR
K. CHOCKALINGAM

Justice V.R. Krishna Iyer

A Man for All Seasons

SOLI J. SORABJEE

Infallibility is not vouchsafed to ordinary mortals. Fallible human beings do at times make errors of judgment. But none can surpass the monumental error I made in opposing Krishna Iyer's appointment as a judge of the supreme court in a letter jointly signed by eight other leading lawyers of the Bombay High Court and published in the *Indian Express* on 2 July 1973. The occasion for this impetuous action was the apprehension that in the wake of the pernicious doctrine of a committed judiciary propagated at that time, the appointment to the supreme court of a self-confessed political animal who had exhibited feathers of deep crimson, would be a disaster.

Soon after the publication of the letter, I had occasion to appear before Krishna Iyer in the supreme court. I was a bit anxious about his reaction to my appearance. The worries were unfounded. There were no stern looks, no sarcastic remarks. Like the 'true gentleman' portrayed by Cardinal Newman, 'he had too much good sense to be affronted by insults and was too well employed to remember injuries'. I publicly acknowledged my mistake at the time of his retirement by an article in the *Statesman* published in January 1981.

It was after my appointment as a law officer in 1977, that I came to know Krishna Iyer closely and developed a rapport or rather kinship with him. I have vivid memories of the arguments in *Mohinder Gill*.[1] The case involved the extent of the powers of the Chief Election Commissioner and whether natural justice required him to give a prior

---

[1] *Mohinder Singh Gill* v. *Chief Election Commr* (1978) 1 SCC 405: AIR 1978 SC 851.

hearing before cancelling the whole poll of 13 Ferozepur constituency. Krishna Iyer vastly expanded the frontiers of natural justice and evolved the doctrine of post-decisional hearing, a salutary development in public law. However, he characteristically warned that natural justice 'is not a bull in a china shop, nor a bee in one's bonnet. Its essence is good conscience in a given situation; nothing more—but nothing less.'

Appearance in the case of *Maneka Gandhi*,[2] the second passport case, was an exhilarating experience. The issue was whether the right to travel abroad and obtaining a passport for that purpose was implicit in the ambit of 'personal liberty' guaranteed by Article 21 of the constitution. Krishna Iyer's conclusion in his concurring judgment is brilliant. '... the water-shed between a police state and a people's *raj* is located partly through its passport policy... the policing of a people's right of exit or entry is fraught with peril to liberty unless policy is precise, operationally respectful of recognised values and harassment proof.

In the cases of *Sunil Batra*[3] and *Charles Sobhraj*,[4] his concern for the rights of prisoners was overwhelming. He outlawed the degrading punishment of solitary confinement. He deprecated the practice of placing iron bars or fetters on prisoners when transporting them from jails to courts unless it was imperative for security reasons which had to be recorded in writing.

Thanks to Krishna Iyer's judgments, 'jail birds' will no longer have to rot under degrading and inhuman conditions. The horrors of solitary confinement have been banished. No more will the jailer and his minions be the monarchs of all they survey, because prisoners now have rights and remedies to combat prison arbitrariness and assert their human dignity. Krishna Iyer's portrait should find a prominent place in every penal institution as the benefactor of numerous prison inmates. My appearance in these cases was a unique experience. It was a joint endeavour or perhaps a conspiracy between the bench and the bar to protect the fundamental rights of prisoners.

Krishna Iyer's opposition to capital punishment, which he regards as official murder springs, essentially from his deep reverence for the dignity and worth of every individual, however downtrodden and despised. He has not minced words to express his abhorrence of society snuffing out the life of one of its members on the ground of retributive justice.

[2] *Maneka Gandhi v. UOI* (1978) 1 SCC 248: AIR 1978 SC 597.
[3] *Sunil Batra v. Delhi Admn.* (1978) 4 SCC 494: AIR 1978 SC 1675.
[4] *Charles Shobraj v. Supdt., Central Jail* (1978) 4 SCC 104: AIR 1978 SC 1514.

His deep attachment to personal liberty revolts at the prospect of persons being detained on mere suspicion without a trial. Preventive detention is an anathema to him. But he did not experience great difficulty in upholding detention of saboteurs and sophisticated smugglers who played havoc with public safety and the economy of our country.

And that is only one instance of the paradox of Krishna Iyer. What could be more paradoxical than Krishna Iyer, a Marxist steeped in dialectical materialism and its dogmas later becoming an ardent believer in life after death? Listen to his judicial plea for simplicity of language in legislative drafting. 'Incomprehensible law annoys the administration and estranges the citizen...the command of the law can claim the allegiance of the law only by simplicity in legislation.' Again, the paradoxical Krishna Iyer at times overlooked the need for simplicity also in judicial pronouncements, which must be intelligible and comprehensible to all courts, authorities, and persons.

It is impossible to recount Krishna Iyer's judgments in a single article. One of his significant judgments is the famous case, In *Re: S. Mulgaokar*,[5] which raised the issue of the use of contempt power against the press for highly critical and derogatory articles about the judiciary. Krishna Iyer deprecated judge-baiting. He warned that the court shall not 'hesitate but shall do stern justice to such "professional" contemners'. Soon thereafter he paradoxically observes, 'Even so, to be gentle is to be just and the quality of mercy is not strained. So, it is that a benign neglect, not judicial genuflexion, is often the prescription'.

To my mind, his greatest contribution to our constitutional jurisprudence is his landmark judgment in *Shamsher Singh*,[6] which was delivered under trying domestic circumstances on account of his wife's illness. Krishna Iyer recognizes that 'the president, like the king, has not merely been constitutionally romanticized but actually vested with a pervasive and persuasive role' but 'he is not a rival center of power in any sense'. Then in stentorian tones he declares the law to be that, 'the president and governor shall exercise their formal constitutional powers only upon and in accordance with, the advice of their ministers, save in a few well-known exceptional situations like (a) the choice of prime minister (chief minister), restricted though this choice is by the paramount consideration that he should command a majority in the House; (b) the dismissal of a government which has lost its majority in the house

---

[5] AIR 1978 SC 727.
[6] *Shamsher Singh* v. *State of Punjab* (1974) 2 SCC 831: AIR 1974 SC 2192.

but refuses to quit office; (c) the dissolution of the house where an appeal to the country is necessitous.'

His judgment in the case of *C.B. Muthamma*[7] dealt a salutary blow to gender discrimination in the Indian Foreign Service Rules. One of the rules required that 'at any time after marriage, a woman member of the service may be required to resign from service, if the government is satisfied that her family and domestic commitments are likely to come in the way of the due and efficient discharge of her duties as a member of the service'. According to Krishna Iyer, 'Discrimination against women, in traumatic transparency, is found in this rule.... This misogynous posture is a hangover of the masculine culture of manacling the weaker sex forgetting how our struggle for national freedom was also a battle against woman's thralldom. Freedom is indivisible, so is justice'. Later on in the judgment, he made it clear that, 'We do not mean to universalize or dogmatize that men and women are equal in all occupations and all situations and do not exclude the need to pragmatise where the require-ments of particular employment, the sensitivities of sex or the peculiarities of societal sectors or the handicaps of either sex may compel selectivity. But save, where the differentiation is demonstrable, the rule of equality must govern'.

Nothing rankled Krishna Iyer more than confronting injustice. To him, law was the instrument to secure social justice. And if in this noble quest he crossed rigid legalistic boundaries, so be it. He is in the good company of Chief Justice Earl Warren of the US supreme court and Lord Denning and other bold judicial souls whose judicial unorthodoxy has ultimately led to the advancement of social justice and promotion of fundamental freedoms.

For a true assessment of Krishna Iyer, do not turn to learned authors on constitutional law and carping critics who indulge in making dispar-aging remarks about the language of his judgments and totally miss their substance. Do not turn also to bumptious bureaucrats and insolent ad-ministrators who are understandably annoyed by his insistence on the observance of the principles of fairplay in all areas of decision-making. Nor seek the opinion of pseudo-intellectual capitalists puffing their pipes in five-star hotels who are angered by his judicial pronouncement advancing the rights of labour. Seek the answer from 'the lowly and the lost'. For instance, from Jolly George and the tribe of debtors who have been spared the degradation of imprisonment for their genuine inability

---

[7] *C.B. Muthamma, IFS v. Union of India and Others* (1979) 4 SCC 260.

to satisfy money decrees passed against them because, according to Krishna Iyer's judgment, 'to cast a person in prison because of his poverty and consequent inability to meet his contractual liability is appalling, because to be poor in this land of poverty is no crime'.

There are judges who are more erudite than Krishna Iyer, judges who have an excellent memory for supreme court and House of Lords citations, judges who can master the record of a case in a few minutes. But the one essential quality which distinguishes him from his judicial brethren and puts him in a class of his own is compassion. He took human suffering seriously and dispensed justice with compassion, which he possessed in abundance.

After retirement from the bench, his zest for service to his fellow beings has intensified. You will find him on a platform in different parts of India and abroad, raising his voice fearlessly for the exploited segments of humanity. He tirelessly fills the unforgiving minute with sixty seconds' worth of distance run, though in the process, he exhausts himself.

His mission in life can be summed up in the moving poem by Emily Dickinson:

> If I can stop one heart from breaking
> I shall not live in vain.
> If I can ease one life the aching or cool one pain
> Or help one fainting robin unto its nest again
> I shall not live in vain.

Krishna Iyer is past ninety years at present. These ninety years have not been spent in hankering after fame and fortune, but in the service of humanity; not with pomp and glory, but with transparent sincerity and true humility. This is what makes Krishna Iyer truly a 'man for all seasons', who has planted indelible footprints on the sands of time.

A Historian's Reflections on the Indian Constitution

GRANVILLE AUSTIN

The reach of the judiciary and of the Supreme Court of India, especially, has been in contention nearly constantly since the Indian constitution's inauguration in January 1950.[1] From the start, two issues have embroiled the judiciary with the executive and legislative branches of government: fundamental rights, and custody of the constitution.

As far as the fundamental rights are concerned, the pre-eminent issue has been promoting the social revolution and, within this, 'socialism' as embodied particularly in the property issues of zamindari abolition and nationalization. Regarding custody, the supreme court held in the 1951 *Shankari Prasad* case[2] that parliament had unlimited authority to amend any part of the constitution. However, this decision lay uneasily upon the brows of other judges, and contention over judicial versus parliamentary supremacy in interpretation of the constitution would persist for decades. All the while, the courts would hold unconstitutional much of the social revolution legislation.

The constitution is the radical document its mothers and fathers intended it to be. The Nehru wing of the Congress Party had made this clear since 1928. It was dedicated to democracy and to social revolution—inseparable because social revolution had to be pursued democratically, and without social-economic reform, the country would not

---

[1] For further reading to understand the working of the Indian constitution, see Granville Austin, *The Indian Constitution: Cornerstone of a Nation*, Oxford University Press, New Delhi (1966); and Granville Austin, *Working a Democratic Constitution— The Indian Experience*, Oxford University Press, New Delhi (1999).

[2] *Shankari Prasad Singh Deo* v. *Union of India* AIR 1951 SC 458.

be democratic. The third strand of what I have named the constitution's seamless web was national unity, whose achievement was dependent on social-economic reform and democracy, and whose preservation was essential to sustaining national democracy and to pursuing reform. The administrative bedrock of the constitution, of course, is the 1935 Government of India Act.

The principal constituents of the constitution's radicalism are:

- Adult suffrage.
- The Fundamental Rights, which contain not only negative rights but also the positive rights to equality under law and to liberty.
- The inclusion of social-economic desiderata in the directive principles of State Policy: The state should strive to promote the welfare of the people through a social order in which justice—social, economic, and political, informs all the institutions of national life.
- The many provisions devoted to special protections for the Schedule Castes and Tribes, minority groups, and the weaker sections of society.

For a society hierarchical and repressive for thousands of years, where the principle of equality was almost unknown, and where scripturally enjoined responsibility to self and to one's in-group almost precluded care for the commonwealth and growth of civic responsibility, these provisions truly are radical. The framers drew from a variety of foreign constitutions—especially from the Irish constitution for the directive principles—and were much affected by the social democratic trends of the period.

During the years 1950–1, the pattern appeared of the government and parliament excluding the courts from fundamental rights matters involving the social revolution and the unity and integrity strand of the seamless web, even at the expense of the democracy strand.

- Preventive detention was used to curb free speech and anti-society activities. Because detention is an executive action, the judiciary was excluded from ruling on any violations of fundamental rights in a detention's early stages—or much longer if parliament so legislates.
- The First Amendment in 1951 created a new Ninth Schedule to the constitution in which state and central laws could be placed beyond judicial review—particularly if they were not consonant with the right to property. In reality, the schedule established a law beyond the constitution.

• This amendment inaugurated the practice of amending the constitution to get around judicial decisions.

The supreme court decisions that evoked the amendment arose from constitutional provisions inadequately drafted in the constituent assembly; from unforeseen conflicts among constitutional provisions; and government compensation for takings of property that arguably was unfair. Yet, the Nehru government's dissatisfaction with judicial decisions did not cause it to attack the judiciary's independence, although some in the Congress Party would have done so. With a clap like thunder, the custody issue reappeared in 1967, when a five-judge bench led by Chief Justice Subba Rao declared that the fundamental rights were entrenched and unamendable[3] by parliament.[4]

Although no judicial decision is irrelevant to politics, this one was overtly political, made in fear of further abridgement of the rights by a parliament dominated by a Congress Party no longer led by Nehru. Prime Minister Indira Gandhi—blaming the courts' intransigence and invoking the social revolution—four years later led her enthusiastically socialist parliament to reverse this situation:

• The twenty-fourth amendment provided that parliament could amend the constitution by way of addition, variation, or repeal and that the president 'shall' assent to such a bill when presented with it.
• The twenty-fifth amendment, among other things, made two of the non-justiciable directive principles supreme over the fundamental rights to equality, to the 'freedoms' of Article 19, and to the right to property.

The pattern established in innocence by Nehru had come to dangerous fruition under his daughter. Gandhi was done neither with the custody issue nor with the court she despised and feared. In the spring of 1973, plans had matured to supersede three judges of the court to appoint her own choice as Chief Justice of India. Although justified in the name of social revolution, this primarily was the 'personalization of government'. She had acted to remove a judge who might rule against her in her pending election case, which, if lost, would bar her from

---

[3] I.C. *Golak Nath* v. *State of Punjab* AIR 1967 SC 1643.

[4] See generally, Granville Austin, 'The Supreme Court and the Struggle for Custody of the Constitution', in *Supreme but not Infallible—Essays in Honour of the Supreme Court of India* (B.N. Kirpal *et al.*, eds), Oxford University Press, New Delhi (2000).

office for six years. A day earlier, the supreme court had reasserted the essence of its custody of the constitution by ruling, in the *Kesavananda Bharati* case,[5] that parliament could amend the Constitution so long as it did not alter its 'basic structure or framework'.

When the supreme court's *Kesavananda* Review Bench[6] would not overturn the basic structure doctrine, Mrs Gandhi's parliament, at the end of 1976, amended the constitution to bar judicial review of constitutional amendments. She already had turned democracy on its head with the emergency proclamation she had inspired in June 1975. Also, parliament had amended the constitution retrospectively to make not illegal the practices at issue in her election case that previously had been illegal. 'Government' had been reduced to the Prime Minister, her son Sanjay, and his 'extra-constitutional authority'. The Janata government between 1977–9 restored and repaired the constitution. And the supreme court, recovering from its quietude during the emergency, showed a new assertiveness in expanding the meaning of the fundamental rights through 'public interest litigation' and 'social action litigation'.

The greatest enemy of individual liberty in India is not government—despite the extreme use of preventive detention, police brutality and corruption, and incarceration without trial—but the hierarchical, survival society, which has also contaminated the performance of bench and bar. Nor can the constitution's 'negative' rights and the courts, themselves, be the citizen's primary protectors. This must come from the executive branch fulfillment of two promises in the constitution:

- 'No person shall be deprived of his life or personal liberty except according to procedure established by law' (Article 21), and,
- 'The state shall not deny to any person equality before the law or the equal protection of the laws within the territory of India' (Article 14).

The courts cannot do what government will not do, and the contempt power is an inadequate persuader. Government inaction when citizen oppresses citizen makes it complicit in the denial of citizen rights as much as its actions may directly deny rights. And so long as judicial processes continue being inordinately slow and may be subject to corruption, the courts, themselves, provide all too little protection for citizens' fundamental rights.

In practice, does Article 14 exist?

---

[5] *Kesavananda Bharati v. State of Kerala* (1973) 4 SCC 225.
[6] Ibid., see Austin, *Working a Democratic Constitution*, op cit., pp. 328–33.

Introduction

Rights, Justice, and Empowerment

C. RAJ KUMAR

Worldwide, the human rights discourse has become a powerful tool for enforcing accountability in governance.[1] Human rights have not only expanded vertically to ensure the protection and promotion of human rights during the interaction of states with all actors, but also expanded and developed horizontally by making human rights the basis for good governance and interaction, even among the citizenry.[2] Human rights have come to acquire a certain degree of legitimacy in the interaction of states in the international arena, an example of which may be the universally accepted right to freedom from torture.[3] At the international level, the role of the United Nations has been to bring human rights to the centre of UN activities by what is known as the 'mainstreaming of human rights'. There are various ways by which international human rights law is enforced, both at the national and international levels.[4] The activities of the UN (not only the work of the UN Office of the High Commissioner for Human Rights, but also other organizations) have now been oriented towards formulating rights-based approaches to development and governance.

[1] For further reading, see Henry Steiner and Philip Alston, *International Human Rights in Context* (2nd edn) Oxford University Press, New York (2000).

[2] See generally, Yash P. Ghai, 'Human Rights and Governance: The Asian Debate', 1995 *Australian Yearbook of International Law*, pp. 1–34.

[3] See generally, Philip Alston and James Crawford (eds), *The Future of UN Human Rights Treaty Monitoring*, Cambridge University Press (2000).

[4] For further reading, see Harold Hongju Koh, 'How is International Human Rights Law Enforced?' (1999) 74 Ind. L.J. 1397.

Rights have become powerful tools to compel states and non-state actors to ensure that their obligations are fulfilled. International human rights NGOs have become more active and vibrant in promoting human rights advocacy. While globalization and its impact on human rights have resulted in numerous instances of impoverishment, simultaneously, there has been a globalization of human rights advocacy by NGOs. Public spirited individuals and institutions engage more easily and are able to develop strategies and methods for creating standards and seeking accountability. The use of the Internet and the development of transnational civil society in global interaction has also helped the cause of human rights as human rights violations are no longer confined to national jurisdictions, but have acquired international significance. The quick flow of information and the possibility of shaming both by the governments of various states and international civil society, including the media and human rights NGOs, have indeed served as a mild deterrent for states bent upon human rights abuse. At the institutional level, human rights have acquired newer meaning and the traditional notions of sovereignty and non-interference have been undermined. This development has been aided by the formation of human rights institutions such as the United Nations Human Rights Committee, which enquires into the human rights situations of various states. When states have ratified the First Optional Protocol to the International Convention on Civil and Political Rights (ICCPR), even individuals may initiate such enquiry.[5] The European Court of Human Rights is also playing an important role in Europe in ensuring that the countries in Europe adhere to the principles and practices of human rights and alter their legal structures to ensure the protection and promotion of human rights.

At the national level, these developments have significantly changed the human rights landscape. Most countries have, in their own constitutions or other legislation, provisions on fundamental rights that are similar to the Universal Declaration of Human Rights (UDHR), the ICCPR and the International Covenant on Economic, Social and Cultural Rights (ICESCR).[6] The international human rights discourse has profoundly influenced various national policies relating to human

---

[5] International Covenant on Civil and Political Rights, G.A. Res. 2200A (XXI), 21 U.N. GAOR, Supp. No. 16, at 52, U.N. Doc. A/6316 (1966), 999 U.N.T.S. 171, entered into force 23 March 1976.

[6] International Covenant on Economic, Social and Cultural Rights, G.A. Res. 2200A (XXI), 21 U.N. GAOR, Supp. No. 16, at 49, U.N. Doc. A/6316, entered into force 3 January 1976.

rights.[7] Traditionally, human rights have been protected and promoted by the national courts through the use of the constitution or other domestic legislation. The national courts have started to use international human rights law more frequently and creatively interpreted various provisions of the constitution to expand the notion of human rights.

In the Indian context, as rightly pointed out by Granville Austin, the chapters on fundamental rights and directive principles of state policy in the constitution were deeply influenced by the struggle for independence and they were 'included in the Constitution in the hope and expectation that one day the tree of true liberty would bloom in India'.[8] The people who drafted the Constitution of India[9] had always intended to include a chapter on rights within the constitutional framework. The members of the Constituent Assembly were key participants in the freedom struggle and were fully aware of the problems that arise when rights are left to the discretion of the government. The rights that were included in the constitution were meant to be fundamental and also enforceable by courts by invoking the writ jurisdiction and judicial review.[10]

Since independence, significant efforts have been made to strengthen the legal, constitutional, and institutional framework to protect, promote, and institutionalize human rights in India. This work has been supported by an active and sensitive judiciary, in particular the Supreme Court of India,[11] through numerous judgments dating from the 1980s, limiting the powers of government, enforcing accountability of the police, custodial institutions, and other enforcement machinery, while simultaneously expanding the notions of freedom and liberty to include civil and political rights as well as economic and social rights. These rights were developed by invoking a broad and purposive interpretation

[7] See generally, C. Raj Kumar, 'International Human Rights Perspectives on the Fundamental Right to Education—Integration of Human Rights and Human Development in the Indian Constitution' (2004) Vol. 12 *Tulane Journal of International and Comparative Law*, pp. 237–85.

[8] Granville Austin, *The Indian Constitution: Cornerstone of a Nation*, Oxford University Press, New Delhi, India (1966), p. 50.

[9] For further reading, see Mahendra P. Singh, *Constitution of India* (V.N. Shukla) (10th edn Eastern Book Company 2001, with supplement (2003).

[10] For an excellent reading to understand the working of the Indian constitution, see Granville Austin, *Working a Democratic Constitution—The Indian Experience*, Oxford University Press, New Delhi (1999).

[11] For further reading, see B.N. Kripal, Ashok H. Desai, Gopal Subramanium, Rajeev Dhavan, Raju Ramachandran (eds), *Supreme But Not Infallible—Essays in Honour of the Supreme Court of India*, Oxford University Press, New Delhi (2000).

of fundamental rights and in particular, Article 21 of the constitution. The courts recognized the need for non-discrimination and non-arbitrariness in decision-making through expanding the various provisions of the constitution to give effect to various aspects of freedom. Even directive principles in the constitution were used to give meaning to the rights guarantees.[12] The development of constitutional provisions relating to liberty and equality were followed by liberal use of the provisions of international human rights treaties. India became a signatory to a number of conventions.

The formation of the National Human Rights Commission (NHRC) in India in 1993 and the creation of various State Human Rights Commissions (SHRCs) in a few states have created certain social expectations, and it is yet to be seen how far these expectation will be fulfilled.[13] The work of the SHRCs is commendable to the extent that human rights have been made into a focal point for assessing governance at the federal and state levels, and human rights accountability of the executive is attempted to be ensured.[14] But the task of human rights enforcement in India, as in other places, is gigantic for any one institution to achieve. It will remain an ongoing struggle. The more support it gets from the various civil society actors, such as human rights NGOs, public-spirited individuals, and the media, the better are the chances it can deliver on the promises of ensuring the protection and promotion of human rights. Human rights violations committed by the law enforcement machinery in India have been taken up by national and international human rights NGOs and also addressed through some useful interventions of the supreme court, various high courts, the NHRC and the SHRCs. The human rights violations committed by a state and its institutions have been brought to the forefront by both the judiciary and the NHRC. Some of these violations have been addressed by granting compensation

[12] For a very interesting perspective on this, see generally, Mahendra P. Singh, 'The Statics and Dynamics of the Fundamental Rights and Directive Principles: A Human Rights Perspective', (2003) 5 SCC (Jour) 1 at http://www.ebc-india.com/lawyer/articles/2003v5a4.htm accessed 20 October 2006.

[13] See generally, Vijayashri Sripati, 'India's National Human Rights Commission: A Shackled Commission?' (2000) 18 B.U. Int'l L.J. 1.

[14] See generally, C. Raj Kumar, 'National Human Rights Institutions—Good Governance Perspectives on Institutionalization of Human Rights' (2003) Vol. 19, No. 2 *American University International Law Review*, pp. 259–300; see also, C. Raj Kumar, 'National Human Rights Institutions and Economic, Social and Cultural Rights: Toward the Institutionalization and Developmentalization of Human Rights' (2006) Volume 28, Number 3 *Human Rights Quarterly*.

to victims of crime and abuse of power and in certain cases, pursuing disciplinary action against erring officials.[15] Liberalization of the rule of *locus standi* resulted in the development of public interest litigation (PIL).[16] PIL was used to effect changes in the criminal justice system with a view to infuse accountability in the prison administration and the management of various custodial institutions.[17]

Realizing the role of law in social engineering, the supreme court expanded the rights jurisprudence to include a variety of civil and political rights and economic and social rights. The suffering of the Indian citizenry became the focus of judicial discourse on human rights and constitutional empowerment became the vehicle of human rights development. The judiciary started to play a direct and important role in governance so as to ensure that the other wings of the government discharged their constitutional obligations in a suitable manner. This activist role of the judiciary was not always appreciated. At times, it was subject to criticism on the grounds that it was interfering in the affairs of the executive. However, the judiciary did not shy away from its constitutional responsibilities and continues to remain an institution that enjoys tremendous moral legitimacy and constitutional status to adjudicate on various issues that come before it, either through the normal channels of the appeal process or through the exercise of writ jurisdiction by way of PILs.

Notwithstanding the progress made relating to human rights in India, it remains an important area of concern. The contemporary realities of executive governance demonstrate the weaknesses and inadequacy of various measures. Human rights violations continue to be committed by the police, custodial, and other law enforcement institutions and military and paramilitary forces. Human rights accountability enforced by the courts or human rights commissions continues to be sporadic and all forms of victimization take place on account of abuse of power and arbitrariness and discrimination in decision-making. Corruption is omnipresent in governmental functioning and institutions that are supposed to uphold the rule of law, like the police and other law

---

[15] See also for the assessment of the torture practice in India by the Supreme Court of India, *D.K. Basu v. State of West Bengal* (1997) 1 SCC 416.

[16] Upendra Baxi, 'Taking Suffering Seriously: Social Action Litigation Before the Supreme Court of India', in Upendra Baxi (ed.), *Law and Poverty: Critical Essays*, N.M. Tripathi, Bombay (1999), pp. 387–415.

[17] A.S. Anand, 'Public Interest Litigation as Aid to Protection of Human Rights', M.C. Bhandari Memorial Lecture (2001) 7 SCC (Jour) 1.

enforcement machinery, are no exception. This underscores the need for developing a culture of respecting human rights amongst law enforcement officials as a *sine qua non* for the preservation of the rule of law. The enforcement of certain laws aimed at protecting national security in India has prompted efforts to better understand human rights in a constitutional sense. It has also resulted in the granting of significant powers to the Indian executive, giving greater scope for abuse and violation of fundamental rights in the form of draconian legislation like the Prevention of Terrorism Act (POTA)[18] and its predecessor, the Terrorist and Disruptive Activities Act (TADA).[19]

This book is a collection of essays by distinguished scholars, criminal justice practitioners, and academic lawyers who have expertise in the fields of human rights, criminal justice, and constitutional law. The issues relating to human rights have been linked to the concerns of the criminal justice system so that human rights of the accused, convicts, as well as victims are duly protected and promoted. The work of the criminal justice system and the victim justice system has been integrated by interpreting human rights as a legal and constitutional apparatus for empowerment. The essays have broadly focused on India, with international and comparative experiences being used to interlink the issues. The theme of the book being 'Human Rights, Justice and Constitutional Empowerment', all efforts have been made by the authors and the editors to ensure that the book reflects the academic discourse and practical and policy implications for addressing the issue of human rights within the criminal justice system from both national and international perspectives. The constitution has been effectively used in India to promote human rights policies in the process of social and political empowerment of the citizenry. The book has also critically examined the extent of constitutional empowerment that has been attained in India and how far the experiences of a few other countries

[18] See V.Venkatesan, 'POTA under Challenge' *Frontline*, Vol. 20, Issue 03, 2003 at http://www.flonnet.com/fl2003/stories/20030214004102600.htm accessed 20 October 2006, see also Fali S. Nariman, 'Why I Voted against POTO', *The Hindu* (24 March 2002) at http://www.hinduonnet.com/thehindu/2002/03/24/stories/2002032402140800.htm accessed 20 October 2006.

[19] See generally, C. Raj Kumar, 'Human Rights Implications of National Security Laws in India: Combating Terrorism while Preserving Civil Liberties' (2005), Vol. 33, Issue 2 *Denver Journal of International Law & Policy*, pp. 195–222. See also, 'Government Decides to Play Judge and Jury' (2001), a critical examination of the Prevention of Terrorism Ordinance 2001, South Asia Human Rights Documentation Centre (SAHRDC), New Delhi.

can help India in understanding the process of promoting consti-tutionalism. The book is divided into three sections: 'Constitutionalism, Human Rights, and Social Empowerment'; 'Governance, Development and Human Rights'; and 'Criminal Justice, Victim Justice, and Women's Empowerment'.

CONSTITUTIONALISM, HUMAN RIGHTS AND SOCIAL EMPOWERMENT[20]

Constitutions provide an elaborate framework for the protection and promotion of human rights and fundamental freedoms.[21] Conventional wisdom states that when rights and freedoms are written into the consti-tutions of different countries, they are given a higher legal status and become central to the political discourse in a society. Constitutions at their best may provide the political and institutional venue for this discourse. Constitutions are also written at a time when momentous political changes take place in a country or society and the framers of the constitution objectively attempt to transform the society. Constitutional guarantees of human rights cannot successfully ensure that these rights are protected, however, unless they succeed in engaging the democratic processes in the society, an empowering function that should be the goal of constitu-tionalism.[22] It is important that there are independent democratic insti-tutions that function effectively in ensuring that the governance system adheres to the principle of the rule of law and the constitution.[23]

Constitutionalism should be understood to encompass all such institutions. The judicial system ought to ensure that the human rights and fundamental freedoms guaranteed under the constitution are vigorously protected and any violation is duly redressed. Independence of the judiciary is expected to overcome any intrusions upon individual rights by other branches of the government.[24] The fact that the judiciary

---

[20] This section is drawn from a previous work, C. Raj Kumar, 'Moving Beyond Constitutionalization and Judicial Protection of Human Rights: Building on the Hong Kong Experience of Civil Society Empowerment' (2003) 26 *Loyola of Los Angeles International and Comparative Law Review* 281.

[21] L.W.H. Ackermann, 'Constitutional Protection of Human Rights: Judicial Process' (1989) 21 Colum. Hum. Rts. L. Rev. 59, pp. 59–71.

[22] See Michael C. Davis, 'Constitutionalism and Political Culture: The Debate over Human Rights and Asian Values' (1998) 11 Harv. Hum. Rts. J. 109, 125.

[23] William C. Whitford, 'The Rule of Law', 2000 Wis. L. Rev. 723, 724.

[24] Linda Camp Keith, 'Judicial Independence and Human Rights Protection Around the World' *Judicature*, January–February 2002, Vol. 85, No. 4, pp. 195–200.

has to protect the rights of the people and also protect against infringement of these rights by other branches of the government means that it has to be given a certain degree of independence and autonomy in its functioning.

Constitutionalism is a principle that encompasses a variety of political theory ideals, demonstrating a framework of governance that is based upon human rights, fundamental freedoms, and human dignity. Michael Davis has argued that constitutionalization is an empowering aspect in engaging civil society.[25] Stephan Holmes argues that the measure of constitutional success is its capacity to create public empowerment.[26]

Constitutional scholars often see constitutionalism in more limited and constraining terms. Walter F. Murphy argues that constitutionalism 'enshrines respect for human worth and dignity as its central principle. To protect that value, citizens must have a right to political participation, and their government must be hedged in by substantive limits on what it can do, even when perfectly mirroring the political will'.[27] Emphasizing this constraining feature of constitutionalism may undermine its empowering role. It is possible to conceive that even with a right to political participation and substantive limitations on the powers of the government, the citizenry may not be able to actively engage in political discourse. In such a case, constitutionalism will have failed. The active engagement of civil society with constitutional political institutions can actually shape and develop good governance policies within a country or a society. In the Indian context, if we fail to appreciate and develop this empowering role, constitutionalism may fail to effectively work in dormant civil society situations.

The relationship between constitutionalism and civil society[28] is profoundly significant for the preservation of the rule of law and for understanding the roles they play in ensuring the protection and promotion of human rights. To develop a viable relationship between civil society[29] and constitutionalism, it is necessary to recognize that 'constitutionalism is a dynamic, political process, rather than a fixed mode

---

[25] See Michael C. Davis, 'Constitutionalism and Political Culture: The Debate over Human Rights and Asian Values' (1998) 11 Harv. Hum. Rts. J. 109, 125.

[26] Ibid.

[27] Walter F. Murphy, 'Constitutions, Constitutionalism, and Democracy' in Douglas Greenberg (ed.), *Constitutionalism and Democracy: Transitions in the Contemporary World*, Oxford University Press, New York (1993).

[28] Gordon A. Christenson, 'World Civil Society and the International Rule of Law' (1997) 19 Hum. Rts. Q., pp. 724–37.

[29] Michael Clough, 'Reflections on Civil Society' (1999) 268 *Nation* 17.

of distributing power, rights and duties'.[30] It is not merely about constraint but about empowerment: '[Constitutional] legitimacy thus is more often validated by political and social realities than by formal legal criteria.'[31] It is persuasively argued that: 'Broad-based political socialization, generally expressed as the creation of civil society, is a prerequisite to stable constitutionalism. A theory of constitutional literacy has emerged that contends that the polity must be educated about the idea of limited government before such a government can succeed. This view is based, in part, on the principle that constitutionalism imposed from above, rather than being allowed to develop from below, is actually authoritarianism and has insufficient basis in civil society to be considered 'genuine' constitutionalism.'[32] In India, this framework needs to be further developed to include civil society[33] and democratic governance perspectives within the constitutional and human rights framework of public administration.

Chapter 1 by Upendra Baxi critically analyses the promises and social expectations generated by the transcendental jurisprudence of Justice V.R. Krishna Iyer. In a way, this chapter sets the tone of the book and other essays written in it. The chapter focuses on the impact of human rights violations in India, the judicial responses initiated by Iyer and how far they are relevant for the transformation of Indian society. This chapter also helps us understand how judicial activism and human rights are used for empowerment and whether they are successful in empowering people.[34]

Chapter 2 by Mahendra P. Singh examines an important theme which has remained the basis for developing human rights in India: 'Constitutionalisation of Human Rights'.[35] Singh has covered various issues relating

[30] Stanley N. Katz, 'Constitutionalism, Contestation, and Civil Society' (2002) 8 *Common Knowledge*, pp. 287–303.

[31] Ibid.

[32] Greenberg (n. 27), pp. xix–xx.

[33] Larry Diamond, 'Rethinking Civil Society: Toward Democratic Consolidation' (1994) 5 J. Democracy 4, 8.

[34] See generally, Upendra Baxi, 'The Avatars of Judicial Activism: Explorations in the geography of (In) Justice', in S.K. Verma and Kusum (eds), *Fifty Years of the Supreme Court of India: Its grasp and Reach*, Oxford University Press and Indian Law Institute, New Delhi (2000), pp. 156–209.

[35] For understanding the incorporation of human rights in a few selected Constitutions of certain countries, see Yash Ghai, 'Universalism and Relativism: Human Rights as a Framework for Negotiating Interethnic Claims', (2000) WL 21 CDZLR 1095. For an understanding of the relationships between constitutionalism

to human rights from the standpoint of the development of constitutionalism in India. The chapter also discusses the relationship between
fundamental rights and directive principles of state policy and how their
integral interpretation has contributed to the development of human
rights. The importance of a balanced interpretation of civil and political
rights and economic and social rights remains the key focal point of
discussion throughout the chapter. The rights discourse has been used
by Singh to examine how an analysis of the jurisprudence of the Indian
judiciary and the development of a theory of rights in India can pave
ways for social empowerment.[36]

Chapter 3 by Sudhir Krishnaswamy addresses a contemporary theme
within human rights discourse worldwide: horizontal application of
human rights. It examines the issue of horizontal application of human
rights in India within the constitutional framework, taking abundant
support from Indian jurisprudence to develop such arguments. The focus of the chapter remains the recognition of the expansionary notion of
human rights within the Indian constitution and various examples have
been given to address this issue. Specifically, the author addresses the
development of sexual harassment law and the demand for affirmative
action in the private sector as two illustrative examples of the development of horizontal application of human rights.

Chapter 4 by N. Ravi examines the relationship between the freedom
of press and the human rights discourse from an international perspective.
He primarily bases his arguments on the Indian situation and argues
that international human rights law recognizes the importance of a free
media in promoting democracy and citizenship. However, the human
rights discourse has over the years tended to undermine the freedom of
press due to tensions on account of different values systems, development
of laws relating to privacy protection in various jurisdictions, enactment
of laws relating to defamation, and other issues relating to hate speech.[37]
Ravi has argued that the biggest challenge that confronts the media and
the human rights community is to ensure that the democratic institutions

---

and state reform in the context of East Asia, see 'East Asia After the Crisis: Human
Rights, Constitutionalism and State Reform' (2004) Vol. 26/1 *Human Rights Quarterly*,
pp. 126–51.

[36] For further reading, see M.P. Singh, 'Securing the Independence of the Judiciary: The Indian Experience' (2000) 10 *Indiana International and Comparative Law
Review*, pp. 245–92.

[37] See generally, Venkat Iyer (ed.), *Media Ethics in Asia: Addressing the Dilemmas in
the Information Age*, AMIC, Singapore (2002).

respond sensitively and safeguard human rights in difficult situations when national security concerns come to the fore, particularly in the context of terrorism.

Chapter 5 by Vikram Raghavan develops the theme of freedom of speech and its implications for broadcasting in India. While focusing on the Indian constitution's guarantee of free speech and how it influences broadcasting policy in India, Raghavan underlines the human rights implications of these policies through a critical examination of Indian jurisprudence.

Chapter 6 by Parmanand Singh discusses the issue of affirmative action as a facet of equality and compensatory discrimination. Singh has given a contemporary analysis of the issue of reservation from the constitutional standpoint, critically examining the social and political implications of the reservation policy. He has also dealt with at length the various cases that have come up before the Indian judiciary and explicates how the contemporary law and policy relating to affirmative action in India has been developed in the context of a highly divisive issue of reservation. Singh has carefully examined the implications of the policy of reservation on scheduled castes and scheduled tribes and the other backward classes.

Constitutionalisation of human rights creates a theoretical framework for the protection of human rights, and from it flows the various legal, judicial, democratic, and institutional mechanizms that ensure the protection and promotion of human rights. When rights are guaranteed within the national constitutional framework of various countries, there are numerous implications for such guarantees.[38] The provision of such rights within the constitution demonstrates the state's acceptance of the importance of protecting these rights at a conceptual level.

It is possible that such rights, even after being constitutionally provided, may not be protected in practice. Under those circumstances, the other democratic institutions in a country may intervene. It is in this context that the judiciaries of various countries have started to interpret the constitution in exercising their powers of judicial review.[39] The

---

[38] See generally, Yash Ghai, 'Universalism and Relativism: Human Rights as a Framework for Negotiating Interethnic Claims', (2000) 21 Cardozo L. Rev. 1095 (discussing the incorporation of international human rights in a few selected constitutions of certain countries).

[39] See Christopher McCrudden, 'A Common Law of Human Rights?: Transnational Judicial Conversations on Constitutional Rights', (2000) 20 Oxford J. Legal Stud., pp. 499–532.

history of the recognition of the basic principle of judicial review, from United States Supreme Court Chief Justice John Marshall's opinion in *Marbury v. Madison*[40] to the contemporary and progressive formulations in the courts of India and South Africa[41] that recognize economic and social rights for citizenry, has been a long and arduous journey.[42]

The role of the constitution and the judiciary to protect and promote human rights, while extremely important and undoubtedly necessary, needs to be understood in different political contexts. The judiciary is able to best perform its constitutional functions only when the independence of democratic institutions is guaranteed and the government of the country adheres to certain principles of constitutional governance. Human rights and constitutional freedoms are too important for the judiciary to be the exclusive custodian of their protection and promotion, and most liberal constitutions typically do not envision that.

Further, the formal mechanizm of protection of human rights through the constitutional apparatus and the enforcement of human rights by the judiciary may fail, particularly when these institutions operate under limitations. There should be further space provided for democratic dissent and resistance to intrusions on human rights. This space is also typically addressed by liberal constitutions both in rights guarantees and democratic commitments. It should be an autonomous space for the citizenry to take upon themselves the task of protecting and promoting human rights and fundamental freedoms. It is possible that resistance from the citizenry can actually serve as a check upon the democratic branches of the government to ensure that the human rights of people are duly protected and that violations of any nature would be met with serious criticism in the form of democratic dissent. Importantly, people's resistance and movements to ensure the protection and promotion of human rights empower the judiciary in performing its constitutional obligations of protecting the rights and freedoms of the citizenry.[43]

[40] 5 US (1 Cranch) 137 (1803). See Larry Alexander & Frederick Schauer, 'Defending Judicial Supremacy: A Reply', (2000) 17 Const. Comment. 455, 459. See also Larry Alexander & Frederick Schauer, 'On Extrajudicial Constitutional Interpretation', (1997) 110 Harv. L. Rev. 1359, 1360.

[41] See Christina Murray, 'A Constitutional Beginning: Making South Africa's Final Constitution', (2001) 23 U. Ark. Little Rock L. Rev. 809, 837.

[42] See Christopher McCrudden, 'A Common Law of Human Rights?: Transnational Judicial Conversations on Constitutional Rights', (2000) 20 Oxford J. Legal Stud., pp. 499–532.

[43] See Michael C. Davis, 'Constitutionalism and Political Culture: The Debate over Human Rights and Asian Values' (1998) 11 Harv. Hum. Rts. J. 109, 125.

Organized people's movements to ensure the protection and promotion of human rights can actually educate branches of the government in lessons of true democratic governance so that people's views are heard and listened to while formulating policies relating to good governance.[44]

GOVERNANCE, DEVELOPMENT, AND HUMAN RIGHTS[45]

The United Nations Development Programme ('UNDP') views governance as 'the exercise of economic, political, and administrative authority to manage a country's affairs at all levels. It comprises mechanizms, processes, and institutions through which citizens and groups articulate their interests, exercise their legal rights, meet their obligations, and mediate their differences'.[46] Governance encompasses the shape that civil and political societies will take in the process of economic, social, and political development. National human rights instituitions (NHRIs) should play a central role in developing good governance policies in states. Reif explains the role of NHRIs, perceiving good governance, as 'the responsible use of public authority to manage a nation's affairs'.[47] According to Reif, good governance includes numerous practices such as '... a professional civil service, elimination of corruption in government, a predictable, transparent, and accountable administration, democratic decision-making, the supremacy of the rule of law, effective protection of human rights, an independent judiciary, a fair economic system, appropriate devolution and decentralization of government, appropriate

[44] See Thomas M. Franck, 'The Emerging Right to Democratic Governance' (1992) 86 Am. J. Int'l L. 46, 52.

[45] This section is drawn from two previous works: C. Raj Kumar, 'National Human Rights Institutions: Good Governance Perspectives on Institutionalization of Human Rights' (2003) 19 *American University International Law Review* 259; and C. Raj Kumar, 'National Human Rights Institutions and Economic, Social and Cultural Rights: Toward the Institutitonalization and Developmentalization of Human Rights' (2006) 28 *Human Rights Quarterly*, pp. 755–79.

[46] See Sakiko Fakuda-Parr & Richard Ponzio, Governance: Past, Present, Future—Setting the Governance Agenda for the Millennium Declaration, U.N. Development Programme Paper, at 1 (2002) (defining various international organizations' definitions of governance).

[47] See Linda C. Reif, 'Building Democratic Institutions: The Role of National Human Rights Institutions in Good Governance and Human Rights Protection' (2000) 13 Harv. Hum. Rts. J. 1, 2 (quoting Clarence J. Dias & David Gillies, 'Human Rights, Democracy and Development', paper presented at the International Centre for Human Rights and Democratic Development, Montreal (1993).

levels of military spending, and so on'.[48] An expansive understanding of good governance helps to recognize the mandate of NHRIs and how they should function.[49] The effectiveness of NHRIs depends upon numerous factors, including the mode and method of establishment, mandate, level of independence, availability of financial and human resources, scope of powers, and integrity of NHRIs' members.[50]

The United Nations Economic and Social Commission for Asia and the Pacific ('UNESCAP') observed that eight major characteristics constitute good governance:[51] participation, rule of law, transparency,[52]

[48] See Reif, ibid. (noting the many ways in which people understand good governance). See generally, Ndiva Kofele-Kale, 'The Right to a Corruption-Free Society as an Individual and Collective Human Right: Elevating Official Corruption to a Crime under International Law' (2000) 34 *Int'l Law*. 149, 152 (maintaining that in countries where transparency and accountability are lacking, corruption flourishes); Balakrishnan Rajagopal, 'Corruption, Legitimacy and Human Rights: The Dialectic of the Relationship' (1999) 14 *Conn. J. Int'l L.*, 495–6 (examining the relationship between corruption, legitimacy, and human rights and how it restructures political action); Nihal Jayawickrama, 'Corruption—A Violator of Human Rights', Transparency Int'l Working Paper, June (1998) at http://www.transparency.org/working_papers/jayawickrama/jayawickrama.html accessed 20 October 2006, (discussing the different ways that a country's corruption violates the protection and promotion of human rights); Lawrence Cocksroft, 'Corruption and Human Rights: A Crucial Link', Transparency Int'l Working Paper, October (1998) at http://www.transparency.org/working_papers/cockcroft/cockroft.html accessed 20 October 2006, (maintaining that the elimination of corruption and strengthening of human rights are interdependent); C. Raj Kumar, 'The Benefit of a Corruption-Free Society', [2002] 12 *H.K. Law*. 39 (arguing that an imminent need exists to formulate a fundamental human right to corruption-free government).

[49] See generally, Sakiko Fakuda-Parr & Richard Ponzio, Governance: Past, Present, Future—Setting the Governance Agenda for the Millennium Declaration, U.N. Development Programme Paper, at 1 (2002) (providing a general understanding of good governance).

[50] See Kamal Hossain, 'Human Rights and Development', in Kamal Hossain (ed.), *Human Rights Commissions and Ombudsman Offices: National Experiences Throughout the World*, Kluwer Law International, The Hague (2000), 55, 61–2 (reciting the features to examine when measuring the effectiveness of NHRIs).

[51] See 'U.N. Economic & Social Commission for Asia & the Pacific, What is Good Governance?' at http://unescap.org/huset/gg/governance.htm accessed 20 October 2006, (spelling out detailed definitions of each characteristic).

[52] See Saladin Al-Jurf, 'Good Governance and Transparency: Their Impact on Development' (1999) 9 Transnat'l L. & Contemp. Probs., 193 (supporting UNESCAP's opinion that governments cannot engage in good governance without promoting transparency).

responsiveness, consensus-oriented, equity and inclusiveness, effectiveness and efficiency, and accountability.[53] The functions of the NHRIs discussed earlier do not fully reflect this approach. Thus, in order to promote a good governance agenda for human rights, NHRIs should alter their present structure to include a more participative, accountable, and transparent approach.[54] Because an NHRI, in its functioning and in its dealing with the government, would stress the fulfilment of these principles, it is important that its own conduct be in conformity with the good governance agenda.[55] Linking human rights and good governance promotes greater transparency and accountability, which may provide more effective communication and engagement between NHRIs, governments, civil society, and victims of human rights violations.[56] In reality, the only way to achieve promotion of human rights is by building national capacities through the expansion of NHRIs' functions to include the governance approach.[57]

One could establish such expansion by mainstreaming human rights, which refers to 'the concept of enhancing the human rights programme and integrating it with a broad range of United Nations activities',[58] including development, governance, and administration of the states. In 1997, the UN Secretary General designated human rights as a crosscutting issue in his reform programme.[59]

---

[53] See Saladin Al-Jurf, Ibid. (explaining generally how to implement good governance through transparency and accountability).

[54] See Philip Alston, 'Towards a Human Rights Accountability Index', (2000) 1 Hum. Dev. J. 249, 250 (asserting that a composite index could help achieve good governance).

[55] See Linda C. Reif, 'Building Democratic Institutions: The Role of National Human Rights Institutions in Good Governance and Human Rights Protection', (2000) 13 Harv. Hum. Rts. J. 1, 2 (explaining how NHRIs should build good governance by being participatory, transparent, and accountable).

[56] See Linda C. Reif, Ibid. (indicating that NHRI's accountability establishes lines of communication with the public).

[57] See Mary Robinson, 'From Rhetoric to Reality: Making Human Rights Work', 2003 E.H.R.L.R. 1, 6–7 (defining national capacities as national protection systems that encompass entire institutional arrangements functioning under national law to ensure human rights).

[58] UN Office of the High Commissioner for Human Rights, 'Mainstreaming Human Rights', at http://www.unhchr.ch/development/mainstreaming-01.html accessed 20 October 2006, (describing the concept of mainstreaming human rights).

[59] Ibid. (referring to how the Secretary General wished to enhance the human rights programme and better blend it into the range of UN activities).

In Chapter 7, I examine the problem of corruption in India and its impact on human rights and the rule of law from a governance perspective.[60] I argue that institutionalized forms of corruption that are widely prevalent in India, besides violating laws, rules and regulations, also violate human rights and constitutional norms and pose a great threat to the rule of law.[61] The chapter underlines the need for integrating the anti-corruption discourse with the human rights discourse so that the right to corruption-free governance becomes a constitutionally protected right. It also examines the development of the right to information and various attempts at civil society empowerment that have taken place in India for the purpose of developing corruption-free governance.

Chapter 8 by Arjun Sengupta examines the importance of the right to development and its implications for reforming the governance system in India.[62] Sengupta underscores the need for an integrated approach towards protection of civil and political rights and economic and social rights. At the international level, the move towards integration of both these sets of rights is taking place at a faster pace. In the Indian context, the Supreme Court of India has interpreted the directive principles of state policy, which include mostly social and economic rights, to provide for an expansionary notion of fundamental rights. Sengupta has also examined the human rights discourse that takes place within the United Nations and the level of consensus that has been reached by the international community for formulating rights-based approaches to development in improving governance.[63]

Chapter 9 by Balakrishnan Rajagopal reflects on the theme of judicial governance and its implications for the human rights discourse from

[60] See generally, C. Raj Kumar, 'Corruption and Human Rights—Promoting Transparency in Governance and the Fundamental Right to Corruption-Free Service in India' (2003), Vol. 17, No.1, *Columbia Journal of Asian Law*, pp. 31–72.

[61] For further reading, see Ndiva Kofele-Kale, 'The Right to a Corruption-Free Society as an Individual and Collective Human Right: Elevating Official Corruption to a Crime under International Law' (2000), Vol. 34 *International Lawyer* 149; Balakrishnan Rajagopal, 'Corruption Legitimacy and Human Rights: The Dialectic of the Relationship' (1999), Vol. 14 *Connecticut Journal of International Law* 495.

[62] See generally, Stephen Marks, 'The Human Right to Development: Between Rhetoric and Reality', (2004) Vol. 17 *Harvard Human Rights Journal*, pp. 137–68.

[63] For further reading, see Arjun Sengupta, 'On the Theory and Practice of the Right to Development' (2002), Vol. 24, No. 4 *Human Rights Quarterly*, pp. 837–89.

a critical perspective, drawing on social movements.[64] While essentially focusing on the role of the Indian judiciary in protecting and promoting human rights and developing good governance mechanizms, Rajagopal critically examines the judicial governance that is prevalent in India. He underlines the inherent weaknesses of judicial activism and critiques the ideological character of the court's approach to human rights.

Chapter 10 by Surya Deva confronts the issue of globalization and its impact on the realization of human rights in India. This issue has assumed significance in light of the shrinking of national sovereignty due to the impact of global actors, multilateral institutions, and multinational corporations exerting tremendous influence on governance at the domestic level.[65] Deva discusses the subject of globalization and its relevance for human rights from a multidimensional perspective by evaluating the impact this process will have on national, regional, and international institutions.[66] The formation of the World Trade Organization (WTO) and the active participation of various developing and developed countries have profound implications for human rights, particularly when public opinion in numerous developing countries is increasingly disfavouring the negative impact of globalization on human rights.

Chapter 11 by Arun Thiruvengadam focuses on the social rights jurisprudence of the Supreme Court of India and its implications for developing constitutional jurisprudence.[67] The author addresses this issue by way of comparative constitutional law and in particular draws experiences from the Supreme Court of India and the South African Constitutional Court. The chapter addresses the impact of transnational judicial communications in developing comparative constitutional law

[64] For further reading, see Balakrishnan Rajagopal, *International Law from Below: Development, Social Movements and Third World Resistance*, Cambridge University Press, (2003), 360; see also Balakrishnan Rajagopal, 'International Law and Social Movements: Challenges of Theorising Resistance' (2003), Vol. 41, Issue 2 *Columbia Journal of Transnational Law*, pp. 397–433.

[65] Fur further reading, see Surya Deva, 'Human Rights Violations by Multinational Corporations and International Law: Where from here?' (2003) 19 *Connecticut Journal of International Law*, pp. 1–57.

[66] See generally, Upendra Baxi, *The Future of Human Rights*, Oxford University Press, New Delhi, India (2002).

[67] See generally, Vijayashri Sripati and Arun Thiruvengadam, 'India: Constitutional amendment making the right to education a Fundamental Right' (2004) Volume 2, Issue 1 *International Journal of Constitutional Law*, pp. 148–58.

with reference to the different approaches adopted by the courts for promoting social rights jurisprudence.[68]

Chapter 12 by Charu Sharma examines the impact of environmental wrongs on human rights and the various ways to integrate the right to environment and developmental justice within the Indian constitutional framework. Sharma also brings into focus the impact of international law and the development of Indian environmental law. The chapter provides for a useful understanding of the jurisprudence developed by the Indian judiciary in integrating human rights and environmental justice with a view to developing a right to a clean environment within the ambit of the right to life and liberty under Article 21 of the constitution. The author reiterates that the achievement of objective human rights is directly linked with the achievement of meaningful environmental rights.

In Chapter 13, Venkat Iyer raises fundamental questions relating to the human rights movement.[69] While mindful of the success of the human rights movement in bringing certain accountability of the governments in the exercise of power, the chapter confronts the attempts of certain human rights activists to push a certain ideological agenda even though there is no universal acceptance of the same.[70] The author emphasizes that the consensus relating to human rights worldwide is still evolutionary and will continue to be problematic when international human rights law is enforced selectively. This chapter serves as an internal critique of the human rights movement while accepting the notion of human rights as an empowering dimension of international relations and international law.

The developmentalization of human rights, which insists on a rights-based approach to development, requires a deep understanding of both civil and political rights (CPR) and economic, social, and cultural rights (ESCR). The 1986 Declaration on the Right to Development is a first step in linking a human rights-based approach to development to the

[68] For further reading, see Christopher McCrudden, 'A Common Law of Human Rights?: Transnational Judicial Conversations on Constitutional Rights' (2000), Vol. 20, No. 4, *Oxford Journal of Legal Studies*, pp. 499–532.

[69] For a critical view on human rights, see Makau Wa Mutua, 'The Ideology of Human Rights' (1996), 36 *Virginia Journal of International Law* 589.

[70] For a critical perspective on the effectiveness of international human rights, see Douglass Cassel, 'Does International Human Rights Law Make a Difference?', (2001) Volume 2 *Chicago Journal of International Law* 121. See also an interesting article by David Kennedy, 'The International Human Rights Movement: Part of the Problem?' (2002) Volume 15 *Harvard Human Rights Journal* 101.

governance agenda.[71] Domestically, NHRIs should be key players in the process of developmentalization of human rights. The issue of national security poses a particular human rights conundrum, implicating both CPRs and ESCRs. After 11 September 2001, a number of countries passed various forms of anti-terrorism laws with a view to protecting national security.[72] These laws have on numerous occasions violated domestic and international human rights norms and have indeed intruded into civil liberties.[73] NHRIs are ideally suited to intervene in these matters as they can engage with government to ensure that national security legislation does not violate civil liberties.

NHRIs should be pioneers in developing domestic human rights discourses. This would require being kept abreast of important discussions taking place worldwide in the field of human rights and taking steps to determine how to integrate these matters into the domestic legal, constitutional, and institutional framework. National security will remain a key human rights issue in a number of countries worldwide, and the potential consequences for human rights and civil liberties are obvious.[74] The UN Secretary General's famous report, *In Larger Freedom*, focused on the relationship between security, development, and human rights in the international context.[75] Domestically, NHRIs should take a leadership role in this debate, as a number of issues relating to terrorism and human rights are currently addressed in a manner that does not take into consideration all aspects of the problem. NHRIs are best suited to understand the relationship between CPRs and ESCRs, not only from a legal standpoint but also from a practical, implementation standpoint.

[71] Declaration on the Right to Development, adopted 4 December 1986, G.A. Res. 41/128, U.N. GAOR, 97th Sess., U.N. Doc. A/RES/41/128 (1986).

[72] For an extensive discussion of the question of what constitutes terrorism, see Emanuel Gross, 'Legal Aspects of Tackling Terrorism: The Balance Between the Right of a Democracy to Defend Itself and the Protection of Human Rights' (2001) 6 U.C.L.A. J. Int'l L. & Foreign Aff. 89.

[73] For an interesting reading on the impact of these acts on human rights, see Philip B. Heymann, 'Civil Liberties and Human Rights in the Aftermath of 11 September' (2002) 25 HARV. J.L. & Pub. Pol'y 440.

[74] See C. Raj Kumar, 'Human Rights Implications of National Security Laws in India: Combating Terrorism while Preserving Civil Liberties' (2005) 33 Denver J. Int'l L. & Pol'y 195.

[75] See In Larger Freedom: Towards Development, Security and Human Rights for All, Report of the Secretary General, UN GAOR, 59th Sess., Agenda Items 45 & 55, U.N. Doc. A/59/2005 (2005).

CRIMINAL JUSTICE, VICTIM JUSTICE, AND WOMEN'S EMPOWERMENT[76]

Unfortunately, an overtly legalistic approach to human rights[77] has failed to recognize that access to justice is a critical component of effective legal systems and, as such, should be one of the criteria evaluated in human rights performance assessments.[78] While access to justice in a procedural sense does involve issues relating to locus standi and legal aid, the jurisprudential foundations of access to justice rest on the capability of people to approach the courts of law or other governance institutions for seeking justice. ESCRs, if properly enforced, serve as empowering tools that will enable the protection of access to justice as a human right.[79] The citizenry of a state will be able to access the civil and criminal justice systems for the protection of their CPRs better if their ESCRs are protected, promoted, and fulfilled.

The modern understanding of the 'rule of law' includes the supremacy of the law, a concept of justice, restrictions on the exercise of discretionary powers, the need for an independent judiciary, and the protection and promotion of human rights.[80] While scholars continue to debate the exact meaning of the rule of law and societies reinvent themselves on different notions of the rule of law, there is no doubt that countries worldwide have recognized the need for the protection of the rule of law as a fundamental fabric of their society.[81]

In Chapter 14, Smita Narula gives a comprehensive analysis of the communal violence in India and the lack of sufficient responses from

[76] This section is drawn from two previous works: C. Raj Kumar, 'National Human Rights Institutions and Economic, Social and Cultural Rights: Toward the Institutionalization and Developmentalization of Human Rights' (2006), 28 *Human Rights Quarterly*, pp. 755–79; and C. Raj Kumar, 'Developing a Human Rights Culture in Hong Kong: Creating a Framework for Establishing an Independent Human Rights Commission' (2004), 11 *Tulsa Journal of Comparative and International Law* 407.

[77] See Laurence R. Helfer, 'Overlegalizing Human Rights: International Relations Theory and the Commonwealth Caribbean Backlash Against Human Rights Regimes' (2002) 102 Colum. L. Rev. 1832.

[78] See Upendra Baxi, 'Voices of Suffering and the Future of Human Rights' (1998) 8 Transnat'l L. & Contemp. Probs. 125.

[79] Jeanne M. Woods, 'Justiciable Social Rights as a Critique of the Liberal Paradigm' (2003) 38 Tex. Int'l l. J. 763, 792.

[80] See generally, Richard H. Fallon, Jr., '"The Rule of Law" as a Concept in Constitutional Discourse' (1997) 97 Colum. L. Rev. 1.

[81] See William C. Whitford, 'The Rule of Law' 2000 Wis. L. Rev. 723.

the criminal justice system, resulting in massive human rights violations during the various episodes of communal violence in India. Narula provides a critical perspective on the role of the police in these riots and their partisan approach sometimes resulting in the undermining of constitutional norms and institutional mandates. She also discusses the ineffectiveness of the prosecution in handling cases against those implicated in the violence, resulting in institutionalized travesty of justice in many trials. Narula argues that judicial activism and public interest litigation can be ways by which the injustices that take place within the criminal justice system can, to a certain extent, be corrected. She also recognizes that there is a need for police reform and reform of the criminal justice system so that the rights of the victims of communal violence are duly protected and promoted.[82]

Chapter 15 by B.B. Pande critically examines the nature of criminality of marginalized sections in India and its impact on the criminal justice system. Pande discusses the social implications of marginal criminality from a legal and criminological standpoint.

Chapter 16 by N.R. Madhava Menon examines the need for making criminal justice human rights-friendly by analysing the policy choices and institutional strategies that are needed. Menon discusses the implications of balancing security concerns with human rights. The role of the NHRC is also discussed, with specific reference to its work in promoting human rights within the criminal justice system. Menon has developed a thematic framework for a human rights-based approach to the implementation of criminal justice policies. The rights of victims within the criminal justice system are also duly addressed. He refers to the positive recommendations of the Malimath Committee Report on Criminal Justice Reforms in recognizing victim's rights.

Chapter 17 by K. Chockalingam examines the growth of victimology and victim justice by tracing certain national and international developments. The author analyses the subject of victimology and the need for bringing victims to the central focus within the criminal justice system from a human rights perspective.[83] He examines the Indian jurisprudence relating to reparation for victims of crime and abuse of power. The Indian judiciary has primarily used certain creative

[82] For further reading, see Smita Narula, 'Overlooked Danger: The Security and Rights Implications of Hindu Nationalism in India', (2003) Volume 16 *Harvard Human Rights Journal*, pp. 41–68.

[83] See generally, Dr. Justice A.S. Anand, Shri P. Babulu Reddy Foundation Lecture, 'Victims of Crime—The Unseen Side', (1998) 1 SCC (Jour) 3.

approaches to develop victim justice perspectives in granting reparation to victims. The author critically examines the recommendations of various commissions and, in particular, the National Commission to Review the Working of the Constitution and the Malimath Committee on Reform of the Criminal Justice System, which have provided for certain specific rights for the victims in the criminal justice system.

Chapter 18 by Lutz Oette focuses on India's international obligations for providing reparation for victims of human rights violations.[84] Oette examines the right to reparation for human right violations in international law and domestic practice with a view to emphasize the need for legal, constitutional, and institutional reform that would recognize the rights of victims of human rights violations. The chapter evaluates the present status of the right to reparation within the criminal law and constitutional law framework, along with a critical appraisal of the jurisprudence that has been developed over the years.

Chapter 19 by D.K. Srivastava discusses the problem of sexual harassment and other forms of violence against women in India. The primary focus of the chapter is to underline the efforts of the Indian judiciary in responding to the various forms of violence against women and in particular invoking the constitutional protection as a remedial measure for proving compensation to victims of sexual harassment. Srivastava critically examines Indian jurisprudence in a comparative perspective, analysing how the law relating to sexual harassment has been developed by the judiciary with a view to providing remedies to the victims of sexual harassment.

The challenges of governance posed in India due to the unique and distinctive development of constitutionalism and political culture can be confronted only through the development of a sustainable human rights culture. Any society based on the rule of law ought to develop its governance apparatus on the basis of laws, rules, regulations, and institutions that ensure adherence to the principle of the rule of law. In the Hong Kong context, the constitutional foundations, democratic, cultural, and institutional contributions, including the role of judiciary, have helped in developing a sound normative framework for the development of human rights. But the challenges to the implementation of human rights are profoundly affected due to the lack of entrenchment of the basic principles of the rule of law.

---

[84] See generally, C. Raj Kumar, 'State Torture in India: Strategies for Resistance and Reparation', (2003) Vol. 5, No. 2 *The Australian Journal of Asian Law (AJAL)*, pp. 160–83.

It is notable that the desires of the Indian populace to pursue democratic governance vigorously in recent years have resulted in constitutional and law reforms in developing the 'right to education'[85] and the
'right to information'.[86] Civil society movements in India need to
be further galvanized to drive home the idea that India needs the
development of a human rights culture. The development of a culture
of human rights goes beyond the work and mandate of laws, rules,
regulations, work of government departments, functioning of institutions, and the work of the judiciary. For human rights to become part of
the civil culture in India, it needs to be inculcated within the social and
political psyche of the people. Existing institutions, in particular the
judiciary and the human rights commissions, can play a vital role in
developing a human rights culture in India. However, the judiciary, by
virtue of its status as an official body that is involved in developing
jurisprudence in all aspects of law, may not be the most effective
institution engaged in the development of human rights culture.

India should continue its work in creating an independent civil
society that is engaged in developing a human rights culture. The fact
that the people of India are increasingly seeking accountability from the
government in all its actions is an important step in the right direction
for promoting a human rights culture. A culture of human rights
shall flourish only in a society that does not fear to dissent.[87] Freedom
from fear is an important freedom, which people should be in a position
to pursue.

Human rights education has great relevance for promoting a human
rights culture in India.[88] A culture of human rights[89] ought to be promoted

[85] C. Raj Kumar, 'International Human Rights Perspectives on the Fundamental Right to Education—Integration of Human Rights and Human Development in
the Indian Constitution' (2004), Vol. 12 *Tulane Journal of International and Comparative
Law*, pp. 237–85.

[86] C. Raj Kumar, 'Corruption and Human Rights—Promoting Transparency in
Governance and the Fundamental Right to Corruption-Free Service in India' (2003),
Vol. 17, No.1, *Columbia Journal of Asian Law*, pp. 31–72.

[87] See generally, Janet L. Hiebert, 'Parliament and the Human Rights Act: Can
the JCHR Help Facilitate a Culture of Rights', January 2006, 4 *International Journal of
Constitutional Law* 1.

[88] See generally, Upendra Baxi, 'Human Rights Education: The Promise of the
Third Millennium?', at http://www.pdhre.org/dialogue/third_millenium.html#
notes accessed 20 October 2006.

[89] See generally, Jose Ayala Lasso, 'A Culture of Human Rights, UN Chronicle'
(1997) Volume 34, Issue 4 *Academic Search Premier* 02517329.

through human rights education. Human rights education in India is extremely important, given the fact that general awareness of the constitution and its human rights framework among the Indian populace is marginal. Awareness relating to rights is very important for empowering the people to seek good governance policies from the government. The strategy for inculcating human rights culture among the people needs to be based upon a number of factors: social, legal, political, judicial, and institutional. Human rights education has been a focal point of UN activities in creating the United Nations Decade for Human Rights Education (1995–2004) in December 1994. In this process, the United Nations General Assembly (UNGA) defined human rights education as 'a life-long process by which people at all levels of development and in all strata of society learn respect for the dignity of others and the means and methods of ensuring that respect in all societies.'[90] The international significance of this is demonstrated by the fact that the UNGA sought the support of the international community and civil society during 1995–2004 in its efforts to promote a culture of human rights worldwide through human rights education and training.[91] Further, the role of human rights education was fully recognized by the World Conference on Human Rights held at Vienna in 1993. 'The Conference considered "human rights education, training and public information essential for the promotion and achievement of stable and harmonious relations among communities and for fostering mutual understanding, tolerance and peace."'[92]

Human rights education in India needs to go beyond the frontiers of academic learning or, for that matter, professional pursuit. Human rights education should aim to forge social transformation and promote a worldview based upon respect for the rights and freedoms of humanity. Shulamith Koenig has in her essay referred to the views of Upendra Baxi,[93] for whom no single phrase in recent human history 'has been

[90] See Office of the High Commissioner for Human Rights, 'Human Rights Education: Lessons for Life' (November 1998), at http://www.unhchr.ch/html/50th/50kit4.htm#Human%20rights%20education accessed 20 October 2006.

[91] Ibid.

[92] Ibid.

[93] See Upendra Baxi, 'Random Reflections on the [Im]possibility of Human Rights', at http://www.pdhre.org/dialogue/reflections.html accessed 20 October 2006. See also Upendra Baxi, 'Acquisitive Mimesis in the Theories of Reflexive Globalization and the Politics of Human Rights' at http://www.pdhre.org/dialogue/mimesis.html accessed 20 October 2006, (paper presented at Chicago Humanities Institute, 9–10 May 1996).

more privileged to bear the mission and burden of human destiny than [the phrase] 'human rights.' In his view, the greatest gift of classical and contemporary human thought is the notion of human rights. Indeed, more than any other moral language available to us at this time in history, the language of human rights is able to expose 'the immorality and...barbarism of the modem face of power'.[94]

Thus, the need for empowering the people of India cannot be better achieved than by developing varied components of human rights education. A sustained development of human rights education can result in the promotion of a culture of human rights. In the case of India, what needs to be examined is how human rights education can be promoted and to what extent the promotion of human rights education can actually facilitate the development of a human rights culture. Interestingly, the International Consultation (IC) on the Pedagogical Foundations of Human Rights Education has formulated a pedagogy of human rights education at a meeting held at the Center for Democratic Studies in La Catalina (CEDAL), Costa Rica, in 1996. At this meeting, it was observed, '...formal education (schools, universities, vocational and technical schools, professional schools, etc.) and other learning environments can be and sometimes are places where faculty, students and staff have the opportunity to search for meaning, to pursue the search for justice and to develop their unique beings in an atmosphere of safety, caring, and compassion. We strongly believe that students who are fully engaged in such an educational process are much more likely to challenge social and cultural domination. Vested interests, persistent habits, and bureaucratic [attitudes] can be obstacles to the incorporation of a human rights pedagogy into formal education.'[95]

India needs to overcome such hurdles in its efforts to develop a system of human rights education that ensures the development of a human rights culture in all its forms and manifestations. The starting point

---

[94] Shulamith Koenig, 'Human Rights Education, Human Rights Culture and the Community of Non-Governmental Organizations: The Birth of a Political Ideology for the Twenty-First Century', The People's Movement for Human Rights Education (PDHRE), at http://www.pdhre.org/dialogue/ideology.html#political accessed 20 October 2006.

[95] 'Towards a Pedagogy of Human Rights Education, International Consultation on the Pedagogical Foundations of Human Rights Education, Center for Democratic Studies in La Catalina, (CEDAL), 22–6 July 1996', The People's Movement for Human Rights Education (PDHRE), at http://www.pdhre.org/dialogue/costarica.html accessed 20 October 2006.

can be to develop knowledge and capacity-building in imparting greater awareness of the constitution and other domestic and international law relating to human rights in India. These efforts can be further developed to identify particular groups from different strata of the society to develop skills and expertise in pursuing training programmes in human rights education ('training of trainers' is an activity that several local and international NGOs perform). The IC has further observed, '...the pedagogy required for such a process will undoubtedly involve a wide variety of methods and approaches that should reflect and be guided by the principles that are basic to in [sic] the human rights movement. These principles include:

- Full respect for all people regardless of class, caste, sexual preference, race, gender, religion, income, ability, age, or other condition;
- Participation of students in their own education and sharing in the decision-making process;
- The celebration of human experience as an expression of diversity and uniqueness as well as an important source of knowledge and wisdom; and
- The vital importance of social responsibility.'[96]

In the process of promoting a culture of human rights,[97] human rights education can also ignite human rights activism. Contemporary India has witnessed a particular type of human rights activism that hopes to seek transparency and accountability of the government. Human rights activism is thus another facet of accountability-seeking endeavours. Commenting on the interaction of human rights and politics, Michael Ignatieff has observed, 'Human rights activism means taking sides, mobilizing constituencies powerful enough to force abusers to stop. As a consequence, effective human rights activism is bound to be partial and political. Yet at the same time, human rights politics is disciplined or constrained by moral universals. The role of moral universalism is not to take activists out of politics but to get activists to discipline their partiality—their conviction that one side is right—with an equal commitment to the rights of the other side.'[98]

[96] Ibid.

[97] See generally, Tom Campbell, 'Human Rights: A Culture of Controversy' (1989) 26 J.L. & Soc'y 6.

[98] Michael Ignatieff, 'Human Rights as Politics' in Michael Ignatief and Amy Gutmann (ed.), *Human Rights as Politics and Idolatry*, Princeton University Press, New Jersey (2001), pp. 9–10.

This is the kind of tolerant conviction that human rights education hopes to promote in India. It is consciously different from dogmatic and fundamentalist viewpoints of values which are intolerant of other variants and understandings of human rights and human values. The culture of human rights that we are seeking to achieve in India also necessitates rights education that informs the way by which governance policies affect human rights and the responses required by civil society to participate in the decision-making process.

While India's legal and human rights frameworks are created by the rights guaranteed under the constitution and their enforcement by the courts and government processes, it is important for other social control mechanizms to play their role in promoting human rights culture. Media organizations should conduct activities in a free and fair manner. While the Indian media is by and large fair in its reporting, there are legitimate concerns about its freedom. A society that hopes to promote a human rights culture should ensure that its media is given due protection under the law for exercising its freedom of speech and expression.

Human rights culture means a number of things to different people. There is no need for essentializing what constitutes human rights culture. The dynamic role that the media has played in other democracies and societies to develop a human rights culture needs to be borne in mind while determining and assessing the potential of the media in India. It is the social responsibility mandate of the media to promote a human rights culture. In this regard, it is also useful to refer to the impact of international human rights NGOs[99] and transnational civil society in ensuring the protection and promotion of human rights in other countries.[100] It is important for India to develop a transparent and sensible approach for deepening democracy so that the concerns and frustrations of the people of India are channelled and indeed regulated so that justice is achieved. This is extremely important in order to protect the rule of law and social stability in India. Promoting a human rights culture is directly related to justice, constitutional empowerment, and development of democracy. Human rights and justice have a profound relationship. They mutually complement each other and support the

---

[99] See generally, Peter Van Tuijl, 'Entering the Global Dealing Room: Reflections on a Rights-Based Framework for NGOs in International Development', (2000) 21 *Third World Quarterly* 617.

[100] See generally, Gordon A. Christenson, 'World Civil Society and the International Rule of Law', (1997) 19 *Human Rights Quarterly* 724.

development of good governance. In the Indian context, it is important to underline that we cannot wait for one to achieve the other. Hence, efforts ought to be taken, in particular by the media and wider civil society to ensure that human rights culture is promoted and sustained. The sustainability of such a human rights culture is possible only in a good governance framework that is based on the protection of the rule of law.

PART I

CONSTITUTIONALISM, HUMAN RIGHTS, AND SOCIAL EMPOWERMENT

The Promise and Peril of Transcendental Jurisprudence

Justice Krishna Iyer's Combat with the Production of Rightlessness in India

UPENDRA BAXI

The political is the horizon of the revolution, not terminated but continued, always reopened by the love of time.... The dynamic, creative, continual, and procedural constitution of strength is the political. This definition is neither empty nor neutral; it is subjected to the determinations of subjectivity and tendency, that is in which multitude and strength crisscross as figures of productive cooperation. But the expression of the multitude and continual creation of a new world of life remain its fundamental element. To take this element away from the political means to take everything away from it; it means to reduce it to pure administrative and diplomatic mediation, to bureaucratic and police activity—that is exactly to that against which the constituent power, as the origin of the political, continually struggles in order to emerge as strength. Indeed, all those activities that would like to present themelseves as the nature of the political do not belong to the political but, rather, to the routine of unchanged repetition. They are the effects of dead labour, perverse inversions of constituent power, and cannot be used to define the political.

INSURGENCIES

Thus ends more or less, the magnificent treatise of Antonio Negri entitled *Insurgencies* (Negri 1999: 334–5). It provides indeed a creative guide to understanding the Herculean jurisprudential labours of Justice Krishna Iyer. He emerged on the landscape of Indian jurisprudence with an elemental seismic force. His decisions remain acts of serial insurgency from the High bench.

Krishna (as he fondly allows me to call him and I here refer to him by his first name) may not have read Negri but enacts each one of the several themes exemplified in the above quotation. He seeks to bring the voice of the multititude to the task of articulation of judicial power and prowess. He combats ceaselessly the 'perversion' of constituent power and inveighs against forms of bureaucratization of human rights. His judgments, and voluminous extra-judicial writings, open up to the ineffable 'love of time' in which the renewal of the political is always a task inviting an activist judge to re-enunciate the 'dynamic, creative, continual, and procedural constitution of strength.' But there is more to Krishna. His indefatigable judicial and juridical praxes authorize him also to reconstruct that which he devastates. In this lies his true genius, which many a judicial biography,[1] *festschriften* and related treatises[2] may describe but never fully exhaust.

This essay does not examine in any detail scores of his judicial opinions; I have contributed often[3] to the tradition of ongoing exploration of his judgments, which has wavered between critique and applause.[4] Nor do I explore the question of Krishna's impact on the Indian adjudicatory and human rights cultures, which need further empirical exploration. Even when there is no doubt that Krishna led the renaissance of the Indian judicial process and power, he did so in the luminous companionship of Justices P.N. Bhagwati, O. Chinnappa Reddy, and D.A. Desai,[5]

---

[1] I invite in particular your attention to Justice Hari Swaroop's adoring judicial biography (1981).

[2] Rajeev Dhavan, Salman Khurshid, and R. Sudarshan (1985).

[3] See Upendra Baxi (1979, 1985, 2003, and 2006). See also, S.P. Sathe (2002), treatises on constitutional/administrative law by A.T. Markose, S.N. Jain, M.P. Jain, I.P. Massey, M.C. Jain Kagzi. B.B. Pande, P.N. Singh, and M.P. Singh (among other eminent scholars) have also explored aspects of Krishna's jurisprudence. See, for a recent analysis, Wouter Vadenhole (2002). No fully fledged Indian feminist critique of his often 'politically incorrect' diction has yet emerged.

[4] The Supreme Court Cases (SCC) *Case Finder* database (July 2004) mentions at least 64 articles in its Journal (I exclude here those authored by Krishna) discussing Krishna's contribution; of this rough count, perhaps the most well-crafted contribution remains that of Professor K.M. Sharma (1981). A full archive of scholarly analyses of his work on, and off, the High bench is yet, after nearly a quarter century of his retirement, to be assembled! Sharma's lament at the absence of the genre of judicial biography also remains unfortunately unheard.

[5] The question of impact must, of course, extend beyond the supreme court 'brethren' and extend to a wider judicial fraternity inclusive of appellate and even district judiciary.

each of whom stood in critical relationship with him.[6] We do not quite know how the fraternal dynamic and difference among them, as well as their colleagues on the high bench, affected the judicial choices that he made from case to case.

[6] The differences among these Judges remain notable. Justices Krishna Iyer and Chinnappa Reddy read widely beyond law and jurisprudence, more than can be said of their other companion Judges. And Chinnappa Reddy was even a little more finely grounded in Marxian theory than Krishna. D.A. Desai was clearly of the Left persuasion and a strong champion of the working classes; he, however, disdained theory. So did Justice Bhagwati, who, unlike Justices Chinnappa Reddy and D.A. Desai, was clearly not of any Marxian persuasion; Krishna was closer to the latter two in ideological orientation. Judicial pragmatism was a virtue with Bhagwati; he tried to achieve what was prudent and will endure in time. Each sought the right moment for historic verdict and almost always found his. But the quest of the right moment differed as Krishna, and to some extent Desai and Reddy, did not have as a long a tenure as Bhagwati. Accordingly, the pace of judicial valour reached varied *inter se*, though they collectively and individually never missed to attack the tenets of legal liberalism. Bhagwati was perhaps the most astute among them in terms of craftspersonship; he channeled his challenges to legal liberalism within its own confines, whereas the other three chose distinctly radical pathways of interrogation. All put together expanded the bounds of judicial activism but Krishna alone strove to accelerate its historic future time.

These are no mere *impressionistic* observations; my own writing has frequently testified to these commonalities and differences on the specific styles of activist justicing these Four Musketeers so richly and fortunately brought to the apex court. But it needs saying that the differences among them remain as significant as the common ground they shared. This essay does not allow space for tracing internecine strife. However, it is significant that Desai was more frequently embattled with Bhagwati than the other two Judges. Reddy used Marxian insights often more subtly than Krishna. The three rarely differed with Krishna in terms of judicial outcomes but each pursued reasoned judicial elaboration in very distinctive modes. They adored Krishna's messianic jurisprudence but found different ways and means of enacting it, and in the process, re-defining it.

In my tribute to D.A. Desai on his first death anniversary, I articulated their camaraderie thus:

How do we celebrate him as a part of the judicial triumvirate, the Trimurti? In many a way, he is inseparable from Krishna Iyer and Chinnappa Reddy. Together, they stormed the citadel of the Indian bourgeois jurisprudence. Together, they installed new icons of socialist justice and progressive law. Together, they gave shape to new rights and enforced vigorously the old ones. Together, they valiantly strove to discipline the capitalist classes to the discipline of human rights and the rule of law. Together, they nurtured the constitutional distance between Shastri Bhavan (the official seat of the Law Ministry) and Bhagwandas Road (siting the Apex court). But Dhirubhai (Desai) alone invented the art of judicial 'terrorism' and put it to stunning wise use.

Krishna himself was to describe the emerging difference in overall terms that contrasted judges who were 'populist activists' and those merely the 'shopkeepers of legal justice'. But both 'populists' and 'shopkeepers' differed among themselves and with each other. Uneasy coalitions among these brethren also remained necessary; the 'populists' had to as often carry the 'shopkeepers' with them, as they had also to allow to be carried by them; within such exigencies of judicial coalition, necessary for agreed and stable outcomes, it is vain to look for a high order of ideological consistency. Considerations of institutional integrity and prestige often mutate, though almost never silence the power of the activist judicial voice.

Not to be ignored is the ambition to speak beyond the inevitably finite future of constitutional interpretation. Both the 'shopkeepers of justice' as well as the 'populist activists' remain afflicted by this high judicial ambition. Both understand their roles as exceeding the production of fungible decisional outcomes that somehow 'settle' the instant case or controversy. Apex Justices aspire always and everywhere, a degree of interpretive immortality. However, only the activists volubly articulate this ambition in terms of crafting a legacy that fosters their own distinctive pre-commitment to higher constitutional values, virtues, and visions. Other Judges seek to speak rather inaudibly to the future of interpretation but their gentle resignation to the imperatives of institutional integrity of the judicial process and power is not always to be readily assimilated with judicial restraintivism, passivism, or even abdication. They craft the future legacy through the discipline, and force, of *stare decisis*, within which alone their own versions of constitutional values may find a secure niche into future histories. Both sorts of Judges routinely accept that their demise from the high bench exhausts their power to speak to the future of interpretation; upon retirement they rarely articulate the guardianship of their interpretational legacy. Krishna furnishes the *only* Indian exception; he has emerged as an articulate public critic and invigilator of his successors. For him life *off* the bench is as important, perhaps even more, as life *on* the bench because populist activism is not exhausted by the act of political grace that elevates a citizen to an apex Judge; rather, he believes that judging the judges is a perennial constitutional estate of all conscientious citizens. This contribution seeks to emplot Krishna's complex legacy in terms of messages that it may still carry for India's eminent contemporary Judges, who incline towards a *structural adjustment* of judicial activism, in tandem with the macroeconomic changes that now, for weal or woe, define the Indian globalization.

THE PROMISE OF THE TRANSCENDENTAL

Somewhat unusually, I take as my starting point not just the landmark judgments by Krishna but rather the text of one of his several speeches,[7] which most articulately sums up his judicial 'philosophy', which I here name as 'transcendental jurisprudence.' In this text, Krishna defends his own cherished positions against the fierce attack on judicial activism launched most notably by Chief Justice Hidyatullah on the one hand[8] and H.M. Seervai on the other.[9] Neither of these iconic figures responded to Krishna's rebuttal. They had, as it were, *finally* stated their case against judicial activism, which they somehow believed to be *unanswerable*.

Krishna's text exemplifies his very own imagery of transcendental jurisprudence. Even the rudimentary sense of 'transcendence' as going 'beyond' entails understanding, not always readily at hand, and invites difficult labours of understanding that which has in turn to be also transcended. The subtlety of textual moves remains forbidding, indeed. At times, this going 'beyond' means simply transcending the colonial inheritance; at times, it signifies reverence owed to the variously constructed justice potential of the Indian constitution; and at times, it also requires the Judges to go beyond the constitution itself, a form that Negri evokes in his *Insurgencies*. But the passage from where we are to where we all ought to be poses the question beloved of philosophers: to transcend is to go beyond 'appearance' to 'reality,' the phenomenal to the noumenal, the particular to the universal, error to truth, expedient to the essential, contingent to the necessary. In sheer jurisprudential terms, this move marks the passage from the positive law (law that is posited by the will of the 'sovereign') to 'natural law' (law posited by the reason of God, by 'nature', or by human reason). A ceaseless quest for the 'higher law' defines Krishna's endeavours at juridical and juristic transcendence.

Krishna's categorical imperative for postcolonial constitutional justicing understandably remains bewildering to most of his erstwhile and contemporary brethren as also for epistemic communities. I know it as a fact (from numerous conversations with supreme court Judges, some of whom I remain privileged to claim as constitutional and personal friends) that they remain rather innocent of the extraordinary

---

[7] See, Krishna Iyer (1984). Incidentally, all page references to this text are in terms of print copy because I rely here on the 'download' pagination available at the SCC *Case Finder*.

[8] See, M. Hidyatullah (1984).

[9] See. H.M. Seervai (1987), pp. 1871–80, 2026–9; and Upendra Baxi (1983b).

discourse, in literary and cultural theory, constituting the 'postcolonial' (see, especially Hallward 2001). Nor do many Indian appellate Judges have the enormous good fortune (the time and the energy) to pursue conceptual and social histories of colonialism. Krishna himself does not quite explore the unsettled relationship between 'colonialism' and 'imperialism' (Young 2001: 1–43). The default setting of Indian legal scholarship necessarily brings 'home' (to their students—the future leaders of the bar and bench) the oblivion of these crucial discourses. The theoretic indigence of Indian legal education and research entails the unfortunate consequence where the bar and the bench remain satisfied with quotational jurisprudence as a badge of erudition, and even wisdom.

The massive and populous Anglophiles (or may one even say Anglo-philistines?) of the bar and the bench do not quite understand the pleni-tude of the Krishna indictment. They see nothing intrinsically wrong in the tradition of the common law, which entails a large measure of uncritical deference to the executive and the legislature. In their under-standing, adjudicatory cultures site, as well as mime and mine, justice according to the law as a fulsome resource for respect for the separation of powers and the constitutive ambiguities of *stare decisis*. They thus see nothing wrong in approaching the tasks of constitutional interpretation *as if the constitution itself was a statute*, even if an oxymoronic 'higher law' statute, inviting practices of reading guided by the canons of statutory construction.

They understand, of course, that British colonialism was wrong, even obnoxious, but think of the legacy of the common law as a kind of liberation theology. The dominant discourse does not regard the reception of the common law tradition of justicing as any vicious aspect of colonization; rather, it salutes the great constitutional corpus of a Durga Das Basu or H.M. Seervai as testimonials to colonial legal liberalism. Indeed, it justifies pursuit of interpretive practices of a constitution within the common law traditions of justicing. Put another way, the world-historic Indian constitution is then read in these modes of iconic servitude, as a mere unfoldment of the Government of India Act, 1935, and much else besides. In this imagery, precociously activist Indian judges emerge as no more than pale replicas of the common law judicial activism of a Denning or a Scarman! This sort of reading indeed further consolidates, and masks and marks, the abiding forms of juridical and judicial re-colonization.

All this thus evolves the fashioning of a hermeneutic monster: *consti-tutional common law*. One would ordinarily think that the constitution required rather the creation of an *uncommon law*, that is, the invention of a whole series of *sui generis* interpretive traditions in which even judicial deference to legislative policy enactment was to be firmly disciplined by the inherent logics of fundamental rights and human freedoms, outside the 'chain of precedent' (to echo the felicitous phrase of Julius Stone). Of course, that code has to be ultimately evolved by judicial interpretation. The question still remains: does deference to co-ordinate branches require Judges to apply principles of statutory construction in adjudging the validity of legislative and administrative action challenged as violative of basic human rights and freedoms guaranteed by Part III of the constitution? Should even the iconoclastic plenitude of constitutional human right to remedies for the redressal of fundamental rights violation (Article 32) be made subject to the doctrines of constructive *res judicata*, and the law of *laches* (that immunizes human rights violations because petitioners bring the cause too late, under the temporal calculus of the Indian Limitation Act)?[10]

Krishna wholesomely combats this judicial reductionism by decrying the common law colonial bequest as 'imperial legal culture.' His critique remains at home with the discursive formation now phrased (by contemporary eminent Canadian constitutional scholarship) as 'the unity of public law', which primarily suggests that 'the rule of law is the rule of fundamental legal values of a society that are located in various sources, written and unwritten, international and domestic', values that in turn direct near-obliteration of distinctions between 'constitutional' and 'administrative' law and jurisprudence and 'standing' and 'justiciability'.[11]

[10] I desist munificent case law citations and references to my writing, I urge interested readers to revisit this discourse. As concerns *res judicata*, a word of explanation is in order. Because Article 226 endows state high courts with a co-equal jurisdiction to monitor human rights-violative administrative and legislative performance, the supreme court has often held dismissal of the cause as preventing further recourse to it. This ignores a constitutional fact: the Article 226 powers of high courts are discretionary, whereas Article 32 confers a fundamental right to constitutional remedies. I have addressed this problem as early as the 1970s in my writing.

[11] David Dyzenhaus (2004) 1. His claim that the Canadian supreme court's performance obligating administrative/quasi judicial action/actants with a duty to give reasons is inaugural in the common law constitutional adjudication remains both inaccurate and wounding by its comprehensive inadvertence to the Indian juristic and juridical feats. To what extent then Judges constitute a 'hegemonic bloc', constituting the visages of the 'Postmodern Prince' (Gill 2003) remains a question inviting further pursuit in inter-/multi- disciplinary settings.

The notion of 'imperialism' has many histories; and the relationship between 'colonialism' and 'imperialism' is not yet fully understood (Young 2001). Krishna's use of both the terms remains polemicist, in the best sense of that word. Krishna does not quite distinguish the 'colonial' from the 'imperial' in this text[12] but it is clear that he has in full view the role that the law and lawyers, courts and judges, play in terms of fostering economic exploitation and political domination. 'Imperial legal culture' constitutes various interlocking and intertwined sites of articulatory practices of reproduction of 'class bias' of the makers, interpreters and enforcers of the law, and even the acts of making/remaking/reading the constitution itself. He describes (borrowing an expression of Franklin D. Roosevelt) appellate judges and lawyers as 'the royalists of the economic order' (p. 3) who continue to reproduce 'the Raj vintage adversary system pickled in Austinian jurisprudence' (p. 8.) Judges and lawyers who everyday operate the colonial legal codes and statutes participate also in the perpetuation of the 'imperial legal culture', and thus continue to promote 'procedural bigotry, traditional construction, remedial rigidity, and legal justice escapism'. They reproduce the divorce between the law and justice through 'exotic adjectival orthodoxies, statutory mystiques, and expensive, formalistic excesses' (p. 9).

Postcoloniality, in Krishna's view, stands inaugurated by the Indian constitution, which summons Judges in particular, and other lawpersons, to the tasks of liberation—liberation at least from the British Raj imperial legal culture. But they may not receive this summons, or default in response, when they perceive the 'paramount parchment with hangovers of a Victorian vintage'.[13] Rather, the constitution marks, and Krishna endlessly reiterates in his judicial opinions, the Nehruvian phrase 'tryst with destiny'. For him then, the constitution does not signal the point of arrival but rather the infinite amplitude of points of departure that jurisprudentially combat the encyclopedic forms of production of the distinctively Indian human rightlessness. Krishna urges Judges (and hopefully the lawpersons as well) to fully understand that theirs is the *portfolio* of social transformation, not the everyday *ledger* upon which may

---

[12] But his other speeches and writings (too voluminous to be cited here), especially in relation to 'The Uruguay Round and India's Accession to WTO', inveigh against the emergence of a new impartial global law and culture.

[13] The turn of phrase is interesting. Krishna himself, being an absolute teetotaler, can never testify to the experience of a hangover! But even when he does not know *inebriation*, surely he knows what *intoxication* is.

stand inscribed miscellaneous quotidian details of lawyerly registration of democratic legitimation of power and also its staggering deficits. Ledger-keeping produces *accounts* but what is required is the politics of production of *accountability*, in which judicial actors and their choices must play a significant, at times decisive, role. Only on such a reading, his call for a 'national accountability' of judges, entailing 'activist sensibility' (p. 2) furnishes a clarion call. Krishna urges Indian judges to go beyond the functional role of that which likens 'the common law judicial review' (in Mary Ebert's luminous phrase) to the 'canary in the coal mine, warning of impending disaster but unable to deal with it' (Dyzenhaus 2004: 15).

All this involves, for Krishna, a reflexive reading of the constitution as indeterminate forms of engagements by the multitudes that (again in Negri's words) address the 'fundamental element' of the *'continual creation of a new world'*. Judicial and juridical performativity re-casts Judges as partners in this 'productive cooperation.' Krishna luminously insists, and exemplifies, the Negri-like re-definition of the 'political' wherein the constitution, far from being 'the routine of unchanged repetition'— an enervating discourse concerning the original intention that signifies but so many effects of 'dead labour'—instead and forever seeks to redefine 'the political'. That phrase names, for Krishna, the very being of judicial process and power. No judicial personage in the long lineage from a Cooke to Cardozo, and beyond, has found such rhetorical amplitude that contrasts the living judicial praxis with forms of dead judicial (and juridical) labour, that define the 'political' in the 'judicial' as 'unchanged repetition' without difference.

Antonio Negri's dissipation of the Marxian 'classes' into amorphous 'multitudes' has caused manifold erudite post-Marxian production of anxieties (see, Passavant and Dean 2004; but see now Hardt and Negri 2004), which I do not revisit here except to say that the changing patterns of Indian fifty-plus constitutionalism, testify precisely to the prowess of the *multitude* against the *minuscule*. On this register many an erudite critique of the activist judicial archive remain somewhat 'ahistorical' in the postcolonial timespaces. Regardless of this discourse, Krishna invites never-ending labours of forms of postcolonial readings of the text, and context, of Indian constitutionalism.

His hermeneutic odyssey forbids any simple summation, at the same time raising a crucial question: How may regime-anointed Judges transcend the *reason* of the state, and the human rights *treason* of the state? Put another way, how may apex Judges give voice to the multitude against the minuscule in their myriad struggles to re-shape the social and historic meaning of 'constituent' power? The formidable daring that Krishna thus offers, contests the mode of essentialist reading of the Indian constitution, a reading that assumes, after all, that Judges *interpret* a given text of the constitution, rather than *create* it by acts of construction. Krishna is not so naïve to deny that there exists an official text named as the Constitution of India; surely it does. But he remains astute enough to say that it is a text by itself and does not generate imperatives of meaning and signification that always necessarily bind Judges except insofar as they choose to regard it as binding; that is, in the exact proportion in which Judges may not conceive their judicial *vocation* as judicial *vacation*. Put another way, a 'populist activist' Judge is never on judicial and juridical *vacation*; her *vocation* summons the constant obligation to re-draft/re-imagine the constitution. Under this conception, constitutional justicing almost always re-casts the figure of a judge into a single-person constituent assembly, an assembly that articulates the voices of the past and present multitudes and their aspirational struggles for liberty, equality, dignity, and justice.

This insurgent reading (given all its exigent enactments from the high bench) entails accentuation of the *spirit* over the *corpus*. The body political in the constitutional text, and context, is indeed gross and corrupted, especially in the Augustinian sense of that term. For Krishna, the judicial role, task, power, and process find their future in the discovery (even invention) of the 'Kingdom of Ends' (to evoke a Kantian phrase) of a secular 'fighting faith and founding creed' (p. 2). Krishna insists that constitutional judicial interpretation promote, even proselytize, a secularist, and secularizing, socialist imagery that constantly *reinvents* the forms of human rights as languages, logics, and paralogics of *justice*. As he says, memorably: 'To defy or deny social justice to the humblest Indian, even from the highest court, is to act not only *extra-constitutionally* but *contra-constitutionally*' (p. 2).

In terms of sheer judicial pragmatics, this entire summons requires Judges to respond to social demands for 'interpretational creativity', device 'remedial realism, and procedural non-formalism', and regard judicial process as a mode of 'impregnating old laws with constitutional value meanings'. It confronts a difficulty and a challenge: the overall 'bench bar ethos' does not favour that the supreme court of India 'fulfill... partnership in the value revolution' inaugurated by the constitution. Krishna then remains not altogether bewildering when he suggests that human rights (here construed in a unique conflation, a creative assemblage of the Preamble, Part III embodiment of fundamental rights, Part IV constitutional obligation to further the directive principles of state policy, and IV-A mandated fundamental duties of Indian citizens) ought to be taken *seriously* in diminishing, even demolishing, the vestiges of colonial law and jurisprudence; that the great colonial codifications of civil and criminal procedure, and of evidence, must be subjected to a continual vigilant discipline of cascading strict constitutional scrutiny.

Krishna leads, by exemplary interpretation, the pathways of progress. He has thus no difficulty in converting *statutory* right of bail into a *constitutional* right; constitutionally outlawing solitary confinement; monitoring the mandatory death sentences and the forms that manifest extreme arbitrariness of judicially imposed death sentences; even interrogating executive clemency in capital offences, and facilitating a remarkable conversion of Article 21's rights to life and liberty from the disciplinary regime of 'the procedure established by law' (the domain of parliament) into a judicially empowered re-writing that now insists on expanding 'substantive due process'(the ever-expanding domain of activist judicial review). In this sense, 'transcendence' germinally evokes the notion of *bringing back the constitution in the everydayness of the routine careers of interpretivism*. Krishna seeks to *normalize* judicial activism, in ways that invoke practices of résistance by 'legalist'/'fiedlist' brethren. He de-problematizes activist justicing by recalling Chief Justice Earl Warren's evocative metaphor: 'Our judges are not monks or scientists but participants in the living stream of national life' (p. 1).

This lumping weirdly fascinates! The monk and scientist, far from the mere life of contemplation, belong together in many ways that shape and reshape the ideology and materiality of the world; each indeed produces separately and individually, complexly interlinked sacred and secular utopias, even dystopias! Krishna is surely mistaken when he thinks that monks and scientists are not 'participants in the living stream of national life.' But he is surely right in saying that Judges ought to attend differently the modes of production of social reality. The communities of monks and scientists may indeed produce human rightlessness whereas Judges ought to produce/reproduce conditions of the politics of production *of*, and *for*, human rights. Thus, he invites not jurisprudence of *retreat* but a jurisprudence of *engagement* with the future of human rights in a globalizing India.

Beyond this, Krishna's successors may justly remain confused, even ambivalent, concerning his call to 'Destination Justice'. To be sure, Krishna here evokes the imagery of *means* and *ends*. But this dialectic assures no sure passage negotiating, on the one hand, the notion that the law is 'the *means* and justice is the *end*' and, on the other, the rather compelling notion that in the 'constellation of values, in the Indian constitutional setting, *ends* are *means*' (p. 1). By this rhetoric, of course, Krishna signifies a 'creed of the constitution' that affirms 'socio-economic justice' that 'binds' both 'social justice and legality'. Aspirationally wholly worthy, this message falls unevenly, even if understandably, and not only on the summit court hearing-impaired appellate extra-ordinary judicial ears.

Krishna evokes the 'transcendental' through myriad, even reverential, recourse to iconoclastic elements in the constitution. All this involves manifold serial acts of insurgent interpretation. At times, this also symbolizes going beyond constitutionalism itself. Krishna's quest for a higher law cannot be divorced from transgression, described recently by Duncan Kennedy (1997: 342–3) as transgressive 'artifact' or 'perform-ance' that 'shatters' the forms of 'proper' expression in order to express that something that those forms suppressed. It thus specializes in a language of a 'particular kind of disruption'. Krishna's minting of a wholly new style of judicial prose is probably the most spectacular example, in contemporary judicial annals, of transgressive artifact/performance. Those who complain about his use of language entirely miss the nature of his quest for transcendence.[14] Krishna's all too frequent assaults on conventional judicial habits of writing remain inseparable from his search (as Kennedy describes this in altogether a different context) 'for intense experience in the interstices of a disrupted rational grid.' For Krishna, transformative praxes require that more than any other set of constitutional actors, adjudicative personages ('actants') display a 'higher functional loyalty' to the 'command of the constitution'. Here, the task of jurisprudential (though not only in that form) as transcendence entails remarkable discursive feats that articulate the visions of postcolonial constitutionalisms and their law-ways.

But the constitution, and this is the second trope in Krishna's disruptive performance, is not just a history of power, its apparatuses, and effects. Rather, it remains an ineffable *future* history of Indian peoples in struggle against these, always a work in progress. Krishna constantly asks us to re-position the dialectic between *subjects* and *citizens* by asking a simple-looking question '... *who* are the people' whom the constitution and the law, the Judges and the jurists, ought to serve in a distinct *fiduciary*

---

[14] See, K. Nambyar (1974) for a vigorous defense of 'judicial gobbledygook'.

capacity? His answer is simple and direct: peoples always must mean and refer to peoples condemned to a state of human rightlessness, or the *'les miserables'* (sic). These are the Indian *Atisudras*, as Babasaheb Ambedkar named the Indian social and economic proletariat. Krishna articulates the communities of suffering as 'the tongueless, tattered, battered, police-hunted, poverty-bitten', 'raped adivasi belles and dowry-burnt brides', 'the tortured prisoners, degraded slum dwellers, homeless pavement-dwellers, bonded labourers, sweated labourers, and discriminated gender...' (p. 5). In sum, these constitute the distinctive Indian *Homo Sacer* (Agamben 1998), or as Marx put this as the 'vast industrial reserve army' and what contemporary post-Marxian languages describe as the 'disposable peoples'.

No Judge of an apex court in any contemporary world of justicing has so poignantly articulated the principal task of constitutional develop-ment in terms of the amelioration of the 'weight of suffering' (to invoke Pierre Bourdieu's moving phrase). No Indian supreme court Judge, before and after Krishna, has found ways of articulating the Indian peoples' sufferings with such poignant, though occasionally dense, investment of high intendment. He rightly insists that no postcolonial constitutionalism or jurisprudence can take human *rights* seriously when it fails to take human/social *suffering* seriously. The Krishna legacy remains thus (in the Derridean idiom; Derrida 1994), profoundly *hauntological*.

The coupling of the colonial inheritance with the challenge of trans-formative praxes poses some extraordinary challenges. Krishna typically frames this in terms of a massive interrogation: 'Should the court pyramid be cornered by the Propriteriat and judicial business be converted into Private Justice Limited painted Public Justice Unlimited?' The question thus posed is historically immense: any truthful answer furnishes a clarion call to Judges that they should transcend their own latent class bias, and further persuade the bar to do likewise. Far from remaining 'legal justice mongers', Judges ought to covert themelseves into knight-errants for a new constitutionalism into the *avatars* of social justice populists. Further, Judges at work should prevent the expropriation of the law and the constitution by special interests that both serve and subvert the ends of a liberal constitutionalism.

Understandably, not all the 'brethren', constituted severally across the high turnover judicial generations,[15] may agree with this understand-

[15] The supreme court Judges retire at the age of sixty-five years. This even means rather vexatious ordination of Judges as Chief Justices of India for constitu-tionally exacerbated tenures of a few days, weeks, or months!

ing of the tasks fashioning a postcolonial jurisprudence of India. And most conspicuously disagreed, in Krishna's own lifetime at the apex court; Krishna understood sagaciously that the labours of transcendence have to be performed within forbidding institutional cultures and contexts. Unsurprisingly, then, his decisional postures, as many of his critics have demonstrated, as often remain mired in 'legalism' he himself describes.[16] Krishna remains historically mindful of this corpus of constraints, which he describes in vivid prose, birthed by the very angst of working with his brethren, thus:

The Indian judiciary is passing through a crisis of identity, split personality, and ideological ambiguity... (t)he institutional imbroglios, compounded by internal antagonisms, aggravated by para-political latencies and exacerbated by perspectival and perceptual divergences. [This] has horizontally and vertically affected the functionalism of judicial process [manifest] in the other pathologies which make the court-system, from the base to the apex, an instrument of escalating incredibility and stultifying disutility (p. 2).

This extraordinary reflexivity is not pervasively characteristic of Indian, nor southern, judicial and juridical performance. In the specific setting of the Indian Supreme Court, the pathologies assumed forms of internecine intra-court sniper warfare between Chief Justice Chandrachud and Justice Bhagwati, which I for once successfully mediated (Baxi 1983a). Characteristically, Krishna seeks here to transcend histories of intra-brethren hurts by translating its social costs of human rightlessness that thus betrays the 'social hopes of the robbed brethren healing people's injustices, suffered for long under feudal-colonial legal orders....'

PERPLEXITIES

When Krishna issues the further summons against the 'reactionary resistance movement,' these new forensic forces fighting 'progressive remedial jurisprudence fleshing out social justice' incarnating a defense of 'bygone faith and imperial juridcalise, forsaking those values of human dignity and equal rights promised to the common millions', it is not possible to deny constitutional love to him, at least by those who treasure futures of human rights. Even so, we need to unravel, on this register, some deep perplexities.

[16] One has just to read H.M. Seervai's analyses of some of Krishna Iyer decisions; but see the more thoughtful observations in K.M. Sharma (1981).

First, and as already noted, there is the problem of 'essentializing' Indian constitutionalism that offers some rather quaint summations of its hopefully redemptive potential as a best possible reading of it. Do we read Krishna's radical jurisprudence as a performance of theoretically indigent reading of Dworkin's thesis concerning law as integrity or instead read it as offering a veiled critique? (Baxi 2003). Or, better still, as a deeply southern experientially grounded non-mimetic and inaugural posture towards the end of the north jurisprudential hegemony?

Second, what difference all this may make to acts of reading the nascent comparative constitutionalism forms of talk? Krishna himself complicates an approach to an answer to this question by his penchant for quotational jurisprudence; even his very best disruptive performances remain littered with explosively abundant references to both major and minor authorial figures in the northern jurisprudential landscape that invite further thought, which I do not here pursue, that southern cannibalization of northern discourse may merely avenge the latter. Krishna's multitudinous evocation of north judicial decisions and writings reveal, in their context, both the pathos and bathos of this genre, when transported to some rather extraordinary Indian contexts.

Third, Krishna's transcendentalism provides a narrative of multiple origins that oscillate across such diverse universes signified by names so incommensurate as Marx, Mahatma, and Maharishi Mahesh Yogi![17] 'Transcendental' thus sublimates, in variegated fusions, in Krishna's feeling prose, the forms of dialectical materialism with heady cocktails of diverse Indian spiritualities that complicate any analytic endeavour. Unraveling this mix presents a formidable challenge naming both its 'promise' and 'peril.'

FRIENDS AND ENEMIES

Fourth, Krishna's notion of the divide in the Indian supreme court separates 'deadly enemies' from *caring* friends of constitutional justice and rights. But this binary remains highly, even dangerously, indeterminate (as we know from difficult passages/negotiation that mark many a

---

[17] I apologize for the fact that Krishna's co-equal devotion to Sri Sai Baba thus escapes my alliteration! The abundant references to the Buddhist figure *karuna* (compassion), *daya* (pity), *prem* (love), and *manavatva* (humanism) [See, *Maru Ram v. Union of India* (1981) 1 SCC 107 at 135–6]—to the Indian genre of 'radical humanism'-define this syncretic mix of spiritual and secular ethic.]

movement of discourse from Carl Schmitt to Jacques Derrida) especially when we distinguish the 'normal' from the 'extraordinary' time of
constitutional adjudication. Is then the distinction invidious that celebrates the dissent of Justice H.R. Khanna's in the infamous *Habeas Corpus
Case* during the mid-time of the Indian emergency of 1975–6 and faults
Krishna's ambivalent performance historically paving, by his refusal
to 'stay' the continuation in office of Prime Minister Indira Gandhi in
the face of a judicially declared electoral disqualification? What shall we
say of Krishna's further gratuitous judicial advice that the election law
may be set right by a 'quick acting' legislature that would amend the
Representation of People's Act retroactively to cure this 'venial' vice?
(See the analysis in Baxi 1979; Austin 1999).[18] Of course, the ending
of the emergency rule also provided an astonishing platform for the
enactment of Krishna's *programschrift* for activist judicial populism.
But things may have been *otherwise*, prolonging the political time and
circumstance of emergency to an indefinite future. We would then
have had to revisit any historic evaluation of Krishna's judicial 'activism.' Only the occurrence of judicial luck may then provide a historic
escape route.

It remains true nonetheless that the 'enemies' need not monopolize
the potential for subversion of constitutional 'democracy', 'friends' often
turn out to be 'enemies' of democracy: peoples' representatives frequently
also accomplish this with rather astonishing felicity! Democratic subversion, the worm's eye of the repressed peoples, is unhappily almost as
often the handiwork of friends as well as enemies of 'democracy'.

Krishna engaged in heroic struggles for the transcendence of the
Indian adjudicature before the advent of a hyper-globalizing world, and
the place of India within it. The very terms of discourse that conveyed
his mighty impact have now almost become politically incorrect! Friends
and enemies of democracy now also stand globalized by forces of global
politics, global capitalism, and a new international military order, now
already installed by the 'war on terror'. New conceptions of 'democracy'

[18] In an interview with Chanchal Sarkar and me, in the now discontinued publication *Facets*, Krishna explained to us why he so decided. Although not quite endorsing the propagandist maxim that Indira Gandhi stood between 'order' and 'chaos',
Krishna's best explanation remained that judicial pragmatics, not heroism, was possibly the best move ahead in the political turmoil because he was acting as a single
Judge during the court's summer vacation and he did remit the matter for further
consideration by a constitutional bench. While factually correct, I remain unpersuaded, then and now, by this defensive posture.

and 'good governance' are now fostered in ways that all too often reduce the plentitude of the idea of 'democracy', even jeopardizing the emergent cultures of human rights-friendly governance.[19] The processes, and the prowess of the contemporary north has favoured processes of the emerging global economic constitutionalism (Gill 2003; Schneiderman 2000), now contribute (as much the Cold War) to 'failed decolonization' (as Gayatri Spivak [1999] now terms this). All this raises questions concerning the future of Krishna jurisprudential endowment in a globalizing India.

How may postcolonial judicial activism speak, if at all, to transnational practices of the hegemon as signifying global militant democracy? How may Judges work in close partnership with the anti-globalization global civil society movement, now fully in place? No matter howsoever labeled, how do these practices relate both in terms of cause and effect of within-nation practices of militant democracy? I cannot pursue this theme here except to cryptically recall with Agamben that the 'idea of inner solidarity between democracy and totalitarianism' at a 'historico-philosophical level' manifests itself in the potentiality of the political that at once makes 'it possible both to protect life and authorize the holocaust' (Agamben 1998). Further, it is not entirely clear how Krishna himself would have responded to the specificity of the 'political' aspect of the hyperglobalizing of India in the south, which always constitutes itself as insurgent'. No doubt, his eminent support, upon superannuation, against WTO-TRIPS agreement catalyzed activist opposition to drastic changes in the radical Indian Patent Act (now unfortunately almost fully accomplished). But the complex question indeed remains: How would have Krishna adjudged, from the high bench, the constitutionality of the various macroeconomic measures of disinvestment, denationalization, and deregulation?

---

[19] Highly indebted South States and those whose national economies are continually structurally adjusted by international financial institutions, as well as the three imperatives of globalization (denationalization, disinvestment, and deregulation) quite often lead to mass protests, inviting a substantial measure of state repression. In such South societies, further, multilateral trade agreements such as the WTO, and NAFTA, entail obligations to protect the rights of the 'community' of direct foreign investors, even at the cost of marginalizing civil and political, as well as democratic rights, of citizens. I have described this elsewhere (Baxi 2006: Chapter 8) as the emergent paradigm of trade-related market-friendly human rights at odds with the paradigm of the Universal Declaration of Human Rights.

SUBALTERN VERSUS DOMINANT CONSTITUTIONALISM

One way to understand Krishna's complex theses concerning the judicial role is to say that he has pioneered the discourse of (what I here name as) subaltern Indian constitutionalism that crystallizes citizen practices of *reimaging* democracy, politics, and the fullness of democratic citizenship. Opposed to these are the forms of dominant constitutionalism that enforce these conceptions from the above. Of course, neither notion is monolithic; forms of domination and subalternity remain heterogeneous and they become fluid and porous in concrete historical settings. Like all binary contrasts, this too is an easy prey to techniques of deconstruction; all we may approximate here are Weberian ideal type constructs.

Briefly put, dominant liberal democratic constitutional theory and practice remain primarily concerned with the power to *rule*, its scope, and justification. It structures scope for agency and choice for individuals and groups through languages of human rights and proceduralist notions of democracy. It organizes fields of power/force that sustain possibilities of deliberative politics around representative institutions and processes, where the elected officials play a key role in promoting conceptions of 'development' and national integration/unity amidst the inevitable conflicts of rights and conflicts between sovereign power and dissenting citizens. Citizenship thus emerges, in lived reality, as a freedom to choose forms of subjection.

Dominant constitutionalism serves its distinctive ends through the architecture of the power, in which (as Carl Schmitt memorably urged us to always recall) articulate sovereignty consists not so much in the power to enunciate *rules*, but to pronounce *decisions* concerning the state of *exception*. The ultimate choices celebrating the reason of state authorize supreme executive power to suspend constitutionalism in times of public emergency or through deployment of war or defense power; normative suspension of constitutional order, often beyond the arc of efficacious judicial review power and process, is always writ large in the theory and practice of the dominant liberal constitutionalism. This ideal type description of dominant constitutionalism of course allows a whole range of historical variation.

Subaltern constitutionalism furnishes a multitudinous register of diverse citizen practices; it above all transcends the dominant notions of constitutional fidelity. For what a constitution is, and may mean, is here a mark of the prowess of citizen interpretation claiming a co-equal authoritative status with the 'official' one and often seeks to override the latter. It often constitutes resistance to 'governance' under dominant constitutionalism. The practices of citizen interpretation may be pacific or violent, often admitting negotiation between these two massive forms. Pacific subaltern constitutionalist practices (PSCP) usually respect the major premises of representation and rights woven into the fabrics of the dominant constitutionalism (DC). Yet, the distinction between pacific intent and violent outcomes remains as problematic as any judgment concerning democracy-reinforcing or destructive dimensions of any PSCP formation, which I do not address here. Broadly put, PSCP at least:

a. Constantly interrogate dominant constitutionalism notions of integrity and the unity of state formative practices, and unmask the foundational and reiterative violence (Derrida 1991) of 'nation building'/'national integration' state constitutional practices and promises.
b. Problematize ways of instituting biopolitics (Agamben 1998).
c. Articulate radical reinterpretation of posited visions of rights, development, and justice and speak to the modes of production of human rightlessness and seek to combat this.[20]
d. Renew and reinforce 'constitutional faith';[21] in this even when PSCP produce occasions and bouts of governance legitimation deficits, these remain legible in terms of their constant vulnerability to risks of co-optation by competitive party politics under the DC signatures.
e. Constitute performances (in the Gramscian sense) of 'passive revolution'; their counter hegemonic profile and potential in negotiating state, law, policy, and administration amelioration often end up enhancing the recalcitrance of dominant constitutionalism.[22]

Subaltern constitutionalism, in its different histories, contests concentration of legitimate force monopoly in the state apparatuses and at times speaks to an order of *co-equal* and *legitimate* decentralization of means

---

[20] These practices of subaltern resistance vary enormously in real life of the actually existing dominant liberal constitutionalisms.

[21] To borrow an insightful phrase regime of Sanford Levinson (1988).

[22] Notably available to view in some recent critiques of the rate and nature of compliance with the *Brown v. Board of Education* and the assorted peregrination of its normative progeny; in effect, effete attainments of dismantling the peculiar forms of American apartheid.

of violence under the auspices of non-state actors. The circuits of use and exchange values thus entailed forbid any facile summation, in terms of 'terrorism' and 'state terrorism.'

No incumbent Judge, or constellations of judges, may find it possible to consistently articulate the values and virtues of subaltern constitutionalism; however, Krishna's performance on the summit court exemplifies preciously how far judicial commitment may service subaltern constitutionalism. I here invoke his many-sided juridical and judicial feats (without burdening this contribution by the citational details, readily available in scholarly writings already indicated thus far). *First*, he enshrines, in several decisions, democratization of access to judiciary, especially the supreme court, as a fundamental human right from which all other human rights derive their rationale. *Second*, he is not content with authorizing access (what lawyers call 'standing') but with the real life attainment of justice and rights-oriented outcomes (what public lawyers call 'justiciability'). *Third*, while submitting to collegial judicial discipline that renders capital punishment constitutionally valid in the 'rarest of rare cases', Krishna consistently favours its commutation into life sentences; what he perforce concedes as constitutional, he also finds way to evacuate the retributivist logics at the bar of the life and liberty rights under Article 21. *Fourth*, he confronts the sites of the microfacism of the local state by opening up the 'British Raj' prisons and custodial institutions to practices of a vigilant judicial gaze, contributing to decisional outcomes that outlaw solitary confinement, and related practices of human, and human rights, deprivations in custodial institutions. *Fifth*, he sculpts carefully the human right to compensation for violation of human rights. *Sixth*, Krishna constantly abridges the originary constitutional distance between Part III (declaring fundamental rights) and Part IV (the inherently non-justiciable directive principles of state policy), thus ever ready to use judicial power to translate *basic human needs* into fundamental *rights* and *freedoms*. *Seventh*, in a luminous decision, he affirms, even sanctifies, citizen discretion to disobey manifestly 'illegal' state decisions /orders /actions. The discourse in *Nawab Khan v. State of Gujarat*[23] asserts a citizen disobedience right, without any sure anticipation of judicial validation, as a fundamental human right, which strikes then at the root of state arbitrary power.

All this (and this remains a non-exhaustive register of Krishna's fecund judicial creativity) signifies an extraordinary jurisgenerative

---

[23] *Ahmedabad Municipal Corporation v. Nawab Khan Gulab Khan* (1974) SCC 121.

(Cover 1987) potential of subaltern constitutionalism in its mortal combat with forms of dominant constitutionalism. It variously combats what a leading Ghanian thinker names as 'democratization of disempowerment' (Ake 1994).

In Lieu of a Conclusion

No narration concerning Krishna's exuberant and prolific judicial and juridical contribution towards practices of re-democratizing India may ever truly end! But this much needs to be said: judicial re-democratization of India via transformative judicial praxes is, by no means, a linear process. As Reinhart Kosselleck (2000: 126–8) helps us understand, the 'categories of the space of experience and the horizon of expectations' necessarily diverge in that constitutional conceptions of rights, justice, and development did not possesses at the time of their creation much 'content in terms of experience'; yet, these embody a movement in which '[p]olitical and social concepts become the navigational instruments of the changing movement of history' (p. 128). Understanding Krishna's insurgent jurisprudence then invites 'practices of conceptual history', those that consist in 'timing histories, spacing concepts', if only because they 'themselves become factors in the formation of consciousness and control of behavior' (p. 129).

References

Agamben, Giorgio (1998), *Homo Sacer: Sovereign Power and Bare Life*, translated by Daniel Heller-Roazen, Standard University Press, Stanford.

Ake, Claude (1994), *Democratization of Disempowerment*, Malthouse Press, London.

Austin, Granville (1999), *Working a Democratic Constitutionalism*, Oxford University Press, New Delhi.

Baxi, Upendra (2003), 'A Known But an Indifferent Judge: Situating Ronald Dworkin in Contemporary Indian Jurisprudence', 1 *ICON: International Journal of Constitutional Law*.

————— (2002), *The Future of Human Rights*, Oxford University Press, New Delhi; second edition (2006).

————— (2000), 'The (Im)possibility of Constitutional Justice: Seismographic Notes on Indian Constitutionalism', in Zoya Hasan, E. Sridharan, and R. Sudershan (eds), *India's Living Constitutionalism*, Permanent Black, New Delhi.

————— (1985), *Courage, Craft, and Contention: The Indian Supreme Court in Mid-Eighties*, N.M. Tripathi, Bombay.

————— (1983a), 'Judicial Terrorism: Some Reflections on Mr Justice Tulzapurkar's Pune Speech', *Mainstream* (January 1).

————— (1983b), 'On How Not to Judge the Judges: Notes Towards Evaluation of Judicial Role', *Journal of the Indian Law Institute*.

————— (1979), The *Indian Supreme Court and Politics*, Eastern Book Co., Lucknow.

Cover, Robert (1987), 'Foreword: Nomos and Narrative', 97 *Harvard Law Review*.

Derrida, Jacques (1994), *Scepters of Marx: The State of Debt, the Work of Mourning, and the New International*, Routledge, London.

————— (1991), 'Force of Law...,' 11 *Cardozo Law Review* 919–1045.

Dhavan, Rajeev, Salman Khurshid, and R. Sudershan (eds) (1985), *Judges and Judicial Power: Essays in Honour of Justice V.R. Krishna Iyer*, Sweet & Maxwell, London.

Dyzenhaus, David (2004), *The Unity of Public Law*, Hart Publishing, Oxford and Portland.

Gill Stephen (2003), *Power and Resistance in the New World Order*, Palgrave/ Macmillan, London.

Hallward (2001), *Absolutely Postcolonial: Writing Between the Singular and the Specific*, Routledge, London.

Hardt, Michael and Antonio Negri (2004), *Multitudes*, Penguin, New York.

Hidyatullah, Mohamed (1984), 'Highways and Bylanes of Justice', (1984) 2 *Supreme Court Cases* 1–7.

Iyer, Krishna (1984), 'Democracy of Judicial Remedies', (1984) 4 *Supreme Court Cases*.

Kennedy, Duncan (1997), *A Critique of Adjudication (fin de siecle)*, Harvard University Press, Massachusetts, Cambridge.

Koselleck, Reinhardt (2002), *The Practice of Conceptual History: Timing History, Spacing Concepts*, translated by Todd Samuel Presner *et. al.*, Stanford University Press, Stanford.

Levinson, Sanford (1998), *Constitutional Faith*, Princeton University Press, Princeton.

Negri, Antonio (1999) *Insurgencies: Constitutional Power and the Modern State*, translated by Mazurizia Boscagli, University of Minnesota Press, Minnesota.

Nambyar K.B. (1974), 'Mr Jethmalani and "Judicial Gobbledygook"', (1974) 1 *Supreme Court Cases* 68.

Passavant, A. Paul and Jodi Dean (2004), *Empire's New Clothes: Reading Hardt and Negri*, Routledge, London.

Sathe, Satyaranjan (2002), *Judicial Activism in India: Transgressing Border and Reinforcing Frontiers*, Oxford University Press, New Delhi.

Schneiderman, David (2000), 'Investment Rules and the New Constitutionalism', 25 *Law and Soc. Enquiry*.

Seervai, H.M. (1979), *Constitutional Law of India* (2nd edn), N.M. Tripathi, Bombay.

Sharma, K.M. (1981), 'The Judicial Universe of Mr Justice Krishnan Iyer', (1981) 4 *Supreme Court Cases* 38.

Spivak, Gayatri Chakraborty (1999), *A Critique of Postcolonial Reason: Toward a History of Vanishing Present*, Harvard University Press, Massachusetts, Cambridge.

Swaroop, Hari (1981), *For Whom the Law is Made*, Veena Publications, New Delhi.

Vadenhole, Wouter (2002), 'Human Rights Law, Development, and Social Action Litigation In India', 2 *Asia-Pacific Journal on Human Rights and the Law*.

Young, Robert (2001), *Postcolonialism: An Historical Introduction*, Blackwell, Oxford.

2

Constitutionalization and Realization of Human Rights in India

MAHENDRA P. SINGH

Constitutionalization of human rights is not a new theme. The US Constitution introduced human rights in its text in 1789. Since then, especially since the end of World War II, the constitutions of almost all the countries around the world have incorporated such rights in their text. The War gave special reason and impetus to human rights internationally. Amongst its first major acts, the United Nations adopted the Universal Declaration of Human Rights in 1948, and in pursuance of it, the two Covenants—ICCPR and ICSECR—in 1966. Together they are known as the International Bill of Rights. The Covenants took too long and got bifurcated into two primarily because of the difference of approach to human rights between the capitalist and socialist countries. For the former, human rights inhere in every human being by virtue of his being so, the state must be debarred from interfering in them. For the latter, they are more than non-interference insofar as the state must also ensure or take the responsibility of ensuring that every human being has the opportunity to realize or enjoy these rights. The former argue that if human rights precede state and are not a gift from it, let people be free to enjoy them without state interference. Such non-interference is their best guarantee. The latter do not agree with this argument because according to them, not all people in society have the opportunity to enjoy their inherent rights for reasons of existing inequalities, especially of resources, which are sustained, perpetuated, and increased if the state lets them operate freely. They would, therefore, expect the state to take the responsibility of redistributing or rearranging the resources of the society in a manner that every one is ensured at least a minimum human existence. In short, the former requires non-interference while the latter requires non-interference in some but action in other matters from the state.

Though the two differing political camps have ceased to exist with the demise of socialism in Europe in 1990, the debate about the two views of human rights persists. The rich, industrialized west still supports the former non-interference model while the poor, non-industrialized rest supports the latter active role of the state. It is not that there are no dissents in the west or the rest, but the divide continues. That division sometimes reaches the level of questioning the entire ideology of human rights as a cloak for maintaining the dominance of the rich industrialized countries over the rest. As in the rich industrialized west, the playing field has generally been leveled for most of the people to the extent that they can avail of the opportunities of life almost equally and contribute their best to the society and to themselves, the argument of non-interference from the state becomes and remains attractive.[1] But in poor non-industrialized countries where only a few enjoy most privileges, leaving no possibilities of any opportunities for the rest to get out of their pathetic sub-human existence, the argument of non-interference engenders distrust in the human rights ideology.[2] Therefore, if the human rights ideology is to be successfully universalized it must take into account the realities of all societies around the world. Ignoring that reality generates natural suspicion about the bona fides of the ideology and it is taken to be an invasion of the west on the rest or of the rich over the poor. Many in the west are aware of these dangers and argue for a more rounded concept of human rights.[3] In addition to the social welfare schemes that have been operating in most of the western countries, they are also asking for the

[1] For the proposition that basic needs are no longer an issue in the west, see D. Conrad, 'The Human Right to Basic Necessities of Life', in J. Luett and M.P. Singh (eds), *Zwischen den Traditionen*, Flener, Stuttgart (1999), 289 at 301; also Ulrich K. Preuss, *Constitutional revolution*, Humanities Press International, Atlantic Highlands, 110 ff. (1995).

[2] See, for example, A. Pollis and P. Schwab, 'Human Rights: A Western Construct with Limited Applicability', in A. Pollis and P. Schwab (eds), *Human Rights: Cultural and Ideological Perspectives*, 1 New York Praeger (1980).

[3] See, for example, Ibid., and A.A. An-Naim (ed.), *Human Rights in Cross-Cultural Perspectives*, University of Pennsylvania Press (1992); C.M. Cerna, 'Universality of Human Rights and Cultural Diversity: Implementation of Human Rights in Different Socio-Cultural Contexts', 16 *Human Rights Quarterly* (1994); F.S. Nariman, 'The Universality of Human Rights', 50 *The Review of Int'l Commission of Jurists*, 8 (1993); A. Supiot, 'The Labyrinth of Human Rights Credo or Common Resource', 21 *New Left Review*, 118 (2003).

constitutionalization of social and economic rights in the same way as the civil and political rights have been constitutionalized. For example, relying upon the philosophy of rights as well as the constitutions of mostly non-western countries, Cécile Fabre convincingly makes out a case for the constitutionalization of social rights.[4] Among the social rights he includes 'adequate minimum income, housing, health care, and education'.[5] Differences may exist on the list of these rights but the fact of realization that these rights too need to be listed in the constitution is important. As western countries are slashing age-old welfare schemes at will, possibilities exist for a demand for constitutionalization of these rights even in the west in the near future.[6]

Realizing that the western model of human rights of restraining the state from interfering in the affairs of the individual alone will not get the desired results of ensuring a life with human dignity to a large majority of people in India, the Constitution of India conceived of socio-economic rights from its very inception. The realization had started much before the inception of the constitution, which may have its roots in Indian traditions.[7] We need not go too far into the past but let us examine the immediate background of the constitution, its provisions, their working, and impact upon the human rights situation in India.

INDIA'S STRUGGLE FOR INDEPENDENCE[8]

Like every other society, India may have passed through experiences and developments not shared by others. For well over one hundred years it was under British rule until 1947. But it had started expressing its

[4] *Social Rights under the Constitution*, Oxford University Press, Oxford (2000).

[5] Ibid., at 4.

[6] Reference may be made to European Charter of Social Rights as well as the demand and debate on this issue among other western countries including the US. See, for example, F.I. Michelman, 'The Constitution, Social Rights, and Liberal Political Justification', in *International Journal of Constitutional Law* (2003) and T. Daintith, *The Constitutional Protection of Economic Rights*, ibid., 56 (2004). Also J. Kothari, 'Social Rights and the Constitution', (2004) 6 SCC (J) 31.

[7] For Indian tradition of Human Rights, see M.P. Singh, 'Tracing the Human Rights to Ancient Indian Tradition—its Relevance to the Understanding and Application of the International Bill of Rights', 1 *Indian journal of juridical sciences*, 137 (2003) and M.P. Singh, 'Human Rights in the Indian Tradition—Alternatives in the Understanding and Realization of the Human Rights Regime, 63 *Zeitschrift fuer auslaendisches oeffentlisches Recht und Voelkerrecht* (*Heidelberg Journal of International Law*), 551 (2003).

[8] Matter in this and some of the subsequent parts has been taken from M.P. Singh, 'Human Rights in the Indian Perspective', 25 *Kansas University Review of Law and Politics*, 17 (2004).

rejection of that rule even before it was formally established in 1858.[9] Well before the close of the century its leaders had started organizing movements for freedom and for human rights.[10] Firstly, they claimed that independence from British rule was their birthright and secondly, until that claim was met, they asked for the same rights as the British had in Great Britain. In the light of the emergence of socialistic ideology and the acceptance of the concept of a social welfare state from the middle of the nineteenth century in Great Britain and several other parts of Europe, as well as their understanding of India and its needs, the leaders of the independence movement started demanding the positive rights of the people along with their negative rights before the end of the nineteenth century. Thus in the Constitutional Bill of Rights of 1895, along with the right to freedom of speech, assembly, etc. they also demanded the right to free education.[11] These demands were multiplied in the subsequent demands for constitutional reforms in the early twentieth century including in Mrs Annie Besant's Constitutional Bill of 1925, the Nehru Report on Constitutional Reforms in 1928, the Karachi Resolution of 1931, and the Sapru Report on the future Constitution of India in 1945. Finally, under the Cabinet Mission Plan of 1946, the British rulers accepted their demand and gave them the opportunity to make, through their elected Constituent Assembly (CA), their constitution which should have a bill of rights.[12]

As the Assembly first met at the beginning of December 1946, it decided to appoint an Advisory Committee on the constitution as envisaged by the Cabinet Mission Plan. Among the first tasks the Advisory Committee performed was the creation of the Fundamental Rights Sub-committee with the responsibility of preparing a list of fundamental rights (FRs). Even before the declaration of independence, the Sub-Committee produced its report on the FRs in the early part of 1947. The most notable feature of the report was the inclusion of both the negative as well as the positive rights of the individual. However, it titled the former as justiciable and the later as non-justiciable rights.[13] In course

[9] In 1857 there was an unsuccessful violent revolt against the British.

[10] The Indian National Congress, the political organization that ultimately led to freedom from British rule, was founded in 1885.

[11] See Shiva Rao (ed.), *The framing of India's Constitution*, vol. I, p. 5, Indian Institute of Public Affairs, New Delhi (1966).

[12] For details see ibid.

[13] For details see ibid., vol. II, 21ff. On the relevance of justiciability, see M.P. Singh, 'The Statics and the Dynamics of the Fundamental Rights and the Directive Principles—A Human Rights Perspective', (2003) 5 SCC (J), p. 1ff.

of time, with necessary adjustments and changes, the former became the FRs and the latter the directive principles of state policy (DPs) in Parts III and VI respectively of the constitution.[14] Emphasising that this division was the creation of the CA and not of 'the leaders of the independence movement [who] had drawn no distinction between the positive and negative obligations of the state', Granville Austin notes:

> The Fundamental Rights and directive principles had their roots deep in the struggle for independence. And they were included in the Constitution in the hope and expectation that one day the tree of true liberty would bloom in India. The Rights and Principles thus connect India's future, present and past, adding greatly to the significance of their inclusion in the Constitution, and giving strength to the pursuit of the social revolution in India.[15]

FUNDAMENTAL RIGHTS AND DIRECTIVE PRINCIPLES

To mention briefly the scheme of the FRs and DPs, the former are included in Part III of the constitution comprising Articles 12 to 35. They were originally divided into seven parts consisting of the right to equality, the right to freedom, the right against exploitation, the right to freedom of religion, the rights of the minorities, the right to property and the right to enforce the FRs. The right to property was deleted from the FRs in 1979 and placed in a new Article 300A. Interesting aspects of FRs for the present purpose are that some of them are available not only against the state but also against private persons or groups. Further, some of them impose positive obligations on the state to take affirmative actions for the realization of the rights of those, particularly the former untouchables and the aborigines designated as the Scheduled Castes (SCs) and the Scheduled Tribes (STs) respectively in the constitution, who could not avail of them in the ordinary course and in the absence of such action.[16] Finally, special care is bestowed upon religious and linguistic minorities.[17]

As regards the DPs, they are placed in Part IV of the constitution comprising Articles 36 to 51. Their spirit is expressed in Article 38, which reads:

(1) The state shall strive to promote the welfare of the people by securing and protecting as effectively as it may, a social order in which

[14] See Granville Austin, *The Indian Constitution: Cornerstone of a Nation*, Oxford University Press, New Delhi, 50ff. (1966).

[15] Ibid., at 50.

[16] See for example, Articles 15(3) & (4) and 16 (4), (4A) & (4B).

[17] See Articles 29 and 30.

justice, social, economic and political, shall inform all the institutions of the national life.

(2) The state shall, in particular, strive to minimize the inequalities in income, and endeavour to eliminate inequalities in status, facilities and opportunities, not only amongst individuals but also amongst groups of people residing in different areas or engaged in different vocations.

The other DPs include right to adequate means of livelihood, equal pay for equal work, distribution of ownership and control of material resources so as to best subserve the common good, operation of the economic system in a way that it does not result in the concentration of wealth and means of production to the common detriment, protection and development of children, free legal aid, right to work, education and public assistance, maternity relief, living wages, suitable conditions of work and a decent standard of life, free and compulsory education for children up to the age of fourteen years, promotion of educational and economic interests of SCs, STs, and other weaker sections of the people, raising the level of nutrition and standard of living and improving of public health, etc.

In addition to FRs and DPs, the constitution has several provisions on human rights providing for negative rights as well as for positive obligations. For example, the equal right of all to participate in the political process on the basis of adult franchise is provided in Articles 325 and 326 and the fairness of electoral process is ensured in Articles 324 to 329. Part XVI, comprising Articles 330 to 342 makes special provisions for the representation of SCs, STs, and the Anglo-Indians in the national parliament and state legislatures by reserving certain number of seats for them. It also makes provision for special educational grants and representation in certain state services for the Anglo-Indians and also for the SCs and STs.[18] Other provisions in that part provide for elaborate machinery for the protection of the SCs, STs, and other backward classes, including the appointment of commissions from time to time for the STs and other backward classes and a permanent national commission for all of them.[19] Special safeguards and machinery are also provided for the linguistic minorities in Part XVII of the constitution.[20] For the better administration of the predominantly tribal areas special provisions are

---

[18] Articles 335–7.
[19] Articles 338–40.
[20] Articles 350–1.

made in Articles 244 and 244A and in Schedules V and VI of the constitution. Provision is also made for the appointment of a tribal welfare minister in some of the states.[21] On the same lines some amendments of the constitution have introduced special provisions for the SCs, STs, women and other weaker sections of the society. For example, Part IVA comprising Article 51A introduced in 1976, imposes certain fundamental Duties (FDs) on the citizens which, among others, ensure dignity of women, common brotherhood among people and protection of environment. Parts IX and IXA, introduced in 1992, make special provisions for the representation, including in the chief executive positions, of the SCs, STs, and women in the village panchayats and the municipalities respectively. Discussions have long been going on for the amendment of the constitution to provide representation to women in the national parliament and the state legislatures.

From this brief description of the elaborate provisions in the constitution, it is clear that almost coinciding with the Universal Declaration of Human Rights and much before the ICCPR and the ICESCR, the Constitution of India had expressed all that is covered in those documents and more. The most notable aspect of the constitution is the recognition of state's obligation to ensure human rights to everyone and not only to those who can make full use of them.

INTERPRETATION AND APPLICATION OF RIGHTS

It is generally felt and admitted that the constitution has not been able to achieve as much on the human rights front as was expected of it. There may be numerous reasons for it including the lack of adequate political will. But as a student of law, when I examine the constitutional interpretation and application over the last half a century, I come to the conclusion that if there has been any lack of understanding of the spirit of the constitution and its makers, it has been more on the part of the lawyers and judges than on the part of the policy makers—the legislators and the executive. To take only two examples in this regard, I may mention the cases of application of special obligation of the state to promote the social, economic, and educational interests of the weaker sections of the society provided in one of the DPs and the distribution of economic resources of the society in such a way as to best serve the common good provided in another.[22] In both the instances, when the courts invalidated

[21] Article 164.
[22] Articles 39 (b) & (c) and 46.

the state actions and legislations just after the commencement of the constitution, making the DPs subordinate to the FRs, the provisional parliament, which was only the new name for the CA, amended the constitution to ensure harmony between the FRs and the DPs.[23] Later, the supreme court also decided that harmony between the FRs and the DPs is one of the basic features of the Indian constitution, which cannot be changed even by an amendment of the constitution.[24] Similarly, on the issue of land reforms, which sought to abolish the numerous intermediaries between the state and the tiller of the land, and of the industrial and other economic regulations including nationalization of major resources of the society—which were declared invalid by the courts because they conflicted with the individual's right to property—the provisional parliament changed the situation by the same amendment.[25] On the issue of property, however, the controversy persisted until, in 1979, the right to property was deleted from the FRs.[26] It is not that the right to property is no more protected; it is argued that it is better protected than ever before.[27] The relevant legislation on expropriation of property has also been so amended as to meet the international standards.[28] But the message of the constitutional amendments is clear: the positive obligations of the state cannot be taken less seriously than its negative obligations and if at any point there appears any conflict between the two they have to be so reconciled and harmonized that both are given effect without undermining the position of either.

When, after more than two decades of the commencement of the constitution and positive state action, it became clear that the position of the weaker sections of the society had not sufficiently improved, the state reinforced these measures from the middle of the seventies.

[23] See *State of Madras* v. *Champakam Dorairajan* AIR 1951 SC 226 and the introduction of Article 15(4) by the Constitution (1st Amendment) Act, 1951.

[24] *Minerva Mills Ltd.* v. *Union of India* AIR 1980 SC 1789.

[25] See *Kameshwar Singh* v. *State* AIR 1951 Pat. 91, *Charanjit Lal Chowdhury* v. *Union of India* AIR 1951 SC 41 and the introduction of Articles 31A and 31B by the Constitution (1st Amendment) Act, 1951.

[26] The Constitution (44th Amendment) Act, 1978 deletion of Article 31 and introduction of Article 300A.

[27] P.K. Tripathi, 'Right to Property after Forty-Fourth Amendment: Better Protected than ever Before', 66 AIR (Journal) 49 (1980).

[28] See the Land Acquisition Act, 1894 and M.P. Singh, 'Expropriation in India', in G.M. Erasmus (ed.), *Compensation for Expropriation: A Comparative Study*, (Jason Reese in association with the United Kingdom National Committe of Comparative Law) Oxford, 1990.

By now, the courts had also started upholding them. A major political doubt arose about the advisability of such measures when in 1990 the central government implemented the recommendations of the Backward Class Commission on the quota for the backward classes in state jobs. Interestingly, when the then main opposition party in parliament won the elections a few months later, instead of withdrawing the disputed action of its predecessor, it broadened its scope. The supreme court upheld the original action of the outgoing government but invalidated the broadened version of it because it diluted the objective of positive obligation by favouring those whom the Constitution did not intend to include within that obligation.[29] Some aspects of the judgment, which were likely to be interpreted against the interest of the backward classes, particularly SCs and STs, were remedied by constitutional amendments.[30] While on this issue the supreme court was for long going along the dominant understanding of the constitutional provisions and policy, pending mid-term elections to parliament in 1999, it gave at least two decisions, which were out of tune with the constitutional developments and against the constitutional commitment to the weakest sections of society.[31] After the elections, parliament again abrogated these decisions by suitably amending the constitution.[32] It has also extended the period of political representation for the SCs, STs, and the Anglo-Indians until 2010.[33] It is notable that the amendments were carried out unanimously.

Apart from these two areas, which involved the balancing of the so-called civil and political rights on the one hand, and of the social and economic rights on the other, the other notable development in human rights is the supreme court's widening approach to fundamental rights, particularly the right to life under Article 21, since 1978. In *Francis Coralie Mullin*, the court held:

We think the right to life includes the right to live with human dignity and all that goes along with it, namely, the bare necessaries of life such as adequate

[29] See *Indra Sawhney* v. *Union of India* AIR 1992 SC 477.

[30] See the Constitution (77th Amendment) Act, 1995, S. 2 inserting cl. (4-A) in Art. 16 and the Constitution (81st Amendment) Act, 2000, S. 2 inserting cl. (4-B) in Art. 16.

[31] See *Preeti Srivastava (Dr)* v. *State of M.P.* (1999) 7 SCC 44 and *Ajit Singh (II)* v. *State of Punjab* (1999) 7 SCC 209.

[32] See the Constitution (81st Amendment) Act, 2000, S. 2 and the Constitution (85th Amendment) Act, 2001, S. 2 amending cl. (4-A) of Art. 16 retrospectively w.e.f. 17 June 1995.

[33] See Art. 334 and the Constitution (79th Amendment) Act, 1999, S. 2.

nutrition, clothing and shelter over the head and facilities for reading, writing and expressing oneself in diverse forms, freely moving about and mixing and commingling with fellow human beings.[34]

Since then, in a number of cases the court has held that the right to life includes the right to clean environment,[35] health and medical care,[36] livelihood,[37] right to access to resources of livelihood,[38] right to education,[39] right to shelter,[40] right to food,[41] and so on. Similarly, under the concept of liberty, it has evolved several rights for accused persons such as speedy trial,[42] free legal aid,[43] good prison conditions and freedom from torture in custody,[44] freedom from cruel and unusual punishment,[45] etc. For the enforcement of these and many other rights the court has also expanded the concept of locus standi or standing and it permits any person having sufficient interest in the matter to invoke the jurisdiction of the court for the enforcement of the rights of those who cannot for any reasons, including social and economic, approach the court.[46] The court can also take *suo motu* action on the basis of information received from newspaper reports or otherwise.[47] It also encourages writing of letters to the court on the violation of human rights and treating those letters as petitions for remedying such violations.[48] It can also give any remedy in matters that it considers appropriate, including the restoration of *status quo ante* and payment of compensation.[49] Consequently, social

[34] *Francis Coralie* v. *Union Territory of Delhi* AIR 1981 SC 746, 753.

[35] See a large number of cases starting with *RLEK* v. *State of UP* AIR 1987 SC 2426.

[36] See, for example, *Paschim Banga Khet Mazdoor Samity* v. *State of W.B.* (1996) 4 SCC 37.

[37] *Olga Tellis* v. *Bombay Municipal Corporation* AIR 1986 SC 180.

[38] *State of H.P.* v. *Umed Ram* AIR 1986 SC 847.

[39] *Unni Krishnan* v. *State of A.P.* (1993) 1 SCC 645.

[40] *Gauri Shankar* v. *Union of India* (1994) 6 SCC 349.

[41] *PUCL* v. *Union of India* 2003 (9) SCALE 835.

[42] See catena of cases starting with *Hussainara Khatoon* v. *Home Secretary, Bihar,* AIR 1979 SC 1369.

[43] *M.H. Hoskot* v. *State of Maharashtra* AIR 1978 SC 1548 and several other later cases.

[44] See several cases starting with *Sunil Batra* v. *Delhi Administration* AIR 1978 SC 1675.

[45] *Parmanand Katara* v. *Union of India* (1995) 3 SCC 248.

[46] See *S.P. Gupta* v. *Union of India* AIR 1982 SC 149 and *Bandhua Mukti Morcha* v. *Union of India* AIR 1984 SC 802.

[47] *M.C. Mehta* v. *Union of India* AIR 1987 SC 1086.

[48] Ibid.

[49] Ibid.

action groups and NGOs frequently approach the supreme court and the high courts for the enforcement of human rights of the vulnerable sections of the society. Such actions quite often involve major issues such as positive action for environment protection and direction to stop large projects having an injurious effect on the rights of the people such as displacement by the construction of big dams and the rights to work and food.[50] Thus, barring the issues that involved the balancing of conflicting rights mentioned in the beginning of this section, the courts have been playing an important role in the creation of a human rights culture. It is notable that the state has not resented courts' expansion of human rights. It has rather supported them as it recently did, for example, by incorporating the court-created right to education into the constitution by an amendment.[51]

The state has also been consistently taking legislative and administrative measures for the realization of the rights of large sections of society comprising weaker sections such as SCs, STs, backward classes, and women. Legislations like the Civil Rights Act, 1955, Equal Remuneration Act, 1975, Bonded Labour Abolition Act, 1976, Contract Labour Act, 1976, Atrocities Against Harijans Act, 1989, Indecent Depiction of Women Act, 1989, and a host of other legislations in support of the rights of the weaker sections of the society have been enacted.

For effective safeguard, enforcement, and realization of human rights of all and of the vulnerable sections of society the state has also established a few commissions. Among them are the National Commission for Women, the National Commission for Minorities, the National Commission and State Commissions for Backward Classes, the National Commission for the SCs and STs, and finally, the National and State Commissions for Human Rights. While the other commissions are for the specific purposes for which they are created, the National and State Commissions for Human Rights take care of the general enforcement and realization of human rights in all walks of life. These commissions have wide powers of enquiries and investigations of the violations of human rights and of making necessary recommendations including the recommendations for interim relief and monetary compensation. They

---

[50] See, for example, *Narmada Bachao Andolan* v. *Union of India* (2000) 10 SCC 664.

[51] The Constitution (86th Amendment) Act, 2002 inserting Article 21-A. The Amendment also inserts a fundamental duty in clause (*k*) of Article 51-A to provide opportunities for education to children between the age of six and fourteen years. It may, however, be pointed out that in some ways the right introduced by amendment is narrower than the right recognized by the court.

also undertake human rights education and awareness programmes under which human rights courses have been introduced in the universities, particularly in the law faculties. The commissions also collaborate with NGOs in promoting and protecting human rights. The recommendations of these commissions are taken seriously and generally implemented by the governments.

As regards the international arena, India is a signatory to most of the international declarations, conventions, and covenants on human rights, including in particular, the UDHR, ICCPR, and ICESCR. Although as a general rule, international law does not prevail over the national law, in the arena of human rights the courts have repeatedly held that unless there is anything to the contrary in the national law, the international standards of human rights apply and are part of the law of the land.[52]

A Theory of Human Rights for India[53]

The foregoing discussion should leave no doubt about India's concern for human rights through their constitutionalization and otherwise. But the ground realities of human rights in India are far from satisfactory. For this unsatisfactory situation, blame is sometimes assigned to Indian tradition which is supposed to be anti-human rights. Even if it is not disputed that the current idea of human rights is a product of the west, it should not automatically lead to the conclusion that Indian tradition is opposed to it.

Maybe a few practices in Indian tradition were not consistent with the idea of human rights. But its leaders and true followers have successfully denounced such practices as corruption of the tradition. To take only recent examples, Swami Dayananda, a firm believer in the Vedic tradition, denounced the caste system and subordination of women as manipulation of that tradition. Rammohan Roy, Vivekananda, Gandhi, and many others did the same. Gandhi even threatened to renounce Hinduism if anyone could prove that untouchability was one of its tenets. That such practices were corruptions of the tradition is evident from their rejection in the constitution, which not only prohibits caste and sex based discriminations and the practice of untouchability but also provides for remedial action against their past impacts. If caste or sex based discriminations and practice of untouchability still continue, the

---

[52] See, for example, *Visakha v. State of Rajasthan* AIR 1997 SC 3011.

[53] Matter in this part has been taken from M.P. Singh, 63 *Heidelberg Journal of International Law* cited in n. 5 above.

blame cannot be assigned to tradition. They are not part of any authoritative and binding tradition, either past or present. If any justifications are cited for them in tradition, they are the same as the privileged and powerful in any society find in their self-interest. Compared to similar justifications in many other traditions and societies, they are, however, much milder. Examples of religious traditions not treating non-believers as human beings and of traditions excluding human beings from that category in the name of slaves or even treating women as less than human beings are not unknown.[54] Indian tradition never went to that extent. Therefore, tradition is no excuse for the poor record of human rights in India. It could at the most be a pretence not to face a much more complex issue. Blaming the tradition serves no purpose either. Tradition can neither be created retrospectively nor can it be disowned or even discarded overnight.[55] Experiments such as change from Hinduism to Christianity, Sikhism, Buddhism, or Islam to overcome the caste system or untouchability yield no results because the same practices become part of these latter religions too. The only possible solution could be the unearthing of the best in tradition, which has been buried deep by the vested interests, and to use it to the realization of the human rights of each and every one of us as the constitution does and the persons named above and many others before and after them have done or are doing.

Following such an approach to human rights in India, I find historians doubting the authenticity of the social history of India drawn entirely on the *Dharmasastra* and other extant literature.[56] The lived history is yet to be known from the archaeological surveys and other findings made possible by scientific and technological innovations in the research methods. However, the consideration of human rights cannot be postponed until the availability of such findings. It must be addressed with whatever information we have. Broadly speaking, available history gives us the picture of the king or ruler in India, before the establishment of Islamic rule, as the creation of the requirement of *dharma* in order to uphold it. Drawing one coherent picture of society operating under dharma, which bound every one including the ruler, the *Dharmasastra* did not differentiate between the religious and temporal power beyond

[54] See, for example, on caste system, untouchabilty, status of women, and slavery see V.P. Nanda, 'Hinduism and Human Rights', V.P. Nanda and S.P. Sinha (eds), *Hindu Law and Legal Theory*, 237 (New York University Press, 1996).

[55] Even revolutions take a long time to make a dent in it, see H.J. Berman, *Law and Revolution*, 18 (Harvard university Press, 1993).

[56] See, for example, R. Thapar, *Ancient Indian Social History* (1978).

creating an additional branch of dharma called *rajdharma* assigning some special powers and responsibilities to the ruler for the administration of the state.[57] Society in India did not experience conflict and subsequent separation between these two powers. Nor could the rulers exercise unlimited powers and become autocrats or tyrants.[58] Beyond taking law and order matters into their own hands, Islamic rulers also did not disturb this arrangement. Islamic rulers were not bound by dharma as expounded in the Indian tradition, but generally they did not interfere in matters of dharma. The British rulers also did not disturb this arrangement except to the extent necessary for their trade interests or as demanded by the Hindus or Muslims in their own matters respectively. Society in general, mostly rural, did not come much in touch with the state. It also did not pass through the stages experienced by western societies, such as the fight for supremacy between the church and the state and their subsequent separation as two independent institutions, religious reformation, feudalism, manorial system, mercantilism, creation of a powerful state, industrial revolution, imperialism and colonialism, and the creation of a civil society primarily representing liberal values.[59] All these factors along with material prosperity made western societies rights-conscious. In the absence of these factors, Indian society did not develop that consciousness.[60] Such a consciousness seems to have come for the first time to the leaders of independence movement from their dealings with the British government and contact with the west. But it did not percolate into the masses beyond the consciousness of self-rule and getting rid of the foreign power. Consequently, the masses remained unaware of current ideas of human rights. The incorporation of that idea in the constitution or other laws and the endorsement of the International Bill of Rights also make little difference for them.

As the state, until its independence from British rule, performed limited functions and the masses did not have much contact with it, their dealings remained confined to themselves perhaps more under the customary practices than even under the norms laid down in

[57] For details, see P.V. Kane, *History of Dharmasastra*, vol. III, 56ff. (1962) and R. Lingat, *The Classical Law of India*, 207ff. (1998).

[58] See J.D.M. Derrett, 'Hindu Law', in J.D.M. Derrett (ed.), *An Introduction to Legal Systems*, 80ff. (1968).

[59] For details of these developments in the west, see Berman, above n. 50.

[60] See R. Kothari, 'Human Rights—A Movement in Search of a Theory', 5 *Lokayan Bulletin*, 17 (1987). Also see A. Varshney, *Ethnic conflict and civil life*, 2002, 23 ff.

Dharmasastra.[61] These practices also determined their rights and duties. Any deviation from these practices met social sanctions and excepting rare cases they were enforced through social pressure and not through litigation. If social pressure did not work in someone's case, primarily because of his weaker position in society, he also invoked the curse of the divine powers that should punish the wrong doer if not in this life, in the next.[62] Roughly this is the background in which the Indian state, after its independence from British rule, took over the responsibility of protecting the rights of the people on the western model. Naturally, in this background, the masses either have little idea of these rights or consider the state as their creator and protector and not as their violator. The state appears to them as restorer of their due in society. In the west on the contrary, from the Magna Carta through the Bill of Rights, the French Declaration of Rights of Men and the Citizen, the US Bill of Rights and even later, the privileged sections of the society claimed their rights against the state. The position of the individual vis-à-vis the state in India is just the reverse of the west. The individual as a privileged person did not ask the state to refrain from disturbing his privileges but like the ancient ruler consecrated in dharma the creators of the Indian state decided to restore to the individual what was his due. They decided that not only shall the state refrain from interfering in his autonomy and dignity but also take positive steps to secure to him his autonomy and dignity.

Thus, the realization of human rights in India is not as much a question of the individual's claim against the state as of the responsibility of the state. Whether the individual asks for his rights or not, the state must secure them to him. The state must know that the people have rights irrespective of their demand for them and that not only has it to honour them by non-interference but has also to secure them to each and every person by positive action. It is not merely an expectation from the state based on any principle of morality, fairness, or international law but a constitutional command.[63] The state and its apparatus can appreciate this command far more easily than the masses appreciating

[61] See W.F. Menski, 'Comparative Law in Global Context: The Legal Systems of Asia and Africa', 156 (Platinum, London, 2000) that people were governed more by *sadachara*, which means custom, than by *dharmasastra*.

[62] See R.S. Khare, 'Elusive Social Justice, Distant Human Rights: Untouchable Women's Struggles and Dilemmas in Changing India', M.R. Anderson and S. Guha (eds), *Changing Concepts of Rights and Justice in South Asia*, 198 (Oxford University Press, 1998).

[63] See the Constitution of India, inter alia, Parts III, IV, IV-A, and XVI.

the idea of their claims. Of course, such an understanding of human rights may not be consistent with the theories of rights in the west, but it is fully consistent with the Indian tradition that the state is subject to its dharma and it must observe it. If it does not, it has no justification to exist and must be replaced. We need not invoke tradition for this purpose because the constitution is the law that binds the state. This kind of understanding of human rights, however, raises the questions: Firstly, why should the state care for the rights of the people unless they demand them? And secondly, what can people do if the state does not care for their rights? The questions are germane and must be answered. My argument is not that the people may sleep over their rights and that it does not matter whether they demand them or not. It matters. Vigilance is the price of liberty. They must be vigilant and keep the state alert that they care for their rights and will not let it deny or curtail them. They must have provision for legal as well as political action if the state tries to deny them their rights. As the masses in India lack adequate rights consciousness as well as the means to enforce their rights, legal awareness alone is not and cannot be enough and effective. Legality is the *sine qua non* for the rule of law, but it does not mean that it is attained only through court action without regard for it by state and political action. The rule of law itself is a consequence of and dependent upon political action.[64] In India, as we have noted above, the constitution clearly sanctions political rather than legal action for the realization of at least social and economic rights. Indian tradition, which speaks of the duties and justifications of the state only in terms of the welfare of the people, could also be invoked in support of the constitution for political action.[65] Such an action is far more effective in the creation of rights consciousness as well as the conditions for their realization than legal action. But as every person is not in a position to invoke political action, he cannot be left at the contingency of such action. Each and every person must be in the position of defending one's rights all the time. Therefore, effective individual action must also be available to him. Political action is, however, a condition precedent even for the provision of individual action. It cautions the state against the dangers of any infraction of his rights. Political action is also required for the realization of human rights in India through the western strategy of litigation because firstly, the courts are also part of state machinery and need to be sensitized about the rights

[64] J. Waldron, *The Law*, 29ff. (1990).
[65] For the justification of state in the Indian tradition, see among others the works cited in n. 52 above.

of the people, and secondly, the existing courts are utterly inadequate and incapable of ensuring the realization of rights.[66]

Further, unlike the west where people in general have reached a level of economic and social well being which they need to defend and promote through civil and political rights, in India most of the violations of these rights occur because of the absence of such well being. Therefore, in India, the question is not whether the social and economic rights are rights or not but whether the conditions precedent for the realization of such rights exist. Unless those conditions exist, violations of the rights cannot be effectively dealt with. These violations are not as much by the state as by the privileged and powerful elements within the state. The rights of the people need to be protected more from these elements than from the state. Such protection cannot be afforded just by restraining the state from interference in the affairs of the individual; it requires positive action from the state not just in the form of policing the individual but through his empowerment. The pattern of violations of human rights in India is a clear indicator that empowerment of the weak and the vulnerable is the key to the improvement of the human rights situation. Such an empowerment is not possible without state support and action. Therefore, while there are a few matters in which the state must keep off, there are many more matters in which positive state action is required. Unless the state undertakes the responsibility of taking such action, the human rights situation cannot improve. It does not mean that either the state must be left free to do whatever it likes or that the individual must be totally dependent upon the state. What is needed is that the individual and the state in close cooperation with each other work out a strategy that ensures empowerment of the weak and vulnerable and also guards against the misuse of the state by the privileged and powerful. A kind of state which Gandhi had envisaged before independence which will not simply be a transfer of power from one ruler to the other but a state that cares for its citizens.[67] This is not an argument of any new theory of human rights but an effort to understand the reasons for the current poor situation of human rights in India and to find suitable solutions for it. The empowerment of the weak by at least satisfying his basic necessities of life is the most apparent solution, and cannot be brought in just by

[66] See, for example, Conrad's lamentation that India does not meet the essential conditions of rule of law because it does not provide enough courts for the enforcement of law. D. Conrad, Die Zukunft des indischen Rechtsstaates, in n. 1 above at 135.

[67] This idea is being realized and promoted by the state. See n. 75 below and the 15 August 2004 speech of the Prime Minister of India.

the strategy of litigation and adversarial action but requires an understanding on the part of the state that it must take certain positive steps.

Again, morality is the basis of all rights.[68] Every right needs a moral justification. Any claim that lacks such a justification cannot acquire the status of right. Tradition may not supply the moral basis in specific details for all the rights that we have today but it provides the germs for most of them, if not all. Morality has been the basis of all the rights and duties in all the traditions expressed in religious texts, philosophical writings or otherwise. Dharma in the Indian tradition supported by the Islamic and Christian traditions, which joined it later, creates the moral base for the rights expressed in legal language today. In a tradition-bound society like India, the language of morals has greater receptivity than the language of law or rights. Therefore, morals must also be resorted to, to improve the position of human rights. Everyone, especially the state and its apparatus, as well as the privileged and the powerful in society must be reminded of their moral obligations towards the underprivileged and deprived masses. This is what the men named above successfully did for securing rights to the people more than any declaration of rights and their legal enforcement has done so far. Among them, particularly Gandhi, as political leader at the forefront of the independence movement and visionary of the future India propounded, inter alia, the concept of trusteeship in which the haves held material resources of the society in trust for the have-nots and not for their self enjoyment and aggrandizement.[69] Others dug out similar moral bases from tradition for uprooting birth and sex based discriminations and other social injustices. In Indian society, where the modern state has been a latecomer and detached from the masses, moral obligations appeal more effectively than the legal. Even though the moral standards of the common man may not be very high they enjoy a higher place than the legal ones. For him, the moral duties of compassion, truth, non-injury, and non-interference with the person or property of others or of support and help to the needy and weak as cherished virtues hailed by tradition appeal more than mere legal obligations without such a moral base. Moral duty could also be fortified with the religious belief that good deeds in this life lead to *moksha* or a better life in the next. The argument of morality is, however, not a

---

[68] See generally, Ronald Dworkin, *Taking Rights Seriously*, Harvard University Press (1977) (reprinted 1996); J. Waldron, *Theories of Rights*, Oxford University Press, New York (1984) and *The Law*, 92 (1990).

[69] See Conrad, n. 1 above at 191.

substitute for legality; it is a supplement to it for the realization of human rights in India.

Finally, though human rights are conceived primarily as protection against the tyranny of the majority even in a constitutional democracy, the ultimate hope for those rights lies in the democratic process. Apparently India is projected as a Hindu majority state, but neither are the Hindus a monolithic unit nor is religion the basis for the political minorities and majorities. India is famously called a country only of minorities and of no majorities.[70] There are other bonds stronger than religion among the Hindus that keep them divided and sometimes also bring them in identity with non-Hindus. Even though at times it appears as if the people are becoming united along religious issues, political surveys and researches prove that in politics, social and economic issues stand above religion.[71] As the majority of people whose rights are most frequently violated are from the poor and deprived sections of society, democratic process is the most potent and promising weapon for the protection of their rights. A healthy democracy alone can ensure that the privileged and the powerful do not exploit the state and its apparatus in their self-interest. As Rawls suggests, a healthy democracy is also the best assurance of determining the priorities and contents of rights and justice.[72] The national elections in May 2004 have established this point to the extent that in spite of good performance of the government on economic front, it was defeated because it did not care for the basic rights of the masses. The masses, therefore, voted for those who promised a better deal to them.

Summing Up

In this brief statement on the position of, and strategies for, the realization of human rights in India, I have tried to establish that in spite of the claim of universality of Human Rights, their content, perspectives, and priorities may differ from society to society.[73] During colonial rule, people of India had experienced the lack of recognition of negative obligations of the state and reliance of the state on the privileged sections of society

[70] S. Tharoor, *India*, 112 (1997).

[71] For a recent survey see A.K. Jha, 'NDA On a Slide', in: *India Today*, 28 (25 August 2003).

[72] J. Rawls, *Political Liberalism* (Columbia University Press, New York, 1993).

[73] Even the concept of universality itself is subject to differing interpretations. See A. Sharma, *Hinduism and Human Rights*, 122ff. (Oxford University Press, 2003).

including the princes, feudal lords, property owners, and high caste or class of people. These sections of society had a hold on its vast resources without regard to the interests of the masses. The leaders of the independence movement were fully aware of the enormous inequities and injustices in society, some of which existed even before colonial rule, but others either created or perpetuated during that rule. Their struggle for independence was not merely for freedom from colonial rule, but also for the removal of the existing inequities and injustices. On the attainment of independence in 1947, they had the choice of achieving their goal either by authoritarian rule or through the rule of law and constitutionalism of the western style. Consciously and after due deliberation, they decided in favour of the latter. But they knew well that conditions in India were not the same or similar as in the west. Therefore, they could not leave the individual and his enterprise unregulated. For that would have amounted to perpetuation of existing inequities and injustices in the society at the cost of denial of the very basic human rights of its vast masses. It is for that reason that they gave as much importance to the positive obligations of the state as to the negative. They required the state not only to not violate the civil and political rights of the people but also to take affirmative action for the realization of social and economic rights necessary for the enjoyment of the former. Had they not done so, the constitution and the rule of law on which it is based and which it promotes would have failed even before the take-off stage. At the time of the adoption of the Constitution, the Chairman of the drafting committee, Ambedkar, had warned the assembly that the political democracy envisaged in the constitution could not last long if economic and social democracy were not brought about.[74] The national elections, especially the latest ones in May 2004, constantly remind us of this prophetic but obvious statement. 'A kinder, gentler, inclusive India is not only a moral imperative but also a practical necessity.'[75]

It is this aspect of human rights, which dominated constitution making in India and which, in my view, must dominate until the goal of social and economic democracy is achieved. That is the reason and justification for India to emphasize social and economic rights as much as civil and political rights in the international arena as in the national.

[74] See Shiva Rao, above n. 34, vol. IV, 943.

[75] A. Varshney, 'Towards a Gentler India', in *India Today*, 36 (7 June 2004). For a detailed analysis of the 2004 elections also see the survey conducted by the Centre for the Study of Developing Societies, Delhi, published in The *Hindu* of 20 May 2004.

We all know that one of the major concerns of human rights recognized in the international instruments was maintenance of international peace. We also acknowledge that poverty anywhere on earth is a threat to peace everywhere. If this is so, human rights must ensure removal of poverty and want everywhere. At the national level, India is trying its best to remove the poverty of its masses through affirmative action consistent with the civil and political rights of the people. At the international level also it has been arguing for this. Therefore, it supports rights like the right to development of all people on the globe. It is expected that the developed nations appreciate the international concern in this regard. They must take care that the political and economic policies are so oriented that at least the most basic rights such as basic necessities of life for people everywhere are realized. India's argument in this regard is not merely utilitarian; it is an argument of justice as much in the international arena as in the national. I believe the average enlightened Indian lives by the ideal of the age-old philosophy of *Sarve Bhavantu Sukhinah, Sarve Santu Niramaya*. Let there be happiness everywhere. Let no one suffer from want. Indian state and society must ensure the realization of that ideal.

3

Horizontal Application of Fundamental Rights and State Action in India

SUDHIR KRISHNASWAMY[*]

[T]he charter is far from irrelevant to private litigants whose disputes fall to be decided at common law. But this is different from the proposition that one private party owes a constitutional duty to another...

RWDSU v. *Dolphin Delivery*[1]

The 1990s inaugurated new ideas about the proper role for the Indian state. For one, the state began to radically restructure itself through the tools of privatization and contracting out, and secondly, indicated that it will vacate the 'commanding heights of the economy' where it once positioned itself.[2] Simultaneously, the appellate courts increasingly apply various constitutional obligations beyond the state to private citizens in public law actions. The rapid development of sexual harassment law and the right to strike decisions[3] are evidence of this trend. This essay explores what these twin movements mean for Indian constitutional law. I will argue that we need a better understanding of the horizontal application of fundamental rights and the doctrine of state action if the constitutional aims and aspirations are to remain relevant in the future.

[*] Sruti Chaganti, Vth Year Student at NALSAR, Hyderabad, provided valuable research assistance.

[1] [1986] 2 SCR 573, 605 (McIntyre J).

[2] The Electricity Act 2003 provides us with a glimpse of what this new 'policy making' state will look like. The core responsibility of the state will be to announce an electricity policy which the state-appointed Regulatory Commission will consider, before regulating the market by incentivizing and penalizing market forces.

[3] *Communist Party of India* v. *Bharat Kumar* (1998) 1 SCC 201.

Implicit in the movements discussed above, is a reapportionment of the proper domains of private and public law. This distinction has had a long and often controversial history[4] as some writers argue that this distinction is unworkable, whether it is grounded in the substantive content of rules or in a jurisdictional division of disputes.[5] The debate about the public-private distinction proceeds at two levels. First, a descriptive argument about whether the distinction should rest on the institutional actors involved—state or non-state—or on the nature of activity being considered—public or private functions. A second prescriptive dimension suggests a normative ordering of social life into public and private spheres, each governed by a different set of normative assumptions[6] though it is unclear what these different normative frameworks might be.[7] At all times, those who propose or oppose this prescriptive distinction are motivated by a fuller account of the proper role of the state and the levels of public participation and accountability that a democratic society must ensure.

Though aware of the rationale and basis for this distinction, this is not the primary focus of this essay. By taking the public-private distinction to be not as categorical and clear-cut as previously supposed, we are ready to reconsider the traditional doctrinal approaches to the scope of application of fundamental rights and the doctrine of state action adopted by the Indian courts. We will no longer assume that fundamental rights necessarily apply only in a 'vertical' fashion to the relationship between the state and citizens and will be open to the view that such rights may have an effect on the 'horizontal' relationship between citizens inter se

---

[4] For a spirited exchange in the *Modern Law Review*, see Carol Harlow, '"Public" and "Private" Law: Definition Without Distinction' (1980) 43 MLR 241; Geoffrey Samuel, *Public and Private Law: A Private Lawyer's Response* (1983) 46 MLR 558; Sir Harry Woolf, *Public Law-Private Law: Why the Divide? A Personal View* MLR 220.

[5] *Carol Harlow* (n. 4) 242.

[6] See P Cane, 'Public Law and Private Law: A Study of the Analysis and Use of a Legal Concept' in J Eekelaar and J Bell (eds) *Oxford Essays in Jurisprudence*, Clarendon Press, Oxford (1987) 57 for a comprehensive analysis of the debate on Public and Private Law against the background of liberal political philosophy and the theoretical inheritances in English Public Law. Peter Cane distinguishes between descriptive and prescriptive versions of the public law—private law distinction in a slightly different fashion from its use in this essay.

[7] D. Oliver 'Common Values in Public and Private Law and Public/Private Divide' PL (1997) 630 argues that both realms of law should be governed by the same normative framework.

in a direct or indirect fashion. The rest of the essay explores how a careful reading of the constitutional text and the doctrines developed by the supreme court would support a restatement of the horizontal effect of fundamental rights in the Indian constitution.

Before we conclude this section, I will briefly sketch two concrete problems which allow for a theoretical and practical assessment of the circumstances in which arguments about the horizontal effect of human rights may be considered. This is particularly important as problems which could potentially be resolved by private law or criminal law are continuously articulated through public law litigation.

CONTRACT WORKERS IN BANGALORE

The Bangalore Mahanagara Palike Guttige Powrakarmikara Sangh is a Union which represents over 2000 Powrakarmika contract workers in Bangalore. Powrakarmikas are garbage collectors and street cleaners working in the 187 wards of Bangalore city and are employed by registered contractors of the Bangalore Mahanagara Palike (hereafter BMP), or City Corporation. Despite its best efforts, the labour union has been unable to get the corporation or its contractors to pay the minimum wage or observe basic service conditions over the last three years and is therefore contemplating legal action.

The union will consider carefully the option to engage the courts as cases like these present difficult legal problems for the courts to resolve. The union, as a third-party beneficiary to the contract entered into between the BMP and the contractors, cannot claim any contractual remedies. It is unlikely that the union will proceed directly against the contractors in a public law action as Indian courts have not recognized the potential for such direct action against private actors in the past. It is most likely that the union will proceed against the BMP, together with the contractors, in a single public law action. By naming both state and non-state parties as respondents to the petition, they may be able to assert that the BMP would be responsible for non-payment of minimum wage either because the activity of cleaning the streets is a 'public function' or on the principle of vicarious liability for contractors' actions. Irrespective of their chances of success in this litigation, this phenomenon of the contracting out of governmental functions is on the rise and poses substantial theoretical problems for our understanding of the scope of public and constitutional obligations of the state and private citizens.

Affirmative Action
in the Private Sector

With the formation of the Congress-led United Progressive Alliance government, there have been renewed demands for the extension of affirmative action programmes to the non-state sector of the economy. These demands are phrased in two legal formats: first, to extend existing reservation policy as practiced in the state sector to the private sector or second, to devise a modified affirmative action policy which responds adequately to the constitutional obligations of the state and private actors.[8] The existing affirmative action programmes applying exclusively to state institutions are designed under the shadow of the guarantee of equality under the constitution and put into place by several executive orders made by the union and State governments. The fundamental constitutional objection to such an extension is grounded in a limited application of the equality guarantee which is circumscribed by the prevailing understanding of the scope of the principle of state action, an issue we will revisit at a later point in this essay.

The two problems discussed above address different social problems but are united in that they present us with the problem of the proper division of the scope and application of public law and private law. Identifying the constitutional basis of sexual harassment law or the relationship between copyright law and the constitutional free speech guarantees of citizens raise similar concerns. Moreover, these problems are not exceptional or unique to the Indian context. Other common law courts have responded to similar problems in a complicated and nuanced fashion. Justice McIntyre, speaking for a three-judge bench of the supreme court of Canada, worked out such a nuanced compromise in the quotation at the start of this essay. By considering the diverse ways in which fundamental rights values may inflect the private common law, McIntyre abandons a rigid vertical-horizontal polarity to the application of horizontal rights. He suggests that Charter rights have an impact on the actions of private citizens, though it may not impose constitutional obligations on them. This essay explores this nuanced position on the applicability of fundamental rights and relies on primary and secondary literature from these jurisdictions insofar as they enhance our understanding of Indian law.

---

[8] The Bhopal Declaration: Charting a New Course for Dalits in the 21st Century, 2002 at http://www.ambedkar.org/news/thebhopaldeclaration.htm

The argument in the essay is conducted in three steps. We first analyse how individual rights may be understood to have an impact on the relations between private citizens. We unpack the distinction between direct and indirect horizontal effect and assess whether the approach of the courts to fundamental rights guaranteed by the Indian constitution support this horizontal extension of the scope of individual rights. Then we analyse the 'state action' principles that regulate the range of actors who may be bearers of the obligations of fundamental rights. We will carefully reconsider if the constitutional text and its interpretation by the courts offer any support for the horizontal application of fundamental rights. The essay concludes by coming back to our preliminary analysis of the public-private law distinction to fashion a revised account which more fully accounts for the current state of Indian constitutional law. Further, we will recognize that the Indian courts have developed a principle of horizontal indirect effect, and I will argue that they may go further to allow for horizontal direct effect to certain fundamental rights in the constitution. This analysis enables practitioners and courts to develop a theoretical background to tackle problems of such a complex nature.

Before I go any further, I must clarify that this essay does not attempt to provide a comprehensive and exhaustive analysis of the Indian case for two reasons: first, as it would involve a tortuous re-rendering of judgments delivered within a different conceptual frame and second, the essay focuses on an illustration of the central ideas of the essay at the cost of a detailed account on the present state of the law. Moreover, concerns of time and space keep me to judgments delivered by the supreme court.

HORIZONTAL RIGHTS

Among the most intensely debated issues in constitutional law today is the scope of application of fundamental rights provisions.[9] The central question posed in these debates is whether rights regulate the relationship between the state and the individual—vertical application—or whether they apply to relations between private individuals—horizontal application. Arguably, the vertical or horizontal application of a right is contingent on the nature of the right and its particular phrasing in a

[9] Stephen Gardbaum, 'The "Horizontal Effect" of Constitutional Rights', 102 Michigan L Rev (2003); Mark Tushnet, 'The Issue of State Action/Horizontal Effect in Comparative Constitutional Law', 1 ICON 79–98 (2003).

constitutional document. So let us turn to the particular rights in the Indian constitution.

Fundamental Rights in the Indian Constitution

Part III of the Indian constitution adopts a varied approach to the phrasing of fundamental rights guarantees. First, are those rights guaranteed to citizens in Part III of the constitution which are expressly directed at the state. The equality and anti-discrimination guarantees under Article 14: 'The State shall not deny to any person equality before the law...' are instances of state directed rights.[10] A majority of the rights are expressed in broad and general terms and ambivalent about who they are addressed to. For example, Article 21 which guarantees the right to life reads: 'No person shall be deprived of his life or personal liberty except according to procedure adopted by law'.[11] Similarly, Article 15(2) provides that 'No citizen shall...' suffer from disability arising out of religion, race or caste, among others. These Articles make no reference to the persons against whom such a right may be claimed. It may be, and often is, argued that the scope of such widely-phrased rights are controlled by the definition of 'state' in Article 12 and the powers of judicial review under Article 13. This argument will be examined in greater detail in the next section on state action.

In a third category are Articles 17, 18, and 23 which expressly impose constitutional obligations on non-state actors. Article 17 abolishes the practice of untouchability and prohibits its practice in any form. The Protection of Civil Rights Act, 1955, implements this prohibition by creating an offence of untouchability and instituting a mechanism of prosecution. Article 18 seeks to abolish civil titles in two ways: by preventing the state from conferring them,[12] and by imposing direct constitutional obligations on citizens from accepting them from foreign states.[13] Article 23 prohibits trafficking in human beings and certain forms of forced labour and any contravention of this provision is to be punishable by law.[14] Though this provision is silent about the persons who are subject to its command, the courts have held this article to be applicable to private persons.[15]

[10] Article 14, Constitution of India.
[11] Article 21, ibid.
[12] Article 18(1), ibid.
[13] Article 18(2), ibid.
[14] Article 23(1), ibid.
[15] *People's Union for Democratic Rights* v. *Union of India* AIR 1982 SC 1473.

Horizontal Rights and the Supreme Court

Though Indian courts have not developed a comprehensive approach to horizontal rights, they have had the opportunity to deal with the three types of rights identified above: those rights which expressly cast obligations on the state, others which are ambivalent about the persons they impose obligations upon, and those rights which are expressly horizontal. Let us analyse carefully the approach of the court to each type of right.

Rights that Impose Obligations on the State

In *Vishaka v. State of Rajasthan*,[16] the petitioners complained about the brutal gang-rape of a social worker to highlight the hazards of working women and the absence of a legal alternative to the moribund criminal justice system. They argued that the failure of the state to establish a legal framework to tackle sexual harassment in the workplace resulted in the violation of a woman's right to equality and against discrimination under Articles 14 and 15, her right to life under Article 21, and her right to 'practice any profession...' protected by Article 19(1)(g). Chief Justice Verma announced a set of guidelines and rules aimed at preventing sexual harassment in the workplace under Article 32 for the enforcement of fundamental rights, read with Article 141, power of the supreme court to 'declare' law.

Sexual harassment in the workplace results in a violation of the rights of a person by other private individuals who are fellow employees or superiors. Though the writ petition was phrased in the idiom of the state's failure to enact a suitable legislation, the intervention sought was to remedy several unfortunate developments in the relationships between private citizens ordinarily resolved by tort, contract, and criminal law. Unfortunately, the court did not investigate the scope and nature of the rights being violated, and whether these rights cast constitutional obligations on the citizen as well as the state. Of particular importance is the scope of equality guarantee in Articles 14 and 15, as these rights expressly cast obligations on the state. Rights which expressly cast obligations on the state need not, for that reason, be disabled from having any horizontal effect on private action, though it is likely that such an argument may be pressed in the courts.

Verma's opinion signals three possible reasons in support of the view that sexual harassment in the workplace by private actors was a

---

[16] AIR 1997 SC 3011.

constitutional wrong. Firstly, we may identify a positive obligation on the state to ensure that women enjoy the benefits of the rights guaranteed to them under the constitution. As it is the legislature's and executive's 'primary responsibility for ensuring...'[17] that women are not subject to sexual harassment, the inability or unwillingness of these organs of the state to fulfil these responsibilities obliges the third organ of the state—courts—to step in and protect these rights. The structure and form of the writ proceedings, where the state of Rajasthan was named as respondent, supports such a positive dimension to fundamental rights, besides allowing for orders passed to bind these respondents. By combining state and non-state actors among the respondents, such petitions allow for widening the scope of application of rights as the court enforces a positive obligation on the state to intervene and decisively alter the relationship between private parties. Often this procedural device shields the court from examining substantive arguments about the scope and application of fundamental rights. We will examine this approach critically in the next section on state action.

Secondly, Verma refers to the fundamental duties of citizens set out in Article 51-A which provides that it 'shall be the duty of every citizen of India...to abide by the constitution and respect it's ideals and institutions...'[18] He does not go on to explain whether constitutional duties include a legally enforceable duty to respect other citizen's rights. If this is the logical extension of the reference to fundamental duties then this provision may provide a unique constitutional basis in the Indian constitution for the horizontal application of several provisions of the constitution. In *Vishaka* this means that all citizens are under the constitutional obligation not to engage in sexually discriminatory behaviour in the workplace.

At first glance, this is a radical doctrinal innovation which mobilizes the concept of fundamental duties of citizens in support of a comprehensive horizontal application of fundamental rights irrespective of the particular phrasing of a right. Existing judicial opinions on the status of fundamental duties do not support such a view. The supreme court has refused to grant a writ of mandamus to enforce a fundamental duty[19] but is willing to use such duties as an interpretive aid while construing other provisions of the constitution.[20] The latter, more modest reading,

[17] *Vishaka* (n.).
[18] Article 51-A (a), Constitution of India.
[19] *Surya Narain v. Union of India* AIR 1982 Raj 1.
[20] *Bijoe Emmanuel v. State of Kerala* AIR 1987 SC 748.

of Part IV of the constitution is insufficient to sustain the full horizontal application of fundamental rights but may provide some support for indirect horizontal effect of fundamental rights. Despite not having worked out the overall implications of such a view, the potential of this argument is promising.

Thirdly, the court relied on the provisions of the International Convention on the Elimination of All Forms of Discrimination against Women, 1992. As the Indian government had ratified the convention and undertaken to implement its obligations, Verma had no hesitation in 'construing the nature and ambit of (the) constitutional guarantee of gender equality in our constitution'[21] as accommodating these obligations. This justification for the horizontal application of the equality guarantee is curious: is it the court's intention to broaden merely those rights in the constitution regarding which the state has undertaken broader treaty obligations? Such an approach draws on emerging methods of interpretation of Commonwealth courts where International Human Rights obligations are used as an aid to interpretation.[22] However, this provides us with a poor theoretical basis for understanding the imposition of constitutional obligations on citizens by the horizontal application of rights.

Ambivalent Rights

In *PD Shamdasani* v. *Central Bank of India*[23] the petitioner was aggrieved by the bank's sale of his shares to recover a debt owed by him. He petitioned the court by a writ action to enforce his fundamental right to acquire, hold, and dispose of his property protected under Article 19(1)(f) and his rights against unlawful 'deprivation' of his property under Article 31(1) against the Central Bank of India, then a private bank incorporated under the Companies Act, 1882. Chief Justice Patanjali Shastri dismissed the petition on the preliminary ground that the petitioner had misconceived his remedy as 'the language and structure of Article 19 and its setting in Part III of the constitution clearly show that the article was intended to protect those freedoms against state action...'.[24] It was self evident to the court that 'violation of rights of property by individuals is not within the purview of the Article.'[25] Moreover, as Article 31, like

---

[21] AIR 1997 SC 3011.

[22] See 'The Bangalore Declaration and Plan of Action', 25 October 1995, at http://wwwlaw.murdoch.edu.au/icjwa/bangalore.html.

[23] AIR 1952 SC 59.

[24] Ibid.

[25] Ibid., 60.

Article 21, qualifies its protection to permit violations of procedures established by law, he concluded that they targeted the 'prohibition of unlawful governmental action'.[26]

While it is right to assert that law-making is a governmental function, both these Articles are concerned with violations of procedures established by law and not with the body making a law. Both state and private citizens are capable of such violations and the court should have considered whether there are good reasons to exclude private actor violations from the scope of these Articles.[27] Further, as these Articles do not expressly impose obligations on the state, as distinct from private citizens, the proposition calls for closer reasoning.

As neither Article 19(1)(f) nor Article 31 survive in the constitution today, being replaced by Article 300-A, it is not useful for our purposes to engage in a detailed textual analysis of these Articles. Shastri fails to provide substantive reasons for his conclusion and instead relies on the obviousness of this proposition. However, he adopted a useful approach by analyzing the fundamental rights provisions individually instead of deciding the issue wholesale by making some assumption about the nature of rights itself! In this context, it is particularly important to distinguish arguments related to the doctrine of state action from those related to the nature of rights which the court failed to do.

In *Vidya Verma* v. *Dr Shiv Narain Verma*,[28] the supreme court was presented with a habeas corpus petition by the husband of the petitioner to release his wife from the custody of her father, alleging a violation of her fundamental right to life and liberty protected under Article 21. Justice Vivian Bose endorsed the finding of the court in *Shamdasani* to fully apply to a petition under Article 21:[29]

> [I]t is clear that the declaration of the fundamental right of private property is in the same negative form in which Article 21 declares the fundamental right to life and liberty. There is no express reference to the state in Article 21. But could it be suggested on that account that that Article was intended to offer protection to life and personal liberty against violation by private individuals?

Rather than engaging with this precise analytical question, Vivian Bose went on to conclude that the words 'except by procedure established

---

[26] Ibid., 61.

[27] See generally, Raju Ramachandran, 'Article 21 and the Ghost of *Shamdasani*', (1987) 1 SCC Journal 42.

[28] AIR 1956 SC 108.

[29] Ibid., at [7] citing *Shamdasani* (n. 5).

by law' in Article 21 excluded such a possibility. Neither of these cases offers any convincing reasons why this requirement of procedural compliance applies only to the state. Bose concluded by reiterating Shastri's conclusion in *AK Gopalan v. State of Madras*: 'as a rule constitutional safeguards are directed against the state and its organs and that protection against violations of rights by individuals must be sought in the ordinary law.'[30] This stipulative and unreasoning approach fails to pay attention to the constitutional text and the theoretical basis for deciding the scope and applicability of fundamental rights.

Expressly Horizontal Rights

In *People's Union for Democratic Rights v. Union of India*[31] the supreme court entertained a writ petition, by petitioners in the public interest, seeking to enforce existing labour laws in the construction work for the Asian Games in Delhi. Our analysis of Justice Bhagwati's opinion in this case will focus on two distinct elements: first, the scope and application of the different rights in the constitution—rights which are expressly horizontal and those which are not—and second, the form of the litigation and the remedies ordered.

Government contractors executing the project engaged in pernicious forms of labour practices which were violations of the constitutional rights to a life with dignity[32] and equality[33] and the constitutional prohibitions against forced[34] and child labour.[35] While the equality guarantee was directed to the state, the right to life is ambivalent about its addressees and the prohibitions against forced and child labour are general in their scope. In this case, the petitioners alleged violations of all these rights by private contractors in their employment contracts as well as by the state which had failed to enforce labour statutes. Bhagwati did not distinguish between the phrasing of different rights violated in this case which kept him from examining the horizontal application of these very different rights. However, he did propose a significant horizontal aspect to Articles 23 and 24 but found that that Article 14 had a much narrower scope.

[30] Ibid., at [6] citing Justice Patanjali Shastri in [1950] SCR 88, 204.
[31] (1982) 3 SCC 235 AIR 1982 SC 1473.
[32] Article 21, Constitution of India.
[33] Article 14, ibid.
[34] Article 23, ibid.
[35] Article 24, ibid.

Article 23

Article 23 prohibits the trafficking of human beings, begar and similar forms of forced labour. It was argued that the failure of the contractors to pay their workers minimum wage resulted in conditions of labour which approximated to begar. There was a substantial argument about the precise meaning of 'begar'—whether it was restricted to the extraction of forced labour or service with no remuneration or whether it could be extended to other similar forms of forced labour where some remuneration was paid? As in *Maneka Gandhi* v. *Union of India*,[36] Bhagwati took the view that the court should take an expansive view of the scope and reach of fundamental rights. He found it inconceivable and unreasonable that the 'constitution-makers' would have sought to exclude forms of labour where minimal wages were paid. By ignoring the fundamental distinctions between feudal modes of extraction of labour and services and the unequal bargaining positions in an unregulated market economy, Bhagwati concluded that the expression 'forced labour' would apply irrespective of the payment or non-payment of remuneration. Irrespective of the merits of this particular conclusion, this essay focuses solely on the horizontal application of rights by the supreme court.

Bhagwati took the view that 'many of the fundamental rights enacted in Part III operate as limitations on the power of the state and impose negative obligations on the state. But there are certain fundamental rights conferred by the constitution which are enforceable against the whole world and are found, *inter alia*, in Articles 17, 23, and 24.'[37] Thereby he identified some rights in the constitution which may be horizontally applied while plausibly others may not. We will examine this distinction in greater detail when we look to the interpretation of Article 24 below.

Despite finding that Article 23 imposed constitutional obligations on citizens, Bhagwati devised a remedy that contemplated a modest indirect horizontal effect of fundamental rights. He emphasized that 'whenever any fundamental right...is enforceable against private individuals...it is the constitutional obligation of the state to take the necessary steps for the purpose of interdicting such violation and ensuring the observance the fundamental right by the private individual who is transgressing the same'.[38] His recognition that the cause of the

[36] AIR 1973 SC.

[37] AIR 1982 SC 1473 (n. 35) 252–3.

[38] Ibid., (n. 35) 260.

constitutional injury was a private actor, did not prompt him to follow through to devise a remedy that was directed at such a private actor.

Article 24

Article 24 provides that no 'child below the age of 14 shall be employed to work in any factory or mine or engaged in any other hazardous employment'.[39] Applying this constitutional prohibition '*proprio vigore*', even in the absence of enabling legislation, he concluded that Article 24 'embodies a fundamental right which is plainly and indubitably enforceable against everyone'.[40] The horizontal application of the Article 24 prohibition may give rise to two corresponding duties: the constitutional duty 'on the contractors not to employ any child below the age of 14 years'[41] and a corresponding obligation on the state to ensure that this obligation is obeyed by the contractors. In other words, the court could have concluded that Article 23 had direct and indirect horizontal application giving rise to these multiple duties. Instead, Bhagwati surprisingly highlighted only the state's responsibility to 'ensure that this constitutional mandate is not violated in any part of India'.[42] Even this proposition was supported, not by holding the state responsible for the private contractor's actions, but only by the general obligation of the state to effectively implement existing laws.

Bhagwati, less convincingly, extended the range of constitutional duties that may be imposed on the state with respect to payment of minimum wages and the payment of equal remuneration for male and female workers. He was of the view that the latter obligation drew support from the constitutional guarantees of equality and non-discrimination under Article 14. Although the imposition of obligations on the state to ensure the implementation of statutory obligations seems to assume some sort of indirect horizontal effect of the equality guarantee we must be careful not to extrapolate too strong a principle beyond a general obligation to implement laws. Moreover it may be a mistake to consider every instance of failure to implement statutory duties as an instance of a constitutional rights injury.

While doing well to identify the direct horizontal effect of the constitutional guarantee under Articles 23 and 24 and suggesting an indirect horizontal effect of the equality right under Article 14, Bhagwati did not

---

[39] Article 21, Constitution of India.
[40] AIR 1982 SC 1473 (n. 35) 250.
[41] Ibid., (n. 35) 250.
[42] Ibid., (n. 35) 246.

fashion corresponding remedies for these constitutional wrongs. He did not extend the reach of the traditional writ remedies to private actors, nor did he fashion a new remedy for constitutional torts committed by state and private actors. The presence of the public interest petitioner obscured the adversarial character of the proceeding, distracting the court from concrete constitutional injuries in this case.[43]

The second limb of analysis of *People's Union* focuses on the particular procedural form of the case and the nature of remedies conceived by the courts. Bhagwati paid special attention to the difference in form and focus of public interest litigation and noted that unlike ordinary writ petitions which seek to enforce fundamental rights against the state, 'public interest litigation intended to promote and vindicate public interest which demands that violations of constitution or legal rights of large number of people',[44] who are otherwise unable to enforce their rights. Bhagwati, partially blinded by the public service ideals that such cases vindicate, failed to go beyond the form of the action to appreciate the rights involved and the remedies demanded. He vehemently denied that the 'purpose of this writ petition was to find fault with any particular authority for not observing the labour laws in relation to workmen employed in the projects which are being executed by it, but to ensure that in future the labour laws are implemented and the rights of the workers under the labour laws are not violated.'[45] Thus, Bhagwati juxtaposed the rhetorical force of his opinion with an emaciated account of constitutional injury and avoided an essential enquiry into the scope and protection of horizontal fundamental rights. Having absolved all state authorities from any constitutional duties with respect to the horizontal application of fundamental rights and failing to recognize any constitutional duties on private actors, he presented a hollowed, ineffectual account of the nature of constitutional rights. A sober, well-reasoned approach would recognize the horizontal character of the rights violated in this case and might have developed a public law action against private parties.

In this case, a coherent response to the respondent's two preliminary objections would have assisted the court to develop the idea of horizontal

[43] See Carol Harlow 'Public Law and Popular Justice' 65 *Modern Law Review* 1 for an argument about how allowing groups standing in public law litigation process not only changes the nature of issues agitated but may also alter the style of adjudication and remedies ordered.

[44] AIR 1982 SC 1473 (n. 35) 240.

[45] Ibid., 244.

rights further. The respondent's first objection was that as the persons whose rights were violated had not approached the court, standing should be denied to the public interest petitioner seeking to represent them. The court proposed a radical shift from the standing rules in 'western jurisprudence', where only those whose rights were violated were entitled to standing, towards a relaxed standing rule whereby 'any member of the public acting bona fide and not out of any extraneous motivation' may move the court to represent the interests of parties who are not able to approach the courts by reason of 'poverty, disability, or socially or economically disadvantaged position'.[46] Though this widening of access to the courts is undoubtedly a laudable goal, it seems to encourage the court to mould the writ petition into a public complaint procedure devoid of its remedial role. The presence of intermediaries acting in the public interest alters the form of litigation and obscures the nature of the constitutional injuries being complained against, thereby distracting the court from its primary duty of constitutional judicial review for discrete and identifiable constitutional injuries. In this case, by responding to the petitioner's concerns rather than those of the right holder, the court avoided any significant analysis of the constitutional injuries and appropriate remedies for such injury.

The second preliminary objection of the respondents had two parts: first, that the employees are not employees of the state authorities but those of the contractor and second, that the writ petition needs to show the violation of a fundamental right and not merely violation of labour law provisions. The first aspect was easily overcome by ruling that the labour laws governing contract labour recognize that the obligations cast on the contractor for the benefit of the workmen apply equally to the principal employer—in this case, the state. Though Bhagwati engaged with the obligations of contractors under a horizontally applicable fundamental right earlier in his opinion, when it was posed directly he chose to impose obligations on the state, relying on its statutory liabilities as the principal employer. The second aspect of this objection requiring the petitioner to show the violation of a fundamental right met with an elaborate response. Bhagwati clarified that Articles 23 and 24 were violated by the actions of the contractors while Article 14 was violated by the state which had failed to implement the statutory provisions preventing discrimination. By identifying the violation of fundamental rights with precision, Bhagwati provides us with a clear idea of how rights may

---

[46] Ibid., 249.

be applied horizontally. If some fundamental rights create horizontal constitutional obligations borne by ordinary citizens, it follows that such citizens may violate fundamental rights. However, remedies for such violations need not necessarily be sought from the violator and the state may be indirectly held responsible to ensure that its citizens do not violate fundamental rights.

We conclude this section by noting the several remedies granted in this case. Bhagwati directed the contractors to pay the workmen minimum wages and the Delhi Development Authority to take action against such contractors who failed to do so. Further, the court recommended that the Delhi Development Authority should hereafter insert a clause in their contracts to ensure that their contractors complied with all labour laws.[47] Lastly, the court appointed three independent ombudsmen to make periodical inspections to ensure that the labour laws were implemented and wages and benefits accrued to the workmen. Despite holding that it was the primary responsibility of the state to ensure compliance with the applicable labour laws, the court issued directions to the private actors. Though Bhagwati did not establish any direct correspondence between the scope and violation of the right and the remedies, we may rightly assume that where fundamental rights are horizontally applied, remedies may be granted against private actors.[48]

So far we have considered the approach of the supreme court to the differently phrased rights in Part III of the Constitution. The first insight we may draw is that the Indian Supreme Court has given fundamental rights some horizontal effect by imposing a wider range of constitutional duties on state actors and by accommodating private and state actors as respondents to a writ petition. The application of fundamental rights to disputes between private citizens in this fashion relies more on the doctrine of state action than the idea of a horizontally applicable right. We examine in this in the next section.

Secondly, we recognize that differently phrased rights may apply horizontally to a different extent and in a different manner. Thereby, the otherwise conflicting decisions of the court in *Shamdasani, Vishaka,* and

---

[47] Paul Craig 'Contracting Out, The Human Rights Act and the Scope of Judicial Review' 118 *Law Quarterly Review*, 551–68 for recent developments in the remedies offered by English administrative law in cases of contracting out of public services.

[48] For a skeptical account of the remedies designed by the supreme court in the bonded labour cases, see Arun Shourie 'The Courts and its Judgments' Oxford University Press, New Delhi (2003).

People's Union may be reconciled. So we may conclude that the right to property, previously protected as a fundamental right, does not have horizontal effect, the equality guarantee as well as the right to life have indirect horizontal effect and the prohibitions against forced and child labour have both direct and indirect horizontal effect. Such a graded approach to the horizontality of different rights recommends itself as it pays attention to the constitutional text, the nature of the right, and the context in which the right is claimed.

Section 8(2) in the Bill of Rights chapter of the South African Constitution 1996, adopts a similar approach to the rights guaranteed in the South African Constitution. It provides that:

A provision of the Bill of Rights binds a natural or juristic person if, and to the extent that, it is applicable, taking account of the nature of the right and the nature of any duty imposed by the right.

Such an approach allows the court to calibrate its intervention using public law techniques, as many disputes between private parties may best be settled by existing private law. By mapping the distinction between private and public law domains and remedies finely, the court avoids the risk of shifting all disputes into the province of public law while recognizing that constitutional obligations on private citizens may have an impact on the scope of protection that the private law affords their interests, choices, and actions.

STATE ACTION

The horizontal effect of fundamental rights may be affected through the doctrine of state action. We consider three ways in which the doctrine of state action may accommodate the horizontal application of fundamental rights below. While one of these modes accommodates direct horizontal effect, the other two are concerned with indirect horizontal effect. We will look at each of these in turn.

Applying Fundamental Rights to Private Actors— Direct Horizontal Effect

In this section, we investigate the high court and supreme court's powers to control the circumstances under which fundamental rights may be applied to private actors. Besides the language of the right itself, there are two further conditions which regulate how fundamental rights may be horizontally applied: First, the scope of the obligation imposed on the state in Article 13 read with Article 12 and second, whether the power of rights-based judicial review and writ jurisdiction of the supreme court and high courts, under Articles 32 and 226 respectively, allow it to issue directions to private parties. We first examine the scope of the Article 13 obligation.

Article 13 on judicial review regulates the law-making powers of the state, as defined in Article 12, by allowing the court to strike down any 'law',[49] which takes away or abridges fundamental rights, as unconstitutional. A broad interpretation of the phrase 'other authorities within the territories of India or under the control of the Government of India' in Article 12 has brought within the term 'state' a wide range of non-departmental bodies considered to be an 'agency or instrumentality'[50] of the state. These non-departmental bodies may be public corporations controlled by the state or bodies that are recognized, regulated, or aided by the state.[51] The rationale for an expansive interpretation of 'other authorities'—that the state should not avoid the rigour of fundamental rights by adopting a different legal form—may justify the application of fundamental rights to contractors carrying out recently privatized public functions. Though the inclusive definition of 'law' in Article 13(3) accommodates a wide range of legislative and executive action, the rationale for this provision is undoubtedly to place fetters on 'state activity' and it is difficult to extend these obligations to private actors.[52]

We now examine the range of remedies available to the supreme court and high courts and who these orders may be addressed to. Article 32 which guarantees the right to move the supreme court for the enforcement of fundamental rights, is silent about the authorities or persons to whom such an order may be made. Arguably such rights may be enforced against those parties who have violated a particular fundamental right. Our analysis of the differential horizontal impact of particular rights, in the section above, helps us to identify the persons who are subject to constitutional obligations. Unlike Article 32, Article 226

[49] Article 13(2), Constitution of India.

[50] Justice Bhagwati set out these principles in *Ajay Hassia* v. *Khalid Mujib* AIR 1981 SC 847.

[51] For a more recent judgment on this point, see *Mysore Paper Mills Limited* v. *Mysore Paper Mills Employees Association* (2002) 2 SCC.

[52] See Udai Raj Rai 'Reach of Fundamental Rights' 36 Journal of the Indian Law Institute (1994) 292–301 for a more optimistic account of how the state action doctrine may accommodate private actors.

offers us more clarity on this point. It confers on every high court the power to 'issue to any person or authority, including in appropriate cases, any government' suitable orders to enforce fundamental rights thereby anticipating the enforcement of fundamental rights against non-state actors. Several high courts have utilized the power to make such orders, in writ actions where state and non-state parties are respondents, but have seldom offered a theoretical argument to support such an exercise.

To unlock the potential of constitutional remedies under Articles 32 and 226 the courts must liberate the scope of fundamental rights from the state-focussed rights based judicial review under Article 13. If fundamental rights may be violated in circumstances other than those anticipated by Article 13, the court may then devise suitable remedies under Articles 32 and 226. This shift opens up the availability of remedies against private actors which is crucial to secure the direct horizontal application of fundamental rights. There are other circumstances where an indirect horizontal effect of fundamental rights may be achieved without the court issuing remedies against private actors. We will now move on to consider two circumstances where this is possible.

Court as the State or Public Authority

Sir William Wade, in 'The Horizons of Horizontality',[53] argues that the Human Rights Act 1998 has full horizontal effect on the sphere of private action between citizens. He suggests that by including 'courts' in the section 6(3) definition of 'public authority', the legislature intended that the courts must, while adjudicating disputes, act compatibly with convention rights protected under the Act. This obligation would apply uniformly, irrespective of whether the courts were adjudicating disputes between two private parties or between public and private parties. By doing away with the distinction between direct and indirect effect, he proposes that the 'court must be an effective agent in all cases alike'.[54] By including courts in its definition of public authorities, Sir Wade argues that the Act renders the precise definition of public authorities, as a controlling factor on the scope of human rights, irrelevant.

Lester and Pannick respond with a more 'sophisticated' approach to the horizontal application of rights.[55] While they do not deny that the

[53] Sir William Wade QC 'Horizons of Horizontality' (2000) 116 LQR 217.
[54] Ibid.
[55] Anthony Lester and David Pannick 'The Impact of the Human Rights Act on Private Law: The Knight's Move' 116 LQR 380 (2000).

convention rights, interpreted and applied under the terms of the Act by British courts and tribunals, would significantly influence private law, they argue that this will not happen in the dramatic way suggested by Sir Wade. The legislative scheme and purpose of the Human Rights Act, 1998, makes a careful distinction between public law wrongdoing in breach of the convention rights and other cases in which the convention rights may be relevant. The obligation on the courts to interpret statutes and declare the common law in a way that is compatible with the convention rights will exert a powerful indirect influence on private law without giving direct horizontal effect to these rights. Therefore, the Human Rights Act does not create new causes of action for constitutional wrongs committed by persons other than public authorities but enjoins the court to reach conclusions in private law in conformity with human rights principles set out in the convention.

At the core of this dispute[56] is an argument about whether the Human Rights Act recognizes a concept of horizontal rights which creates legal obligations between citizens or whether the Act puts in place a modified doctrine of state action which includes the interpretive role of the judiciary. Earlier in this chapter we recognized that the Indian constitution accommodates the horizontal application of fundamental rights. We now consider whether the constitutional text offers any support for a state action doctrine which obliges courts to apply human rights norms while resolving private law disputes.

The only phrase in Article 12, which defines the 'state' wherever such a term is used in specific Articles, that may plausibly accommodate the courts is 'other authorities'. The rest of the Article clearly picks out the legislative and executive organs of the state. The expression 'other authorities' is qualified by two criteria: 'within the territory of India' and 'under the control of the Government of India.'[57] Courts would satisfy the first criterion but are constitutionally assumed to be independent of the control of the government. The 'instrumentality or agency' test which gives meaning to the phrase 'other authorities' fails to accommodate the courts. This is unsurprising as the test evolved in response to the problem of imposing human rights obligations to non-departmental bodies which carry out 'public duties'.

---

[56] For a different and more comprehensive view on horizontal application of human rights in English law, see Murray Hunt 'The "Horizontal Effect" of the Human Rights Act' *Public Law* (1998) 423.

[57] Article 12, Constitution of India.

One may identify two types of cases where court orders have been challenged for fundamental rights violations by writ petitions. Where the challenge is to rules made by high courts or the supreme court for the administration of the courts, these are subject to rights-based review under Article 32.[58] The courts have applied fundamental rights to the internal administrative functions of the judiciary where the service conditions of subordinate judges and the administrative personnel of the courts are challenged.[59] However, the position is not as clear where a writ challenges a judicial decision pronounced by a judge of competent jurisdiction. While early authority holds that the appropriate challenge to judicial decisions is an appeal and not a writ,[60] the supreme court has diluted that position. In *A.R. Antulay* v. *R.S. Nayak*[61] the court granted a remedy for the violation of the petitioner's fundamental rights by the lower court's order but failed to offer a coherent justification under Articles 32 or Article 12.

So, until the supreme court evolves a different interpretation of the phrase 'other authorities' we are reasonably certain that the courts cannot be the vehicle for the full horizontal effect of fundamental rights as proposed by Sir William Wade. Moreover, given the convincing arguments advanced by Lester and Pannick for a limited view of the interpretive obligations of the court, the courts should not be burdened with this role.

Indirect Horizontal Effect

We had noted earlier that while some constitutional rights do not expressly cast obligations on private actors, even where constitutional rights are expressly horizontal or ambivalent the courts seldom give direct horizontal effect to constitutional rights. In this section we consider whether Indian courts are more enthusiastic about indirect horizontal effect to fundamental rights in the constitution.

In *MC Mehta* v. *State of Tamil Nadu*,[62] the petitioner complained about child labour in Sivakasi and requested the court to stop this practise and institutionalize a rehabilitation scheme. He claimed that child labour

[58] *Prem Chand Garg* v. *Excise Commissioner* AIR 1963 SC 996.

[59] *Supreme Court Advocates on Record Association* v. *Union of India* AIR 1994 SC 268.

[60] *Naresh* v. *State of Maharashtra* AIR 1967 SC 1.

[61] (1988) 2 SCC 602.

[62] (1996) 6 SCC 756.

violated the constitutional prohibition against child labour in hazardous industries, the directive principles which direct the state to ensure adequate nutrition and education to children below the age of six, besides other constitutional provisions, international commitments and statutory provisions. The respondents included the State of Tamil Nadu and private parties who employed the children. Justice Hansaria did not enquire into who was responsible for these violations but fashioned a ten-point action plan which required all state governments to enforce legal obligations against private employers and private employers to contribute to a welfare scheme for children taken out of the labour market. The court did not distinguish between the Article 24 right against employment of children in hazardous employment, which may apply vertically or horizontally, and the directive principle under Article 45 which imposes legal obligations on the state. Without finding that these rights cast obligations on private parties or concluding that courts were 'state', for the purposes of Article 12, the court swiftly translated such matters into public law actions through two critical shifts: first, by imposing positive obligations on the state even where fundamental rights are violated by non-state parties and second, by adopting liberal rules of standing and procedure to allow public interest petitioners to name both state and private parties as respondents.

In such cases, the courts allow fundamental rights to have an indirect effect on private action by allowing these constitutional values to influence the entire legal system—both common law and statutory law—by giving them proper weight but not necessarily determining all private law disputes. It is beyond the scope of this paper to develop an exhaustive and elaborate account of the use of these techniques by the court. For the moment it is sufficient for me to demonstrate that this is no isolated instance.

In *People's Union* and *Vishaka*, the Union of India and the state of Rajasthan respectively were named as respondents together with private parties. Though the court was confronted with violations of fundamental rights by private actors, it cast positive obligations on the state to prevent such violations. These obligations are stronger where the state fails to enforce law on private parties or where the employers are beneficiaries of public contracts.[63] In *People's Union*, Bhagwati held that 'if the Union of India, the Delhi Administration or the Delhi Development Authority at any time finds that provisions of the Equal Remuneration

---

[63] *People's Union for Democratic Rights* (n. 31) 250.

Act, 1946, are not observed and the principles of equality before the law enshrined in Article 14 is violated by its own contractors, it cannot ignore such violation and sit quiet by adopting a non-interfering attitude' and argue 'the the violation is being committed by the contractors and not by it.'[64] Though one may identify traces of a vicarious liability principle in *People's Union*, this is certainly not applicable in *Vishaka*, as no contractual relationship between the violators of fundamental rights and the state exists.

In *Vishaka*, the court held that the judicial power under Article 32 and the executive power of the union have to protect 'working women from sexual harassment and to make their fundamental rights meaningful. Governance of the society by the rule of law mandates this requirement as a logical concomitant of the constitutional scheme.'[65] In the absence of domestic legislation in this field, the court stepped in to issue 'guidelines and norms'[66] to be complied with in all work places and other institutions till such legislation is passed. This extraordinary remedy was justified as an exercise of the court's power to design suitable remedies under Article 32 and to declare law under Article 141 of the constitution. At this point, we will not engage with a theoretical investigation of whether such norms and guidelines may be issued in exercise of the constitutional powers claimed by the court. Instead, we pay attention to the technique by which the court has found fundamental rights to be applicable horizontally albeit indirectly through the state.

Earlier we noticed that *Vishaka* did not develop any reasonable argument about the horizontal dimensions of fundamental rights. However, Verma did articulate an overarching obligation of the institutions of state, including the court, to develop and give effect to legal regimes which protect its citizen's fundamental rights. He extracted this universal obligation from the 'rule of law', but did not specify the different roles of the executive, legislature and judiciary. Though such an obligation raises separation of powers concerns, for this chapter it is sufficient to notice the indirect horizontal effect which arises from the positive obligation of the state to ensure the maintenance of fundamental rights in the private sphere.

Two significant differences may be observed between these two cases. While *People's Union* dealt with indirect horizontal effect where the executive failed to enforce statutory rules, in *Vishaka* the legislature

[64] Ibid.
[65] *Vishaka* (n. 16) 9.
[66] Ibid., 16.

had failed to legislate with respect to sexual harassment. In other words, these opinions related to the horizontal effect of fundamental rights on statutory law and common law respectively. Secondly, one must notice the institution which bears these obligations. While the positive obligation to ensure that fundamental rights had impact on the private sphere was imposed on the executive branch of government in the *People's Union*, the court and the legislature were enjoined by the same obligation in *Vishaka*.

These two developments in *Vishaka*, significantly broaden the scope and application of fundamental rights guaranteed by the constitution. These extensions of the indirect horizontal application of fundamental rights are logical extensions of the reasoning in *People's Union*. One may consistently apply indirect horizontal effect to legal relations governed by common or statutory law and there appear no special reasons why the executive should be the sole institutional vector for indirect horizontal effect, as the legislature and judiciary may adequately respond to these positive obligations even if in very different ways. The Canadian Supreme Court offers a good example when applying the Canadian charter. This court adheres to the vertical position requiring 'governmental action' before constitutional rights are triggered, but recognizes horizontal effect on private individuals through the inherent power of the courts to develop the common law in line with charter values.[67]

In this section we have investigated whether Indian courts have developed a suitable model of state action which accommodates the horizontal application of fundamental rights. We considered three alternative possibilities. First, we enquired into whether the court directly applied fundamental rights to private actors by recognizing them as parties, and the targets of remedies, in public law writ actions. Although the constitutional provisions support such a view, the court has not developed a doctrine of direct horizontal effect. It is argued that the court should use direct horizontal effect where there is a violation of an expressly horizontal right.

Second, we considered the argument that courts may be brought within the scope of the expression 'state' in Article 12. Drawing on the English debate on section 6 definition of 'public authority' in the Human Rights Act, 1998, which expressly includes courts, we enquired if the courts are under an interpretive obligation to apply human rights norms in public and private law actions. As the supreme court has not

[67] Murray Hunt (n. 56).

developed a clear-cut approach to applying Articles 12 and 32 to a court exercising judicial functions, this aspect is unlikely to develop in India.

Lastly, we examined the development of indirect horizontal effect through modifications of the public law writ action coupled with a wider conception of the fundamental rights obligations of the state. In *People's Union* and *Vishaka* the court has applied fundamental rights norms in the sphere of private action, regulated by statutory law or common law, even where no rights violation is demonstrated. By requiring all three organs of government—the executive, legislature and courts—to take these norms into account, the court has applied these rights expansively.

We began this essay by exploring the nature of the distinction between public and private law. We understood this distinction not merely to be one about jurisdictional boundaries into which legal problems may be divided into but also about the normative frameworks which should apply to relationships between citizens, and between the state and citizens. We are aware that it is no longer possible to assert that this distinction could apply with a great deal of precision and that several social problems—sexual harassment in the workplace and affirmative action in the private sector—destabilize this categorical approach.

We then carefully reconsidered the constitutional text and the supreme court's approach to the fundamental rights guaranteed by the constitution and the 'state action' requirement. A close reading of the fundamental rights encourages us to abandon the conventional understanding in Indian constitutional theory that these rights are addressed exclusively to the state. The rights contained in Part III are phrased differently: while some articles are expressly addressed to the state, others are unambiguously addressed to all citizens or are ambivalent about their addressees. Despite not developing a rationale for the phrasing of rights in this fashion we may conclude that these rights have a differential horizontal impact. Though the courts have not acknowledged the significance of these differentially phrased rights, they have recognized that some rights in the constitution may apply horizontally. I argue that the phrasing of a right, in particular who it is addressed to, helps us identify the bearer of the obligations that such a right imposes. Where rights are addressed to the state, the aggrieved citizen may only approach the state for a remedy and where the rights are addressed to fellow citizens, one may address one's claims directly upon such a citizen who violates these obligations. Such an argument would conclude that where rights are ambivalent about who they are addressed to, citizens may enjoy the option of proceeding against either the state or citizen. As the horizontal effect of constitutional rights need not always directly impose legal obligations on citizens, we consider the 'state action' requirement in the constitution to develop a comprehensive account of the horizontal effect of rights.

There is no clarity in Indian constitutional theory and practice about the roles played by the Article 12 definition of 'state' read with the Article 13 power of judicial review and its relation to Articles 32 and 226 which provide for constitutional remedies. Most existing constitutional literature suggests that the Article 12 definition of 'state' controls the scope of application of all the rights in Part III of the constitution. Our analysis of the addressees of the fundamental rights reveals that not all rights are addressed to the state. This must mean that the Article 12 definition of 'states' at best circumscribes the range of actors who will bear the obligations for those rights which are addressed to the state. The supreme court has adopted the 'agency or instrumentality' test as the standard metric by which it will assess if an entity will carry the obligations of the state. This test accommodates a range of non-departmental public bodies and private bodies in contractual relationships with the states but will not go far enough to accommodate the courts, private entities, or individual citizens. Unless the court develops a new standard in interpreting the scope of the term 'state' in Article 12, there is a minimal scope for direct horizontal effect of those rights which are addressed to the state.

Articles 32 and 226 set out special constitutional remedies which may be sought by a person aggrieved by the violation of fundamental rights.[68] Article 32 is silent about whom such a remedy would lie against while Article 226 expressly allows the high court to issue such remedies against 'any person or authority, including... any government.'[69] Though the courts have not embraced the width of these provisions, they have over the last three decades developed a method by which they have adapted the public law writ action to mould the relations between private parties. This method has two ingredients: first, by regularly including both state and non-state actors as parties to a writ petition and second,

---

[68] Article 226 provides that these remedies may be invoked for 'any other purpose' besides the enforcement of fundamental rights. It is beyond the scope of this paper to examine the breadth of this expression and whether it applies merely to other cases of administrative judicial review or a range of other cases. See *State of Orissa v. Ram Chandra Dev* AIR 1964 SC 685 for the supreme court's view on the scope of the phrase.

[69] Ibid.

by imposing a broad affirmative obligation on the state to ensure that the outcomes regulated by private law are consonant with constitutional values. The courts have not developed an overarching theoretical or doctrinal justification for developing this indirect horizontal effect of fundamental rights. Moreover, they have used this technique irrespective of the right being enforced.

We are now in a position to pull together the various arguments considered above. The horizontal effect of fundamental rights guaranteed by the Indian constitution may be achieved in a complex and nuanced fashion if we take account of the nature of the right and then provide for its particular remedy. While expressly horizontal rights may be directly enforced against private citizens, ambivalent and state focussed rights may either have a direct effect on those entities who are an agency or instrumentality of the state or have an indirect horizontal effect through the techniques developed by the court in public law writ actions. Such a nuanced approach has the advantages of developing a theoretically coherent approach which responds both to the constitutional text and court practice.

4

Freedom of the Press and the Human Rights Discourse

Managing the Tensions[1]

N. RAVI

While international human rights documents emphasize the intrinsic value of a free media, the human rights discourse has over the years tended to relegate it to the background because of tensions arising from divergent value systems, privacy protection and hate speech issues. While the most serious source of tension, the balance that needs to be struck between protection of minority groups from hate speech on the one hand and freedom of expression on the other, is difficult to reconcile at the level of abstract concepts or universal values, most nations have struck a proper balance suited to their own experience and specific circumstances. A free media with its impact on public opinion and institutions in a democratic system can be of great instrumental value in promoting human rights observance. Its effectiveness, however, varies depending on the nature of the human rights violations, with the remedial impact being the greatest in routine cases of custodial violence and the like and the least in insurgency type of situations where state policy seeks to suppress a terrorist or secessionist group. The greatest challenge before the human rights community and the media is to get the democratic system to respond sensitively and safeguard human rights in difficult situations when national security concerns come to the fore.

[1] This paper is based on my work as a Visiting Fellow at the Human Rights Program of the Harvard Law School in the spring of 2000. I am thankful to Henry Steiner, Director of the Human Rights Program and to Peter Rosenblum, Projects Director, for their guidance and suggestions.

FREEDOM OF THE PRESS IN INTERNATIONAL HUMAN RIGHTS DOCUMENTS

Freedom of the press and the media, which forms part of the larger right of freedom of speech, is an important, though over the years somewhat diminishing, component of international human rights documents starting from the Universal Declaration of Human Rights and through the International Covenant on Civil and Political Rights (ICCPR) and the regional covenants. The Universal Declaration elevates it to the preamble that states, 'The advent of a world in which human beings shall enjoy freedom of speech and belief and freedom from fear and want has been proclaimed as the highest aspiration of the common people.' Article 19 specifies, 'Everyone has the right to freedom of opinion and expression; this right includes freedom to hold opinions without interference and to seek, receive, and impart information and ideas through any media and regardless of frontiers'.

The ICCPR in Article 19 elaborates: '(2) Everyone shall have the right to freedom of expression; this right shall include freedom to seek, receive, and impart information and ideas of all kinds, regardless of frontiers, either orally, in writing or in print, in the form of art, or through any other media of his choice.' In Article 19(3), it also allows limits to be imposed on the right: 'The exercise of the rights provided for in paragraph 2 of this Article carries with it special duties and responsibilities. It may therefore be subject to certain restrictions, but these shall only be such as are provided by law and are necessary:

(a) For respect of the rights or reputations of others;
(b) For the protection of national security or of public order (*ordre public*) or of public health or morals.'

Apart from allowing states to impose restrictions on specific grounds, the ICCPR also requires states to ban certain types of speech and Article 20 enjoins: '(1) Any propaganda for war shall be prohibited by law. (2) Any advocacy of national, racial or religious hatred that constitutes incitement to discrimination, hostility or violence shall be prohibited by law.'

In the European convention for the Protection of Human Rights and Fundamental Freedoms and in the American Convention on Human Rights, the basic right of freedom of expression is guaranteed in a way similar to Article 19 of the ICCPR. The European Convention in Article 10 is somewhat more elaborate on the grounds on which restrictions may be imposed: '(2) The exercise of these freedoms, since it carries with it duties and responsibilities, may be subject to such formalities, conditions, restrictions, or penalties as are prescribed by law and are necessary in a democratic society, in the interests of national security, territorial integrity, or public safety, for the prevention of disorder or crime, for the protection of health or morals, for the protection of the reputation or rights of others, for preventing the disclosure of information received in confidence, or for maintaining the authority and impartiality of the judiciary.'

The American Convention (in Article 13) seeks also to protect freedom of the press and the media from indirect controls: '(3) The right of expression may not be restricted by indirect methods or means, such as the abuse of government or private controls over newsprint, radio broadcasting frequencies, or equipment used in the dissemination of information, or by any other means tending to impede the communication and circulation of ideas and opinions.' It allows censorship of certain categories of expression: '(4) Notwithstanding the provisions of paragraph 2 above, public entertainments may be subject by law to prior censorship for the sole purpose of regulating access to them for the moral protection of childhood and adolescence.' Like the ICCPR, it enjoins on the parties to ban propaganda of hate and incitement: '(5) Any propaganda for war and any advocacy of national, racial, or religious hatred that constitute incitements to lawless violence or to any other similar illegal action against any person or group of persons on any grounds including those of race, colour, religion, language, or national origin shall be considered as offenses punishable by law.'

In the delineation of the right of freedom of expression in international human rights documents, the following six aspects are noteworthy, though not all of them find place in any single document. First, the right to seek, receive, and impart information and ideas both within the country and in the outside world ('regardless of frontiers') is protected. Second, this right extends to all modes of expression: oral, print, electronic, or art form, though some forms may suffer more of direct (for example, censorship of films) or incidental (for example, communications regulations and band allocation for television and radio broadcasts) restrictions. Third, this right may be restricted only by law and only to the extent considered necessary and tolerable in a democratic society. Fourth, the grounds on which the right to freedom of expression may be restricted generally include national security, public order, public health and morals, protection of the reputation of others and safeguards during the judicial process against public exposure of children and victims of some crimes, against disclosure of national security secrets, and protection of the integrity of the judicial process itself. Fifth, as a norm, the restricted categories entail penalties after their expression but in some cases such as cinema and entertainment where the impact is immediate, prior restraint or censorship may be allowed in the interest of protecting morals, particularly of children. Sixth, apart from the permissible restrictions on specific grounds, states are required to prohibit and penalize certain categories of speech including propaganda for war and speech that promotes hate and incites people towards discrimination and violence based on race, religion, language or national origin. It is significant that over the years human rights documents have tended to build in more qualifications to free speech, with the later documents veering towards a more restrictive approach that would protect vulnerable groups against certain forms of speech.

FREEDOM OF THE PRESS IN THE HUMAN RIGHTS DISCOURSE

The growing body of what may be regarded as the human rights discourse comprising books, journals, papers, theses and other publications, material on Internet websites, conferences and seminars, and generally the work and delineation of issues by human rights organizations tends to focus on groups such as children, women, victims of torture, conflict and crime, dissidents, prisoners of conscience, and others whose liberty is curtailed, and refugees. Organizations such as the Committee to Protect Journalists focus specifically on the issue of freedom of expression and report on the state of human rights. The US State Department's annual reports generally contain an assessment of press freedom in different countries.

The delineation of free press and freedom of expression issues in the human rights discourse shows that the concern is largely over aggravated forms of assault on freedom of expression including killing and imprisonment of journalists and writers and physical attacks on newspaper premises. Heroic defiance of censorship and restrictions that entail penalties and suffering is highlighted while silent compliance is hardly noticed. It would seem that restrictions on the freedom of expression coupled with restrictions on liberty or violations of physical security are taken seriously, not just restrictions on freedom of expression *per se*. When marking World Press Freedom Day on 3 May 2000, the Committee to Protect Journalists compiled a list of ten 'worst enemies of the press' ranging from Foday Sankoh of Sierra Leone to Slobodan Milosevic of Yugoslavia to Fidel Castro of Cuba and Mahathir Mahamad of Malaysia.[2] They had all resorted to aggravated forms of assault on freedom of expression and were rightly condemned. At the same time, those who resort to more subtle measures to muzzle the press hardly come under such scrutiny.

This may be in part because of rights touching on life, physical well-being, and freedom being accorded a higher priority. Also, the press and the media are not seen as disadvantaged, needing as much support as other groups do. In an interesting paper on the debate on a new broadcasting bill in India,[3] Mark N. Templeton notes that there was no discussion from the human rights perspective in terms of the fundamental freedoms and the right to seek, receive, and impart information. He suggests, 'Perhaps they (human rights activists) think that the satellite broadcasters and cable operators will fight for media freedoms and that the human rights community can spend its limited time and energy elsewhere.' The fact that substantial sections of the press and the electronic media are associated with large and profitable groups would only go to reinforce this attitude.

TENSIONS BETWEEN FREE PRESS AND HUMAN RIGHTS

There are, however, sources of tension as well between a free press and human rights advocates. In the first place, human rights advocacy demands a certain commitment and a passionate espousal of good causes that cannot be found in the disembodied, neutral voices of journalists. Journalism tends to be value-neutral, with its insistence on getting all sides of a story and while there is still plenty of room to write with a great deal of sensitivity and feeling and make a deep impact on public opinion, the demands of objectivity need to be kept in mind.

It is not uncommon for human rights advocates to express their disappointment over the media which they see as reflecting human rights concerns inadequately or not at all. Justice Rajinder Sachar, a noted civil liberties proponent in India has this to say of the role of the Indian press in relation to its coverage of human rights abuses:[4] 'This attitude (of the media) was disappointingly reflected in the passive, even negative, role

---

[2] http://www.cpj.org/enemies/enemies_00.html.
[3] *Cardozo Journal of International and Comparative Law*, Fall 1997.
[4] The *Hindu*, 10 February 1999.

the media played when dealing with the working of the Terrorists and Disruptive Activities (Prevention) Act.... Governments conveniently invoke the sensitive ground of national security to silence the media from reporting human rights violations in affected areas. Unfortunately, the media, by and large, has a tendency to accept this gratuitous advice without much demur.'

Secondly, human rights advocacy leans towards greater privacy protection, especially in the case of victims of rape, violence and accidents, and children. Some of the more blatant cases of violations of privacy by the media that have been brought up before the courts include the case of reporters entering the hospital room and photographing the nine-year-old son of a famous French actor who had been injured in an accident,[5] a story with photographs in *Time* magazine of a woman with a severe eating disorder (under captions such as 'She eats for ten'),[6] and photographing and interviewing in the hospital room an English actor who was semi-conscious after having suffered a severe head injury.[7]

The biggest source of tension, however, arises from the third category, namely the abuse of the press and the media in aid of some of the worst human rights abuses that has at times tended to set press freedom in opposition to human rights advocacy. In such cases, the media has served as a vehicle for propaganda, for fanning hatred and for inciting some groups to violence against others. Such propaganda has ranged from direct attacks and calls for the elimination of some groups considered undesirable or inimical to the dominant group to more subtle forms that seek to create insecurity among the dominant group and spur it to violent attack against some minority group. The use of the media for hate propaganda by the Nazi regime is one of the earliest modern instances.[8] In Bosnia, the antagonists used radio to incite ethnic hatred against one another.[9]

It was in Rwanda, however, that radio was used most insidiously and blatantly in the service of genocide. The official government station, Radio Rwanda, initially 'played a pernicious role in instigating several

[5] Cass 2e civ., 12 July 1966.

[6] *Barber v. Time Inc.*, 159, S.W. 2d 291 (Mo. 1942).

[7] *Kaye v. Robertson* [1991] F.S.R 62 (Eng. C.A.).

[8] Robert Edwin Herzstein, *The War That Hitler Won: The Most Infamous Propaganda Campaign*, New York: Putnam (1978).

[9] Francoise J. Hampson, 'Incitement and the Media', Human Rights Centre, University of Essex, Papers in the Theory and Practice of Human Rights, No. 3, 1993.

massacres', according to the Special Rapporteur to the UN Commission on Human Rights, B.W. Ndiaye.[10] When Radio Rwanda was brought under the control of moderates as part of the reforms aimed at reconciliation, the extremists among the officials in the military and in business started the Radio-Television Libre des Milles Collines (RTLM) which gained a large audience for its popular talk show format. It operated in conjunction with the ruling party's private militia, Interhamwe, and typically it would name and criticize an individual and immediately Interhamwe groups would find and attack him. It became even more active in instigating genocide after April 1994 when it started organizing roadblocks ('RTLM radio is with the people manning the roadblocks' was a constant announcement) and naming 'enemies' who were then stopped and killed by militias. Typical of its propaganda was a broadcast on 15 April 1994, when an announcer exhorted the listeners: 'If you do not want to have Rwandans exterminated... stand up, take action... without worrying about international opinion.'[11]

The response under international law to such extreme forms of hate speech is still evolving and has not so far proved to be effective. In times of war, jamming of radio broadcasts has been resorted to routinely. During the Cold War, Radio Liberty and Radio Free Europe were the voices of Western propaganda aimed at the people in the Soviet Union and Eastern Europe, and were extensively jammed by the governments. In internal conflicts, however, the international community did not generally consider jamming or other preventive means to stop incitement, though in the case of the RTLM, there was a debate on whether jamming would be justified.[12] The US Committee for Refugees (USCR), which along with Human Rights Watch-Africa was pushing for the jamming of the RTLM broadcasts, had this to say midway during the crisis:[13] 'The USCR urges the US to use immediately its technical capability to 'jam' the radio broadcasts of Radio Milles Collines, which Rwandan extremists have used to disseminate their racist, hate-filled violence. In recent days this radio station has broadcast messages to the militias and to the public exhorting them to accelerate the slaughter.' The US Assistant Secretary

[10] UN Doc. E/CN.4/1994/7/Add.1 at 10–12.

[11] Article 19, Broadcasting Genocide: Censorship, Propaganda and State Sponsored Violence in Rwanda 1990–4 (1996).

[12] Jamie Frederic Metzl, 'Rwandan Genocide and the International Law of Radio Jamming', 91. A.J.I.L 68.

[13] US Committee for Refugees, Responding to the Rwanda Crisis (3 May 1994) cited by Metzl.

of State for African Affairs, George Moose, told the Sub-Committee on Africa of the US House Committee on Foreign Affairs on 4 May 1994,[14] 'One of the things we were looking at very seriously over the weekend was whether we could and should deploy assets of our own to try and shut down or block out transmissions of...RTLM.' However, he went on to add that the broadcasts had ceased during the week.

The law of humanitarian intervention even in the middle of a crisis is in a troubled state and intervention anticipating a humanitarian crisis is even more problematic. While the United Nations Security Council can authorize the use of force in situations where international peace and security are threatened—a major humanitarian crisis would be such a situation—preventive action against hateful propaganda and incitement including radio jamming remains a little-examined area. Metzl notes in an article in the *American Journal of International Law*[15] that the traditional US interpretation of international law was that jamming was banned as violative of freedom of expression. This interpretation dates back to the Cold War period when the US claimed the right to broadcast radio programmes without interference into the Soviet Union and the Eastern Bloc countries. The Soviet Union and many of the developing countries, on the other hand, considered foreign broadcasts from across their borders as violations of national sovereignty that could be countered by jamming. In the event, neither approach was of help in dealing with the situation in Rwanda.

The helplessness of the international community in the face of what was a most heinous abuse of free expression in the cause of genocide only heightened the tensions between free press advocacy and human rights. Yet if the international community was unwilling to bear the costs of intervention in the Rwandan genocide, it did seek to bring the more prominent perpetrators to book. After the International Criminal Tribunal for Rwanda was set up, Jean-Bosco Barayagwiza, founder of the extremist Hutu CDR party and ranking member of RTLM was brought before it and charged with inciting murder. In November 1999, he was initially discharged by the Tribunal's appeals chamber for repeated violations of his fundamental rights including the detention for 19 months without charges after his arrest in Cameroon, the Tribunal's failure to hear his habeas corpus petitions, and his delayed appearance before the Tribunal

[14] The Crisis in Rwanda: Hearings Before the Sub-Committee on Africa of the House Committee on Foreign Affairs, 103rd Congress 15 (1994) cited by Metzl.

[15] Rwandan Genocide and the International Law of Radio Jamming 91 A.J.I.L. 628.

96 days after his transfer to its custody. In March 2000, the chamber reversed its decision and decided that the Tribunal should try him. It still found that his rights had been violated but on a considerably smaller scale than had been found in its November 1999 decision. It ruled that the violations would be taken into account in his trial. If found not guilty by the trial chamber, he would be entitled to financial compensation; if, on the other hand, the trial chamber found him guilty, the violations would be taken into account in determining his sentence. He has since been indicted on nine counts including crime against humanity and violations of the Geneva Conventions. The prosecution has alleged that in an interview broadcast by RTLM, Barayagwiza had called for the extermination of Tutsis and moderate Hutus opposed to the then government. He is set to join Hassan Ngeze, editor of the anti-Tutsi publication, *Kangura*, and RTLM co-founder, Ferdinand Nahimana, in what has been described as a media trial before the Tribunal that was to begin in September 2000.

In a larger context, freedom of speech needs to be reconciled with equality and the tolerance of diversity needed in a liberal, pluralist democracy. The human rights movement generally tends to come to the aid of ethnic and religious minorities and women who are very often the targets of hate speech. For instance, Article 4 of the International Convention on the Elimination of All Forms of Racial Discrimination says:

'State Parties condemn all propaganda and all organizations which are based on ideas or theories of superiority of one race or group of persons of one colour or ethnic origin, or which attempt to justify or promote racial hatred and discrimination in any form, and undertake to adopt immediate and positive measures designed to eradicate all incitement to, or acts of, such discrimination and, to this end, with due regard to the principles embodied in the Universal Declaration of Human Rights and the rights expressly set forth in Article 5 of this convention, inter alia:

(a) Shall declare as an offence punishable by law all dissemination of ideas based on racial superiority or hatred, incitement to racial discrimination, as well as all acts of violence or incitement to such acts against any race or group of persons of another colour or ethnic origin, and also the provision of any assistance to racist activities, including the financing thereof...

The convention notes the conflict between prohibition of hate speech and the right to freedom of expression and calls for 'due regard' for rights enumerated in the Universal Declaration including the rights of freedom of speech, association, and conscience. The actual balance that is struck between the need to protect vulnerable ethnic or religious minority groups and the right to free speech varies widely among nations.[16] The United States' approach tends to be the most tolerant of free speech. Europe, Germany, France, Austria, and the Netherlands maintain broad restrictions on racist speech including Holocaust denial while the United Kingdom generally emphasizes the public order aspect. Some other countries, including India, prohibit the wounding of religious or ethnic sentiments and impose wide restrictions in this area. Broadly, the extent of freedom of speech allowed and the degree of protection for vulnerable groups against hate speech reflect the experience and the specific circumstances in the individual countries. Countries that have seen the impact of hate propaganda have put in place a regime more restrictive of free speech and more protective of minority groups.

A detailed discussion of hate speech laws is beyond the scope of this paper but it is clear enough that one could lean towards greater protection of ethnic and religious groups from hate propaganda or towards allowing a greater latitude for free speech. At one end of the spectrum is an enumeration of differences that may reflect and reinforce prejudice and at the other is speech which incites immediate, hateful violence. The human rights movement leans towards providing a greater protection to the groups targeted by hate speech while media organizations and free speech advocates would prefer a greater latitude, allowing restrictions on only the more aggravated forms of hate speech. If both human rights groups and free press advocates were to seek universal standards, their approaches may be difficult to reconcile. However, if the balance that is struck in individual countries is examined in the light of the specific circumstances prevailing in them, the safeguards against hate speech would seem to be adequate in most cases.

CHECKING VALUE OF PRESS FREEDOM

While cases of abuse of press and media freedom loom large in the human rights discourse, there are certain tales of heroism as well which seem for the moment to be confined to the discourse on press issues, unable to get over the barrier that seems to separate the two areas. In serious and more brutal conflicts, the traditional role of the war correspondent takes on

[16] Dominic McGoldrick and Thérèse O'Donnell, 'Hate-Speech Laws: Consistency with National and International Human Rights Law' (Legal Studies, Vol. 18, Issue 4, pp. 453–85, Dec. 1998).

a more sensitive character as the reporting of the massacres in Rwanda, Pol Pot's genocide in Cambodia, and the ethnic conflicts in the Balkans has brought out. Journalists are very often the first to record for the international community the brutality and the trampling of human rights in such situations. From the professional standpoint, Roy Gutman and David Rieff, in the book, *Crimes of War: What the Public Should Know* provide valuable material, seeking to sensitize journalists covering conflicts to international law relating to war crimes, providing legal definitions as well as practical advice. Recognising the positive role that radio, for instance, can play, Western governments and NGOs have funded private stations in the Balkans to promote peace and reconciliation. The role of Studio Ijambo in Burundi offers valuable lessons on ways that journalism could help stem bloodshed even in times when passions and anger seem uncontrollably on the rampage.

Of the traditional rationales for free speech and freedom of the press—the search for the truth, individual autonomy, and self-expression and democratic participation—the individual's right to self-expression has gained prominence in the more recent period. That is no doubt of great substantive value but press freedom can also be seen as an instrumental right in furthering observance of human rights. What Vincent Blassi terms the 'checking value' of press freedom would seem to be of great significance for the human rights discourse. The press' exposure of abuse of power and atrocities provides the decision-making public in a democratic and responsive system with information on which they can act to remedy situations. John Milton in *Areopagitica* stressed the importance of the remedial aspect, though in a different context of getting his plea for unlicensed printing heard: 'For this is not the liberty which we can hope, that no grievance ever should arise in the Commonwealth— that let no man in this world expect; but when complaints are freely heard, deeply considered and speedily reformed, then is the utmost bound of civil liberty that wise men look for.' Routine exposés and stories of injustice and suffering play a valuable role in helping people to remain conscious of their rights and in the search for remedies and these are very much a part of sensitive journalism. There are also dramatic instances that bring out the effectiveness of the media's watchdog role forcefully in the international arena as well as in the purely domestic sphere.

Even in the early part of the twentieth century, this role was demonstrated in the context of King Leopold II's colony in the Congo.[17] In the

---

[17] Adam Hochschild, *King Leopold's Ghost: A Story of Greed, Terror and Heroism in Colonial Africa*, Houghton Mifflin (1999).

race to colonize Africa, Leopold seized for himself the territory 75 times the size of Belgium around the Congo river and started what Joseph Conrad termed, 'the vilest scramble for loot that ever disfigured the history of human conscience.' With a brutal 19,000-men army, he held whole villages hostages and forced them to collect rubber and also used forced labour to build roads and railways. His men were ruthless with those who did not work to their satisfaction and 10 million people—half the population of Congo—died of hunger and exhaustion while working for him. The slaughter was exposed by a British shipping line worker-turned-journalist, Edmund Morel, a diplomat, Roger Casement, and some concerned missionaries. With the support of such figures as Mark Twain and the Archbishop of Canterbury, Morel mounted a vigorous campaign in both Europe and the United States. When on 10 December 1906 Hearst's *New York American* joined the campaign with an expose of Leopold's attempt to bribe American Congressmen to look the other way, public opinion and the attitude of governments in the US and Europe shifted so dramatically that Leopold was forced to hand over his personal colony to Belgium in 1908, though the near-genocidal deaths continued for a decade thereafter and forced labour for much longer.

In 1984, the Palestinian hijackers of a bus filled with Israelis were killed and the hostages rescued. According to the initial account by the Israeli government, the terrorists had been killed in a gun battle with the security services. However, the Israeli newspaper, *Hadashot*, uncovered and published the truth that the account of the gun battle was a fabrication and that the Palestinians had been executed after their capture by the security services. A huge public scandal ensued and safeguards against such executions were later put in place. It is a different matter that the newspaper's license to publish was suspended for four days for publishing material endangering the public peace and the Israeli Supreme Court upheld the suspension.

The prison in Bhagalpur in the northern Indian state of Bihar was the scene of horrific happenings in 1982.[18] Frustrated with the delays in the criminal court system, the police in the district engaged in a most brutal campaign against suspects. They took it upon themselves to pierce the eyes and blind with acid several prisoners facing charges—a court-ordered investigation later found at least 17 blinded under-trial prisoners. Some of the prisoners petitioned the local magistrates in the district who only ignored their pleas. This story was uncovered by the *Indian*

[18] *Anil Yadav v. State of Bihar* (1981) 1 SCC 622.

Express newspaper and was published nation-wide, creating a storm of protest and indignation. The blindings were later taken before the Supreme Court of India by some public-spirited lawyers. The court ordered an immediate medical examination and treatment for the blinded prisoners and launched a detailed enquiry which found the account of blinding by the police to be substantially true.

EFFECTIVENESS OF THE PRESS IN DEMOCRACIES

Turning to the mechanisms through which a free press could operate to check human rights abuses, the impact of its findings on public opinion and on the democratic political system is obviously of the greatest importance. Public opinion, however, tends to be roused only by the more outrageous incidents and small, day-to-day violations are often ignored. Here, one may usefully draw upon the insight of Amartya Sen that a free press and the democratic system are most effective in spurring public action to tackle emergencies such as famines where sympathy is immediate. This they do by imposing political costs on tardy response or inaction by public officials. On the other hand, they do not generate similar responses in the case of persistent problems of hunger, malnutrition, ill health, and illiteracy. Writes Sen,[19] 'Democracies have been particularly successful in preventing disasters that are easy to understand, in which sympathy can take an especially immediate form. Many other problems are not quite so accessible. Thus India's success in eradicating famine is not matched by a similar success in eliminating non-extreme hunger, or in curing persistent illiteracy, or in relieving inequalities in gender relations. While the plight of famine victims is easy to politicize, these other deprivations call for deeper analysis, and for greater and more effective use of mass communication and political participation—in sum, for a fuller practice of democracy.'

In the spectrum ranging from galvanized public action in times of famines and emergencies to apathy towards persistent poverty-related problems, the case of human rights would seem to fall somewhere in between. The experience in India shows that even here, one has to distinguish between different types of human rights abuses and how the democratic system tends to deal with them. In the more routine cases that are not politically sensitive such as instances of custodial violence in police stations and prisons by lower level functionaries, sexual harassment

---

[19] Sen, 'Freedom and Needs', *The New Republic*, 10 January 1994.

and rape, the political executive and the higher levels of the administration are usually quick to launch action to penalize the offenders once the violations are brought to their notice. These indeed are the staple of the human rights discourse in much of the media.

There is, however, another category where human rights violations take place in the execution of a tough state policy directed towards terrorists or groups wanting to break away—the typical response of states to some group within seeking self-determination. Here, the democratic system even with a free press tends to look the other way. This is true of the experience of India which has faced insurgencies in the states of the north-east, Punjab, and Andhra Pradesh Extra-judicial executions by the police of the suspected terrorists and insurgents and fabricated accounts of 'encounters' or gunfights in which they ostensibly lost their lives have become common in such situations.[20] The mainstream political parties whether in government or opposition hardly take up such human rights violations in the public arena. There is even a certain measure of judicial latitude as demonstrated by the supreme court's decisions upholding the constitutional validity of draconian laws such as the Terrorists and Disruptive Activities Act and the Armed Forces Special Powers Act which curb due process rights and confer arbitrary power to the security forces.[21]

There is a third category of human rights violations where the democratic system tends to be even more tolerant of state sponsored violence, and that is when a foreign element comes in—by way of a dispute with another nation and intrusion by outsiders as in Kashmir. Here, not merely is the democratic political system under challenge, but the nation as a whole is seen as threatened and there is a subtle appeal to patriotic sentiment. Where the nation's integrity itself is seen to be in peril, human rights concerns recede to the background and extraordinary measures, including the curtailment of liberty and fair trial rights and even a greater latitude in the use of force by police and security personnel, are very often sought to be justified in the name of national security and public order. Still, accounts of human rights violations and contrary viewpoints of civil liberties groups and non-government organizations at times find expression in the media, even if its checking value stands diminished. The larger challenge equally before the human rights movement and the media is to get the democratic, administrative, and judicial systems including the

[20] 'Encounters: National Human Rights Commission to issue notice', The *Hindu*, 6 August 1997; 'Punjab resorted to secret cremations', The *Hindu*, 23 July 1999.
[21] *Kartar Singh v. State of Punjab* (1994) 3 SCC 569.

relatively new institutions like human rights commissions to respond effectively to protect human rights in such difficult circumstances.

Outside of the formal democratic system, two other kinds of pressures seem to operate with the aid of a free press. The first is the civil society and the community of NGOs who bring together individuals and groups whose rights are violated and collect a critical mass of data for an effective campaign. In the area of human rights, the NGOs have developed a symbiotic relationship with the press, providing the media with information from the field and also using independent press reports as a major source of information. The second is the international community and the moral pressure it can bring to bear on a recalcitrant country, as the experience in the Balkans and in Africa has repeatedly shown. Here, as the international media report human rights abuses, public opinion outside tends to come to the aid of the victims, often pushing governments to sanction or act in some way against the violating countries. Just as images of starvation have raised public support for carrying out relief programmes, reports of human rights violations could help in gathering support for diplomatic efforts, economic sanctions, and even for humanitarian intervention if warranted.

In seeking to manage the tensions arising from hate speech and propaganda, international human rights documents have over the years veered towards a greater protection to minority groups even at some cost to freedom of speech, and the protective regime in most countries is by and large satisfactory. Both the human rights community and the media can profit from a closer interaction and exchange of information and views. The media could take a greater interest in human rights issues and human rights organizations would gain a better understanding of the role and working of the media. Quite apart from its intrinsic value, the instrumental value of a free media in promoting human rights observance needs to be realized in a fuller measure.

Developments in India

Developments in India subsequently confirm the mixed feelings over the role of the media in promoting human rights even as the media itself continued to face legal pressures. Human rights as an issue is no longer a novelty in the media, and most newspapers and magazines as well as television channels carry news reports and features on the rights of women and children and prisoners, for instance. Pre-natal tests to determine the sex of children as a prelude to aborting female fetuses, female infanticide in some parts of the country, deaths caused by disputes over dowry, sexual harassment at the workplace and in public places, rape and the casual approach of the lower judiciary to the crime, ill treatment of the mentally ill have all been highlighted by the media, leading to public policy changes and strong public action even if attitudinal change remains a very slow process. Deaths in police custody in many states and deaths in 'encounters' with the police (an euphemism for cold blooded extra-judicial execution) particularly in Andhra Pradesh and Kashmir but also sporadically in other states where it has been extended from insurgents to criminal gangs, continue to be covered by the media. The media as a whole is sensitive to the brutal fallout of caste prejudice taking the form of torture and physical degradation at the hands of informal village groups inflicting punishment on some hapless transgressor of their codes, and the ill-treatment of dalits who are subject to indignities and in some places to blatant discrimination in restaurants and tea shops—in some villages in Tamil Nadu, for instance, the two tumbler system is in vogue in which dalits are served not in reusable glass or metal tumblers but in mud cups which are later destroyed. The emergence of active human rights groups and non-governmental organizations has in many ways brought the media into closer touch with the happenings on the ground and secured a greater visibility for human rights issues.

In the area of governance, the media continue to focus intensively on the issue of corruption and transparency in administration. The most dramatic illustration of this trend was of course the exposé by the *Tehelka* website of the corrupt tendencies in defence deals, with some officials and public figures caught accepting money on camera. A more recent instance was the exposé in the *Indian Express* of the Union Minister of State for Environment and Forests, Dilip Singh Judeo, who was alleged to have accepted money in return for clearing a mining lease for an Australian firm.

On the negative side, sections of the media at times lapse into hate speech themselves or become vehicles of hate speech targeting specific religious and caste groups, endangering their person, livelihood, and their very lives. The most obvious illustration of this tendency was in Gujarat during the post-Godhra riots in which several hundred Muslims were killed in retaliation for the brutal burning of returning pilgrims in railway carriages at the Godhra railway station. Several unofficial enquiries speak of the local press instigating the rioters through exaggerated and even false reports. On the other hand, the media outside Gujarat focused on the passivity, and in some places even the complicity, of the state administration during the riots and the killings. The Muslim minority, because of the dispute over building the Ram temple at Ayodhya and the Christian minority, because of the evangelical activities and the debate over religious conversions, have in the last decade and half emerged as the targets of attacks through the media.

Areas for Reform

Extent of Free Speech—Not for Print Alone

While in theory, freedom of speech and expression includes freedom of the media as a whole, in practice it does not seem to reach the electronic media, radio, and television. Terrestrial television and much of radio are still in the hands of the government though under a notionally autonomous public broadcasting body, the Prasar Bharati. For long, state monopoly over broadcasting not only negated the idea of a pluralistic media but also denied voice to large sections of critical opinion and diverse viewpoints. The old mindset which justified censorship of films on the ground of the audio-visual medium's unique and deep impact persists among the judiciary. Thus in the *Cricket Association of Bengal* case,[22] the supreme court (Jeevan Reddy J) observed, 'It is a powerful instrument which can be used for greater good as also for doing immense harm to society.' There is also the notion that a society as fragile as India's cannot quite free public broadcasting from controls: 'Ours is a nascent republic. We are yet to achieve the goal of a stable society. This country cannot afford to read into Article 19 (1) (a) an unrestricted right to licensing of broadcasting.'[23]

The idea that the state could impose a more stringent regulation on the electronic media was also based on the reasoning that the airwaves are public property, transmission bandwidth was limited, and needed to be allocated carefully through a system of licensing of the use of specific frequencies. Even in conditions where bandwidth was limited, there was no justification for a complete ban on private broadcasting stations even if a regulatory system was needed to allocate the bands. With the opening up and the spread of satellite television and cable channels, even the limited bandwidth argument which was the only passable rationale for regulation is no longer valid.

---

[22] (1995) 2 SCC 161.
[23] Ibid.

The control mindset is persistent though, as the statement of objects and reasons of the Cable Television Networks Act, 1995, makes clear: 'There has been a haphazard mushrooming of cable television networks all over the country during the last few years as a result of the availability of signals of foreign television networks via satellites. This has been perceived as a 'cultural invasion' in many quarters since the programmes available on these satellite channels are predominantly Western and totally alien to our culture and way of life. Since there is no regulation of these cable television networks, lot of undesirable programmes and advertisements are becoming available to the viewers without any kind of censorship.'

So long as the legal basis remains weak and the right of the private electronic media is not brought squarely under Article 19 (1) (a), media freedom will remain incomplete. This needs to be redressed through public policy changes to permit private broadcasting and by a review of judicial decisions to strengthen the constitutional basis of freedom of the electronic media.

Free Speech, National Security, and Terrorism

Meanwhile, laws on secrecy, defamation, contempt of court, and breach of legislative privilege reflecting the colonial mindset that the governed have no right to criticize those who govern, continue to restrain free speech. A dramatic illustration of the misapplication of the Official Secrets Acts is the case of Iftikar Geelani, a Kashmiri journalist who was imprisoned pending charges that he was in possession of material on Indian troop deployment in Kashmir that was in the public domain and which he had downloaded from the Internet. A provision of the Prevention of Terrorism Act that requires journalists to pass on to the police any information on terrorist activity on penalty of imprisonment is a new source of pressure on journalists, particularly those operating in the troubled areas of the north-east and in Kashmir and are in touch with insurgent groups and their political representatives and spokesmen who function with different levels of official recognition.

In the midst of such disquieting developments comes the heartening news of the repeal of POTA though present indications are that cases pending under the old law would continue. Free speech gained when the section of the Act making it an offence to express support for a terrorist organization was read down by the Central POTA Review Committee in the case of the Marumalarchi Dravida Munnetra Kazhagam (MDMK) leader, Vaiko, who was detained under the law for over a year and a half pending trial. It held that speeches in support of Sri Lankan Tamils and opposition to the extradition of the LTTE leader, V. Prabhakaran, were part of the political philosophy of the MDMK and went on to say that such speeches 'cannot be said to be speeches made for the purpose of encouraging support for the LTTE or to further its activities'.

Criminal Defamation

In the area of defamation, while the supreme court has laid down that in civil defamation a public official suing has to prove that a publication was made in 'reckless disregard for the truth' (*R. Rajagopal v. State of Tamil Nadu*),[24] there is no such mitigating provision in the criminal defamation law which exerts a tremendous pressure on the press. India continues to be one of the few jurisdictions in the democratic world where the criminal defamation law is used with a disturbing regularity. Truth *per se* is not a defence in a criminal defamation case, it has to further pass the test that it was published in the public interest. And the standard to be applied in the case of defamation of a public official is the same as that of a private individual. Very often, criminal defamation cases that require personal appearances, at times at distant places, are launched to harass rather than seriously proceed to trial. The Tamil Nadu Government had, on behalf of the Chief Minster, filed over a 100 criminal defamation cases against newspapers and the media. The inefficiency of the judicial system where a criminal case could go for over five years and the possibilities of obtaining stay orders at different stages tax the stamina of the complainant as much as that of the accused and mitigate the harshness of the law. However, one persistent complainant and one conviction can have a chilling effect on the press as a whole.

Contempt of Court

Another law invoked against the press is the Contempt of Courts Act in which the judge acts as the prosecutor, judge, and the hangman rolled into one. The courts themselves have set out the rule that this extraordinary jurisdiction is not to be invoked lightly but only rarely to protect the institution of the judiciary from being scandalized. However, once invoked, there is no defence, not even the truth, and the only way out is an apology. Often, the courts levy a token penalty to make the point, but at times the penalty could be serious as in the case of Jayashree Khadilkar-Pandey who was sentenced to seven days imprisonment for a series of

[24] AIR 1995 SC 264; (1994) 6 SCC 632.

editorials in the Marathi daily, *Navakal*, attacking Justice Srikrishna who was heading a commission enquiring into the Hindu-Muslim riots in Mumbai. The question whether truth could be invoked as a defence to a charge of contempt of court is pending determination since 1990 by a Constitution bench of the supreme court. A large scale application of this law was in the matter of three Karnataka High Court judges, who were alleged in news reports to have misbehaved in a resort in Mysore—14 newspapers and over 50 journalists and publishers were charged with having committed contempt of court. The supreme court, declaring it wants to give a quietus to the case has stayed the proceedings as of now. The larger issues of judicial accountability and invoking the power to punish for contempt of court as well as the defences available are still to be addressed. Following the suggestion of the Constitution Review Commission, the Government of India has proposed an amendment to the Contempt of Courts Act which would make truth a defence to a charge of contempt of court provided it is being put forward bona fide and is in the public interest. The proposed amendment to the Contempt of Courts Act reads, 'Provided that the court may permit the defence of justification by truth on satisfaction as to the bona fides of the plea and it being in the public interest'.[25] It needs also to be examined if the offence of scandalizing the court which is vague and allows of arbitrary interpretation and use should remain on the statute book at all.

Privileges of Legislatures

Another device at times used in an arbitrary and unrestrained manner against the press is the power to punish for breach of legislative privilege and contempt of the legislature. The most dramatic use of this power was in November 2003 by the Tamil Nadu Legislative Assembly in the case of *The Hindu* where this writer and four others were sentenced to 15 days imprisonment for publishing three reports describing proceedings in the Assembly, and an editorial critical of what it said was an intolerant attitude. The supreme court has since stayed the arrests and the issue of reconciling legislative privilege with freedom of expression under Article 19 (1) (a) and personal liberty under Article 21 of the constitution is to be decided by a constitution bench of the court. Meanwhile, the Tamil Nadu Assembly has rescinded the sentence through another resolution.

[25] The Contempt of Court (Amendment) Act 2006 received the absent of the President on 17 March 2006 (ed.).

The legislators enjoy the same privileges that the British House of Commons enjoyed at the time of commencement of the constitution in 1950. The House of Commons has since given up many of its privileges in tune with the more liberal times but the privileges of the Indian parliament and the state legislatures remain frozen in time. This position was meant to be temporary as the Constituent Assembly did not have the time to get into the details of codification of the privileges. However, legislators as a whole have resisted codifying their privileges and would seem to prefer the vagueness and flexibility that permits unrestrained use. The law as pronounced by the supreme court is to the effect that uncodified privileges may override some fundamental rights such as freedom of expression under Article 19 (1) (a)—but not personal liberty under Article 21—but once codified, the privileges will be examined in the light of all the fundamental rights including Article 19 (1) (a) and the grounds on which reasonable restrictions may be imposed on the rights.

Protection from the Moral Police

If a critical test of free speech is the extent to which ideas and concepts that shock and dissenting views far out of the mainstream are allowed free expression, the country seems to be slipping into more illiberal times. Themes deemed to be provocative (the Bombay riots, the Gujarat violence), unusual, shocking, and supposedly alien to the nation's culture (Deepa Mehta's 'Fire' which explores a lesbian relationship in a conservative family) or even challenges to a widely accepted notion (a call for the reform of the system of reservations, in 'Ore Oru Gramathile') are sought to be suppressed either by officialdom or by an intolerant group, or by a combination of both. Typically, when an organized group threatens an agitation against a film or a book or a play, the administration intent on avoiding trouble seeks to suppress the work rather than protect free expression.

Strangely, in the case of Ore Oru Gramathile, it was the Madras High Court which had imposed the ban when the state of Tamil Nadu challenged the grant of a censor certificate for the film. Its reasoning was that an attack on the reservations system would create enmity among different caste groups, leading to large-scale violence. This argument was rejected by the supreme court (Shetty J) which stressed, 'it was not necessary that every one sing the same song'. It went on to quote an earlier judgement of the court, 'It is our firm belief, nay, a conviction which constitutes one of the basic values of a free society to which we are wedded under our constitution that there must be freedom not only for the thought that we cherish, but also for the thought that we hate' (1989) 2 SCC 574. It was also emphatic in rejecting the usual law and order grounds that administrations advance in seeking a ban on provocative speeches and performances: 'Freedom of expression cannot be suppressed on account of threat of demonstration and processions or threat of violence. That would tantamount to negation of the rule of law and a surrender to blackmail and intimidation. It is the duty of the state to protect the freedom of expression since it is a liberty guaranteed against the state. The state cannot plead its inability to handle the hostile audience problem. It is its obligatory duty to prevent it and protect the freedom of expression'.

This categorical pronouncement should have put a halt to the activities of the moral and the political police who are too quick to seek a ban or to prevent the publication or exhibition of books, films, plays, and works of art that they feel would be objectionable. That unfortunately has not been the case, and protests, violence, calls for bans continue even as the state looks on, hesitant to protect the right of a lone artist or film maker or writer from the undemocratic instincts of intolerant and vociferous groups. It is time the supreme court's edict against allowing intolerant groups to suppress dissenting voices was enforced in letter and spirit.

5

Reflections on Free Speech and Broadcasting in India

VIKRAM RAGHAVAN*

In the past two decades, broadcasting has emerged as the dominant means for communications in India.[1] Since the early 1990s especially, this important sector of the economy has been radically transformed by deregulation and liberalization. A stifling state monopoly over radio and television has ended. A large number of private television and radio stations have emerged. Their colourful, provocative, and very diverse programme content has replaced the stale and insipid offerings of state-run broadcasting agencies. Today, broadcasting in India is a powerful tool to spread news and information, debate and discuss issues, entertain and amuse, and engage people to action. The multiple uses and enormous

* I am grateful to several friends and colleagues, who read this essay. They are Upendra Baxi, David Fontana, N.S. Gopalakrishnan, Promod Nair, Patrick Roberts, Thomas Sebastian, V. Suresh, Arun Thiruvengadam, and Benjamin Yong. Their comments and insights greatly improved my writing and analysis. I am not sure Justice Krishna Iyer will agree with everything I say here. But, to paraphrase Ronald Dworkin, controversy is at the heart of our great legal tradition to which Krishna Iyer has contributed so much. See Ronald Dworkin, 'Political Judges and the Rule of Law' in *Comparative Constitutional Law: Festschrift in Honour of Professor P.K. Tripathi* 3, M.P. Singh (ed.), Eastern Book Co., Lucknow (1989). Paragraph references for judgments cited here are from Manupatra, the online legal database. Finally, I write this essay in my personal capacity, and the opinions I express here are entirely my own. They do not represent the World Bank's position on any issue.

[1] For a general account of these changes, see *Broadcasting Reform in India*, Monroe E. Price and Stefaan G. Verhulst (eds), Oxford University Press, New Delhi (2000). When using the term 'broadcasting', I am referring to the radio and the television (in all its species: terrestrial, satellite, and cable).

influence of radio and television raise a variety of legal and regulatory challenges. Prominent among them, is the extent to which the Indian Constitution's guarantee of free speech influences broadcasting policy and regulates programme content. I propose examining these subjects using the following outline.

The first part of this essay is a primer on India's constitutional framework for free speech protection. It explains the textual basis for freedom of speech and expression in the constitution and surveys the supreme court's early cases. Before broadcast deregulation began, the supreme court's free speech docket did not include very many radio and television cases. However, in some remarkable pre-deregulation decisions, the court held that citizens have a fundamental right of access to government broadcasting facilities.

The next part focuses on an important supreme court decision with profound implications for free-speech and broadcasting. In it, the court ruled that Indian citizens enjoy a fundamental right to transmit and receive information through audio-visual means, and that the government has no monopoly over broadcast frequencies. The concluding part of this essay analyses whether greater restrictions should be imposed on broadcasting compared to other expressive forms, such as books, newspapers, or even ordinary speech, because of its powerful impact on audiences.

Freedom of Speech and the Indian Constitution: An Overview

Articles 19 (1) (a) and 19 (2)

Freedom of speech and expression is a sacred icon in the constitution's inner sanctum, the fundamental rights chapter. This freedom is a central tenet of India's constitutional faith. Textually, it is recognized in Article 19, which also lists certain other fundamental freedoms that Indian citizens enjoy. Clause (1) (a) of that Article protects free speech and it reads:

'All citizens shall have the right; (a) to freedom of speech and expression'

In drafting this provision, India's founders were influenced by the First Amendment to the United States Constitution. That amendment says, 'Congress shall make no law abridging the freedom of speech, or of the press.'[2] It assures, in relatively absolute terms, freedom of speech and

[2] US Constitution, Amendment I.

the press.[3] But, under the Indian constitution, this freedom is a lot more qualified. Article 19 (2) contains a list of various grounds that permit the government to impose reasonable restrictions on the freedom. These grounds are India's sovereignty and integrity, state security, foreign relations, public order, decency, morality, contempt of court, defamation, and incitement of offenses.

Constitutional History

During the constitutional debates, there was hardly any doubt whether the constitution should explicitly protect free speech. Several members of the Constituent Assembly vividly recalled, and had even experienced, the colonial British administration's attempts to stifle the freedom movement using oppressive anti-sedition laws.[4] Based on that experience, they strongly believed that the constitution must explicitly recognize various fundamental freedoms, including free speech and expression.[5] However, there was considerable division about whether to include specific grounds that would enable the government to curtail or restrict those freedoms.

Some members argued that including restrictive grounds would significantly affect or even negate the general content of the freedoms. Others, however, favoured incorporating them because they feared that absolute freedom would be dangerous given India's enormous poverty, illiteracy, and economic problems.[6] Ultimately, it appears that many members voted to include the grounds influenced by the 'needs of the time'.[7]

Early Cases Involving the Print Media

When India's Constitution was inaugurated in 1950, freedom of speech was a relatively novel concept. But the courts were quickly filled with

[3] See William O. Douglas, *We the Judges: Studies in American and Indian Constitutional Law from Marshall to Mukherjea*, 307, Doubleday Carden City, New York (1956) (noting that, unlike the Indian constitution, the First Amendment does not permit legislative innovations).

[4] See P.K. Tripathi, 'Free Speech in the Indian Constitution: Background and Prospect', 67 *Yale L.J.* 384, 391–3 (1957–8) (discussing the importance of free speech to Gandhi and the Indian national movement).

[5] See B. Shiva Rao, *Framing of India's Constitution: A Study*, pp. 222–3, Indian Institute of Public Administration, New Delhi (1968).

[6] See ibid., at 223–5.

[7] See ibid., at 223.

cases in which citizens invoked the new freedom. Most actions involved newspapers or magazines. Plaintiffs were usually newspaper publishers or editors, who alleged that the government had restricted what they wanted to print or publish. Unlike the more recent South African Constitution, India's Constitution does not expressly recognize press or media freedom.[3] But this omission did not stop the supreme court from declaring that freedom of the press is an integral part of Article 19 (1) (a).

Romesh Thapar v. Madras was the court's first free speech decision.[9] It arose from a government order forbidding the circulation of a journal, Crossroads. The order was made under a state law enacted to protect public safety and public order. Thapar, Crossroads's editor and publisher, complained that the order violated his freedom of speech. The supreme court, which had barely opened for business, agreed. Writing for the majority, Justice Patanjali Sastri ruled that free speech includes the right to propagate ideas, which is ensured by circulation.[10] Public order was not a constitutional basis to restrict free speech.[11] The law was declared unconstitutional and the order set aside.

On the same day as Romesh Thapar, the court also decided Brij Bhushan v. Delhi, another free speech case.[12] At issue was an order requiring publishers to submit 'all communal matter and news and views about Pakistan including photographs and cartoons....'[13] Relying on Romesh Thapar, Patanjali Sastri had little hesitation in holding the order invalid. But, in more forceful language than his Romesh Thapar opinion, he wrote that liberty of the press is an essential part of Article 19(1)(a).[14]

[8] See South African Constitution, section 16 (1) (a) ('Everyone has the right to freedom of expression, which includes—(a) freedom of the press and other media[]').

[9] AIR 1950 SC 124: (1950) SCR 594.

[10] Ibid., at para 4. See Burt Neuborne, 'The Supreme Court of India' 1 International Journal of Constitutional Law 476, 508 (2003) (Romesh Thapar anticipated the US Supreme Court's over-breadth doctrine).

[11] Romesh Thapar and certain other developments led to the First Amendment enacted in 1951. Among other things, this amendment retroactively broadened the scope of permissible free speech restrictions in Article 19 (2). For an account of its legislative history, see Granville Austin, Working a Democratic Constitution, The Indian Experience, pp. 38–50, Oxford University Press, New Delhi (1999).

[12] (1950) SCR 605.

[13] Ibid., at para 1.

[14] Ibid., at para 4 (italics mine). The judge did not offer any reasons for this interpretation other than to cite Blackstone's commentaries. His opinion suggested that press freedom flows inexorably from the freedom of speech. During the Constituent Assembly debates, Ambedkar, chair of the drafting committee, was not

The supreme court explored this theme again in *Express Newspapers* v. *Union of India*.[15] The court strongly emphasized the importance of media freedom. It held that the press could not be oppressed with laws that abridge free speech, curtail circulation, or undermine its independence by driving it to seek government aid.[16] The court reiterated this view in *Sakal Papers* v. *Union of India*, where it struck down the government's page and price limitations on newspapers.[17] It emphasized that citizens have a fundamental right to propagate their views and to reach any class and number of readers they choose.[18]

Absence of Broadcasting from the Court's Free Speech Docket

Few, if any, of the supreme court's early free speech cases involved broadcasting. In large part, this was because the government tightly controlled radio and television services. Radio was the principal electronic media in India through the 1950s and 1960s.[19] Television services commenced in the early 1970s, and during the 1980s, they gradually emerged as an important communications medium. But, until the early 1990s, All India Radio, the government's radio monopoly, and Doordarshan, the state-run television entity, enjoyed exclusive control over all broadcast services. Very early in its history, the supreme court emphasized the importance of an independent press free from government interference. It had no hesitation in linking this concept to the freedom of speech. Yet, it is striking that, until the late 1980s and early 1990s, the court

---

in favour of including a separate provision. No special recognition was required, he declared, because individuals, such as editors and managers, run the press. These persons could express themselves freely when writing or publishing. Therefore, it was unnecessary to provide separate protection for the press. See 7 *Constituent Assembly Debates* 780 (2 December 1948). Apparently convinced by this explanation, the Assembly rejected a proposal to expressly include freedom of the press in the Constitution. See ibid., at 784.

[15] (1959) SCR 12.

[16] See ibid., at para 207.

[17] AIR 1962 SC 395: (1962) 3 SCR 842.

[18] See ibid., at para 27.

[19] For an historical account of Indian radio, see Pon Thangamani, *History of Broadcasting in India: With Special Reference to Tamil Nadu 1924–1954*, pp. 223–8, Ponnaiah Pathippagam 2000; and Sevanthi Ninan, *History of Indian Broadcasting Reform 3 in Broadcasting Reform in India*, supra n. 1.

never considered (or was never explicitly petitioned to consider) whether the same rationale should also extend to broadcasting, which remained completely dominated by the government.[20]

There could be several reasons for this phenomenon. First, state control of broadcasting was rather common even in many western liberal democracies (excluding the United States). There seemed no compelling need for India to be different by allowing private ownership of broadcasting. Second, from the mid-1970s onward, there were significant political and legislative attempts to make broadcasting autonomous. The court may have been content with leaving broadcast reform to the legislative and political process without interfering in a highly charged partisan battle. Third, the court may have been unwilling to take on the government on this important policy issue. During 1970s and 1980s, when the Congress party was in power, it adamantly opposed any autonomy for broadcasting.[21] The court may have wanted to preserve its capital for more important battles with the government. And finally, and quite simply, the court may have just not been presented with an appropriate case to consider the issue.[22]

Facing no competition from the private sector, government bureaucrats generally decided what programmes to broadcast on both All India Radio and Doordarshan.[23] They, in turn, were often influenced by their

[20] Before deregulation began in the 1990s, government control over broadcasting was an issue in at least three cases. But the courts declined to interfere. See *Prakash Vir Shastri* v. *Union of India* AIR 1974 Del. 1 (declining to issue direction that All India Radio avoid favouring ruling party in its coverage); *A.B. Shorawal* v. *L.K. Advani* AIR 1977 All. 426 (refusing independent candidate's petition challenging government decision to restrict election broadcasts to only those candidates fielded by political parties); and *P.L. Lakhanpal* v. *Union of India* AIR 1982 Del. 167 (upholding government control over broadcasting).

[21] See Venkat Iyer, *Mass Media Laws and Regulations in India*, p. 68, Asian Media Information and Communication Centre (2000) (Prime Ministers Indira Gandhi and Rajiv Gandhi argued that, as a developing country, India was not ready for independent broadcasting); David Page and William Crawley, *Satellites over South Asia*, p. 63, New Delhi: Sage Publications (2001) (the Congress government consistently ignored recommendations to allow state governments [often controlled by opposition parties] to operate their own broadcasting services).

[22] I have not found any record of the court having declined to hear appeals from the three high court cases mentioned in note 20, above.

[23] See Lloyd I. Rudoph and Susanne Hoeber Rudolph, *In Pursuit of Lakshmi: The Political Economy of the Indian State*, p. 82. University of Chicago Press (1987) (noting complaint that, on account of frequent transfers and reassignments, Indian Administration Service officers lacked technical expertise to run Doordarshan).

political superiors on important programming decisions, especially the content of news bulletins. Radio and television became full-fledged propaganda machines for successive Indian governments. Thus, in the first few decades following India's independence, free speech, as a means to ensure diversity of view-points, had little direct relevance to broadcasting.[24]

Free Speech and Film Censorship

There was, however, one important exception to the general dominance of the print media in free speech matters: censorship cases involving films and documentaries. They involved film producers and directors who challenged government censorship of their productions. Film censorship usually takes place under the Cinematograph Act (No. 37 of 1952). This statute established the Board of Film Censors, which later became the Board of Film Certification, (the 'Film Board'). Section 4 (1) requires every film scheduled for public screening to obtain a certificate from the Film Board. Section 5B (1) declares that a film shall not be certified if it violates certain provisions. These provisions are a word-for-word reproduction of the permissible restrictions on free speech under Article 19 (2).

K.A. Abbas v. *Union of India* is the leading supreme court decision on film censorship.[25] It gave the court its first opportunity to discuss constitutional protection for free speech in the media outside the traditional context of newspapers and magazines. Abbas, the petitioner, was an award-winning film producer. The Film Board refused unrestricted screening of his documentary, *A Tale of Four Cities*, because it included scenes from a Bombay (now, Mumbai) red-light district. The board asked Abbas to edit certain scenes if the documentary was to qualify for a screening certificate. Abbas refused and complained to the supreme court that the board was violating his freedom of expression.[26]

[24] Free speech was a major casualty during the infamous emergency of the mid-1970s. Prime Minister Indira Gandhi's government misused radio and television to propagate its achievements, while censoring the newspapers that sought to carry alternative views or criticism. The courts tried to intervene in some newspaper cases, but they did not consider the government's blatant abuse of broadcasting.

[25] AIR 1971 SC 481: (1970) 2 SCC 780. There were a few film censorship cases before *Abbas*. But they did not produce any significant outcomes. See, for example, *P.N. Films* v. *Union of India*, AIR 1955 Bom. 381 (declining to address validity of Cinematograph Act because court lacked jurisdiction to hear the matter).

[26] At oral argument, the government made a dramatic concession. The film would receive a screening certificate without requiring any further edits. The case

Chief Justice Hidayatullah wrote a well-reasoned and artful judgment for an unanimous constitution bench. Tracing the evolution of film censorship, the Chief Justice noted that the Indian film industry lacked a professional self-regulatory body like the Motion Picture Association of America. Therefore, if the content of films was to be regulated, only the government could do so.[27] As a matter of practice, Hidayatullah observed that censorship existed all over the world in some form or the other.[28] Although motion pictures in the United States generally enjoyed a significant degree of First Amendment protection, they were not completely free from restrictions. Restrictions could also be imposed on films in England.[29] Censorship, he concluded, is a valid exercise of power in the interests of public morality and decency. It is in society's interest and does not violate freedom of speech and expression.[30] The Chief Justice also upheld certain government-issued guidelines used by film censors to certify films.[31]

An important dimension of *Abbas* is Hidayatullah's suggestion that films can be treated differently from other mediums of expression. Cinema is a powerful media, he wrote, combining sound, light, and movement to create a powerful impact.[32] For this reason, he readily

should have ended there. Instead, at Abbas's request, the court continued the proceedings to decide whether pre-censorship of films, itself, was constitutional. Justifying this unusual manoeuvre, the court explained that film producers required clear guidance on censorship. See *Abbas* at para 7; see also H.M. Seervai, 1 *Constitutional Law of India*, 792; N.M. Tripathi 1991 (criticizing this procedure because it resulted in the court rendering an advisory opinion).

[27] See *Abbas* at para 11.

[28] The Chief Justice found, with some apparent satisfaction, that even Abbas, the petitioner, supported censorship, having written in favour of it. See ibid., at para 20.

[29] In any case, the Chief Justice wrote, American and British practices on film censorship are not decisive because the Indian constitution allowed reasonable restrictions on the free speech. See ibid., at para 39.

[30] See *Abbas* at paras 40–1.

[31] But the Chief Justice complained that these guidelines did not contain anything that would preserve or promote art. To remedy this situation, he announced additional standards for censors to ensure that films were not unreasonably edited. These directions were taken from an earlier Hidayatullah opinion in *Ranjit D. Udeshi v. State of Maharashtra* (1965) 1 SCR 63. In that case, the directions were formulated as a guide to determine obscenity in literature. They could also be used, the Chief Justice believed, to assess films. See *Abbas* at para 48.

[32] To illustrate, the Chief Justice helpfully volunteered his own reaction to suggestive content in different media. One could view erotic tableaux in ancient temples

upheld film censorship on the grounds of public morality, decency, and the interests of society. But he declined to consider whether censorship could also be imposed on other forms of expression.[33] Thus, Hidayatullah was inclined to treat electronic productions, such as films and documentaries, differently from other media like newspapers. But he did not reveal how far this difference in treatment could go.

RELATIONSHIP BETWEEN ARTICLE 19 (1) (A) AND GOVERNMENT BROADCASTING

As I mentioned earlier, until rather recently, broadcasting in India was under complete state control. Because of this dominant position, All India Radio and Doordarshan enjoyed virtually unlimited control over what Indians watched or listened. If you were a programme or documentary producer and you wanted to broadcast your productions, you were at the government's complete mercy. All India Radio and Doordarshan could easily decline to consider your productions or impose onerous terms for broadcasting them. If you were refused, you had nowhere else to go. Government domination of broadcasting was complete. There were no private broadcast companies.[34]

As discussed earlier, it is remarkable that, in stark contrast to its rich Article 19 (1) (a) jurisprudence on the print media, the supreme court did not explore the inter-relationship between free speech and broadcasting for a substantial period. Gradually, however, in the late 1980s, judges came to realize that state domination over broadcasting is at odds with India's liberal and democratic polity. This change in judicial thinking led to two important cases in which the supreme court fashioned an important right of access for citizens to government broadcasting using Article 19 (1) (a). In a successive line of cases, the court ruled that

---

or read the *Kamasutra*, he declared, with relative equanimity. But he would consider abhorrent any documentary on those works that was a practical sex guide. See *Abbas* at para 50.

[33] *See* ibid., at paras 40–1. Each form, the Chief Justice noted, had 'a different context and importance'.

[34] You could not broadcast your production privately either. Until the Cable Networks Act (No. 7 of 1995) was enacted, private cable networks that independently transmitted programmes using videotapes or satellite feeds were illegal. See *Restaurant Lee* v. *State of Madhya Pradesh* AIR 1983 MP 146 (holding that local video networks cannot operate without a licence) under the Telegraph Act (No. 13 of 1885).

government-owned broadcasting agencies, notably Doordarshan, must not act arbitrarily in making broadcast decisions.[35]

Right of Access to Government Broadcasting

The first supreme court case to discuss the relationship between broadcasting and freedom of speech was *Odyssey Communications v. Lokvidyan Sangathan*.[36] It arose from a public interest petition against a television serial, *Honi Anhoni*, which was being telecast on Doordarshan. The petitioners, a voluntary organization, alleged that the programme would promote blind beliefs and false superstitions. Like evangelical Christians terrified by the *Harry Potter* series, the petitioners argued that the serial would create fear in children through ghost stories. Apparently convinced by this ridiculous submission, the Bombay High Court granted an interim injunction. But the supreme court easily reversed it. On behalf of the court, Justice Venkataramiah ruled:

It can no longer be disputed that the right of a citizen to exhibit films on Doordarshan, subject to the terms and conditions to be imposed by Doordarshan, is a part of the fundamental right of freedom of expression guaranteed under [A]rticle 19 (1) (a) of the Constitution of India which can be curtailed only under circumstances which are set out in clause (2) of [A]rticle 19 of the Constitution of India. The right is similar to the right of the citizen to publish his views through any other media, such as newspapers, magazines, advertisement hoardings, etc., subject to the terms and conditions of the owners of the media.[37]

Although Venkataramiah gave the impression that he was not saying anything new, this holding was a bold, new development in India's free speech jurisprudence. The court had created an entirely new right of access to government-owned broadcasting facilities, which it traced to Article 19 (1) (a). It was also the first time that broadcasting was explicitly acknowledged as an element in Indian free speech jurisprudence.

Venkataramiah compared this new right of access to what he claimed was the right to publish in newspapers, magazines, and advertisement hoardings. But his analogy was clearly wrong. Neither the constitution nor the court's prior jurisprudence (at least until *Odyssey*) supports such

[35] See *generally*, C.M. Jariwala, 'An Emerging Frontier of Speech and Expression: Freedom of Doordarshan', 38 *Journal of the Indian Law Institute* 149 (1996).

[36] AIR 1988 SC 1642: (1988) 3 SCC 410.

[37] See ibid., at para 5.

a right. Moreover, Article 19 (1) (a) is traditionally understood to apply only to entities that constitute the state under Article 13. Most newspapers, magazines, and advertisement hoardings in India are in private hands. Their publishers and owners do not constitute the 'state' under Article 13.[38] Therefore, strictly speaking from a constitutional angle, they were not required to offer their facilities to other citizens on demand. One could argue that Justice Venkataramiah was only referring to a citizen's right to use government-owned newspapers, magazines, and hoardings. If this *is* true, then the judge should have said so.

Fairness in Government Broadcasting Decisions

If it remained standing by itself, *Odyssey*'s novel right of access could have been easily dismissed as *obiter*. The underlying case did not involve any government actions that denied access to broadcasting facilities. The court could have easily decided the matter without formulating a new right.[39] As it turned out, however, the supreme court affirmed *Odyssey*'s right of access in a subsequent decision, *Life Insurance Corporation* v. *Shah*.[40] This case arose, in part, from Doordarshan's refusal to screen an award-winning documentary on the Bhopal gas disaster.[41] The

[38] Most fundamental rights, including the freedom of speech, are enforceable only against the executive (government agencies, departments, or other authorities) and the legislative. Collectively, these entities are called the 'state'. See Constitution of India, Articles 12 and 13. Private entities are generally not bound to observe fundamental rights.

[39] Unlike the typical free speech case, in *Odyssey* the government and the producer were actually on the same side. They both wanted telecast of the serial to proceed. There was no violation of any fundamental rights, in the ordinary sense, because these violations usually involve some infringing governmental action—and in this case, there was none. But Justice Venkataramiah still found a violation had taken place. According to him, the violation lay in the high court's order enjoining Doordarshan from telecasting the programme. The injunction abridged the producer's rights. *See Odyssey* at para 6. This reasoning, while attractive at first blush, ignores a binding nine-judge precedent, *Naresh Mirajkar* v. *State of Maharashtra*, AIR 1967 SC 1. There, the supreme court held that a judicial order from a high court *could not* be challenged as a fundamental rights violation. See ibid., at para 38 ('it is singularly inappropriate to assume that a judicial decision pronounced by a judge of competent jurisdiction in or in relation to a matter brought before him for adjudication can affect the fundamental rights of the citizens under [Article 19 (1) (a))]').

[40] (1992) 3 SCC 637.

[41] The decision's cause title is derived from a separate case involving the Life Insurance Corporation ('LIC'), a state-run agency like Doordarshan. The LIC case

producer challenged this action, and, in its defense, Doordarshan argued that the film lacked moderation and restraint. The high court set aside Doordarshan's action and found that Article 19 (1) (a) had been violated.

The supreme court upheld the high court's judgment. On behalf of the court, Justice Ahmadi noted the importance of free speech and expression in the constitutional scheme. Article 19 (1) (a) must be broadly construed, Ahmadi declared, to include the freedom to circulate one's views by mouth, in writing, or through audio-visual instrumentalities. It includes the right to propagate one's views through the print media or through any other communication channel, including the radio and television.[42]

Discussing case law, Ahmadi noted that citizens are entitled under Article 19 (1) (a) to communicate their ideas or thoughts through a newspaper, a magazine, or a movie.[43] This right is only subject to reasonable restrictions under Article 19 (2). On this basis, he concluded that the documentary producer had the 'unquestionable' right to convey his perception of the Bhopal gas disaster. He noted that the documentary had won an important award and received a screening certificate from the Film Board. It accurately portrayed events during the Bhopal gas disaster even though it was critical of the government's handling of the situation. Doordarshan had acted incorrectly by refusing to air the documentary.

Then, came the opinion's dramatic conclusion. As a state agency using public funds, Ahmadi ruled, Doordarshan could not refuse to screen the documentary without valid grounds. He did not accept Doordarshan's reasons for rejecting the documentary, and he agreed with the high court that Doordarshan must telecast it.[44]

---

arose from the agency's refusal to publish a rejoinder to a column in its in-house magazine. The Gujarat High Court ordered the publication on free speech grounds. LIC appealed to the supreme court. The court delivered a common judgment in that case and in the case against Doordarshan because they raised the common constitutional issue of free speech in government-owned facilities.

[42] See *Life Insurance Corp.* v. *Manubhai Shah* (1992) 3 SCC 637 at para 8.

[43] See ibid., at para 21.

[44] See *Manubhai Shah* at para 23. Ignoring the uneasy relationship between *Odyssey*'s facts and legal conclusions, Ahmadi referred to it approvingly in his survey of free speech case law. But, interestingly enough, he did not cite *Odyssey* as the underlying basis for holding that citizens have a fundamental right to communicate through movies (from which he went on to conclude that Doordarshan could not arbitrarily deny screening of movies).

Manubhai Shah's factual moorings placed *Odyssey*'s right of access doctrine on a much stronger footing. In *Odyssey*, Doordarshan and the producer were on the same side. They both wanted the programme aired. Yet, as we saw earlier, the court chose to declare a fundamental right of access to Doordarshan subject, of course, to certain terms and conditions. *Manubhai* applied this doctrine to a much more relevant case: one in which Doordarshan had decided *not* to screen a privately produced documentary.

Manubhai's holding that Doordarshan's broadcasting decisions must be based on 'valid grounds' is significant. But Ahmadi did not reveal how these decisions ought to be taken. That question is more elaborately considered in *Fasih Chaudhary* v. *Director General, Doordarshan*, a decision roughly contemporaneous to *Manubhai* and *Odyssey*.[45] There, a screen-writer argued that Doordarshan must accept his script for a television series on national integration. Doordarshan had unfairly rejected the script, he alleged, for another proposal. The supreme court was unpersuaded. It dismissed the case and upheld Doordarshan's selection. But, in its judgment, the court observed that Doordarshan must act in a fair and legitimate manner when considering broadcasting proposals. Doordarshan must show no malice, affection, favouritism, or nepotism. Thus, *Manubhai* and *Fasih Chaudhary* establish an important principle that government-broadcasting agencies cannot act arbitrarily or capriciously.

Odyssey, Manubhai Shah, and *Fasih Chaudhary* are all remarkable decisions. They are intelligent judicial innovations that gave new meaning to Article 19 (1) (a) by interpreting it to include broadcasting and requiring government broadcasting agencies to act responsibly. At a time when there was complete government domination over broadcasting, these cases offered citizens a meaningful opportunity to utilize this important medium of expression. The right of access to government broadcasting is India's homegrown version of a 'fairness' doctrine (although it is so

[45] (1989) I SCC 89: AIR 1989 SC 157. *Manubhai's* focus on Article 19 (1) (a) and the freedom of speech could be a reason for Ahmadi's reluctance to expand further on Doordarshan's decision making. Substantive and procedural aspects of government decision-making are usually addressed under the right to equality guaranteed by Article 14. This Article, and its requirement of non-arbitrariness in administrative matters, were not prominently discussed in *Manubhai*. By contrast, *Fasih Chaudhary* was more like a standard administrative-law decision. But this fact does not diminish its significance in complementing *Manubhai* and *Odyssey*'s right of access doctrine.

far confined only to government agencies).[46] In the post-liberalization era, the importance of these principles may have slightly diminished. With the proliferation of private satellite channels and cable networks, citizens now have a variety of opportunities to express their views without relying on Doordarshan. Yet, taken together, the three cases represent an important breakthrough in the evolution of India's free speech jurisprudence as it relates to broadcasting and they have been repeatedly affirmed.[47]

But the story is far from over. In the long run, there is likely to be considerable pressure to extend the doctrine of access rights to private entities. Although Indian broadcasting has not been completely deregulated, there are a considerable number of private players in the sector today. In the past few years, several large private broadcasting companies have emerged. They have become important and influential avenues for news and analysis, debate, and discussion. Thus, a key regulatory challenge for the future will be to find innovative and unburdensome (from a free speech perspective) ways to ensure diversity of information and opinions in a medium that is increasingly offered by private entities.

[46] The fairness doctrine was evolved by the Federal Communications Commission (FCC) in the United States. It imposes a two-pronged obligation on private broadcasters. First, they must cover important and controversial community issues. And second, they must offer a reasonable opportunity for contrasting viewpoints on such issues. See *Fairness Doctrine Report*, 102 FCC 2d 145 (1985). This doctrine was upheld by the US Supreme Court in *Red Lion Broadcasting Co.* v. *FCC*, 395 US 367 (1969). But the FCC repealed the fairness doctrine in 1987 because it found that the doctrine's net effect was to actually reduce, rather than increase, diversity of viewpoints. See in *Re Complaint of Syracuse Peace Council*, 2 FCC Rcd. 5043 (1987).

[47] See *C. Gopalakrishnan* v. *Union of India* AIR 1996 Ker. 333 (cites *Odyssey* to hold that citizens have a fundamental right to exhibit films on Doordarshan; and orders local station to complete telecast of a popular television serial for which an extension had been refused); *Prime Channel* v. *Union of India*, 1996 (38) DRJ 106 (public interest should be paramount in Doordarshan's programmes; it must carefully and critically examine all television serials before entering into agreements with producers); *Home Communication* v. *Union of India*, Civil Writ Petition No. 3104 of 1993, (Delhi High Court, 21 September 1993) ('first-come first-served' scheme to allot off-time programming slots on Doordarshan's satellite channels is arbitrary and invalid); and *cf. Bhim Vakanki* v. *Union of India* AIR 1999 Guj. 113 (upholding Doordarshan's selection of programmes commemorating fifty years of independence and stressing that government entities [like Doordarshan] must have scope for 'free play in the joints').

Free Speech in Government-Produced Programmes

A relatively unexplored dimension of Article 19 (1) (a) involves its application to programmes, such as news, current affairs, or political commentaries, broadcast by government stations. This dimension of free speech was analysed by the Bombay High Court's decision in *Indira Jaisingh* v. *Union of India*.[48] The petitioner, a leading constitutional lawyer, complained that Doordarshan had deleted important portions of her television interview. These portions contained criticism of a bill pending in parliament affecting Muslim women's rights.

Justice Sujata Manohar, then a high court judge, frowned on this action. She held that citizens interviewed on government television should be free to express their views and opinions. Censorship or deliberate distortion of what they say violates their freedom of speech.[49] An uninhibited market place of ideas is necessary, Justice Manohar ruled, especially when television is a state monopoly.[50] She ordered Doordarshan to give Indira Jaisingh a 'proper and reasonable' opportunity to express herself.

Indira Jaisingh is a unique case. It blends elements of a traditional free speech controversy, like *Romesh Thapar* where the Supreme Court rejected the government's attempt to restrict the press, with relief based on the access doctrine by requiring the government to provide the petitioner an opportunity to express her views. There are few, if any, reported cases that are similar to it.[51]

CRICKET ASSOCIATION CASE: USING FREE SPEECH TO REFORM BROADCAST REGULATORY FRAMEWORK

Perhaps, the most important case on free speech and broadcasting is the supreme court's 1995 decision in *Secretary, Ministry of Information and*

---

[48] AIR 1989 Bom. 25.

[49] See ibid., at para 13.

[50] See ibid., at para 16.

[51] In this respect, *Indira Jaisingh* is slightly different from *Manubhai*. In that decision, Doordarshan was ordered to screen an existing privately produced documentary. Justice Manohar's order in *Indira Jaisingh*, however, required Doordarshan to give the petitioner a fresh opportunity in a future Doordarshan programme. I am grateful to my friend, Tom Sebastian, for alerting me to this dimension of *Indira Jaisingh*.

Broadcasting v. *Cricket Association of Bengal* ('*Cricket Association*').[52] In this landmark ruling, the court held that every citizen has a fundamental right to impart as well as to receive information through the electronic media. It ruled that frequencies or airwaves are public property, and that the government enjoys no monopoly over them. Calling for significant reforms in broadcast regulation, the court ordered the government to take immediate steps to set up an independent and autonomous public authority to regulate frequencies.[53] Freedom of speech and expression played an important role in this decision.

Facts

Cricket Association's factual matrix is long and complex.[54] The decision is actually a common judgment for two different cases that arose independently of each other. But they share some similar elements and raised common questions of law. Both matters relate to international cricket tournaments organized by professional cricket bodies. In each case, Doordarshan and the tournament organizers were unable to agree on contractual terms for live telecasts of the matches. Consequently, the organizers sold their broadcasting rights to foreign broadcasting companies. It was alleged that Doordarshan, angered by these decisions, influenced other government agencies to interfere with the foreign broadcasters' preparations to telecast the matches. Among other things, the companies were denied uplinking rights and necessary import clearances.

Aggrieved by these developments, the tournament organizers sought legal relief. In the first case, the government and the organizers

---

[52] AIR 1995 SC 1236: (1995) 3 SCC 619. The principal opinion in *Cricket Association* was written by Justice Sawant for himself and Justice Mohan. Justice B.P. Jeevan Reddy wrote a separate, but concurring, opinion. In their opinions, Sawant and Jeevan Reddy indicated that they did not agree on any issue. Indeed, Jeevan Reddy noted that he agreed broadly with Sawant's conclusions. See ibid., at para 26. Yet, a careful reading of their opinions reveals significant differences on some important issues. For this reason, Sawant's opinion should be regarded as the Court's majority position, while Jeevan Reddy's views represent the minority opinion.

[53] For comment, see Sharad Varma, 'Air Waves: Public Property', 10 *The Lawyers* 4, May 1995; Shreyas Jayasimha and Shuva Mandal, 'Freeing the Airways', 9 *National Law School Journal* 150 (1997); M.P. Jain, *The Supreme Court and Fundamental Rights in Fifty Years of the Supreme Court of India*, p. 47, S.K. Verma and Kusum (eds), Oxford University Press (2000).

[54] A detailed account of the facts is available in Justice Jeevan Reddy's opinion. *See Cricket Association* at paras 29–45.

engaged in a very contentious round of interlocutory proceedings in the Calcutta High Court before taking the matter to the supreme court. In the second case, the organizers directly approached the supreme court through a writ petition. The court passed interim orders in both matters reserving its final judgment on the merits for later. When this decision was handed down, all the matches had been played and both tournaments were over. Aside from the factual disputes, the principal issues that the court addressed involved: (i) the scope of Article 19 (1)(a) vis-à-vis broadcasting; (ii) the extent of government control over frequencies and broadcasting; and (iii) the nature of the regulatory framework governing broadcasting.

Is There A Fundamental Right to Broadcasting?

In defending their decisions to award telecast rights to foreign companies, the tournament organizers, in both cases, relied strongly on Article 19 (1) (a). Freedom of speech and expression, they argued, includes the right to disseminate information. This meant that they could decide how, and in what manner, the matches should be telecast. Justice Sawant agreed. His long opinion includes a detailed survey of leading Indian decisions, US case law, and scholarly work on free speech and the media.[55] After an extensive survey of these authorities, Sawant held:

The freedom of speech and expression includes [the] right to acquire information and to disseminate it... the right to communicate, therefore, includes [the] right to communicate through any media that is available whether print or electronic or audio-visual, such as advertisement, movie, article, speech, etc.... This freedom includes the freedom to communicate or circulate one's opinion without interference to as large a population in the country as well as abroad as is possible to reach.[56]

The right to free speech, Sawant ruled, includes right to educate, inform, and entertain. It also includes the right to be educated, informed, and entertained.[57] This right is only subject to reasonable restrictions under Article 19 (2). If the government makes any restrictions, it must bear the burden of justifying them.[58]

Although Sawant clearly recognized the right to communicate through *any* media, his opinion does not explicitly say that there is a

[55] See ibid., at paras 4–10.
[56] See ibid., at para 11.
[57] See ibid., at para 11.
[58] See ibid., at para 2.

fundamental right to broadcasting. In fact, it is a bit confusing on this important issue. At one point, Sawant noted that the case did not involve the rights of private broadcasters. Yet, in another place, he admitted that the right to telecast is implicit in the right to educate, inform, and entertain, which is an extension of the freedom of speech and expression.[59] Ultimately, given Sawant's broad interpretation of Article 19 (1) (a) (in the quotation above), it is difficult to argue that, after *Cricket Association*, the right to communicate does not include a right to broadcast.[60]

This interpretation is especially compelling because Sawant went on to hold, in relation to the underlying facts, that the tournament organizers, as telecasters of matches, enjoyed free speech rights under Article 19 (1) (a).[61] They could telecast the matches using a method or agency of their choice. But the degree to which their rights were available, he cautioned, would depend on their underlying character and objectives. In the cases before the court, the tournament organizers were professional sporting bodies that promote cricket. They did not intend, Sawant assumed, to earn a large profit from telecasting the matches. Rather, they would use proceeds from the telecast contracts to develop the sport.

Justice Jeevan Reddy, on the other hand, was unwilling to recognize any explicit constitutional right to telecast for private entities, including the tournament organizers. But he had limited room to maneuver. The court in *Odyssey* and *Manubhai Shah* had already held that private citizens have a fundamental right to access government broadcasting facilities based on Article 19 (1) (a). These decisions made it difficult for Reddy to hold that broadcasting is not covered by the freedom of speech. Faced with these precedents, and after surveying other comparative materials, he conceded that Article 19 (1) (a) includes the right to receive and impart information.[62] Citizens are entitled to a plurality of views and a range of opinions on all issues, he acknowledged.

Then, Reddy reached an astonishing conclusion. Diversity of views and information, he argued, can only be ensured by a public broadcasting corporation—not private or government-controlled services. Broadcasting requires airwaves or frequencies, he reasoned, and these elements

[59] See ibid., at para 17.

[60] This is how at least one subsequent decision has interpreted *Cricket Association*. See *Union of India* v. *Association for Democratic Reforms* AIR 2002 SC 2112 at para 44 (citing *Cricket Association* for the proposition that there is a fundamental right to telecast sporting events).

[61] See ibid., at para 17.

[62] See ibid., at para 94 and 97 (3) (b).

are public property. They must, therefore, be utilized only for the public good. For this reason, there is no fundamental right under Article 19 (1) (a) to impart information using radio frequencies.[63]

Jeevan Reddy's interpretation of Article 19 (1) (a) is clearly much narrower than those of Sawant. Therefore, Sawant's opinion is the supreme court's majority view. Despite the ambiguity in his language, Sawant's recognition of a fundamental right to impart information and communicate through audio and visual means is very significant. This must surely mean that there is a fundamental right to broadcast, even if its scope depends on the underlying entity exercising the right.

This outcome was a giant leap forward in Indian Constitutional law. But, in some sense, it was an inevitable development in the progression of Indian free speech jurisprudence. Four months after the constitution's inauguration, the supreme court unhesitatingly declared in *Romesh Thapar* and *Brij Bhushan* that Article 19 (1) (a) includes the freedom of the press. This freedom, the court ruled, includes the right to print, publish, and circulate news and opinions without government interference.[64] As a consequence, for almost fifty years, Indian print media enjoyed the full plenitude of free speech protection. Thus, when broadcasting emerged as an important expressive medium, it was only fair for the supreme court to provide broadcasting with similar protection as the print media. A denial of free speech in broadcasting would have caused an unhealthy constitutional disequilibrium among different modes of expression. A person would have a fundamental right to say, write, and publish something, but not to telecast or broadcast it. That position would have been unfair and unjust.

What, then, is included within the fundamental right to broadcast under Article 19 (1) (a)? As Sawant himself explained, this right includes the freedom to disseminate views and information in India and abroad. It permits artists and performers to express themselves through dramas, songs, dance, and productions.[65] It must enable commentators and analysts to reflect on political developments and to criticize governments and public officials. It should provide a meaningful avenue for political

---

[63] See ibid., at para 90.

[64] See text accompanying notes 9–22.

[65] See *Usha Uthup* v. *West Bengal* AIR 1984 Cal. 268 (Article 19 (1) (a) includes the right to sing disco music and dance); and *Ruchika Theatre Group* v. *Delhi* AIR 1985 Del. 324 (freedom of speech includes the right to stage plays and dramas).

discussions and debate.[66] It ought to protect broadcast journalists who carry out investigations and report their findings.[67] And it must allow satirists and comedians to lampoon and parody contemporary events and people.

Finally, it is unfortunate that Sawant linked the fundamental right to broadcast to the underlying nature or business motives of the entity exercising the right. After the *Bank Nationalization* and *Bennett Coleman Cases*, it is now well settled that Indian citizens may exercise their fundamental rights through companies or other corporate entities.[68] Many fundamental freedoms cannot be meaningfully exercised individually or in isolation. Therefore, to make full and efficient use of these freedoms, it may be necessary for citizens to organize commercially. By its very nature, broadcasting is not a cottage industry or a small-scale undertaking. It requires extensive financial, human, and technical resources. In an increasingly global and competitive world where broadcasting has become the dominant means of communication, it would be unfortunate if broadcasting freedom in India depends on some pious assessment of the purpose or motives of those seeking to exercise that freedom. The constitution certainly does not require such an assessment when guaranteeing the fundamental freedoms.

No Government Monopoly Over Frequencies or Airwaves

Another important issue that *Cricket Association* discussed was whether the government enjoys a broadcast monopoly. As a general argument in

[66] See *Telugu Desam Party* v. *Election Commission*, 1995 (5) ALD 631 (Election Commission stipulation that political parties refrain from campaigning through the electronic media unreasonably interferes with the right to communicate and discuss political issues).

[67] See *M. Hasan* v. *Andhra Pradesh* AIR 1998 AP 35 (prison officials' action preventing journalists from conducting video interview with prisoners violates Article 19 (1) (a)).

[68] Read literally, the free speech protection in Article 19 (1) (a) is only available to citizens. But, in *Bennett Coleman* v. *Union of India*, AIR 1973 SC 106, the supreme court held that a company can sue for fundamental rights violations if it is joined by editors, directors, or shareholders, who are citizens. For this principle, the court relied on its decision in the *Bank Nationalisation* case where it upheld a shareholder's standing to challenge the government's takeover of commercial banks. See *R.C. Cooper* v. *Union of India* (1970) 1 SCC 248. For comment, see M.P. Jain, 'Article 19 (1) (a): Freedom of the Press', 15 *Journal of the Indian Law Institute* 154 (1973).

both cases, the government asserted that it had a complete control over all frequencies or airways in India. It had the unilateral right to decide how they should be used. The supreme court, however, categorically rejected this submission. Sawant held that the constitution forbids any monopoly in both the print and electronic media.[69] He acknowledged that broadcast frequencies are public property and noted the traditional argument for government control—to prevent the rich and wealthy from manipulating public opinion. But this argument lost its force, Sawant observed, in two circumstances. First, where a section of society is unreasonably denied access to broadcasting or the government claims an exclusive right to prepare and relay programmes. And second, if access is sought to frequencies not used by the government.[70]

Sawant was sympathetic to the argument that, if private broadcasters acted irresponsibly, it would be impossible to repair the damage. But, he countered that there are several regulatory provisions to handle such a situation. The judge seemed troubled by the fact that the government enjoyed virtually unbridled discretion to grant or refuse a broadcast licence. This situation could result, he warned, in the government suppressing speech, instead of protecting it.[71] In any case, the tournament organizers in the underlying cases had not asked for any frequencies used by the government. There were other frequencies that could be allotted to them. The government could refuse their applications for frequencies only on the grounds in Article 19 (2).[72]

[69] See *Cricket Association* at para 13. According to Sawant, the constitution only permits monopolies in the general-public interest. See ibid.

[70] See ibid.

[71] See ibid.

[72] See ibid., at para 17. Sawant was unimpressed by the government's submission that the tournament organizers were using their fundamental rights to benefit foreign companies (which did not enjoy such rights). The right to free speech, Sawant wrote, includes the right to disseminate information by the best possible method through an agency of one's choice. The organizers could choose the best avenue to obtain maximum revenues for their sport. See ibid. Jeevan Reddy appears to dissent on this point. He noted that, in both cases, the tournament organizers sold their telecast rights to foreign entities. Thus, they had effectively parted with their rights to broadcast the matches. Therefore, it was really the foreign companies, and not the tournament organizers, that were seeking to telecast the matches. The government's alleged actions in refusing them up linking did not violate the tournament organizers' rights because they had none! See ibid., at para 92. This reasoning suffers from a vital flaw. If the freedom of speech, and by implication, the right to telecast (which, in any case, Reddy was ambivalent about), is available only to Indian citizens, how could they be regarded as having sold this right to a foreign

Jeevan Reddy's opinion took a slightly different course on this issue. As a basic proposition, Reddy posited that frequencies or radio spectrum are public property. They cannot be concentrated in the hands of a few—whether government or private entities. A monopoly over broadcasting is inconsistent with free speech. Government control over the broadcast media effectively means control by the political party in power.[73] Yet, Reddy declined to recognize that private citizens or entities have a fundamental right to use broadcast frequencies.

Although they both held that frequencies were public property, Sawant and Reddy differed substantially on what this meant in practical terms. According to Sawant, as public property, frequencies must be used in the best interests of society. For this purpose, a central agency could either establish its own broadcasting network *or it could license private users*. He acknowledged that only a few persons could own frequencies because of the enormous costs involved. But to overcome this problem, he noted, the US FCC had evolved its fairness doctrine to impose access requirements on private broadcasters.[74] A similar arrangement was available in India through the Press Council, which enforces a right to reply.[75] Thus, Sawant, while endorsing the public nature of frequencies, clearly indicated that private citizens and entities could also utilize them.

Reddy was far more restrictive. He was strongly in favour of establishing a public broadcasting corporation that would use the frequencies to promote the public good. Private broadcasters could not be trusted to perform this function because they are primarily motivated by profits.[76]

Changes to the Regulatory Framework for Broadcasting

Both *Cricket Association* opinions extensively discussed the regulatory framework for broadcasting. This aspect of the case is important because it affects the manner in which the freedom to broadcast is exercised. When *Cricket Association* was decided (and as is the case even today), the

---

entity? It appears that Jeevan Reddy confused the contractual rights to telecast matches, which the organizers validly assigned to foreign companies, with their constitutional freedom to telecast sporting events.

[73] See ibid., at para 90.

[74] Unbeknownst, perhaps, to Sawant, the FCC repealed its fairness doctrine in 1987. See supra n. 46.

[75] See *Cricket Association* at para 17. It is unclear whether Sawant was suggesting that a right of reply should also be enforced against private broadcasting services.

[76] See ibid., at para 90.

Telegraph Act of 1885 formed the principal regulatory basis for broadcasting. This law establishes an 'exclusive privilege' for the government over all telecom and broadcasting services. As we saw earlier, Sawant was quite categorical in holding that the constitution forbids a monopoly in the print or electronic media.[77] Yet, inexplicably, he chose not to discuss whether the Telegraph Act was unconstitutional for this reason. Instead, he dispassionately analysed the statute, and acknowledged that it created a government monopoly over broadcasting.[78] He noted that the Act also permitted the government to grant broadcast licences. This power to license, he suggested, must be exercised consistently with Article 19 (2). In other words, any restrictions or conditions placed on licensees must be based on the grounds indicated in that provision.[79] What prevented Sawant from discussing the constitutionality of the statute is unclear from the opinion.

Sawant returned to this issue in his summary of conclusions where he issued a remarkable order to the central government. He directed it to take *immediate steps* to establish an independent autonomous public authority to control and regulate use of airwaves or frequencies. This authority, Sawant wrote, should be representative of all sections and interests in society.[80]

Like Sawant, Reddy favoured creating an independent corporation(s) or authority for broadcasting. But he prescribed a much wider role for this corporation than Sawant did. Reddy wanted this entity to not only manage frequencies, but also control all broadcasting. It was the 'command implicit' in Article 19 (1) (a), he wrote, that broadcasting should be controlled by a statutory corporation.[81] Only such a structure could ensure fair and balanced presentation of news and public issues.[82]

[77] See text-accompanying note 69.

[78] See *Cricket Association* at para 13. Section 4 (1) of the Telegraph Act of 1885 confers an exclusive privilege on the central government to establish and operate telegraphs. The Act's definition of a 'telegraph' is wide enough to include most forms of broadcasting.

[79] See ibid., at para 13.

[80] See ibid., at para 24.

[81] See ibid., at para 97 (3) (b). Jeevan Reddy fails to explain the basis for his conclusion. There is clearly nothing in the wording of Article 19 (1) to suggest such an implicit command.

[82] Reddy did concede, however, that more than one public corporation could be established to ensure sufficient competition in broadcasting. See ibid., at para 96. The primary role that Sawant envisaged for the authority was allocation and regulation

Is There a Fundamental Right to Establish a Broadcasting Station?

If, as Sawant held, citizens enjoy a fundamental right to transmit information through audio-visual means and there is no government monopoly over frequencies, can private citizens claim the right to establish a radio or television station? Venkataramiah anticipated such a question in *Odyssey*, but he left it open to be considered in an appropriate case.[83] With its lengthy discussion of broadcasting rights, one could have expected that *Cricket Association* to discuss this question. But Sawant declined to do so holding that private broadcasting was not at issue before the court.[84] Jeevan Reddy, on the other hand, felt no such compunctions. He was categorical that no private person or individual had a fundamental right to establish a broadcasting station. Private broadcasters, Reddy warned, were more likely to manipulate news and opinions than government-controlled media.[85] He agreed that private broadcasters could always set up stations abroad if they were not allowed to do so in

---

of frequencies. In one part of his opinion, he did suggest that the authority could also establish its own broadcasting network or it could grant licences to other entities, including private ones. But he did not include this point in his summary of conclusions. See ibid., at para 24.

[83] Venkataramiah clarified that his articulation of a right of access to Doordarshan did not imply a fundamental right to establish a private broadcasting station or a television centre. See ibid., at para 5. This question was also considered in two cases before *Odyssey*. It was first discussed by Justice Das in his separate opinion to *A.K. Gopalan v. State of Madras* AIR 1950 SC: (1950) 1 SCR 88. Analyzing Article 19 (1) (a), he raised hypothetical question whether an Indian citizen could establish a station for broadcasts to foreign territories. The answer, according to him, was 'clearly no.' See ibid., at para 279. Das's view is, of course, only *dicta* because *Gopalan* did not involve any broadcasting issues. But the question squarely arose before the Delhi High Court in 1982. A petitioner complained that the government had denied his application to start a private ratio station. He argued that strict government control over the electronic media prevented the opposition from expressing their views. The high court found that the freedom of speech includes the right to broadcast. But it declined to recognize that this right extends to establishing broadcasting stations because there would be chaos if everyone wanted to have their own stations. See *P.L. Lakhanpal v. Union of India* AIR 1982 Del. 167. This case is not cited in either *Odyssey* or in *Cricket Association*.

[84] See *Cricket Association* at para 17.

[85] Jeevan Reddy seemed particularly bothered by developments in Italy. There, the constitution was interpreted to imply a right to establish private broadcasting stations at the local level. This development subsequently led to the rise of giant media oligopolies. See ibid., at para 62.

India. But this fact did not change his reading of Article 19 (1) (a). According to Reddy, the article implicitly required public broadcasting—not private broadcasting.[86]

Since Sawant's majority opinion does not endorse Reddy's position on this matter, this issue remains unresolved. But it does seem illogical to suggest that the right to broadcast does not also include the right to establish a broadcasting station. It is true that, in the prevailing techno-logical and regulatory circumstances, there are some limitations on this right because broadcast frequencies are considered scarce. But, in strict economic terms, there is really nothing that is not scarce, other than, perhaps, fresh air. All goods are, in some sense, limited and finite. Scarcity, therefore, is not a legitimate basis to say that there is no right.[87]

[86] On this point, Reddy's opinion suffers from a contradiction. Despite his claim that Article 19 (1) (a) implicitly requires public broadcasting, he went on to concede that parliament could permit private broadcasting. He then added that a court should not rule on this issue because it involved a 'policy' matter. If this last statement is true, why did Reddy posit a constitutional basis for public broadcasting in Article 19 (1) (a)? If private broadcasting is, as he claimed, a policy matter, he should have refrained from offering a gratuitous opinion on the subject.

[87] To be sure, not everyone who wants to establish a broadcasting station may actually be able to do so. Under the present mechanics of spectrum usage, only certain applicants may be able to obtain frequency allocations. They have to undergo a competitive process and satisfy certain technical and financial qualifications. Once selected, they have to comply with certain terms and conditions to operate their stations. But the presence of a selection process, eligibility qualifications, and operating conditions does not mean that there is no right to establish broadcasting stations. The scarcity aspect to frequency regulation has another dimension. Some legal scholars argue that the present 'real property' model for frequency management, which assumes airwaves are scarce, is no longer valid. They argue that modern technology, called spread spectrum, enables high-tech transmitters or devices to use the same frequency to communicate without interfering with each other. See Yochai Benkler and Lawrence Lessig, 'Will Technology Make CBS Un-constitutional?', *The New Republic* 12–14, 14 December 1998. Thus, spectrum is potentially unlimited and no longer scarce. Interestingly enough, Reddy referred to this argument. *See Cricket Association* at para 81. But it did not affect his conclusion that airwaves are public property and must be utilized for the greatest public good. See ibid. It is also regrettable that, by focusing exclusively on terrestrial broadcasting, both Sawant and Reddy ignored another broadcast medium: cable television. Cable networks can efficiently transmit a large number of programmes without imposing additional demands on frequencies. When the supreme court decided *Cricket Association,* cable networks had emerged and were rapidly expanding across India. Yet, the opinions completely ignored this development. See Ninan, supra n. 19 at 13–14.

There are two other dimensions to this question that were not explored by either Sawant or Jeevan Reddy. First, assuming, that there is no right to establish a broadcasting station in Article 19 (1) (a), one could possibly argue that this right resides, instead, in Article 19 (1) (g). That provision gives citizens the freedom to practice any trade, profession, occupation, or business. The only permissible restrictions are those imposed in the 'interests of the general public.' Why would it be against the general public interest to have more radio and television stations? More stations will result in increased competition for broadcasting services. This will result in greater diversity of opinions, entertainment, and information.[88]

A second aspect to this right to establish broadcasting stations relates to the constitutional protection for religious and minority rights. Article 25 (1) gives all persons the right to freely profess, practice, and *propagate* their religion, and Article 29 (1) assures minorities the right to conserve their distinct language, script, or culture.[89] The court has interpreted these articles to recognize that religious communities and minorities may establish their own educational institutions to foster their religious and cultural heritage.[90] If this is true, why can't communities or minorities also operate broadcasting stations for this purpose? For minorities especially, it is hard to imagine a more effective way to preserve their language and culture than to establish a radio or television station.

[88] It is possible to say, as Reddy did, that a private broadcaster motivated only by profits may take advantage of this fundamental right to manipulate opinions and information. But this logic is applicable to any activity, which involves private industry. Distortions or misrepresentation of information can also take place through the print media, which is largely owned by private individuals and companies. Yet, no one has seriously suggested that, because of this danger, the right to establish newspapers and magazines should be limited. Education is another example of an information-intensive activity involving entities. One could argue that private educational institutions, motivated by the desire for profits or parochial interests, may manipulate knowledge and information they impart to students. Yet, as the court has affirmed, citizens enjoy a distinct fundamental right to establish private educational institutions (as a trade or occupation) under Article 19 (1) (g). See *T.M.A. Pai Foundation* v. *State of Karnataka* (2002) 8 SCC 481 at paras 18–26 (establishing and running an educational institution is an occupation under Article 19 (1) (g)) (majority view of Chief Justice B.N. Kirpal). If this is true, it seems illogical to maintain that there is no similar right to establish broadcasting stations.

[89] See *Stainislaus* v. *State of Madhya Pradesh* AIR 1977 SC 908 at para 20 (holding the right to propagate one's religion includes the right to transmit or spread its tenets).

[90] See ibid., at para 89.

Few cases in India's constitutional history have captured public and activist attention as *Cricket Association*. The decision was widely welcomed, especially the holding that the government had no monopoly over radio frequencies. This ruling and the court's direction that the government must place frequencies under the control of an autonomous public agency were bold, radical, and ground breaking. *Cricket Association* reinvigorated and breathed new life into Indian free speech law. It also forced government officials and policy makers to consider establishing a district regulatory framework for broadcasting.[91]

SCOPE OF RESTRICTIONS ON BROADCASTING SERVICES

Programme content on radio and television is subject to various restrictions enumerated in Article 19 (2). As the *Abbas* case reveals, the most significant and frequently invoked restrictions on the electronic media are those based on public morality and decency. Yet, as Indians increasingly turn to the radio and television for news and current affairs, other restrictions, such as state security, public order, contempt of court, and India's sovereignty and integrity, may increasingly affect broadcasting. It is tempting to explore each of those restrictions in detail. However, this essay has space limitations. Therefore, I will focus on a more general question. Can the government impose a greater degree of restriction on broadcasting services than it does on other expressive media, such as newspapers or a public speech?

This question has been considered in some detail by the US Supreme Court. Despite its robust defense of free speech, that court has explicitly held that terrestrial broadcasting (not cable) is entitled to a lesser degree of First Amendment protection.[92] This reduction is justified

[91] *Cricket Association* was followed by a Calcutta High Court order that directed the central government to take appropriate steps to implement the Prasar Bharati Act (No. 25 of 1990). This law was enacted in 1990 to provide organizational autonomy to All India Radio and Doordarshan under a single corporate umbrella. But it was not brought into force immediately. A writ petition was filed in the Calcutta High Court demanding enforcement of the statute. The government offered various justifications for the delay. But the high court was unconvinced and ordered the government to take necessary action. See *Peoples' Union for Civil Liberties* v. *Union of India* AIR 1996 Cal. 89. As is its wont in such matters, the government constituted a committee to study the issue. It was only in 1999 that the Act was finally brought into force.

[92] See *Red Lion Broadcasting Co.* v. *FCC*, 395 US 367 (1969) and *FCC* v. *Pacifica Foundation*, 438 US 726 (1978).

on the ground of spectrum scarcity and the unique nature of broad-casting.[93]

In India, however, the position is not very clear even after *Cricket Association*. As we saw earlier, in his *Abbas* opinion, Hidayatullah suggested that films could be treated differently from other media. But he did not indicate to what extent audio-visual expression or the electronic media could be treated different from other media.[94] Sawant addressed this issue in *Cricket Association*. But a careful reading of his opinion reveals inconsistent views on how it should be resolved.

At one stage in his judgment, Sawant categorically rejects the government's argument that broadcasting can be subject to additional restrictions because of spectrum scarcity. 'The virtues of the electronic media', he argued, 'cannot become its enemies'.[95] For this reason, he opposed enlarging restrictions beyond those already listed in Article 19 (2). Yet, when summarizing his conclusions, Sawant wrote that *additional* restrictions could be imposed on the electronic media because they use frequencies or airwaves that are public property.[96] Reddy was firmly of the view that broadcasting cannot claim the same degree of free speech protection as the print media because it was 'inherently different.'[97]

Perhaps, this question will be conclusively settled through an appropriate case in the future. But, as a conceptual matter, are greater restrictions on broadcasting justified? I believe they are not for several reasons. First, there is no textual basis in the constitution for subjecting one medium to greater restrictions than others. Article 19 (2) establishes no caste system among various forms of expression, and it would be ludicrous to judicially engraft one. Free speech should be protected regardless of the forum or medium in which it is espoused. Second, the United States' First Amendment does not specifically indicate what restrictions may be validly imposed on free speech. Permissible restrictions, and their scope and effect, have gradually evolved through

[93] See generally, Christopher S. Yoo, 'The Rise and Demise of the Technology-Specific Approach to the First Amendment', 91 *Georgetown Law Journal* 245 (2003).

[94] See text accompanying notes 32–3.

[95] See ibid., at para 17.

[96] See ibid., at para 24 (ii). Perhaps, this confusion arose because Sawant believed that the scarcity argument was factually inapplicable to the underlying cases. Neither tournament organizer had asked for a permanent allocation of spectrum. They only wanted frequencies for a temporary duration to telecast the matches.

[97] See ibid., at para 97 (1) (c).

case law. Thus, the US Supreme Court's lower protection for free speech in broadcasting emerged in the absence of specific textual benchmarks. Article 19 (2), on the other hand, contains a long list of widely-worded grounds for the government to restrict free speech. As Sawant noted (even if he contradicted himself later) it is illogical to increase this list just because broadcasting has a wider reach and greater impact.

Third, greater restrictions are sometimes justified because broadcasters use frequencies, which are public property, to transmit information. But this argument is weak. Other expressive media also use public goods to disseminate their content. Newspapers are delivered through public streets. Books and periodicals are transported using national highways and railways to various parts of India. Even the most basic examples of exercising free speech—a roadside speech, public meeting, or demonstration—all involve the use of public property.

Finally, broadcasting restrictions are defended on the ground that India is still a developing country.[98] The poor and illiterate, it is argued, are vulnerable to the dramatic appeal of radio and television. They must be protected. This paternalistic assumption suggests that the poor and illiterate have no capacity for thought, reasoning, or rational judgment. Being poor or unable to read does not mean one is unable to think. In fact, the poor and illiterate in India are called upon to perform important functions: voting in elections, giving evidence in court, and serving in legislatures.

A constitutional provision like Article 19 (1) (a) 'is never static, it is ever-evolving and ever-changing and therefore does not admit a narrow, pedantic, or syllogistic approach.'[99] As more Indians turn to the radio and television to express themselves, they must have the ability to fully utilize this media. Indeed, they have a fundamental right to do so. And in order to be meaningful, this right must include the ability to establish broadcasting stations.

Almost a decade after *Cricket Association* was decided, there is still no comprehensive legal and regulatory framework governing Indian

---

[98] See *Union of India* v. *Motion Picture Association* AIR 1999 SC 2334 at para 17 (noting that a substantial portion of India's population is illiterate in justifying 'must-carry' provisions that require film exhibitors to screen government-produced scientific and educational films).

[99] See *S. Rangarajan* v. *P. Jagjivan Ram* (1989) 2 SCC 574.

broadcasting (with the limited exception of cable networks).[100] The government continues to issue broadcast licenses. That function presents a serious conflict of interest, because the government also controls All India Radio and Doordarshan, which are competitors to private broadcasting licensees. Moreover, the government has failed to comply with the supreme court's directions in *Cricket Association* to establish an independent and autonomous entity to regulate frequencies. Prasar Bharati, a broadcasting corporation established in 1999, functions largely as a holding company for Doordarshan and All India Radio. It is not an independent and autonomous regulatory agency, nor does it have any control over frequencies. It is not what the supreme court called for in *Cricket Association*.[101]

The lingering question is how deeply India's institutions, especially the judiciary, have internalized the importance of free expression in the electronic media. It is my earnest hope, and I am sure Justice Krishna Iyer will agree with me, that freedom of speech has become an indelible value of India's polity. It nourishes and fosters the vibrant civil society and thriving democracy, which has made India the envy of many parts of the world. It is especially important that this important constitutional guarantee is fully available to broadcasting as it grows and expands. Without it, an increasingly important sphere of Indian life and activity will not receive the bright sunshine of the constitution's fundamental freedoms.

[100] *Cf.* M.P. Singh, *Constitution of India* 112 (Lucknow, Eastern Book Co. 2001) (arguing that the Prasar Bharati is 'taking care' of the issue raised in the *Cricket Association Case*). In early 2004, the government gave the Telecom Regulatory Authority of India (TRAI), the independent regulator of telecom services, jurisdiction over broadcasting and cable services as well. See Ministry of Communications and Information Technology, Government of India, *Additional Functions Entrusted for Telecom Regulatory Authority of India,* Order No. S O45 (E); and *Broadcasting Services and Cable Services Notified as Telecommunication Service,* Notification No. S O44 (E) (9 January 2004). At the time of writing, it is unclear whether TRAI is to be a permanent broadcasting regulator or whether the notification is merely an ad hoc administrative arrangement.

[101] In the absence of a permanent autonomous broadcast regulator, Indian courts will have to decide broadcasting disputes, especially those between government-controlled and private entities. See, for example, *Ten Sports* v. *Citizen Consumer and Civic Action Group* (2004) 5 SCC 351 (dispute between Prasar Bharati and a foreign company involving rights to telecast India-Pakistan cricket matches).

6

Equality and Compensatory Discrimination

The Indian Experience

PARMANAND SINGH

THE EMERGING DEBATE

The issue of reservations has divided Indians in unaccustomed ways. Reservations are blamed for generating a variety of social evils. Caste-based reservations are seen as perpetuating the evils of caste system and accentuating caste consciousness, besides impeding the goals of secularism. It is widely believed that the benefits of reservations are snatched away by the elites among the backward classes at the expense of the truly needy and deserving. Many people believe that compensatory policies have failed to achieve the goals of participation, representation, integration, and assimilation of the disadvantaged groups in the mainstream of national life. The system tends to engender a spirit of self-denigration and increases the dependency of the beneficiaries on state patronage, thereby undermining their self-development and self esteem.

Then, those who are excluded complain that they are no better off than those preferred. They argue that in a setting of scarce resources and opportunities, it is an unfair way of distributing valued public offices and professions on the basis of group identity. The quota system places an unfair burden on the merited applicants who have to stake their careers as a price for the collective good. The excluded ones are, therefore, very much doubtful about their ethical, moral, or social obligation to repair the disadvantaged for the handicaps they actually did not cause. Is it compensation for centuries of invidious discrimination? Can reparation be made in any real sense for these kinds of historical injuries, they ask.

Most Indians are supportive of affirmative action schemes aiming at helping the disadvantaged enabling them to catch up to the standards of competition set up by the larger society. Reservations, on the other hand, provoke resentments as they involve suspension of standards and alteration of the rules of competition and constrict the chances of merited applicants.

It is argued that even if reservations are socially desirable for the Scheduled Castes (SCs) and Scheduled Tribes (STs) on the ground of the redressal of past injustices, there is no justification to extend the principle of historical compensation to the Other Backward Classes (OBCs) who have never been subjected collectively to historical contempt, insult, or prejudice. OBC comprehensively refers to a huge mass of many millions of people clamouring for special treatment. The vagueness of constitutional promises for these categories has led to unending litigation, political manipulation, and violent disturbances.[1] There is little doubt that in post-independence India, caste has served as a readymade traditional channel of political mobilization. Politics has afforded to the lower castes a symbol to achieve upward mobility through reserved positions. This has resulted in struggles for power equation. It cannot be disputed that social and educational backwardness of OBC has sufficiently been lightened by the post-independence agrarian reform measures and these people have acquired enormous political clout as a result of suffrage. The OBC reservations have become a tool of self-aggrandizement on the part of politically dominant castes who are able to influence those who hold power. Even those in power see the advantage in the system of caste quotas to maintain balance of power.

We arrive, then, at an ironic tension. The constitutional commitment to discourage caste is overshadowed by increasing resilience of caste in public life. Since the conferral of privileges is essentially a political act, the reservation policies are designed more as a matter of political expediency than in conformity with constitutional imperatives. It may, however, be pointed out at the outset that the elaborate system of compensatory discrimination for the Scheduled Castes and Scheduled Tribes, has never been a source of intense social conflicts, court cases, or political stalemate. There is a constitutional presumption of their social, economic, and cultural backwardness. The judiciary has taken a consistent view that there is a firm constitutional commitment for the economic betterment of these classes who are constitutionally

[1] See Parmanand Singh, 'Reservation, Reality and the Constitution—Current Crisis in India' in P. Leelakrishnan (ed.), *New Horizons of Law* 62–96, Cochin University of Science and Technology, Cochin (1987).

defined and centrally designated.[2] The Other Backward Classes (OBCs), however, are nowhere defined in the constitution and are left the determination of the state governments.

JUDICIAL RESPONSES

Scheduled Castes and the Scheduled Tribes

The Constitution of India accords a special status to SC and ST for compensatory treatment. *Thomas*[3] represented a significant doctrinal shift on the meaning of equality by reaffirming a special constitutional commitment for the economic betterment of the SC and ST due to their dismal social milieu and utter historical backwardness. It is in this context that the supreme court held that Articles 14 to 16 themselves proclaim a regime of substantive equality for these categories. Article 16(4) was not an exception to Article 16(1) as the state was authorized to adopt any method to achieve proportional equality for these people and was not limited only to job reservations as a means to achieve equality for them. That the new concept of equality did not empower the state to create new favoured groups for compensatory discrimination was very clearly articulated by Justice Krishna Iyer:[4]

Article16(4) covers all backward classes but to earn the benefit of grouping under Article 16(1) based on Articles 46 and 335—the twin considerations of terrible backwardness of the type *harijans* have to endure and maintenance of administrative efficiency must be satisfied.

He then clarified that the new reading of equality will prevent politically powerful castes from taking advantage of compensatory benefits:[5]

Not all caste-backwardness is recognized in this formula. To do so would be subversive of both Article 16(1) and (2). The social disparity must be so grim and substantial as to serve a foundation for benign discrimination. If we search we cannot find any large segment other than the Scheduled Castes and

---

[2] See Articles 341, 342, 366(24) and (25), Constitution of India. The courts have refused to review Presidential notification and held that the SC and ST are presumed to be backward and deserve massive compensatory benefits. For detailed discussion see, Parmanand Singh, 'Social Justice For Harijans: Some Socio-legal Problems of Identification, Conversion and Judicial Review' 20 *Journal of the Indian Law Institute* 355 (1978).

[3] *State of Kerala v. N.M. Thomas* (1976) 2 SCC 310.

[4] Ibid., at 369.

[5] Ibid., at 371.

Scheduled Tribes. No class other than harijans can jump the gauntlet of 'equal opportunity'. Their only hope is in Article 16(4).

Krishna Iyer very correctly recognized the distinction between the SC and the OBC and held that the distinct social history of the former justified preferences for their upward mobility by choosing any method of preference apart from reservations but for OBC, reservation was the only permissible method of preference. Iyer provided a conceptual framework for departing from the merit principle only for remedying historic wrongs. The opinion contributed by Iyer in *A.B.S.K. Sangh* v. *Union of India*[6] is commendable for its appeal to a 'result-oriented reservation'[7] for the SC and ST and for its social science approach to the problem of offsetting inherited inequalities. He graphically highlights the ineffectiveness of the sterile system of reservation which has made almost no impact on the economic and social problems of these depressed masses 'who are still slumbering despite inducement to awaken'.[8] Rather, the system has generated caste-politics with a tendency to convert Article 16(4) into a 'super fundamental right to continue backward all the time'.[9] If democracy itself played 'into the hands of hostile forces, the jurisprudence of keeping backward as backward and perpetuation of discrimination as vested interest may prevail as a rule of life'.[10] Iyer endorsed a higher percentage of reservation for these categories in view of the yawning gap between the legitimate expectation of these people and their utter under-representation in services except in menial jobs as scavengers and sweepers for which no one else is forthcoming. Iyer stated that in view of the microscopic representation of SC and ST at all levels of services it will only be a statistical jugglery to say that the 'carry forward' rule would create a monopoly of *harijans* and *girijans* in services.[11] *Shoshit Sangh* proposed to examine the whole question of reasonableness of reservations by looking at the overall position of SC and ST in employ-ment. It is clear that there is a clear constitutional commitment and national policy to pursue the group concept of proportional equality for the SC and ST. Justice as proportionality demands that that SC and ST are represented at all levels of income and achievement in proportion to their ratio in the population. This is why places are reserved for them in

[6] *A.B.S.K. Sangh* v. *Union of India* (1981) 1 SCC 246.
[7] Ibid., at 264.
[8] Ibid., at 298, 299.
[9] Ibid., at 264.
[10] Ibid., at 301.
[11] Ibid., at 294.

legislative bodies, services, and educational institutions in proportion to their ratio in the population. In my view the recent constitutional amendment inserting Article 16(4)(b) to a great extent supports the approach of Iyer that reservation for the SC and ST must be viewed in terms of its impact on these people. This amendment has nullified the rule declared by the supreme court in *Indra Sawhney*[12] that the ceiling of 50 per cent shall apply to backlog vacancies for the reserve categories (SC and ST) which could not be filled in any previous year for any reason. The new clause provides that such unfilled vacancies would not be combined with the vacancies of the year in which they are being filled up to determine the ceiling of 50 per cent on total number of vacancies in that year.

Other Backward Classes: From *Balaji* to *Indra Sawhney*

The reservation policies for OBC have been subjected to close judicial scrutiny ever since the famous case of *Balaji*.[13] *Balaji* had struck down a Mysore reservation scheme on many counts. The Mysore order suffered from many vices—excessive reservations, exclusive use of caste test, classification of backward classes into backward and most backward classes, inclusion of about 90 per cent of the population as the eligible beneficiary and many others. The supreme court viewed wholesale reservation as undermining standards and efficiency in professions. Reservations should be 'reasonably below' 50 per cent so that sufficient places are available for merit competition.[14] Only those communities could be treated as educationally backward who were 'well below' the state average of literacy implying that the number of beneficiaries should be less than half of the population.[15] For determining social backwardness, it should be ensured that the backward classes in the matter of their backwardness are comparable to the ST and ST.[16] The court agreed that in relation to Hindus, caste status of a person could be one of the possible measures of backwardness to be used in conjunction with non-communal tests such as poverty, occupation, place of habitation, etc.[17] Caste status,

[12] *Indra Sawhney v. Union of India* AIR 1993 SC 477.

[13] *M.R. Balaji v. State of Mysore* AIR 1963 SC 649.

[14] Ibid., at 662–3.

[15] Ibid., at 660.

[16] Ibid., at 658.

[17] Ibid., at 659.

could however, in no circumstance, be the sole determinant of social backwardness.[18] Social backwardness was, in the ultimate analysis, the result of poverty to a very large extent and social backwardness which resulted from poverty was likely to be aggravated considerations of caste to which the poor citizens might belong but that only showed the relevance both of poverty and caste in determining social backwardness.[19] The court showed its hostility to the creation of layers or strata among the backward classes and emphasized the element of absolute backwardness so that really backward classes were the beneficiaries.[20] Since the aim of compensatory discrimination was to overcome rooted inequalities, the backward classes should be both socially and educationally backward.[21] All these guidelines were supplied by the court to prevent the reservation clauses from expanding into a regime of caste and communal allotments.

Balaji undoubtedly opposed the exclusive reliance on caste standing in determining backwardness but it tolerated communities including caste groups as 'classes' under Article 15(4):[22]

It is for the attainment of social and economic justice that Article 15(4) authorizes the making of special provisions for the advancement of the communities therein contemplated, even if such provisions may be inconsistent with fundamental rights.

It seems clear that *Balaji* allowed caste and communities as classes or units of classification whose social backwardness could be measured by multiple tests, caste standing being only one of the tests. But in *Chitralekha* v. *State of Mysore*[23] the supreme court 'explained' *Balaji* by saying that 'castes' could not be 'classes' in any circumstance:[24]

If the makers of the constitution intended to take caste also as a unit of social and educational backwardness, they would have said so as they said of the Scheduled Castes and Scheduled Tribes. The juxtaposition of the expression ' Backward Classes' and 'Scheduled Castes' in Article 15(4) also leads to a reasonable inference that the expression 'classes' is not synonymous with 'castes'.

[18] Ibid.
[19] Ibid.
[20] Ibid., at 658.
[21] Ibid.
[22] Ibid., at 664.
[23] AIR 1964 SC 1823.
[24] Ibid., at 1833.

In approving an arrangement based on income and occupation, the supreme court modified *Balaji* by saying that caste was not a compelling test of backwardness and therefore backward classes could be designated by exclusive economic tests. The notion propounded by *Chitralekha*, was, however, short lived. In *P. Rajendran* v. *State of Madras*[25] the court upheld a caste based classification of OBC and asserted that the aim was not merely to eliminate economic inequalities but to overcome disabilities arising out of past discrimination:[26]

It must not be forgotten that a caste is also a class of citizens and if the caste as a whole is socially and educationally backward, reservation can be made in favour of such caste...

In *Periakaruppan* v. *State of Tamil Nadu*[27] and *State of A.P.* v. *U.S.V. Balram*,[28] *Rajendran* was applied in full vigour. The concern expressed in *Chitralekha* to exclude the prosperous segments from the OBC list, was also diluted in *Balram* where the court observed that caste as a whole could be treated as backward class 'notwithstanding the fact that few individuals in that group may be both socially and educationally above the general average'.[29] Contrary to *Balaji* 'well below the state average' test of educational backwardness, the supreme court in *Balram* upheld the inclusion of several communities in the list whose educational attainments were higher than the state average.[30] Not only this, the court also disputed *Balaji's* comparability with SC/ST standard and relaxed it by saying that the OBC need not exactly be similar to SC and ST.[31] Only a year later, the supreme court in *Janki Prasad* v. *State of J&K*[32] quickly reverted to the *Balaji* posture, holding that comparability requirement was a fundamental requirement as the SC and ST exemplified the real social and educational backwardness and served as a model for classifying OBC.[33] The court was willing to commend the income tests and the income ceiling applied to caste and communal units but it rejected the notion that poverty could be the conclusive test of social and educational backwardness.[34]

[25] AIR 1968 SC 1012.
[26] Ibid., at 1014–15.
[27] AIR 1971 SC 2303.
[28] AIR 1972 SC 1374.
[29] Ibid., at 1395–6.
[30] Ibid., at 1397.
[31] Ibid., at 1395–6.
[32] AIR 1973 SC 930.
[33] Ibid., at 938–9.
[34] Ibid., at 937.

An exclusive economic test was again rejected in *State of U.P.* v. *Pradip Tandon*[35] in reply to an argument that all people from rural areas of Uttar Pradesh were uniformly backward. The court reiterated the view that poverty was rampant in the whole of India and even in sections which are recognized as socially and educationally advanced there are large pockets of poverty. In *Pradip Tandon* the court remarked that caste should not be even one of the criteria of backwardness.[36] Only a year later in *K.S. Jayasree* v. *State of Kerala*[37] the court changed its view and held that caste standing could be one of the measures of backwardness and both caste and poverty were relevant. The court highly commended Kerala's means-cum-caste/community test of backwardness and agreed that with economic advancement, social disabilities were also dispelled and the state should, therefore, strive to eliminate the well-off from the listed groups by fixing an income ceiling.[38]

All the rival readings of the reservation clauses were neatly crystallized in the debate within the supreme court in *K.C. Vasanth Kumar* v. *State of Karnataka*.[39] Chief Justice Chandrachud commended means-cum-caste/community test of backwardness and wanted that the OBC should be comparable with SC and ST.[40] Justice Desai interpreted *Balaji* as recommending exclusive economic tests.[41] He believed that caste test entailed a lion's share of problems and also impeded the goals of secularism. He recommended economic test of backwardness.[42] Justice Sen also deplored 'caste-oriented policy of reservations' and wanted it to be economic-based.[43] Justice Chinnappa Reddy equated social and educational backwardness with low social position and equated *castes* with *classes*. He held:[44]

One may without hesitation say that if poverty be the cause, caste is the primary index of social backwardness so that social backwardness is often readily identifiable with reference to a person's caste.

Justice Venkataramiah was also critical of *Balaji* for not giving 'adequate importance to the evils of caste system'[45] and to the history of reservation

[35] AIR 1975 SC 563.
[36] Ibid., at 566–7.
[37] AIR 1976 SC 2381.
[38] Ibid., at 2386.
[39] AIR 1985 SC 1495.
[40] Ibid., at 1498–9.
[41] Ibid., at 1500, 15005.
[42] Ibid., at 1507.
[43] Ibid., at 1530.
[44] Ibid., at 1512.
[45] Ibid., at 1546.

clauses. He attributed the meaning of 'classes' to the expression 'class' in Article 366(24)[46] which was in the nature of the explanation to the definition of SC and ST.[47] Applying the rule of *ejusdem generis*, he defined OBC as castes, communities and races.[48] He argued that this interpretation was confirmed by the history of Article 16(4) where Ambedkar equated classes with castes and communities.[49]

The above analysis reveals a variety of judicial opinions on the meaning of OBC. On the question of determining socially and educationally backward classes, the supreme court has vacillated; sometimes allowing communal quotas, at other times preventing them, sometimes emphasizing the elimination of historic disparities, at other times emphasizing elimination of economic inequalities. The constitutional commitment in favour of OBC, thus remained ambiguous and dithering and continued to be a source of dismay and resentment.

The implementation of the Mandal Commission Report by the V.P. Singh government in August 1990 gave rise to unprecedented violent disturbances and political warfare. Article 340 of the constitution provides for the appointment of a Commission by the president to investigate the conditions of socially and educationally backward classes. In 1953, the Kaka Kalelkar Commission was appointed by the president, and it submitted its report in 1955 in which a majority of the members recommended caste test of backwardness. The Chairman, Kaka Kalelkar, however, gave his dissent emphasizing economic tests and completely eschewing caste criterion in identifying backward classes. The government did not act upon this report. In 1978, the Janata government appointed the second Backward Classes Commission under the chairmanship of B.P. Mandal. The V.P. Singh government issued an Office Memorandum in 1990 reserving 27 per cent vacancies in civil posts and services under the government of India in favour of socially and educationally backward classes. Reservations had to be provided only in initial recruitment and not in promotions. The National Front government headed by V.P. Singh did not survive for long. The Congress government headed by Narshimha Rao came to power. The Congress government stood by the Office Memorandum issued by the National Front government but

---

[46] Article 366(24) reads: Scheduled Castes means such castes, races or tribes or parts of or groups within such castes, races and tribes as are deemed under Article 341 to be Scheduled Castes for the purpose of this Constitution.

[47] Supra n. 39 at 1546.

[48] Ibid.

[49] Ibid., at 1545.

made two additions to the reservation policy. One was that within 27 per cent of the vacancies in civil posts reserved for backward classes, preference would be given to the candidates belonging to poorer sections of the backward classes. In case sufficient number of such candidates was not available in a particular category of backward class, the unfilled vacancies would be filled in by other categories. Another addition was that 10 per cent of the vacancies would be reserved for economically backward sections of the people who were not covered by any of the existing schemes of reservation. This was to be in addition to 27 per cent of the posts or appointments reserved for socially and educationally backward classes.

In *Indra Sawhney* v. *Union of India*[50] a nine judge bench of the supreme court examined the validity of the government order reserving 27 per cent of jobs for socially and educationally backward classes in government services. Six judges (M.H. Kania CJ, B.P. Jeevan Reddy, M.N. Venkatachaliah, A.M. Ahmadi, S.R. Pandian, and S.B. Sawant JJ) upheld the government order providing the well-off from among the backward classes were eliminated from the benefits of job reservation. Three judges (Kuldip Singh, T.K. Thommen, and R.M. Sahai JJ) wrote dissenting opinions fully rejecting the Mandal Report and its reasoning. Space does not permit me to dwell in detail on all aspects of the *Mandal* case. I attempt here to comment on the main principles laid down in this case.

Backward Classes as Castes and Communities

Justice Jeevan Reddy (with whom Kania CJ, Venkatachaliah and A.M. Ahmadi JJ, concurred) traced the history of the Hindu caste system and observed that caste determined the social status. Caste-occupation nexus were the key to measure social backwardness. His lordship held that since caste is a social class, caste as a whole could be designated as a backward class under Article 16(4).[51] The majority took the view that caste is a predominant test of backwardness among Hindus. For non-Hindu communities, occupational groups could be the units of classification. These judges would prefer to start with caste groups as units of classification and then apply to them other relevant criteria of social backwardness such as income, occupation, place of residence, educational achievements, etc.[52] Sawant in his concurring opinion agreed with Reddy

[50] *Indra Sawhney* v. *Union of India,* supra n. 12.
[51] Ibid., at 553.
[52] Ibid., at 556–7.

and said that while classification on the basis of caste was forbidden by clause (2) of Article 16, the use of caste was permissible for identifying backward classes. Pandian also endorsed the caste groups as units of classification for designating backward classes and held that caste could not be the sole test of backwardness. Thommen, dissenting, held that caste could be one of the tests of backwardness but could not be the sole criterion. Kuldip Singh, rejected the use of caste as even one of the measures of backwardness. Sahai, also agreed that backwardness could not mean backward caste. All backward class people could not be given reservation. They must be severely under represented in services in order to be considered for reservation. In *Mandal* the majority of the judges have upheld the use of caste groups as the basis of backward class classification and have also approved caste standing as the predominant test of social backwardness.

Article 16(4) not Similar to Article 15(4)

Until *Mandal*, the expression 'backward class of citizens' in Article 16(4) and 'socially and educationally backward classes' in Article 15(4) meant the same thing, and the meaning ascribed to socially and educationally backward classes in *Balaji* was applied in all cases of job reservations under Article 16(4).[53] In *Mandal*, the majority held that the beneficiaries of Articles 15(4) and 16(4) are not the same. The accent of Article 16(4) is on social backwardness rather than on educational backwardness.[54] The argument of the majority is that Article 340 which uses the expression 'socially and educationally backward classes' is related to Article 15(4) as was clarified by Jawaharlal Nehru in his speech in parliament while introducing the First Amendment in 1951. Since Article 16(4) uses the expression 'backward class of citizens' and there is no reference in Article 340, the former Article would cover a wider category of socially backward classes who are severely under represented in the services under the state. Reddy and Pandian, therefore, approved the Mandal Commission's approach in giving 12 out of 22 points to the factor of social backwardness.[55] The implication of *Mandal* will be to empower the government to make an expansive category of backward classes for job reservation policies.

[53] See *Triloki Nath Tikku* v. *State of Jammu and Kashmir* AIR 1967 SC 1283 at 1286, *Janki Prasad* v. *State of Jammu and Kashmir* AIR 1973 SC 930 at 936.

[54] Supra n. 12 at 556–7.

[55] Ibid., at 558.

Comparabiiity of Backward Classes with SCs and STs

Balaji and subsequent decisions had applied the requirement of comparability of OBC to SC and ST in order to resist the expansive listing of OBCs. *Mandal* overrules *Balaji* on this point and fully endorses the Mandal Report's approach.[56] This is, in my respectful submission, a retrogate step. *Balaji's* insistence on conjunctive reading of social and educational backwardness and also on the comparability of OBC with SC and ST was intended to identify the really backward classes which has been nullified by *Mandal*.

Creamy Layers to be Eliminated

The supreme court in *Mandal* insisted on the elimination of creamy layers from among the designated backward classes.[57] According to Reddy the very concept of a class denotes a number of persons having certain common traits which distinguish them from the others. In the backward class under Article 16(4) if the connecting link is social backwardness, it should broadly be the same in a given class. If some of the members are far too advanced socially, the connecting thread between them and the remaining class snaps. After excluding them alone, would the class be compact. Therefore, the exclusion of the advanced sections from the benefits of reservation will help the truly backward classes. Reddy asked a question, suppose a member of the backward class goes to the Middle East and earns a lot of money as a carpenter, is he to be excluded from the backward classes? Are his children to be excluded from the benefit of reservation? The income limit must be such as to mean and signify social advancement. On the other hand, there were certain positions, the occupants of which could be treated as socially advanced without further inquiry. For example, if a person belonging to backward class gets appointed to an All-India Service like the Indian Administrative Service or Indian Police Service 'his status in society rises'[58] and such person is no longer socially disadvantaged. His children should not get the benefit of reservation. It was, however, clarified that such exclusion of creamy layer would not apply to the SC and ST. In my submission, there is no valid reason why the creamy layer from among the SC and ST should not be excluded from the benefit of reservation. The court

---

[56] Ibid., at 560–1, 629–30, 648.
[57] Ibid., at 558–60, 667–9.
[58] Ibid., at 893.

directed the government to set up a commission for identifying the criteria for the elimination of creamy layer. In compliance of the court's direction, the government appointed the Justice Ram Nandan Committee which submitted its report in 1993. The central government also identified the criteria for such elimination. When the states of Bihar and Uttar Pradesh defied the central government's criteria, the supreme court quashed the schemes formulated by these states on the ground that the criteria laid down by these states were inconsistent with *Mandal*.[59] Kerala followed the footsteps of Bihar and created a farcical criteria, which would circumvent the requirement of excluding the creamy layer. The court set aside Kerala's scheme as violating the principle of equality and rule of law which is the basic structure of the constitution. The court stated that non-exclusion of creamy layer or inclusion of advanced castes in the OBC list is unconstitutional.[60]

Article 16(4) Classification of 'Backward' and 'More Backward' Classes

On this issue also *Balaji* was overruled by the majority of the judges in *Mandal*. In *Balaji* it was held that classification of backward classes into 'backward' and 'most backward classes' would entail several layers of backward classes each of which might claim the benefits of reservation. Such 'relative tests' would be impermissible as they would substantially deprive the really backward classes from the benefit of compensatory discrimination. In *Mandal*, the court recommended sub-classification on the ground that even among the backward classes some may be more backward than the others.[61] I agree with this view. If the backward classes have to be protected against open competition, there is no reason why the most disadvantaged should not be protected against relatively advanced sections of the backward classes.

Article 16(4) not an Exception to Article 16(1)

Mandal reaffirms *Thomas* that Article 16(4) is not an exception to Article 16(1) but an instance of classification implicit in Article 16(1).[62] But the majority also held that Article 16(4) is exhaustive of the power of

---

[59] See *Ashok Kumar* v. *State of Bihar* (1995) 5 SCC 403.
[60] *Indra Sawhney* v. *Union of India* (2000) 1 SCC 168.
[61] Supra n. 12 at 562–3, 586.
[62] Ibid., at 539–41, 619, 643.

reservation in favour of backward classes and no preference of any kind would be permissible for them under clause (1) of Article 16.[63] This, in my submission, goes against *Thomas* which permitted employment preferences such as test exemptions, age waivers, fee concessions, etc. for backward classes under Article 16(1). *Mandal* in fact overrules *Thomas* and accepts the dissenting opinion of Justice Beg in *Thomas* that Article 16(4) exhausted all exceptions made in favour of backward classes and no preference can be given to them under Article 16(1). *Mandal* expands the meaning of reservation to align this concept with the existing practice about age waivers, test exemptions, fee concessions, relaxation in minimum qualifications, and so forth.

Reservations Impermissible in Promotions

In *Mandal*, eight out of nine judges[64] held that Article 16(4) does not permit reservations in promotions. Overruling a leading decision,[65] the court held that reservations at every stage of promotion would inevitably undermine the efficiency in administration mandated by Article 335. Reddy held that once the backward class of citizens enter the service through reserved quota, the efficiency of administration demands that these member too compete with others and earn promotions like others. Crutches cannot be provided throughout one's career.[66] Pandian held that reservations are concerned with initial recruitment or at the initial stage and not at the time of promotions.[67] Sawant believed that reservation in promotions would result in unnecessary frustration, demoralization, lack of interest in work, and constant hostility in administration.[68] Kuldip Singh argued that the aim is to provide reservation to a class and not to individuals. In promotions, backward class as a collectivity are nowhere in the picture, only individuals are.[69] Sahai gave an example of a medical student who had been admitted through reserved quota but had to pass the medical examination without any relaxation in standards.[70]

---

[63] Ibid.
[64] Justice Ahmadi did not express any opinion on this point.
[65] *General Manager, S. Railways v. Rangachari* AIR 1962 SC 36.
[66] Supra n. 12 at 569–74.
[67] Ibid., at 632.
[68] Ibid., at 673.
[69] Ibid., at 715.
[70] Ibid., at 757, 762.

With respect to SCs and STs *Mandal* has been rendered ineffective by a constitutional amendment in 1995. This amendment adds a new clause 4(a) to Article 16 which provides:

Nothing in this article shall prevent the state from making any provision for reservation in matters of promotions to any class or classes of posts in the service of the state in favour of Scheduled Castes and Scheduled Tribes, which in the opinion of the state, are not adequately represented in the services under the state.

This clause, however, does not affect the decision of *Mandal* on the issue of promotions in respect of OBC but makes the decision inapplicable as regards SC and ST. Despite the above amendment authorizing reservation in promotions for the SC and ST, the decision of the supreme court in *Ajit Singh II* v. *State of Punjab*[71] had come as a set back for the SC/ST employees who were promoted but not given seniority from the date of their promotion. In this case it was held that the roster point promotees (reserved category) cannot count their seniority in the promoted category from the date of their continuous officiation in the promoted post *vis-à-vis* the general candidates who were senior to them in the lower category and who were later promoted. On the other hand, a senior general candidate at the lower level, if he reaches the promotional level later but before the further promotion of a reserved candidate, he will have to be treated as senior at the promotional level, to the reserved candidate, even if the reserved candidate was earlier promoted to that level. In so holding the court overruled its earlier decisions in *Union of India* v. *Virpal Singh*[72] and *Jagdish Lal* v. *State of Haryana*.[73] In *Ajit Singh II* declaring the right to equality as a personal right, the court observed:[74]

Article 16(1) provides to every employee otherwise eligible for promotion or who comes within the zone of consideration, a fundamental right to be 'considered' for promotion. Equal opportunity here means the right to be 'considered' for promotion. If a person satisfies the eligibility and zone criteria but is not considered for promotion, then there will be a clear infraction of his fundamental right to be 'considered' for promotion, which is his personal right.

Most significantly, the court in *Ajit Singh II* reaffirmed the principle that Articles 15(4) and 16(4) do not confer any fundamental right to reservation. These provisions do not impose any constitutional duty to provide for reservations: they simply enable the state to depart from the merit

---

[71] *Ajit Singh II* v. *State of Punjab* (1999) 7 SCC 209.

[72] (1996) 2 SCC 715.

[73] (1997) 6 SCC 538.

[74] Supra n. 71 at 227.

principle of selection and provide reservations for backward classes. Right to be considered for promotion is a fundamental right of every individual. Affirmative action according to the court, should not result in reverse discrimination. The need therefore is to balance the fundamental right under Article 16(1) and the reservations under Article 16(4) and 16(4)(a). Since a reserved candidate does not compete under merit, he cannot claim seniority over the general category candidate even if the reserved category candidate has been promoted earlier in time.

This judgment gave rise to widespread resentment among the SC/ST employees which led parliament to further amend Article 16(4)(a). By the 85th Amendment Act 2001, it has been clarified that the seniority of reserved category promotees will be counted from the date of their continuous officiation in the promoted post *vis-à-vis* the general category candidates who were senior to them in the lower category but were promoted later. The reversal of *Ajit Singh II* has been made effective from 17 June 1995, the day Article 16(4)(a) came into force.

Amendment to Article 16(4)(a) reads:

In Article 16 of the Constitution in clause 4(a) 'in matters of promotion to any class' the words 'in matters of promotion with consequential seniority to any class' be substituted.

The Poor Among the Advanced Sections

The court in *Mandal* made it abundantly clear that the aim of compensatory discrimination is to remedy historic wrongs and not to eliminate economic inequalities by helping the poor from the forward sections of the society. The court's reasoning is that all poor people from the forward sections are not socially backward due to caste inequities and past discrimination. There is a difference between a poor who has been a barber and a poor who has been a priest. The latter did not suffer from those disabilities, in addition to poverty, from which the former suffered. Mere poverty could not be decisive of backwardness. Reddy held that classification on the basis of poverty could not be related to clause 4 of Article 16. Sawant also said that all economically disadvantaged were not backward for the purposes of Article 16(4). He said:[75]

Economic backwardness is the bane of the majority of the people in this country. There are poor sections in all the castes and communities. Poverty runs across

[75] Supra n. 12 at 705.

all barriers. The nature and degree of economic backwardness and its causes and effects, however, vary from section to section of the populace. Even the poor among the higher castes are socially as superior to the lower castes as the rich among the higher castes. Their economic backwardness is not on account of social backwardness.

Sawant said that the reservation policy under Article 16(4) was not aimed at 'economic upliftment or alleviation of poverty'.[76] Job reservations were 'specifically designed to give a due share in the State power'[77] to the backward classes. Consequently, the court quashed the office memorandum issued by Narshimha Rao's government providing for reservation of 10 per cent vacancies for economically backward classes of people not covered by the existing schemes of reservations.

Reservations not to Exceed 50 per cent

In *Mandal*, the judges quoted with approval the speech of B.R. Ambedkar in the Constituent Assembly in which he had stated that reservations should be confined to a minority of posts and appointments. Jeevan Reddy observed that reservation of a majority of posts and services could not have been envisaged by the framers of the constitution. He, therefore, held that reservation should not exceed 50 per cent of the vacancies. This could, however, not be an inflexible rule and in certain circumstances reservation could exceed 50 per cent. The judge said:[78]

While 50 per cent shall be the rule, it is necessary not to put out of consideration certain extraordinary situations inherent in the great diversity of this country and the people. It might happen that in far-flung and remote areas the population inhabiting those areas might, on account of their being out of the mainstream of national life and in view of conditions peculiarly characteristic to them, need to be treated in a different way, some relaxation in this strict rule may be imperative. In doing so, extreme caution is to be exercised and a special case made out.

Mandal also ruled that in making reservations, a year should be taken as the basis or unit , as the case may be, for applying the rule of 50 per cent and not the entire cadre strength.[79] In other words, the ceiling of 50 per cent will apply to backlog vacancies for the reserved categories which could not be filled in any previous year for any reason.

[76] Ibid., at 706.
[77] Ibid.
[78] Ibid., at 566.
[79] Ibid., at 567–9.

Mandal has now been nullified by the 81st Amendment Act 2000, by insertion of clause (4)(b) in Article 16 which reads:

Nothing in this Article shall prevent the state from considering any unfilled vacancies of a year which are reserved for being filled up in that year in accordance with any provision for reservation made under clause (4) or clause (4)(a) as a separate class of vacancies to be filled up in any succeeding year or years and such class of vacancies shall not be considered together with the vacancies of the year in which they are being filled up for determining the ceiling of 50 per cent reservation on total number of vacancies of that year.

The result of this amendment is that carry-forward vacancies shall always remain separate from the vacancies falling in a particular year. They are not to be clubbed together for finding out whether the quota of 50 per cent has been exceeded.

ADMISSION TO PROFESSIONAL COURSES AND NATIONAL INTEREST

In *Dr. Preeti Srivastava* v. State *of M.P.*[80] a five judge bench[81] of the supreme court has held that at the level of super specialization in medicine there cannot be any reservation because any dilution of merit at this level would adversely affect the national interest in having the best possible people at the highest level of professional and educational training. The court went on to say that reservation in favour of backward classes was as much in the interest of the society as in the interest of the protected group. At the same time there may be 'other national interests, such as promoting excellence at the highest level and providing best talent in the country with the maximum available facilities to excel and contribute to society which have also to be borne in mind'.[82]

Justice Sujata V. Manohar referred to the observations of Justice Jeevan Reddy in *Mandal* against reservations in certain higher echelon posts and services under Article 16(4) read with Article 335. Article 335 requires that the claims of the SC and ST in public services will be considered by the state consistent with the maintenance of efficiency in administration. No consideration of efficiency in professions is required under Article 15(4). Her lordship, however, ruled that admission to super

---

[80] *Dr Preeti Srivastava* v. State *of M.P.* AIR 1999 SC 2894.
[81] Chief Justice A.S. Anand, and Justices Sujata V. Manohar, K. Venkataswami, V.N. Khare and S.B. Majumdar.
[82] Supra n. 80 at 2920.

specialities courses in medicine amounted to recruitment to posts and services in the hospitals and therefore the principles embodied in Article 335 equally applied to Article 15(4) reservations.[83]

She maintained that 'even otherwise, under Article 15(4) the special provisions which are made at this level of education have to be consistent with the national interest in promoting highest level of efficiency, skill, and knowledge amongst the best in the country so that they can contribute to national progress and enhance the prestige of the nation.'[84]

Preeti is also notable for prescribing norms for relaxation of standards for reserved category candidates in the admission test for admission to the post-graduate courses in medicine. The supreme court ruled that the minimum qualifying marks are mandatory even for reserved category candidates and there should not be much disparity between the qualifying marks fixed for the general category candidates and reserved category candidates. The difference in minimum qualifying marks should be the same as for admission to MBBS courses e.g., 35 per cent for reserved category and 45 per cent for the general category.

The court has propounded a new principle for reservations under Article 15(4) thus:[85]

Any special provision under Article 15(4) has to balance the importance of having at the highest level of education students who are meritorious and who have secured admission on their merit as against social equity of giving compensatory benefit of admission to the Scheduled Castes and Scheduled Tribes candidates who are in a disadvantageous position. The same reasoning which propelled this court to underline reasonableness of a special provision and the national interest in giving at the highest level of education, few seats at the top of the educational pyramid only on the basis of merit and excellence, applies equally to a special provision in the form of lower qualifying marks for the backward at the highest level of education.

Most importantly, the supreme court in *Preeti* overrules its two earlier decisions[86] which held that prescribing no minimum qualifying marks for the reserved category candidates would have no impact on standards of education and a reserved category getting even zero mark could be

[83] Ibid., at 2921. On this point Justice Majumdar dissented holding that the principle of Article 335 cannot be applied to Article 15(4) and is relevant for Article 16(4) only Ibid., 2939.

[84] Ibid., at 2921.

[85] Ibid., at 2906.

[86] *State of M.P.* v. *Kumari Nivedita Jain* (1981) 4 SCC 296, and *Ajai Kumar Singh* v. *State of Bihar* (1994) 4 SCC 401.

admitted. The court also rejected the argument that if minimum marks for the reserved category were insisted, many reserved seats would remain unfilled. The purpose of higher medical education, according to the court, was not to fill the reserved seats by lowering the standards, but to 'ensure that the reserved category candidates having the requisite training and calibre to benefit from post-graduate medical education, are not denied this opportunity by competing with general category candidates'.[87] The supreme court's ruling in *Preeti* will have a far reaching consequence for the schemes of admission to post-graduate courses like law, management, and engineering courses. At present, the reserved category candidates in these courses are getting reserved seats even on zero mark so that the reserved seats do not go unfilled. It is quite likely that on the strength of *Preeti* it might be asserted that no candidate of reserved category should be admitted to these professional courses without securing minimum qualifying marks.

The judgment of the supreme court during August 2005 in *P.A. Inamdar v. State of Maharashtra*[88] holding that with respect to private unaided educational institutions, the state has no power to enforce its reservation policy, gave rise to widespread criticism of the court for legitimizing and promoting privatisation of education and making education accessible only to the rich and powerful and denying the chances of the students of backward classes to avail the benefits of reservations in unaided minority or non-minority educational institutions. This ruling was seen as adversely affecting the interests of the backward classes. Parliament again decided to amend the constitution to enable the state to make appropriate laws to provide for reservations in private educational institutions in favour of socially and educationally backward classes and the Scheduled Castes and Scheduled Tribes.[89] The Central Government's move in April 2006 to introduce reservations for Other Backward Classes in pursuance of

---

[87] Supra n. 80 at 2918.

[88] 2005 (5) SCJ 746.

[89] Article 15(5) was added by the Constitution (Ninety-Third Amendment) Act 2005 (with effect from 20.1.2006) which reads as follows:

Nothing in this article or in sub clause (g) of Article 19 shall prevent the State from making a special provision , by law, for the advancement of any socially and educationally backward classes of citizens or the Scheduled Castes and Scheduled Tribes in so far as such special provisions relate to their admission to educational institutions including private educational institutions , whether aided or unaided by the state, other than minority educational institutions referred to in clause (1) of Article 30. .

Article 15(5), in elite institutions of higher and professional educational institutions, popularly called *Mandal II,* has once again led to widespread protests, resentments and political stalemate like that which happened in 1990–1 during the anti-Mandal agitations. The leading opponents of the OBC quota have been the doctors across the country. At the time of this writing there seems to be no respite from the ongoing agitation, the anti-reservation protestors having rejected the government's formula of increasing the seats for general category so that the merit principle is not unduly constricted by OBC quota of 27 per cent in such institutions.

In contributing to the meaning of equality as mandating substantive equality or equality of results, the supreme court has not considered the question whether the vast compensatory responsibilities bestowed by it on the government will give rise to the problem of resources and priorities in fulfilling competing commitments. The departure from merit principle is permissible not only for overcoming historic disparities but for overcoming all kinds of inequalities arising out of personal or circumstantial handicaps and misfortunes. Justice Bhagwati, while defending regional preferences in medical school admissions observed:[90]

Now the concept of equality…is a dynamic concept. It takes within its sweep every process of equalization and protective discrimination…. The state must resort to compensatory state action for the purpose of making people who are factually unequal in their wealth, education or social environment equal in specified areas.

It means that the state can enlarge the criteria of selection, not merely for inducting the members of the lowest social categories in services and professions, but for the pursuit of any governmental solicitude or state interest. Even *Mandal* approves the preferential job policies, including reservations for children of defence personnel, political sufferers, physically challenged, and other groups under Article 16(1). As a matter of principle of constitutional law, the state has a plenary power to utilize classification to remedy any kind of inequalities and conditions of unfairness and this is desirable also. Indian society is afflicted by several ailments and there are many victims requiring remedial attention. But the framers of the Indian constitution directed attention and priority to be accorded to the SC and ST. The new reading of equality value and of compensatory discrimination as mandating a general regime of substantive equality largely diffuses the priority accorded to the SC and ST.

[90] *Pradeep Jain* v. *Union of India* (1984) 3 SCC 654 at 677.

Marc Galanter very rightly reacts:[91]

In a setting of chronic shortage, an enlarged commitment to remedy all undeserved difficulties betokens a commendable generosity of spirit. But it also raises
the question of priorities and allocation of scarce resources, including attention. Government's authorization to pursue substantive equality is vastly greater
than will conceivably be available to it...will not the commitment to the lowest
social group—especially where these are perceived to receive massive benefits—
be overwhelmed by governmental response to the better-placed claimants on
its compensatory attention? *The sense of the regime of formal equality qualified by a
singular exception to alleviate disparities derived from position in the traditional social
hierarchy is liquidated or dissolved into a general and unfulfillable commitment to substantive equality.*

Justice Krishna Iyer in his opinion in *Thomas* visualized the possibility of
runaway expansion of compensatory principle and attempted to provide
a conceptual framework for confining the principle only for remedying
historic wrongs:[92]

The distinction would seem to be between handicaps imposed accidentally by
nature and those resulting from societal arrangements such as caste structures
and group suppression. Society being, in the broad sense, responsible for these
latter conditions, it has also the duty to regard them as relevant differences
among men and to compensate for them whenever they operate to prevent
equal access to basic, minimal advantages enjoyed by other citizens.

The enlarged commitment to equality and removal of social disparities
will not automatically transform Indian society. The court can only erect
broader notions of policy and produce doctrines favourable to the
disadvantaged and the deprived. Still the beneficiaries have to depend
upon state patronage. The judges cannot take the initiative to compel
the government to live up to its commitments. The reservation issue
simply dramatizes that it is beyond the court to rescue the reservation
power from political abuse and distortions.[93] The multiple and competing

---

[91] Marc Galanter, *Competing Equalities: Law and the Backward Classes in India* 392
Oxford University Press, New Delhi (1984).

[92] Supra n. 3 at 338.

[93] For example, the State of Tamil Nadu did not accept *Mandal* and nullified the
restraint imposed by the judgment by enacting Tamil Nadu Reservation etc. Act,
1994, authorizing it to make reservations up to 69 per cent. By the 76th constitutional amendment, this Act has been placed in the Ninth Schedule to protect it
from attack. The central government has also not accepted *Mandal* and has inserted
16(4)(a) and 16(4)(b) discussed above.

principles of equality and compensatory discrimination have facilitated selective reading of the legal doctrines and have enabled the commissions and governments to choose those that are favourable to them.

Reservations involve social costs and impinge heavily on the careers of merit applicants, provoking resistance and resentment. Much of the resistance and resentment can be minimized either by diluting or widely spreading the social costs by measures aiming at the overall competitiveness of the beneficiaries (like added educational facilities, measures to improve favourable home environment, coaching, training. etc.). But the political leadership has not found the improvement in the existential conditions of the poor and the deprived to be of much electoral advantage. The obsessive fascination of the political class to expand the OBC category for electoral gains has nothing to do with social justice for the historically deprived groups. Rather, the aim is to include new claimants to the OBC pool in order to maintain caste equations. The political practice is solely degenerating the entire policy into absurd results. Certain communities including the members of the forward castes are trying to enter the reservation pool. The harsh reality, however, is that reservations produce illusory benefits. In the age of privatization and the influence of global capital, the government posts are almost non-existent or very scarce. The government's reservation policy does not extend to jobs in private sectors. The system of reservations has succeeded in creating a small elite among the backward classes and has not helped in achieving group mobility. Group mobility can be achieved only when a group possesses a high degree of cohesion and its leadership is able to perceive the interest of the whole group. But the individuals who move up through the reservation schemes suffer from an identity crisis and are quite often reluctant to identify themselves with the members of their own community and thus fail to play the representative role.

The Indian experience teaches us that the quota system is only a short cut and crude strategy of social reconstruction, which if mismanaged, will lead society to traumatic tensions. In democracy, groups wield political power and a government confronted with demands and pressures for reservations from all sides cannot withstand a fierce onslaught without giving something. Once a society decides to distribute scarce resources and opportunities on the basis of group identity, groups are strengthened, and benefits once given can never be withdrawn. More and more groups will proliferate and public patience will be exhausted by the runaway extension of the reservation pool. By definition, reservation is a temporary measure to achieve equality, to be complemented by long range developmental measures which, when begin to produce results, the reservations can slowly be withdrawn. What is needed today is that the state divert more and more of its resources to increase the overall competitiveness of the members of the backward classes rather that stick to reservations as the only best means to promote equality. Unless the number of beneficiaries is reduced and bounded, the system will always carry the threat of expanding into a regime of caste and communal quotas.

PART II

GOVERNANCE, DEVELOPMENT, AND HUMAN RIGHTS

7

Corruption and its Impact on Human Rights and the Rule of Law

Governance Perspectives

C. RAJ KUMAR

Corruption is one of India's most nagging problems impeding growth and development.[1] Corruption is institutionalized in India. Every sector of the governance apparatus is marred by this problem with only certain variations in the level of corruption. Though the social, economic and political consequences of corruption are immense for India, there is very little political consensus on taking serious measures to address this problem. In fact, politicians are perceived to be among the chief perpetrators of this problem, and efforts made by state institutions, in particular by the judiciary, are invariably met with stiff resistance. Corruption violates human rights as it discriminates against people.[2] Corruption violates the principle of equality and fairness as decisions are taken in an arbitrary manner favouring bribe-givers, as opposed to people who are legitimately entitled.

The problem of corruption in India is writ large in the various institutions entrusted with the task of governance. Democratic governance is about people exercising choices to elect their representatives

---

[1] See generally, N. Vittal, *Corruption in India. The Roadblock to National Prosperity*, Academic Foundation, New Delhi, 2003.

[2] For further reading on human rights based approaches to developing corruption-free governance in India, see C. Raj Kumar, 'Corruption and Human Rights—Promoting Transparency in Governance and the Fundamental Right to Corruption-Free Service in India', *Columbia Journal of Asian Law*, Vol. 17, No. 1, Fall 2003, pp. 31–72.

and also participating in the governance process. While basic principles of democracy are well established in India, there are serious concerns as to the nature of democratic governance due to corruption and other forms of abuse of power that are widespread in every sector of the administration. Undoubtedly, the form of corruption in India and its adverse effects on human rights have shaken the foundations of the rule of law upon which a modern society rests. Gradually, Indian people have lost faith in the governance system and developed a scepticism as corruption affects their survival. The constitutional foundation, legislative framework, the judiciary, and institutional mechanisms available for anti-corruption work such as the media, civil society, and other governance systems in place have been unable to significantly reduce corruption or, for that matter, develop a culture of respect for law. Corruption creates a vicious atmosphere of lack of respect for law and democratic institutions. As a consequence, civil, political, economic, social, and cultural rights of Indians are violated. This situation has undermined the democratic foundations of the Indian state as the trust of the ruled towards the rulers has been significantly undermined.

The rule of law is protected only when there is a fairly predicable legal system that responds to problems in a fair, non-discriminatory, and effective manner. In the Indian context, institutionalized corruption has undermined all institutions, and has threatened the rule of law. The time has come for Indian society to tackle the problem of corruption head-on, as corruption has come to attack the very basis of democracy and the rule of law. While there is no single solution or approach to the problem, it is important to recognize that anti-corruption efforts of any nature should primarily be intended to empower the citizenry. This means that all legal, institutional, judicial, and even constitutional measures to eliminate corruption should be oriented toward empowering the Indian citizenry. The best avenue to fight corruption is public vigilance backed by strong and transparent institutions.

In this context, the rights-based approaches to development and governance assume significance as rights are meant to empower people. There are two facets of empowerment that have to take place in India for promoting effective anti-corruption strategies. First, the people of India need to be empowered by providing a right to corruption-free governance or other rights that will enable them to fulfil their right to corruption-free governance. This should be supplemented by providing forums and institutions that work to ensure the protection and promotion of this right. Access to justice remains a priority for the enforcement of this right. The judiciary and other institutions should develop mechanisms so that access to victims of corruption is available and remedial measures are quick and effective in fulfilling their rights. Secondly, institutions that are already working in the field of anti-corruption need to be duly empowered so that political interference or other forms of vested interests do not creep into the system and affect anti-corruption work. For this to happen, transparency, institutional autonomy, and functional independence of the anti-corruption institutions become mandatory. This inevitably means that there has to be political will at the highest level of the government so that anti-corruption becomes an important policy of the government not only in terms of words, but also deeds.

This article first provides an overview of the problem of corruption in India and its various consequences for governance. Second, it examines the problem of corruption from a human rights perspective to recognize that the kind of corruption that prevails in India violates human rights.[3] Third, it argues that corruption has a profound effect on the rule of law and democracy in India. It is useful to understand that corrupt practices not only violate a number of laws but also create an environment of lawlessness and lack of respect for law. As a consequence of this threat to the environment of the rule of law, the foundations of Indian democracy are threatened. Fourth, it examines the need for anti-corruption measures to focus on empowering the Indian citizenry. Whatever strategies are adopted for eliminating corruption should bring the Indian citizen to the central focus of political discourse. In this context, rights-based approaches to governance and need for a fundamental right to corruption-free governance in India are critically examined. Fifth, various

---

[3] For further reading of similar arguments at the international level, see Ndiva Kofele-Kale, 'The Right to a Corruption-Free Society as an Individual and Collective Human Rights: Elevating Official Corruption to a Crime under International Law', *International Lawyer*, Spring 2000, WL 34 INTLLAW 19. For further reading, see Balakrishnan Rajagopal, 'Corruption Legitimacy and Human Rights: The Dialectic of the Relationship', *Connecticut Journal of International Law*, Fall 1999, WL 14, CTJIL 495; Nihal Jayawickrama, 'Corruption—A Violator of Human Rights?', *Transparency International Working Paper*, 1998, web: http://www.transparency.de/documents/work-papers/index.html (last visited: 31 May 2006); Lawrence Cocksroft, 'Corruption and Human Rights: A Crucial Link', *Transparency International Working Paper*, 1998, web: http://www.transparency.de/documents/work-papers/index.html (last visited: 31 May 2006); See also, United Nations Development Programme (UNDP), 'Fighting Corruption to Improve Governance', February 1999; C. Raj Kumar, 'The Benefit of a Corruption-Free Society', *Hong Kong Lawyer*, December 2002, pp. 39–46.

institutions in India and their effectiveness in ensuring corruption-free governance will be assessed. It is important that the mandate of Human Rights Commissions be expanded to include corruption-free governance as a medium for protecting and promoting human rights. Sixth, the role of the judiciary in protecting the right to corruption-free governance of the Indian citizenry needs to be strengthened. The fact that the judiciary is still perceived to be fair and less corrupt makes its interventions on cases concerning corruption very important. It needs to be impressed upon the judiciary that corruption is not just a criminal law violation, but also a far more significant issue that affects human rights and the rule of law in India. On this basis, the judiciary can develop a jurisprudential and constitutional foundation for anti-corruption work. This may be aided by a special appellate bench of the judiciary or a more aggressive mandate to tackle this problem in the National Human Rights Commission. Seventh, the functioning of civil society, including the media, needs to be galvanized. The development of the right to information in India had a lot to do with the consistent work of civil society. It is important to keep up this momentum for further gains.

CORRUPTION AND ITS CONSEQUENCES FOR GOVERNANCE

Corruption has become so deeply institutionalized in India that there is not a single institution that is said to be free from it.[4] The National Commission to Review the Working of the Constitution in its Consultation Paper on Probity in Governance has observed:

The paradox of India, however, is that in spite of a vigilant press and public opinion, the level of corruption is exceptionally high. This may be attributed to the utter insensitivity, lack of shame, and the absence of any sense of public morality among the bribe-takers. Indeed they wear their badge of corruption and shamelessness with equal élan and brazenness...Corruption today poses a danger not only to the quality of governance but is threatening the very foundations of our society and the State.[5]

[4] For a comprehensive analysis of the problem of corruption in India, see Krishna K. Tummala, 'Corruption in India: Control Measures and Consequences', *Asian Journal of Political Science*, Vol 10, No. 2 (December 2002).

[5] National Commission to Review the Working of the Constitution, a consultation paper on 'Probity in Governance', 21 August 2001, Vol. II, Book 1, New Delhi, India. Web: http://lawmin.nic.in/ncrwc/finalreport/v2b1-12.htm (last visited: 31 May 2006).

These observations are truly significant coming from a very high-powered commission that was recently established. Corruption has systematically affected every institution of governance in India. Politicians and bureaucrats have figured prominently in various allegations of corruption that have been levelled against government by the citizenry. Corruption has also undermined the development and growth impact of social and economic policies that India has adopted.[6] It is correctly observed that 'most government offices typically present a picture of a client-public bewildered and harassed by opaque rules and procedures and inordinate delays, constantly vulnerable to exploitation by employees and touts'.[7] While corruption by itself poses a variety of problems relating to abuse of power and arbitrary decision-making, the direct consequences of corruption and its impact on the state machinery include issues like 'a determined denial of transparency, accessibility and accountability, cumbersome and confusing procedures, proliferation of mindless controls, and poor commitment at all levels to real results of public welfare.'[8]

Corruption is an ubiquitous scourge in Indian society. Corruption undermines fairness in governance.[9] The institutions of governance make decisions not on the basis of what is best suited to fulfil socio-economic objectives. Rather, decisions are made on the basis of how to maximize the corrupt interests of a few. Power holders work to abuse power in such a manner that they can earn money through illegal means and wield this power in a socially detrimental manner. Good governance is based upon a number of factors.[10] The United Nations Development Programme (UNDP) views governance as 'the exercise of economic,

---

[6] For a comprehensive reading on the subject of corruption from a historical and contemporary perspective, see S.S. Gill, *The Pathology of Corruption*, Harper Collins, New Delhi (1998).

[7] Harsh Mander and Abha Joshi, 'The Movement for Right to Information in India—People's Power for the Control of Corruption', Commonwealth Human Rights Initiative (CHRI), New Delhi. Web: http://www.humanrightsinitiative.org/programs/ai/rti/india/articles/The%20Movement%20for%20RTI%20in%20India.pdf (last visited: 31 May 2006).

[8] Ibid.

[9] See generally, Report of the National Commission to Review the Working of the Constitution, A Background Paper on 'Some Ideas on Governance', Vol. II, Book 3, New Delhi. Web: http://lawmin.nic in/ncrwc/finalreport/v2b3-2.htm (last visited: 31 May 2006).

[10] See generally, C.P. Barthwal (ed.), Good Governance in India, Deep and Deep Publications Pvt. Ltd., New Delhi (2003), p. 302.

political, and administrative authority to manage a country's affairs at all levels. It comprises mechanisms, processes, and institutions through which citizens and groups articulate their interests, exercise their legal rights, meet their obligations, and mediate their differences.'[11]

Reif has observed that good governance includes a number of practices such as,

professional civil service, elimination of corruption in government, a predictable, transparent and accountable administration, democratic decision-making, the supremacy of the rule of law, effective protection of human rights, an independent judiciary, a fair economic system, appropriate devolution and decentralization of government, appropriate levels of military spending, and so on.[12]

There is little doubt about the extent of corruption in India, as it is a well-known fact that without paying bribes, it is difficult to get anything done at any office or institution. In a study of petty corruption, India prominently figures among the 30 most corrupt nations in the world. Transparency International (TI) conducted a study in which 16 states were scanned and it sampled around 5000 rural and urban families. It estimated that every year ordinary Indians pay as much as US$ 6 billion (1.5 per cent of India's GDP) as bribes. Noting this, Rakesh Kalshian has observed that, 'be it birth and death certificates, admission to schools and universities, bank loans, passports, ration cards, driving licences, electric, water or telephone connections, legal or illegal, you name it, and the corruption "yellow pages" have them all'.[13]

In the Global Integrity Report, 2004 prepared by the US-based Center for Public Integrity after a year-long study of 25 nations around the world, India has been rated as a 'weak democracy' on account of corruption and lack of accountability in its public institutions.[14] The

[11] Sakiko Fakuda-Parr and Richard Ponzio, 'Governance: Past, Present, Future—Setting the Governance Agenda for the Millennium Declaration', U.N. Development Programme Paper. Web: http://www.undp.org/governance/eventsites/PAR_Bergen_2002/gov-past-present-future.pdf (last visited 31 May 2006).

[12] See Linda C. Reif, 'Building Democratic Institutions: The Role of National Human Rights Institutions in Good Governance and Human Rights Protection', 13 *Harvard Human Rights Journal*, 2000.

[13] Rakesh Kalshian, 'India: Corruption Notebook', The Center for Public Integrity, USA. Web: http://www.public-i.org/ga/country.aspx?cc=in&act=notebook (last visited: 31 May 2006).

[14] See *Times of India*, 23 May 2004. Web: http://timesofindia.indiatimes.com/articleshow/692836.cms (last visited: 31 May 2006).

report has put India in the 'weak' category on a 'public integrity index', which is a measure of the existence and effectiveness of laws and institutions that promote accountability and limit corruption. The report provides that a major bottleneck in the Indian democratic and legal framework has been lack of transparency about the functioning of the government. It notes that, 'this lack of transparency empowered the bureaucracy in significant ways and paved the way for abuse of power'.[15] As is the case with enforcement of many other laws in India, the report recognizes that while powerful anti-corruption laws are in place, the challenges are in their effective implementation. It adds that the system as a whole does not seem to have effective checks in place to prevent or tackle corruption. As far as efforts to curb corruption are concerned, the report observed that there is no comprehensive effort at eliminating corruption from the governance machinery. As of now, 'the war against corruption is largely waged by a few isolated individuals, select citizen groups, a sprinkling of committed officers and the judiciary'.[16]

It is clear that corruption of any form and in particular the type of institutionalized corruption that prevails in India will not allow good governance. In fact, corruption is an anathema to good governance and it is important that Indian society moves toward reforming the governance system with a view to eliminating corruption. The consequences of ignoring this problem would mean that all other efforts in social and economic development would be adversely affected in a serious manner. Moreover, development of any kind is possible only in a free society. A society cannot be said to be free in which the governance institutions and the individuals who operate it are corrupt and decisions are made not on the basis of merit, but on the basis of vested interests, where bribery is the rule and integrity is an exception.

CORRUPTION AND ITS IMPACT ON HUMAN RIGHTS

Human rights have traditionally been understood to be rights relating to life, liberty, equality, and dignity. In the Indian context, Section 2(d) of the Protection of Human Rights Act, 1993, has defined 'human rights' to mean, 'the rights relating to life, liberty, equality, and dignity of the individual guaranteed by the constitution or embodied in international

---

[15] Ibid.
[16] Ibid.

covenants and enforceable by courts in India.'[17] Human rights in India have also been given a strong constitutional foundation and have developed through innovative judicial interventions over the decades. Public interest litigation[18] is one of the ways by which traditional rules relating to standing have been liberalized and justice has been taken to people who are not in a position to approach the court directly for various reasons.[19]

The interventions of the Indian judiciary to protect and promote both civil and political rights and economic, social, and cultural rights have been remarkably successful in numerous areas of law, but have not yielded positive results in certain areas. The Indian judiciary's activism was ignited by a number of factors, including the failure of the legislature and the executive in promoting good governance policies and sound administration. This compelled the judiciary to intervene in matters that are traditionally perceived to be the domain of other wings of the government. This process of judicial governance is obviously not without controversy or problems as it raises issues relating to the role of judiciary in a democracy and how judiciary as an institution should position itself in promoting human rights and justice. It also raises the systemic question of separation of powers among the three organs of state—legislative, executive, and judiciary.[20]

It is notable that the issue of corruption, whenever it has come up for adjudication in a court of law, has been approached as a criminal law enforcement issue as opposed to a human rights issue. The legislative framework for anti-corruption laws in India is sound and indeed a useful basis for developing other legal, institutional, and enforcement mechanisms for anti-corruption action. However, it is important to recognise that corruption of the nature prevailing in India is far deeper than what a criminal legislation could achieve by prohibiting the act and punishing

[17] The Protection of Human Rights Act, 1993, National Human Rights Commission, New Delhi.

[18] See A.S. Anand (2001), 'Public Interest Litigation as Aid to Protection of Human Rights', M.C. Bhandari Memorial Lecture, (2001) 7 SCC (Jour) 1. Web: http://www.ebc-india.com/lawyer/articles/2001v7a1.htm (last visited 31 May 2006).

[19] See Upendra Baxi, 'Taking Suffering Seriously: Social Action Litigation Before the supreme court of India', *Law and Poverty: Critical Essays*, N.M. Tripathi, Bombay (1999), 387–415.

[20] See generally, Paul O. Caresse, *The Cloaking of Power: Montesquieu, Blackstone, and the Rise of Judicial Activism*, University of Chicago Press, Chicago (2003), pp. xiv, 335.

the wrongdoers. It is necessary to recognise that corruption in India violates human rights. The human rights discourse should be directly involved in anti-corruption initiatives so that corrupt acts of individuals and institutions are no longer mere violations of criminal law and tax law but also human rights violations. This framework of corruption-human rights interface is valuable to understand the implications of violation of constitutionally entrenched rights due to corruption

There are several ways by which corruption can be presented in the trellis of human rights.[21] First, corruption by the nature of its actions discriminates against people. Bribe givers receive more unwarranted favoured treatment than people who do not give bribes. This discriminatory treatment leads to violations of laws, rules, and regulations by the power holders as they obtain some illicit benefit from the bribe receivers. The discrimination that takes place on account of bribery is a direct human rights issue. Equality and non-discrimination are the basic foundations of human rights jurisprudence and they are given a strong constitutional basis in India. Second, corruption promotes unfairness in decision-making. Governance decisions that are made by the power holders are not on the basis of any principle of fairness, but on the basis of the bribe given to them. Unfairness in decision-making violates equality and promotes arbitrariness in administration. The purpose of adjudication in India and elsewhere is to ensure that decisions that are made by power holders are subject to judicial scrutiny on the basis of principles of fairness and accountability. Corrupt actions and decisions taken on account of bribery will not stand such judicial scrutiny and are bound to be set aside. Third, corruption violates a whole set of civil and political rights. In a study conducted by Transparency International (TI), it was revealed that the police as an institution was considered most corrupt in society's perception, accounting for US$ 391 million in bribes. The study also noted that besides the bribes which policepersons receive, ordinary citizens are subjected to severe harassment and all forms of humiliation for securing their basic constitutional rights—14 per cent have to pay bribes for filing a First Information Report (a preliminary record of an alleged crime), 7 per cent for avoiding false arrests, 6 per cent

[21] See C. Raj Kumar, 'Corruption and Human Rights', *Frontline*, Vol. 19, Issue 19, 14–27 September 2002, Chennai; Web: http://www.flonnet.com/fl1919/19190780. htm (last visited: 31 May 2006); C. Raj Kumar, 'Corruption and Human Rights—II', *Frontline*, Vol. 19—Issue 20, 28 September–11 October 2002; Web: http://www. frontlineonnet.com/fl1920/stories/20021011008607500.htm (last visited: 31 May 2006).

for police verification of passports, 6 per cent for arresting accused in a case, 5 per cent for taking cognizance of complaints, and 3 per cent for sending charge-sheets to the courts.[22]

The statistical figures clearly demonstrate the profound and significant human rights implications of corruption. Corruption in police and other similar law enforcement institutions violates the civil and political rights of Indians. This demonstrates not only the failure of the criminal justice system[23] in India but also that institutionalized corruption in India directly violates human rights. Corruption in police typically violates civil rights, but there are also cases of corruption in the election system that have affected political rights. Despite the fact that the Election Commission of India is reputed for its independence, autonomy, and efficiency, the mammoth size of a country like India has only made enforcement of law extremely difficult. This has created problems for human rights, since violations occur first and then the process of institutional redressal begins *reactively, not preventively*. In the case of corruption, it is far more difficult as most corrupt acts do not come into the public domain and remain shrouded in secrecy. But when impoverishment and deprivation is a byword in a country like India, which has a large share of people who are uneducated and unaware of their rights, corruption poses a serious threat to their human rights. Corruption also violates economic, social, and cultural rights. There are numerous instances of government officials and institutions not protecting the rights to food, health, and other economic and social rights. Most of the cases involve bribery, as there is misallocation of resources due to vested interests operating at every level. Corruption affects both economic and social development. Officials who receive bribes do not implement development policies on the basis of governance needs. Rather, development policies become tools and fertile grounds for promoting bribery and other forms of corruption that disempower the poor and the vulnerable.

A former Prime Minister of India estimated that 85 per cent of public funds do not reach the intended beneficiaries due to corruption. Further, the funds that are actually spent on public works and development projects are most often spent on projects that maximize the

---

[22] Rakesh Kalshian, 'India: Corruption Notebook', The Center for Public Integrity, USA. Web: http://www.public-i.org/ga/country.aspx?cc=in&act=notebook (last visited 31 May 2006).

[23] For further reading, see Rajeev Dhavan, 'The Criminal (In)justice System', *Journal of the NHRC*, Vol. 2, 2003, New Delhi, pp. 60–87.

possibility of bribery.[24] Corruption in India is a serious concern for human rights as it violates economic and social rights in a manner that does not receive adequate response. The TI study noted that the public establishment in India is highly corrupt, extorting as much as US$ 1.6 billion each year in bribes, followed by power utilities, educational institutions, and the judiciary in that order.[25]

The fact that corruption disempowers people in India and subjects them to all forms of violations means that the responses to corruption should also be human rights-based and should result in empowering the Indian citizenry. Human rights relating to corruption-free governance need to be recognized through the constitution or other human rights legislation so that the anti-corruption cause does not remain only the responsibility of law enforcement officers (who are themselves corrupt), but also of citizens. Since bureaucratic and political corruption is rampant in India, it is important to broaden the anti-corruption discourse and involve the people. People ought to be sensitized to the discourse that corruption is a serious violation that must be treated not simply as illegal action and breach of law but also as an attack on human rights and dignity.

CORRUPTION AND ITS IMPLICATIONS
FOR THE RULE OF LAW

As corrupt acts are primarily violations of law, they have serious implications for the protection of the rule of law.[26] The rule of law is based upon the belief that a society should be built around people conducting their activities in a lawful and predictable manner; the government acting on the basis of law; rules and regulations and their enforcement being done in a non-discriminatory, fair and reasonable manner. Corruption of the kind that prevails in India threatens the rule of law fabric prevailing in society. The laws that are constantly violated

[24] Prashant Bhushan, 'Fighting Corruption: The Critical Role of Civil Society'. Web: http://www.unodc.org/pdf/crime/corruption/merida_e.pdf (last visited 31 May 2006).

[25] Rakesh Kalshian, India: Corruption Notebook, The Center for Public Integrity, USA. Web: http://www.public-i.org/ga/country.aspx?cc=in&act=notebook (last visited 31 May 2006).

[26] For a very interesting reading on the impact of corruption on the rule of law in India, see Christophe Jaffrelot, 'Indian Democracy: The Rule of Law on Trial', *Indian Review*, Vol. No.1, January 2002, pp. 17–121.

have created a vicious cycle of bribery and influence-peddling, resulting in a cynical attitude towards law enforcement. Even the anti-corruption laws that are occasionally enforced have become political ploys on the part of politicians to settle scores against the opposition. This has further accentuated the twin problems of 'criminalization of politics' and 'politicization of crime'. The Vohra Committee Report, commenting on this problem, observed that:

A network of mafias is virtually running a parallel government pushing the state apparatus into irrelevance…there has been a rapid spread and growth of criminal gangs, armed senas, drug mafias, smuggling gangs, and economic lobbies in the country, which have over the years developed an intensive network of contacts with bureaucrats, government functionaries at local level, politicians, media persons, and strategically located individuals in non-state sector.[27]

It is useful to understand the jurisprudential foundations of the rule of law to relate it to the issue of corruption. In its Rule of Law Project, the International Commission of Jurists defines the rule of law as: 'The principles, institutions, and procedures, not always identical but broadly similar, which the experience and traditions of lawyers in different countries of the world, often themselves having varying political structures and economic backgrounds, have shown to be important to protect the individual from arbitrary government and to enable him to enjoy the dignity of man'.[28] Summarizing the various conceptions of the rule of law given by modern theorists, Hernandez-Truyol has observed that, 'there are three characteristics central to a cogent notion of the rule of law: (1) absence of arbitrary power on the part of the government; (2) administration of ordinary law by ordinary tribunals; and (3) existence of general rule of constitutional equality resulting from the ordinary law of the land. With these characteristics, the rule of law serves three purposes: (1) it protects against anarchy; (2) it allows persons to rely on laws and plan their lives in a way in which they can predict what

[27] R. Upadhyay, 'Political Corruption in India: An Analysis', South Asia Analysis Group, Paper no. 219, 30 March 2001. Web: http://www.saag.org/papers3/paper219. htm (last visited 31 May 2006).

[28] 'The Dynamic Aspects of the Rule of Law in the Modern Age', International Commission of Jurists, Report on the Proceedings of the South-East Asian and Pacific Conference of Jurists, Bangkok, 15–19 February 1965, at 17 (citing the working definition of the rule of law as a dynamic concept, adopted by the Commission at the New Delhi Congress in 1959). This was referred to in n.10 of Berta Esperanza Hernandez-Truyol, 'The Rule of Law and Human Rights', *Florida Journal of International Law*, March 2004.

consequences will flow from their actions; and (3) it protects against arbitrary and capricious action of the government'.[29]

From the above conceptions of the rule of law, it is useful to specifically see how corruption affects the fulfilment of the rule of law and thereby undermines law and justice in Indian society. The following are the specific circumstances generated due to bribery and other forms of corruption negatively impacting on the rule of law:

Arbitrariness in Decision-Making *Violates* the Rule of Law

Bribery is inescapable in government decision-making in India. The state and its instrumentalities, which are entrusted with the responsibility of distributing resources in a fair and non-discriminatory manner, conduct their activities in an arbitrary manner. The arbitrariness is further promoted by irrelevant criteria infused into the decision-making process on account of corruption. This violates the rule of law and leads to the Indian citizenry losing faith in the administrative system. Arbitrariness on account of corruption has been institutionalized. This means that decisions are taken in a fair manner only as an exception like a Pavlovian reflex. The impact this effect has on the citizenry is profound, as people do not have faith in the legal system, the criminal justice and the civil justice systems.

Discrimination in Administration *Undermines* the Rule of Law

One of the important consequences of corruption is that there is widespread discrimination of people. The power holders exercise their discretion to discriminate against people with bribe givers receiving favourable treatment and the people who do not give bribes being unfairly victimized. This victimization of people who do not give bribes is extremely discriminatory and undermines the rule of law on the basis of which all democratic societies are governed. Discrimination in administration due to bribery and other forms of corruption promotes a sense of frustration and helplessness among the victimized as there are no effective mechanisms for redressal. Inevitably, the victims of this

---

[29] Berta Esperanza Hernandez-Truyol, 'The Rule of Law and Human Rights', *Florida Journal of International Law*, March 2004.

discrimination tend to be the poor, whose capacity for bribing is far less than the middle or upper classes.

Abuse of Discretionary Powers *Violates* the Rule of Law

Corruption takes place on account of abuse of the discretionary powers vested with the government in decision-making. Notwithstanding the fact that economic reforms have removed some of the traditional rules relating to exercise of discretion by government officials under the licence-quota Raj, there are still a number of areas in which the government remains the sole authority for exercising discretion. While privatization is not the only answer to removing corruption, it is important to infuse enforceable mechanisms of transparency and accountability that will promote fair, non-discriminatory, and reasonable exercise of discretion. Discretionary power for government officials becomes fertile ground for abuse and corruption becomes a norm. In a country like India which is vastly uneducated and where a significant section of the populace is ignorant of rights and is impoverished due to a number of factors, it is important to ensure that abuse of discretion does not take place. Even if the corrective mechanisms in the form of institutions and anti-corruption agencies are in place and are effective (which is not the case), it is important to create accountable structures for the administrators, particularly when they have discretionary power. Further, as far as possible, these discretionary powers should be limited and in due course made on the basis of objective and determinable criteria so that opportunities for bribery and other forms of corruption are reduced, if not altogether eliminated.

Unpredictability in Law Enforcement *Affects* the Rule of Law

Institutionalized corruption in India has created a lot of uncertainty and unpredictability in law enforcement with regard to anti-corruption laws.[30] Also, due to lack of independence of anti-corruption institutions, the level of uncertainty when it comes to cases relating to investigation, prosecution, and conviction of people who are charged on grounds

[30] For an elaborate commentary on the anti-corruption law in India, see P.V. Ramakrishna, *A Treatise on Anti-Corruption Law in India*, 9th edn, S. Gogia and Company, Hyderabad, p. 1563.

relating to corruption is high. This has affected the rule of law as the basis for criminal justice, as it has been replaced by other extraneous factors like the political importance of the particular anti-corruption case to the government in power, and the availability of manpower, expertise, and experience of the investigating authority in investigating the particular case. For instance, the Tehelka scandal that shook the ruling party of its time is still being investigated without any sign of conclusive determination of guilt. These factors have infused a lot of unpredictability in corruption cases, which ought to be investigated with a sense of professionalism, integrity, and fairness. Much of this was due to the lack of institutional autonomy and the haphazard manner in which different agencies were dealing with cases relating to corruption. The conferral of statutory status to the Central Vigilance Commission (CVC) in the wake of the supreme court judgment in *Vineet Narain* v. *Union of India*[31] is a step in the right direction to ensure that investigative agencies like the CVC are not directly subjected to pressures from the political class while dealing with cases of corruption. This judgment also endowed the CVC with wider powers including supervision over the Central Bureau of Investigation (CBI) and the Enforcement Directorate (ED). This will help reduce to a certain extent the unpredictability surrounding the investigation of corruption cases and the effects on the rule of law. Rule of law is based upon a certain level of predictability that violations of law will be met with certain consequences. This predictability has not been supported in cases relating to corruption in India and hence, it is important to take steps to reform the criminal justice system and the civil justice system with a view to infuse predictability and remove uncertainty in the protection of the rule of law. The success of the Independent Commission against Corruption (ICAC) in Hong Kong in making Hong Kong one of the least corrupt societies in the world is a useful case in point for India to examine with regard to the need for ensuring independent institutions that fight corruption.[32]

---

[31] (1997) 7 SCALE 656; AIR 1998 SC 889.

[32] See generally, 'Human Rights Approaches of Corruption Control Mechanisms —Enhancing the Hong Kong Experience of Corruption Prevention Strategies', *San Diego International Law Journal*, Vol. 5, 2004, pp. 323–51; see also, Alan Lai, 'Building Public Confidence in Anti-Corruption Efforts—The Approach of the Hong Kong Special Administrative Region of China', *Forum on Crime and Society*, Vol. 2, No. 1, December 2002. Though the ICAC is highly respected, the lack of democratic development in Hong Kong has been a lingering problem that, if not addressed, may have long-term implications.

RIGHTS-BASED APPROACHES TO
ANTI-CORRUPTION MEASURES

Having recognized that corruption affects human rights and the rule of law, it is important to develop the right to corruption-free governance through a number of right-based strategies in India. Rights-based approaches to governance are those strategies that rest on the conceptual foundation that social and economic goals do not remain policy objectives, but get transformed into rights that are vested with the citizenry—increasing incentives for public vigilance. In this conception there are 'right-bearers' and 'duty-holders'. The people will have the rights relating to various social and economic goals that were hitherto described as policy objectives. The representatives of the government are vested with the duty of ensuring the protection and promotion of the particular rights.

It is not that the rights-based approaches to anti-corruption measures will automatically ensure corruption-free governance, nor is this approach free from problems relating to enforcement. Rights by their very nature are claims on the government or its representatives to act in a particular manner. There are numerous legal, jurisprudential, and philosophical bases for rights to be in the constitution or for that matter to be used effectively for promoting democratic governance. By the same token, there are criticisms of rights-based approaches to constitutional governance, particularly in the area of economic, social, and cultural rights.

The bone of contention is with regard to whether rights ought to be expanded so as to include economic and social rights. Some commentators have observed that it is important to limit rights so that expanding the notion of rights and their attendant non-enforceability does not result in dilution of traditional rights. But in the context of India, the judiciary has significantly developed the notion of rights without diluting traditional rights. While the success of the judiciary in enforcing economic and social rights has been mixed, there is very little scepticism or doubt in the mind of the judiciary to continue its interventions when these rights are violated either in a constitutional sense or for that matter by legislation. In fact, the development of the 'right to life' jurisprudence under Article 21 of the Constitution of India[33] is one such example in which the courts have not hesitated to include new rights as a part of the evolving nature of human rights and human dignity. The fundamental right to education was also initially recognized

---

[33] Mahendra P. Singh, 'Constitution of India', V.N. Shukla, Tenth Edition (2001), with supplement (2003), Eastern Book Company, Lucknow.

by the Supreme Court of India followed by a constitutional amendment that specifically incorporated this right into the constitution.[34]

Notwithstanding these developments relating to 'rights jurisprudence' in India and elsewhere, the notion of rights-based approaches to development and governance is not one without controversy or criticism. However, the conceptual basis for such an approach is indeed useful for formulating various effective anti-corruption measures. In this regard, it is useful to propose that there should be a fundamental right to corruption-free service in Indian society. The formulation of such a right along with the development of other rights-based approaches to development will help in eliminating corruption and promoting integrity and good governance in the following specific ways:

Corruption-Free Administration as a Facet of Constitutional Governance

The recognition of the right to corruption-free governance as a constitutionally recognized fundamental right has the potential to bring the problem of corruption to the central focus of political discourse. This will ensure that the state and all its instrumentalities act in accordance with the constitution and do not engage in any form of corrupt actions that will violate the fundamental rights of the Indian citizenry. Constitutional governance means that the governance system is based upon the underlying ideals, goals, objectives, aspirations, and values of the constitution. Unfortunately, corruption has undermined all these constitutional values. The right to corruption-free governance has the potential to bring the corruption issue to the forefront of administration and all individuals and institutions within the government will be expected to take the necessary steps to fulfil this fundamental right.

Empowerment of the Judiciary to Ensure Corruption-Free Governance

The recognition of the fundamental right to corruption-free governance will quickly empower the judiciary to bring forward the integration of anti-corruption discourse and the human rights discourse. Both these discourses are about increasing legitimacy of the state and ensuring

[34] For further reading, see C. Raj Kumar, 'International Human Rights Perspectives on the Fundamental Right to Education—Integration of Human Rights and Human Development in the Indian Constitution', *Tulane Journal of International and Comparative Law*, Vol. 12, 2004, pp. 237–85.

accountability of the administration. The judiciary is best suited to continue this role as it has attempted in the past to create greater transparency and infuse institutional autonomy and independence to investigative agencies that engage in anti-corruption work. With the recognition of this right, the judiciary is in a far better position to develop jurisprudence relating to good governance.

Galvanizing Social Consciousness for Corruption-Free Governance

The formulation of the right to corruption-free governance will help in galvanizing social consciousness on issues relating to bribery and other forms of corruption. It is necessary to garner the support of the citizens, as it is their apathy and indifference to abuse of power that has resulted in a deep-rooted sense of institutionalized corruption in India. Political morality cannot be brought about without the development of individual morality. The particular right can help in creating greater support for corruption-free governance and also result in the citizens valuing integrity and rectitude as important criteria for electing their representatives. At the same time citizens will feel a greater sense of urgency in reporting on corrupt activity.

Expanding the Mandate of National Human Rights Institutions

There are various institutions in India that are engaged in the task of protecting and promoting human rights. The National Human Rights Commission (NHRC), the National Commission for Women (NCW), National Commission for Minorities (NCM), National Commission for Scheduled Castes and Scheduled Tribes, the various State Human Rights Commissions, etc., are examples of institutions that work on certain issues relating to human rights. Besides these institutions, the judiciary, by virtue of its constitutional responsibilities, is committed to protecting human rights. It is proposed that for anti-corruption work to be broadened and for it to become a mainstream governance issue, there is need for various institutions to broaden their mandate to include human rights work as a focal point for promoting good governance.[35]

---

[35] See generally, C. Raj Kumar, 'National Human Rights Institutions—Good Governance Perspectives on Institutionalization of Human Rights', *American University International Law Review*, Vol. 19, No. 2, 2003, pp. 259–300.

The good governance agenda includes protection and promotion of human rights and rule of law. Both these functions will not be fully accomplished if corruption is rampant in the government. It is important that institutions like the NHRC provide a framework on the basis of which corrupt acts of individuals and institutions that result in human rights violations are given due cognizance by the NHRC. It is recognized that the NHRC is overloaded with human rights cases that come before it. However, it is important that the corruption problem, when it takes a human rights contour, be duly recognized and steps taken in that direction. The NHRC should attempt to understand the implications of corruption for human rights not only from a theoretical perspective but also from a practical standpoint. It is useful to examine from the various cases that come before the NHRC how many of them are due to some act of bribery or other forms of corruption. Further, the Research Division of the NHRC may consider supporting studies and researches conducted to examine both the human rights consequences of corruption and how far the human rights discourse can help in ensuring corruption-free governance.

One of the important developments that have taken place due to the institutionalization of human rights in India through establishing certain commissions is that human rights have come to take certain democratic space within the domestic political discourse. However, the existence of democratic institutions does not necessarily mean that human rights violations do not occur or that their incidence is reduced. What it means is that there are institutional mechanisms available for victims of human rights violations to seek justice.[36] The effectiveness of these institutions in India is still a matter of opinion, but by and large, the NHRC has come to acquire a certain reputation because of its indispensability, impartiality, and independence. Of course, it needs to be noted that the powers of the NHRC are limited and their opinions on human rights issues are recommendations, though they carry a lot of legitimacy and persuasiveness due to the composition of the commission.

The law enforcement agencies that are engaged in the task of anti-corruption work (such as the CVC, the CBI, and the ED) may be truly empowered if institutions like the NHRC take cognizance of cases relating to corruption when it is a human rights issue. This will bring

[36] See generally, C. Raj Kumar, 'Role and Contribution of National Human Rights Commissions in Promoting National and International Human Rights Norms in the National Context', *Indian Journal of Public Administration* (*IJPA*), Vol. XLVII, No. 2, April–June 2001, pp. 222–36.

the corruption problem to the centre of governance discourse in India as it will be a human rights violation and the consequences of such actions will be significant. The recognition of corruption as a human rights issue does not warrant any amendment to the Protection of Human Rights Act, 1993. The definition of 'human rights' given in Section 2 and the functions of the NHRC given in Section 12 are wide enough to include corruption as a violation of human rights. Speaking about the role of NHRCs at the 59th Session of the UN Commission on Human Rights on 16 April 2003, Justice A.S. Anand, the NHRC Chairperson, observed:

It is our view that national institutions are both catalysts and monitors of good governance within their respective jurisdictions and can play a unique role in the defence and furtherance of human rights if they are pro-active, if they take preventive measures to stave-off or mitigate violations, if they are fearless in bringing to book those who have violated human rights.[37]

The fact that the NHRC has recognized its role to be that of 'catalyst and monitor of good governance' is a step in the right direction for increasing the institutional mandate of the NHRC to recognize corruption as a human rights issue and to promote corruption-free governance. This statement should be supplemented by taking serious steps to understand the problem of corruption in India and to evolve human rights-based approaches to tackle this problem. In this regard, it is encouraging to note that the NHRC has been developing right-based approaches to development in the area of population stabilization and combating HIV. The NHRC can also engage with other anti-corruption agencies such as the CVC, the CBI, and the ED, which are most of the time on the 'other side' when it comes to the NHRC's work relating to human rights. However, this institutional engagement must be a facet of good governance because if the NHRC has to take a proactive role in promoting good governance policies, it is necessary for it to understand the problem of corruption from a criminal law enforcement perspective as well.

JUDICIAL ENFORCEMENT OF
CORRUPTION-FREE GOVERNANCE

The Constitution of India has provided for the separation of powers in the Indian governance system and the judiciary is entrusted with the

[37] Important Statements/Decisions/Opinions of the Commission, *Journal of the NHRC*, Vol. 2, 2003, pp. 148–75.

work of ensuring that the actions of the legislature and the executive are in accordance with the constitution. The preamble to the constitution underlines the fundamental tenets of the constitution-makers to build a new socio-economic order where there will be social, economic, and political justice and equality of status and opportunity for all. This basic objective of the constitution mandates every organ of the state—the executive, the legislature, and the judiciary—to work harmoniously to realize the objectives concretized in the chapters on the fundamental rights and the directive principles of state policy.[38] However, the institutionalized corruption that is prevalent in India has shattered these objectives and the various organs of the state have abused power, become corrupt, and acted for self-interest and not on the basis of public interest. The entire governance machinery is tainted with regularity of scams and allegations of corruption coming to the forefront. The Indian judiciary needs to understand that fundamental rights cannot have any meaning for a large number of people in India, until policies are reformed to ensure corruption-free governance built on the foundation of the directive principles. Bribery and other forms of corruption have resulted in an almost illusory access to justice for weaker sections of Indian society for protection of their fundamental rights. In this regard, a TI study made the following observations:

The survey also revealed that the greatest sufferers of this petty corruption are not the middle classes, who often have the ability to grease greedy palms (even if grudgingly), but the urban poor—hawkers, rickshaw-pullers and small tea-shop owners, small-time mechanics, poor migrants labourers, slum-dwellers: in one word, the city's underbelly, bravely trying to eke out a living in the most heartless and trying circumstances. As for rural poor, consider this: the government spends US$ 8.5 billion annually on them but most of it disappears on the way.[39]

Corruption in implementing development policies has culminated in the creation of poverty, lack of education, health care, etc. To the majority of the Indian populace, rights and benefits conferred by the constitution and enforced by the judiciary means nothing. Because of their handicap, they lack the capacity to assert their rights. The constitution has indeed

[38] See C. Raj Kumar, 'The Development of International Human Rights Law in National Judiciaries—The Indian Experience', *Annual Report of The Institute of Jurisprudence*, Vol. 19, July 2003, pp. 75–91.

[39] Rakesh Kalshian, 'India: Corruption Notebook', The Center for Public Integrity, USA. Web: http://www.public-i.org/ga/country.aspx?cc=in&act=notebook (last visited: 31 May 2006).

shown a great concern for the underprivileged, conferred on them many rights and entitlements and laid obligations on the state to take measures for improving the conditions of their life. Towards that end, laws were enacted and administrative programmes formulated by the state for bringing about social and economic change and ensuring distributive justice to the people. The judiciary regarded it as its duty to come to the rescue of the underprivileged, to help them reap the benefits of economic and social entitlements. However, the problem of corruption has undermined the various steps that were taken to promote social and economic development.

The Indian judiciary ought to recognize that one of the drawbacks of the justice delivery system in India is the denial of access to justice to the common men and women because of corruption. Just as the court liberated itself from traditional methods of judicial process and made creative use of judicial power by developing a variety of techniques, including PIL to make access to justice a reality, it should also take up the corruption issue directly and recognize the human rights consequences of corruption. Thus, through judicial innovation, cases relating to corruption need to be approached from a human rights standpoint. Lack of legislative thinking and executive inaction on issues relating to corruption coupled with exploitation of the masses by the power holders requires the judiciary to work towards ensuring corruption-free governance.

While the judiciary has not yet recognized corruption as a human rights issue in India, there are a few instances where it has intervened on corruption matters. It is useful to refer to the decision of the Supreme Court of India in the case of *Vineet Narain* v. *Union of India*[40] in which the court conferred statutory status on the CVC and decided to insulate the CBI and the ED from political control and pressures. Further, the court referred with approval the recommendations of the Lord Nolan Committee on Standards in Public Life in the United Kingdom. The following seven principles of public life stated in the Report by Lord Nolan and commended by the court are: selflessness, integrity, objectivity, accountability, openness, honesty, and leadership.[41] The supreme court observed further:

These principles of public life are of general application in every democracy and one is expected to bear them in mind while scrutinizing the conduct of every

---

[40] (1997) 7 SCALE 656; AIR 1998 SC 889.
[41] See Vol. I of Lord Nolan's Report (1995).

holder of a public office.... Any deviation from the path of rectitude by any of them amounts to a breach of trust and must be severely dealt with instead of being pushed under the carpet. If the conduct amounts to an offence, it must be promptly investigated and the offender against whom a *prima facie* case is made out should be prosecuted expeditiously so that the majesty of law is upheld and the rule of law vindicated.[42]

The fact that the judiciary in India has taken a proactive role in ensuring good governance by intervening on issues that are traditionally within the domain of the executive has received a lot of attention. The judicial intervention has been due to the fact that the legislature and the executive have failed in certain key areas and the governance machinery needed to be tuned to ensure that the rule of law is protected. It is important for the judiciary to take a strong position when it comes to corruption recognizing that widespread bribery and other forms of corruption promote a culture of disrespect for law and the various institutions that are established for protecting law and order and promoting justice. Until this is recognized, the work of the judiciary, like other institutions, will be crippled by the challenge of enforcement of human rights that arise due to corruption in government functioning. While corruption at the higher level of judiciary may not be rampant, the lower levels of judiciary in India are notorious for their own acts of corruption.[43] This is indeed a dangerous trend and poses a serious threat to the rule of law, social stability, and democracy in India. The judiciary has a difficult task cut out for itself as it should not only ensure that other wings of the government are not corrupt, but develop mechanisms of accountability for itself so that corruption within the judiciary does not get institutionalized. It may be wise for the judiciary to develop its own internal mechanism of oversight concerning judicial corruption, perhaps with a designated bench of Justices of Appeal to receive public complaints concerning corruption in the judiciary. This may operate as an oversight panel to consider allegations of corruption and make recommendations

---

[42] AIR 1998 SC 889, at p. 917.

[43] See generally, Rajeev Dhavan, 'Judicial Corruption', The *Hindu*, Chennai, India, 22 Feburary 2002. Web: http://www.hinduonnet.com/2002/02/22/stories/2002022200031000.htm (last visited: 31 May 2006); see also, P.P. Rao, 'The Judiciary', The *Hindu*, Chennai, India, 15 May 2003. Web: http://www.hinduonnet.com/thehindu/2003/05/15/stories/2003051500361000.htm (last visited: 31 May 2006); Rajeev Dhavan, 'Judicial Propriety and Tehelka', The *Hindu*, Chennai, India, 29 November 2002. Web: http://www.hinduonnet.com/thehindu/2002/11/29/stories/2002112901181000.htm (last visited: 31 May 2006).

separate from, though perhaps in aid of, the ordinary processes of appeal or for reference to law enforcement agencies. In *Common Cause, A Registered Society* v. *Union of India*, the supreme court observed that:

It is high time that the public servants should be held personally responsible for their malafide acts in the discharge of their functions as public servants.... We take it to be perfectly clear, that if a public servant abuses his office either by an act of omission or commission, and the consequence of that is injury to an individual or loss of public property, an action may be maintained against such public servant.... No public servant can arrogate to himself the power to act in a manner which is arbitrary.'[44]

The judiciary as an institution still commands a lot of respect among the people of India and there are legitimate social expectations generated due to the judicial interventions when there has been maladministration. The judiciary has also created a sense of accountability in government institutions by its interventions. This accountability of the government to the people needs to be established through developing jurisprudence relating to corruption-free governance as a part of human rights commitments and constitutional governance.

CIVIL SOCIETY ACTIVISM AND THE RIGHT TO INFORMATION

Civil society has come to occupy a predominant role in ensuring corruption-free governance.[45] One of the important objectives of human rights-based approaches to corruption-free administration is to empower civil society to ensure that transparency and accountability become the norm for governance. India is such a vast country that corruption-free governance cannot be established purely by relying upon the various investigative agencies and institutions. Civil society, including the media, has to be involved in a significant manner to ensure that corruption-free governance does not remain a policy goal or an institutional aspiration. Civil society is best suited to perform this role as it can devote itself to ensuring that the decisions of the government are made in a transparent and socially accountable manner. Further, civil society in India is part of the vibrant democratic set-up and is able to be involved in both rural and

[44] AIR 1996 SC 3539 at p. 3551 (paragraph 25).

[45] See generally, Sunil Sodhi, 'Combating Corruption in India—The Role of Civil Society', paper prepared for the XVIII World Congress of International Political Science Association, 1–5 August 2000, Quebec City.

urban India at the grassroots levels. The problem of most human rights commitments has been the existence of a gap between theory and practice; policy and reality. Corruption-free governance should be part of civil society activism so that the people are empowered to seek transparency and accountability from decision-makers. Prashant Bhushan, a senior Advocate of the Supreme Court of India, has observed that:

...a corruption free society must have a) strong and adequate laws such as Anti-corruption Acts, Right to information law, and laws to protect whistle blowers; b) Strong, independent, and properly functioning institutions to enforce account-ability and criminal justice such as investigative agencies, vigilance commissions, and the judiciary; and c) an organized and vigilant civil society which monitors the conduct of public officials and exposes corrupt ones.... Ultimately, it is only a powerful civil society movement, which can break the vicious cycle of corruption in any society.[46]

It needs to be noted that the right to information is a powerful tool for formulating the right to corruption-free governance. The right to information is the first step in checking governmental corruption, as the people of India ought to be empowered by the availability of information on the decisions taken by the government that affect their lives. Commenting upon the relevance of the right to information for the control of corruption, Harsh Mander and Abha Joshi have observed that:

the right to information is expected to improve the quality of decision making by public authorities, in both policy and administrative matters, by removing unnecessary secrecy surrounding the decision-making process.... The cumulative impact on control of corruption and the arbitrary exercise of power, of the availability of such information to the citizen, would be momentous.[47]

The constitutional foundation of the right to information rests on Part III of the Constitution of India, dealing with fundamental rights. Even though there is no specific right to information or for that matter right to freedom of the press as such in the constitution, the right to

---

[46] Prashant Bhushan, 'Fighting Corruption: The Critical Role of Civil Society'. Web: http://www.unodc.org/pdf/crime/corruption/merida_e.pdf (last visited 31 May 2006).

[47] Harsh Mander and Abha Joshi, 'The Movement for Right to Information in India—People's Power for the Control of Corruption', Commonwealth Human Rights Initiative (CHRI), New Delhi. Web: http://www.humanrightsinitiative.org/programs/ai/rti/india/articles/The%20Movement%20for%20RTI%20in%20India.pdf (last visited: 31 May 2006).

information has been creatively interpreted and read into the constitution by the judiciary.[48] The constitution has a sound framework for protecting human rights in the form of the right to equal protection of laws and the right to equality before the law (Article 14), the right to freedom of speech and expression (Article 19(1)(a)) and the right to life and liberty (Article 21). This is further supported by the right to constitutional remedies provided in Article 32, which is the right to approach the high courts and the supreme court through their writ jurisdiction for remedies in cases of violation of these rights.

The various efforts to curb corruption at all levels of governmental decision-making have acquired the form of efforts to promote transparency and enforce accountability through developing the right to information at the state and central levels. It initially started with the work of a grassroots mass-based organization, known as the *Mazdoor Kisan Shakti Sangathan* (Labour Farmer Strength Organization-MKSS), in the state of Rajasthan. The origin of MKSS was so nondescript that it did not invite much attention. Members of the MKSS walked from village to village asking simple questions: did the people know the amount of funds that were coming to their village for development? How was the money that came from different sources actually spent? Although these questions were simple, the poor and impoverished of India had never dared to ask.[49]

When this information was collected, the MKSS went to the Government Block Office, which is the authority that administers development funding in about 100 villages, with a request to provide detailed information on development expenditure.[50] In response, they were told that there was no government rule that would allow villagers to demand such information and receive it.[51] This culminated in the MKSS launching a people's campaign in the state of Rajasthan. The aim of the campaign was to conduct numerous public hearings in which cases of corruption and misappropriation of public funds were shared with a lot of people.[52]

---

[48] See Granville Austin, *The Indian Constitution—Cornerstone of a Nation*, Oxford University Press, New Delhi (1966). See also, Granville Austin, *Working a Democratic Constitution—The Indian Experience*, Oxford University Press, New Delhi (1999).

[49] Bunker Roy, 'The Power of Information—A Grassroots Organization in India Defeats Corruption', D+C Development and Cooperation, Deutsche Stiftung fur internationale Entwicklung (DSE), Frankfurt. Web: www.dse.de/zeitschr/de202-11.htm (last visited: 31 May 2006).

[50] Ibid.

[51] Ibid.

[52] Ibid.

Aruna Roy of the MKSS has observed that the right to information in Rajasthan was aimed at ending the arbitrary use of power.[53] The campaign of MKSS had focused on demanding transparency of official records, a social audit of government spending and redressal machinery for people who had not been given their due.[54] The result of this powerful, mass-based, grass-roots civil society activism in the form of social struggle resulted in the state of Rajasthan passing a law on the right to information, besides creating an environment in which corruption is tolerated less and accountability of the government officials is enforced.[55] The MKSS movement to seek the right to information came about due to large-scale, rampant embezzlement of public funds. The consequences of these corrupt actions were 'non-employment of, or under-payment to, the local workforce, and non-existent or bad quality assets on the ground, which were meant for education, housing, or health facilities for the rural poor.'[56] The linkage between the human rights violations on account of institutionalized corruption and the lack of transparency and accountability[57] in governance led the MKSS to establish a 'connection between the manipulation of official records and denial of life opportunities to the rural poor'.[58] This resulted in the movement to seek the right to access to official records as a part of the right to life and livelihood.[59]

This civil society activism was followed by a nationwide movement to seek national legislation on freedom of information through the work of the MKSS in Rajasthan. The important link between lack of transparency, absence of accountability, and institutionalized corruption gave

[53] Kalpana Sharma, 'Right to Information will check Corruption', The *Hindu*, 24 February 2002, National Page. Web: http://www.hinduonnet.com/2002/02/24/stories/2002022400251200.htm (last visited: 31 May 2006).

[54] Ibid.

[55] Ibid.

[56] Ibid.

[57] For further reading, see Karnataka Working Group's 2002 Report, 'Improving Accountability in Panchayati Raj' (2003) at www.indiatogether.org/2003/jan/gov-karpri02.htm (last visited 12 April 2006). See also, Prashant Bhushan, 'India Approves Freedom of Information Law—The Freedom of Information Bill 2002', National Campaign for the People's Right to Information, December 2002. Web: www.freedominfo.org/news/india/ (last visited: 31 May 2006); Neelabh Mishra, 'A Battle Half Won', *Combat Law*, Issue 6, India Together. Web: www.indiatogether.org/bin/pfriend/cgi (last visited: 31 May 2006).

[58] Ibid.

[59] Ibid.

the social and political impetus to seek the formulation of the right to information.[60]

The relevance of the right to information[61] in India is much more than allowing the free flow of information from the government to the public. It is about people exercising their right to seek necessary information from the government so that the government and its representatives are held accountable to the public. The right to information ensures that governmental decisions are made in a transparent manner and that the people have the right to be informed of decisions that affect them. Interestingly, the right to know, 'receive, and impart information has been recognized within the right to freedom of speech and expression'[62] under Article 19 (1)(a) of the constitution.[63] The right to information law has now been enacted in a few states in India, including Rajasthan, Madhya Pradesh, Maharashtra, Goa, Tamil Nadu, Karnataka, Delhi, and Andhra Pradesh.[64] The Freedom of Information Bill, 2002, was passed by the Lok Sabha (lower house of the Indian parliament) on 3 December 2002 and by the Rajya Sabha (upper house of the Indian parliament) on 16 December 2002.[65] Further, for ensuring greater and more effective access to information, the Government of India resolved that the Freedom of Information Act, 2002, be made more progressive, participatory, and meaningful.[66] This was done after the proposals by the National Advisory Council suggested a number of changes. To facilitate these changes, the government decided to repeal the Freedom of Information Act, 2002, and adopted a new legislation, namely, The Right to

[60] For further reading, see Karnataka Working Group's 2002 Report, 'Reinventing Rural Governance', January 2003. Web: www.indiatogether.org/2003/jan/gov-karpri01.htm (last visited: 31 May 2006).

[61] Bela Bhatia and Jean Dreze, 'Freedom of Information is Key to Anti-Corruption Campaign in Rural India' (1998), at http://www.transparency.org/working_papers/bhatia-dreze/bhatia-dreze.html (last visited 12 April 2006).

[62] *S.P. Gupta* v. *Union of India* AIR 1982 SC 149 at 234; *Secretary, Ministry of I&B, Government of India* v. *Cricket Association of Bengal* (1995) 2 SCC 161.

[63] Mahendra P. Singh, *Constitution of India*, V.N Shukla (ed.), Eastern Book Company, 10th edn. 2001 and Supp. 2003.

[64] Prashant Bhushan, 'India Approves Freedom of Information Law—The Freedom of Information Bill 2002' (2002), at www.freedominfo.org/news/india/ (last visited 31 May 2006).

[65] Neelabh Mishra, 'A Battle Half Won', at www.indiatogether.org/bin/pfriend/cgi (last visited 8 May 2006).

[66] Shalu Nigam, *Right to Information Law and Practice*, JBA Publishers, 2006, p. 155.

Information Act, 2005 (Act No. 22 of 2005).[67] This was published in the Gazette of India (Extraordinary) Part II—Section I, on 21 June 2005, and the Act received the assent of the president on 15 June 2005.[68]

The preamble to The Right to Information Act, 2005, notes: 'An Act to provide for setting out the practical regime of right to information for citizens to secure access to information under the control of public authorities, in order to promote transparency and accountability in the working of every public authority, the constitution of a Central Information Commission and State Information Commissions and for matters connected herewith or incidental thereto....'[69] Noting the specific issue of corruption, the Preamble to the Act states, '...And whereas democracy requires an informed citizen and transparency of information which are vital to its functioning and also to contain corruption and to hold Governments and their instrumentalities accountable to the governed....'[70]

Various departments, including some of those notorious for rampant corruption (such as the Delhi Development Authority), have created information supplying mechanisms. These legislative and administrative successes owe their impetus, drive, and culmination to civil society activism.

The empire of corruption has done seminal damage to good governance and rule of law. Corruption is discriminatory and an assault on human rights of the Indian people, not merely a criminal offence. We must view corruption from the angle of human rights so that public institutions can be held accountable for abuse of power. We must encourage institutions like the NHRC to begin taking cognizance of corruption cases to raise the profile of this linkage with human rights. We must also evolve a new language including the right to corruption-free governance as a fundamental human right, which is non-derogable so that the ideal of constitutional governance is upheld. There are various ways and means by which the judiciary can step in to correct the malaise of corruption in the light of inaction or apathy by the legislative and executive branches of the state. Corruption *within* the judiciary, mainly at the lower levels, ought to be an important target for elimination. Anti-corruption work must involve grassroots civil society organizations,

[67] Ibid.
[68] Ibid., p. 156.
[69] Preamble of The Right to Information Act, 2005, Ibid.
[70] Ibid.

on the lines of the MKSS that succeeded in getting a law enacted for
the people's right to information. Since corruption is a disempowering
force, the most effective way to root it out is through empowerment of
citizens, both through popular self-initiative and through institutional
mechanisms that exist in the legal system. A holistic war against
corruption through legal and social action has been long due. Until such
a movement comes about, corruption will continue to eat into the socio-
economic development of India, and take a heavy human toll.

8

The Right to Development and its Implications for Governance Reform in India

ARJUN SENGUPTA[*]

The Indian economy has made significant progress in all sectors of development in the last fifty years since it started its planning process. In the initial years the overwhelming concern of Indian policy makers was to protect its newly earned independence and to succeed in the new experiment of building a nation. The independence was threatened— at least that was the widely shared perception of people in India—by international political and military alliances, which were not tolerant of our autonomous development, or for that matter of other newly independent countries. It was also threatened economically because those countries, which had dominated our economy and similarly the economies of the other newly independent countries for centuries, were reluctant to withdraw their hold.

The threat to nation-building was even more serious, because India was engaged in an experiment of binding a diverse and fractious community of religious, linguistic, ethnic, and social groups into the common identity of a nation. Politics and economics were intertwined. While the identity of a nation was supposed to be mainly political, it was necessary that different groups constituting the nation should have a stake in the development of the economy. It was necessary that all people and each

* This essay is an extension of a paper by the author in the *Journal of The National Human Rights Commission*, India Vol. 2, 2003. Five Reports of the author as the Independent Expert on the Right to Development have been brought out in *The Right to Development* by the Franciscans International, Geneva. This volume also contains a number of articles by distinguished scholars on the subject.

group consider that developing together, as a part of India, would satisfy their interests more than from splitting away into separate entities.

It is easy to forget the difficulties of the earlier years when group identities based on language, caste, or religion were fomented all over the country towards separation into small autonomous national units. The genius of the policy makers in those days was to persuade these groups to develop their linguistic and ethnic identities through political changes and economic development, but still keep them committed to the unity of the Indian nation. The federal structure of the country helped, and also developed over the years in that process. But more importantly, it was the economic development with new industries, infrastructure as well as transport and communication, agricultural development, irrigation projects, and innovation in the financial sector backing up unified domestic markets, which made all to commit themselves to the unity of an Indian nation.

One implication of this was giving the state not only a major role in Indian development, but also the notion that it was to be guided by political and often non-commercial motivation for keeping the country together. It led us to deviate from the free play of the market forces, which always protect and promote those who begin with an initial advantage of assets and incomes. Whether the markets would have accentuated the inequalities and encouraged the trends of divisiveness in an already unequal society, cannot be easily demonstrated. However, the perception was that markets left alone would not get us out of the quagmire of the colonial rule. It was widely felt that the state, with democratically elected governments, would work more in the interest of all the peoples in the country, and guide the markets rather than be guided by them.

Mistakes were made in those years in economic policies dominated by the state, with intervention and created inefficiencies. However, the policy makers did succeed in maintaining the country's independence and national unity. Together with that, there were major advances in the development of our infrastructure, industries, science and technology, and in restructuring our rural economy and land relations. The overall growth of the economy in the first 30 years was not much more than 3.5 per cent a year, although there were periods when the growth rates recorded 5 to 6 per cent per annum. Even that average growth rate was definitely much higher than the growth rates of the previous 30 years of colonial period. But they were by all accounts much less than what we needed and probably much less than we could have secured, if we had followed a fully market oriented development.

Thinking on development in that period, however, was mainly centred around economic growth, and the emphasis on industrialization and the Indian way of development was very much consistent with the mainstream view about economics of development. There were some countries in South-East Asia and for a limited period Latin America, which had grown at much higher rates than India by following more market related, outward oriented economic policies. But none of them had the complex political-economic structure of India and the overwhelming demand from its democratic polity was for retaining the country's independence and for following a process of economic growth, which all sections of its peoples at least perceived as promoting their well-being.

Over the last 25 years, however, development thinking has undergone a substantial change. Economic growth is no longer the focal point of economic development. It is the concern with accelerating improvement of well-being of the people, which came to be recognized as the principal purpose of development. Economic growth would at best be a necessary condition for such a sustained development over a long period. But it was not sufficient to guarantee that it would result in the improved well-being of all sections of people. This shift in the paradigm of economic thinking is associated with the rise and spread of the notion of human development. Amartya Sen was a principal proponent of this new thinking. The Human Development Reports of the UNDP, brought out by his friend, the famous Pakistani economist Mahbub-ul-Haq, spelt out the statistical implications of that approach in its successive yearly publications. Human development became the name of the game of economic development.

The right to development is a new phase of human development, that combines the human rights approach with the programmes and policies of human development. In a nut shell, as Sen has described, human development means expansion of freedom, peoples' ability to lead lives of their choice, with the removal of obstacles such as hunger, malnutrition, ill-health, illiteracy, and economic insecurities. Development is then defined as expansion of freedoms. Human rights on the other hand are claims that people make for certain privileges and advantages as rights, which the society must provide as first priority, because these rights are the foundational norms of the society. When those freedoms whose expansion is defined as development are claimed as rights of the people of the country, we have the right to development. As all rights entail obligations on the part of the duty-bearers like the state and other authorities, the right to development entails obligations of formulating and implementing appropriate development policies, by the state, supported by cooperation of the international community.

Human rights are expressions of basic freedoms, which require access to and availability of, basic necessities for all people to be reached through processes that are built on the notion of equity, non-discrimination, participation, and empowerment. So a human right based development policy has to be equitable and participatory, accountable and non-discriminatory. If a human right of development is accepted by the people of India it will change the whole approach to development policy in this country.

In the following pages are presented the outlines of the logic of human right to development. I do not go into the details of how concretely it can change Indian economic policy. That is a subject of research in which many are now involved. But what this essay intends to do is to explain the rationale of this approach so that support for it can develop in this country as widely as possible. Human rights in history had been based on popular movements leading up to constitutional changes. This essay is aimed at creating a basis of such popular discussion, scrutiny, and debates leading up to public action.

HUMAN RIGHT TO DEVELOPMENT

Human rights have been recognised as standards of achievement and norms of behaviour of all members of a society, in particular of those in authority like the governments or other agencies who have the power to influence the behaviour of others. They form the foundations of a society and they are inviolable, as society would disintegrate otherwise. These rights are claimed by the people as their entitlement to certain objects or privileges or interests which they value—what they want to have and to be—to protect and promote their dignity as human beings. The society is formed to ensure through its laws, constitution, and institutions that every one enjoys these rights. The states, according to this perspective, derive their authority over society from their responsibility to safeguard these rights.

Traditionally, the rights language had the power to mobilize public action to compel the social authorities, whether they were kings or sovereign rulers or nation states, to protect these rights, at least not to violate them if not promote them. Initially, whether it was for the magna carta, for the American war of independence, or the French revolution, these rights were formulated essentially as negative rights when the authorities were charged to abstain from interfering with, or preventing the enjoyment of these rights. These were all presented in the form of freedoms which were considered basic to human dignity and which were threatened by the possible actions of the authorities. Indeed, the American declaration was categorical about the rights of the people to rebel against and overthrow the state, if it failed to ensure the enjoyment of these freedoms.

After the Second World War, when attempts were made to rebuild the international system so that the experience of the holocaust was not repeated, these rights were presented as civil and political rights that the nation states were obliged to protect and all other actors in the international society, the states, international agencies as well as non-state actors, were obliged to help protect. But at the same time, the international community started talking about a system of positive rights, essentially in the form of economic, social, and cultural rights with respect to which the nation states and other actors of the international community had the obligation of not only protecting, but also of promoting and fulfilling. These were positive rights requiring positive actions, involving the use of resources and changing institutions, and taking measures to realize these rights in a step-by-step, progressive manner. The Universal Declaration of Human Rights which was adopted by the United Nations in 1948 included both civil and political rights, as well as economic, social, and cultural rights and they formed the basic norms for all the nation states, as the foundation of the civilized international society that the world community was trying to reconstruct. The economic, social, and cultural rights were regarded as fundamental as the civil and political rights.[1]

Soon, it was realized that the distinction between civil and political rights and economic, social, and cultural rights was extremely artificial. Protecting the rights directly from violation might not require any use of resources involving what the states were not supposed to do or interfere. But if that protection had to be sustainable, adequate steps needed to be taken to build up mechanisms to safeguard these rights, to promote them, and to prevent them from being violated by other non-state actors. These required positive actions absorbing resources and changing institutions. So, even civil and political rights were to become a combination of negative and positive rights. Economic, social, and

---

[1] Paul Gorden Lauren, *The Evolution of International Human Rights*, University of Pennsylvania Press (1998), pp. 205–80.

cultural rights would also be seen as integrally dependent on many of the negative civil and political rights, such as the right to life, freedom of movement, of information, of association, and basic liberties. Human rights came to be recognized as totally interdependent, the level of realization of one right depended on the levels of realization of other rights.[2]

Besides interdependence, another major characteristic of human rights is their integrity, which follows from the premise that human rights are entailed by the concept of human dignity. Their fulfilment preserves human dignity and their violation destroys it. That human dignity is by its nature indivisible—one cannot lose it at one place and compensate that by increasing it at another. From this follows the integrity of human rights, a violation of one human right cannot be overcome by enhancement of another. If one is not free from hunger or one's right to education and health are violated, they cannot be compensated by an expansion of the rights to free speech or the freedom of association. Similarly, one can be well-fed and physically healthy but the right to food or the right to health, which relate to the dignity with which one can access food and health services, cannot be fulfilled if one is denied the rights to basic liberties and freedoms.[3]

The importance of these characteristics of human rights, related to interdependence and integrity, has not always been fully appreciated. People have gone around with the task of fulfilling individual rights, whether they are civil and political rights like free speech, free association, or freedom from torture or economic and social rights to food, health, education, or shelter, without bothering so much about the consideration that the fulfilment of any one of these rights depends on the fulfilment of the other rights and that the violation of any one of them, violates all of them. This was also the reason why an artificial distinction was made between first generation rights (civil and political rights) and second generation rights (economic, social, and cultural rights), one which became a simple but misleading way of differentiating between the political stand of the first world and of the second and Third World countries. Because of cold war politics, the first world industrial countries appeared to defend the civil and political rights while the second world, pro-socialist and the Third World, developing countries seemed to be primarily concerned with economic, social, and cultural rights. This political difference was

[2] See Sengupta, Arjun, *Development and Change*, Vol. 31, No. 3, Institute of Social Studies, Blackwell Publishers, The Hague, June 2000.

[3] The Fourth and Fifth Report of the Independent Expert on the Right to Development, in *The Right to Development*, Franciscans International, Geneva, 2002.

projected to the conceptual plane, contradicting the principles of inter-dependence and integrity of human rights.[4]

The right to development, in the United Nations discourse, also came to be identified mainly with the Third World developing countries, who wanted to carve a niche for themselves in the cold war politics, asking for a right that would give them a status equal to others in international relations. The concept of the right to development, however, was much broader and would apply to any society where there were sections of people lacking in development, either absolutely or relatively to other sections of society. The 1986 Declaration of the Right to Development, which was adopted by the United Nations with an overwhelming majority, defined development as a composite right, as a process of development where all human rights, civil, political, economic, social, and cultural (as well as other rights such as those of children and women which came to be recognized later) are realized. The notion of a composite right explicitly recognizes the interdependence of all rights and their integrity in the sense that if any one of these rights is violated, it cannot be sustained that any other right may be enhanced.

A New Approach to Development

A distinction was clearly made between rights and the supply of any particular object of value. Rights would depend not only on the availability of corresponding goods and services but also the nature of access to them in a manner that is consistent with human rights standards. Development was described as a comprehensive economic, social and political process where all rights can be and are realized over time, when the level of realization of any one right at a particular point of time, depended upon the levels of realization of all other rights at that time as well as the realization of that right over the successive periods. The availability of and access to these rights are to be secured, consistent with human rights standards. The different instruments of human rights laws and the associated jurisprudence, have spelt out those standards in terms of principles of equity, non-discrimination, transparency, account-ability and participation of the beneficiaries in the decision making and in the implementation of the measures for realizing these rights. These standards set the nature of the access to the objects of value,

[4] Karl Vasak, 'For the Third Generation of Human Rights: The Rights of Soli-darity', Inaugural Lecture at the Tenth Study Session of the International Institute of Human Rights, 2–27 July 1979.

supplementing their availability in order to be reckoned as human right. Development then becomes a process. The outcomes of the process and entitlements of the people of a country fulfilling which will be the highest priority of all state actions, and supporting which would be the obligation of all members of international community are both claimed as human rights.[5]

Let me elaborate this point a little further. There are two major implications of recognizing development as a human right. First, no kind of development can qualify as a human right. It is not an expansion of GDP or industrialization, or export promotion or increasing the volume of employment. It is a particular process of realizing that development has to be equitable, that is, it is realized without increasing inequalities and with a fair sharing of the benefits of development. There cannot be any discrimination in the sharing of benefits and in the activities producing the benefits between different people, irrespective of gender or caste, religion or ethnicity. The decision making and product sharing will have to be fully participatory where the process will have to be accountable and transparent. These characteristics of the process would be applicable both at the micro and at the macro level and the policies for development will have to be adopted to fulfil these requirements. A top-down centralized planning process will have no role in that development, just as an unfettered market mechanism that increases the inequalities based on the initial distribution of wealth and asset, can no longer be the only method of development. It does not of course mean that there is no more role of markets or of plan coordination of policies and actions. It only emphasizes their instrumental role—neither the market nor the plan coordination by the states are goals in themselves, and as instruments for realizing development they have to be subjected to constraints of human rights standards.

Second, this particular process of development becomes the fundamental concern of all those who have the obligations to fulfil development. Human rights imply obligations. If a right is claimed, legitimately and justifiably, by any agent in society, then all other agents in society whose actions have influence on the fulfilment of that right will have an obligation, to the maximum extent possible, to take measures to fulfil them. This is the strength of the human rights discourse. As we have mentioned at the very beginning, the human rights claims 'trump'

---

[5] Sengupta, Arjun, 'On the Theory and Practice of the Right to Development', *Human Rights Quarterly*, Vol. 24, No. 4, November 2002.

over all other claims of policies or social action, particularly of the state authorities which have the highest influence, through laws, legislation, administration, and public policies, to enable the fulfilment of those rights.[6] The state authorities cannot escape from using their resources, whether financial or administrative or institutional, in meeting this first priority claim rather than devoting them to other objectives of administration, defence, corporate profits or sectional interests. The state authorities not only have to pursue the policies to realize these rights but also must submit themselves to a system of accountability through a legislative, judicial, and administrative process. They have to justify in concrete terms that they are devoting their maximum efforts to fulfilling these rights and the people would have every right to overthrow the authorities if they do not satisfy the standards of accountability.

DEVELOPMENT POLICY AS OBLIGATIONS

The state authorities have the primary responsibility of taking every measure to realize these rights, because of their command over the resources and activities within their area of jurisdiction. But in the human rights discourse all other agents are also responsible to help and cooperate with the state and the other agencies to fulfil these rights. This allows the invoking of the principle of international cooperation, which has been recognized in the different covenants of the Bill of Rights and also by the United Nations Charter, where all members of the international community have pledged to do their best to fulfil these rights. In other words, if a state adopts policies that would enable fulfilment of these rights, all members of the international community, nation states of the industrial countries, international institutions like the World Bank, the IMF, WTO, and multinational corporations would have the obligation to cooperate to the maximum extent possible with the state. This cooperation can take the form of resource transfer, debt rescheduling, opening up trade barriers, dispensation of intellectual property rights or any other way that can help the fulfilment of these rights.

All these would follow if development can be recognized as a human right. The fact that the 1986 Declaration on the Right to Development was adopted by the United Nations and that a full consensus of all nations was created in 1993 at Vienna in favour of regarding this as a human

[6] Ronald Dworkin, 'Rights as Trumps' in *Theories of Rights*, Jeremy Waldron (ed.), Oxford University Press, New York, 1995.

right, goes a long way to this recognition in terms of human rights law. It does not have the status of a treaty as the conventions of civil and political, and economic, social, and cultural rights have. But since the right to development is a composite of all those rights, recognized by treaty, it will have all their force of implementation, as if it was a treaty right itself. In terms of positive law, therefore, the right to development can be said to have full recognition as a human right. But that recognition is not enough to ensure its implementation. It will be necessary to incorporate these obligations in domestic laws and in the legal procedures of international institutions. That would require movements and campaigns to persuade all members of society to accept the legitimacy of this right to development.

There will be several issues of controversy related to this concept of a human right to development, which I like to touch upon. First, a claim to be recognized as a human right must satisfy two tests. The legitimacy test and the coherence test.[7] The legitimacy test is related to establishing the claim as derivative of some basic moral principles which are universally acceptable. The notion of preserving human dignity has been used as the basis of human rights that lends a moral authority to such claims which supersede all other competing demands of the sates' and other agencies' command over physical, administrative and financial resources. Can development be given the same status? The contribution of Amartya Sen here has been seminal. Development discourse that was carried out earlier in terms of expanding gross domestic product or the supply of some basic need of commodities and services has been changed into a process identified with expansion of freedom—freedoms of people to do or to be what they value, in order to fulfil their potential as full human beings. All the ingredients of development process are formulated as expansion of freedom and development is claimed as a right when those freedoms are claimed as a right. This moral legitimacy, together with the procedural legitimacy of getting this right recognized through the United Nations process, should be sufficient to establish that development as a human right qualifies the legitimacy test.

The coherence test implies a matching of the right with the obligations or specifying the agents who would have the obligations of taking the necessary measures that would fulfil that right. Once the agents with obligations and the duties or measures that they should adopt can

---

[7] Amartya Sen, *Development as Freedom*, Oxford University Press, New Delhi, pp. 226–32.

be specified, it should be possible to subject them to a system of account-ability, which is essentially required for any legal right. One should be able to say who should do what, and establish a mechanism to take remedial action if the duty holders do not perform the duty. It is not necessary that this accountability should be tested only in a court of law. There are administrative, legislative, and international treaty bodies mechanism including those of the Human Rights Commissions which could monitor this accountability and enforce the remedies. But in order to identify the duty holder and the exact duties, it should be necessary to establish the feasibility of this right. If the rights cannot be realized or are not feasible even with appropriate institutional changes, legal processes, and public policies, then there can be no duty which can be specified to deliver the rights.

It is important to appreciate the implications of this notion of feasibility. It does not mean that the rights should be immediately realizable or that they should be entirely subjected to the existing institutions and arrangements. Indeed, the conditions of feasibility would often imply changing the institutions and social arrangements so that at least in principle, it can be demonstrated that if those changes take place then there would exist specific duties, to be carried out by the duty holders, which would fulfil these rights. Indeed, without such demonstra-tion of feasibility, the rights remain 'manifesto' rights or 'background' rights. Establishing the feasibility would contribute to their becoming 'valid rights' or 'concrete rights'.[8] Sen has invoked a concept of meta rights in that context, which says that if such rights are not realizable within a time frame or in a particular institutional set-up but if there exists a set of policies which would have a high likelihood of realizing these rights, within a reasonable period, then these policies can be regarded as rights, as valid objects of claims, with concomitant obligations and accountability.[9]

The right to development is obviously something which cannot be realized immediately. As a composite of all rights of food, health, education, employment, standards of living as well as freedom of speech, association and movement, etc., it has to be realized progressively in a phased manner, and the most important constraint on that process would

[8] These issues have been elaborated in Sengupta, Arjun, 'On the Theory and Practice of the Right to Development', (n. 5). Also Sen: Martin E. Winston (ed.), The Philosophy of Human Rights, Belmont, 1989.

[9] Sen, Amartya, 'The Right not to be Hungry' in Alston and Tomasevski (ed.), The Right to Food, SIM, Netherlands.

be the availability of resources—financial, material, and international. So, a necessary condition, for making these rights realizable, would be economic growth, which expands gross domestic product, changes institutions and technology and allows the resource constraints on the realization of these rights to be relaxed. It is in this sense that economic growth is essential for a sustainable realization of the right to development. This treatment of economic growth in the right to development has often been misunderstood. Economic growth has not been demanded as a human right but as a necessary instrument for realizing the human right to development. Economic growth is not sufficient for realizing that right, but it is necessary at least over a period of time. It is possible to realize some of the rights even without economic growth, if there is no slack in the use of resources due to inefficiency and misallocation. But if all the rights have to be realized together, then at some time or other, they will hit the resource constraint if the resources do not expand. As we have seen earlier, that realization of the right requires both increase in the availability of goods and services, corresponding to the rights, as also the access to those goods and services. This is true of all rights whether civil, political, economic, social, or cultural. So, if resources do not expand, then continuous improvement of some rights making increasing demand of resources would lead to a short-fall of resources, for fulfilling some other rights which would then be violated. Since no right can be violated in the realization of the composite right to development, the result would be that the right to development itself would be violated.

The process of economic growth which is considered as essential should also meet the standards of human rights. It should be equitable, participatory, accountable, and transparent. Because if it were not so and a process of economic growth increased inequities or violated the principle of participation, the fulfilment of individual rights according to the standards of human rights would not be possible. So, the economic growth that is admissible in the rights discourse should be achieved with equity and social justice.

If these arguments are accepted, it should be clear that the right to development would require the state authorities to adopt a development policy carried out with equity, participation, and accountability at both the micro and macro level. That has to be designed in coordination with the policies of sectoral development related to the different rights, but in the context of overall development and economic growth. That would have to be sustainable and carried out in response to the existing financial, technological, and institutional constraints. One of the most important requirements of that kind of sustainable growth would be macro economic stability, with fiscal and monetary discipline. The human rights community must be prepared to accept the imperatives of that concern. However, it also brings out the importance of harmonizing that process of growth with sectoral policies specifically aimed at realizing the different rights. Just economic growth is not enough and is definitely not consistent with the claims of development as a human right. Economic growth that ignores or violates the principles of human rights in different areas is not admissible in the discourse of human right to development.

CONTENTIOUS ISSUES

One of the contentious issues, that is still raised in some quarters is whether the right to development has been recognized as a human right under international law. With the adoption of the Declaration on the Right to Development in 1986 and through subsequent declarations and resolutions of international and intergovernmental meetings and summits and through practices, proclamation of norms, and developing jurisprudence, it can be said to have gathered the status of customary law, and is consistent with the general principles of law. Further, because it is a composite of rights which are a part of the international legal system, such as the civil and political rights and the economic, social, and cultural rights, which are recognized by international treaties as covenants, the right to development is composed of phased realization of all the covenant rights. If the component elements are legal rights, then the composite would also be a legal right. In other words, the contention about the legality of the right to development is not different from the contention about the legality of all other recognized rights. If the civil, political, economic, social, and cultural rights are accepted as legal rights, the right to development would also be a legal right.[10]

A relatively less contentious issue is whether there is any value addition to the existing recognized rights, of further recognizing another composite right. If there is no value addition, why should one talk about a new and distinct right such as the right to development? The answer to this is to appreciate that the composite right is not just the aggregate

[10] See Philip Alston and Brumo Simma's paper. 'The Sources of Human Rights Law: Custom, Jus Cogens, and General Principles', *Human Rights Law*, New York University Press.

or the sum of all the rights. It is something more than that, because of the interdependence of these rights, which leads to a positive feedback to each others' realization. The right to education is easier to realize if it is complemented by the right to food or right to health. Similarly, the right to the freedom of expression is more effectively realized if the right to education is also ensured. The implications for fulfilling the obligation of realizing the rights are more straightforward, when the different rights are implemented together as a composite rather than when they are implemented separately as different component rights. For example, sequencing the realization of the rights, or the pace of fulfilment of each of them could be so designed as to improve the realization of all of them in a coordinated manner, within a target time horizon. Similarly, the total cost of realization of all the rights could be much less when they are realized together in a coordinated manner, than when each of them is realized separately.

So, if the right to development is the right to a process of development, which is a composite of the phased realization of all the rights, then the phasing and sequencing of the different rights would depend upon the manner in which the realization of different rights are coordinated. The Maastricht Guidelines[11] have described this outcome or the results of this process as targets for different rights over a period. It is like the Millennium Development Goals to be reached by 2015. If these targets were to be realized as human rights, then there is the right to development as a process. The intermediate year's targets of fulfilling the different rights will then have to be fixed, on the basis of recognizing their interdependence and coordinating their achievements, in the best possible manner, given the constraints of the objective situations. That process of development, therefore, is not just a simple aggregation of different rights but will be a phased and sequenced composite of different rights.

There are two implications of identifying this process. First, it will be necessary to arrive at a consensus not only for determining the terminal value of the targets, that is, the extent to which the different rights are supposed to be fully realized by the end of the time period, but will also be necessary to have a consensus about the intermediate values of the achievements of the rights. This is because fixing the terminal values of targets does not yield a unique set of intermediate targets. There will be

[11] See Maastricht Guidelines on Violations of Economic, Social, and Cultural Rights, Maastricht, 22–6, January 1997 http://www.law.uu.nl/english/sim/instr/maastr.asp.

choices of different paces of fulfilling the different rights. For example, some countries may like to fulfil the right to food first, leaving the fulfilment of several other rights, that of education, shelter, or freedom of association at different paces over the same period. Similarly, some other countries may choose to take up education and health first, or the right of freedom of expression. This does not mean that choosing some rights would neglect other rights or there could be a violation of some rights, while fulfilling one or other rights. In a process of development claimed as a human right, no human right can be violated.[12] There is no trade off between the rights in that sense, as accepted in the human rights discourse. But there can be trade off between the speed or the pace of the realization of different rights. It is important to allow such possibilities of trade off in any country where all rights cannot be realized instantly or even within a short period. This is the distinct value-addition of considering the composite of all the rights as a process of development.

The second implication is the emergence of the development policy, which would be the obligation of the state and other duty-bearers, as a counterpart of the right to development, an approach that would be substantially different for realizing each of the rights separately and in isolation from each other. Such a development policy has to be worked out, coordinating the sectoral policies; policies associated with the access and availability of facilities, corresponding to each of the rights. It must also include a policy for relaxing the resource constraint in the economy through a rights based process of economic growth, as otherwise all the rights which use up resources cannot be realized together. If the resources do not expand, then increased use of resources for realizing some rights would reduce the resources available for the realization of other rights, leading to a regression or violation of some rights. Therefore, such a development policy must include a well designed macro-economic policy for raising the country's economic growth. In the rights framework, however, such economic growth must be consistent with the human rights standards—which have been identified with equity, non-discrimination, participation, accountability, and transparency.[13]

[12] See, the Reports submitted by the Independent Expert to the Human Rights Commission, Geneva: First Report: E/CN.4/1999/WG.18/2, 27 July 1999. Fourth Report: E/CN.4/2002/WG.18/2, 20 December 2001. website: http://www.unhchr.ch/html/menu2/7/b/mdev.htm.

[13] See, Reports submitted by the Independent Expert to the Human Rights Commission, Geneva: Second Report: A/55/306, 17 August 2000. Third Report: E/CN.4/2001/WG.18/2, 2 January 2001.

This leads us to another, and possibly the most contentious issue, namely the obligation of international cooperation. Articles 55 and 56 of the United Nations Charter spell out this obligation of international cooperation, which all states have pledged to fulfil. But in the case of right to development that obligation has been given very precise formulation. The primary obligation for fulfilling the right to development, vests with the state parties to which the people claiming their rights belong. The state has to design a proper development policy, as mentioned above, coordinating the sectoral policies and an overall policy for economic growth. The international community both in terms of the United Nations Charter, which is a United Nations Treaty, with binding obligations, as well as in terms of the Declaration on the Right to Development, has the obligation of cooperation with the state authorities to enable them to realize the right to development.

The content of that international obligation in the current situation of the globalization of the world economy has now become clearly identifiable. No state today can pursue an economic policy with the same degree of freedom of manoeuvrability, as they could even 20–30 years back. The results of their economic policies are circumscribed by the operation of the international markets of goods and services, of finance, energy, transport, and of technology, as well as the functioning of international institutions affecting these activities. If a state is trying to implement a development policy that includes not only sectoral policy but also a policy of economic growth, so that all the rights can be realized as a right to a process of development, the international community then must cooperate in the fields of trade, aid, debt, financial flows, technology, etc., so that the efforts of that state are not frustrated. There are some general areas of international cooperation in which all member states and international institutions must engage, such as trade liberalization, debt re-scheduling, orderly flows of finance capital and technology transfer and intellectual property protection, so that all developing countries benefit and are able to adopt the rights-based policies of development. But for those states who actually try to implement policies and programmes for realizing the right to development, the international cooperation must be much more specific, removing the bottlenecks obstructing such development policies. In other words, the obligations of international cooperation will have to be contextualised, responding to the specific needs of the country. Furthermore, mechanisms will have to be set up to monitor and review the process, so that remedial steps can be taken by all the parties concerned, if the process of realizing the right to development is disrupted. For that purpose, proposals have been made for designing and operationalizing 'Development Compacts' between the countries implementing the right to development, and the representative institutions and members of the international community.[14]

The fundamental contribution of the discourse on the right to development is to highlight the obligations of the state authorities and the international community, that derive their legitimacy from the fulfilment of human rights. Development has been identified as a process of realization of fundamental freedoms—the freedoms that enhance the dignity and integrity of the peoples of different countries. When these freedoms are claimed as rights, development is identified as a process of realizing those rights. And as rights, they entail obligations on the part of the state authorities and the international community, who have accepted human rights as the foundational norms of their societies and their standards of achievement. It spells out a new paradigm of governance, firmly instituting the notions of accountability and obligation, in terms of the principles and practices of human rights.

[14] Reports submitted by the Independent Expert to the Human Rights Commission, Geneva, especially the Second Report: A/55/306, 17 August 2000.

9

Judicial Governance and the Ideology of Human Rights

Reflections from a Social Movement Perspective

BALAKRISHNAN RAJAGOPAL[*]

Social movements[1] in India have depended heavily upon the Indian Supreme Court since it began its activist phase in the late 1970s. Human rights groups and concerned citizens have approached the court for

[*] Sections of this essay were originally presented as a summer lecture at the Institute for International Judges at Brandeis University on 13 June 2002 and at the Institute for Development Studies at Sussex on 16–18 October 2003. I am grateful for the comments of the various participants in these events, especially Justice Richard Goldstone, Justice Rajinder Sachhar, Celestine Nyamu and Peter Houtzager. I also wish to thank Upendra Baxi, Rajeev Dhavan, Bhairav Acharya, Frank Michelman and Duncan Kennedy for very useful comments on a previous draft. Responsibility for all errors is mine.

[1] I do not use the term social movements here with a single, precise definition, but as a way to talk about collective struggles over resources, values, and identity. The definitions are much contested in the very rich literature on social movements. For an overview, see e.g. *The Blackwell Companion to Social Movements* (David A. Snow, Sarah A. Soule and Hanspeter Kreisi (eds), 2004), chapter 1. I have extensively discussed and reviewed this literature earlier especially as it relates to international law. See Balakrishnan Rajagopal, *International Law from Below: Development, Social Movements and Third World Resistance*, Cambridge University Press (2003); 'International law and Social Movements: Challenges of Theorizing Resistance', 41 *Columbia J. Transnat'l L.* 397 (2003); 'From Resistance to Renewal: The Third World, Social Movements and The Expansion of International Institutions', 41(2) *Harv. Int'l L.J.* 529 (Spring 2000).

remedy and the court has responded impressively. It has sneaked in 'due process' into Indian jurisprudence to curb detention without trial,[2] expanded the meaning of right to life under Article 21 to include livelihood[3] and environment,[4] defended the freedom of the media,[5] guarded the rights of employees,[6] read some directive principles in Part IV such as basic education into fundamental rights,[7] taken measures to advance gender justice[8] including through a progressive incorporation of international law into domestic law and innovated procedural measures such as an expansive concept of standing, continuing mandamus and court-appointed commissions of enquiry.[9] Indeed, it will not be an exaggeration to say that most social movements in India since the 1970s have actively used the courts—especially the supreme court—as part of their struggles, whether it be the women's movement, the labour movement, the human rights movement or the environmental movement. Despite this activism, it is now increasingly recognized that the impact of the court on ground reality has not been consistent. In the area of human rights for instance, studies show that the court's seminal rulings are often not translated into reality for a range of reasons.[10] In addition, the court's activism, especially under the umbrella of social action litigation (SAL), has itself come under criticism for its undemocratic nature, lack of effectiveness, and judicial grandstanding as well as its alleged violation of separation of powers. As one distinguished observer of judicial activism puts it, 'judicial activism is at once a peril and a

[2] *Maneka Gandhi* v. *Union of India* AIR 1978 SC 597.

[3] *Olga Tellis and others* v. *Bombay Municipal Corporation* AIR 1986 SC 180.

[4] *Center for Environmental Law WWF-I* v. *Union of India* (1999) 1 SCC 263.

[5] *R. Rajagopal* v. *State of Tamil Nadu* (1994) 6 SCC 632.

[6] *Bangalore Water Supply & Sewerage Board* v. *R. Rajappa* (1978) 3 SCR 207.

[7] *J.P. Unni Krishnan* v. *State of Andhra Pradesh* (1993) 1 SCC 645.

[8] *Vishaka* v. *State of Rajasthan* (1997) 6 SCC 247.

[9] For a discussion, see Upendra Baxi, 'Taking Human Suffering Seriously: Social Action Litigation Before the Supreme Court of India', in Neelan Tiruchelvan and Radhika Coomaraswamy (eds), *The Role of the Judiciary in Plural Societies*, St. Martin's Press (1987); Ashok H. Desai, and S.Muralidhar, 'Public Interest Litigation: Potential and Problems' in B.N. Kirpal, Ashok H. Desai, Gopal Subramanium, Rajeev Dhavan and Raju Ramchandran (eds), *Supreme But Not Infallible: Essays in Honour of the Supreme Court of India*, Oxford University Press, New Delhi (2000); S.P. Sathe, *Judicial Activism in India: Transgressing Borders and Enforcing Limits*, Oxford University Press, New Delhi (2002).

[10] Charles Epp, *The Rights Revolution: Lawyers, Activists and Supreme Courts in Comparative Perspective*, University of Chicago Press (1998), chapters 5 and 6.

promise, an assurance of solidarity for the depressed classes of Indian society as well as a site of betrayal'.[11]

In this essay, I join this critique and call attention to the limitations of judicial activism, as it has been practised more recently, for a progressive social movement politics.[12] Rather than criticizing judicial activism for its counter-majoritarian character or its lack of effectiveness on the ground, I focus attention on the ideological character of the court's particular approach to human rights. In particular, I suggest that the court's activism increasingly manifests several biases—in favour of the state and development, in favour of the rich and against workers, in favour of the urban middle class and against rural farmers, and in favour of a globalitarian class and against the distributive ethos of the Indian constitution—that, when taken together, result in an ideological interpretation of human rights.[13] This ideological interpretation is the result, I suggest, of at least two dynamics: the first one internal to the court itself that grows out of the particular history of the evolution of the court since the 1970s, as an organ of state governance thereby leading to the emergence of what I call 'judicial governance'; and second, a

[11] Upendra Baxi, 'The Avatars of Indian Judicial Activism: Explorations in the Geographies of (In)Justice' in S.K. Verma and Kusum (eds), *Fifty Years of the Supreme Court of India: Its Grasp and Reach*, Oxford University Press, New Delhi, (2000) at 161.

[12] This essay is not intended, by any means, to be a critique of judicial activism per se. Rather, its goal is to explore the limits and possibilities of deploying judicial power as part of larger social movement struggles, an area in which the Indian Supreme Court has been a world leader for a long time. This essay is part of an on-going larger project of mine that seeks to compare the place of judicial activism in social movement struggles in southern democracies.

[13] By saying that the court's interpretation of human rights is 'ideological', I do not mean the more common understanding that it is either dogma, or simply not neutral. Interpretations of human rights can hardly be neutral. Nor do I use the word 'ideology' in a Marxist sense to mean false consciousness. Rather, what I mean by an ideological interpretation of human rights is that the meaning of human rights that emerges from the court's jurisprudence is systematically sustaining and repro-ducing forms of domination in Indian society. For my understanding of the role of ideology and domination through judicial practice, I rely on Duncan Kennedy, *A Critique of Adjudication* (1998), especially 290–4. I also rely on John Thompson's defi-nition of ideology, lucidly explained in Susan Marks, *The Riddle of all Constitutions: International Law, Democracy and the Critique of Ideology*, Oxford University Press, Ox-ford (2000) at pp. 8–15. In this sense, an ideological interpretation of human rights means simply an interpretation that defends and favours the status quo and the relations of domination that constitute the status quo.

dynamic that is external to the court and the result of the human rights discourse itself, especially as it has been constructed at the international level and reproduced at the domestic level. The first dynamic neutralizes the transformative potential of the court, while the second dynamic shows the inherently elitist and anti-poor nature of international human rights. These dynamics produce a constrained court-centered approach to human rights, despite the occasionally inspiring judgments that emanate from the court. I argue that this constrained approach by the court to human rights is primarily due to its concern that its decisions are compatible with an overall 'logic of the state' in which the higher judiciary plays its appointed role as an instrument of governance much more often than its traditional role as an institution of justice. This notion of 'judicial governance' imposes inherent limitations on the extent to which the court can be expected to be an active part of social movement struggles for realization of human rights, particularly those rights that are sought to be exercised in conflict with statist and developmentalist ideologies.

The following part of this essay provides a brief overview of the Supreme Court of India's mixed record in protecting human rights including through the incorporation of international legal norms. I then explain that this mixed record in protecting human rights is the complex product of several factors including the evolution of the Indian Supreme Court as an organ of governance, its historical tensions with the legislature, its expansion of the human rights agenda due to its prominence as a site of movement politics and the political and class alignment of individual judges. The next part discusses the ideological biases that are inherent in the discourse of human rights itself, including the biases against economic, social, and cultural rights, which operate to render the court as marginal to social movement struggles even when it tries to incorporate international norms into domestic law. In particular, I focus on the way the realization of economic and social rights under international law is seen to be dependent upon either state capacity or greater free market-led consumption and argue that this conceptualization is part of the reason why the court has been biased. Further, I discuss some recent dissident strands of comparative and international jurisprudence on human rights, which have had a much more active relationship with social movement politics, and ask whether the supreme court can learn any lessons from this experience. I conclude by arguing that the court must abandon its ideological approach to human rights and refashion its jurisprudence in ways that strengthen social movement struggles of the poor.

THE SUPREME COURT AND HUMAN RIGHTS:
A MIXED RECORD[14]

The human rights record of the supreme court is, by and large, a product of the post-emergency period in Indian politics. Partly due to its desire to atone for its mistake in deciding the infamous *Habeas Corpus* Case,[15] and to thereby recover the moral ground that it had lost among the public, the supreme court began an activist phase, liberally interpreting constitutional rights to expand the domain of freedom. Its focus on human rights was also politically acceptable given that the Janata government in power between 1977 and 1979 could only favourably look upon a court which was trying to address some of the worst legacies of the emergency such as the abuses in prisons. Thus, in a series of cases the court expanded the legal rights of detainees and undertrials,[16] addressed custodial deaths[17] and extra-judicial killings, awarded compensation for violations of fundamental rights[18] and expanded the substantive meaning of equality through affirmative action.[19] The court has also expanded the rights of women including rape victims,[20] as well as the rights of children.[21] Its commitment to human rights continues to inspire public admiration as the public reaction to the recent Best Bakery Case[22] shows. In many

---

[14] This section is not by any means, intended to be a comprehensive historical survey of the supreme court's vast jurisprudence over more than half a century. Far more qualified jurists and practitioners have already done a superb job of surveying and assessing the court's record. See e.g., S.P. Sathe, supra n. 9. Nor is it a verdict on the court's undoubted value as a resource for realizing rights, like some other recent studies. See Epp, supra n. 10. Rather, the purpose of this section is only to outline the broad directions that the court has taken recently given its historical evolution, and to assess evidence of judicial bias. The goal of this exercise is the expectation that the court's activism can be nudged towards a more subaltern direction.

[15] *A.D.M. Jabalpur* v. *S.S. Shukla* (1976) 2 SCC 521.

[16] *Hussainara Khatoon* v. *State of Bihar* (I to VI), (1980) 1 SCC 81; *Sunil Batra* v. *Delhi Administration* (1980) 3 SCC 488; *Citizens for Democracy* v. *State of Assam* (1995) 3 SCC 743.

[17] *D.K. Basu* v. *State of West Bengal* (1997) 1 SCC 416.

[18] Ibid., at 439.

[19] *State of Kerala* v. *N.M. Thomas* (1976) 1 SCR 906.

[20] *Delhi Domestic Working Women's Forum* v. *Union of India*, 1994 (4) SCALE 608; *Vishaka*, supra n. 8; *Chairman, Railway Board* v. *Chandrima Das* (2000) 2 SCC 465.

[21] Supra n. 7.

[22] *Teesta Setalvad & Others* v. *State of Gujarat & Others*, 2004 SCCL.COM 404 (decided on 12 April 2004); *Zaheera H. Sheikh & Others* v. *State of Gujarat & Others*, 2004 SCCL.COM 507 (decided on 12 April 2004).

of these cases, the court has liberally interpreted the constitutional provisions, reading international law into domestic law.[23] Many of these human rights rulings were made possible through a procedural revolution that is a unique Indian contribution to the world, through the democratization of standing to sue and through such innovative devices as a continued mandamus, and judicial commissions of enquiry. The court has converted an ordinary list of fundamental rights into a veritable weapon of the weak through creative judicial interpretation. In this, the court was doubtlessly riding a human rights wave, driven by a range of social movements that were sprouting all over India in the aftermath of the emergency, which were seeking refuge in the court after finding that bureaucratic and traditional political avenues of action were proving to be more intractable.

Despite this laudable activism in human rights, the court's record is characterized by a serious measure of substantive ad hocism. In particular, the court's record on economic, social, and cultural rights remains deeply unsatisfactory. With some notable exceptions such as a recent judgment dealing with the right to education,[24] the record of the Indian Supreme Court in enforcing internationally recognized economic, social, and cultural rights is patchy and is getting worse especially when compared to the heyday of its activism when Judges such as Krishna Iyer and Chinnappa Reddy were on the bench. In the area of labour rights, despite the impression that the Indian courts remain sympathetic to labour due to India's pro-labour laws, the record of the court shows an inconsistent approach without affording protection to crucial rights such as the right to strike though it has passed several important judgments relating to the abolition of forced, bonded and child labour.[25] Though many of these latter judgments remain current law, they were all issued in the early 1980s and not after the economic liberalization began in earnest in 1991. Indeed, a judgment that reflects current judicial trend is the court's decision in the *T.K.Rangarajan* case, declaring that the Tamil Nadu government employees had no legal, moral, or equitable right to strike.[26] While individual judges in the past have shown a great deal of sympathy to labour, including Desai and Krishna Iyer,

[23] Supra n. 8.

[24] Supra n. 7.

[25] *People's Union for Democratic Rights v. Union of India* AIR 1982 SC 1473; *Sanjit Roy v. State of Rajasthan* AIR 1983 SC 328; *Bandhua Mukti Morcha v. Union of India* AIR 1984 SC 802.

[26] *T.K. Rangarajan v. Government of Tamil Nadu and Others*, 2003 SOL Case No. 429.

the more recent crop of judges appear to display less sympathy. This change in the attitude of the judges towards labour rights cannot be divorced from the broader socio-economic context of liberalization, privatization, and World Bank and IMF demands for reform of labour laws since 1991.

Even in the case of land rights as a distinct category of human rights, the court's record is far from satisfactory.[27] The record of the court during the first two decades of its existence could only be described as a grudging and resigned support as it struggled to contain the political branches from carrying out the agrarian/land reform that was seen to be necessary to realize the vision of the constitution. Thus the court frequently held that such land reforms violated aspects of the constitutional right to property, especially the requirement to pay compensation, even as it upheld the protection of land reform laws from judicial scrutiny.[28] The attitude of the court began to change in the early 1970s as more pro-poor judges such as Krishna Iyer and Bhagwati joined and the court began to uphold agrarian reform especially under the new constitutional amendments that had been adopted to shield land reform laws from judicial scrutiny. As Krishna Iyer said in *State of Kerala* v. *Gwalior Rayon Silk Mfg. (Wvg.) Co. Ltd.*[29] while upholding the constitutional validity of a land reform law from Kerala,

the concept of agrarian reform is a complex and dynamic one promoting wider interests than conventional reorganisation of the land system or distribution of land. It is intended to realize the social function of the land and includes—we are merely giving, by way of illustration, a few familiar proposals of agrarian reform—creation of economic units of rural production, establishment of adequate credit system, implementation of modern production techniques, construction of irrigation systems and adequate drainage, making available

[27] It must be noted that land rights are not protected as a special sub-species under the constitution. Rather, it must be read as a structural feature of the constitution resulting from the commitment to agrarian reform in general under Article 31 (4) and (6) as enacted in 1950. Further, the status of land rights as a species of human rights under international law is also far from clear and must also be read to be implied from the 'vision' of the post-colonial, Third-World and Soviet influenced international law, that began to take shape from the late 1960s.

[28] For example, compare *Shankari Prasad Singh Deo* v. *Union of India* AIR 1951 SC 458 (upholding the validity of the first amendment to the constitution that shielded land acquisition laws from legal challenge under Part III) with *State of West Bengal* v. *Bela Banerjee* AIR 1954 SC 170 (ruling that the meaning of 'compensation' in Article 31(2) meant just equivalent for the property acquired).

[29] (1973) 2 SCC 713, at page 731 (Krishna Iyer J., concurring).

fertilizers, fungicides, herbicides and other methods of intensifying and increasing agricultural production, providing readily available means of communication and transportation, to facilitate proper marketing of the village produce, putting up of silos, warehouses, etc., to the extent necessary for preserving produce and handling it so as to bring it conveniently within the reach of the consumers when they need it, training of village youth in modern agricultural practices with a view to maximizing production and help solve social problems that are found in relation to the life of the agricultural community. The village man, his welfare, is the target.

This nuanced understanding of the importance of agrarian reform and land rights was, however, limited to some justices and temporally limited between the early 1970s to the early 1980s. On the whole, the record of the court has been more in favour of property rights, narrowly construed, and not land rights. The agonized and complex balance that the court struck in *Kesavananda Bharati*[30] between the amendment power and the structural integrity of the constitution could also be seen, from one angle, as a balance between property rights and human rights. Indeed, with the repeal of the property rights clause in the constitution through the 44th amendment in 1978, it could be said that the role of the court in securing land rights (as opposed to property rights) has been almost negligible. This was so even during the 1970s when political focus was on the issue of land, when compared to the more activist role of the political branches at the federal and state levels. Since the mid-1980s, and especially since economic liberalization began in 1991, land issues have not been at the top of the political or judicial agenda.

In cases relating to housing rights or right to health, the court has rarely shown the kind of aggressive public policy interventionism that it exhibits in other areas such as environment. Even in landmark rulings such as *Olga Tellis*, the court has never ruled that the slum dwellers actually had a right to housing but only that an eviction without a notice and a hearing would amount to an arbitrary violation of their right to livelihood which is part of right to life under Article 21.[31] What is affirmed thus is a right to a process and not a remedy for the structural violation itself. The removal of the right to property as a fundamental right by the 44th amendment to the constitution in 1978 has also made it more difficult to advance a claim of right to housing understood substantively as a spatial assertion by any individual, despite the presence of Articles 31A and 300A. Though the court has not hesitated from using even soft law

[30] See infra n. 46.
[31] Supra n. 2 at 194.

sources such as resolutions of the UN or even the International Law
Commission to reinterpret Indian constitutional provisions relating to
environment, sustainable development, or workplace gender discrimination, it does not show the same kind of adventurism while dealing
with socio-economic rights such as housing. This is surely not because
of lack of legal sources. For example, in the infamous case of *Narmada
Bachao Andolan* in 2000,[32] the court put its seal of approval on the largest
court-sanctioned forced eviction in the world though abundant
international legal material existed to show that the raising of the height
of the Sardar Sarover dam was contrary to current legal standards.[33]
Though the counsel in that case argued that the forced eviction of tribal
people was a violation of Article 21 read with ILO Convention 108,
to which India is a party, the court rejected the argument.[34] But it is
remarkable that the counsel did not argue that several economic, social,
and cultural rights of the tribal people were violated under the
International Covenant on Economic, Social, and Cultural Rights[35]
(ICESCR) to which India is a party, showing perhaps how much salience
the language of socio-economic rights has before the court. Nor did the
counsel argue that the Narmada tribals had a constitutional right to carry
on a trade or business according to Article 19(1)(g) of the constitution
or that the tribals had a property right under Articles 300A and 31A. In
effect, this has meant that constitutional rights—to trade, do business,
or to property—are recognized by the court only for the rich and not for
the poor who are often outside the formal legal system and therefore
lack any formal entitlements under state law.

After dragging the case through the court for another five years,
followed by an apparently favourable ruling in 2005 for the displaced
people on procedural grounds,[36] the court has once again ruled against
the rights of the displaced people in the Narmada valley, by allowing the

---

[32] *Narmada Bachao Andolan* v. *Union of India & Others*, 10 SCC 664.

[33] For a critique of the judgment, see Balakrishnan Rajagopal, 'Limits of Law in
Counter-hegemonic Globalization: The Indian Supreme Court and the Narmada
Valley Struggle', in Boaventura de Souza Santos and César A. Rodríguez-Garavito
(eds), *Law and Globalization from Below: Towards a Cosmopolitan Legality*, Cambridge
University Press, Cambridge (2006).

[34] See ibid.

[35] International Covenant on Economic, Social and Cultural Rights, 16 December 1966, Art. 11(2), 993 UNTS 3.

[36] *Narmada Bachao Andolan* v. *Union of India and Others*, 15 March 2005, available
at http://narmada.aidindia.org/docs/narmadaverdict.pdf

further raising of the height of the main dam in the project even though most of the displaced people have not been resettled according to the court's own previous orders.[37] This troubling failure of justice has occurred despite a finding of utter failure by the authorities to fulfil the terms of resettlement, according to a confidential report prepared by a Group of Ministers appointed by the Prime Minister,[38] as well as an unprecedented 20-day fast by the leaders of the affected community in New Delhi.[39]

This could be contrasted to other recent cases wherein the court has displayed remarkable activism in upholding the rights of urban landlords under Article 19(1)(g) and struck down the Bombay Rent Control Act.[40] Only a fierce agitation by the tenants in the aftermath of the judgment prevented the government from revising the rents upwards. On top of this the court ordered the government of Maharashtra to change the law forthwith, intruding into the legislative domain through activism which learned observers see as a violation of separation of powers.[41]

In addition, unfortunately the court's decisions may be construed as having an urban and elitist bias against the poor and the countryside. In a range of cases involving conflicts between protection of the environment and workers' rights/tribal rights/housing rights, the court has chosen the former, without bothering much to balance the two objectives.[42] When polluting industries are ordered to be closed by the court, the workers and their families who are directly affected are rarely heard before orders are issued. The court's remarks often display much attention to the environmental issues that are of importance to urban dwellers such as pollution, while showing relatively less attention to rural livelihoods, which are often intricately tied to the land and forests. In the *Narmada* case, for instance, the court showed complete callousness to the plight

[37] Ibid., 8 May 2006, available at http://narmada.aidindia.org/content/view/49/26/. For a critical commentary on the Court's judgment, see Ramaswamy Iyer, 'Abandoning the displaced', The *Hindu*, 10 May 2006.

[38] See the text of the report in the *Hindu*, 17 April 2006, available at http://www.hindu.com/2006/04/17/stories/2006041705231100.htm

[39] For coverage, see http://www.narmada.org/index.html

[40] *Malpe Vishwanath Acharya* v. *State of Maharashtra* (1998) 2 SCC 1. See also *Joginder Pal* v. *Naval Kishore Behal* (2002) 5 SCC 397.

[41] See Sathe, supra n. 8 at 282–3.

[42] See, for example, *M.C. Mehta* v. *Union of India* (1997) 11 SCC 227; *F.B. Taraporawala* v. *Bayer India Ltd.* (1996) 6 SCC 58; *M.C. Mehta* v. *Union of India* 1996 (1) SCALE SP-22; *Pradeep Krishen* v. *Union of India* (1996) 8 SCC 599; *Animal & Environmental Legal Defence Fund* v. *Union of India* (1997) 3 SCC 549.

of the rural and tribal people targeted for displacement and declared that 'the displacement of the tribals and other persons would not per se result in the violations of their fundamental or other rights. The effect is to see that on their rehabilitation at new locations they are better off than what they were. At the rehabilitation sites they will have more and better amenities than which they enjoyed in their tribal hamlets. The gradual assimilation in the mainstream of the society will lead to betterment and progress'.[43] Implicit in this is the notion that rural and tribal livelihoods are inferior and bound to be displaced through urbanization and modernization. Likewise, the court's activism in the area of environment is also characterized by a readiness to protect the environment and health of the rich while ignoring the structural poverty and governmental failure that causes these health problems in the first place. For instance, in *Ratlam Municipal Council* case,[44] the court was ready to rely on section 133 of the Criminal Procedure Code to order a municipality to abate public nuisance caused by open drains and public excretion by slum-dwellers, reading environmental protection broadly to include health and injecting that reading into Part III. But the court's order did not concern the rights of the slum dwellers themselves whose recourse to public excretion was the result of lack of infrastructure which is the responsibility of the municipality though Krishna Iyer pointed out that 'decency and dignity are non-negotiable facets of human rights and are a first charge on local self-governing bodies'.[45] Nor did it concern the rights of those *dalits* who are socially condemned to perform the odious practice of manual cleaning of public toilets, despite the fact that it has been outlawed.[46] Indeed, in several cases, the state courts have also ordered specific measures such as construction of extra public latrines for protecting human health and sanitation under Article 21, while ignoring the rights of the dalits who are employed to clean them manually.[47] To point out these facts is not to belittle the valiant record of the court in protecting the environment or in attempting to shore up processes of governance, but it must be recognized that the court's record has much room for improvement.

[43] Supra n. 24 at 702–3.

[44] Infra n. 34.

[45] Ibid., at 1629.

[46] Employment of Manual Scavengers and Construction of Dry Latrines (Prohibition) Act, 1993.

[47] See e.g., *Dr. K.C.Malhotra* v. *State of M.P.* AIR 1994 MP 43; *L.K.Koolwal* v. *State of Rajasthan* AIR 1983 Raj.2; *Kinkri Devi* v. *State* AIR 1988 HP 4.

To sum up, the court's approach to human rights enforcement could be said to overemphasize civil and political rights at the cost of economic, social, and cultural rights.[48] The result of this overemphasis is that the court has tended to relatively neglect those rights that are of most importance to the vulnerable segments of Indian society, often organized in the form of a multitude of social movements. To put it this way may be seen as somewhat unfair to the court and some objections could be raised. First, it could be contended that the court is constrained by the language of the constitution, which makes fundamental rights in Part III judicially enforceable and leaves the directive principles of state policy in Part IV as policy aspirations. Given that many socio-economic rights are contained in Part IV, it could be argued that the court cannot enforce them as robustly as it does the rights contained in Part III. That claim is not well-founded because the court has not hesitated from reading several other directive principles into fundamental rights, such as the policy of environmental protection in Article 48A into Article 21. The court could, if it wishes, do the same with regard to housing, redistribution of wealth and health. Second, it could be argued that the court may have been constrained by a need to respect the boundary between law and policy, or that it could have been concerned about its own function and role vis-à-vis other branches of government or that it wanted to ensure that its orders had a reasonable prospect of being implemented. None of these arguments hold any water since the court has rarely paid much attention to these issues in its impressive career of judicial activism.[49] For example, in the area of environment, the court has issued orders for closing tanneries, shut down polluting industries and closely supervised enforcement of statutes, rarely constrained by a concern to respect the boundary between law and policy.[50] Even when it was clear that the enforcement of these judicial orders had financial implications that only the government and the legislature had the power to sanction, the court has treated this issue as having no juridical basis.[51] This could be contrasted to the attitude of the court relating to housing rights when it

[48] For an earlier statement, see Balakrishnan Rajagopal, 'The Supreme Court and Human Rights', The *Hindu* (6 December 2000).

[49] For a discussion of these possible limits to judicial activism, see Desai and Muralidhar, supra n. 9 at 176–83.

[50] For a discussion, see Harish Salve, 'Justice between generations: Environment and social justice' in *Supreme But Not Infallible,* supra n. 9.

[51] For example, see the remarks of the court in *Municipal Council Ratlam* v. *Vardichan* AIR 1980 SC 1622; *M.C. Mehta* v. *Union of India* AIR 1988 SC 1037.

suddenly discovers that financial implications do matter for enforcement.[52] What could explain this inconsistency?

EXPLAINING THE MIXED JUDICIAL RECORD

What then can explain why one of the most activist courts in the world is biased in favour of some rights while ignoring the rest? What can explain the urban or class bias? For one answer, I suggest that we look to what I call 'judicial governance'. By this, I mean *the emergence of governance functions assumed by the court in the face of a failing or failed state apparatus that proves unwilling or is incapable of carrying out its mandate under the law and the constitution.* The supreme court has increasingly assumed this function since the early 1970s and in that process, come to share many of the biases that are inherent in the process of governance itself.[53] Let me explain.

During the first two decades of its history, the court was largely positivistic, strictly interpreting the constitution using the traditional canons of statutory interpretation. As the legal expert Rajeev Dhavan puts it, 'there was never any great dissonance between Nehru's developmental plan for the Indian people and the positivist theory of law that the British had bequeathed to the courts of independent India. The fact that the Constituent Assembly had scripted a judicially enforceable Bill of Rights into the text of the constitution did not disturb the positivist credentials of Indian law. The fundamental rights guaranteed to the citizen had been perceived as essentially 'legal rights' granted by a super statute: each one of the rights had been hedged in by limitations and was interpreted like any other statute'.[54] This positivist approach could be seen, for instance in *A.K.Gopalan*[55] while interpreting Article 21 in a

[52] *Olga Tellis*, supra n. 3 at 194 ('The State may not by affirmative action, be compelled to provide adequate means of livelihood or work to the citizens.').

[53] It could be argued that there has always been a contradiction between the court's deference to the role of the state in the development process (including its welfare function) and its need to discharge its obligation to uphold the law when the developmental state acts contrary to the law and constitution. This contradiction is perhaps more manifest after evidence of pervasive state failure began appearing in the 1970s.

[54] See Rajeev Dhavan, 'Judges and Indian Democracy: The Lesser Evil?' in Frankel Franncine *et al.* (ed.), *Transforming India: Social and Political Dynamics of Democracy*, Oxford University Press, Delhi (2000) at 322.

[55] *A.K. Gopalan* v. *State of Madras* AIR 1950 SC 27.

legalistic and narrow manner. This positivist approach to law began to change somewhat during the mid-1960s as can be seen in the *Golaknath* case,[56] once it became obvious that the courts were slowing down needed economic and social reform through their positivist methodology, leading to great tensions between the judiciary and the government. As Subba Rao, CJ, said in *Golak Nath*, '...Articles 32,141 and 142 are couched in such wide and elastic terms as to enable this court to formulate legal doctrines to meet the ends of justice.... To deny this power to the supreme court on the basis of some outmoded theory that the court only finds the law but does not make it is to make ineffective the powerful instrument of justice placed in the hands of the highest judiciary of this country'.[57] Enunciating the 'basic structure' doctrine in *Kesavananda Bharati*[58] was yet another instance of judicial craft that repudiated its positivist legacy. But the true turn-around came after the emergency, when the court turned away from formalism and positivism entirely, as witnessed in the *Maneka Gandhi* case[59] where the court fully repudiated *A.K.Gopalan* and launched Article 21 in a new expansive direction.

The court was doing this against the background of a widespread failure of the state to do socio-economic justice, resulting in the emergence of a multitude of social movements across the country, among farmers, peasants, and women.[60] The moral credibility of the Congress party, the grand old party of independence, had collapsed, and the government had lost its legitimacy due to the repression during the emergency. The Janata government which followed in 1977 was weak. These circumstances, coupled with the court's own attempt at *mea culpa* for its role during the emergency, led to the consecration of the judiciary— no doubt self-imagined to some extent[61]—as the preferred branch of governance. The court's willingness to assume powers of governance, as witnessed in the growth of SAL, also compelled the court to share the *goals* of governance and tolerate the *methods* of governance, much more than in the past.

[56] *I.C. Golak Nath* v. *State of Punjab* AIR 1967 SC 1643.

[57] Ibid., at 1668–9.

[58] *Kesavananda Bharati* v. *State of Kerala* AIR 1973 SC 1461.

[59] *Maneka Gandhi* v. *Union of India* AIR 1978 SC 597.

[60] For a discussion of the emergence of social movements from the 1970s, see Gail Omvedt, *Reinventing Revolution: New Social Movements and the Socialist Traditions in India* (1993).

[61] For an extended and sophisticated argument that links judicial power, activism and self-image of the judges, see Upendra Baxi, supra n. 11.

One such goal was sustainable development, a concept of development laced with environmentalism. The court's activism in the environmental area from the early 1980s was not happening in a vacuum, but as part of a state-making process that was reconfiguring the goals of the Indian state itself. Following the 1972 Stockholm UN Conference on the Environment, the regulatory authority over forests was transferred from the state list to the concurrent list in the constitution in 1976, allowing shared federal and state authority. The Prime Minister issued a directive in 1980 mandating environmental impact assessments by federal agencies for medium and major irrigation projects. Parliament passed the Forest Conservation Act in 1980 and the federal environmental department was upgraded to the Ministry of Environment and Forests in 1985.[62] Several Indian environmental NGOs were also established in the 1970s, including the Center for Science and Environment and Kalpavriksh, while environmental movements had been witnessed in parts of the country such as the Silent valley agitation and the *Chipko* movement.[63] Against this background, the court's environmental activism must be seen as a result of the contestation between different social actors over the meaning and direction of the goals of the Indian state itself.

As a result of the court's assumption of governance functions, its approach to human rights is determined by its congruence, at any given time, with the overarching ideologies of *statism* and *developmentalism* which remain dominant ideologies of governance. Put differently, the court is generally loath to find for a petitioner who is asserting rights that openly contradict with either the dominance of the state or with the vision of socio-economic and cultural change that is implied in the grand vision of development. This is because, the court, as a governance mechanism, shares the ideologies of statism and developmentalism. The meanings of these ideologies do not remain fixed; rather, they change over time,

[62] For a discussion of these developments, see Sanjeev Khagram, 'Restructuring the Global Politics of Development: The Case of India's Narmada Valley Dams' in Sanjeev Khagram, James V. Riker and Kathryn Sikkink (eds), *Restructuring World Politics: Transnational Social Movements, Networks and Norms*, University of Minnesota Press (2002) at 218–19.

[63] On the growth of environmental movement in India, see Ramachandra Guha, 'The Environmentalism of the Poor' in Richard G. Fox and Orin Starn (eds), *Between Resistance and Revolution* (1997) at 17–39; Harsh Sethi, 'Survival and Democracy: Ecological Struggles in India', in Poona Wignaraja (ed.), *New Social Movements in the South* (1993) at 122–48.

reflecting the dominant theories and social relations of the day. Thus, developmentalism has meant many things from state-led industrial growth to sustainable development to rights-based development to neoliberal development. Indeed, many of these meanings coexist in tension within the ideological matrix of the state and the judiciary is not free from them. These ideologies enable the court to justify the sacrifice of some human rights for others and the social costs imposed on some in the interest of others, but to do so for different reasons at different times. Thus, in the *Narmada* case, the court derisively characterized the *Narmada Bachao Andolan*, the petitioner, as an 'anti-dam organization' and declared that the 'displacement of these people would undoubtedly disconnect them from their past, culture, custom and traditions, but then it becomes necessary to harvest a river for the larger good'.[64] This is one reason why the court is biased in favour of some rights over others.

A second reason why the court may be biased in favour of some rights over others has to do with the particular history of the court's long tussle with the legislature over the question of property rights. This complex story has been well told elsewhere by scholars,[65] but for our purposes, it must be noted that the court's conflict with the legislature starting with the First Amendment to the constitution and extending until the 1970s did not completely end with the *Kesavananda Bharati* case, but has cast its long shadow over the relationship between Part III and Part IV and the future of socio-economic rights. Since most socio-economic rights are listed as policy aspirations under Part IV, the only legitimate measures that may be taken to enforce them are by the government unless the court decides to read a Directive Principle into Part III, thus enabling individuals to claim their rights, which is something the court has done often. But that creates a problem as the court has had a bitter history of conflict with the government over whether the measures taken to enforce directive principles must themselves comply with Part III rights. To put it differently, the court has come to see itself, for historical and textual reasons, principally as the defender of Part III rights especially when weighing governmental measures that seek to give effect to the principles in Part IV. This has resulted in creating a structural bias in favour of civil and political rights which dominate Part III unless the court decides to read the principles of Part IV into Part III.

[64] Supra n. 24 at 765.
[65] See Granville Austin, *Working a Democratic Constitution*, Oxford University Press, New Delhi (1999).

This could be evidenced, for instance, in the way in which almost all implied rights—livelihood, environment, education—have been read into Article 21 and therefore translated as a civil or political right. Given this history, it is not surprising that the bar so often frames its arguments in terms of the rights in Part III.

A third reason for the bias of the court in favour of some rights over others has to do with social movement politics itself. Social movements in India, as elsewhere, tend to be highly suspicious of courts and law because of their perception as elite defenders of the status quo. In the Indian context, this perception is not without reality. As such, social movements tend to approach courts relatively rarely unless they stand to gain immediately either through publicity, or to stave off disasters. Given that social movements tend to be a primary driving force behind the enforcement of most socio-economic rights, this has the result of keeping these rights issues off the court's agenda. Instead, the court is faced with issues that tend to dominate the mainstream NGO agenda, such as torture, custodial deaths, environment and more recently, women's rights.

A fourth reason for the bias of the court can be found in the individual class and political alignments of judges, as well as their individual training and outlook towards socio-economic issues. The social philosophy of the individual judges often determines the outcomes of cases in India (as elsewhere), where the court does not sit *en blanc* as in the US, but rather constitutes itself in 2 and 3 judge benches. These benches are also not constant as judges retire very often even as the cases drag on for years. This may mean that a single case may see several judges deciding different aspects. The individual ideology of judges becomes extraordinarily important as a result. A case in point is *Narmada*, where Justice Barucha was the only judge who stayed on the bench from 1994 (when the case was initiated) to 2000 (when the judgment was delivered). It is not coincidental that he was the sole dissenting judge who found in favour of the NBA. In addition, individual judges often dramatically differ on the extent to which they are receptive to arguments about constitutionalizing socio-economic rights including by reliance on international law. For example, a survey of the supreme court judgments shows that the majority of cases in which the court has referred to the ICESCR have been decided by one judge, K. Ramaswamy, and most of them have been decided since the mid-1990s.[66]

[66] Survey on SCC CD-ROM, July 2004.

A final reason for the bias of the court in favour of some rights has to do with the role of the bar itself. The Indian bar, while tremendously talented, has not aggressively pushed for adjudication of socio-economic rights and does not seem to draw on the most current trends in international and comparative law. As pointed out earlier, the counsel for *Narmada Bachao Andolan* made few, if any, references to the extensive international and comparative jurisprudence on forced eviction. As a result, even in the field of environmental law, the court has tended mostly to rely on domestic Indian legal sources, and not on the most current comparative and international legal materials.[67] The judgments themselves are often confusing and show a breezy familiarity with international law[68] and do not draw on the experience of some of the most progressive constitutional courts in the world adequately, such as the South African court. The responsibility for this lies, ultimately, with the bar which lacks adequate representation from oppressed groups such as Dalits.

THE IDEOLOGY OF HUMAN RIGHTS DISCOURSE

A second set of explanations for the bias of the court against socio-economic rights are to be found within the discourse of human rights itself. This discourse, which is international in origin, is generally taken to be neutral in which all rights are equal, indivisible, and interdependent. Far from this, the conceptualization of socio-economic rights within the human rights discourse is deeply problematic and constrains any judiciary that is mandated to enforce it. It is not my claim here that civil and political rights are more privileged in the language of the human rights treaties than economic, social, and cultural rights. That familiar claim,[69]

[67] C.M. Jariwala, 'The Directions of Environmental Justice: An Overview' in S.K. Verma and Kusum (eds), *Fifty Years of the Supreme Court of India: Its Grasp and Reach*, Oxford University Press, New Delhi (2000) at 492.

[68] For instance, many judgments describe that India is a *signatory* to this or that treaty, when what they mean is that India is a state party. There are serious differences in the international legal obligations that accrue after signature as opposed to ratification. In addition, sometimes the court wrongly refers to international treaties on human rights, and often fails to analyse (as opposed to merely declaring) how the treaty comes to be part of domestic law. For an example, see *LIC of India v. Consumer Education Research Centre* (1995) 5 SCC 482 (referring to the European Convention of Social, Economic and Cultural Rights and the convention on the Right to Development for Socio-Economic Justice, which does not exist), para 49.

[69] For a discussion, see Martin Scheinin, *Economic and Social Rights as Legal Rights*, in Economic, Social and Cultural Rights 41, 42, Asbjorn Eide *et al.* (eds) (1995).

while true, captures only part of the problem. The other part of the problem relates to the way socio-economic rights are conceptualized, and the specific problems that a court is said to encounter while attempting to enforce such rights.[70] To state my argument in a nutshell, socio-economic rights tend to be conceptualized in the international legal lexicon in specific ways that make their realization depend on either *state capacity* to provide such rights or on the availability of market mechanisms that can ensure constantly increasing 'standards of living' (as the ICESCR puts it[71]) through greater *consumption*. The choice for realizing socio-economic rights then, is between increasing state capacity on the one hand and a culture-ideology of consumerism, led by market fundamentalism, on the other. In the context of most post-colonial states, increasing state capacity is not an attractive option as it assumes that the state will not be predatory. Markets, by themselves, have no track record of ensuring the socio-economic rights of the poor by encouraging greater consumption.[72] Within this constrained framework, socio-economic rights lose their emancipatory potential, and the court, no matter how heroic, cannot overcome this framework easily. The ideologies of socio-economic rights in the international legal lexicon overwhelm the constitutional ideologies of equality or justice which may in fact provide space for social movement struggles for realization of rights.

This is distinct from the broader charge that violations of economic and social rights are systematically ignored when compared to violations of civil and political rights. As the UN Committee on Economic, Social and Cultural Rights has put it, 'the shocking reality...is that States and the international community as a whole continue to tolerate all too often breaches of economic, social and cultural rights which, if they occurred in relation to civil and political rights, would provoke expressions of horror and outrage and lead to concerted calls for immediate remedial action. In effect, despite the rhetoric, violations of civil and political rights continue to be treated as though they were far more serious, and more patently intolerable, than massive and direct denials of economic, social and cultural rights.' World Conference on Human Rights, Preparatory Committee, Contribution Submitted by the Committee on Economic, Social and Cultural Rights, UN Doc. A/CONF.157/PC/62/Add.5, para. 5 (1993).

[70] A critical, yet sympathetic, approach to socio-economic rights has been thoughtfully engaged by other scholars before. See, for example, Craig Scott, 'Reaching Beyond (Without Abandoning) the Category of "Economic, Social and Cultural Rights"', 21 *Hum. Rts. Q.* 633 (1999).

[71] ICESCR, supra n. 32, Article 11.

[72] In India, there has never been a widespread belief in the idea that markets, by themselves, can ensure socio-economic rights or ensure equitable distribution of resources. If any thing, the constitution envisages serious state intervention in the

First, what are socio-economic human rights and what were states' attitudes towards them? Socio-economic rights including education, health, standards of living, trade union rights, housing, water, food, cultural identity, etc., are contained in the ICESCR. As is well-known, unlike the ICCPR,[73] which mandates that all rights should be immediately implementable, the ICESCR subjects the guarantee of rights to two conditions: that they should be 'progressively realizable' and that the realization should be subject to 'available resources'. So-called third generation rights are collective or solidarity rights such as the rights to development, environment, and peace. The Universal Declaration on Human Rights[74] (UDHR) makes no distinctions between rights, but due to the ideological rivalry during the Cold War, two different covenants were adopted in 1966—ICCPR and ICESCR. Underlying each was a deep division over the appropriate role of the state in the economy. The debates during drafting show that while many, if not most western states were in support of Second generation rights in principle, there were serious divisions over the responsibilities of states.[75] Indeed, the covenants, being treaties, were drafted as the legal responsibilities of states. As such, the concern during the drafting of the covenants was not so much whether socio-economic rights were important for human dignity (a major goal of the effort) but whether the states could afford to guarantee them. In other words, the human rights debate became one about *state capacity* rather than human dignity.[76] In the context of the 1960s, this was then a debate about the appropriate developmental role of the state—a proxy war between the dirigist and market-oriented models of economy.

In this debate, so-called developing countries—at least those that were decolonized—were mostly supportive of a strong role of the state

economy. This belief in the market's capability, which is widespread among US legal academics, especially of the 'law and economics' variety, is heavily contested now. For an analysis, see Martha McCluskey, 'Efficiency and Social Citizenship: Challenging the Neoliberal Attack on the Welfare State', 78 *Ind. L.J.* 783 (Summer 2003).

[73] International Covenant on Civil and Political Rights, 1966.

[74] Universal Declaration of Human Rights, GA Res. 217A (III), Art. 25 (1), UN Doc. A/810, at 71 (1948), at http://www.unhchr.ch/html/menu3/b/69.html.

[75] Farroukh Jhabvala, 'On Human Rights and the Socio-Economic Context', in Frederick E. Snyder and Surakiart Sathirathai (eds), *Third World Attitudes Toward International Law*, Martinus Nijhoff, Dordrecht (1987).

[76] For a longer discussion of the points outlined here, see Balakrishnan Rajagopal, *International Law From Below: Development, Social Movements and Third World Resistance*, Cambridge University Press (2003), Part III.

in the economy. The reason was that these newly independent countries were terribly interested in nation building and saw the state as the main instrument for achieving economic and social development, so that they could 'catch up' with the west. India was no exception. Vesting the state with the obligation to ensure housing, education, or standard of living for its citizens, gave a moral justification for the developmental role of the state. This is important to bear in mind, as the developmental role of the state has been substantially delegitimated now both due to the miserable record of the developmental state in the Third World (its violence) and the triumph of neoliberal ideology that dictates the almost complete withdrawal of the state from the economy.[77] In this context, a state that is fully committed to the entire panoply of human rights including socio-economic rights appears to stand a better chance of ensuring development and progressive state building—as is evidenced by South Africa—but it would require that socio-economic rights be recast first.

So-called third generation rights began emerging in the context of intense North-South politics in the 1970s. The failure of the Non-Aligned Movement and the G-77 group of countries to push the New International Economic Order (NIEO) debate to any real results during the 1970s meant that the Third World states needed some other ideological basis for contesting the power and influence of the west. They turned to human rights discourse to resignify the debate about development. Starting with the Declaration of Tehran of 1967, this gained momentum and agencies such as UNESCO and ILO played a key role in pushing the debate on human rights and peace and human rights and development during the 1970s. After the articulation of the right to development in the 1970s and after almost a decade of intense transformation in UN practice, the UN General Assembly adopted the Declaration on the Right to Development in 1986. By that time, a right to peace had been already declared.

Thus the ideological debate about development had shifted terrain and now had fully arrived in the area of human rights. It is well-known that the 1986 Declaration on Right to Development was ideologically polarized (The US voted against it, with some other western countries abstaining) and has proved to be controversial ever since. The impact of the new developmentalization of human rights was quite profound. First,

---

[77] See Ashis Nandy, 'State' in Wolfgang Sachs (ed.), *Development Dictionary: A Guide to Knowledge as Power*, Zed Books, London (1992).

it was during the 1970s that the UN doctrine on the 'interdependence, indivisibility, and interconnectedness of all human rights' became official. This meant that officially at least, the debates about the hierarchy of human rights, and tradeoffs between human rights, had been settled. Second, the embrace of human rights by Third World states at the diplomatic level, and the entry of new Third World states into the UN Commission on Human Rights in 1979, had domestic repercussions and led to demands for more democracy and human rights within states. This political background to socio-economic rights is crucial for appreciating the criticisms levelled at socio-economic rights as well as the limitations inherent in their conceptualization due to their historical trajectories.

What are some of the traditional criticisms of socio-economic rights? Traditionally, mainstream international lawyers in the west have been rather dismissive of socio-economic rights and western state practice has also been often hostile to these rights[78] though there is now an attempt to engage in revisionist history wherein the US in particular,[79] was only promoting economic and social rights when it pushed for free markets during the Cold War. Leading NGOs such as Amnesty International and Human Rights Watch have also begun recasting their mandates to deal more directly with economic and social rights, though they continue to express doubts.[80] I list some well-known and oft-discussed criticisms of economic and social rights here that seem most relevant to the context in India, including the following, while providing my assessments of those critiques:

a. A first criticism is that socio-economic rights do not fit conceptually within the idea of rights, which are generally taken to mean negative liberties rather than positive entitlements. Never highly persuasive,

---

[78] I am not flooding this paper with too many citations for much of what follows as its broad arguments are well rehearsed in the field of human rights. For one example of some traditional tensions in the field of socio-economic rights, see J. Oloka-Onyango, 'Beyond the Rhetoric: Reinvigorating the Struggle for Economic and Social Rights in Africa', 26 Cal. W. Int'l L.J. 1 (Fall 1995).

[79] Thus, according to the Attorney Advisor to the Department of State, 'during the Cold War, Western governments championed democratic institutions and the operation of the free market as the means to implement economic and social rights'. See Michael J. Dennis, 'Human Rights in 2002: The Annual Sessions of the UN Commission on Human Rights and the Economic and Social Council', 97 A.J.I.L. 364 (April 2003).

[80] See, for example, Kenneth Roth, 'Defending Economic, Social and Cultural Rights: Practical Issues faced by an International Human Rights Organization', 26 Hum. Rts. Q. 63 (2004).

this criticism has two major problems. First, the idea of rights as negative liberties alone is a highly narrow and almost ethnocentric one that reflects a particular western tradition and cannot therefore, serve as the basis of universal rights. Second, even negative liberties turn out to have positive entitlements—for example, the right to fair trial requires the provision of legal representation to those who cannot afford any under the ICCPR. So, conceptually, the idea that human rights are the rights to be left alone does not hold much water even if we take classic civil and political liberties.[81]

b. A second critique is that socio-economic rights are not rights, but aspirations of what a desirable society looks like. Proponents of this critique, who include many American Constitutional lawyers such as Cass Sunstein,[82] criticized the Eastern European states for enshrining socio-economic rights in their constitutions. The major problem with this critique is that it equates socio-economic rights with the welfare state, a massive statist enterprise to provide public housing, free education, health and massive subsidies for food, etc. This has a rich tradition even in human rights scholarship, which often conflates socio-economic rights with the welfare state, as *rights to government programmes*.[83] Reducing socio-economic rights to welfare statism or government programmes simply re-enacts the same flaw that characterized the birth of the covenants in 1966 when the debate about rights became a debate about state capacity. In addition, a strand of this critique also equates socio-economic rights with the freedom to acquire goods, or simply greater consumption. In areas like health or housing for example, one can see a clear evidence of this tendency. In this guise, socio-economic rights simply become equated with marketization and the freedom to 'choose' goods in the market. This is how, for example, the World Bank has conceived its own role vis-à-vis socio-economic rights in recent years.[84] If the former strand of

---

[81] For a discussion, see Herman Schwartz, 'Do Economic and Social Rights Belong in a Constitution?', 10 *Am. U. J. Int'l L. & Pol'y* 1233, 1233 (1995).

[82] Cass Sunstein, 'Against Positive Rights', 2/1 *East. Eur. Const. Rev.* 35 (1993). He has since changed his position and is now a supporter of economic and social rights. See Cass Sunstein, *The Second Bill of Rights: FDR'S Unfinished Revolution and Why We Need It More than Ever* (Basic Books, 2004).

[83] E. Vierdag, 'The Legal Nature of the Rights Granted by the International Covenant on Economic, Social and Cultural Rights', 9 *Netherlands Ybk. Int. L.* 69 (1978).

[84] See e.g., *Human Rights and Development: The Role of the World Bank*, World Bank (1998).

this critique aims at supply-side solutions to violations of socio-economic rights, the latter strand offers demand-side solutions. If we stop seeing rights-holders as passive recipients of government benefits or as inexorable consumers, but rather as active shapers and enforcers of their own rights through vigorous democratic participation, the hollowness of this critique is exposed. In fact, *a really meaningful socio-economic rights agenda must rest on a strong critique of welfare statism, market fundamentalism and the culture-ideology of consumerism.* I would suggest that this is in fact the emerging meaning of socio-economic rights as can be seen from recent dissident strands of constitutional and international jurisprudence as well as the practice of social movements that are discussed in the next section.

c. A third critique is that socio-economic rights are not justiciable or as the ICESCR puts it, the rights are 'progressively realizable' within 'available resources'.[85] The argument is that this is both because it costs money to implement them, and also because judges lack the legitimacy, competence, and the power to meaningfully address them. I deal with the latter part of the critique in the next section. Regarding the first part, it can be easily rebutted. As Henry Shue and others have shown, it takes a lot of money to implement most civil and political rights such as the right to vote simply because the enjoyment of these rights requires a sophisticated infrastructure of state agencies and civil society actors.[86] Socio-economic rights are no different. Besides, it is increasingly recognized that the enjoyment of socio-economic rights rest not so much on resources as in the lack of voice/power. In Amartya Sen's language, the entitlements depend on capabilities, which in turn are a product of disabilities imposed by race, gender, class, ethnicity, and a variety of other social, political, economic, and cultural dimensions of life.[87] As Sen has pointed out, the life expectancy of American blacks is lower than the people in

[85] Article 2(1). The key issue in international human rights law concerning economic and social rights today is the issue of justiciability, but at the international level. Thus, the Commission on Human Rights and the ECOSOC have authorized the creation of a Working Group to consider the conclusion of an Optional Protocol to the ICESCR that could receive individual complaints. See CHR Res. 2002/24 (22 April); ECOSOC December 2002/254 (25 July). The focus of my article is more on the domestic judiciary.

[86] Henry Shue, *Basic Rights: Subsistence, Affluence, and US Foreign Policy* (2nd edn), Princeton University Press (1996).

[87] Amartya Sen, *Development as Freedom*, Oxford University Press, New Delhi (1999), chapter 1–4.

Kerala, even though the US is so much wealthier than India in per capita terms.

d. A fourth criticism is that there is a hierarchy among rights and socio-economic rights do not rank at the top. The idea of hierarchy of rights comes in different forms in international law. It can be seen in the notion of *jus cogens* for example, that confines its meaning to certain massive human rights violations such as genocide or even prohibition of torture, but does not include other massive human rights violations as hunger or forced eviction/destruction of housing. It can also be seen in the idea that certain rights are core rights while others are not. Even in specialized areas of human rights such as those relating to labour, the idea of core standards is prevalent.[88] If we look at what these are, they invariable turn out to be civil and political rights (freedom to organize for instance) but not socio-economic rights (such as occupational health). The idea of core rights is not only arbitrary, ideological and biased, it is also dangerous, as it shows a green signal for violation of other rights by states and other actors.

In addition to the problems that are inherent in the conceptualization of socio-economic rights, it is also often suggested that there are specific problems relating to their enforcement by courts. What are some of these problems? So-called third generation rights have rarely come before the courts though, as I have noted earlier, the right to environment has been interpreted by the court to be part of right to life under Article 21 of the constitution. Socio-economic rights have been litigated for years before domestic courts. Learning from this experience, one can reflect on some additional criticisms of socio-economic rights that are traditionally made from the perspective of judging.

These criticisms are three-fold.[89] First, it is mentioned that judges lack the legitimacy to adjudicate socio-economic rights because they are not elected representatives of the people. The reason why this is important is that the determination of socio-economic rights is said to

[88] See ILO Declaration on fundamental principles and rights at work, June 1998, at www.ilo.org.

[89] See Sunstein, supra n. 57. For an illuminating description of the major objections to the judicialization of social rights, see Frank Michelman, 'The constitution, social rights, and liberal political justification', *I-CON (International Journal of Constitutional Law)*, Volume 1, Issue 1, January 2003 at pp. 13–34. See also Craig Scott and R. Macklem, 'Constitutional Ropes of Sand or Justiciable Guarantees: Social Rights in a New South African Constitution?' 141 *U. Penn. L. Rev.* 1 (1992).

require decisions of a budgetary nature, which are supposed to be left to other branches of government. Ordering the enforcement of a right to housing will, in this view, unnecessarily intrude into the domain of the legislature and the executive by shifting resources from other areas. Second, it is alleged that judges lack the technical competence to adjudicate socio-economic rights as they require mastery of complex social and economic policies and often massive amount of data. It is advised that judges should leave this complex task to administrative agencies that have the competence to do it. A third critique is that a judicial approach to the enforcement of socio-economic rights is not the right way to their realization as it is too fragmentary, sporadic and lacks the scale required to address massive problems such as illiteracy or slums.

None of these critiques hold much water. First, while adjudicating civil and political rights, judges make decisions that have serious budgetary implications as well. For example, ordering an improvement in prison conditions or mandatory legal representation costs money and may not reflect the existing law. If judges can do this, why can they not order improvements in socio-economic rights that have budgetary implications? Also, the elected representatives themselves often lack legitimacy and courts may be no more or less legitimate than undemocratic or corrupt representative institutions. Finally, legitimacy is not simply a product of elections, but could also be seen as a product of fidelity to core constitutional values or global ethics. A court may in fact be upholding this conception of legitimacy when it decides that the constitution requires the enforcement of socio-economic rights even against existing law or policy.

Second, the question of competence of judges over economic and social policies is also a ruse. Administrative agencies and often legislators are often equally incompetent over the details of economic and social policy, and yet they take crucial decisions that shape public policy. Besides, adjudication of commercial and related matters such as antitrust or tax requires a great deal of technical skill that judges are allowed and even expected to have. If they can do so in commercial matters, why can they not do the same in adjudicating socio-economic rights?

Third, the problem of scale, that an adjudicatory approach to socio-economic rights is not by itself adequate, is a serious critique. An excessive reliance on the judiciary to realize socio-economic rights is certainly bad and will not address systemic problems such as chronic health crises, massive poverty, homelessness, etc. However, this critique wrongly assumes that countries put all their policy eggs in the judicial basket. No country in the world does so and India certainly does not do so. In fact, most countries have massive social and economic programmes geared to address chronic problems in society that constitute socio-economic rights violations. These are often supported and expanded by many civil society actors such as NGOs. The role of the court is by definition, a limited and supplementary one even in countries such as India, where massive public-private programmes are put in place to address poverty, homelessness, AIDS crisis and so forth, and the court must often take on an administrative law model of judging to monitor the delivery of government programmes.

While the traditional criticisms of socio-economic rights continue to matter, there are a whole range of new issues that have arisen regarding the conceptualization and enforcement of these rights, as well as the actors on whom liability may be imposed for violations. The context for these new issues lies in greater social movement struggles over socio-economic rights. These new issues must be properly understood and appreciated by judges, if socio-economic rights are to be successfully and sustainably realized.

By now it is obvious that one of the major reasons for the weakness of socio-economic rights is the extent to which these rights have been reduced to either building state capacity or to consumerism. Put differently, socio-economic rights have been the victims of the ideology of development and so-called third generation rights have especially become a proxy for the frustrations of Third World states due to their failure to achieve a NIEO. This is unfortunate, and the whole regime of human rights needs to be freed from the stifling ideological baggage of the 1960s that continues to bedevil it. That ideological baggage saw development in macroeconomic terms, a matter of large capital-intensive projects, import substituting industrialization, a large state presence in civil society including control of unions, a single party structure, weak judiciaries, a nation-building ideology, a commitment to the rationale of 'catching up' with the west, and the valourization of the national identity over all other identities. *Contesting the ideology of development is central to this task* and it has not truly begun except in the periphery in the form of social movement action in the Third World.[90] In the eyes of social movements, which consist of the most vulnerable and poor populations

[90] For an earlier elaboration, see Balakrishnan Rajagopal, 'International Law and the Development Encounter: Violence and Resistance from the Margins' *American Society of International Law 93rd Proceedings* 16 (1999).

in the Third World, it is the attempt to impose 'development' on them that have made them worse off. Development is, in this view, the disease rather than the cure. Without performing this cathartic task, socio-economic rights will simply continue to be seen as the best way to sneak a gigantic welfare state in, while so-called third generation rights will continue to be seen as a replay of a tired old debate over technology transfer, greater development assistance, and better terms of trade. While a welfare state and the goals of the NIEO may continue to be important, they must be sought elsewhere and through different channels, and not through the human rights discourse.

A second challenge is to reconceptualize the background norms of private law—including property, contracts, and tort—that underlie the operation of the market which produces and perpetuates poverty, domination, and exclusion.[91] This is perhaps the most difficult challenge in making socio-economic rights a reality to those to whom they matter most. The regime of human rights, including socio-economic rights, has traditionally been conceived of as a regime of public law, with very little bearing on private law. Thus, human rights were conceptualized in the classical tradition as rights of individuals against the state and in the absence of any state action, violations of individual rights by other private actors were—and still are—not considered violations of human rights. This nexus with the state, while reflecting its classical liberal roots, makes the classical doctrine of human rights less useful and relevant in a Third World country such as India. Many human rights violations, including most violations of socio-economic rights, occur in the private arena of the market or the family, and the rules that structure social relationships in these arenas have been largely untouched by the moral impulses of the human rights regime. This is particularly true in India where the teaching and the practice of private law follows a very doctrinaire, Blackstonian path with little regard to the outcomes of private law transactions on the most vulnerable. An added source of illegitimacy in the post-colonial context of India is that these private law regimes mostly remain unchanged from the colonial period and perpetuate the exploitation and domination that these regimes were set up to perpetuate.

A third challenge is the clear rise of non-state actors in international politics. Both transnational corporations as well as transnational social movement networks now have profound impact on international law

---

[91] For a discussion in the context of socio-economic rights, see Mark Tushnet, 'State Action, Social Welfare Rights, and the Judicial Role: Some Comparative Observations', 3 *Chi. J. Int'l L.* 435 (Fall 2002).

and politics. The former wield enormous power over national govern-ments while the latter have transformed the space of law making and implementation. During the last decade, social movements have compelled the adoption of a major treaty (Ottawa Convention on Antipersonnel Landmines), created new international institutional innovations (World Bank Complaints Panel, World Commission on Dams, Commission on Sustainable Development, IMF Ombudsman) and other multistakeholder initiatives (Mining Review, Global Compact, corporate social responsibility movement including actors such as Global Reporting Initiative) and transformed compliance mechanisms (especially in environmental law).[92] In addition, social movement action also led to the 1996 advisory opinion of the International Court of Justice on the legality of the threat or use of nuclear weapons,[93] as clearly recognized by international lawyers.[94] Much, if not most, of social movement action has been targeted towards the enforcement of socio-economic rights. This new form of politics will inevitably have a profound impact on the Indian Supreme Court soon if only because Indian social movements are so deeply embedded in transnational networks. It is imperative that judges remain conscious about how their constituency is rapidly changing from an exclusive club of domestic public interest groups suing local authorities to a range of transnational social movement networks that take on transnational actors such as corporations and even international agencies. That is likely to emerge as the frontline of socio-economic adjudication and the court is likely to be a site of contention.

A fourth new issue that must be noted is the rising concern about the increasing incompatibility between fundamental norms of inter-national law relating to human rights and other aspects of international law that promote economic globalization.[95] In particular, conflicts are emerging between the international trade regime on the one hand and norms protecting human rights and environment on the other. Similarly,

[92] See Balakrishnan Rajagopal, 'International Law and Social Movements: Challenges of theorizing resistance' 41 *Columbia Journal of Transnational Law* 397 (2003).

[93] See 'Legality of the Threat or Use of Nuclear Weapons', *I.C.J. Reports* (1996).

[94] Richard Falk, 'The Nuclear Weapons Advisory Opinion and the New Jurisprudence of Global Civil Society', in Richard Falk, *Law in an Emerging Global Village* (Ardsley, New York: Transnational Publishers, 1998) at 165–88.

[95] For an analysis, see Christiana Ochoa, 'Advancing the Language of Human Rights in a Global Economic Order: An Analysis of a Discourse', 23 B.C. *Third World L.J.* (Winter 2003), 57.

conflicts have emerged between the policies of the Bretton Woods institutions and norms of international law in the area of human rights and environment. The court cannot remain oblivious to these developments. As India enforces its obligations under the WTO regime of treaties through the enactment of statutes, the court is likely to see legal challenges to these statutes on the ground, inter alia, that they violate international human rights law and the court must decide that conflict between trade law and human rights law. In other words, the court cannot simply call for incorporating international law into domestic law in cases involving human rights, when there are several unresolved issues concerning the incorporation of other branches of international law into domestic law as well as the relationship between different branches of international law once they are incorporated into domestic law. The supreme court has not begun paying attention to these issues nor has the bar begun engaging with them. In addition, questions are increasingly arising about the legal responsibilities of international institutions such as the WTO, World Bank, and the IMF, which remain oblivious to the broad obligations of all actors under international law to respect human rights. These organizations are not subjected to the jurisdiction of the court. Due to their diplomatic immunity, they cannot be sued in national courts even when they violate human rights norms through their policies and projects. To address this partially, the World Bank established the Complaints Panel in 1993 but that body is not a judicial one. It does not apply international law; rather it simply checks if the projects complained of have violated World Bank's own internal policies known as 'operational directives'. The IMF's Ombudsman is even weaker and does not allow complaints from individuals to be entertained. The WTO has no mechanism for complaints by individuals or groups from states that lose in its proceedings. The impartiality and independence of WTO panels and Appellate Body leave a lot to be desired and poor countries—let alone vulnerable groups within these countries—have very little, if any, say in how WTO is run. Yet, these organizations have profound impact on human rights of poor people, farmers, women, minorities and indigenous groups, fishermen/women, and other vulnerable groups. These impacts are mostly on the livelihoods and cultural identity of these groups and individuals. The last refuge of such groups and individuals is often the supreme court and the court must begin to fashion a jurisprudence of remedies for wrongs that are attributable to overseas entities. Indeed, it is not inconceivable that the decisions of international bodies—whether the Security Council or the WTO—may end up being reviewed by domestic constitutional courts such as the Indian Supreme Court in the future, involving difficult questions of balancing different aspects of international law in domestic enforcement. In many of the new areas of challenge, adjudication is some way off and even if begun, may not immediately and by itself change the profound inequities of the international system with its maldistribution of resources, gender and race oppression, and assaults on cultural identities. On the other hand, an activist judiciary may make an important difference to the politics of reform in many social and economic areas by compelling national states and international agencies to acknowledge that there are limits to what they can do even in the name of 'progress' or 'development'. Judicializing socio-economic rights may also serve to recover human rights from its self-imposed limitations, by aiding the political and social demands of social movements but only so long as socio-economic rights are reconceptualized, as I have argued.

JUDICIAL ACTIVISM ON SOCIO-ECONOMIC RIGHTS AND SOCIAL MOVEMENTS

The first priority is to begin reconceptualizing socio-economic rights and recentering them as mobilizing strategies, as I have argued. Without doing this, entrenching socio-economic rights in the constitution or importing international human rights through judicial interpretation, will only reproduce arguments for state capacity or market fundamentalism. In other words, an unquestioning embrace of socio-economic rights will hardly result in progressive politics.[96] If this task is commenced, courts may actually be able to use the category of socio-economic rights for assisting positive social change. But this task lies far ahead. For example, it is well known that there is little by way of international jurisprudence on socio-economic human rights. This is partly because the institutions that can potentially have the maximum impact on these rights are declining competence while existing international courts are skewed in favour of civil and political rights or confined to specific territorial jurisdiction as in the case of the International Criminal Tribunals for former Yugoslavia or Rwanda (ICTY/ICTR). The ICJ, the Law of the Sea Court as well as the newly established International Criminal Court (ICC) are not much relevant in protecting socio-economic rights, with some exceptions. The ICJ hears only disputes

---

[96] For an example of such an approach, see Andras Sajo, 'Socio-economic Rights and the International Economic Order', 35 (Fall 2002), 221.

between states and with some exceptions (to be discussed below), has not ruled in any significant way on these rights. The Law of the Sea Court could potentially have a major impact on socio-economic rights, but has been established only very recently. The ICC does not concern itself with everyday violations, and is, in any case, unlikely to take up even massive violations of economic or social rights per se, unless it is in the course of armed conflict. The institutions that can have the maximum impact on these rights include the IMF, the World Bank, and the WTO. However, the World Bank has consistently maintained that it is prohibited by its Articles of Agreement from considering 'political' factors though in recent years it has moved to embrace a narrow, market-oriented version of human rights and rule of law as part of its mandate. Its Complaints Panel does not apply any international law to evaluate Bank projects, as I noted earlier, though some of its recent findings show an acute awareness of the ethical basis of critical World Bank policies relating, for example, to indigenous peoples. In a recent finding on the Qinghai project in China, the Panel found that the poverty reduction project had failed to count entire towns of ethnic Tibetan minorities as part of project-displaced.[97] On the whole, however, the Panel remains weak and of little relevance to what the Bank does. The IMF has also consistently refused to consider human rights impact of its policies though it now considers poverty, gender, and environmental impact of its policies. The WTO has explicitly refused to consider human rights impact of its policies and treaties though the purpose of international trade is, according to the Marrakesh agreement that established the WTO, the increase in employment, human welfare, and prosperity. In addition, most of these organizations function in secret and therefore make it impossible to evaluate what sort of factors are taken into account in their decisions.

Existing international mechanisms of a judicial character such as the UN Human Rights Committee (HRC) do not deal with socio-economic rights due to their subject matter jurisdiction. There is in fact no international court right now, which has jurisdiction over these rights. The Committee on socio-economic rights under the ICESCR is not a court and does not receive complaints like the HRC though its general comments and comments on country reports have been very helpful in developing the jurisprudence in this area. The ICJ has had very little to say on these or any rights though some recent judgments give some

[97] World Bank Complaints Panel Report on The Qinghai Project (China: Western Poverty Reduction Project), 28 April 2000, at http://wbln0018.worldbank.org/ipn/ipnweb.nsf.

hope. In *Hungary* v. *Slovakia*,[98] the court was able to expound on the dispute between the two nations over the construction of a dam on the river Danube, and state responsibility for non-performance of treaty obligations. The majority opinion as well as Judge Weeramantry's concurring opinion made an important contribution by rearticulating the legal basis for the principle of sustainable development in international law. By creatively interpreting this principle, the opinion showed the intricate connection between environment, human rights, and cultural survival. Similarly, in the 1996 *Nuclear Weapons* advisory Opinion, the ICJ has explicitly recognized the right to environment, a so-called Third generation right, as a human right.[99] Again, Judge Weeramantry's dissent stands out as a classic in exploring the impact of nuclear weapons on socio-economic rights. Finally, in *Botswana* v. *Namibia*,[100] Weeramantry's dissent shows how even in a matter that is as traditional as boundary delimitation, communal property ownership by indigenous peoples cannot be trumped arbitrarily by international law and how principles of environmental law and equity serve to shape outcomes.

Other international courts such as the ICTY and ICTR, or the HRC, have had little to say about socio-economic rights due to their subject matter or territorial jurisdiction, though the ICTY has, in some judgments, clearly recognized forced eviction of minorities as a gross violation of international law relating to housing, among others.[101] This interpretation, which follows international law as reflected in UN documents (such as the reports of the UN Special Rapporteur on Right to Housing), shows how humanitarian law can be creatively applied to socio-economic rights when there is evidence of massive or gross violation based on race, ethnicity, gender or any of the other prohibited grounds under Article 2 of the ICESCR.

---

[98] *Gabčíkovo-Nagymaros Project (Hungary/Slovakia)*, ICJ, Judgment of 27 September 1997 (Merits) at http://www.icj-cij.org/.

[99] *Legality of The Threat or Use of Nuclear Weapons*, ICJ, Advisory Opinion of 8 July 1996, at http://www.icj-cij.org/.

[100] *Kasikili/Sedudu Island (Botswana/Namibia)*, ICJ, Judgment of 13 December 1999, at http://www.icj-cij.org/.

[101] *Prosecutor* v. *Tadic*, 105 ILR 419 IT-95-17/1 (Appeals Chamber) (21 July 2000) (involving forced eviction and destruction of housing); *Prosecutor* v. *Tihomir Blaskic*, IT-95-14 (Trial Chamber I) (3 March 2000) (involving, inter alia, forced displacement and destruction of housing); *Prosecutor* v. *Goran Jelicic*, IT-95-10 (Trial Chamber) (14 December 1999) (involving, inter alia, forced displacement and destruction of housing); *Prosecutor* v. *Tadic*, 105 ILR 419 (Appeals Chamber) (15 July 1999) (involving, inter alia, forced displacement and forced relocation).

The encouraging trends in the area of socio-economic rights come from at least four directions:

a. Comparative constitutional adjudication: Several domestic courts have recently passed important judgments in the area of rights to health, housing, property, education, environment, livelihood, and other related socio-economic rights. Most prominent among them is the South African (SA) Constitutional Court, which has now achieved a well-deserved reputation for passing landmark judgments in the area of socio-economic rights which are justiciable under the South African constitution, unlike the Indian constitution.[102] In three landmark judgments in recent years, *Soobramoney*,[103] *Grootboom*,[104] and the *HIV Treatment Action Campaign* case,[105] the South African court has made important contributions to the growth of socio-economic rights jurisprudence. I cannot discuss these cases in detail due to lack of space, but one novelty of *Grootboom* and the *HIV Treatment Action Campaign* cases is the indirect endorsement by the court of the idea of core minimum standards for socio-economic rights, by arguing that any housing plan that doesn't provide for the short-term needs of the most vulnerable is not 'reasonable'. The idea of core minimum standards, which had been articulated by the Committee on Economic, Social and Cultural Rights in 1990,[106] postulated that even though socio-economic rights are progressively realizable subject to available resources, there is a core minimum of

---

[102] This does not mean, of course, that the judgments have had a real impact on the ground. The *Grootboom* case, for example, has been criticized for having had very little impact on the families who filed the suit as well as on the housing situation for the poorest, partly because it was not backed by a strong social movement. Contrasted to this is the *HIV Treatment Action Campaign* case which has been backed by a strong social movement and had a major and immediate impact on thousands of lives. The issue of the complex relationship between judicial activism and social movements is beyond the scope of this paper and is the subject of a longer comparative study I am conducting.

[103] *Soobramoney v. Minister of Health (Kwazulu-Natal)*, CCT 32/97, 27 November 1997.

[104] *Government of R.S.A. v. Grootboom*, CCT 11/00, 4 October 2000.

[105] *Minister of Health & Others v. Treatment Action Campaign & Others*, CCT 8/02, 5 July 2002.

[106] General Comment No. 3, Committee on Economic, Social and Cultural Rights, Report on the Fifth Session (26 November–14 December 1990), Economic and Social Council, Official Records, 1991, Supplement No. 3, UN Doc E/1991/23, at para 10.

each right that must be assured to each individual by the states especially when the population concerned is very vulnerable and/or in crisis. The South African court explicitly distanced itself from that position but ended up reaching a similar outcome by its reliance on the notion of 'reasonableness'. Indeed, the *Grootboom* case could be seen to endorse the highly limited traditional framework of human rights law, which reduces socio-economic rights to mean a right to government programmes, as I argued above. Nevertheless, the judgments of the South African court have had a major moralizing influence on discussions about socio-economic rights, partly because the court's activism has been part of a larger social movements-led mobilization for social justice within South Africa. Its opinions carry a great deal of importance not only because South Africa is the world's first human rights-oriented state, but also because its constitution expressly allows the court to consider international law in its interpretation. This has allowed the growth of judicial globalization, as the court freely borrows from the jurisprudence of the UN Committee on Economic, Social and Cultural Rights as well as the jurisprudence of other countries such as India, Canada, or Germany.

b. Constitutionalization of rights: Constitutions or amendments adopted since the late 1980s have often incorporated new rights such as the right to environment (Mongolia, South Africa), communal property rights for indigenous people and rights to cultural identity (Colombia, India), local self government (India, Brazil) and right to education (India).[107] This trend is indicative of a new sensibility about the increasing importance of socio-economic rights as universal human rights. The supreme court could take this development into account especially while interpreting customary international law or general principles of international law, but so far it has not shown that it wants to do so.

c. Regional jurisprudence: Regional courts have been active in pushing the boundaries of human rights to include socio-economic rights. The European Court of Human Rights has decided a number of recent cases on the right to housing, forced evictions, and right to property, especially those that involve discrimination on prohibited grounds—both violations of Article 8 of the convention (right to privacy/home) as well as Article 1 of Protocol No.1 (right to property/

---

[107] See texts of Constitutions at http://confinder.richmond.edu/.

possessions).[108] The Inter American Commission on Human Rights and the Inter American Court on Human Rights have been active in this regard. While several of the latter's opinions remain relevant for the growth of socio-economic rights jurisprudence—such as the *Velasquez Rodriguez* case which established the liability of non-state actors for human rights violations[109]—a recent decision stands out. In *Awas Tingni*,[110] the court declared that Nicaragua had violated the right to property and the right to judicial protection (or *amparo* remedy) under the American Convention by not demarcating and titling the land of Awas Tingni community speedily, by granting a logging concession to a company over their land, and by denying speedy justice when they complained. This decision has profound implications for different areas of international and domestic law including the law of indigenous peoples, the law of sustainable development, human rights, and even on the concept of sovereignty.

d. Social Movements: A fourth trend is the growing strength of social movements domestically and internationally and their greater abil-ity and willingness to use legal forums to wage their battles. In the *Awas Tingni* case for example, a transnational coalition of indigenous rights was actively involved in litigation. Similarly, the *HIV Treatment Action* case in South Africa was part of a global struggle waged by a transnational social movement with strong domestic roots to ensure affordable access to drugs for HIV patients. Domestically, many of the recent trends referred to here (for example, the constitutional reforms in Colombia) have been driven largely by social movement

[108] See e.g., *Selcuk and Asker* v. *Turkey*, App.No. 00023184/94; 00023185/94, Judg-ment 24 April 1998; *Ilic* v. *Croatia*, App.No. 00042389/98, Judgment 19 September 2000; *Brumarescu* v. *Romania*, App.No. 00028342/95, Judgment 28 October 1999; *Kopecky* v. *Slovakia*, App. No. 00044912/98, Judgment 28 October 1999; *Iatridis* v. *Greece*, App. No. 00031107/96, Judgment 25 March 1999; *Akdivar and Others* v. *Tur-key*, App. No. 00021893/93, Judgment 16 September 1996.

[109] *No. 1—Velásquez Rodríguez Case*. Preliminary Objections. Judgment of 26 June 1987. See also Report No. 40/00, Case 10.538 *Isabela Velásquez and Francisco Velásquez*, Case 10.608 *Ronal Homero Mota et al.*, Case 10.796 *Eleodoro Polanco Arévalo*, Case 10.856 *Adolfo René and Luis Pacheco Del Cid*, and Case 10.921 *Nicolás Matoj et al., v. Guatemala* (13 April 2000)); *Enxet-Lamenxay and Kayleyphapopyet (Riachito) Indigenous Communities*, Case 11.713, Report No. 90/99, Inter-Am. C.H.R; *Maya Indigenous Communities and Their Members*, Case 12.053, Inter-Am. C.H.R., OEA/ Ser./L/V/II.111 doc. 20 rev. (2000) (Annual Report 2000).

[110] *The Case of Mayagna (Sumo) Awas Tingni Community* v. *Nicaragua*, Judgment of 31 August 2001, Inter-Am Ct. H.R. (Ser. C) No. 79 (2001).

action. These movements are overwhelmingly focussed on the realization of socio-economic rights. In the face of such energy, courts cannot, for long, resist being engaged in these issues.

I have argued in this essay that the Indian Supreme Court's record in protecting human rights shows a bias against socio-economic rights of the poor and the dispossessed and that this bias may be explained by two sets of factors: a first set of factors, internal to the Indian system, that have positioned the court as an organ of governance, thereby sharing the biases of many of the goals and methods of governance itself; and a second set of factors that derive from the biased nature of the human rights discourse itself. I have also argued that recent international and comparative judicial experience has much to offer the Supreme Court to transform its jurisprudence into a more people-friendly one. Socio-economic rights do not have to remain as second-class rights to which courts pay lip service and even that only so long as they fit into a developmentalist world view. However, in order to do so, these rights must themselves be reconceptualized to move away from market fundamentalism, state fetishism and the culture-ideology of consumerism. They must, instead, be refashioned as counter-hegemonic mobilizing strategies in which the court and social movements partner to achieve social justice. The court must also begin to pay more attention to emerging dimensions of socio-economic rights including the responsibilities of transnational corporations and agencies as well as the relationship between different branches of international law in domestic law. There are creative opportunities for expanding the jurisprudence of the court. There are a number of substantive and procedural areas where the frontiers of law can be pushed to make it more legitimate. The court's legitimacy will depend to a large extent on its ability to offer support to social movement struggles which are primarily focused on the realization of economic and social rights at a time of economic liberalization and globalization.

10

Globalization and its Impact on the Realization of Human Rights

Indian Perspective on a Global Canvas

SURYA DEVA*

> 'Globalization *has* a human face.'[1]
> Another world is possible.[2]

GLOBALIZATION: GIVING IT A MEANING AND CONTEXT

Globalization, both as a description and as a prescription,[3] has provoked several contradictory responses.[4] Though the two opening statements

---

* Several developments have taken place since this chapter was first written in early 2004, and then revised in 2005. A substantially revised and updated version of this chapter has been published in volume 12 of the *Buffalo Human Rights Law Review* (2006). I dedicate this chapter to the ignored sufferings of the victims of globalization, in India and abroad.

[1] Jagdish Bhagwati, *In Defense of Globalization*, Oxford University Press, New Delhi (2004), p. x [emphasis in original].

[2] The slogan of the World Social Forum, http://www.wsfindia.org/. Also the title of a book based on the World Social Forum 2002: William F Fisher and Thomas Ponniah (eds), *Another World is Possible: Popular Alternatives to Globalization at the World Social Forum*, Fernwood Publishing Ltd., Nova Scotia (2003).

[3] James Petras and Henry Veltmeyer, *Globalisation Unmasked: Imperialism in the 21st Century*, Fernwood Publishing, Nova Scotia (2001), 11.

[4] 'Not merely are complex and contradictory events, processes and happenings lumped under this [i.e., globalization] rubric, signifying uneven and indeterminate developments, but also theories about globalization brings to us...a "whole continent of contested conceptions".' Upendra Baxi, *The Future of Human Rights*, Oxford University Press, New Delhi (2002), 133. Braithwaite and Drahos, see 'globalization as a contest of principles—a contest, for example, between the principle of harmonization

amply indicate this contradiction, some illustrations will help in removing any remaining doubts. Globalization demands deregulation and regulation at the same time.[5] One may ask whether globalization is about removing borders or strengthening the existing ones; it has removed borders regarding trade but not regarding several other important issues such as access to food or medicines, labour movement, employment, and immigration.[6] Globalization, which is a matter of celebration and resistance at the same time both in the west and in the 'rest',[7] is either inevitable or irreversible[8] or is an example of western imperialism[9] in an era of neo-liberalism[10] and therefore, whether reversible, is a moot point.[11] Whether globalization poses a threat to human rights[12] or gives impetus

---

and the principle of national sovereignty.' John Braithwaite and Peter Drahos, *Global Business Regulation*, Cambridge University Press, Cambridge (2000), 7, 511–12.

[5] 'It is necessary to regulate, for example, anti-competitive practices. In fact, free markets may not deliver the desired results in the absence of some regulation'. Joseph E. Stiglitz, *Globalisation and its Discontents*, W.W. Norton and Co., New York (2002), 55–8, 84.

[6] See UN General Assembly, Preliminary Report of the Secretary General on 'Globalisation and its Impact on the Full Enjoyment of all Human Rights', A/55/342 (31 August 2000), para 37.

[7] Stiglitz, supra n. 5, 3–4, 247–9; Noreena Hertz, *The Silent Takeover: Global Capitalism and the Death of Democracy*, William Heinemann, London (2001), 1–5; Michael Goodhart, 'Origins and Universality in the Human Rights Debates: Cultural Essentialism and the Challenge of Globalization' *Human Rights Quarterly*, 25 (2003) 935, 960–1.

[8] For example, Stiglitz suggests that abandoning globalization is 'neither feasible nor desirable'. Stiglitz, supra n. 619, 214, 222. Compare Murray Dobbin, *The Myth of the Good Corporate Citizen: Democracy under the Rule of Big Business*, Stoddart, Toronto (1998), 6, 280.

[9] Tony Schirato and Jen Webb, *Understanding Globalisation*, Sage Publications, London (2003), 15–16; William K. Tabb, *The Amoral Elephant: Globalization and the Struggle for Social Justice in the Twenty-First Century*, Monthly Review Press, New York (2001), 31, 79–98.

[10] See, for a critique of neo-liberalism, Noam Chomsky, *Profit over People: Neoliberalism and Global Order*, Madhyam Books, Delhi (1999).

[11] The Western hypocrisy regarding the removal of trade barriers is one of the reasons for such a suspicion. See Stiglitz, supra n. 5, 6–7, 60–2; and generally Petras and Veltmeyer, supra n. 3.

[12] Goodhart, supra n. 7, 935–6; Eloy Casagrande Jr and Richard Welford, 'The Big Brothers: Transnational Corporations, Trade Organizations and Multilateral Financial Institutions' in Richard Welford et. al., *Hijacking Environmentalism: Corporate Responses to Sustainable Development*, Earthscan Publications Ltd., London (1997), 137–55 [hereinafter Welford, *Hijacking Environmentalism*].

to their realization is again not settled.[13] Further, globalization is resulting in *alienation of people by bringing them together*; there is no consensus on whether the bringing of people closer and thus striving for global homogeneity-uniformity-conformity is a good development, or it is at the heavy cost of destroying indigenous or local beliefs and culture.[14] Similarly, whether globalization increases or decreases poverty as well as economic disparity is a hotly debated and contested issue;[15] the same could be said about the impact of foreign direct investment by multinational corporations (MNCs), the *drivers* of globalization,[16] on development[17] and human rights.[18] What is, however, hardly contested is the fact that globalization has serious implications—positive or negative—for the realization of human rights everywhere, but more so in developing countries.[19]

So, what is *it* which is affecting the lives of all—without any discrimination of caste, creed, colour, sex, race, religion, language, or economic status?[20] Globalization, including its various dimensions—from political to economic, social, cultural, and technological—is defined in varied ways. Giddens, for example, conceptualizes globalization as something where 'local happenings are shaped by events occurring many miles away'.[21] Another commentator views globalization as 'an intense

---

[13] Dinah Shelton, 'Protecting Human Rights in a Globalized World' *Boston College International & Comparative Law Review* 25 (2002), 273, 291–9.

[14] Herz, supra n. 7, 13–15. See also Balmurli Natrajan, 'Legitimating Globalization: Culture and its Uses' *Transnational Law & Contemporary Problems* 12 (2002), 127.

[15] Petras and Veltmeyer, supra n. 3, 20–2; Stiglitz, supra n. 5, 4–10, 24–5, 86, Hertz, supra n. 7, 8, 41–51; Shelton, supra n. 13, 278–9.

[16] 'Globalization is powerfully driven by international corporations.' Stiglitz, supra n. 5, 10.

[17] McCorquodale and Fairbrother, infra n. 24, 742–50.

[18] Sherif H. Seid, *Global Regulation of Foreign Direct Investment*, Ashgate, Aldershot (2002), 3–30, 104–10, 125–9, 131–8; Stiglitz, supra n. 5, 67–73; William H. Meyer, 'Human Rights and MNCs: Theory Versus Quantitative Analysis' *Human Rights Quarterly* 18 (1996), 368; Jackie Smith *et. al.*, 'Human Rights and the Global Economy: A Response to Meyer' *Human Rights Quarterly* 21 (1999) 207.

[19] Antony Anghie, 'Time Present and Time Past: Globalization, International Financial Institutions, and The Third World' *New York University Journal of International Law & Policy* 32 (2000) 243.

[20] Globalization is omnipresent in the sense that it affects the lives of even those who are unaware of it or do not want to get affected by it.

[21] Anthony Giddens, *The Consequences of Modernity*, Polity, Cambridge (1990), 64, as quoted by Richard Peet *et. al.*, *Unholy Trinity: The IMF, World Bank and WTO*, SIRD Kuala Lumpur (2003), 1.

interchange of people, ideas, capital and technology across international space'.[22] On similar lines, for Dunning, globalization means 'connectivity of individuals and institutions across the globe'.[23] Though defined variedly,[24] it is not difficult to identify the central tenet of globalization: globalization is about *movement across the natural and/or (mostly) man-made borders/barriers in a speedy, efficient way and with minimum restrictions*. This movement is ensured through the 4-Ds: deregulation, denationalization, disinvestment, and digitalization.

A reference to 'human rights' in this chapter, on the other hand, is taken to mean not only the rights laid down under the Constitution of India,[25] various other statutes[26] and the international conventions ratified by India but also the rights created by the judiciary.[27]

I examine, in the next part, the interaction of the *process* of globalization and human rights, especially those traits of globalization which (could) affect human rights in several ways. The following part first tries to locate the position of the three branches of the Indian government and then offers a snapshot of some of the emerging human rights themes in India. I then suggest some strategies as well as guiding principles which could help in a successful *marketing* of human rights in an era of globalization, and finally sum up the position taken in this chapter, and also suggest how the Gandhian talisman could ensure that the process of globalization is alive to the human rights of *all*.

[22] Peet, Ibid., 28.

[23] John H. Dunning, 'The Moral Imperatives of Global Capitalism: An Overview', in John H. Dunning (ed.), *Making Globalization Good: The Moral Challenges of Global Capitalism*, Oxford University Press, Oxford (2003), 12.

[24] See, for example, Shelton, supra n. 13, 275–6; Robert McCorquodale and Richard Fairbrother, 'Globalization and Human Rights' *Human Rights Quarterly* 21 (1999) 735, 736–9; David Kinley, 'Human Rights, Globalization and the Rule of Law: Friends, Foes or Family?' *UCLA Journal of International Law & Foreign Affairs* 7 (2002–3) 239, 242–4 [hereinafter Kinley, 'Friends, Foes or Family?'].

[25] Articles 12–35 in Part III of the constitution lay down fundamental rights. Moreover, the directive principles of state policy contained in Part IV, though not justiciable, also have important bearing on the scope of human rights. Mahendra P. Singh, 'The Statics and Dynamics of Fundamental Rights and the directive principles: A Human Rights Perspectives' (2003) 5 SCC (Jour) 1.

[26] See, for example, the Human Rights Act, 1993; the Trade Unions Act, 1926; the Payment of Wages Act, 1936; the Minimum Wages Act, 1948; the Maternity Benefit Act, 1961; the Child Labour (Prohibition and Regulation) Act, 1986.

[27] Mahendra P. Singh (ed.), *Shukla's Constitution of India*, 10th edn, Eastern Book Co., Lucknow (2001), 164–81.

But before we proceed further, two signposts for the readers. First, it could be suggested that globalization is not something new;[28] in a way, it predates even the human rights movement in its current form. Though I do not disagree with such suggestions regarding the historical roots of globalization, I assert that the 'globalization of today' has acquired newer/different connotations from the 'globalization of yesterday'.[29] Second, though all the dimensions of globalization, in my view, have some immediate or mediate bearing on the realization of human rights, I do not intend or pretend to examine here all of such dimensions.

GLOBALIZATION AND HUMAN RIGHTS: FRIENDS OR FOES?

Globalization has, undoubtedly, not only influenced the content, nature, and realization of human rights but also the mechanism for their enforcement. This being the case, one should ask a more fundamental question first: what is the nature of globalization, both as a concept and as a process? Is it pro/anti human rights, or a neutral phenomenon? In my view, globalization as a *concept* is neither pro nor anti-human rights; conceptually, globalization could offer opportunities both for the promotion and abridgment of human rights, at the national level as well as internationally.[30] What is, however, critical is the 'way' in which this conception is operationalized, that is, the *process* of globalization. The direction of the way will depend on many factors, including the composition of actors behind it and their objectives. The *apparent* actors are states and states-led international institutions such as the United Nations (UN), World Bank, International Monetary Fund (IMF) and the World Trade Organization

[28] One could, for example, refer to the ancient Indian concept of *Vasudhaiva Kutumbakam* (treat the whole world as your family). See also John Feffer, 'Challenging Globalization: An Introduction', in John Feffer (ed.), *Living in Hope: People Challenging Globalization*, Zed Books, London (2002), 2–4.

[29] Shelton, supra n. 13, 275–6. See also Frank J Garcia, 'The Universal Declaration of Human Rights at 50 and the Challenge of Global Markets: Trading Away Human Rights Principle' *Brooklyn Journal of International Law* 25 (1999) 51, 57–8; Baldev Raj Nayar, *Globalization and Nationalism: The Changing Balance in India's Economic Policy, 1950–2000*, Sage Publications, New Delhi (2001), 16–20.

[30] Dunning argues: 'Globalization is a morally neutral concept. In itself, it is neither good not bad, but it may be motivated for good or bad reasons, and used to bring about more or less good or bad results.' Dunning, supra n. 23. See also McCorquodale and Fairbrother, supra n. 24, 763.

(WTO).[31] On the other hand, the *hidden* (and probably more influential)[32] actors are MNCs and their representative organizations.[33]

In order to find out whether the relationship between globalization, as a process, and human rights is of friends or foes, I first try to map some of the more significant aspects of the process of globalization which have a direct bearing on the realization of human rights, and then examine few ways in which globalization has affected or could affect human rights.

The Process of Globalization: Some Human Rights-related Aspects

At least the following aspects of the process of globalization have a potential to influence human rights jurisprudence:

Changing Role and Position of States

Globalization directly hits at the traditional notion of state sovereignty; 'the project of globalization...lies in "rolling back the state"'.[34] One should not, however, assume lightly that states or their sovereignty are withering away totally.[35] States, in principle, still possess the power of regulation/intervention, but the expectation is that states will exercise their power only when it suits the interests of global capital,[36] even if

[31] See Braithwaite and Drahos, supra n. 4, 27; Stiglitz, supra n. 5, 10. See also Peet, supra n. 21.

[32] Of the 100 largest economies in the world, 51 are corporations and only 49 are countries. Further, 2004 figures show that out of the 100 largest economic entities in terms of their market value, 67 are corporations. Paul Sheehan, 'All Aboard the Big Red Juggernaut', *Sydney Morning Herald* (22–3 January 2005), 41. See also Dobbin, supra n. 8, 85–121, and generally David C. Korten, *When Corporations Rule the World*, Connecticut: Kumarian Press, West Hartford (1995).

[33] See generally Seid, supra n. 18, 138–41; Braithwaite and Drahos, supra n. 4, 488–94.

[34] Baxi, supra n. 4, 139. Hertz also argues that 'the state has been stepping back, and the market has been taking over.' Hertz, supra n. 7, 32. It is worth noting that this change in the role of states is happening because of the decisions taken, voluntarily or otherwise, by states themselves.

[35] Sassen argues that there is not a loss of sovereignty but only a reconstitution/transformation of it. Saskia Sassen, *Losing Control? Sovereignty in an Age of Globalization*, Columbia University Press, New York (1996), 1–30.

[36] Dobbin, for example, paints the picture thus: 'Not only do corporations want more—more cuts to their taxes, more cuts to UI and pension premium, even greater cuts to social programmes, more repeals of environmental laws and protections for workers' health and safety, and more and better ways to squeeze more from their employees.' Dobbin, supra n. 8, 2, and also at 9.

doing so harms the interests of local communities.[37] Moreover, states, even with a democratic set up, might not be able to take an activist position towards fulfilling their human rights obligations under pressure from international bodies or MNCs. Given this scenario, it is doubtful whether states could still be trusted for solely guarding, to the best of their ability, the human rights of their populace.

Rise in the Number and Influence of MNCs

Corresponding to the decay of regulatory states is a rise in the number and influence of MNCs;[38] both our present and future is 'in the hands of large corporations'.[39] However, despite the fact that MNCs of *today* dwarf many modern states in terms of their economic might, their activities by and large are still not subject to concrete, legally binding human rights obligations flowing from either constitutional law[40] or international law.[41] Not only this, but MNCs are also able to influence policy and law making in key areas such as public health, child labour, workers' rights, consumer protection, foreign investment, environment protection, women's rights at workplace, and indigenous peoples' rights.[42]

[37] See Baxi, supra n. 4, 139–43.

[38] See Hertz, supra n. 7, 6–8; Erin Elizabeth Macek, 'Scratching the Corporate Back: Why Corporations have no Incentive to Define Human Rights' *Minnesota Journal of Global Trade* 11 (2002) 101, 103–04.

[39] Richard Welford, 'Introduction: What are we Doing to the World?' in Welford, *Hijacking Environmentalism*, supra n. 12, 3, 6 [hereafter Welford, 'Introduction'].

[40] Though the human rights mandate emanating from most of the constitutions, including that of India, is directed towards states or state actors, courts in different jurisdictions have tried to subject private corporations to human rights obligation by resorting to the doctrine of horizontal effect or otherwise. See, for example, *Guerra* v. *Italy* (1998) 26 EHRR 357; *Visakha* v. *State of Rajasthan* AIR 1997 SC 3011. See also David Kinley, 'Human Rights as Legally Binding or Merely Relevant?' in Stephen Bottomley and David Kinley (eds), *Commercial Law and Human Rights*, Ashgate/Dartmouth, Aldershot (2002), 25, 38–42 [hereafter Kinley, 'HRs as Legally Binding']. But this process has not been either smooth or uniform. It is also fraught with many difficulties. See generally, Mark Tushnet, 'The Issue of State Action/Horizontal Effect in Comparative Constitutional Law' *International Journal of Constitutional Law* 1 (2003) 79.

[41] Surya Deva, 'Human Rights Violations by Multinational Corporations and International Law: Where from Here?' *Connecticut Journal of International Law* 19 (2003) 1; David Kinley and Junko Tadaki, 'From Talk to Walk: The Emergence of Human Rights Responsibilities for Corporations at International Law' *Virginia Journal of International Law* 44 (2004) 931.

[42] See, for example, how BHP influenced the government of Papua New Guinea to enact a law to limit its liability for environmental pollution caused in OK Tedi.

Although it can be argued that the arrival of MNCs in local markets benefits consumers and/or that they could also have some positive impact on human rights,[43] this has not been the case always. The involvement of MNCs in human rights violations[44] or generating environmental hazards is well documented.[45] Corporations undoubtedly produce wealth, but they also produce *risks*[46] both to humans and to the ecosystem.[47] And globalization has facilitated the export of risks to those countries which are least capable or likely to handle them.[48]

Foreign Direct Investment

At a time when development is squarely related to the flow of foreign direct investment (FDI),[49] it is a challenge for developing countries to create an atmosphere conducive to FDI and at the same time ensure that FDI does not work, directly or indirectly, against local developmental needs or the realization of human rights. Investment, undoubtedly, contributes to development, but it is doubtful if states are able to exercise a reasonable amount of control over the two critical aspect of this process—whose development and at what cost.[50] States may, in fact, be

[43] See supra n. 18. Bottomley examines the relationship of corporations and human rights from various perspectives—from corporations as *violators* to *promoters* and *beneficiaries* of human rights. Stephen Bottomley, '*Corporations and Human Rights*' in Bottomley and Kinley (eds), supra n. 40, 47–68.

[44] See, e.g., continuously updated material at http://www.business-humanrights. org/Home; Beth Stephens, 'The Amorality of Profit: Transnational Corporations and Human Rights' *Berkeley Journal of International Law* 20 (2002) 45, 51–3; Jordan J. Paust, 'Human Rights Responsibilities of Private Corporations' *Vanderbilt Journal of Transnational Law* 35 (2002) 801, 817–19; Kinley and Tadaki, supra n. 41, 933–4.

[45] Seid, supra n. 18, 131–5; Greenpeace, *Corporate Crimes: The Need for an International Instrument on Corporate Accountability and Liability* (2002).

[46] Frank Pearce and Steve Tombs, *Toxic Capitalism: Corporate Crime and the Chemical Industry*, Ashgate/Dartmouth, Aldershot (1998), 281. See also the cases of corporate deviance discussed by Maurice Punch, *Dirty Business: Exploring Corporate Misconduct—Analysis and Cases*, Sage Publications, London (1996), 85–212.

[47] Pearce and Tombs, for example, examine in detail the threats posed by chemicals industries to both humans and the environment. Pearce and Tombs, Ibid., 127–215. See also Jack Doyle, *Trespass Against Us: Dow Chemicals and the Toxic Century*, Common Courage Press, Monroe (2004).

[48] '[B]usiness deviance is exported to less regulated societies and business crime disperses to seek out more congenial environment.' Punch, supra n. 46, 249.

[49] Seid, supra n. 18, 3, 10–12.

[50] Surya Deva, 'The *Sangam* of Foreign Investment, Multinational Corporations and Human Rights: An Indian Perspective for a Developing Asia' *Singapore Journal of Legal Studies* 305 (2004).

ready to barter even their power of regulation in favour of short-term economic gains.[51] Over and above, as many developing countries compete for their share of FDI, this often leads to a 'race to the bottom' regarding human rights, including environmental and labour standards.[52]

Technology

'Technology is one of the most prominent of the many areas used to characterize globalization',[53] because it enables 'the "freedom of circulation" of ideas, goods and peoples'.[54] Technology has the potential to shape the nature of human rights,[55] and could have mixed effect on their realization.[56] The Internet, for example, not only enabled the transmission of information to consumers swiftly and in a cost-effective manner, but also allowed NGOs to foster partnerships/alliances across the world[57] to fight against what of globalization is perceived against human rights.[58] But the Internet has also raised thorny issues related to, say, the right to privacy or child pornography. Similarly, digitalization and biotechnology do/could have serious implications for the realization of various human rights.[59]

[51] Kwamena Acquaah, *International Regulation of Transnational Corporations: The New Reality*, Praeger, New York (1986), 66; Steven R. Ratner, 'Corporation and Human Rights: A Theory of Legal Responsibility' *Yale Law Journal* 111 (2001) 443, 462; Robert McCorquodale, 'Human Rights and Global Business' in Bottomley and Kinley (eds), supra n. 40, 89, 97–8; Peter Muchlinski, *Multinational Enterprises and the Law*, Blackwell Publishers, Oxford (1995), 104–7.

[52] Seid, supra n. 18, 120; Macek, supra n. 38, 104; Clare Duffield, 'Multinational Corporations and Workers' Rights' in Stuart Rees and Shelley Wright (eds), *Human Rights and Corporate Responsibility—A Dialogue*, Pluto Press, Sydney (2000), 191, 194; Mahmood Monshipouri et. al., 'Multinational Corporations and the Ethics of Global Responsibility: Problems and Possibilities' *Human Rights Quarterly* 25 (2003) 965, 973.

[53] Schirato and Webb, supra n. 9, 46.

[54] Ibid., 56.

[55] See, on how the right to freedom of speech changes in the digital age, Jack M. Balkin, 'How Rights Change: Freedom of Speech in the Digital Age' *Sydney Law Review* 26 (2004) 5.

[56] McCorquodale and Fairbrother, supra n. 24, 758–63.

[57] Baxi calls this 'cyber-space solidarity'. Baxi, supra n. 4, 127. See also Seid, supra n. 18, 119; Braithwaite and Drahos, supra n. 4, 497.

[58] Hertz, supra n. 7, 145–50; Scott Pegg, 'An Emerging Market for the New Millennium: Transnational Corporations and Human Rights' in Jedrzej G Frynas and Scott Pegg (eds), *Transnational Corporations and Human Rights*, Palgrave Macmillan, New York (2003), 1, 10.

[59] Baxi, supra n. 4, 159–64; UN Report, supra n. 6, para 27.

In sum, though technology could be used to promote human rights, there are reasons to believe, given the economic considerations involved in its production, transfer, and dissemination, that the final balance-sheet might paint a gloomy picture as far as the future of human rights is concerned.[60] This is more so because it is doubtful whether technology is neutral,[61] and it may benefit *some* more than the *many*.[62]

Governance by Regional/International Treaties

Globalization demands a close cooperation amongst states. The result being that the line between municipal and international governance issues is getting blurred;[63] and increasingly more and more issues are being regulated/governed by regional or international treaties. There are two significant effects of this transfer of governance issues, including human rights, from states to supra-states bodies.[64] First, it limits the leeway and discretion, which is a vital attribute, available to states to react to their respective special human rights needs. For example, a member state of the WTO could no longer act, even if demanded by its constitution, to tackle an epidemic or health emergency in disregard to the TRIPs Agreement and the Doha Declaration.[65] Second, the process promotes centralization by going further away from the people.[66] In addition, it is undemocratic in operation; as often the treaty obligations are undertaken by the executive branch of the government, resulting in denial of opportunity to the people and/or their representatives to have their say in the decision making process.[67]

[60] The Human Development Report notes: 'Policies are urgently needed to turn the advances in the new technologies into advances for all of humankind, and to prevent the rules of globalization from blocking poor people and poor countries out of the knowledge economy.' *Human Development Report* (1999), 72.

[61] Tabb, supra n. 9, 169.

[62] Schirato and Webb, supra n. 9, 57–8, 60–1.

[63] See Alex Y. Seita, 'Globalization and the Convergence of Values' *Cornell International Law Journal* 30 (1997) 429.

[64] Baxi, supra n. 4, 135.

[65] WT/MIN(01)/DEC/1 (adopted on 14 November 2001); the *Declaration on the TRIPs Agreement and Public Health*, WT/MIN(01)/DEC/2 (adopted on 14 November 2001); and the *General Council's Decision on the Implementation of Paragraph 6 of the Doha Declaration*, WT/L/540 (30 August 2003).

[66] McCorquodale and Fairbrother, supra n. 24, pp. 746–7.

[67] The working of Article 73(1)(*b*) read with Article 253 of the Indian constitution amply demonstrates this, especially regarding the acceptance of WTO obligations. See also *Maganbhi Ishvarbhai Patel* v. *Union of India* AIR 1969 SC 783, 807; and

(Over)Reliance on Free Market

Globalization relies heavily on both the market and its principles of economic efficiency and welfare, which could in turn promote human rights in several ways.[68] But the market could also work against the realization of human rights. In fact, in view of a deep normative conflict between trade law, which underpins market, and human rights law,[69] it cannot be said with certainty whether free market philosophy will provide enough space for human rights to flourish. This is besides the point that the market is full of pitfalls and therefore, it may be necessary not only for the promotion of human rights but also for the sustainability of the market that state intervention supplements the market and its principles.[70]

Culture of Consumerism

Corporations strive hard and compete fiercely to increase their profit and/or capture more market share. And in this process when consumerism is increasingly used as a device for 'market-creation',[71] the interests of consumers are the obvious casualties. Consumers choices are moulded, even at the cost of their health and safety, through, for example, the use of mega stars or women in sexually explicit advertisements.[72] As 'chick-choco-chips culture',[73] which has started taking its roots even in villages, dictates life priorities, the culture of consumerism poses a serious challenge to the realization of human rights of *all*. In these circumstances, one can only wonder if we need to have a second look at those aspects of globalization which promote a 'culture of consumerism', something incompatible with sustainable development.[74]

---

the Report of the National Commission to Review the Working of the Constitution (2002), para 5.10.3.

[68] Garcia, supra n. 29, pp. 58–9.

[69] Ibid., 63–76.

[70] See generally Seid, supra n. 18, 25–6; Peet, supra n. 21, 33–4.

[71] McCorquodale and Fairbrother, supra n. 24, 735.

[72] Natrajan, supra n. 14, 127–30; Maria Mies and Vandana Shiva, *Ecofeminism*, Spinifex, Melbourne (1993), 135.

[73] See, on how MNCs influence social and cultural traits of people, Krishna Kumar (ed.), *Transnational Enterprises: Their Impact on Third World Societies and Culture*, Westview Press, Boulder (1980).

[74] Richard Welford, *Environmental Strategy and Sustainable Development: The Corporate Challenge for the Twenty-First Century*, Routledge, London (1995), 5–19 [hereinafter Welford, *Environmental Strategy*]; Mies and Shiva, supra n. 72, 251–62; and generally Bradley A. Harsch, 'Consumerism and Environmental Policy: Moving Past Consumer Culture' *Ecology Law Quarterly* 26 (1999) 543.

Role Played by Media and NGOs

Media and various civil society organs such as NGOs and public-spirited lawyers/academics have assumed a greater role in global governance; they influence policy and law making decisions at both municipal and international levels.[75] Although both NGOs and media could play, and have played in the past, a significant part in the promotion of human rights,[76] there is an iota of scepticism involved in their role. For example, NGOs' dependence on donations[77] and a polarization of media in certain corporate hands[78] are matters of some concern, especially if seen from the perspective of developing countries.

How Globalization Affects Human Rights

I argue that globalization has influenced, and could further influence, the *future* of human rights in several respects. Some of those courses are chartered below.

Content and Nature

Globalization has the potential not only to change the nature of human rights but also provide impetus to the evolution of new rights. Though at this stage it is difficult to predict with certainty who are going to derive more benefit out of this change in the nature and (over)-production

[75] Rajagopal, who articulates a theory of resistance in international law, argues that '[c]oncerted social movement action has driven several recent international developments.' Balakrishnan Rajagopal, 'International Law and Social Movements: Challenges of Theorising Resistance' *Columbia Journal of Transnational Law* 41 (2003) 397, 399; and also Balakrishnan Rajagopal, *International Law from Below: Development, Social Movements and Third World Resistance*, Cambridge University Press, Cambridge (2003).

[76] See generally Braithwaite and Drahos, supra n. 4, 497–501. Baxi also explores various techniques such as of reportage, lobbying, global direct action, etc., employed to ensure that human rights survive in a market economy. Baxi, supra n. 4, 127–8.

[77] See Baxi, supra n. 4, 121–5. For a Marxist critique of the role played by NGOs, see Petras and Veltmeyer, supra n. 3, 128–38.

[78] UN Report, supra n. 6, para 44; Dionne Bunsha, 'Media Becoming propaganda Vehicle for Corporates' The *Hindu* (19 January 2004), http://www.thehindu.com/2004/01/19/stories/2004011902161200.htm; and also generally Hertz, supra n. 7, 133–41.

of human rights,[79] there are already strong arguments for according trade-related interests the status of human rights.[80]

Prioritization

Certain human rights, which are the backbone of free market economy, are bound to become more important.[81] What is, however, critical to note is that this prioritization inter se human rights is not always dictated by the interests of humans but market forces and non-humans. The prominence gained by intellectual *property* rights vis-à-vis other socio-economic rights demonstrates this.

Bearers

Humans are no longer the sole bearers of human rights; human rights are claimed by, or on behalf of, several non-humans such as corporations,[82] other corporate bodies and even animals.[83] Out of these, the most notable case is of corporations which, though sceptical to accept legally binding human rights obligations, have shown little hesitation in invoking human rights to subserve their business interests.[84]

[79] Baxi, supra n. 4, 67–76. Ochoa cautions us against the creation/use of alternative language to describe human rights, while negotiating with MNCs and international economic institutions. Christiana Ochoa, 'Advancing the Language of Human Rights in a Global Economic Order: An Analysis of a Discourse' *Boston College Third World Law Journal* 23 (2003) 57.

[80] See, for example, Ernst-Ulrich Petersmann, 'Time for a United Nations "Global Compact" for Integrating Human Rights into the Law of Worldwide Organizations: Lessons from European Integration' *European Journal of International Law* 13 (2002) 621. Contra, Philip Alston, 'Resisting the Merger and Acquisition of Human Rights by Trade Law: A Reply to Petersmann' *European Journal of International Law* 13 (2002) 815.

[81] Baxi argues that the UDHR is being supplemented by 'trade-related, market-friendly human rights'. Baxi, supra n. 4, 132, and also at 144–6, 149–52.

[82] *Autronic AG* v. *Switzerland* 12 (1990) EHRR 485; Michael K. Addo, 'The Corporation as a Victim of Human Rights Violations' in Michael K. Addo (ed.), *Human Rights Standards and the Responsibility of Transnational Corporations*, Kluwer Law International, Hague (1999), 190. Compare Bottomley, supra n. 43, 61–5.

[83] Peter Singer, *Animal liberation*, 2nd edn, Pimlico, London (1995); Paola Cavalieri, *The Animal Question: Why Non-human Animals Deserve Human Rights* (translated by Catherine Woollard) Oxford University Press, New York, (2001). See generally Jens David Ohlin, 'Is the Concept of the Person Necessary for Human Rights?' *Columbia Law Review* 105 (2005) 209.

[84] See Carl J. Mayer, 'Personalising the Impersonal: Corporations and the Bill of Rights' *Hastings Law Journal* 41 (1990) 577.

Violators

Various non-state actors, primarily corporations, are emerging as potential human rights violators, acting either independently or in connivance with states. But it could be suggested that there is nothing novel about it: the involvement of corporations in human rights abuses could be traced as early as to the activities of the British East India Company,[85] a time when the notion of human rights in its present form was unknown. One should, however, note that both the modern corporations[86] and the instances of their role in human rights violations differ significantly from their ancestors.[87] The net result is a situation where a state-centric human rights enforcement mechanism tries, rather unsuccessfully, to tame *stateless*—not only in terms of operation and organization but also appearance—actors.

Enforcement

Globalization is also reducing reliance on state-centered mechanisms for enforcing human rights. In the future, non-state or supra-state bodies are likely to assume a more prominent role in human rights enforcement. In particular, various societal organs such as the media, NGOs, consumers, investors, shareholders, public-spirited social activists, and labour unions would seek to ensure compliance with human rights obligations.

In view of the above analysis, three preliminary conclusions could be offered. First, though globalization as a concept is not inherently anti or pro-human rights, the same cannot be said about globalization as a process. In view of the nature and motive of the actors involved, the process of globalization is widely seen more as a foe than a friend of the human rights of *all*. Second, as globalization offers opportunities both for promotion and abridgment of human rights, at the national level as well as internationally, at a given point of time the position of globalization vis-à-vis human rights will ultimately depend on how effectively human

[85] Donald C Dowling, Jr., 'The Multinational's Manifesto on Sweatshops, Trade/Labour Linkage, and Codes of Conduct' *Tulsa Journal of Comparative & International Law* 8 (2000) 27, 52.

[86] To me one of the most significant differences, in an era of neo-colonization, is that states and MNCs seem to have exchanged their places: from the time of British East India Company acting as the agent of a colonial state, now many states are more than willing to act as agents of MNCs.

[87] There is a difference not only in the nature of human rights violated but also in the *modus operandi* of such violations and the places where such violation are occurring. See Ratner, supra n. 51, 443; Baxi, supra n. 4, xviiii and also at 155.

rights activists are able to utilize those opportunities qua other competing actors. Third, it is highly unlikely that any one interest-constituency will have a long lasting monopoly over the process of globalization so as to derive more benefits out of it. Though, to date it is primarily driven by something else than the human rights of *all*, especially of the poor-oppressed-illiterate masses, this may change in future.

HUMAN RIGHTS REALIZATION IN AN ERA OF GLOBALIZATION: THE INDIAN EXPERIENCE

In this section, I try to first locate the position of the three wings of Indian government vis-à-vis human rights in an era of globalization and then take readers on a quick tour of some of the emerging human rights themes.

Stating the Position of the Indian State

The position and role of states in the process of globalization is critical to the state of human rights realization. But their position/role is complex and full of difficult choices.[88] For example, though the realization of both globalization and human rights demands states' intervention, there is no consensus on when and to what extent states should intervene. In fact, there is a divergence on what globalization proponents/actors and human rights activists would like states to regulate or deregulate. Critics even argue that states might not be serious *on their own* to act and enforce human rights obligations against corporations.[89] How has the Indian state fared on this front? Below is a brief account of this.

Executive-Legislature

Since the time the government launched what is now known as the new economic policy (NEP) in the early 1990s, there has been a debate not only about the constitutionality and propriety of the policy but also about its effects.[90] Although it is reasonable to suggest that liberalization was

[88] Pearce and Tombs, supra n. 46, 284–6.

[89] 'States will do as little as possible to enforce health and safety laws. They will pass them only when forced to do so by public crises or union agitation, strengthen them reluctantly, weaken them whenever possible, and enforce them in a manner calculated not to seriously impede profitability.' Snider, as quoted by Pearce and Tombs, supra n. 46, 286.

[90] See, for example, Parmanand Singh (ed.), *Legal Dimensions of Market Economy*, Faculty of Law, University of Delhi, New Delhi (1997); Mahesh V. Joshi, *Economic*

the need of the hour, it seems that the government did not consistently ensure that the realization of human rights, especially of the poor populace, remained an important variable at the time of law-making or policy decision-taking. Some examples will help in making it clearer. First, the government did not control adequately the *direction* of foreign investment, and probably made bad policy decisions in terms of investment prioritization.[91] This resulted, for example, in a situation where people in villages have access to Pepsi/Coca-Cola but not to safe drinking water, adequate food, health care, electricity, roads, or schools.[92] Second, it also seems that the amendments proposed by the government in laws related to foreign investment, trade union, contract labour, factories, industrial dispute, and monopolistic practices, are having a negative impact on human rights, especially of labourers and women workers.[93]

Third, the government's decision to bypass the authority of parliament to undertake international obligations on important issues is another area of great concern, as it directly hits at the roots of parliamentary democracy.[94] Fourth, the government has shown undue leniency, and thus sent a wrong signal to foreign corporations regarding their human rights responsibility, by not vigorously pursuing the extradition of Warren Anderson, the ex-CEO of Union Carbide Corporation, against whom criminal proceedings are pending before a court in relation to the Bhopal gas tragedy.[95] Fifth, when it was alleged by an NGO that the soft drinks manufactured by Pepsi and Coca-Cola contained toxic pesticides, the government swiftly banned their supply/sale within the parliament

---

Reforms in India: A Critical Evaluation, APH Publishing, New Delhi (1997); Terence J. Byres (ed.), *The State, Development Planning and Liberalization in India*, Oxford University Press, New Delhi (1997).

[91] See McCorquodale and Fairbrother, supra n. 24, 742–50.

[92] See the cover story, 'Is India Shining?', *Frontline*, Vol. 21, Issue 5 (28 February–12 March 2004), http://www.frontlineonnet.com/fl2105/fl210500.htm.

[93] See generally Usha Ramanathan, 'Business and Human Rights—The India Paper', IELRC Working Paper 2001–2, http://www.ielrc.org/content/w0102.pdf (visited 30 March 2004).

[94] Though the constitution empowers the executive to enter into international treaties, it seems that this provision has been improperly utilized by various governments, *supra* n. 67.

[95] See, for example, the opinion of the Attorney General on the extradition of Anderson, http://www.bhopal.com/opinion.htm (visited 6 January 2003). In fact, the government had made an application before the court to dilute the charge to 'death by rash or negligent act' from 'culpable homicide not amounting to murder'. The court, however, rejected this request.

but left the health of ordinary consumers at the mercy of corporate (mis)information.[96]

This is, however, not to suggest that the government has been totally oblivious to the impact of globalization on its constitutional obligation of realizing human rights of all and of the impoverished especially. For example, it launched a social security scheme for the unorganized sector; amended the constitution to provide for free and compulsory primary education;[97] released a charter on 'corporate responsibility for environmental protection'; made environmental clearance mandatory for new big urban projects; and recently proposed an Employment Guarantee Scheme to provide at least 100 days of employment to every household in rural India.[98]

Judiciary

The Indian judiciary, by and large, has been active and vigilant in safeguarding human rights, more so since the late 1970s. In fact, well before the adoption of NEP, the supreme court could foresee the unfolding future event, that is, the impact of liberalization/privatization on fundamental rights.[99] At a more general level, the judiciary is aware of the impact of globalization on constitution and constitutionalism, perceives itself as an institution which has to play a key role in the emerging scenario, and argues for an economic interpretation of the constitution.[100] Courts have been approached constantly for redressing a specific human rights violation or offering a principled policy guideline—from the constitutionality of the policy of privatization[101] and disinvestment[102] to the defacing of rocks by painting of advertisements;[103] from pollution of

[96] Later on, a Joint Parliamentary Committee investigated the issue and suggested framing appropriate guidelines in this regard.

[97] Article 21A, inserted by the Constitution (86th Amendment) Act 2002. See also the newly inserted Article 51A(k), which imposes a fundamental duty on parents/guardians to offer education opportunities to their children/wards, and a change in the ambit of Article 45.

[98] To implement this scheme, a Bill has been introduced in the parliament in December 2004.

[99] See, for example, M.C. Mehta v. Union of India AIR 1987 SC 1086.

[100] State of Punjab v. Devans Modern Breweries Ltd. [2003] 4 LRI 647, paras 320–47.

[101] Delhi Science Forum v. Union of India (1996) 2 SCC 405.

[102] Balco Employees Union v. Union of India AIR 2001 SC 350; Centre for Public Interest Litigation v. Union of India AIR 2003 SC 3277.

[103] 'SC's 5-crore Message: You cannot Get Away', http://www.indianexpress.com/full_story.php?content_id=10061 (visited 1 April 2004).

rivers[104] to the relocation of industries out of Delhi;[105] from starvation deaths[106] to the use of environment-friendly fuel in buses in Delhi;[107] from the extent of right to strike and *bandh*[108] to the right to health[109] and education;[110] from the employment of children in hazardous industries[111] to female foeticide/infanticide through modern technology.[112] In most of the cases, the judiciary has not disappointed the victims of human rights violations and human rights activists. Moreover, the supreme court has also tried to establish a balance between the need for development and the protection of human rights.[113] Though in the majority of such cases the court could reach an equilibrium, doubts could be raised about some cases. For example, serious questions are raised about a decision wherein the apex court held, in unequivocal terms, that there is no fundamental, legal, or moral right to go on strike.[114] It is also suggested that on occasions even the supreme court has been influenced by liberalization and/or business interests of corporations, that too at the cost of human rights.[115]

[104] *Almitra H. Patel* v. *Union of India* AIR 2000 SC 1256.

[105] *M.C. Mehta* v. *Union of India* (1996) 4 SCC 351.

[106] *Kishen Pattnayak* v. *State of Orissa* 1989 Supp(1) SCC 258.

[107] *M.C. Mehta* v. *Union of India* AIR 2002 SC 1696.

[108] *CPM* v. *Bharat Kumar* AIR 1998 SC 184; *T K Rangarajan* v. *State of Tamil Nadu* AIR 2003 SC 3032.

[109] *Parmanand Kataria* v. *Union of India* AIR 1989 SC 2039; *Paschim Banga Khet Mzdoor Samity* v. *State of West Bengal* (1996) 4 SCC 37; *Kirloskar Brothers Ltd.* v. *ESIC* (1996) 2 SCC 682; *Air India Statutory Corporation* v. *United Labour Union* (1997) 9 SCC 377.

[110] *Mohini Jain* v. *State of Karnataka* (1992) 3 SCC 666; *Unni Krishnan* v. *State of Andhra Pradesh* (1993) 1 SCC 645.

[111] *M.C. Mehta* v. *State of Tamil Nadu* AIR 1997 SC 699.

[112] *CEHAT* v. *Union of India* AIR 2001 SC 2007; *CEHAT* v. *Union of India* AIR 2003 SC 3309.

[113] *Vellore Citizens Welfare Forum* v. *Union of India* AIR 1996 SC 2715; *Narmada Bachao Andolan* v. *Union of India* (2000) 10 SCC 664; *AP Pollution Control Board-II* v. *Prof. M.V. Nayudu* (2001) 2 SCC 62; *Goa Foundation, Goa* v. *Diksha Holdings (P) Ltd.* AIR 2001 SC 184.

[114] *T.K. Rangarajan*, supra n. 108.

[115] The Bhopal gas tragedy settlement is a very good example of this. See Jamie Cassels, 'Multinational Corporations and Catastrophic Law' *Cumberland Law Review* 31 (2000/2001) 311, 330. See also Parmanand Singh, 'State, Market and Economic Reforms' in Singh, supra n. 90, 23, 30–1. The following observation of the supreme court in *Devans Modern Breweries* also reflects its support to liberalization and sceptic attitude towards socialist policies: '*Socialism* might have been a catchword from our history. It *may be present in the Preamble of our Constitution. However, due to the liberalization*

In sum, it could be argued that though the different branches of the government have been conscious of their responsibility towards human rights realization under the constitution, their role leaves much to be desired. On several occasions, they seems to have been swayed too much by the argument that economic prosperity will automatically lead to better realization of human rights at all levels, and in that process have fallen into the trap of international financial institutions and global corporate actors. It could, however, be said that this is not something unique about the Indian state; the human rights policies of other states too have been not only inconsistent but also based on economic interests and influenced by corporate actors.[116] This is though no justification for the unsatisfactory performance of the Indian state.

A Snapshot of Emerging Human Rights Themes

Article 12: Who is Subject to Fundamental (Human) Rights Now?

The efficacy of any human rights regime depends, inter alia, upon two interdependent variables: *what* is protected and *against whom*. In the Indian context, though the judiciary has been alive to the changing needs and extended the already wide ambit of both *what* (Parts III and IV)[117] and *against whom* (Article 12),[118] real doubts still persist as to whether the definition of 'state' under Article 12 as well as its judicial extension can bear the strains put by the modern mantras of liberlization, disinvestment and free market economy.[119] The test of 'instrumentality or agency' of

---

policy adopted by the Central Government from the early nineties, this view that the Indian society is essentially wedded to socialism is definitely withering away.' (Emphasis added). *Devans Modern Breweries*, supra n. 100, para 329.

[116] Hertz, supra n. 7, 71–7 and also at 93–101; Peet, supra n. 21, 15.

[117] Singh, *Shukla's Constitution of India*, supra n. 27, 164–81. See also M.P. Jain, 'The Supreme Court and Fundamental Rights' in S.K. Verma and Kusum (eds), *Fifty Years of the Supreme Court of India—Its Grasp and Reach*, Oxford University Press, New Delhi (2000), 1; S.P. Sathe, *Judicial Activism in India—Transgressing Borders and Enforcing Limits*, Oxford University Press, New Delhi (2002).

[118] *Electricity Board, Rajasthan v. Mohan Lal* (1967) 3 SCR 377; *Sukhdev Singh v. Bhagtram* (1971) 3 SCR 619; *R D Shetty v. International Airport Authority* AIR 1979 SC 1628; *Som Prakash Rekhi v. Union of India* AIR 1981 SC 212; *Ajay Hasia v. Khalid Mujib* AIR 1981 SC 487; *Pradeep Kumar Biswas v. Indian Institute of Chemical Bioiogy* (2002) 5 SCC 111.

[119] Surya Deva, 'Concept of "State" in the Era of Liberalization and Withering State—An Analysis' in D.S. Prakasa Rao (ed.), *Constitutional Jurisprudence and*

state faced its first major challenge in 1986 in the form of *M.C Mehta* v. *Union of India*.[120] Although the court made some bold observations, it did not answer the question whether Shriram, a private company manufacturing fertilizers and chemicals, could be considered an 'authority' for the purpose of Article 12.

In fact, this case gave a fair indication of what was in store for the coming years. Now it seems that the test of 'instrumentality or agency' either does not deliver desirable results,[121] or the supreme court itself finds it difficult to apply the test in view of continuous withdrawal of state from public services. The court has enforced fundamental rights against private individuals,[122] granted relief to the petitioner without going into the question whether the violator of the fundamental right was the state,[123] or made general observations that even private corporate actors would be subject to the mandate of both fundamental rights and directive principles.[124] This approach, though defensible jurisprudentially, has not received unqualified praise from all quarters.[125] Moreover, it does not resolve the real question, namely, what difference the expansive interpretation of 'what' will make in view of ever narrowing 'against whom'. For example, the affirmative action provisions[126] are non-existent as far as private corporations are concerned. Similarly, how effective will the protection offered by Article 19(1)(c) be against a private corporation that seeks an undertaking for not forming/joining association or unions

---

Environmental Justice: A Festschrift Volume in the Honour of Professor A. Lakshminath, Pratyusha Publishing Ltd., Visakhapatnam (2002), 175.

[120] AIR 1987 SC 1086.

[121] See, for example, *Zee Telefilms Ltd.* v. *Union of India* [Writ Petition (Civil) 541 of 2004, decided on 2 February 2005].

[122] See, for example, *Bodhisattwa Gautam* v. *Subra Chakraborty* AIR 1996 SC 922; *Vishaka* v. *State of Rajasthan* AIR 1997 SC 3011; *Apparel Export Promotion Council* v. *A.K. Chopra* AIR 1999 SC 625.

[123] See, for example, *Bodhisattwa Gautam*, *Id.*; *'X'* v. *'Z' Hospital* (1998) 8 SCC 296; *M.C. Mehta* v. *Kamal Nath* (2000) 6 SCC 213.

[124] *Kirloskar Brothers Ltd.* v. *ESIC* (1996) 2 SCC 682, 688. Again, in *Air India Statutory Corporation* v. *United Labour Union* (1997) 9 SCC 377 the court observed at 409: 'It is axiomatic, whether or not industry is controlled by Government or public corporations...or private agents, juristic persons, their constitution, control and working would also be subject to the same constitutional limitations in the trinity, viz., Preamble, Fundamental Rights and the directive principles.'

[125] See, for example, Arun Shourie, *Courts and their Judgments—Premises, Perquisites, Consequences*, Rupa & Co., New Delhi (2001), 68.

[126] Articles 15(4) and 16(4)/(4A)/(4B).

as part of the contract? Thus, in my view the shrinking territory of 'against whom' poses a major challenge for the realization of human rights in India, and everywhere generally, in an era of globalization.[127]

Liberalization Policies and Directive Principles

Given that the policies promoting liberalization per se, including privatization and disinvestment, have been declared to be constitutional and are here to stay,[128] it needs to be considered how they impact on the constitutional obligation of the Indian state to promote human rights—whether embodied as directive principles, or in the form of 'converted fundamental rights'.[129] For example, can the Indian government still establish a just social order by minimizing/eliminating inequalities,[130] ensure that there is no concentration of wealth or means of production,[131] secure maternity benefits in private sector,[132] or protect environment and wild life?[133] The same could be said regarding the plethora of rights created by the judiciary by importing directive principles into fundamental rights. For example, it is not clear how the government plan to ensure that various traits of globalization do not unreasonably affect, for example, the right to livelihood[134] or the right to shelter.[135]

Right to Information

The flow of information to and from the consumers of democracy is vital because it enables participation in decision making, ensures transparency in governance, helps in fighting injustice, and facilitates

[127] '[I]f the private sector is continued to be treated as immune from constitutional restraints, it would virtually amount to leaving the entire corporate sector as a protected island where constitutional writs cannot run.' Anil K. Rai, *Concept of State and Fundamental Rights*, Deep and Deep Publications, New Delhi (1996), 155.

[128] Supra n. 101 and 102. See also M.P. Singh, 'Constitutionality of Market Economy' in Singh, supra n. 90, 1.

[129] The term 'converted fundamental rights' refers to the rights evolved by reading directive principles into fundamental rights.

[130] Article 38.

[131] Article 39. See also Parmanand Singh, supra n. 115, 28–9.

[132] Article 42.

[133] Article 48A. See also Ashish Kothari, 'Environment and the New Economic Policies: 1991–6' in Singh, supra n. 90, 57.

[134] *Olga Tellis* v. *Bombay Municipal Corporation* AIR 1886 SC 180; *DTC* v. *DTC Mazdoor Congress* AIR 1991 SC 101.

[135] *Gauri Shankar* v. *Union of India* (1994) 6 SCC 349; *Shiv Sagar Tiwari* v. *Union of India* (1997) 1 SCC 444.

the realization of other human rights.[136] The globalization of various technologies has enabled the flow of information speedily and in an inexpensive way, and has thus, contributed to the protection of human rights. However, despite these positives, we still need to guard against monopolization and/or manipulation of information, and also ensure that a wider population becomes part of the 'information society'.[137]

Right to Education and the Question of Quality/Affordability

How is globalization going to affect access to a reasonable quality of education—both primary and higher—which works as a ladder to the realization of other human rights? No doubt the Constitution *now* mandates the state 'to provide free and compulsory education to all children between the age of six to fourteen years,'[138] but its manner is still to be determined by a law made by the state. In view of the fact that the government is not spending a significant part of its GDP on primary education,[139] it is really a matter of conjecture how one of the Millennium Development Goals—achieving universal primary education by 2015—is going to be realized. Similarly, though 'excellence' in professional education has a role to play in economic development of the country,[140] it is most likely that students belonging to a selected class only will be able to participate in such a development process, given that private professional institutions are free to fix their fees.[141] In sum, although globalization has opened/widened the vista of getting higher education (even from abroad), it has also darkened an already gloomy picture of primary education of, say, girls in remote villages. After all, it does not

[136] In order to strengthen the 'right' to information, the government has introduced the Right to Information Bill 2004 to replace the existing Freedom of Information Act 2002. The Bill, however, suffers from several lacuna.

[137] To overcome the 'digital divide', the Indian government has accepted the report of the 'Working Group on Information Technology (IT) for Masses' and has launched the National IT Mission to oversee the implementation of this report: http://www.mit.gov.in/E-rural/index.asp; http://www.mit.gov.in/E-rural/nitm.asp (visited 4 August 2004).

[138] Supra n. 97.

[139] See data available at http://www.education.nic.in/htmlweb/edusta.htm (visited 10 April 2004). Notably, the government in 2004 imposed a 2 per cent education cess on all taxes to generate extra resources.

[140] *Islamic Academy of Education* v. *State of Karnataka* [2003] 3 LRI 483, para 195.

[141] Ibid., paras 6 and 59; *TMA Pai Foundation* v. *State of Karnataka* (2002) 8 SCC 481. It is important to notice that even government-aided institutions such as IIMs had opposed the government's move to reduce the applicable fees.

look like that many corporations will come forward to spend, and *not invest*, on providing quality primary education.

Yes to Commercial Speech, But No to Strikes/Bandhs/Demonstrations

It is not difficult to identify how globalization is moulding the freedom of speech and expression, taken in its widest forms, in India. As commerce and advertising became more and more important, the supreme court considered it desirable to recognize, by overruling its earlier stand, commercial speech as a fundamental right under Article 19(1)(*a*).[142] On the other hand, as strikes, *bandhs* and demonstrations seem to disrupt, among other things, business activities, the court has not accepted them as part of freedom of speech and expression.[143] These judgments, which directly hit at people's movements which resist globalization and its forces, not only seek to deny a rightful place to strikes-*bandhs*-demonstrations in responsible governance but also fail to take into account those situations when doing so may be part of a fundamental constitutional duty.[144]

Right to Health, (Safe Drinking) Water and Clean Environment

Privatization coupled with gradual retreat of state from public services is also making it harder for the common people to have access to heath care or other basic needs such as (safe drinking) water. As the government run health facilities are deteriorating, private health centres are mushrooming by exploiting poor people's *poor* health.[145] The current scenario is also resulting in 'aqua robbery' by corporations[146] and thus, denying

---

[142] *Tata Press Ltd.* v. *MTNL* AIR 1995 SC 2438, overruling *Hamdard Dawakhana* v. *Union of India* AIR 1960 SC 554.

[143] Supra n. 722. See also a recent ruling of the Calcutta High Court prohibiting processions and rallies on weekdays. 'Muzzling Democratic Expression', *The Hindu* (8 October 2003), http://www.thehindu.com/2003/10/08/stories/2003100802191000.htm.

[144] Article 51A, for example, puts every citizen under a duty 'to cherish and follow the noble ideals which inspired our national struggle for freedom', and 'to protect and improve the natural environment.' It can be reasonably argued that the citizens will only be performing their duties if they take resort to strikes-*bandhs*-demonstrations to oppose government policies which run counter to the above objectives.

[145] Siddharth Narrain, 'Health, for a Price', *Frontline*, Vol. 21, Issue 5, (28 February–12 March 2004), http://www.frontlineonnet.com/fl2105/stories/20040312008112900.htm.

[146] Justice V.R. Krishna Iyer, 'The Right to Water', *The Hindu* (28 January 2004), http://www.thehindu.com/2004/01/28/stories/2004012802471000.htm.

the local population a basic natural right such as access to water—both for drinking and irrigation purposes. Besides, globalization has not only created more opportunities for environmental pollution but also enabled the export of hazardous waste and contaminated materials to developing countries, including India,[147] which are least capable both to say no to such export and contain the harms involved.

Tribal Rights and Sustainable Development

The Indian constitution contains ample provisions to protect the special interests of tribal population.[148] However, there are real fears that their concerns might not get adequate attention under free market economy. Arguably, the policies of general or accumulative development impinge upon the vital rights of tribal people. Displacement of tribal population and lack of adequate rehabilitation due to the construction of large dams, resulting in severance of their ties with their past is a very good example of this.[149] Also, globalization policies, by promoting a culture of consumerism and changing people's life style/habits, are having an adverse effect on sustainable development too.

'MARKETING' HUMAN RIGHTS UNDER GLOBALIZATION

As it looks doubtful, on the basis of the above analysis, if market and its principles alone can ensure the protection of human rights, there is an acute need to look for new strategies which could ensure a successful *marketing* of human rights in an era of globalization.[150] Capitalist-led globalization is, undoubtedly, in need of reforms[151]—reforms which are

---

[147] Supra n. 48.

[148] Part X read with Schedules V and VI; and Articles 15(4), 16(4)/(4A)/(4B), 46, 275, 330, 332, 338A, 339, 342, 371A–371D, and 371G. The Indian government though has not yet ratified the ILO Convention (No. 169) Concerning Indigenous and Tribal Peoples in Independent Countries, 1989.

[149] See Arundhati Roy, 'The Greater Common Good', *Frontline*, Vol. 16, Issue 11 (22 May–4 June 1999), http://www.frontlineonnet.com/fl1611/16110040.htm;]; Mies & Shiva, supra n. 72, 98–107; Suprio Dasgupta, 'Tribal Rights in Free Market Economy' in Singh, supra n. 90, 113.

[150] Baxi poses the question thus: 'Is the contemporary human rights mode of resistance to globalization historically adequate to retrieve the human rights *movement* from the market?' Baxi, supra n. 4, 166 [Emphasis in original].

[151] Stiglitz argues: 'Globalization today is not working for many of the world's poor. It is not working for much of the environment. It is not working for the stability of the global economy.' Stiglitz, supra n. 5, 214. But the issue, for Stiglitz, is not to backtrack on globalization but to ensure that we can make it work. Ibid., 222.

not superficial but fundamental and radical.[152] But how do we go about it? Stiglitz, for example, suggests a 'global collective action' on the part of international institutions on concerned issues.[153] But again the real issue is whether these institutions are going to do it? I argue, instead, that it is those who are suffering adversely from the current process of globalization that will have more incentives to act. However, since such sufferers' *potential to act* is generally dormant,[154] they will require impetus from others—in identifying the real issues, locating actors/their policies responsible for the harmful trend, developing strategies to challenge the status quo, and offering alternatives. Despite their respective short-comings and limitations, I see media, NGOs, human rights activists, socially conscious consumers/investors, and public-spirited lawyers/academicians as the potential catalysts.[155]

I briefly mention three strategies and three guiding principles that might help in ensuring that human rights are neither forgotten nor hijacked by market forces. The three strategies are: question the *inhuman* present; institutionalize resistance (both within and outside the boundaries of a given legal system); and develop advocacy for alternatives. First of all, the existing inhuman decisions/policies, whether domestic, regional, or international, need to be questioned in an assertive manner. Second, it is important to institutionalize the current global but scattered resistance to the process of globalization; commonalities amongst various socio-economic movements must be found and networked. Finally, equally significant is to develop advocacy groups who could offer alternatives to the 'existing', which is often taken as something inevitable/irreversible, to the decision-makers.

These three strategies should try to promote and be guided, inter alia, by the following principles: sustainable development *as a way of life*; the duty of humanity-fraternity; and a corporate culture of human rights. First, there is an acute necessity to promote sustainable development as a way of life—for everyone, at all times, everywhere. As 'infinite growth with a finite pool of resources is impossible',[156] we also need to re-examine

[152] Welford, *Environmental Strategy*, supra n. 74, 1–3.

[153] Stiglitz, supra n. 5, 222–4. He also moots for transparency and effective participation in governance of the international institutions. Ibid., 24–9. See also Dobbin, supra n. 8, 280–308.

[154] There could be several reasons for such a dormant state, e.g., lack of information; mystification of real issues/realties; non-availability of resources.

[155] See Braithwaite and Drahos, supra n. 4, 623–8; Hertz, supra n. 7, 114–23, 126–30, 173–82, 202–4; McCorquodale, supra n. 51, 109–13.

[156] Welford, *Hijacking Environmentalism*, supra n. 12, x.

how we define growth.[157] Growth devoid of, or at the cost of human rights (even of the ignored few) should definitely not be an acceptable option. Second, it should be considered how the duty of humanity-fraternity, if inculcated among the people, could support the realization of human rights. Last but not least, efforts must be made to develop and promote a corporate culture of human rights. But before that the 'dominant corporate culture which believes that natural resources are there for taking and that environmental and social problems will be resolved through growth, scientific advancement, technology transfer..., free trade and the odd charitable hand-out'[158] must be changed.

WHETHER ANOTHER WORLD IS POSSIBLE?

In this chapter, I have tried to demonstrate, with reference to the Indian experience, that globalization had (and could have) a mixed impact on the realization of human rights. The negative effects, however, seem to arise and be felt more in developing and under-developed countries. This is understandable as well as explainable. Although globalization as a 'concept' is neither pro nor anti-human rights, the same cannot be said about globalization as a 'process'. It would be pretentious, in my view, to argue that globalization as a *process* retains its neutrality after it interacts with actors—from human to non-human and inhuman—most of which pursue the agenda of the west and not of the 'rest'.

However, as the fault, in my view, does not lie in globalization but in the *way* it is run, it is important for the human rights activists to bear in mind that the resistance is directed towards the 'way' and not towards globalization per se.[159] Globalization could, in fact, help in the realization of human rights. Nevertheless, what is needed is that the process of globalization is harnessed to suit human rights interests. Needless to emphasize, the primary onus is on the architects/actors of globalization, which presented it as a panacea for everything and for everyone, that globalization not only contributes to the realization of human rights but also *seems* to do so.

---

[157] For example, an aggregate growth does not truly reflect an improvement in the lives of *all* the people. Stiglitz, supra n. 5, 79; Kinley, 'Friends, Foes or family', supra n. 24, 255; Petras and Veltmeyer, supra n. 3, 122–7.

[158] Welford, 'Introduction', supra n. 39, 7.

[159] In fact, it is argued that 'many of the social movements that appear to resist globalization actually resist the *kind* of globalization'. Peet, supra n. 21, 3.

It is also likely that in time to come, the language of human rights is going to be invoked more frequently to fight *what* of globalization is perceived as unfair and unjust.[160] At the same time, global actors will also try to mould human rights so as to subserve their economic interests. This will happen because of the power and status acquired by human rights in relatively recent times.[161] The success of such competing attempts, however, would depend upon the seriousness/vigour shown by the involved participants, and the nature of strategies employed by them to pursue their respective agenda.

In sum, another world, in which the human rights of *all*—even of the poor forgotten spectators of globalization—though difficult to achieve, is possible.[162] One way of ensuring this could be to be guided by the Gandhian talisman while taking decisions which operationalize globalization: 'Whenever you are in doubt, or when the self becomes too much with you, apply the following test. Recall the face of the poorest and the weakest [woman] whom you may have seen, and ask yourself, if the step you contemplate is going to be of any use to [her]. Will [she] gain anything by it? Will it restore [her] a control over [her] own life and destiny? In other words, will it lead to *swaraj* for the hungry and spiritually starving millions?'[163] In my view, only after the least advantaged taste the promised benefits, can one legitimately claim that globalization is an 'unambiguously' good thing, not for the select few but for everyone.

---

[160] Goodhart argues that 'universal human rights are the best tools available for effective political resistance to and reform of globalization.' Goodhart, supra n. 7, 963.

[161] 'Ours is the age of rights. Human rights is the idea of our time, the only political-moral idea that has received universal acceptance.' Louis Henkin, *The Age of Rights*, Columbia University Press, New York (1990), at ix. Compare, David Kennedy, 'The International Human Rights Movement: Part of the Problem?' *Harvard Human Rights Journal* 15 (2002) 99.

[162] See Fisher and Ponniah, supra n. 2.

[163] Mahatma Gandhi, *Last Phase*, Vol. II (1958), at 65, as quoted at http://www.mkgandhi.org/gquots1.htm (visited 13 April 2004).

11

The Global Dialogue Among Courts

Social Rights Jurisprudence of the Supreme Court of India from a Comparative Perspective

ARUN THIRUVENGADAM*

Courts within countries in the British Commonwealth have a long tradition of referring to each other's jurisprudence. In recent years, this trend has spread rapidly to other parts of the world, including civil law countries, making it a phenomenon that is truly global in nature. Another significant departure from the earlier trend is that the current exchange of judicial reasoning and doctrines appears to be more of a reciprocal process, when compared to the one-way traffic that character- ized the practice during colonial times.

There is a growing body of literature which describes and analyses this phenomenon in various jurisdictions.[1] Several authors have focused

* I am grateful to Steven Budlender and Vikram Raghavan for their thorough re- view of earlier versions of this essay. Thanks also to Mayura Baweja, Jayanth Krishnan, and Justice Richard Goldstone for their comments, and to C. Raj Kumar for his diligence as an editor. None of them is, however, responsible for any errors of fact or analysis. This article reflects the law as of May 2004, and does not purport to cover developments since that date.

[1] See generally, Pradyumna K. Tripathi, 'Foreign Precedents and Constitutional Law', 57 COLUM. L. REV. 319 (1957) (focusing on how US judicial precedents are received by courts in Australia, Canada, India, and Israel); Anne-Marie Slaughter, 'A Typology of Transjudicial Communication', 29 U. RICHMOND L. REV. 99 (1994) (describing 'transjudicial communication' generally between nations and specifically between the European Court of Justice and the European Court of Human Rights and individual nations in Europe); Mark Tushnet, 'The Possibilities of Constitutional Law', 108 YALE. L.J. 1225 (1999) (analysing the issue at a theoretical level and focusing on specific instances of borrowing of constitutional doctrine); Sujit

on how the Supreme Court of India has been an important player in this exchange of judicial doctrines.[2] Justice Claire L'Heureux-Dube of the Supreme Court of Canada, while describing several instances where courts in India, Canada, South Africa, and various other countries have borrowed from each other in adjudicating upon human rights issues, has called the phenomenon 'a worldwide dialogue'.[3] Similarly, Justice Michael Kirby of the High Court of Australia has enumerated instances of trans-judicial influence between courts in Australia and India.[4] Raju Ramachandran

Choudhry, 'Globalization in Search of Justification: Toward a Theory of Comparative Constitutional Interpretation', 74 IND. L.J. 819 (1999) (describing, among others, the use of Canadian constitutional jurisprudence by the new South African constitutional court); Christopher McCrudden, 'A Common Law of Human Rights: Transnational Judicial Conversations on Constitutional Rights', 20 OXFORD J. LEG. STUD. 499 (2000) (surveying the borrowing of constitutional and human rights doctrines across the commonwealth and globally); *Symposium*, 1 INT'L J. CONST. L. 181 (2003) (describing and analysing the borrowing of constitutional doctrines and reasoning in Japan, South Africa, Argentina, and the US); Sarah K. Harding, 'Comparative Reasoning and Judicial Review', 28 YALE J. INT'L L. 409 (2003) (focusing on judicial borrowings between Canada and the US); Vicki C. Jackson, 'Comparative Constitutional Federalism and Transnational Judicial Discourse', 2 INT'L J. CONST. L. 91 (2004) (analysing the possibility of borrowing of constitutional doctrines relating to federalism between Canada, the US, and Germany).

[2] For an elaborate analysis of the use of foreign precedents by the Indian Supreme Court from its inception until the mid-1980s, see *Durga Das Basu, Comparative Constitutional Law* 9–101, New Delhi: Prentice Hall (1984) (describing how, after an initial aversion to foreign precedents, the supreme court came around to citing and relying on a host of cases from the US, Australia, Canada and a number of other jurisdictions). The impact of US constitutional precedents on the development of Indian constitutional law has been well documented. It has also been noted that the Public Interest Litigation (PIL) movement developed by the Supreme Court of India, though different in many ways, was essentially inspired by the American public interest law movement in the 1960s, and had the same 'basic philosophy and content'. S.K. Agarwala, *Public Interest Litigation in India: A Critique* 8, Bombay: N.N. Tripathi (1987) (refuting the argument, put forth by Justice Bhagwati and Upendra Baxi, that the Indian PIL movement was completely distinguishable from its American counterpart).

[3] Claire L'Heureux-Dube, 'Human Rights: A Worldwide Dialogue', in *Supreme but not Infallible* 214 (B.N. Kirpal et. al., eds) (2000). This is a revised version of an earlier, influential and oft-cited article, 'The Importance of Dialogue: Globalization and the International impact of the Rehnquist Court', 34 TULSA L.J. 15 (1998) (arguing that the Rehnquist Court has had less global influence than the Warren and Burger courts because it does not engage in trans-judicial dialogue with the major courts of the world).

[4] Michael J. Kirby, 'The Supreme Court of India and Australian Law', in *Supreme but not Infallible* 66 (B.N. Kirpal et al., eds) Oxford University Press, New Delhi (2000).

has documented how the doctrine of 'basic structure', which was evolved by the Supreme Court of India, has spread across its borders into other parts of South Asia.[5]

The phenomenon of trans-judicial influence raises many important normative and jurisprudential concerns, which are, however, not the focus of analysis here.[6] In this essay, I focus on trans-judicial influences between India and South Africa in the area of social rights.[7] Since the basis for this jurisdiction has been ascribed by courts in both countries to provisions in their respective constitutions, such an analysis must begin with a study of the relevant constitutional provisions, and the process by which they were enshrined in the two nations. The essay aims to analyse trans-judicial influences between the two courts by looking closely at the social rights jurisprudence that they have evolved over time.

In the next section of this essay, I examine the manner in which the constitutional texts of India and South Africa deal with social rights, with a view to understanding the motivations of the respective constitutional drafters. The essay then describes some prominent cases involving social rights that have been decided by the Indian Supreme Court. The following part contains an analysis of three major cases involving social rights that have arisen under the 1996 South African constitution. In the concluding section, I record a few observations about the comparative survey undertaken in the essay.

THE DEBATE OVER SOCIAL RIGHTS

The debate over whether social rights belong in a constitution, what textual forms they should take, and how they should be implemented, is

[5] Raju Ramachandran, 'The Supreme Court and the Basic Structure Doctrine', in *Supreme but not Infallible* 107, 126–8 (B.N. Kirpal *et. al.*, eds) Oxford University Press, New Delhi (2000) (describing the adoption of this doctrine by courts in Bangladesh and Pakistan, and in the constitutional text of Nepal, as well as its rejection by the apex court in Sri Lanka).

[6] These issues are the focus of my doctoral dissertation, and are extensively discussed in the literature cited in note 1.

[7] In this essay, I use the term 'social rights' to refer to those rights that protect the necessities of life or, more specifically, are considered necessary for the foundations of an adequate quality of life. These would therefore encompass, at a minimum, rights to adequate nutrition, health, housing, and education. Though the term 'social, economic and cultural rights' or the term 'welfare rights' is usually used in this discourse to cover a broad range of issues, I will use the term 'social rights' to mean these specific issues.

a long-standing one, and has generated a considerable body of literature in various jurisdictions. In this essay, I focus on the manner in which the issue was perceived and resolved by two sets of constitutional actors in India and South Africa: the framers of the respective constitutions (who decided upon the textual provisions relating to social rights) and judges of the apex courts in both jurisdictions (who interpreted and applied these provisions to actual cases). In this section, I first examine the debates in these two contexts to give an overview of the main arguments in the debate. Thereafter, I focus on the common arguments raised both in India and in South Africa, as well as other arguments available in the existing literature, to set the stage for a discussion of the case law in the two jurisdictions.

India

The Constitution of India was drafted by an indirectly elected Constituent Assembly over a period of three years, between December 1946 to December 1949.[8] It contains two separate chapters dealing with rights. Part III of the constitution, titled 'Fundamental Rights' enshrines what are broadly referred to as 'civil and political rights' or 'negative rights'.[9] Part IV of the constitution, called the 'Directive Principles of State Policy' includes what are referred to as 'socio-economic rights' or 'positive rights'.[10] Significantly for our purposes, the directive principles are prefaced by a constitutional provision (Article 37), which clearly states that

[8] For details regarding the constitution-making process in India, see generally, *Granville Austin, The Indian Constitution: Cornerstone of a Nation*, Oxford University Press, New Delhi (1966).

[9] Provisions in this part of the constitution guarantee the right to equality (Article 14), the right against discrimination on grounds of religion, race, caste, sex, or place of birth (Articles 15 and 16), the right to freedoms of speech, association, assembly, movement and location of residence, and of occupation (Article 19), the right to life and personal liberty (Article 21), the right against bonded labour, slavery, and child labour (Articles 23 and 24), and cultural and educational rights (Articles 25, 28–30).

[10] The spirit of the directive principles is captured in Article 38, which outlines the societal goal of the Republic of India when it declares that 'the State shall strive to promote the welfare of the people by securing as effectively as it may a social order in which justice, social, economic and political, shall inform all the institutions of the national life'. To achieve this societal end, the other directive principles urge the state to ensure that citizens have an adequate means of livelihood (Article 39(a)); that the operation of the economic system and the ownership and control of the material resources of the country subserve the common good (Article 39(b&c)); that the health of the workers, including children, is not abused (Article 39(d)); and

they are not justiciable, but are to be, nevertheless, 'fundamental in the governance of the country'.

The circumstances leading to the drafting of these provisions is instructive for the broader context of the essay. The Constituent Assembly was dominated by members of the Indian National Congress, which had been at the forefront of the national struggle for independence from British colonial rule. Despite this, the Assembly was considered to be representative of Indians in general, and took self-conscious steps to ensure diversity within its ranks.[11] Significantly, prior to the deliberations in the Constituent Assembly, discussions about the rights to be guaranteed by the new constitution *never distinguished between the positive and negative obligations of the state*. Both types of rights had developed historically over the period of India's struggle for independence, as a common demand, and reflected the very character of Indian politics.[12]

When the directive principles were included in the draft constitution by the Constitutional Advisor, B.N. Rau, he preferred to adopt the Irish constitutional model of distinguishing between justiciable and non-justiciable rights. B.N. Rau was convinced that the socio-economic rights were less susceptible to judicial enforcement than the civil and political rights, and preferred to include them as non-justiciable rights which would give them the force of 'moral precepts'.[13] Many members of the Constituent Assembly, including influential members such as B.R. Ambedkar and K.T. Shah, were in fact in favour of making the directive principles judicially enforceable as they feared that not doing so would make them mere 'pious wishes' and so much window dressing for the social revolution.[14]

---

that special consideration is given to pregnant women (Article 42). Other provisions seek to ensure, *inter alia,* that workers, both agricultural and industrial, have a standard of living that allows them to enjoy leisure and social and cultural opportunities (Articles 41 and 42); that the state raises the level of nutrition and the general standard of living of the people (Article 47); and that the state reforms Indian society by improving the techniques of agriculture, husbandry, cottage industry, etc. (Article 48).

[11] One major step in this regard was the appointment of B.R. Ambedkar, a representative of the 'untouchables', as the Chairman of the Drafting Committee of the Constituent Assembly.

[12] *Austin*, supra n. 8 at 52.

[13] Ibid., at 77.

[14] B.R. Ambedkar was a strong votary of including detailed socio-economic rights within the constitution. He submitted a lengthy list of fundamental rights that included traditional civil and political rights as well as provisions regarding

It appears that B.N. Rau was able to convince the other members of the Fundamental Rights Sub-committee that to follow the Irish example of making the directive principles non-justiciable would be the most prudent option. Even Ambedkar retreated to supporting the directive principles by reasoning that the political party in power would certainly have to answer for them before the electorate at the time of elections.

It is important to emphasize that the framers of the constitution wanted the directive principles to be implemented in earnest. One has to understand the context within which these provisions were framed. The Constituent Assembly was also the first parliament of the independent nation, and was already enacting a series of laws meant to improve the socio-economic conditions of the Indian people. The framers had no doubt in their minds that any government that was elected would focus primarily on the socio-economic goals enshrined in the constitution, particularly because of the consensus in this regard between all the existing political actors. However, the events which actually transpired were, as will be demonstrated, quite different from the expectations of the framers.

South Africa

The drafting of the 1996 constitution of South Africa was a long and arduous process with several unique features.[15] Because of its long experience with apartheid and the firm conviction of all parties involved

---

social and religious minorities, and a social scheme which was to come into force in ten years. His scheme provided, among other things, that all key industries should be owned and operated by the State, that all land should be nationalized, and that agriculture should be a state industry with organized plots to be formed by villagers. He suggested that insurance should be a state monopoly, and that every adult Indian should be compelled to have life insurance—an idea similar to the US Social Security system. He was supported by K.T. Shah, who believed that there must be a specified time limit within which all the directive principles must be made justiciable. *Austin*, ibid., at 78.

[15] The 'final' South African constitution of 1996 was preceded by the passing of an Interim Constitution by the South African Parliament on 22 December 1993. The text of the Interim Constitution was the product of successful negotiations between the erstwhile white South African government and the liberation movement, and was part of a two-phase transition to democracy. The Interim Constitution set the stage for the drafting of the final constitution after the first democratic elections were held in South Africa in April 1994. The Final Constitution was drafted by a participatory process, and after being approved by the Constitutional Court, was signed by President Mandela, taking effect on 4 February 1997. For literature on the

in the negotiations that South Africa had to be transformed from a racial oligarchy to a well-functioning constitutional democracy, the importance of having constitutionally protected social rights was recognized by important political actors at an early stage.[16]

As some advocates of social rights put it, a bill of rights which only protected civil and political rights would make a mockery of claims that a constitution would promote democracy and that a constitutional government would work in the interest of the impoverished, as South Africa's legacy of apartheid had resulted in severe maldistribution of wealth and resources. According to this view, by leaving out social rights, 'South Africans would be constitutionalizing only part of what it means to be a full person'.[17] By this view, such a result would '[s]ymbolically,

---

process by which the 1996 Constitution of South Africa came to be drafted, and the various stages and difficulties involved, see generally, *The Long Journey: South Africa's Quest for a Negotiated Settlement* (Steven Friedman ed., Johannesburg, Ravan Press (1993); Allister Sparks, *Tomorrow is Another Country*, Chicago, University of Chicago Press (1994); Makau wa Mutua, 'Hope and Despair for a New South Africa: The Limits of Rights Discourse', 10 HARV. HUM. RTS. J. 63 (1997); Hassan Ebrahim, *The Soul of a Nation: Constitution-Making in South Africa* 239–50, Cape Town, OUP (1998); Jeremy Sarkin, 'The Drafting of South Africa's Final Constitution From a Human Rights Perspective', 47 AM. J. COMP. L. 67 (1999); Christina Murray, 'A Constitutional Beginning: Making South Africa's Final Constitution', 23 UNIV. ARK. L.R.L. REV. 809 (2001); and D.J. Brand, 'Constitutional Reform—The South African Experience', 33 CUM. L. REV. 1 (2002–3).

[16] The African National Congress (ANC) which was the premier party in the liberation movement, and has been the party in power since 1996, has long been an advocate for guaranteeing socio-economic rights in a Bill of Rights for South Africa. This is reflected in part in the text of the Freedom charter that it adopted as far back as in 1955. In the early 1990s, the ANC's Constitutional Committee produced the Working Draft Bill of Rights which contained directly enforceable social rights. 'A Bill of Rights for a Democratic South Africa—Working Draft for Consultation', reprinted in 7 S. AFR. J. HUM RTS. 110 (1991). However, it must be emphasized that even within the ANC, there was intense debate over the form and content that social rights would take in the final document. Randal S. Jeffrey, 'Social and Economic Rights in the South African Constitution: Legal Consequences and Practical Considerations', 27 COL. J.L. & SOC. PROB. 1, 11 (1993).

[17] Craig Scott and Patrick Macklem, 'Constitutional Ropes of Sand or Justiciable Guarantees? Social Rights in a New South African Constitution' 141 U. PA. L. REV. 1, 29 (1992). See also, Nicholas Haysom, 'Constitutionalism, Majoritarian Democracy and Socio-Economic Rights', 8 S.AF. J. HUM RTS. 451, 454 (1992) (citing the ANC's view that to have a meaningful place in the hearts and minds of the people, the constitution must address the pressing needs of ordinary people, for which inclusion of social rights was necessary).

but still brutally' exclude 'those segments of society for whom autonomy means nothing without the necessities of life'.[18] Though there were some influential voices who opposed the incorporation of social rights completely,[19] the general position amongst the opponents seemed to be that social rights should be included in a manner similar to the directive principles in the Irish and Indian constitutions, and should not be made judicially enforceable.[20] In elaborating this view, Dennis Davis drew upon the earlier work of American theorists such as Robert Nozick[21] and Lon L. Fuller[22] to contend that the constitution should aim at promoting equality so that popular political participation becomes the true cornerstone of South African society. Davis argued that inclusion of justiciable social rights would place far too much power in the hands of an unaccountable judiciary, which would in turn erode 'the possibility for meaningful public participation in the shaping of the societal goal'.[23]

[18] Scott and Macklem, ibid.

[19] See for example, J.M. Didcott, 'Practical Workings of a Bill of Rights', in *A Bill of Rights for South Africa* (Johann Van Der Westhuizen and Henning Viljoen, eds) 52 (Durban, Butterworths) (1988). Judge Didcott, in rejecting the idea of including social rights in a new South African Bill of Rights, stated: 'A Bill of Rights is not a political manifesto, a political programme. Primarily, it is a protective device. It is a shield, in other words, rather than a sword. It can state, effectively and quite easily, what may not be done. It cannot stipulate, with equal ease or effectiveness, what shall be done. The reason is not only that the courts, its enforcers, lack the expertise and the infrastructure to get into the business of legislation or administration. It is also, and more tellingly, that they cannot raise the money'. Didcott, ibid., at 58. In fact, this is the classic Anglo-American position on social rights. Given the influence of British law on the South African legal system, it was perhaps to be expected that judges trained in that tradition would adopt the classic liberal western view of social rights.

[20] This is the view adopted by scholars such as Davis. Dennis Davis, 'The Case Against the Inclusion of Socio-Economic Demands in a Bill of Rights Except as Directive Principles', 8 S.Af. J. Hum Rts. 475 (1992).

[21] Davis cites the following passage from Nozick: 'The major objection to speaking of everyone's having a right to various things such as equality of opportunity, life and so on and enforcing that right, is that these rights require a substructure of things and materials and actions...No one has a right to something whose realization requires certain uses of things and activities that other people have rights and entitlements over'. Robert Nozick, *Anarchy, State & Utopia*, 238 (Oxford, Blackwell 1974).

[22] Davis cites Fuller's suggestion that the concept of legal adjudication cannot be transplanted successfully into dealing with polycentric tasks. Polycentric tasks are defined as being 'many centred, each crossing of strands is a distinct centre for distributing tensions'. Lon L. Fuller, 'The Forms and Limits of Adjudication', 92 Harv. L. Rev. 353 at 394–5 (1978).

[23] Davis, supra n. 20 at 489–90.

He further argued that by retaining social rights as directive principles, the constitution would provide the framework for meaningful political participation, and would encourage the judiciary to 'do what it does best: engage in review of legislat[ive] and executive action'.[24]

In the early 1990s, when drafts of the South African constitution were being actively considered, several detailed studies of the Indian constitutional experience with social rights were conducted by South African scholars.[25] It is clear, both from the oral and written accounts of significant actors in the constitution-making process, that the Indian constitutional experience with social rights was closely studied in South Africa, with a view to obtaining insights into the manner in which the social rights provisions of the South African constitution should be structured and formulated.

Due to intense differences of opinion both within the ANC as well as more generally within the negotiating parties, the interim constitution of 1993 did not contain any social rights (though it did contain, in Sections 32 and 30 respectively, guarantees in respect of basic education and basic services for children). However, the process of drafting the final constitution witnessed a great deal of lobbying in favour of the inclusion of social rights by individuals, interest groups and influential organizations like the Human Rights Committee.[26] As a result, the text of the 1996 constitution contains enforceable social rights.

What is striking about the thirty-two provisions which constitute the Bill of Rights in the 1996 constitution (Sections 7–39) is the non-hierarchical approach adopted towards different categories of rights. There is no classification between negative and positive rights, and section 7(2) makes it clear that *all* rights in the bill of rights are to be respected, promoted, protected, and fulfilled. Section 8, which sets out the application of the bill of rights, states that it applies to 'all law' and binds

---

[24] Ibid., at 486. Interestingly, Dennis Davis radically altered his view about the enforceability of socio-economic rights, especially after being appointed as a Judge at the High Court of Cape Town. His judgment for the Cape High Court in the *Grootboom* case, which will be analysed later, shows the extent of this transformation.

[25] An example of one such extensive study is the elaborate two-stage survey conducted by Bertus de Villiers. Bertus de Villiers, 'Directive Principles of State Policy and Fundamental Rights: The Indian Experience', 8 S. Afr. J. Hum. Rts. 29 (1992); and Bertus de Villiers, 'The Socio-Economic Consequences of Directive Principles of State Policy: Limitations on Fundamental Rights', 8 S. Afr. J. Hum. Rts. 188 (1992).

[26] Sarkin, supra n. 15 at 77.

'a natural or juristic person if, and to the extent that, it is applicable, taking into account the nature of the right and the nature of any duty imposed by the right'. By so providing, the South African constitution avoids the problems associated with the state action doctrine evolved in the US and other liberal democracies, which does not envisage private actors being bound by the provisions of the bill of rights.[27]

The specific social rights which this essay focuses on are contained in sections 26 (declaring the right to access to adequate housing), 27 (guaranteeing the right to have access to health services, food, water, and social security), and 29 (guaranteeing the right to education). Significantly, however, these rights are not absolute. A standard restrictive clause in several of these provisions is the following: 'The State must take reasonable legislative and other measures, within its available resources, to achieve the progressive realization of this right'. The effect and import of this provision will be analysed when we focus on the interpretation attributed to this clause in successive cases decided by the constitutional court.

It must however be noted, as Cass Sunstein has pointed out, that the language employed in the social rights provisions does not unambiguously delineate the institutional roles of courts and legislatures in implementing these rights.[28] Sunstein points out that a textual interpretation could well lead to an interpretation that enforcement of the social rights is reserved to non-judicial actors within 'the state', thereby rendering the position in South Africa very similar to the Indian position. However, this aspect was clarified by the constitutional court which, while certifying the final constitution, held that socio-economic rights are indeed subject to judicial enforcement, and 'are, at least to some extent, justiciable'.[29] Rejecting the contention that social rights would result in the allocation of resources by the judiciary, the court pointed out that this was true of 'many of the civil and political rights entrenched' in the constitution. The court went on to say that many of the so-called negative rights 'will give rise to similar budgetary implications without compromising their justiciability'. The court did, however, advocate a

---

[27] For a fuller description of the provisions in the Bill of Rights, see Justice Richard J. Goldstone, 'The South African Bill of Rights', 32 Tex. Int'l L.J. 459 (1997).

[28] Sunstein, *Social and Economic Rights? Lessons from South Africa*, John M. Olin Law and Economics Working Paper No. 124, 4–5, at: http://www.law. uchicago.edu/academics/publiclaw/resources/12.CRS.pdf [hereinafter, *Lessons from South Africa*].

[29] *Ex Parte* Chairperson of the Constituent Assembly, 1996 (4) SA 744 at paragraphs 77–8.

cautious approach to the implementation of social rights by concluding that at 'the very minimum, socio-economic rights can be protected
negatively from improper invasion'.[30] As Sunstein notes, this is an
exceedingly narrow use of judicial authority for overseeing social rights.[31]
However, in practice, the court has ventured beyond this cautious
approach, and as will be shown in the next section, has taken concrete
steps to aid the implementation of the social rights.

Arguments Against Incorporation of Social Rights

As noted in the preceding parts, the debates in India and South Africa
witnessed several different levels of arguments against the constitutionalization of social rights. These can be divided, broadly speaking, into two
dimensions (which are not analytically distinct, and sometimes overlap):
the legitimacy dimension and the institutional dimension.[32] The
legitimacy dimension refers to the nature, or character of social rights
and asks whether it would be legitimate to confer constitutional status
on social rights in light of their subject matter. Within this category fall
arguments which hold the constitutionalization of social rights to be
illegitimate because such rights entail the redistribution of wealth and
state intervention in market economies.[33]

The institutional dimension looks more to the nature, or character,
of the judiciary, and addresses whether the judiciary possesses the institutional capacity and competence to adjudicate social rights. Arguments
falling within this category refer not to whether it is legitimate for a
particular matter to be made the subject of judicial review, but rather to
whether a particular matter is capable of being made the subject of such
review. In general, constitutional jurisprudence in many jurisdictions

---

[30] Ibid.

[31] Sunstein, *Lessons from South Africa*, supra n. 28 at 5.

[32] I borrow the use of this distinction, and indeed much of the discussion in this
sub-section, from Scott and Macklem, supra n. 17 at 21.

[33] Friedrich A. Hayek, Law, Legislation and Liberty 112–15 (London: Routledge
and Paul) (1975); Richard Epstein, Takings: Private Property and the Power of Eminent Domain 307–12 (Cambridge: Harvard University Press) (1985). Another category of arguments within this classification expresses concerns about the legitimacy
of empowering the judiciary to overrule the popular will as expressed through legislative activity. See generally, Mark Tushnet, *Red, White and Blue: A Critical Analysis
of Constitutional Law* 70 (Cambridge: Harvard University Press) (1987); Penuell M.
Maduna, 'Judicial Review and Protection of Human Rights Under a New Constitutional Order in South Africa', 21 COLUM. HUM. RTS. L. REV. 73, 76–81 (1989).

tends to adopt the view that the judiciary is an institution that, by virtue of its nature, does not possess the capability to adequately engage in the relatively complex task of delineating the contours of social rights.[34] The argument, in its overall form, is that social rights are problematic because: they are positive rights and require governmental action; are resource-intensive and are therefore expensive to protect; are progressive and therefore require time for realization; are vague in terms of the obligations they mandate; and involve complex, polycentric, and diffuse interests in collective goods.

Breaking up this overall argument of the institutional dimension, two different sets of concerns can be identified.[35] The first is that courts are inappropriate institutions for adjudicating social rights because social rights impose positive obligations on the state which require government to act rather than refrain from acting. By contrast, classical rights are seen as negative rights requiring the state only to refrain from interfering with a pre-defined zone of individual liberty. Negative rights are therefore: cost-free; capable of being satisfied immediately; precise in the obligations they generate; and comprehensible because they involve discrete clashes of identifiable individual interests. The second type of institutional competence arguments focus on the fact that social rights suffer from a high degree of imprecision. Proponents of this view would point, for instance, to the obligation of a state to provide nutritious food to hungry people, as hopelessly vague and indeterminate. They argue that courts would be unable to translate such an abstract aspiration into

[34] These arguments focus their criticism on the ability of courts to find and receive proper information upon which to base their decisions, and upon the ability of the courts to monitor, administer, and implement the changes. They spell out the deficiencies of the judiciary in skill, education, training, and procedure, focusing on the fact that constitutionalization of social rights touches on a complex intersection of issues involving institutional design, policy choice, and contested political aspirations. See generally, Scott and Macklem, supra n. 16 at 23 (referring to the strong body of US constitutional scholarship which argues that the judiciary is ill-equipped for activism and its quasi-policymaking demands); Howard I. Kalodner and James J. Fishman, *The Limits of Justice*, Cambridge: Ballingnet Pub. Co. (1978); Kenneth C. Davis, 'Facts in Lawmaking', 80 COLUM. L. REV. 931, 942 (1980); Fuller, supra n. 25 at 393–405; Fritz W. Schapf, 'Judicial Review and the Political Question: A Functional Analysis', 75 YALE L.J. 517 (1966).

[35] The South African jurist, Etienne Mureinik, also identifies these two sets of concerns, but prefers to call them respectively, the expense argument and the indeterminacy argument. Etienne Mureinik, 'Beyond a Charter of Luxuries: Economic Rights in the Constitution', 8 S. AFR. J. HUM. RTS 464, 465–8 (1992).

enforceable orders in specific cases. As will be demonstrated, the imprecision argument is often bound up in the overall claim that social rights involve positive obligations.

While these distinctions between arguments involving legitimacy and institutional concerns on the one hand, and between distinctions within each of these groups on the other, are significant, one has to acknowledge that there are overlaps between these different strands. As Scott and Macklem note, the various different levels of arguments 'interact with one another to create a powerful web of resistance to the proposition that social rights ought to be included in judicial constitutional discourse.'[36] In a similar vein, Etienne Mureinik argues that all the objections against social rights 'seem to reduce to the same essential difficulty: that a [social] right can be realized in more than one way, and that judges lack the expertise and the accountability which would qualify them to choose among the alternatives'.[37]

The argument that negative rights do not require governmental action, and are cost-free, has effectively been refuted by several scholars, and will not be focused on in this essay.[38] In this respect, it is interesting to consider the views of Cass Sunstein, who is a prominent example of a scholar who has shifted from being an opponent to the idea of constitutionalizing social rights, to being an enthusiastic votary of the concept.[39]

[36] Scott and Macklem, supra n. 17 at 24.

[37] Mureinik, supra note 35 at 468.

[38] Scott and Macklem cite several instances of decided cases involving negative rights (due process and procedural fairness; life, liberty and security of person; the rights to privacy and family life; prisoners' rights; and equality rights) which involve extensive governmental action and allocation of resources to demolish the argument that courts, in adjudicating upon negative rights, do not face such considerations. Scott and Macklem, supra n. 17 at 48–71.

[39] For his earlier view, see Cass R. Sunstein, 'Against Positive Rights', in *Western Rights?: Post Communist Application* 225 at 229, Andras Sajo (ed.) The Hague: Kluwer Law Int'l (1996) (arguing that courts 'lack the tools of a bureaucracy' and 'cannot create government programmes' thereby rendering it 'unrealistic to expect courts to enforce many positive rights'). For his revised view, see, Sunstein, 'Lessons from South Africa', supra n. 27 (contending that the approach of the South African Constitutional Court in the *Grootboom* case 'stands as a powerful rejoinder to those who have contended that socio-economic rights do not belong in a constitution'). Sunstein has pointed out elsewhere that even conventional individual rights, like the right to free speech and private property, require governmental action. In a book co-authored with Stephen Holmes, Sunstein notes that the most important of the negative rights—private property—cannot exist without a governmental apparatus, ready and able to secure people's holdings as such. Their work makes the important

In the next two sections, I seek to analyse how the apex courts in India and South Africa have, in handing down judgments in social rights cases, reacted to, and sought to overcome, these objections.

THE APPROACH OF THE SUPREME COURT OF INDIA

The Supreme Court of India began functioning soon after the adoption of India's new Constitution on 26 January 1950. It now has a substantial body of constitutional jurisprudence comprising over a half-century of decided cases, a good proportion of which deals with the broad issues under consideration in this essay. In this section, I first provide a brief historical overview of this jurisprudence. In subsequent sub-sections, I focus on the court's case law on specific social rights issues (livelihood and housing; education; and public health).

Overview of the Supreme Court's Constitutional Jurisprudence

During its initial years, the supreme court adopted a literal interpretation of constitutional provisions, leading to charges that it was excessively conservative. In case after case, it was required to balance the individual rights guaranteed under the fundamental rights against the societal interests enumerated in the directive principles. In an early case decided in 1952, the supreme court adopted an approach which it would follow for several years: it emphasized the textual wording of Article 37 to conclude that the directive principles codified in Part IV are inferior to the fundamental rights enshrined in Part III of the constitutional text.[40]

---

point that all rights, even the most conventional, have costs. See generally, Stephen Holmes and Cass R. Sunstein, The Cost of Rights, New York: W.W. Norton (1999).

[40] In the words of the court: 'The Directive Principles of State Policy, which by Article 37 are expressly made unenforceable by a court, cannot override the provisions found in Part III. ...The chapter of fundamental rights is sacrosanct and not liable to be abridged by any Legislative or Executive Act or order, except to the extent provided in the appropriate article in Part III.... *The Directive Principles have to conform to and run subsidiary to the chapter of fundamental rights.*' State of Madras v. Champakam Dorairajan AIR 1951 SC 226. (Emphasis added). For details and analysis of the rulings of the supreme court on the directive principles between 1950–73, see generally, Rajeev Dhavan, *The Supreme Court of India: A Socio-Legal Critique of its Juristic Techniques* (Bombay: N.M. Tripathi) 87–95 (1977) (detailing the weak interpretive and legal force accorded to the directive principles by the supreme court in its early years).

Reacting to this decision, P.K. Tripathi, a leading academic of the time, wrote an article criticizing this approach in 1954. His views, though initially ignored by the court, became influential in later years and are said to have partly accounted for its change in attitude.[41]

In the first few decades of its existence, however, the Indian Supreme Court continued to adopt an approach that was not favourable to the implementation of the social rights enumerated in the directive principles. This resulted in the court and the government being locked in an intense battle, the details of which are beyond the scope of this essay.[42]

In 1975, the imposition of a National Emergency by Prime Minister Indira Gandhi led to a severe assault on civil liberties and the power of the judiciary to provide redress. In holding in the *Habeas Corpus* case that preventive detention laws were immune from judicial review, the supreme court was widely perceived to have abandoned its role of guardian of the constitution.[43]

By the late-1970s, the credibility of the judiciary—as represented by the supreme court in particular—was at a considerable low, especially amongst legal scholars and the activist bar. The court, and the judiciary in general, was perceived as an elitist body, seeking to protect the interests of the privileged in society, and as being either uninterested or powerless to aid the causes of the underprivileged.

---

[41] Tripathi argued: 'that the directive principles of state policy do not constitute a set of inferior and subsidiary principles; that they are in fact, by their very origin and history, principles which define and delimit the fundamental rights of the individual; that in the case of an apparent conflict between the scope of a fundamental right of the individual on the one hand and a directive principle on the other, it should be presumed that the conflict is apparent and resoluble when the two conflicting rules are properly interpreted, and in the process of interpretation it would be proper and appropriate to remember that the directive principles of state policy embody a set of social principles that came into existence to check the wild extravagance of the fundamental rights of the individual.... [A]s time passes, our courts and our lawyers will gradually begin to appreciate the value of the directive principles and correspondingly the principles will figure more and more in forensic argument and juristic discussion, and they will exert a greater and more adequate influence on the jurisprudence of this country'. P.K. Tripathi, 'Directive Principles of State Policy: The Lawyers' Approach to them Hitherto, Parochial, Injurious and Unconstitutional', 17 Sup. Ct. J. 7–36 (1954).

[42] For details about this confrontation and the impact it had on several aspects of Indian constitutional law, see generally, *Supreme but not Infallible* (B.N. Kirpal *et. al.*, eds) Oxford University Press, New Delhi (2000).

[43] *A.D.M. Jabalpur v. Shiv Kant Shukla* AIR 1976 SC 1207.

Beginning in the late 1970s, 'spurred on by an inchoate alliance of social activists, lawyers, journalists, and academics',[44] some judges of the supreme court began entertaining a series of Public Interest Litigation (PIL) cases. As a result, the court moved away from its traditional emphasis on civil and political rights, and began focusing on social rights cases, as well as cases involving the civil and political rights of the most oppressed sections of society. There is a body of reputed scholars who believe that the forms of judicial activism exhibited in PIL cases are to be understood as the court's efforts to retrieve a degree of legitimacy after the collapse of its credibility during the emergency.[45]

The supreme court's 1978 decision in *Maneka Gandhi v. Union of India*[46] is generally regarded as having secured a vital breakthrough, which set the stage for later decisions involving the enforcement of social rights. In this case, the court held that Article 21 of the constitution, which guarantees to every person the right to life, must be read expansively. The court insisted that the traditional understanding of Article 21, which had been read as a provision guaranteeing only freedom from personal restraint, was misplaced. The right to life, according to the court, would include a variety of rights that add meaning to the right to life of an individual, and to the blossoming of her personality. In later years, the court read several of the directive principles into this expansive understanding of the right to life, and argued that to have a meaningful 'life', Indians would have to be guaranteed several of the social rights. More importantly, the court began to hold that it was the duty of the government to implement these social rights. For instance, in one case, the court held that the right to life in Article 21 also encompasses 'the bare necessities of life such as adequate nutrition, clothing and shelter

---

[44] This is how Rajeev Dhavan describes the beginning of the PIL movement. Rajeev Dhavan, 'The Republic of India: The Constitution as the Situs of Struggle: India's Constitution Fory Years On', in *Constitutional Systems in Late Twentieth Century Asia* 373, 383 (Lawrence W. Beer, ed., Seattle: University of Washington Press, 1992). For the account of one of the main actors in this movement, see Upendra Baxi, 'Taking Suffering Seriously: Social Action Litigation in the Supreme Court of India', in *Judges and the Judicial Power* 289–315 (Rajeev Dhavan *et. al.*, eds, 1985).

[45] Upendra Baxi, *The Indian Supreme Court and Politics* 122–3, 233–45, Lucknow: Eastern Book Company (1980) (explaining how the supreme court's judicial activism in the post-emergency phase was an attempt to 'bury its emergency past' and describing the steps taken in the area of rights of prisoners); S.P. Sathe, *Judicial Activism in India* (New Delhi: OUP, 2002); Jamie Cassels, 'Judicial Activism and Public Interest Litigation in India: Attempting the Impossible', 37 AM. J. COMP. L. 495, 511 (1989).

[46] AIR 1978 SC 597.

and facilities for reading, writing and expressing oneself in diverse forms'.[47] In this manner (which has been described by one South African judge as 'smuggling social and economic rights in through the back door'[48]) the supreme court has sought to override the textual hurdle of Article 37 of the constitution which specifically states that the directive principles are not judicially enforceable.

Between the late 1970s until the present day, the supreme court's decisions in PIL cases have dominated its docket, and have caused it to engage with virtually every significant issue of public life in India.[49] However, its decisions, though enjoying public support in general, have not been free from controversies. There is no doubt, however, that a quarter century after the first PIL case, the public image of the supreme court has been considerably enhanced by its efforts at tackling issues affecting ordinary Indians. Whether the court has succeeded in resolving these issues or not is, as we shall see, a very different matter.

Cases Dealing with the Right to Livelihood and Housing

One of the first major PIL cases which involved the right to livelihood and indirectly, the right to housing, was *Olga Tellis* v. *Bombay Municipal Corporation*.[50] This case was initiated by a journalist who filed a petition on behalf of several hundreds of pavement-dwellers in Bombay against whom, pursuant to a decision of the Bombay Municipal Corporation to build a freeway on the site, forcible eviction proceedings had been initiated. Drawing upon the reasoning adopted in *Maneka*, the petitioner argued that since the pavement dwellers would be deprived of their livelihood if they were evicted and deported to the rural areas they had migrated from, the eviction amounted to a deprivation of their right to life, and was therefore unconstitutional. The court partly accepted this argument and held that the expression 'life' in Article 21 would necessarily

[47] *Francis Coralie Mullin* v. *Administrator, Union Territory of Delhi*, AIR 1981 SC 746.

[48] Justice Albie Sachs, 'Social and Economic Rights: Can They Be Made Justiciable', S.M.U.L. REV. 1381 at 1384 (2000).

[49] See generally, Sangeeta Ahuja, *People, Law and Justice: A Case Book of Public Interest Litigation*, New Delhi: Orient Longman (1997). For a recent survey of the various issues tackled by the court under its PIL jurisdiction, see generally, Ashok H. Desai and S. Muralidhar, 'Public Interest Litigation: Potential and Problems', in *Supreme but not Infallible* 159–92 (B.N. Kirpal *et. al.*, eds) Oxford University Press, New Delhi (2000).

include the right to livelihood. It also held that *though the state could not be compelled to provide means of subsistence to all its citizens,* it could not deprive a citizen of the means to her livelihood. The court therefore issued an injunction halting all evictions of pavement dwellers for a period of four months. It also ordered that established communities could not be removed where they did not interfere with the public way unless the land was needed for a proper public purpose, that others could not be removed until after the monsoon, and that alternate accommodation should be found (though this was not a precondition).

Though the court's intentions were laudatory, the case became symptomatic of PIL cases where the court's intervention did not actually help improve matters on the ground, as many of the pavement dwellers could not find alternate accommodation and found the period of four months inadequate to find alternate housing. Additionally, the 'right' established by the court had a hollow ring to it, because in the end, the court held that the law authorizing the evictions was reasonable if it was read down to provide for a hearing. This case illustrates the court's institutional limitations for handling problems of immense magnitude such as that posed by the rapid migration of workers from rural to urban areas, and the housing crunch that results. Activists were disappointed that though the court had declared the right to livelihood to be a fundamental right under Article 21, it had not gone so far as to declare that a right to housing was equally a necessary concomitant of the right to life.[51]

In a case decided nearly twelve years later,[52] the supreme court appeared to have developed a more nuanced approach to the issue. There, the court argued that several of the directive principles (Articles 38, 39, and 46 in particular) required the state to evolve 'schemes in a planned manner by annual budgets to provide [a] right of residence to the poor.' The court urged municipal corporations to earmark portions of their annual budgets for implementing the social rights of the disadvantaged

[50] AIR 1985 SC 180.

[51] One commentator has noted that the court might have abstained from doing so for fear of the consequences of its actions: such relief would have substantially affected the overall budgetary resources of the state of Maharashtra, placed the housing needs of Bombay pavement dwellers and slum dwellers above other social needs that might have to be unmet given limited funds, and would have interfered with the state's claimed expertise in planning the future development of the city of Bombay. Clark D. Cunningham, 'Public Interest Litigation in the Indian Supreme Court: A Study in the Light of American Experience', 29 J. IND. L. INST. 494 at 516 (1987).

[52] *Ahmedabad Municipal Corporation v. Gulab Khan Nawab Khan* AIR 1997 SC 152.

in society. Once again, while one can admire the enthusiasm of the court for pursuing the cause of housing for the poor, the wisdom and effectiveness of such declaratory judgments is open to debate.

Cases Establishing a Right to Education

In the early nineties, the supreme court delivered two important decisions on the right to education. Under Article 45 of the constitution, the state is specifically called upon to provide free and compulsory education to children below the age of fourteen. Though the provision was to come into effect within ten years of the commencement of the constitution, even five decades after its inception the right was far from being attained. In *Mohini Jain* v. *State of Karnataka*,[53] which involved a challenge to the system of 'capitation fees' charged by private higher educational institutions, a two-judge bench of the supreme court commented on this failure of the state, and held that the right to education was a fundamental right and that the State was constitutionally bound to provide education at all levels. The court reasoned that to live a life of dignity that was assured by Article 21, every citizen required access to educational facilities, and this was a fundamental right. Accordingly, the court held that private educational institutions that received accreditation from the state could not charge exorbitant fees for educational courses. The court frowned upon the excessive commercialization of education and observed that this practice violated the constitution, while also being repugnant to the Indian cultural ethos.

This decision was modified by the decision of a larger constitution bench of the supreme court in *Unnikrishnan* v. *State of Bihar*.[54] The latter decision, which was decided by a five-judge bench, altered the earlier ruling to the extent that the former made the right to education 'at all levels' a fundamental right. The supreme court noted that though the right to primary education upto the age of fourteen years was a fundamental right, the state could not be fastened with the obligation of providing higher education to all citizens. The court did however conclude that the system of higher education in respect of engineering and medical education was in a pathetic state, and after issuing notices to the bodies responsible for overseeing standards in the two areas, directed the drawing up of an elaborate scheme designed to improve conditions of access to higher education. The decision resulted in a situation where

[53] AIR 1992 SC 1858.
[54] (1993) 1 SCC 645.

for several succeeding years, the court was asked to set the fees for engineering and medical colleges on an annual basis. The wisdom of this measure is also open to question because, by virtually taking over the task of the relevant professional bodies which supervise medical and engineering education, the court was intruding upon areas where it had no expertise and was arguably making matters worse. While there can be no doubt that the problems arose in part because of the inaction of the professional bodies, perhaps a better course of action might have been to mandate that the bodies act under the supervision of the court, a strategy that the court has used to good effect in some other cases. It must, however, be noted that these two cases relating to education were in great measure responsible for an increased demand for a fundamental right to education. That demand ultimately led, in December 2002, to the enactment of a constitutional amendment to the text of Article 21, making the right to education a fundamental right for children between the ages of six and fourteen.[55]

Cases Establishing the Right to Health

The Supreme Court of India has also delivered significant judgements in the area of the right to health. As already noted, there are several provisions in the directive principles which exhort the state to make provision for adequate health facilities. In the first case on this issue, *Parmanand Katara v. Union of India*,[56] the court was confronted with a situation where hospitals were refusing to admit accident victims and were directing them to specific hospitals designed to admit 'medico-legal cases'. The court ruled that while the medical authorities were free to draw up administrative rules based on practical requirements, no medical authority could refuse to provide immediate medical attention to a patient in need. The court relied on various medical sources to conclude that this violated universally accepted notions of medical ethics. More importantly, the court concluded that this measure violated the right to life guaranteed under Article 21 as that right would be rendered illusory if a citizen could be refused emergency medical treatment on account of an administrative arrangement between hospitals.

[55] For a critical overview of the circumstances leading to the adoption of the 86th constitutional amendment, see generally, Vijayshri Sripathi and Arun K. Thiruvengadam, 'India: Constitutional Amendment Making the Right to Education a Fundamental Right', 2 INT'L J. CONST. L. 148 (2004).

[56] AIR 1989 SC 2039.

In a subsequent case, *Paschim Banga Khet Mazdoor Samiti* v. *State of West Bengal*,[57] the court had to deal with a situation where a particular state had woefully inadequate primary health facilities. The facts that gave rise to the case were that a train accident victim, Hakim Sheikh, was turned away from a number of public hospitals in Calcutta on the ground that the hospitals did not have adequate facilities to treat him. Ultimately, he was treated in a private hospital, and the delays aggravated his injuries. Realizing that the situation posed in the case was not a local problem, the court issued notices to all state governments and directed them to undertake the provision of minimal primary health facilities throughout their territories. When confronted with the argument of lack of financial resources, the court reiterated a stance it adopted in an earlier case, and declared that lack of resources could not be cited as an excuse for non-performance of a constitutionally mandated obligation.[58] The court set up an expert committee to investigate the matter and endorsed the final report of the committee which contained a seven-point agenda addressing issues as diverse as upgrading of facilities, to setting up a centralized communications system amongst hospitals to ensure the adequacy of ambulance equipment and personnel.

Analysis and Appraisal of the Supreme Court's Efforts

The supreme court's forays into the uncharted territory of social rights have attracted criticism almost from the very beginning of its efforts. In India, unlike in South Africa, the supreme court has no direct constitutional responsibility for social rights. Under the Indian constitution, that primary responsibility vests in the legislative and executive bodies. An important justification offered by the judges who initiated PIL cases

---

[57] AIR 1996 SC 2426.

[58] The court held: 'It is no doubt true that financial resources are needed for providing these facilities. But at the same time it cannot be ignored that it is the constitutional obligation of the state to provide adequate medical services to the people. Whatever is necessary for this has to be done. In the context of the constitutional obligation to provide free legal aid to a poor accused this court has held that the state cannot avoid its constitutional obligation in that regard on account of financial constraints.... The said observations would apply with equal, if not greater, force in the matter of discharge of constitutional obligation of the state to provide medical aid to preserve life...It is necessary that a time-bound plan for providing these services should be chalked out for ensuring availability of proper medical services in this regard as indicated by us and steps should be taken to implement the same.' Ibid., at 2432.

has been the collapse of responsible government by the political branches, and the need for courts to step in to fill the resulting vacuum. What is interesting is that even within the supreme court, there was intense debate over the novel measures initiated in PIL cases.[59]

Initially, the supreme court's efforts in PIL cases were enthusiastically supported by activists, academics and social groups, but as the nature of the court's jurisdiction in PIL cases underwent a transformation (moving from issues affecting the underprivileged in the late 1970s and early 1980s, to a broad range of issues affecting the middle classes in the 1990s), even supporters of the court's activism expressed scepticism and caution. There is concern that the original mandate of PIL has changed adversely, and that there is a need to steer the court back to the real, deep-seated issues which account for underdevelopment at the grassroots.[60] Such critics note that the court has started focusing on concerns of the middle class, and point to recent cases dealing with environmental issues where the court has on several occasions ruled against the interests of migrant workers. Similarly, as successive Indian governments have moved towards neo-liberal reforms, the supreme court, by adopting a hands-off approach to economic issues, has exposed itself to the accusation that it has abandoned its protective role in respect of indigenous peoples, workers,[61] and other underprivileged sections.

Other critics have focused on the fact that by getting embroiled in political and social problems, the court imperils its own institutional

[59] In 1982, a senior judge of the court, Justice Tulzapurkar, noted in a public speech that the court should not 'in the name of alleviating the grave public injury…arrogate to itself the role of an administrator or an overseer…of all non-functioning or malfunctioning public bodies or institutions'. In making these observations, Tulzapurkar was attacking the main rationale offered by the pro-PIL judges for their interventions. V.D. Tulzapurkar, 'Judiciary: Attacks and Survival' AIR 1982 (Jour.) 14.

[60] See, for example, Usha Ramanathan, 'Of Judicial Power', 19 (6) *Frontline* (16–29 March 2002) at: http://www.frontlineonnet.com/fl1906/19060300.htm.

[61] The supreme court's recent ruling in *K. Rangarajan* v. *Government of Tamil Nadu*, [2003] LRI 850, where it held that government employees have no 'fundamental, legal or equitable right to go on strike', has provoked outrage among labour rights groups who view the ruling as a continuing assault on the rights of workers since the adoption of policies of liberalization in the early 1990s. V. Venkatesan, 'The Judicial Response', 20 (18) *Frontline* (30 August–12 September 2003) at: http://www.frontlineonnet.com/fl2018/stories/20030912005302000.htm (analysing the decision and describing how it flies in the face of several prior holdings of the supreme court).

credibility and future.[62] At an early stage of the development of PIL, Justice R.S. Pathak (who later went to become Chief Justice) wrote a separate judgment in *Bandhua Mukti Morcha* v. *Union of India* in which he took a similar view cautioning his colleagues against venturing into the arena of policy-making while deciding PIL cases.[63] The *Bandhua* case itself had a very interesting role to play in the history of the PIL movement. Being one of the early cases, it was celebrated as a path-breaking legal development, became a kind of torchbearer and symbol for the court's activism, and was cited time and again in every major PIL case that followed. The case was brought to the court by an activist working to end the practice of 'bonded' or forced labour, and focused on the conditions under which quarry workers in Faridabad (near the capital city of Delhi) were made to work. Specifically, the petitioner sought the implementation of a law that sought to codify the constitutional prohibition against forced labour. The court relaxed traditionally strict rules of standing to allow the petitioner to represent the cause of the workers, and passed a series of directions designed to end the oppressive practices. The legal victory in court did not, however, translate into real changes on the ground. As noted by one commentator writing almost ten years after the original judgment, in realistic terms, little changed for the many impoverished Indians who continued to eke out an existence by working in deplorable conditions of forced labour.[64]

[62] T.R. Andhyarujina, *Judicial Activism and Constitutional Democracy in India* 37 Bombay: N.M. Tripathi (1992). In this extensive critique of the Court's activism in PIL cases, Andhyarujina further argues that if courts continue to act as substitutes for responsible government, their continual intervention will cause a deflection of the primary responsibility of the people, the legislature and the executive for self-government and self-correction. He also asserts that indiscriminate and immediate resort to courts aborts the political initiative and the rousing of public opinion, ultimately affecting the quality of deliberative democracy in that society. He also points to the several PIL decisions that have remained on paper, with no real effect, and argues that if the ranks of such cases increases, it will ultimately erode the stability and prestige of the judiciary as an institution. Ibid., at 39–43 and 44–5.

[63] AIR 1984 SC 802. In Pathak's words: '...In the process of correcting executive error or removing legislative omission the court can so easily find itself involved in policy making of a quality and to a degree characteristic of political authority, and indeed run the risk of being mistaken for one. An excessively political role identifiable with political governance betrays the court into functions alien to its fundamental character...'

[64] Oliver Mendelsohn, 'Life and Struggles in the Stone Quarries of India: A Case Study', 29 J. Comm. & Comp. Pol. 43 (1991). Mendelsohn notes: '[D]espite a spectacular success in the form of the supreme court judgment, the Faribadad

Nearly twenty years after the original decision had been rendered, the case was still being heard by the court, which was increasingly frustrated by its failure to make substantive progress. This has led one influential observer to conclude that the court's sustained and detailed attention in this matter has borne little fruit, and this trend is in fact symptomatic of the court's interventions in several PIL cases.[65]

Some scholars have set the court's PIL jurisprudence against the broader context of the extreme inefficiency of the overall judicial system in India, which is described as 'the most crowded of any in the world.'[66] The massive problems of delay, cost, and ineffectiveness have contributed to a situation where 'cases take decades, sometimes generations, to resolve.'[67] One scholar contends, based on an extensive survey of 73 prominent social advocacy groups, that this reality is leading to a situation where the most prominent social advocacy groups tend to avoid litigation as a strategy.[68] Obviously, this is bound to affect the rate and quality of social rights cases brought before the supreme court in future.

Despite such criticisms, the supreme court has consistently found great public support for its intervention in PIL cases, as is regularly confirmed by polls in leading newspapers and newsmagazines. However,

---

campaign had to be counted a failure. Very few workers had effectively been rehabilitated as bonded labourers; wages had risen only moderately; and health and safety conditions were scarcely different from a decade ago.... The reasons for the failure are several but at root is a variation of what one always finds in relation to exploitation of the poor in India; the overwhelming power of large employers and the unreliability of the state as an ally of the poor, despite good intentions of elements within the judiciary and bureaucracy.' Ibid., at 49.

[65] Arun Shourie, *Courts and their Judgements* 16–58, New Delhi: Rupa (2001) (discussing at great length the history and development of the *Bandhua* case).

[66] Jayanth K. Krishnan, 'Social Policy Advocacy and the Role of the Courts in India', 21 AMERICAN ASIAN REVIEW 91 (2003) (citing statistics that indicate that as of 2002, there were 23 million pending court cases—20,000 in the supreme court, 3.2 million in the high courts, and 20 million in lower or subordinate courts). See also, Marc Galanter and Jayanth K. Krishnan, 'Bread for the Poor': Access to Justice and the Rights of the Needy in India', 55 Hastings L.J. 789 (2004) (documenting the huge obstacles that ordinary Indians face in gaining access to courts in India).

[67] Krishnan, ibid.

[68] Ibid. See also, Charles Epp, 'The Rights Revolution: Lawyers, Activists and Supreme Courts in Comparative Perspective', Chicago: University of Chicago Press (1998) (arguing that the 'rights revolution' in India has only been partially successful because it is court-centred, and because the far more crucial support structures— well funded mass-based activist groups and interest group systems—have not developed and matured over time).

this fact must be understood against the context of the existing political situation in the country, where the executive and legislative wings of government have lost much of their credibility with the people over the last two decades. The approval ratings for the supreme court are more properly understood as a negative vote against the functioning of the basic institutions of democratic governance.

Admirers of the court's activism admit that there have been abject failures, but point to the fact that the court has learned from its mistakes, and has sought to develop innovative measures to overcome the early problems.[69] These measures include the evolution of the following innovative strategies: the practice of appointing *amicus curiae* to assist the adjudicatory process of the court;[70] the practice of issuing orders of 'continuing mandamus';[71] issuance of orders forewarning the conse-quences of non-implementation;[72] and avoiding rulings where the court

[69] S. Muralidhar, 'Implementation of Court Orders in the Area of Economic, Social and Cultural Rights: An Overview of the Experience of the Indian Judiciary', Paper presented at the First South Asian Regional Judicial Colloquium on Access to Justice, 4–5 (2002) (Unpublished paper on file with author).

[70] These *amici curiae* usually consist of senior lawyers or noted experts from relevant fields and help the court in sifting out the relevant facts from the documents and pleadings, and in sharpening the focus of discussion, bearing in mind the contingencies of judicial functioning. This practice also ensures that an element of continuity is maintained while implementing the orders of the court, apart from ensuring that the process is not dependent upon the sustained interest of the petitioner. To similar effect, the court has also appointed commissioners and expert bodies for ascertaining facts or for an independent verification of the facts presented by the petitioner or the state.

[71] As part of this practice, the court issues a series of orders at various regular hearings, and after ensuring implementation, proceeds to issue a final judgment. Even after issuing the final judgment, the court often retains the case on its docket, and oversees its implementation. So, for instance, in a case where it sought to ensure that arrests across India followed certain minimum safeguards that protect the rights of the accused, the court monitored the implementation of its orders for nearly seven years after the date of the main judgment in the case. *D.K. Basu* v. *State of West Bengal* (1997) 1 SCC 416 (original judgment). For a sampling of subsequent orders designed to ensure implementation of the original judgment, see (1999) 7 SCALE 222, (2000) 5 SCALE 353 and (2001) 7 SCALE 487.

[72] For instance, in the case relating to vehicular pollution in the city of Delhi, the court warned that violation of its orders would invite action for contempt of court. *M.C. Mehta* v. *Union of India* (1998) 1 SCC 226, 243. Similarly, in the case involving the supervision of environmental regulation of forests, the court has often held recalcitrant state officials guilty of contempt when it found that they were thwarting its orders. *T.N. Godavaraman Tirumulapad* (1998) 3 SCALE 669 and (1998) 9 SCC 672.

is required to formulate policy.[73] The devising of such strategies seems to indicate that the court is aware of the strength of the institutional objections to judicial implementation of social rights, and is actively seeking to overcome traditional obstacles to the functioning of courts in these areas.

It is therefore evident that the Indian Supreme Court's efforts to enter-tain PIL cases generally, and to implement social rights in particular, have been complex tasks inviting a great deal of criticism and causing considerable controversy. Still, the court's PIL jurisdiction continues to draw public support as it is seen as seeking to make genuine (if at times naïve and even misguided) efforts at securing justice to those who approach it for implementation of their constitutionally protected rights. The challenge for the supreme court is to ensure that its orders in social rights cases are monitored and successfully implemented. If judicial orders in social rights cases continue not to be implemented, the court will no doubt see its support, and legitimacy, waning rather quickly.

THE APPROACH OF THE CONSTITUTIONAL COURT OF SOUTH AFRICA

The Constitutional Court of South Africa was inaugurated on 14 February 1995. Since then, it has established a reputation for delivering progressive judgments in several areas of the law. One has to bear in mind that much of the court's attitude and approach is in fact dictated

[73] *Delhi Science Forum* v. *Union of India* (1996) 2 SCC 405 (refusing to interfere or comment upon the policy decision of the Government of India to privatize the telecommunications sector); *Krishna Bhat* v. *Union of India*, (1990) 3 SCC 65 (refusing to intervene in a petition seeking to enforce prohibition of the sale of liquor); *Kanhaya Lal Sethia* v. *Union of India*, (1997) 6 SCC 573 (refusing to intervene in a case seeking the recognition of a particular language as a national language). This approach has particularly been followed in cases relating to economic policy, leading to the accusation that by not interfering with policies which have the effect of adding to the burdens of the most oppressed sections in society, the court was abdicating its constitutional duty to protect and enforce the directive principles. Critics have also commented upon the inconsistent attitude adopted by the supreme court where it does in fact formulate policies in certain areas, whereas in others, it adopts a complete hands-off approach. Upendra Baxi, *Judicial Activism, Legal Education and Research in a Globalizing India* (1996). See also, Upendra Baxi, 'The Avatars of Indian Judicial Activism: Explorations in the Geographies of [In]Justice', in *Fifty Years of the supreme court* (Kusum ed., New Delhi: Oxford University Press, 2000).

by the specific text of the Constitution of South Africa. Because the South African constitution has a specific, *transformative* agenda, the text itself dictates a very active, progressive approach for the new state in general. It could thus be argued that the constitutional court was conceived as an activist court. A review of its jurisprudence must consider how far the court has lived upto this mandate.

A few aspects of the constitutional court must be noted before we analyse its judgments on social rights. First, unlike the highest courts in the US and India, the constitutional court is a specialized body that only considers cases that raise constitutional questions. To that extent, it is separate from the rest of the South African judiciary and is an entirely new institution. Though South Africa has traditionally had a common law system, in this respect, it has decided to borrow from the continental European model of constitutionalism.[74] The eleven-member body thus only deals with a limited number of cases every year (an average of about 20 cases a year), and each case is heard by the entire court.[75] This has the advantage of ensuring consistency in the court's rulings, and also allows the court much more time to deliberate over its decisions. The supreme court of India sits in panels of two and three judges (which has often resulted in inconsistent judgments being delivered by different benches of the court) and decides several thousands of constitutional cases annually. Lastly, while the supreme court is not specifically required to consider either international or comparative law, the constitutional court is constitutionally mandated, when interpreting the bill of rights, to consider the relevant international law. The same provision gives the court the discretion of considering foreign law where relevant.[76] This provision keeps the court engaged in a continuing conversation with

---

[74] Like Germany after the Nazi era, South Africa had to face the problem of what it would do with its judiciary, all of whose members had been appointed during the apartheid era, and a large majority of whom had been active implementers of the policy of apartheid. Instead of dismissing all the existing judges, South Africa followed the German example, and set up an entirely new court at the top of the judicial system. It was hoped that this apex court, staffed by people of unimpeachable qualities, would set the tone for the rest of the judiciary in the new order.

[75] Though the constitution requires that each case be heard before at least eight judges, in practice, all eleven judges hear every case.

[76] Section 39(1), S. AFR. CONST. (Constitution of the Republic of South Africa, Act 108 of 1996). The provision reads: When interpreting the constitution, a court, tribunal or forum: (a) must promote the values that underlie an open and democratic society based on human dignity, equality and freedom; (b) must consider international law; and (c) may consider foreign law.

comparative and international law while reaching its decisions relating to domestic constitutional law.

In the remaining part of this section, I analyse, in some detail, three of the four judgments handed down by the constitutional Court in cases involving social rights. The issues raised in each of these three cases has great resonance in the Indian context (and might well result in similar litigation in India), and studying these cases closely will undoubtedly be of great benefit to scholars, lawyers, and judges in India.

The *Soobramoney* Case:
Right to Health and Emergency Care

The facts of the *Soobramoney* case are compelling and tragic.[77] Thiagraj Soobramoney was a forty-one year old man afflicted with several ailments: diabetes, heart disease, and chronic renal failure. Renal failure is of two types: acute and chronic. While acute renal failure can be remedied (and sometimes cured) by treatment on a renal dialysis machine, chronic renal failure is an irreversible condition, and a patient suffering from this problem requires regular renal dialysis just to stay alive. For such a patient, a kidney transplant becomes the only option, with regular dialysis acting as a survival mechanism until the transplant can be arranged. The tragic aspect of Soobramoney's condition was that, on account of his other health problems, he was deemed ineligible for a kidney transplant.

After exhausting his personal finances in seeking treatment at private hospitals, Soobramoney turned to the state-funded Addington Hospital in Durban. The Addington Hospital had 20 dialysis machines in varying states of repair. Given the expense of the treatment involved, and the scarcity of resources, the hospital's renal specialist, a nationally regarded doctor (who was also the president of the South African Renal Society at the time of the case), had evolved a policy which sought to use the machines in cases where they could make the most difference. The hospital therefore followed a policy of providing renal dialysis auto- matically to *acute* renal failure cases. In cases where patients had *chronic* renal failure, the hospital followed a policy of administering renal dialysis

[77] *Soobramoney v. Minister of Health, KwaZulu-Natal* 1998 (1) SA 765 (CC). The main judgment was delivered by president Chaskalson, with separate concurring judgments by Sachs J. and Madala J. The full text of the judgment is at the website of the Constitutional Court at: http://www.concourt.gov.za/files/soobram/soobram.pdf.

only to those patients who were scheduled to undergo kidney transplants. Since Soobramoney was ineligible for a kidney transplant, and renal dialysis treatment would only serve to prolong his life upto a certain point of time, the hospital refused to provide him access to dialysis treatment.

Soobramoney filed a constitutional application before the high court which was dismissed. His case was heard on an urgent basis by the constitutional court on 11 November 1997. On 27 November 1997, the constitutional court upheld the lower court's ruling and held that the rejection of Soobramoney's application for renal treatment did not violate his rights under the Constitution of South Africa. Shortly after the judgment, Soobramoney died.

Soobramoney's principal claim was based on Section 27 which guarantees the right to health.[78] His lawyers argued that by virtue of Section 27(3), Soobramoney could not be 'refused emergency medical treatment'. The court rejected this argument, holding that Soobramoney's case related not to an 'emergency' or 'catastrophe' but to an 'ongoing state of affairs'. Reacting to the petitioner's reliance on the Indian Supreme Court's ruling in the *Paschim Banga Samity* case, the constitutional court held that that case was distinguishable as there, the petitioner had been denied emergency care by several hospitals where he was taken following his accident. The constitutional court held that the facts relating to Soobramoney were different. Here, the state, represented by the doctors at Addington Hospital who had formulated the policy regarding who was to be accorded priority in access to renal treatment facilities, had made a tragic but necessary choice based on the resources available to it, and the acuteness of the problem faced by patients.[79]

[78] The full text of the provision reads: S.27. Health care, food, water and social security (1) Everyone has the right to have access to (a) health care services, including reproductive health care; (b) sufficient food and water; and (c) social security, including, if they are unable to support themselves and their dependants, appropriate social assistance. (2) The state must take reasonable legislative and other measures, within its available resources, to achieve the progressive realization of each of these rights. (3) No one may be refused emergency medical treatment.

[79] After reviewing the policy in force, the court added its seal of approval to the policy by noting: 'By using the available dialysis machines in accordance with the guidelines more patients are benefited than would be the case if they are used to keep alive persons with chronic renal failure, and the outcome of the treatment is also likely to be more beneficial because it is directed to curing patients, and not simply to maintaining them in a chronically ill condition.' *Soobramoney*, supra n. 77 at paragraph 25.

In providing additional reasons for its holding, the court reasoned that 'if treatment has to be provided to the appellant, it would also have to be provided to all other persons similarly placed'.[80] This, according to the court, was problematic because 'if this principle were to be applied to all patients claiming access to expensive medical treatment or expensive drugs, the health budget would have to be dramatically increased to the prejudice of other needs that the state has to meet'.[81] In a crucial passage, the court noted:

These choices involve difficult decisions to be taken at the political level in fixing the health budget, and at the functional level in deciding upon the priorities to be met. A court will be slow to interfere with rational decisions taken in good faith by the political organs and medical authorities whose responsibility it is to deal with such matters.[82]

The court concluded its judgement with the following observations:

The State has to manage its limited resources in order to address all claims. There will be times when this requires it to adopt a holistic approach to the larger needs of society rather than to focus on the specific needs of particular individuals within society.[83]

Since this was the first case where the constitutional court had to adjudicate upon the social rights in the constitution, and because of the tragic circumstances surrounding it, the case attracted a great deal of scholarly and public attention. While members of the public focused on the sensational nature of the facts of the case, some critics were more concerned about the language employed by the constitutional court. To them, the wording employed by the court signalled deference to the executive authorities bordering on abdication of a reviewing role in assessing the constitutional adequacy of existing state resources for promoting the rights guaranteed in the bill of rights.[84] In a detailed analysis

---

[80] Ibid., at paragraph 28.

[81] Ibid.

[82] Ibid., at paragraph 20. One commentator has termed this approach 'the utilitarian calculus' and has argued that in a rights context, a utilitarian approach is deeply problematic as it is premised on a presumption of fixed and limited resources. Jeanne M. Woods, 'Justiciable Social Rights as a Critique of the Liberal Paradigm', 38 TEX. INT'L L.J. 763, 779–80 (2003).

[83] *Soobramoney*, supra n. 77 at paragraph 31.

[84] One commentator has criticized the court for begging the question 'whether the state should be allowed to treat dialysis as an extraordinary resource that must be rationed for the poor *in a country whose white citizens enjoy one of the highest standards of living*

of the case,[85] two leading scholars, while generally critical of the court's final decision (including its interpretation that the reasoning in the Indian case of *Paschim Banga Khet Samity* was inapplicable to the case at hand) have pointed out that the court may have been influenced by several factors in deciding as it did. They first note that the case was litigated scarcely a year after the final constitution had come into effect, leaving little time for the government to work out the relationship between constitutionalized priorities and policy making in relevant fields. They also point out that the medical profession had made a categorical decision supporting the stance adopted by the government on the issue, and the court would have found it easier to defer to that opinion.

The *Grootboom* Case: Right to Housing

The second major case involving social rights came before the constitutional court nearly three years after the *Soobramoney* case was decided. It involved the vexed issue of housing in post-apartheid South Africa. Like many other social problems, the acute housing shortage in many areas of the new nation can also be attributed to the policies of apartheid.[86] The new democratic government of South Africa had taken steps to arrest the growing housing crisis, but, as the case demonstrates, this did not solve the problem. This case represents a major shift in the court's approach to social rights.

The case in question was brought by a black woman, Irene Grootboom, and others totalling nearly 900 petitioners, of whom 510 were children.[87] All of them had originally lived in squatter settlements in the

---

in the world.' She points out that the majority opinion made no mention of the resources available in the private sector, nor did it suggest that the State should do anything further to respond to the epidemic of kidney disease. Woods, supra n. 82 at 783.

[85] Craig Scott and Philip Alston, 'Adjudicating Constitutional Priorities in a Transnational Context: A Comment on Soobramoney's Legacy and Grootboom's Promise', 16 S. AFR. J. HUM RTS. 206–68 (2000). Scott and Alston identify several problems with the reasoning employed by the constitutional court in *Soobramoney* According to them, the decision renders Section 27(3) a virtually redundant negative right; and reflects a non-application of minds to the issue of relationship between Sections 27(1) and (2). Scott and Alston, ibid., at 233–56.

[86] Years of segregated housing policies had resulted in large sections of the black population being forced to live in shacks and other forms of primitive housing.

[87] *Government of the Republic of South Africa v. Grootboom*, 2000 (1) SA 46 (CC). The unanimous opinion for the court was delivered by Yacoob J. The full text of the judgment is at: http://www.concourt.gov.za/files/grootboom1/grootboom1.pdf.

Wallacedene area. Conditions in the settlements in the Wallacedene area were pathetic: the facilities were overcrowded and diseases such as asthma and flu were rampant on account of water-logging. Several of the squatters had applied to the municipal authorities for low cost housing. They were placed on a waiting list, where they remained for several years. In late 1998, becoming frustrated by the intolerable living conditions in Wallacedene, Grootboom and the other petitioners in the case moved to a vacant area called 'New Rust' where they proceeded to put up temporary shacks. The New Rust land was privately owned and had in fact been marked for low cost housing. The owner of the land obtained orders of eviction against the squatters who resisted the orders. Eventually, the squatters were forcibly evicted, their homes were burnt and bulldozed, and their possessions were destroyed. The squatters found shelter on a sports field where they put up temporary shelters in the form of plastic sheets, and petitioned the Cape High Court. The high court found in their favour, and ordered relief. The government appealed to the constitutional court which heard the matter in May 2000 and delivered its judgment on 4 October 2000, partly overruling the lower court's ruling.

The case primarily involved two constitutional provisions: Section 26 (which guarantees a right to housing)[88] and Section 28 (laying out certain rights of children).[89] The Cape High Court, in its judgment delivered by Dennis Davis J, relied on the provisions of Section 28 to hold that that provision creates a freestanding, absolute right in children to the protections mentioned there, namely, to housing, health care, and other benefits. The high court rejected the claim to shelter based on Section 26 (which right is textually limited by the adequacy of resources available to the state), and instead chose to base its order granting relief to the petitioners on its interpretation of Section 28. By this rationale, the children of the squatters had a constitutional right to housing, and their parents would also have rights to housing through them.

---

[88] Section 26 reads: 26. (1) Everyone has the right to have access to adequate housing. (2) The state must take reasonable legislative and other measures, within its available resources, to achieve the progressive realization of this right. (3) No one may be evicted from their home, or have their home demolished, without an order of court made after considering all the relevant circumstances. No legislation may permit arbitrary evictions.

[89] The relevant part of Section 28 reads: 28. (1) Every child has the right... (b) to family care or parental care, or to appropriate alternative care when removed from the family environment; (c) to basic nutrition, shelter, basic health care services and social services....

In its judgment, the constitutional court reversed this approach—it based its decision on Section 26, and rejected the argument based on Section 28. While discussing the constitutional scheme, the court observed that in the South African context, the question to ask is not whether socio-economic rights are justiciable, but how they are to be enforced. The court noted that this question would have to be carefully explored on a case-by-case basis.[90] Dealing first with the high court's analysis of the claim based on Section 28, the constitutional court pointed out that the reasoning adopted by the high court to grant relief to the squatters resulted in the anomalous situation that people who have children have a direct and enforceable right to housing under Section 28(1)(c), while others with either no children or whose children were now adults would not be entitled to housing, regardless of how dire their circumstances may be. Pointing out other problems with such reasoning, the court dismissed this argument.[91]

Turning to the language of Section 26, which does provide for a right to housing, the court undertook a careful study of its language and import. Its analysis in this respect is significant as it interpreted several terms—'progressive realization', 'reasonable measures', 'within available resources'—which appear in several of the social rights provisions. Reading subsections (1) and (2), the court concluded that there is at the very least, a negative obligation to desist from preventing or impairing the right of access to adequate housing. It held that the conduct of the municipality authorities in forcibly evicting the petitioners a day earlier than announced and burning their possessions fell foul of this requirement. As to the positive obligations that this section imposed on the state, the court noted that these were textually limited to the availability of resources. Significantly, the court observed that 'state policy dealing with housing must...take account of different economic levels in South African society'.[92] The court noted that the state has different obligations towards those who could afford to pay for housing and those

[90] *Grootboom*, supra n. 87 at paragraph 20. This approach of the court is similar to the constitutional theory of 'judicial minimalism' advocated by Cass Sunstein. Cass R. Sunstein, One Case at a Time: Judicial Minimalism on the Supreme Court, Cambridge: Harvard University Press (1999) (arguing that judges should leave significant questions unresolved, decide the particular case on the particular facts, and write opinions narrowly rather than broadly).

[91] *Grootboom*, supra n. 87 at paragraphs 70–9.

[92] Ibid., at paragraph 35. In this regard, it may be recalled that the constitutional court avoided such a line of inquiry and reasoning in the *Soobramoney* case. As will be elaborated upon shortly, this is a significant difference.

who cannot. In respect of the former, the state's obligation lay in 'unlocking the system, providing access to housing stock and a legislative framework to facilitate self-built houses through planning laws and access to finance'.[93] As for the poor, the court held that the state had a special obligation towards providing them access to housing. Again, the court noted that the nature of this obligation would depend on the context: it would differ from province to province, and from rural to urban areas.

Analysing the requirements of subsection (2), the constitutional court noted that the steps taken by the state towards fulfilment of its obligation must be 'reasonable'. Elaborating on what would amount to 'reasonable measures', the court noted that a reasonable programme must 'clearly allocate responsibilities and tasks to different spheres of government and ensure that the appropriate financial and human resources are available'; and 'must establish a coherent public housing programme directed towards the progressive realization of the right of access to adequate housing within the state's available means'.[94] Interestingly, while expounding on how to ascertain whether measures were reasonable or not, the court observed:

A court considering reasonableness will *not enquire whether other more desirable or favourable measures could have been adopted, or whether public money could have been better spent.* The question would be whether the measures that have been adopted have been reasonable. It is necessary to recognise that a wide range of possible measures could be adopted by the state to meet its obligations. Many of these would meet the requirement of reasonableness. Once it is shown that the measures do so, this requirement is met.[95]

This is a crucial insight into the approach of the court in exercising its jurisdiction. It must be noted that though this standard of review is certainly an improvement over that evolved and applied in *Soobramoney*, it is nevertheless a deferential standard of scrutiny. To challenge governmental action, the burden is very clearly on the person alleging a violation of a social right. The court set out some further tests for determining reasonableness. In its view, to be reasonable, '[t]he programme must be balanced and flexible and make appropriate provision for attention to housing crises *and to short, medium and long term needs*'.[96]

---

[93] Ibid., at paragraph 36. Jeanne Woods has criticized the constitutional court for avoiding a similar approach in the *Soobramoney* case. Woods, supra n. 82 at 780.

[94] *Grootboom*, supra n. 87 at paragraph 39.

[95] Ibid., at paragraph 41. (Emphasis added).

[96] Ibid., at paragraph 43.

The court emphasized that a programme that excluded a significant section of society could not be said to be reasonable. Interpreting the words 'progressive realization' in Section 26, the court held that the use of this expression showed that it was contemplated that the right could not be realized immediately. However, it was the duty of the state to progressively facilitate accessibility of the right; as time progressed, housing must be made more accessible not only to a larger number of people but to a wider range of people. To this end, legal, administrative, operational, and financial hurdles should be examined, and, where possible, lowered over time. Turning to the phrase 'within available resources', the court acknowledged that while the measures initiated by the state must be calculated to attain the goal expeditiously and effectively, the availability of resources is an important factor in determining what is reasonable.

Moving on to the details of the housing plan adopted by the legislative and executive authorities, the court undertook a wide survey of the legislative and executive measures undertaken by government, and expressed its appreciation for the earnest efforts initiated in this respect.[97] The court, however, noted that this did not mean that the measures were automatically reasonable within the meaning of Section 26 of the constitution. The court declared that although it was a systematic response to a pressing social need, the programme did not cater to the needs of people in desperate need, and they were left without any form of assistance for an indefinite period of time. This feature of the programme made it deficient in respect of fulfilling the obligations imposed by Section 26. The court therefore concluded that as the state housing programme in the area of the Cape Metropolitan Council did not make any provision for people such as Grootboom who were in desperate need in the short term, it fell short of compliance with the requirements of Section 26. The state was therefore ordered to devise, fund, implement, and supervise measures to provide relief to persons in situations similar to Grootboom and the other petitioners.[98]

While granting this positive relief, the court, in its typically circum-

---

[97] The court noted: 'What has been done in the execution of this programme is a major achievement. Large sums of money have been spent and a significant number of houses has been built. Considerable thought, energy, resources, and expertise have been and continue to be devoted to the process of effective housing delivery.' Ibid., at paragraph 53.

[98] It must be emphasized that the final judgment of the court does not contain specific directions in respect of the petitioners. This is because the court had already issued directions on the specific case of the petitioners. In an order passed nearly a

spect manner, added notes of restraint to its decision. It clarified that neither Section 26 nor Section 28 would entitle persons to claim shelter or housing immediately upon demand. The court also took care to point out that its judgment on Grootboom's petition must not be understood as approving any practice of land invasion for the purpose of coercing a state structure into providing housing on a preferential basis to those who participate in any exercise of the kind initiated by Grootboom and her fellow petitioners.[99]

The *Grootboom* decision has also generated an enormous amount of scholarly literature.[100] Cass Sunstein has hailed the decision as adopting a novel and highly promising approach to the judicial protection of social rights 'in a way that is respectful of democratic prerogatives and the simple fact of limited budgets'.[101] Sunstein points out that the approach adopted by the court is one that is generally unfamiliar in constitutional law, but is the ordinary material of administrative law, governing judicial control of administrative agencies: a requirement of reasoned judgment, including reasonable priority-setting. According to Sunstein, this is exactly the approach adopted by the constitutional court in the *Grootboom* case, and he describes this as 'an administrative law model of socio-economic rights'.[102] Although generally celebratory in his analysis of the case, Sunstein is careful to note that this approach leaves many issues—especially how money should be allocated to competing social rights

---

month before the final judgment, the court had, based on a consent order filed by the parties, issued detailed directions towards improving the temporary accommodation facilities being occupied by Grootboom and the other petitioners. The terms of the order are very detailed (providing for the installation of specified number of toilets and other sanitation facilities, specifying that 200,000 Rand be spent towards making those facilities waterproof, etc.) and lawyers familiar with the similarly detailed directions regularly issued by the Indian Supreme Court will find much common ground in the two approaches. The text of this short order is at: http://www.concourt.gov.za/files/grootboom/grootboom.pdf.

[99] Ibid., at paragraphs 92 and 95.

[100] See generally, Scott and Alston, supra n. 85 (this article contains an extensive analysis of the Cape High Court's judgment in *Grootboom*, but not of the constitutional court's final decision as it was written before that decision was delivered); Pierre De Vos, 'Grootboom, the Right of Access to Housing and Substantive Equality as Contextual Fairness', 17 S. AFR. J. HUM. RTS. 258–76 (2000); Heinz Klug, 'Five Years On: How Relevant is the Constitution to the New South Africa?' 26 VT. L. REV. 803–19 (2002); and Sunstein, 'Lessons from South Africa', supra n. 27.

[101] Sunstein, 'Lessons from South Africa', supra n. 28at 14.

[102] Ibid., at 13.

priorities—unresolved.

Other scholars have doubted whether *Grootboom* was as radical a decision as its supporters have claimed. Heinz Klug notes that *Grootboom* was actually quite a cautious and conservative decision because, as we have noted previously, while recognizing that social rights give rise to positive obligations, the court suggested that the government was free to choose the means through which to implement these positive obligations, even when the reasonableness of governmental measures would depend on the specific context. Klug observes: '[t]he extent of the positive obligation recognised in *Grootboom* was limited to the requirement that the government produce a reasonable plan to address the problem of emergency housing faced by the appellants'.[103] When contrasted with the approach adopted by the Indian Supreme Court, for instance, this approach does seem rather tame, and one wonders why scholars such as Sunstein describe *Grootboom* as an 'unprecedented' decision.

The *Treatment Action Campaign* Case: Expanding the Right to Health

In May 2002, the constitutional court heard a case involving one of the most difficult issues affecting the Republic of South Africa: the HIV/AIDS pandemic. The case required the constitutional court to make some difficult decisions about how far it was willing to go to enforce social rights. This was the first case where it found itself in a situation where its interpretation of what the constitution demanded was directly at odds with the government's policy. Though the court never explicitly acknowledges this in its judgment, one of the main problems at issue was the wide-ranging perception, created in part due to the public remarks of the president of South Africa, that the South African government was not serious in pursuing the battle against the pandemic.

In order to fully understand the import of the case, it is necessary to understand its context and the problems it sought to address. The HIV/AIDS pandemic is rampant in South Africa, and approximately '70,000 children are infected each year through mother to child transmission (MTCT) of HIV'.[104] An antiretroviral drug called Nevirapine offered a relatively simple medical response to this specific problem of MTCT as

[103] Klug, supra n. 100 at 807–8.

[104] *Minister of Health* v. *Treatment Action Campaign*, 2002 (5) SA 721 (CC) at paragraph 19. The court delivered a *per curiam* decision. The full text of the decision is at: http://www.concourt.gov.za/files/tac/tac.pdf.

a 'single dose of 200 mg to the mother during labour and a single oral dose of 2mg/kg to the infant within 48 to 72 hours after birth' significantly reduces the rate of MTCT of HIV, although it may still result from breast-feeding. Even though there were concerns about the long-term side effects of Nevirapine, in January 2001, the World Health Organization recommended the administration of the drug to mothers and infants at the time of birth in order to combat HIV. Following this, in April 2001, the South African Medicines Control Council formally approved the drug for use within South Africa. In July 2000, the manufacturers of Nevirapine offered to make it available to the South African government free of charge for a total period of five years. At the time of the judgment, the government had not accepted this offer. Nevertheless, the cost of the drug in the private sector had dropped to negligible levels.

The South African government had evolved a national policy regarding AIDS/HIV and had accepted a limited provision of Nevirapine in the public health sector by making the drug 'available for the prevention of MTCT' at only a limited number of pilot sites.[105] In support of this approach, the government pointed out its scepticism about the effectiveness of Nevirapine, and its long-term side effects.[106] Ultimately, however, the government's main argument against Nevirapine boiled down to the fact that making it immediately available at all public health facilities was not possible due to a lack of human and financial resources.[107]

The case was initiated primarily by the Treatment Action Campaign, which is an AIDS advocacy group. It was joined by other reputed organizations and individuals working to stem the pandemic's effects.

[105] These sites, which numbered eighteen, would reach only 10 per cent of the population and would be used for the purposes of testing implementation for the next two years.

[106] The government argued that Nevirapine had hidden costs associated with it, and that the prevention of interpartum transmission cannot be separated from the problem of postpartum transmission, especially through breast-feeding. These arguments were advocated with great force before the high court but their emphasis before the constitutional court was reduced, in part because of their implausibility in the face of overwhelming scientific evidence, and the approval of the drug by the relevant governmental authority.

[107] The government insisted that it 'wanted to develop and monitor its human and material resources nationwide for the delivery of a comprehensive package of testing and counselling, dispensing of Nevirapine and follow-up services to pregnant women attending at public health institutions'. Ibid., at paragraph 15.

The applicants pointed out that the factual basis of the government's scepticism of Nevirapine was questionable. The drug had been approved both by the WHO and South Africa's drug control agency, and was being used worldwide as an important weapon in the fight against the pandemic. They pointed out that the drug was freely available in the private sector, and the effect of the government's policy was that most doctors in the public sector were prohibited from prescribing its use. The applicants accepted the government's principal argument that a multi-pronged strategy was required to prevent MTCT, but did not concede that preventing patients at other sites of the benefits of Nevirapine served any purpose. They pointed out that those countless mothers and their babies who could not afford private health care, and did not have access to the limited pilot sites, were being unconstitutionally denied their right to a life-saving drug. In December 2001, the high court granted an order in favour of the applicants, and the government brought the case on appeal to the constitutional court.

The hostile nature of the proceedings was demonstrated by the fact that for the first time in a case involving social rights, the Government of South Africa energetically pursued a formalistic separation of powers argument.[108] The government argued that under the doctrine of separation of powers, the making of policy is the prerogative of the executive, and not of the courts, and that courts cannot make orders which have the effect of requiring the executive to pursue a particular policy. The government therefore argued that the only competent order that the court could make was to issue a declaration of rights—which would leave the government free to pay heed to the declaration made, and to adapt its policies to the extent that it would be necessary to bring them in conformity with the court's judgment.

The constitutional court carefully explained that the specific textual mandate of the South African constitution vested responsibility in the courts for supervising whether governmental policies were in accordance with the rights guaranteed in the bill of rights. The court rejected the distinction sought to be drawn between declaratory and mandatory orders. It noted that even simple declaratory orders against the government or the organs of the state can affect their policy, and may well have budgetary implications. The court held that the government is constitutionally bound to give effect to such orders, whether or not they

---

[108] A weak form of this 'separation of powers' argument was adopted in the *Grootboom* case, but was not pursued by the government, and the court was not required to rule upon the issue.

affect its policy, and it has to find the resources to do so.[109]

To support its stance that the judiciary had the power to issue injunctive relief against the state in appropriate cases, the constitutional court cited examples from the Supreme Courts of the US, Canada, and India, the German Constitutional Court, and the British House of Lords, and noted that in none of these jurisdictions was there any suggestion that the granting of injunctive relief against the state was in breach of the doctrine of separation of powers. The constitutional court expressly relied on the Indian case of *M.C. Mehta* v. *State of Tamil Nadu*,[110] and the fact that the Indian Supreme Court's 'wide-ranging order concerning child labour' included 'highly detailed mandatory and structural injunctions'. It must be noted, however, that despite its reliance on the mandatory and structural injunctions issued by the supreme court, the constitutional court did not in fact issue any such injunctions in its own final decision. Though the court had the option of issuing structural injunctions which would allow it to monitor the implementation of its orders, the court inexplicably did not avail of that option. It may well have been that the court decided to trust the government. However, given that by the time the order in the case was announced, there were already reports in the press that the orders in the *Grootboom* case had not been implemented, as well as the fact that the Minister of Health had publicly refused to implement the order of the high court, such a level of trust and confidence may well have been unfounded.

Nevertheless, the fact remains that the order in the *Treatment Action Campaign* case is, until now, the boldest assertion of its jurisdiction by the constitutional court in cases involving social rights. It is interesting that before this case, the court was never really required to justify its power and jurisdiction in this manner. It may well be that the court

[109] The court was quite emphatic in laying down the law on its jurisdiction and powers in ordering relief regarding social rights issues: 'A dispute concerning socio-economic rights is thus likely to require a court to evaluate state policy and to give judgment on whether or not it is consistent with the constitution. If it finds that policy is inconsistent with the constitution, it is obliged...to make a declaration to that effect. But that is not all.... *The power to grant mandatory relief includes the power where it is appropriate to exercise some form of supervisory jurisdiction to ensure that the order is implemented....* We thus reject the argument that the only power that this court has in the present case is to issue a declaratory order. Where a breach of any right has taken place, including a socio-economic right, the court is under a duty to ensure that effective relief is granted.... *Where necessary this may include both the issuing of a mandamus and the exercise of supervisory jurisdiction.*' Ibid., at paragraphs 101, 104 and 106.

[110] (1996) 6 SCC 776.

felt the need to do so in light of the extremely restrictive and narrow role that the government was advocating for it in cases involving social rights. After laying out the scope of its jurisdiction in such clear terms, the court concluded that the government's policy of not providing Nevi-rapine in public hospitals fell short of the requirements of Sections 27(1) and (2) of the constitution. It ordered the government to immediately remove the restrictions on the administering of Nevirapine to needy patients, and also issued a number of incidental directions to facilitate this process.[111]

Another unusual feature of the *Treatment Action Campaign* judgment is the court's willingness to issue orders on general issues beyond the specific facts of the case. For instance, the court made several general observations on various aspects of the government's HIV/AIDS policy and was generous in handing out suggestions for improvement. Most strikingly, the court declared that as a general rule, the government should seek to evolve decisions in a transparent manner,[112] and should consult and communicate with various care-givers.[113] As noted earlier, in previous cases, the court, far from venturing beyond the narrow facts of the case, was concerned more with narrowing down the implications of its ruling on the facts of the case before it. The difference can be explained by the court's perception of the adequacy of governmental policy. As we have

---

[111] These directions are enumerated at paragraph 135 of the judgment. While the *Treatment Action Campaign* case has generally received wide praise, some scholars have criticized the constitutional court's express rejection of the 'minimum core obligation' approach recommended by the UN Committee on Economic, Social and Cultural Rights. Stated simply, this 'minimum core obligation' approach requires States to immediately marshal available resources to provide the minimum levels of a right—the survival needs of each person—which may be expanded upon later. If States do not meet these basic needs, the omission constitutes a prima facie violation of the International Covenant on Economic and Social Rights, and states are required to justify their failure to fulfill the obligation. The constitutional court rejected this approach, preferring instead to pursue the 'reasonableness' approach it had adopted in *Grootboom* and holding that by not providing access to Nevirapine, the government's policies fell foul of the requirement of 'reasonableness'. For literature that is critical of this approach of the constitutional court and instead advocates the approach of the UN Committee, see generally, Sandra Liebenberg, 'Violations of Socio-economic Rights: The Role of the South African Human Rights Commission', in (Penelope Andrews *et. al.*, eds), *The Post Apartheid Constitutions* 405, 418–20 (Johannesburg Wits University Press, 2001); and David Bilchitz, 'South Africa: Right to Health and access to HIV/AIDS drug treatment', 2. INT'L J. CONST. L. 524, 531–4 (2004).

[112] Ibid., at paragraph 123.

[113] Ibid., at paragraph 133.

noted, in *Grootboom*, the court felt that the government was otherwise sincere and earnest in its efforts to provide housing to the citizens of the Republic. Quite obviously, the court did not feel the same way about the government's efforts with regard to its HIV/AIDS policy.

The Constitutional Court's Approach in Cases Involving Social Rights

In March 2004, the constitutional court delivered its fourth judgement relating to social rights in the case of *Khosa* v. *Minister of Social Development*.[114] The court once again overrode the objections of the South African government to hold that non-citizens in South Africa (who had obtained permanent residence status) would be entitled to receive social security benefits. The court also held that the South African government would have to bear the extra financial costs to arrange for such disbursement.

The South African Constitutional Court has had to grapple with very serious issues concerning social rights, and it has sought to resolve them by adopting a pragmatic and cautious approach. As Craig Scott and Philip Alston have noted, an important factor explaining the restrained approach in *Soobramoney* may well have been the fact that it came up so shortly after the birth of the new republic, giving the South African government very little time to take action to remedy the monumental and lingering problems of four centuries of colonial rule, followed by five decades of apartheid. However, as the years have passed, and the new, democratic government of South Africa has had more time and opportunities to tackle these issues which have been prioritized by the constitution, the constitutional court appears to have changed its attitude and is taking a more proactive role in seeking to enforce social rights. This would help explain the slow yet discernible change in the court's attitude, which is most noticeable in the *Treatment Action Campaign* case where the court ventured beyond its restrained approach in earlier cases, and flexed its muscles to issue wide-ranging directions. A review of this case reveals the court, for the first time, adopting an approach where it considers itself an equal partner in the process of securing to citizens of South Africa the

---

[114] Case No. CCT13/03, at http://www.concourt.gov.za/judgment.php? case_id= 12598 . Constraints of space, as well as the fact that the central issue in this case does not have immediate relevance to the Indian context (where there is no legal entitlement to social security benefits), prevent a close analysis of the facts and reasoning of the case which nevertheless remains a fascinating site for the issues being focused upon in this essay.

social rights guaranteed by its new constitution.

Having said that, one must be careful not to draw too romantic an image of the court's role in making a difference to the lives of ordinary citizens, or even its capacity to do so in the long run. South Africa remains amongst the poorer countries of the world. Its populace is marked by huge differences of wealth, education, and income, and is still recovering from the combined long term effects of colonialism and apartheid. It faces law and order problems of a huge magnitude. The HIV/AIDS pandemic has caught the entire nation in its grip and the risk to its adult population poses a colossal challenge to its economy.

The judges of the constitutional court are well aware of these circumstances,[115] but appear to be inclined towards small and cautious measures in exercising their social rights jurisdiction. They also appear, at least in the cases decided until now, to be willing to defer to the South African government's approach to social rights issues, and seem to give the government a considerable degree of latitude especially when formulating remedies.[116] While some would argue that this is a prudent option, critics have asserted that by doing so, the constitutional court is abdicating its jurisdiction in respect of social rights, leading to a situation where 'the promise of socio-economic rights contained in the constitution has become illusory.'[117]

In future years, the challenge for the South African constitutional court will be to continue to enforce the mandate set out for them by the constitutional text in respect of social rights, while maintaining credibility with, and gaining the trust of, the people at large as well as the other organs of government in South Africa.

---

[115] This awareness is reflected, for instance, in this eloquent passage in president Chaskalson's opinion in *Soobramoney*: 'We live in a society in which there are great disparities of wealth. Millions of people are living in deplorable conditions and in great poverty.... These conditions already existed when the constitution was adopted and a commitment to address them, and to transform our society into one in which there will be human dignity, freedom and equality, lies at the heart of our constitutional order. For as long as these conditions continue to exist, that aspiration will have a hollow ring'. *Soobramoney*, supra n. 77 at paragraph 8.

[116] Marius Peterse, 'Coming to Terms with Judicial Enforcement of Social Rights', 20 SOUTH AFRICAN J. HUM RTS. 383, 414 (2004) (noting that the constitutional court has used the 'remedial arsenal at its disposal' in social rights cases 'most cautiously.')

[117] Lynn Berat, 'The Constitutional Court of South Africa and Jurisdictional Questions: In the Interest of Justice?' 3 INT'L J. CONST. L. 39, 72 (2005).

COMPARATIVE REFLECTIONS

Contrasting the constitutional experiences of India and South Africa in respect of social rights leads to interesting insights. The two nations have many historical links, and share several similarities: among others, a common colonial experience under British imperial rule; and populations that are extremely diverse, and are divided by extreme disparities of wealth as well as social and economic opportunities. In both countries, the drafters of the respective constitutions placed considerable responsibility and power in the newly established judicial systems. However, in respect of social rights, the constitutional models adopted were quite different in the two nations. Part of that can be explained by the different time periods in which the constitutions were enacted, and the different conceptions of constitutionalism that prevailed and motivated the respective drafters of these two major constitutions. While the Indian judiciary had to carve out a social rights jurisdiction for itself, the South African Constitutional Court had express textual mandates in this respect.

Both apex courts have been subjected to criticism for the judgments pronounced by them in the area of social rights. Their experiences would seem to suggest that at least some of the arguments voiced by those raising institutional objections to judicial implementation of social rights might be well founded. Both institutions will necessarily have to improve their track records in respect of monitoring the orders that they issue in social rights cases, and ensuring that they get fully implemented. This will require considerable innovation as the traditional remedies are quite inadequate for the task of overcoming developmental problems. While the Indian Supreme Court has taken some steps in this respect, this is clearly an aspect that will require more ingenuity and application in the future as well.

A survey of the social rights cases decided by the two courts reveals an interesting point. Executive wings of government around the world seem to share the trait of jealously guarding their monopoly over determining the economic policies that their nations follow. In most countries, the only way the people at large can exercise control over the direction of such economic policies is by choosing candidates of their economic persuasion at elections, and hoping that once elected, the candidates will actually stick to their promised policies. The course of action adopted by courts in India and South Africa allows activists and social movements in these two nations to have an additional means to influence national economic policy: by bringing appropriate cases involving social rights before the courts. Although both apex courts have demonstrated a marked reluctance to exercise their social rights jurisdiction to directly impact the economic policies that are being pursued by their governments, there have been some steps (and encouraging dicta) in this regard, and it remains to be seen whether this trend will grow in future years.

The survey also reveals that the South African Constitutional Court has been influenced by the social rights jurisprudence evolved by the Supreme Court of India. As we have noted, the drafters of the South African constitution had taken into account both the textual provisions in the Constitution of India relating to social rights, as well as the PIL jurisprudence of the Supreme Court of India. Thus, the adoption of social rights as enforceable fundamental rights in South Africa, which is the basis for the social rights jurisdiction of the constitutional court, may well have been influenced by the supreme court's social rights jurisprudence. In addition, as noted earlier, the constitutional court has expressly referred to the reasoning adopted in relevant Indian cases to justify its own results in the *Soobramoney* and *Treatment Action Campaign* decisions.

The constitutional court has extensively relied upon precedents of the supreme court to resolve other difficult constitutional issues.[118] However, at least until now, the reverse has not been true.[119] One hopes

---

[118] A survey of cases decided by the South African Constitutional Court in the first three years of its functioning (1995–7) reveals that it referred to Indian precedents in 9 out of the 60 judgments that were delivered during this period. Some of the early major cases where the South African Constitutional Court referred to Indian precedents include: *S. v. Makwanyane*, 1995 (3) SA 391 (CC) (holding the death penalty unconstitutional and referring to the reasoning in *Bachan Singh v. State of Punjab* (1980) 2 SCC 684); *Coetzee v. Govt. of South Africa*, 1995 (4) SA 631 (holding the imprisonment of judgment-debtors unconstitutional and relying on *Kharak Singh v. State of UP*, [1964] 1 SCR 332 and *Maneka Gandhi v. Union of India*, AIR 1978 SC 597) and *Ex. Council Western Cape v. President of RSA*, 1995 (4) SA 877 (laying down the limits of powers that can be delegated by the president, and relying on *Rajnarainsingh v. Chairman, Patna Admn Comm.* [1955] 1 SCR 290).

[119] A *Manupatra* search reveals that the supreme court of India has relied upon a precedent of the South African constitutional court in only one case so far, and even here, the reference can only be characterized as casual rather than a substantive engagement with the reasoning employed by the constitutional court. *State of Punjab v. V.K. Khanna* AIR 2001 SC 343 (this was a case concerning bias in administrative actions, and Banerjee's judgment for the court refers, in passing, to the decision of the constitutional court in *President of the Republic of South Africa v. South African Rugby*

that in future, the supreme court of India too will benefit from analysing the careful reasoning that is so characteristic of the rulings of the South African Constitutional Court. Given the great similarity in the issues that confront their respective nations, one would naturally expect these two stellar judicial institutions to benefit from mutual exchanges of judicial reasoning.

I conclude by taking note of the views of Justice Krishna Iyer, who is widely acknowledged as one of the principal architects of the PIL movement in India. Iyer has been extremely critical of the tendency of Indian jurists and judges to pay blind obeisance to foreign precedents from Britain and the United States, and has urged Indian lawyers and academics to 'initiate a renaissance movement for creative Indian jurisprudence'.[120] While I am sympathetic to Iyer's views on this issue, I am equally confident that he would whole-heartedly extend his support to a project that seeks to increase the exchange of judicial reasoning and learning across countries in the developing world that have much to offer to each other.

Football Union, 1999 (4) SA 147). Since this article was written, the Supreme Court of India has relied on decisions of the South African Constitutional Court in a few more cases. The most prominent example of this trend is to be found in the August 2006 decision in *Kuldip Nayar v. Union of India* (2006) 7 SCC 1, where the Supreme Court of India cited and relied upon the decisions of the South African Constitutional Court in *New National Party of South Africa v. Government of the Republic of South Africa and Anr*, 1999 (3) SA 191, and *United Democratic Movement v. President of the Republic of South Africa and Ors*, 2003 (1) SA 495.

[120] V.R. Krishna Iyer, 'Inaugural Address at the Second State Lawyers' Conference, Andhra Pradesh at Rajahmundry (1976) 2 SCC (Jour) 1. (Our forensic and parliamentary way of life is still washed by the Thames and the Potomac and not the Yamuna, Godavari or Kaveri). See also, *Rattan Lal v. Vardesh Chander* (1976) 2 SCC 103, 114–15 (paragraph 21) ('We have to part company with the precedents of the British-Indian period tying our non-statutory areas of law to vintage English law...British and Indian ways of life vary so much, the validity of an Anglophilic bias in Bharat's justice, equity and good conscience is questionable today...Free India has to find its conscience in our rugged realities—and no more in alien legal thought').

12

Human Rights and Environmental Wrongs

Integrating the Right to Environment and Developmental Justice in the Indian Constitution

CHARU SHARMA

BACKGROUND

The Indian Constitution never recognized that there would be any enforceable or justiciable rights for the environment; that came much later and in the form of fundamental duties imposed upon the citizens under the constitution.

Contrary to the importance accorded to the environment now and amendments to this effect the earlier constitution did not reflect any duties or rights provisions relating to the environment or its protection. Scholars argue that caring for the environment was within the Indian ethos but that was when population levels did not pose such a threat to natural resources and communities and civilizations were short-sighted and did not look beyond their own anthropocentric goals.

Yet in the last fifty-five years, environmental concerns have surfaced as much in India as elsewhere, and accordingly the country has dealt with the concern, conflicts, and repercussions through piece-meal legislation, constitutional interpretation and judicial ingenuity—in tune with national policy and international principles. Compared to other countries, India has done well in terms of recognizing some kind of environmental right implicitly. However, a number of unanswered issues plague a realist; the real questions being:

- will implicit recognition work only until it clashes with major fundamental rights as has been often recorded?;

- how long until unsustainable development patterns continue to exhaust these resources if we don't do something about them urgently?;
- and how long will this new/nascent environmental right to healthy environment which has begun to be placed on the mantle of fundamental rights wrestle with constitutionally-enshrined fundamental rights and basic human needs of a developing country?

There might be a theoretical answer to the above questions but realists will never find a concrete answer because within a spectrum of basic needs and human rights like right to food, to work, to development, etc., in the developing world, environment will always be placed at the low end of the spectrum of fundamental rights and whenever it does receive priority somewhere, the rights of many will be trampled. Instead of carving niche for recognition of environmental rights, the courts will be doing more harm than actual justice.

A number of methods can be examined to solve the present crisis and tide over the major constitutional gap, weak enforcement mechanisms and the perceived conflict between fulfillment of basic human needs, and vindication of right to development and protection of our environment.

This essay explores the link between human rights and environmental justice thus meted out by the courts. In so doing, firstly it looks into the development and recognition of environmental rights, sustainable development, and environmental justice under international law. Secondly, it considers recent case-law to examine the inconsistency between constitutional rights and the difficulty in enforcement of fundamental duties and emphasizes judicial creativity that has created a body of 'environmental rights' in India. Thirdly, it considers how Indian environmental law has been or might be affected by international legal regimes and international principles. Lastly, it looks at some unanswered questions which need immediate answers and major legal reform in order to address the issues of environmental degradation, deprivation of basic human rights, and poverty. The author reiterates that environmental justice may not be possible unless development proceeds on a sustainable basis and recognition of a constitutionally guaranteed right to healthy environment may just be the right thing for socially empowering people to achieve their basic human rights as both such rights are not different from a horse-and-carriage relationship.

The Indian supreme court recognizes that '…hygienic environment is an integral facet of right to healthy life under Article 21 and it would be impossible to live with human dignity without a humane and healthy environment'.[1]

The Constitution of India does not make reference to the environment under its chapter on fundamental rights and freedoms. In 1980, the first emphatic attempt to right and ameliorate the living conditions and living environment of the residents of Ratlam was made by the supreme court through Justice Krishna Iyer for preserving public health and protection of the environment.[2] The court gave directions to remove the nuisance caused due to human waste by compelling the municipal authority to carry out its duties to the community by constructing sanitation facilities.[3] The judgment had two effects. Firstly, the court held that a municipality could not shirk its statutory obligations to provide sanitation facilities by pleading financial constraints. Secondly, the court imposed a mandatory duty on the magistrate to remove any public nuisance wherever one existed by interpreting section 133 of the Criminal Procedure Code. This case was just the tip of the iceberg and the beginning of the plethora of environmental cases, which were to be adjudicated later on before the supreme court on a wide host of issues arising out of environmental protection, human rights violation, and sustainable development. At the same time, ingenious judicial creativity could be seen in exposition of the tool of public interest litigation where citizens robbed of their fundamental rights had been provided appropriate relief by the supreme court by demolishing all technical difficulties in approaching the court for vindication of their rights, an Article 32 writ petition. The court accepted simple applications from public-spirited citizens who came forward to espouse the cause of social justice and empowerment for the right of others who were unable to do so

[1] *T.N. Godavarman Thirumalpad v. Union of India*, Writ Petition (civil) 202 of 1995 decided on 30 October 2002, per Arijit Pasayat J. elaborating the supreme court's view in *Virender Gaur v. State of Haryana* 1995 (2) SCC 577 on how Article 21 had been interpreted in a manner to include right to live with human dignity which encompasses within its ambit, the protection of environment, its preservation, ecological balance free from air and water pollution and that environmental, ecological, air, water pollution, etc., should be regarded as amounting to violation of Article 21 guaranteeing a right to life.'

[2] This does not mean that there were no environmental cases before the courts; rather most of the pre-1980 environmental cases dealt with tort actions or statutory violations under the various environmental statutes e.g., Water Act, 1974, or an offence under the Indian Penal Code 1860, e.g., S. 268 causing a public nuisance.

[3] *Municipal Council, Ratlam v. Vardhichand and Ors* AIR 1980 SC 1622.

themselves.[4] By this time, the scope of right to life under Article 21 of the constitution was expanded to a considerable degree with amazing judicial ingenuity. Yet, as the constitution had never recognized the right to environment, the court never decided any case based on the violation of the right to a healthy environment.

By the mid 1980's, the court was however prepared to consider a creative and unprecedented use of the duty to respect the environment under the directive principles of state policy introduced by the forty second amendment to the constitution in 1972 and to further expand the scope of Article 21 in order to remedy the environmental wrongs arising from mining[5] and quarrying works, building and construction, waste management and escape of deadly gases from chemical plants.[6] In 1987, and then in 1991, the court applied a creative approach to recognize a right to a wholesome environment[7] and interpreted Article 21 to include the right to enjoy pollution, free water and air for the full enjoyment of life.[8] After establishing some fundamental norms while dealing with environmental cases from 1995–2003 the court has further recognized and expanded upon international environmental expositions and has accordingly applied international law principles, e.g., 'polluter pays' which have been held to be a part of the basic environmental law of the land and require that a polluter must bear the costs of remedying a situation created by its industrial activity and pay compensation to the victims of pollution,[9] or the 'precautionary principle' that requires

---

[4] The best attempts of the court to address the environmental issues can be seen in its various orders and decisions regarding the Pollution of Ganges and the Yamuna river ((1998) 1 SCC 226) in a series of cases filed by M.C. Mehta, e.g., in *M.C. Mehta v. UOI* (Ganga pollution and Kanpur tannery cases), see AIR 1991 Supp.(1) SCC 181; 1992 Supp.(2) SCC 637; 1993 Supp.(1) SCC 434 and 1992 Supp.(2) SCC 633.

[5] *Tarun Bharat Sangh v. UOI* (Sariska Case) 1994 2 SCALE 68; AIR 1992 SC 514.

[6] For critical comments on the persistent violation of human rights caused due to the environmental disaster that was 'Bhoposhima', see V.R Krishna Iyer, 'Union Carbide's "Bhoposhima" and Indian Justice in Somno–Coma' in Constitutional Miscellany (2nd edn) Eastern Book Company 2003, pp. 228–58.

[7] *Rural Litigation and Entitlement Kendra, Dehradun v. State of Uttar Pradesh* AIR 1988 SC 2187; *T. Damodar Rao v. The Special Officer, Municipal Corporation of Hyderabad* AIR 1987 AP 171, 181.

[8] *Subhash Kumar v. State of Bihar* AIR 1991 SC 420 at 424.

[9] *Indian Council for Enviro-legal Action v. UOI* AIR 1996 SC 1446, 1446r, *Vellore Citizens' Welfare Forum v. UOI* AIR 1996 SC 2715 ; *S. Jagannath v. UOI* AIR 1997 SC 811. See also Divan, S. and Rosencranz, A., 'Environmental Law and Policy in India: Cases, Materials and Statutes', 2nd edn, Oxford University Press, Third Impression (2002), pp. 41–2.

the state authorities to prevent, solve and anticipate factors that would lead to environmental pollution and subjecting the developer to prove that its action was environmentally useful[10] or 'intergenerational equity'. The court recognizes a duty upon the decision making authorities to give due regard to ecological factors including 'an obligation of the present generation to preserve the natural resources and pass on to the future generations an environment intact as the one we inherited from the previous generation'.[11]

From the above mentioned description it is clear that the Indian Supreme Court has gone far to expand the scope of Article 21 to recognize a right to a wholesome environment as a facet of the right to life under the constitution.

DEVELOPMENT AND RECOGNITION OF ENVIRONMENTAL RIGHTS UNDER INTERNATIONAL LAW

Many scholars would still assert that the status and the link between human rights and the environment has not been clearly established in international law. But such a claim can now be clearly dismissed based on the mounting evidence in the form of international conventions, treaties,[12] accords, and international case-law and legal writings[13] that

[10] *Vellore Citizens' Welfare Forum* v. *UOI* AIR 1996 SC 2715,2721; *A.P. Pollution Control Board* v. *Prof M.V. Nayadu* AIR 1999 SC 812, 819.

[11] *State of Himachal Pardesh* v. *Ganesh Wood Products* AIR 1996 SC 149, 163.

[12] See, for example, Article 1 of the International Covenant on Civil and Political Rights, which declares unequivocally that 'all peoples have the right to self determination—that people have a right of self determination obviously includes that people have right of environmental sovereignty and they have a right to freely dispose of their natural wealth and resources and...in case can they be deprived of its own means of subsistence', Rio Declaration was a further summation of the value of protecting the environment and the human being and the human right to adequate condition of life, in an environment of quality that permits a life of dignity and well-being' Stockholm Decl. Principle 1, UN Doc. A/conf.48/14, at 2–65 (1972); Rio Decl., Principle 4, UN Doc.A/Conf.151/5/rev.1 (13 June 1992).

[13] 'Prof. Nico Schrijver of the Institute of Social Studies at Hague, in his paper Legal Aspect of Sustainable Development and Protection of Environment' has highlighted this right to development or sustainable development and indicated that the same includes a healthy environment' see *M.C. Mehta* v. *UOI* 2001 SOL Case No. 156, per Umesh C. Banerjee, J., para 5; see also *Calcutta Wetlands* judgment AIR 1993 Cal 215 where Banerjee J. states that 'While it is true that in a developing country there shall have to be developments, but that development shall have to be in closest possible harmony with the environment, as otherwise there would be development but no environment, which would result in total devastation'.

recognize a right to healthy and wholesome environment under some facet of right to respect for home and private life,[14] right to life,[15] right to peaceful enjoyment of possession, right to a fair trial, right to freedom of expression, or directly.

The 1972 Stockholm Conference of the United Nations on Human Environment had recognized the link between human rights and environmental protection stressing that human beings had a fundamental right to freedom, equality, and adequate conditions of life, in an environment of a quality that permits a life of dignity and well-being.[16] The International Covenant on Economic, Social, and Cultural Rights, 1966, had also stressed the relationship between environment and development by stating, inter alia, that people had a 'right to enjoy the highest attainable standard of physical and mental health' and that member states needed to advance 'all aspects of industrial and environmental hygiene' in order to achieve this objective.[17]

Similarly in 1981, the African Charter on Human and People's Rights recognized that 'all peoples shall have the right to a generally satisfactory environment favourable to their development'.[18] The World Commission on Environment and Development, or the Brundtland Report, 1987, had stressed the importance of sustainable development which encapsulated two significant concepts stating that member states should

[14] See the decision of the European Court of Human Rights in *Hatton & ors* v. *United Kingdom* (Application 36022/97, 2 October 2001): the case concerned an application by 8 applicants who claimed that the changes in the manner that nighttime flights were regulated in 1993 at Heathrow Airport, UK, had affected them in a serious manner leading to sleeping problems (seeking vindication of their rights under Articles 8 and 13 of the European Convention on Human Rights). Article 8 deals with right to respect for private and family life and Article 13 the right to an effective remedy. The European Court of Human Rights held that the applicants' rights under Article 8 and 13 were violated and regard must be had to a 'whole range of economic considerations and in the particularly sensitive area of environmental protection, mere reference to economic well-being of the country is not sufficient to outweigh the rights of the others.'

[15] Article 2, European Convention on Human Rights: 'everyone has a right to life protected by law'.

[16] See the Report of the United Nations Conference on the Human Environment 'Stockholm Declaration', 1972, UN Doc.A/Conf.48/14.

[17] See International Covenant on Economic, Social and Cultural Rights, e.i.f. 3 January 1976, Art 12, 993 UNTS 3, at http://www.unhchr.ch/html/menu3/b/a_cescr.htm.

[18] African Charter on Human and People's Rights, June 27 1981 at OAU Doc. CAB/LEG/67/3 rev. 5, 21 I.L.M. 58art.2

endeavour to promote giving an overriding priority to the 'needs' of the poor and that if the current state of unsustainable development hampered by technology and social organization goes on unabated, the environment would not be able to meet the needs of the present and the future generations.[19] In 1992, the Rio Declaration emphasized conservation of environment through means of sustainable and equitable use and sharing of the benefits derived from biological resources and international environmental scholars assert that it also spearheaded further sustainable development approach with respect to the environment component and the recognition of community-based rights of the people.[20] From the 1994 Geneva Draft Declaration of the Principles on Human Rights and the Environment, one finds further evidence of the recognition and development of right to a healthy and ecologically sound environment.[21] The Declaration stressed upon the link between human rights and environmental protection recognizing the interdependence and indivisibility of the relationship between environmental right and other human rights, including civil, cultural, economic, political, and social rights. It also stressed that environmental protection was important as upholding fundamental human rights such as right to life, health, and culture and right to participation. In 1998, the Aarhus convention emphasized the right to environment, right of access to information, participation in decision making, and right to access to justice in environmental matters.[22] Similarly, the European Convention on Human Rights also contains provisions that stress upon the applicability of fundamental human rights with respect to the environment.[23]

Apart from other numerous international instruments that reflect the development of a right to environment, over 60 countries worldwide

[19] Our Common Future, Oxford University Press (1987) p. 43.

[20] See CIEL Publications One Specis, One Planet: Environmental Justice and Sustainable Development, Center for International Environmental Law (CIEL), October 2002 at http://www.ciel.org/Publications/onespecies_oneplanet/22oct02.html.

[21] At http://www1.umn.edu/humanrts/instree/1994-dec.htm.

[22] Convention on Access to Information, Public Participation in Decision Making and Access to Justice in Environmental Matters,The Aarhus Convention, 4th UNECE Ministerial Conference, Aarhus, 25 June 1998, UN Doc. ECE/CEP/43 at http://www.unece.org/env/pp/documents/cep43e.pdf.

[23] European Convention for the Protection of Human Rights and Fundamental Freedoms, Article 6, at http://www1.umn.edu/humanrts/instree/z17euroco.html. See also Article 8.

have recognized the right to a healthy environment.[24] Notable amongst them are the Constitution of Philippines that recognizes the right of the people to a balanced and healthful ecology in accord with rhythm and harmony of nature;[25] the Brazilian Constitution which states that everybody has a right to ecologically balanced environment, and imposes on the authorities and the community an obligation to defend and preserve the environment for present and future generations;[26] and the South African constitution which grants, inter alia, the right to an environment that is not harmful to the health and well-being of the people.[27] The significance of including environmental provisions in the constitution is very aptly illustrated in the following paragraph by Okidi quoting Brandl and Bungert:

Constitutional implementation enables environmental protection to achieve the highest rank among legal norms, a level at which a given value trumps every statute, administrative rule or court decisions. For instance, environmental protection might be considered a fundamental right retained by the individual and thus might enjoy the protected status accorded to other fundamental rights. In addition, addressing environmental concerns at the constitutional level means that environmental protection need not depend on narrow majorities in the legislative bodies. Rather, environmental protection is more firmly rooted in the legal order because constitutional provisions ordinarily may be altered only pursuant to elaborate procedures by a special majority, if at all.[28]

From the above exposition, one can clearly see how international legal norms and instruments have provided for the development and recognition of a right to environment.

CONFLICT BETWEEN CONSTITUTIONAL RIGHTS[29]

The decisions by the supreme court of India have been relied upon in a number of instances in the neighboring countries in Asia, e.g., by the

[24] See Ksentini, F.Z., Human Right and the Environment: Final Report, Annex III, UN ESCOR, Hum. Rts. Comm., at 81–9, UN Doc. E/CN.4/Sub.2/1994/9.

[25] See Article II, section 16 of the Constitution of Philippines.

[26] See Article 225 of the Constitution of Federative Republic of Brazil at http://www.senado.gov.br/bdtextual/const88/const88i.pdf.

[27] See Chapter 2, section 24 of the Constitution of South Africa.

[28] See Okidi, C.O., International Perspective on the Environment and Constitutions at http://www.kenyaconstitution. org/html/fsig5.htm.

[29] This section of the paper draws upon an earlier work presented at the International Conference on Human Rights and Basic Needs: From Theory to Practice in India at The Wissenschaftskolleg zu Berlin, February 2003.

supreme court of Pakistan in solving its own environmental problems and providing justice to those whose rights have been infringed.[30] The Human Development Report, 2002, states that the Indian supreme court has been 'the cornerstone of India's democracy since independence' and 'a renewed judicial activism can be seen in the vigorous decisions of the court defending citizens' fundamental rights and safeguarding environmental and other public goods.' These cases have also led to protection of public goods such as clean air and water and uncontaminated blood supplies. The Report recognizes the supreme court's efforts which can be seen emerging parallel to the emergence of civil society organizations and social movements dedicated to providing social justice and human rights goals.[31] Similar praise and credit has been given to the supreme court by judges and international legal scholars all over the world as an institution 'that has established itself as one of the indisputably great courts of the world and the guardian of the Indian constitution.'[32] Among the more striking features has been the 'court's active acceptance of responsibility for the pursuit of objects well outside the bounds of conventional litigation'.[33]

Most of the cases recognizing the human right to a 'wholesome environment'[34] have been accepted by the supreme court and various high courts as a writ petition under Articles 32 and 226 of the constitution.[35]

[30] See *Ms Shehla Zia and others* v. *WAPDA* Human Rights Case no 15-K of 1992 supreme court of Pakistan where the court has interpreted Articles 9, 14 and 184(3) of the constitution of Pakistan to interpret 'Life' to include 'more than vegetative or animal life or mere existence from conception to death ... [it] enables man not only to sustain life but also to enjoy it' and applied precautionary principle in the instant case.

[31] See the Human Development Report 2002, p. 72 at http://stone.undp. org/hdr/report/global/2002/en/pdf/chapterthree.pdf

[32] 'On 50 years of the Indian Supreme Court', Vigyan Bhavan, Delhi, India, 26 November 1999. Lord Bingham of Cornhill, Speech at the Golden Jubilee celebrations to mark fifty years of the Indian Supreme Court.

[33] Ibid.

[34] See, for example, *Rural Litigation & Entitlement Kendra* v. *State of Uttar Pradesh* AIR 1988 SC 2187; *Subash Kumar* v. *State of Bihar* AIR 1991 SC 420; *M.C. Mehta* v. *UOI* 1992(3) SCC 256.

[35] Article 32 of the constitution provides a right to constitutional remedies. It guarantees the right to move the supreme court by appropriate proceedings for the enforcement of the rights conferred by Part III of the constitution. Under this Article, the supreme court can issue directions, orders or writs including the writs in the nature of habeas corpus, mandamus, quo warranto, and certiorari for any of the rights conferred by part III. Similarly under Article 226, the high court of a state has power to issue writs concurrently to any person, authority, or government for the enforcement of any of the rights conferred by Part III and for any other purpose. The

But it was with the judicial innovation notably of Justice Bhagwati and Justice VR Krishna Iyer as mentioned above that the tool of public interest litigation (PIL)was creatively used to ameliorate the conditions of those whose fundamental rights had been affected due to various actors including state agencies.[36]

It was after the Bhopal gas disaster that the court was swamped with petitions relating to environmental harms[37] and consequent deprivation of fundamental rights of an individual. This was due to the fact that the tool of PIL could be easily used after the precedent set by PIL cases involving human rights of the poor and the powerless people were decided, especially those relating to police brutality and administrative abuse which action under PIL took care of the interest of the common public who had no access to judiciary and were largely unrepresented. According to Divan and Rosencranz the path for multiple number of petitioners affected by any environmental disaster was open and the court started addressing environmental problems looking at community rights instead of individual rights and most of the time the approach adopted by the court was proactive and amicus environment.[38] Secondly, 'this type of litigation in the supreme court was characterized by being non-adversarial, pro bono, and in public spirit'.[39] Further, apart from PIL and locus standi relaxation, the supreme court also used its power under Article 142 to mould its decision in order to do complete justice.

Judicial recognition of environmental rights was achieved in India starting from the supreme court's decision in *Rural Litigation and*

---

courts have a wide latitude thus to grant relief to the aggrieved persons but there are certain limits on the court's power. Primary among them is the issue of 'locus standi' or the petitioner's standing to institute proceedings before the court. Previously, only a person who was injured or aggrieved could move the court by appropriate proceedings for any remedy. In other words, only a person who was directly affected by administrative inaction or whose fundamental right had been affected could petition the court: *Calcutta Gas Co. Ltd.* v. *State of West Bengal* AIR 1962 SC 1044, 1047.

[36] See for example *People's Union for Democratic Rights* v. *Union of India* (AIR 1982 SC 1473); *Bandhua Mukti Morcha* v. *Union of India* (AIR 1984 SC 802); *Hussainara Khatoon* v. *Home Secretary, State of Bihar* AIR 1979 SC1360; *Dr. Upendra Baxi* v. *State of UP* (1983) 2 SCC 308.

[37] Early cases involving environmental problems which were brought to the courts as PILs: *Janaki Nathbhai Chhara* v. *Sardarnagar Municipality* AIR 1986 GUJ 49 and *Citizens Action Committee* v. *Civil Surgeon, Mayo General Hospital* AIR 1986 BOM 136.

[38] See Divan, S. and Rosencranz, A., *Environmental Law and Policy in India: Cases Materials and Statues*, 2nd edn. (Oxford University Press, Third Impression 2002), chapter 4 Section E, pp. 133–41.

[39] Ibid.

Entitlement Kendra v. *State of Uttar Pradesh* or the *Doon Valley Quarrying* case.[40] The court gave five orders in this case based on its understanding that environmental rights were to be implied into the scope of fundamental right to life and personal liberty guaranteed under Article 21 of the Constitution. In *M.C. Mehta* v. *Union of India*[41] (the *Shriram gas leak* or the *Oleum gas leak* case) the supreme court ordered the closure of an industrial plant in Delhi. The court introduced an important legal rule of 'strict liability' and 'polluter pays'. The defendant was allowed to reopen the factory only after agreeing to 'prudent ownership and management of its facilities and accepting to be personally responsible for compensation for any injuries or deaths caused by escaping chlorine gases, and after having accepted to establish a compensation fund for any victims of future gas emissions'.[42] *MC Mehta* v. *Union of India* (*Ganga pollution and tanneries cases*)[43] and the *Taj trapezium* case,[44] the supreme court took pioneering measures for preventing pollution of the river Ganga, and the Taj Mahal and ordered closing down of several industries which caused pollution in Kanpur and in Agra. Obviously, in so doing, the court would have realized that many industry and factory owners would be forced to close down their factories and/or incur unwanted costs to install pollution control equipment. One can see that in these cases environmental protection took priority over a right to trade and business.

The following section elaborates upon the judicial creativity on the development of a right to healthy environment by interpretation of the fundamental rights under the constitution and incorporation of international legal principles and instruments to which India is signatory.

CONSEQUENCES OF INTERNATIONAL
LAW ON INDIAN ENVIRONMENTAL LAW[45]

The Right to Life under Article 21 and the Right to Environment

The most significant contribution of the judiciary has been to interpret by ingenious means and bring environmental protection within the

---

[40] AIR 1985 SC 652, AIR 1988 SC 2187.

[41] AIR 1987 SC 1086 or the *Shriram gas leak/oleum gas leak* case.

[42] See n. 9 Divan and Rosencranz at p. 41

[43] AIR 1987 SC 965.

[44] *M.C. Mehta* v. *UOI* AIR 1997 SC 734.

[45] The following section closely reflects the views and comments of the author presented at International Conference on Human Rights and Basic Needs: From Theory to Practice in India at The Wissenschaftskolleg zu Berlin, February 2003.

purview of the inviolable fundamental rights, especially of the right to life and personal liberty under Article 21. Initially, the judiciary had relied upon Articles 48A and 51A of the constitution to remedy the constitutional gap or the lack of an enforceable and clear right to environment. Such a path was evidently fraught with many conflicts and the difficulties of enforcement and meaningful implementation. Such problems were bound to happen and arose because of the fact that hardly anything could be done as the provisions under the constitution were non-self executing principles and only enjoined a duty upon the state and a duty upon the citizens for working towards preservation and protection of the environment. However, this did not provide any relief. The judiciary looked askance to the fundamental rights chapter. One could imagine that the imperative of environmental protection had been recognized since 1972. India's participation at the UNCED and its role in recalling its ancient environmental traditions and culture would have been forever hovering in the minds of the higher judiciary and thus when presented with potential and actual environmental catastrophes, the judges working within the restrains of the constitution, carved a path for interpretation of fundamental rights read with fundamental duties of the state and the citizens to at least mention the right to environment in the *Limestone Quarrying* or the *Doon Valley* case in 1988.[46] One must remember that this was also the time when the Bhopal gas disaster had already claimed thousands of lives and the folly of not having or enforcing environmental protection programmes for potentially hazardous and in this case deadly gases within close proximity of dwellings had sensitized every individual's capacity to think, plan for the future, and seek justice. The *Doon Valley* case, was the first time that the supreme court had referred to the right to life and healthy environment under Article 21. It was also faced with a cruel choice between closing the quarries whereby many would have lost their jobs over the detrimental harm that was being caused by the illegal limestone quarrying to the water drainage system of Dehradun and nearby areas. But the court did make a choice and it also accepted that its decision would cause the quarries to be closed, but it stated that ' it is a price that has to be paid for protecting and safeguarding the right of the people to live in a healthy environment.' Having given such a decision and thus setting a path for future environmental actions, the court, in the 1990s, clearly stated what it had alluded to earlier in the *Doon Valley* case and other cases following it. In *Subhash Kumar* v. *State of Bihar*[47]

---

[46] AIR 1985 SC 652, AIR 1988 SC 2187.
[47] AIR 1991 SC 420.

the supreme court held that 'right to live is a fundamental right under Article 21 of the constitution and it includes the right to enjoyment of pollution-free water and air for full enjoyment of life. If anything endangers or impairs that quality of life, in derogation of laws, a citizen has a right of recourse to Article 32 of the constitution'.[48] The path thus opened by the supreme court led the state high courts to follow suit.[49] In *T. Damodar Rao* v. *Special Officer, Municipal Corporation, Hyderabad*,[50] as well as *L.K. Koolwal* v. *State of Rajasthan*,[51] the right to life under Article 21 was stated to include an environmental right. In the former case the court refused permission to the Life Insurance Corporation and the Income Tax Department for building residential houses in a recreational zone. The high court held that... 'environmental law has succeeded in unshackling man's right to life and liberty from the clutches of common law theory of individual ownership...it would be reasonable to hold that enjoyment of life and its attainment and fulfillment guaranteed by Article 21 embraces protection and preservation of nature's gifts without which life cannot be enjoyed...the slow poisoning of the atmosphere by polluted atmosphere can also be regarded as violating the right under Article 21.' The court further held that 'under the powerful but nascent law of environment, the unbridled right of the owner to enjoy his piece of land granted under the common law doctrine of ownership was substantially curtailed.'

In the latter case, the petitioner had represented the citizens of Jaipur in the matter of inadequate sanitation of Jaipur city. Ordering the sanitation department to provide adequate sanitation, the court, inter alia, held that 'maintenance of health, preservation of sanitation and environment falls within the purview of Article 21.... Sanitation [as it] adversely affects the life of the citizen and it amounts to slow poisoning and reducing the life of the citizen because of the hazards created, if not checked'.

In expanding the scope of the right to life and personal liberty, the court has isolated and identified specific principles from within the

[48] Ibid., 424.

[49] The high court of Kerala in *Attakoya Thangal* v. *Union of India* 1990 (1) KerLT 580 held that: 'Right to life is much more than the right to animal existence and its attributes are manifold, as life itself. A prioritization of human needs and a new value system has been recognized in these areas. The right to sweet water and the right to free air are the attributes of the right to life. These are the basic elements which sustain life itself.'

[50] AIR 1987 AP 171.

[51] AIR 1988 RAJ 2.

specific environmental legislation, constitutional interpretation, and internationally acknowledged environmental doctrines applied in other countries. With the help of these principles the court has evolved and expanded upon the scope of the emerging human right to a healthy environment in India. Often the court has justified the application of new principles by virtue of reading from the legislation itself or deriving validity from India's international obligations.

Using the Right to Equality to Protect the Right to Environment

In many instances where the issue has related to environmental protection or a web of issues relating to the conflict between builders, industrialists, and timber factory owners who encroach upon forest land and whose activities detrimentally impact not only the forests and the environment but also the forest dwellers, the petitioners, especially many non-governmental organizations have invoked Article 14. Such organizations have petitioned the court for declarations and orders invalidating construction permits which have been granted by various municipal corporations or state agencies. This has largely been the case where petitioners have challenged permissions which have been arbitrarily granted by state agencies without adequate consideration of environmental impacts.[52] Article 14 of the constitution deals with the right to equality and empowers a person who has been unequally dealt with to question the arbitrary decision made by a government authority.[53] It provides that the state shall not deny to any person equality before the law or the equal protection of the laws within the territory of India. Government authorities including and administrative bodies have often been questioned whether they have been reasonable and not arbitrary in making the decisions and granting permissions. The test applied by the court within Article 14 has been the test of reasonableness and unequal treatment. A governmental decision that fails to take into account relevant considerations that affect the environment has been held to be invalid.[54] In *Enviro- Legal Action* v. *Union of India*, the *CRZ* case,[55] the court has held that the principle of intergenerational equity (the right of each

---

[52] *Kinrki Devi* v. *State of HP* AIR 1988 HP 4.

[53] Article 14 strikes at arbitrariness—see n. 9, Divan and Rosencranz at p. 53.

[54] *State of HP* v. *Ganesh Woods Products*, supra n.; See also *Pleasant Stay Hotel* v. *Palani Hills Conservation Council* (1995) 6 SCC 127, 136, 139, 140.

[55] AIR 1996 (5) 281.

generation to benefit from past natural inheritance and the obligation of the present generation to preserve such heritage for future generations) would be violated if there was a substantial adverse ecological effect caused by industry.[56] The court stated that environmental statutes were enacted to ensure good quality of life for unborn generations since it is they who must bear the brunt of ecological degradation.[57]

Conflict between Environment and Right to Trade

In *Sushila Saw Mills* v. *State of Orissa*,[58] the petitioner had challenged a section of the Orissa Saw Mills and Saw Pits (Control) Act of 1991, which prohibited saw mills from operating in a forest or within a buffer of 10 kilometers from a forest. The law in this case had been enacted to protect a forest and stop illegal felling of trees. The supreme court dismissed the petition and held that the right to carry on trade and business was subject to statutory regulation and in this case the regulations were for protecting the forest area from illegal felling. The court explained that it was in the public interest that certain restrictions may be applied statutorily and those under Article 19(1)(g) might in certain cases include total prohibition of trade or business activity, and that it was a class legislation and did not offend Articles 14 or 301 of the constitution.

Although Article 19(1)(g) guarantees the fundamental right to a person to carry on any occupation, trade, or business, such a right to carry on business may be restricted when it conflicts with another person's right to safe and clean drinking water. In cases where such conflict is evident, the court has tried to balance the environmental interest with the right to trade or carrying on business. In some instances, the judiciary has had to prioritize the preservation of environmental resources, the right of a community, and the right of an industry to carry on business. In *Abhilash Textiles* v. *Rajkot Municipal Corporation*,[59] the High Court of Gujarat decided an apparent conflict between the right of a textile industry to carry on business with the danger to public health by discharge of dirty water onto public roads and drains.[60] The court held, inter alia, that 'the right under Article 19(1)(g) was a fundamental right but it

[56] Ibid.
[57] Ibid., 281, 293. See also n. 9 Divan and Rosencranz at pp. 53–4.
[58] AIR 1995 SC 2484.
[59] AIR 1988 GUJ 57.
[60] See Divan and Rosencranz, supra n. 9 at 54.

was subject to reasonable restrictions in the interest of the general public as provided under sub-clause(6) of Article19. No one has the right to carry on business if it is a nuisance to the society.' The court said that 'if a business activity became a health hazard to the society such an activity could not be allowed'. Further, the court also held that the petitioners were violating their fundamental duty under Article 51A (g) and although the Municipal Commissioner had issued them a notice of reminder, the petitioner had continued with activities disregarding its fundamental duty.[61]

Right to Better Quality of Environment

In the *Ratlam* case[62] Justice Krishna Iyer had stated that there was a relationship between environment and development and that the government should be conscious of the environmental impact while considering development. Following this approach many judges from various state high courts and those in the supreme court have adopted a more holistic approach towards the environment. In cases where there is an apparent conflict over environment and developmental actions, the courts have made detailed orders and appointed monitoring committees to supervise and inform the court of the factual situation. This kind of monitoring can be seen from the decision of the supreme

[61] Divan and Rosencranz comment that the court in this case had pre-judged the issue. Instead of making a determination that the petitioners had no right to carry on trade and business if they did not comply with the municipal regulations, the court should have used its privilege under Article 226 of the constitution and sent the petitioners for a personal hearing before the commissioner. See Divan and Rosencranz, supra n. 9 at 57. To justify the action taken by the court and in making the determination that it did, one should keep in mind that the problem which the petitioners and the defendants were embroiled in was one which had a number of entangled legal issues, requiring a determination. In the author's opinion, had the matter been resent to the commissioner it would not have seen the light of day and status quo would have been maintained unless something drastic would have happened. This is stated not to undermine the authority of the commissioner but the issue at hand where 165 petitioners were afraid of the restrictions on their right to trade and the discharge of dirty water which was polluting in a manner which would be health hazard to the public at large. Moreover, the supreme court by 1995 had had a history of being environmentally sensitive and an activist. Dealing with environmental cases of such kind the court's conscience seems to have veered towards making a sound environmental decision and in being able to constitutionally justify the reasonable fetters on the fundamental right to trade and business.

[62] AIR 1980 SC 1622.

court in *Municipal Council, Ratlam* v. *Vardhichand*[63] and the *Olga Tellis* v. *Bombay Municipal Coprn* cases.[64] In *Olga Tellis*, the court expanded the right to life as including the right to livelihood. The right to life, explained Justice Bhagwati, included the right to livelihood and since the petitioners would be deprived of their livelihood if they were evicted from the slums and pavement dwellings, their eviction would be tantamount to deprivation of their life and was hence unconstitutional. In *Free Legal Aid Cell* v. *Government of NCT Delhi*,[65] the Delhi High Court dealt with the high levels of noise pollution during festivals and marriages and held that noise pollution was wrongful contamination of the environment and resulted in nuisance and affected the health of a person and therefore violated Article 21 if it exceeded reasonable limits. It also stated that the effect of noise pollution deserved full attention of the judiciary.

In *M.C. Mehta* v. *Union of India*,[66] (Mehta 1998) the petitioner filed a PIL concerning the deterioration of the environment and the duty of the state government under Article 21 to ensure better quality of environment. The court ordered the central government to show steps they had taken to achieve this goal through national policy and to restore the quality of environment.

In the recent *Delhi Air Pollution* case dealing with tackling the hazards of air pollution in the city of Delhi, the court dealt with the number one cause of air pollution—that caused by automobiles operating in the city on diesel fuel. The number of orders passed in *M.C. Mehta*[67] show the new trend adopted by the supreme court to mould remedies in order to provide justice and reach a positive result. The court directed the entire fleet of buses to adapt their vehicle engines to emit low sulphur and use clean fuel. The court also directed the Ministry of Environment and Forest and the Delhi government to comply with the court's orders but relaxed the rules in view of the hardships and the problems faced by the commuters and the school going children. The court noted that as 'the existing ground realities show[ed] a near breakdown of the transport system in Delhi, primarily due to inaction on the part of the Delhi administration to take timely and effective steps, the citizens should not be made to suffer for somebody else's follies.' Further, the court stressed upon the government and the administration to act in aid of the

[63] Ibid.
[64] AIR 1986 SC 180.
[65] CWP no. 4683 of 2000 D/23-7-2000.
[66] (1998) 9 SCC 589.
[67] AIR 2001 SC 1846.

supreme court directives under the constitutional duty imposed by Article 144 and cautioned the authorities that the apex court would take any failure seriously.

In many cases, the court has held that in certain situations the right to environment needed to be prioritized over development where a specific situation has called for exposition and interpretation of an immediate and specific policy structure. In *Vellore Citizens Welfare Forum v. Union of India*,[68] the court recognized that precautionary principle is a principle of Indian environmental law. Then, in *AP Pollution Control Board v. Prof M.V. Nayudu*,[69] the court discussed the development of the precautionary principle, and in the *Narmada Bachao Andolan* case,[70] the court held that 'when there is a state of uncertainty due to lack of data or material about the extent of damage or pollution likely to be caused then, in order to maintain the ecological balance the burden of proof that the said balance will be maintained must necessarily be on the industry or the unit which is likely to cause such pollution'. A recent expansion of the right to life has been the recognition of the public trust doctrine by the supreme court as part of law of the land in the case of *MI Builders Pvt Ltd. v. Radhey Shyam Sahu*.[71] The court has applied this doctrine to protect and preserve public land and related it to sustainable development, precautionary principle, environmental impact assessment and biodiversity protection.[72] In *M.C. Mehta v. Kamal Nath & Ors*[73] (*Span resort* case), Span Resort Motels had established an illegal tourist resort near the banks of the Beas river in Kulu Manali, in the state of Himachal

[68] AIR 1996 SC 2715.

[69] AIR 1999 SC 812.

[70] AIR 1999 SC 3345.

[71] See *MI Builders Pvt. Ltd. v. Radhey Shyam Sahu* AIR 1999 SC 2468.

[72] Ibid. (the court applied the public trust doctrine in order to preserve a municipal park which had historical importance. The court stated that the municipal corporation had failed in its duty to protect and maintain the part under the Municipal Act and the permission given to the builders to construct a shopping area and a parking lot did not constitute to serve the alleged stated public purpose and was away from environmental interest. As a trustee of the natural resources the municipal corporation had acted otherwise. The court relied on *M.C. Mehta v. Kamal Nath (Span Resort* case) (1997) 1 SCC 388 and observed that the public trust doctrine was a part of law of the land. See also *Majra v. Indian Oil Corporation* AIR 1999 J&K 81.For a comment on MI Builders and the public trust doctrine, see Jona Razzaque, 'Application of the Public trust Doctrine in Indian Environmental Cases', 13(2) *Journal of Environmental Law*, 2001, 221.

[73] (1997) 1 SCC 388.

Pradesh. The court found the motel guilty of building an illegal wall and a bund restricting the flow of the river and damaging the ecology of the area. After taking into account Joseph Sax's public trust doctrine,[74] the court reiterated the duty of the state acting as a trustee to protect natural resources and gave directions to the polluter to pay compensation by way of cost for rectifying the damage to the environment and reversing the affected ecology of the area it had occupied illegally. The court stated that the 'public trust doctrine primarily rested on the principle that certain resources like air, sea, water, and forests have such great importance to the people as a whole that it would be unjustified to make them subject of private ownership'. In reaching its decision and recognizing inter-national principles as part of the Indian environmental law, it had also relied on American cases[75] and the common law concept as expounded by academics in the US and UK and directly applied Article 130-r(2) of the Treaty of Rome. In doing this, the court has set a precedent and in fact changed the nature of such international legal instruments and their applicability for the future irrespective of such instruments having no binding force. In the follow up action, the court cancelled the lease that was granted to Span Motels and in the year 2002, upholding the 'polluter pays' principle asked Span Motels to pay exemplary damages amounting to 1,000,000[76] and an additional fine. This instance of imposition of exemplary damages upon a polluter reflects the seriousness with which the supreme court regarded the issue of natural resources protection and protection of the affected people under that ecosystem. The court also took to task the state government for the patent breach of trust it had committed by leasing such an ecologically fragile land to the motel.

Thus the supreme court has expanded the scope of right to life to a right to safe and healthy environment by applying the public trust doctrine. And it is most likely that this case will set a precedent to be followed and applied in other cases when there is conflict between right to environment and right to development or other fundamental rights covered under Article 21 of the constitution. This clearly evidences the higher judiciary's commitment for environmental protection based on a sustainable development concept. By adopting this doctrine, the court

[74] See generally, Joseph Sax, 'The Public Trust Doctrine in Natural Resources Law: Effective Judicial Intervention' (1970) 68 Mich LR 471. See n. 72, Jona Razzaque at p. 228.

[75] *Illinois Central Railroad Co.* v. *People of the State of Illinois* 146 US 387.

[76] *M.C. Mehta* v. *Kamal Nath* (2002) 3 SCC 653.

has skillfully used it as a tool to protect and preserve the natural resources and the environment in many instances where an authority has acted in excess of the powers given under a specific act or where an authority has abused its power and not acted in accordance with its duty under the directive principles of state policy, such as under Article 48A.[77]

OTHER CONFLICTING ISSUES UNANSWERED

Marginalization of Citizens: Backlash and the Downside[78]

Based on the above, one would agree that the judiciary has given actual meaning to the concept of sustainable development and has helped solve many current controversies. The court used it in the *Narmada* case[79] and upheld the plan for development of the sardar sarvovar dam, saying such development would mean material or economic development but all those who were displaced had to be rehabilitated.[80] In many instances

[77] See also *M/s Stella Silks Ltd.* v. *State of Karnataka* AIR 2001 Kar 219, Water prevention and Control of Pollution Act, s. 33A, discharge of contaminated water by the industry, put on notice by the statutory authority but continued flouting the Act, all activities of the industry ordered to be stopped and electricity and other facilities license cancelled. The supreme court held that the interest of a particular person or industry is not the concern with which the Act has been enacted by the legislature. It is for protecting the interest of society and for ensuring the ecological preservation of nature that such enactments are made. If the petitioner flouts the legislation for their own private benefit such acts shall not be entertained and the court imposed costs as a measure of deterrence.

[78] This section would not have been complete without acknowledging my views in another paper 'Human Right to a Healthy Environment in India', a paper which I presented in a conference on Human Rights and basic Needs Theory and Practice in India in Berlin Institute of Advanced Studies, Germany on February 2003. In this section I have reiterated my views stated in , 'The Evolution and Scope of the Human Right to a Healthy Environment' Human Rights and Basic Needs—Theory and Practice in India, Prof. M.P. Singh and Prof. Helmut Goerlich (eds), 1–22 at pp. 16–17, Forthcoming book chapter.

[79] *Narmada Bachao Andolan* v. *UOI* AIR 1999 SC 3345 and the earlier Writ Petition (Civil) No. 319 of 1994. There have been a number of orders in this case, the most recent being in February and March 1999.

[80] The Sardar Sarovar Dam project involved a number of legal issues. According to most of the academics and social activists none of the issues relating to rehabilitation and resettlement or human rights violation has been satisfactorily been dealt with either by the government or by the supreme court. While the government and supporters of the dam in Gujarat argue that the water and the power it will provide

the court has tried to balance the conflicting interests of the people and of the environment per se. On other occasions the court has stepped into the shoes of the administrator and has filled up a number of gaps left by absence of clear governmental policy.[81] But in other instances, apart from judiciary's pro-environmental and public-spirited stance, the court has stepped back and held that it is not in public interest that the court should delve in areas that are the function of the executive.[82] However, many of the decisions have marginalized the people affected by detrimental and unplanned development, superficial enforcement of environmental protection laws and technical decision making. In recent disputes between the governmental authorities' actions, for protection of the environment,[83] relocation[84] and rehabilitation of uprooted citizens one can see some downsides of the environmentalist stance.

will be crucial for the entire region, spread over all four states in the west of the country (Gujarat, Rajasthan, Madhya Pradesh, and Maharashtra), a well known social activist Medha Patkar, India's well known writer, Arundhati Roy, and others who have strong reservations about the dam say that more than 200 villages would be submerged under the water and nearly one million people would be displaced by the dam waters. The protestors have argued over rehabilitation, resettlement issues, and human rights abuses that the affected persons have been subjected to over the course of ten years. The project has also been severely criticized by the international community for human rights violations in the form of repressive police force to silence the protestors, intimidate the activists, violent police beatings, and abuse. See, for example, 'People Struggle against mega(lomanic) Dam Project', at http:// www.nadir. org/nadir/initiativ/agp/free/dams/narmada/ See, for example, Sacrifice at the Temple of India: Narmada, International Dams Newsletter, Vol. 1, Winter 1985–6. See also 'NBA Satyagraha Update, 10 August 2003 at http://www.nadir.org/ nadir/initiativ/agp/free/dams/narmada/2003/0810Narmada_update.htm.

   [81] However see Sierra/Amnesty Report 2000 1/19/00, p. 14 at http://www.amnesty. org/allib/aireport/ar99/asa20.htm.

   [82] *BSES Ltd. & Anr v. UOI* AIR 2001(1) Bom CR 394.

   [83] See, for example, the decision of the Kerala High Court in *Executive Engineer, Attappady Valley Irrigation Project v. Environmental & Ecological Protection Samithy* AIR 1993 KER 320 finding the single judge's findings on merits of case inadequate; see also Rural Litigation and Entitlement Kendra, *Dehradun v. State of Uttar Pradesh* AIR 1988 SC 2187, court did not provide for the rehabilitation of the mine-owners elsewhere in the state.

   [84] *M.C. Mehta v. UOI*, 1996(4) SCC 351; 1998(2) RRR 575 (SC), see also *M.C. Mehta v. UOI* 2001 SOL Case No. 156 judicial review of the orders passed to shift 'H' categories industries(hazardous pollution causing factories and industries) outside the National Capital Territory of Delhi in order to create 'green lung spaces' in Delhi where earlier such factories and industries had stood and to clear Delhi's reputation as being the most polluted city. Although the petition was a public interest litigation and treated by the court with the best interests of the citizens of Delhi

In *BSES Ltd,*[85] the Bombay High Court has held that 'while public interest litigation is a welcome development there are nevertheless limits beyond which it may as well cease to be public interest any further... environmental issues are important and deserve serious consideration but the need of the environment needs to be balanced with the needs of the community at large and with the needs of a large developing country.'

In *Almitra Patel* v. *Union of India,*[86] the supreme court dealt with the question of eviction of urban encroachers (informal sector laborers) from public land. In giving its decision the court issued a warning against encroachment of public lands and stated that 'establishment or creating of slums...appears to be a good business and well organized...large areas of public land, in this way, are usurped for private use free of cost.... Rewarding an encroacher on public land with free alternate site is like giving a reward to a pickpocket.'[87] Academic scholars have criticized the labeling of the 'encroachers'—the labourers from the informal sector who are outside the organized labour market but make a significant contribution to the urban economy. Labourers, hawkers, and vendors comprise the most visible segment of the informal sector; legal academics pose a question whether in the name of protection of public spaces and parks this segment of workers is being denied the fundamental right to their life and livelihood. This decision of the supreme court of India and other recent decisions[88] by the Bombay[89] and Delhi High Court,[90] seem to have marginalized this population and denied to them justice in order to ensure clean and obstruction-free pavements and public places in order that pedestrians should have a superior claim to the pavements and maintaining the aesthetic grandeur of a public place. A look at the various reports where academics and professional have examined the potential

---

at heart, yet hundreds of factory owners and thousands of workers and labourers find themselves in a quandary as the relocation sites provided by the government authority for many of these people mean demise of their livelihood. Although the decision to relocate was made in 1996 even after eight years the fate of many of the labourers and factory owners is uncertain as they have not been able to establish themselves comfortably in the new sites (if already allocated) because of shortage of water and power and lack of infrastructure facilities amongst others.

[85] AIR 2001 (1) Bom CR 394.

[86] 2000(1) SCALE 568.

[87] Ibid., at 570–1.

[88] See, for example, *Ahmedabad Municipal Corporation* v. *Nawab Khan* AIR 1997 SC 152- regarding encroachment.

[89] *Bombay Hawker's Union* v. *Bombay Municipal Corp.* AIR 1985 SC 1206.

[90] *MCD* v. *Gurnam Kaur* AIR 1989 SC 38.

impacts and consequences of the construction and development of the Sardar Sarovar Dam Project on the Narmada river also indicates that large populations of the affected people in the area rather than being benefited have been marginalized. The 1994 Resettlement and Development World Bank Reports indicate that resettlement and rehabilitation of the uprooted villagers has been unsatisfactory.[91] In fact, some reports and non-governmental organizations assert that environmental judicialism has driven many individuals to misery as development and in many places environmental protection has taken precedence over the individual's right to life and livelihood.[92]

An Alternate Legal Framework

In order to examine whether there is a necessity to have 'environmental rights' that need to be included as fundamental right and be enforceable as other fundamental rights are in India, the first method is to let the current legal framework remain as it is but more effort requires to be put into planning and environmental problem solving. Judges should be making decisions based on economic tools[93] as that will be more practicable and in tune with sustainable development in the true sense keeping in mind the international principles of good governance, especially the precautionary principle, polluter pays, and public participation principle. This in turn further requires the recognition of the parallel customary law framework which has been relegated to a minimalist level by the regulatory use and extraction laws on natural resources management in India. In traditional Indian jurisprudence, custom constituted an independent source of law in contrast to religious

[91] See Human Rights and the Environment: International Campaigns: 'Take Action Against the Narmada Dam' at Sierra Club's Environmental Update (on file with author) at http://sieraclub.org/human-rights/india.

[92] Ibid., see also 'People Struggle against mega(lomanic) Dam Project', at http://www.nadir.org/nadir/initiativ/agp/free/dams/narmada/; 'Sacrifice at the Temple of India: Narmada', International Dams Newsletter, Vol. 1, Winter 1985–6, 'NDA Satyagraha Update', 10 August 2003 at http://www.nadir.org/nadir/initiativ/agp/free/dams/narmada/2003/0810Narmada_update.htm.

[93] Economic tools have been used in many countries to grapple with environmental pollution including the United States and in India amongst others. e.g., see 'The United States Experience with Economic Incentives for Pollution Control' USEPA publication at http://yosemite.epa.gov/ee/epa/eed.nsf/webpages/USExeprienceWithEconomicIncentives.html. United States National Center for Environmental Economics.

laws or those imposed through royal commands or texts. This led to a system of decentralized governance that is currently being revived as people all over the world have understood its importance. Inclusion of custom and traditional practices is all the more significant at the very basic level of use and preservation of forest, water, and land resources. It is this custom which still exists within practices or local laws in many parts of our country.[94] Many scholars assert that 'such customary legal frameworks provide a wealth of information on sustainable natural resource use and management'.[95] It is only when natural resource management laws enacted with community-based interests in mind are backed with substantive rights and procedural laws using equitable means, can relative success in fighting against environmental degradation and changing the levels of poverty and deprivation be achieved.[96] Scholars in India have stressed the recognition and revival of customary law in order to have decentralized governance frameworks, 'that include the functions of law making, law enforcement, dispute resolution, etc., based on localized control of resources.' Such a framework they argue, needs to be supported by procedural laws that declare and protect the rights of socially disempowered people.[97]

The Constitution of India has been effectively used to promote human rights policies in the process of social and political empowerment of the citizens. As a corollary to the above and in furtherance of providing substantive right as with the 93rd amendment to the constitution by introduction of the right to education, there is a need for another amendment with respect to a right to a healthy and wholesome environment backed by substantive right to community-based natural resources and procedural laws for equitable sharing, management, and preservation of such resources.

As an alternate method for the long-term conservation of natural resources, we should recognize and advocate rights to the environment per se as distinct from anthropocentric protection, so much so that once

[94] This may be observed in current forest use practices, traditional water use and extraction technologies, landholding patterns, agricultural practices, fisheries, common land uses for agricultural and non-agricultural purposes, etc.

[95] Vani, M.S., 'Customary Law and Modern Governance of Natural Resources in India—Conflicts, Prospects for Accord and Strategies', paper for the Commission on Folk Law and Legal Pluralism XIIIth International Congress, Chiang Mai University, Thailand, April 2002.

[96] Ibid.

[97] Ibid.

there is relative equilibrium within the ever changing natural and social environment, basic needs and human rights can be taken care of and there would not be any actual or perceived conflicts between environmental protection or right to development or basic human needs.

Of course, there may be certain other alternatives, but at the moment, India needs to opt for the most practical solution of prioritizing environmental rights and basic needs to tide over the debate between basic human needs divorced from a right to healthy environment.

The above analysis makes it clear that the Indian judiciary has contributed towards the development of an environmental jurisprudence aided by environmentally-spirited lawyers, scholars, and NGOs and that the link between human rights and environment has been clearly established in the form of recognition of a right to healthy and wholesome environment. Yet, many scholars argue that unless more is done by way of major structural and substantive reform to environmental protection, such as by amending the use-extraction laws and recognition of customary traditions and empowerment of local people's representatives such as the Panchayats,[98] environmental degradation and harm arising out of unsustainable practices of development, and the conflict between environmental rights and other human rights cannot be righted.[99] The author reiterates that the achievement of objective human rights is directly linked with achievement of meaningful environmental rights. Obviously, this places a huge responsibility upon the government, statutory authorities, judges, NGOs, and not the least, private citizens. A supreme effort by all who are concerned with human rights protection is needed to build and revive a consensus for promoting inherent respect for the environment, otherwise human rights and environmental wrongs would never be righted and millions of people would be denied access to complete justice.

[98] See n. 94.
[99] Some of the above concerns have been addressed by the Draft National Environmental Policy, 2004, see The *Hindu*, 29 August 2004 at http://www.hinduonnet.com/2004/08/30/stories/2004083004131200. htm.

13

The Human Rights Movement

Time to Turn the Searchlight Inwards

VENKAT IYER[*]

'Human rights' has become one of the fashionable phrases of our time. The concept has been elevated to the status of a 'global religion'.[1] Seldom does a week pass without some new report or initiative or campaign being launched on the subject somewhere in the world. The concept has also given rise to a whole new 'industry'—one which has grown in leaps and bounds in recent years, defying economic downturns and recessions, wars, and natural calamities. At the same time, however, human rights remain a deeply controversial issue—an issue which has divided people as much as it has united them. Given this reality, it is, I believe, necessary to take a hard look at the state of the human rights movement today and to examine the many challenges that it faces.

There is, clearly, much to be celebrated in the achievements of the human rights movement over the decades. The movement has a respectable pedigree. One only has to reflect on the horrors of the two world wars to realise how essential it was to get rid of the doctrine that how a country treats its inhabitants is a matter exclusively for its own determination. Today, few countries would subscribe to that doctrine, and the world has, by and large, been a better place for it.

[*] Many of the arguments canvassed in this essay were first articulated by the author in his Justice Bal Memorial Lecture, delivered at the ILS Law College, Poona, on 4 January 2003.

[1] A. de Waal, review of T. Evans (ed.), *Human Rights Fifty Years On: A Reappraisal*, Manchester University Press, Manchester (1999), in *The Times Literary Supplement*, 2 July 1999, at p. 32.

Much has also been achieved, over the years, in the area of standard-setting. The Universal Declaration of Human Rights (UDHR) is a good example of a document which lays out, in general but inspiring terms, the benchmarks that people everywhere ought to aspire to if they are to avoid what the Declaration describes as 'the barbarous acts which have [in the past] outraged the conscience of mankind'. The ideals enshrined in the UDHR have been given more concrete shape in a number of subsequent documents, notably in the International Covenant on Civil and Political Rights (ICCPR), adopted in 1966. No less impressively, these standard-setting endeavours have also been replicated, with considerable enthusiasm and on a regional basis, through such instruments as the European Convention on Human Rights, the American Convention on Human Rights and the African Charter on Human and Peoples' Rights.

There is a need to recognize the progress that has been achieved in the trans-border enforcement of human rights, particularly through the regional mechanisms and institutions that have been put in place during the past three to four decades. The European Court of Human Rights, for example, is now capable of receiving complaints from individuals about human rights violations committed against them by the governments of some 44 countries that are member-states of the Council of Europe. This system of international justice, imperfect though it may be, is nevertheless a remarkable achievement in a world where the sovereignty of individual states is, rightly or wrongly, so fiercely protected. Comparative constitutional law—and in particular, the practice of courts referring to each other's cases in human rights matters—has produced a rich corpus of human rights jurisprudence.

All these advances have led, slowly but inexorably, to a greater awareness among the general public around the world about the importance of protecting and promoting human rights, which is a positive outcome of the post-war human rights movement. One of the reasons why, I believe, these positive developments have come about is that those who were at the forefront of the human rights movement, especially in the 1950s, 1960s, and 1970s, adopted a measured and balanced approach in their campaigns. They realized that although human rights is an evolving concept, any change, if it is to command public confidence, has to be gradual rather than revolutionary.

That approach, alas, appears increasingly to be ignored by many of the contemporary human rights activists, who have given greater importance to forcing the pace of change, and who have also, it has to be said, at times acted in pursuit of certain ideological goals which do not enjoy universal support. This has led to legitimate suspicions as to the utility of the human rights discourse in many parts of the world.

The problem has been compounded by a belief on the part of some human rights activists in the infallibility of their own judgments and prescriptions. These activists see human rights 'as a cause that is above justifying itself', as one commentator recently put it.[2]

FRAGILE CONSENSUS

It is not sufficiently understood by many members of the contemporary human rights movement that the global consensus on human rights is still rather fragile. The importance of a domestic and international commitment to human rights is not in doubt, nor is its relevance to the formulation of policies on governance. But the consensus breaks down when we begin to go into the details, for there is much disagreement globally over the actual content of human rights. The disagreement cannot, it must be said, always be attributed to bad faith on the part of the protagonists. The truth is that the way one looks at human rights is usually coloured by one's own experiences; it is also determined by the harsh realities prevailing in any given place and at any given time.

The situation is not helped by the zealotry, the self-righteousness and the glaring inconsistencies of some of the leaders of the human rights movement. In taking a critical look at their shortcomings, I do not wish to detract from the good work that is being carried out by a large number of dedicated, conscientious, and level-headed human rights campaigners around the world. My aim, rather, is to offer constructive criticism, as I do believe that it is healthy, occasionally, to turn the search-light inwards.

In referring to the 'human rights movement', I am not suggesting that this movement is a centrally commanded monolithic entity with an immutable set of characteristics. I recognize the many and complex motivations that impel people to join human rights groups or work in other ways for the promotion of human rights. Like all generalizations, my use of the phrase 'human rights movement' is necessarily imprecise, but in the absence of a better alternative I have decided to stick with this shorthand term.

[2] Thomas Brudholm, 'Conviction and Critique: Addressing the Sceptic', in Kirsten Hastrup (ed.), *Human Rights on Common Grounds*, Kluwer, The Hague (2001), at p. 36.

Dogma and Inconsistency

Like other social movements, the human rights movements has a fair share of individuals, institutions, and many professional human rights activists who are driven by ideology and dogma, rather than by a sense of genuine commitment to the notion of human rights, familiarity with social realities, and a sense of pragmatism and common sense. There are often inconsistencies in the articulation of the human rights ideas and principles, which lead to myriad problems and which threaten the credibility of the movement. It is important for human rights professionals to recognize that human rights are subject to interpretations. It is entirely possible for different cultures and societies to interpret human rights differently, in accordance with the values that underpin those societies. The unwillingness of many in the human rights movement to accept this reality has manifested itself, first and foremost, in glaring inconsistencies in their approach to fundamental issues—inconsistencies which most ordinary people find very difficult to understand or overlook.

Most human rights groups are, on their own admission, committed to democratic governance, that is to say, respect for the wishes of the majority. In the United Kingdom, for example, human rights activists have been in the vanguard of the campaign to reform the House of Lords, on the grounds that the hereditary element in the House was anti-democratic. However, confronted with strong democratic majorities on issues with which they disagree, they are often reluctant to accept the wishes of the majority.

A case in point is the response of some human rights groups to the last presidential elections in France. One recalls the large-scale rioting that followed the results of the first round of those elections in which Jean-Marie Le Pen, the leader of the right-wing National Front, secured the second highest number of votes. The election was free and fair, yet, some people, including human rights activists, did not accept the verdict, and instead resorted to violent demonstrations. While electoral democracy may not be the only way to ensure democratic governance, it does provide a certain degree of legitimacy to the governance process and ought to be respected by all, including the human rights community. This is the only way by which we can ensure the protection of the rule of law, which is a cornerstone of every democracy. It is the responsibility of the human rights community to ensure that their actions reflect a certain degree of ideological, political, and moral coherence, and that they do not engage in partisan politics. This is important for protecting the legitimacy of the human rights discourse.

The State Government elections in Gujarat, India, in 2003, demonstrated issues relating to political governance and electoral reforms where reasonable people can disagree. We can have a serious disagreement on the wisdom of one or another party being elected to power,[3] but since electoral democracy is the basis of choosing the government, it is incumbent upon all concerned to accept the result unless it can be shown that the result was vitiated by large-scale corruption or fraud. The human rights movement would be justified in identifying the weaknesses and deficiencies in the policies of a government, but there is need for objectivity in this analysis and very few human rights groups are ready and willing to show such objectivity.

In this context, it is useful to refer to the words of the renowned philosopher, F.A. Hayek, who warned many years ago that an over-reliance on democracy can often be dangerous. Such reliance, argued Hayek, 'is largely responsible for the misleading and unfounded belief that so long as the ultimate source of power is the will of the majority, the power cannot be arbitrary.'[4] Indians will remember the assault on human rights and democracy by the country's Emergency Parliament (1977–9), which demonstrated that an elected government with unchecked powers can also pose threat to democracy and the protection of the rule of law. The challenge to the human rights movement lies in advancing its goals without alienating large numbers of ordinary, law-abiding citizens.

Economic ideology often plays a deleterious role in the actions of the human rights movement. An examination of some prescriptions handed down by human rights activists for the real or imagined ills of

[3] Many respectable people would, for instance, hold the view that the Narendra Modi government that was brought into power was unfit for public office in view of what they believe was its complicity in the anti-Muslim violence that engulfed the State in 2002; others would argue that the proper response to the Gujarat carnage was the sustained and even-handed prosecution of each and every offender, not denial to the government as a whole of the democratic mandate earned by it in freely contested elections. The fundamental tenet of a rule of law society is that however high a person is, the law is above him or her and that the legal system ought to ensure that the offenders are brought to justice. Unfortunately in India, the gap between the normative legal and human right framework and the enforcement of laws is wide.

[4] F.A. Hayek, cited in T. Campbell, J. Goldsworthy and A. Stone, *Protecting Human Rights*, Oxford University Press, Oxford (2003), at p. 136.

the world would show an unmistakable bias towards the re-distributionist philosophy. This is a relatively new phenomenon, because considerations of social equality or material equality were never traditionally considered a legitimate part of any prevailing creed of human rights. However, there has been a fundamental transition in the approach of the human rights movement, the benefit of which is questionable. Consider this statement by Amnesty International in one of its recent annual reports: 'As globalization spreads, bringing greater wealth to some and destitution and despair to others, human rights activists must promote not just legal justice, but also social justice'.[5]

Such generalizations by the proponents of the human rights community may not entirely capture the reality. Globalization is far too complex a phenomenon and there is a need for a far more rigorous analysis to examine its specific negative implications for human rights. As for the arguments in favour of greater social spending, it needs to be noted that each new demand for largesse on behalf of an allegedly disadvantaged group means an increased burden on other tax-payers who may not necessarily find the case for the largesse convincing, but the tax-payer is not always offered a choice in the matter.[6] Oftentimes, the pleas for increased spending by human rights campaigners may reflect a well-intentioned desire on their part to use the tax system as a mechanism to transfer wealth from the relatively well-off to one or more constituencies favoured by the campaigners, but there may not be a broad consensus in society as a whole that the potential beneficiaries are deserving of such transfers. Another unfortunate effect of such pleas for non-voluntary redistribution of resources is increasing government encroachment on economic decisions which are best left to individuals,

[5] *Amnesty International Report 2002.* Amnesty International, London (2002), at p. 8.

[6] Many human rights activists show insufficient understanding of the potential impact that large-scale public expenditure may have on the ordinary tax-payer. Take, for example, the following statement made by a lawyer-activist from India who called for a radical—and potentially expensive—overhaul of the Indian legal system not so long ago: 'The systemic shift that the situation demands does not depend so much on availability of resources as on the willingness to adapt and change' (S. Muralidhar, 'Access to Justice', Seminar, New Delhi, January 2005, at www.india-seminar.com/2005/545%20muralidhar1.htm, accessed on 6 June 2005). It does, of course, depend on the availability of resources, and the resources can only, eventually, come from the tax-payer. It is important to provide a balanced perspective on such issues so that people can make informed choices and decisions on matters that affect society at large.

and a corresponding diminution of personal freedom. In relation to inequalities in society, greater intervention on the part of the state on economic matters may not be the best approach.

While there could be legitimate disagreements as to the kind of economic policies a country ought to adopt, it is important that the human rights groups provide a fuller picture of the debate and take into account the views of the wider society in such matters. This would reflect a far more serious and objective attitude, rather than a one-sided approach to economic decision-making. It will also reflect a better approach to democratic governance.

While there is nothing inherently wrong in the advocacy of social justice, many people would question the appropriateness of human rights agencies to undertake this task. At the root of the problem lies a contestable ordering of priorities and a confusion of rights with *aspirations*. As Michael Ignatieff has noted in the context of economic, social and cultural rights, 'To confuse rights with aspirations, and rights conventions with syncretic syntheses of world values is to destroy the very meaning of rights as a way of protecting human beings from injustice and tyranny'.[7]

It is important to recognize that poverty, deprivation, and perceived unfairness in society are serious matters that deserve urgent attention, but they cannot be allowed to excuse wrongdoing. As Frank Field, a British Labour MP notes in a recent monograph on anti-social behaviour, 'Much of the unacceptable behaviour is caused less by any sense of rising up against injustice, than by human nature reacting as it will when there is no clear framework within which it should operate. Injustices should be tackled, but it would be wrong to think that such reforms will of themselves counter anti-social behaviour.'[8] Obviously, there are multiple approaches to the elimination of social injustices, and democratic governance is about discussing these approaches freely and frankly, and to evolve acceptable solutions to the problem. It should not be assumed by the human rights community or other social movements that a particular approach has greater moral validity, because reasonable people still disagree on the best approaches to good governance.

Part of the problem is that many in the contemporary human rights movement are not sufficiently willing to engage in an objective analysis of the present state of human rights realities. An undue reliance on, and strained interpretations of, international human rights instruments may

[7] Michael Ignatieff, 'Whose universal values? The crisis in human rights', *Praemium Erasmianum* Essay, The Hague, 1999, at pp. 36–7.

[8] Frank Field, *Neighbours from Hell*, Politico's, London (2003), at p. 46.

not help their cause, unless there is genuine popular consensus in support of those instruments.[9] Frank Field believes that the operation of the European Convention on Human Rights, for example, needs 'to be radically rebalanced for the operation of the law to match more closely the clear sense of fairness that most voters possess'.[10]

The issue of development and other infrastructural projects has become a central issue of contestation for many human rights campaigners. It is not sufficiently acknowledged by the human rights community that a number of these projects are aimed at the larger social good, even if they involve some—usually temporary—hardship to a few. Again, this is an area that requires far more incisive analysis than that is being currently offered by the human rights movement. Both domestic and international non-governmental organizations have engaged in activism —and not always peaceful activism—with a view to undermining the development goals of projects and in that process most of the time, there is often only one view that emerges, namely that development projects are against the interests of the people. Unfortunately, this may not be the case as there may be a good number of beneficiaries—for example, in terms of new employees—for these projects, and the human rights movement should provide the necessary space for other viewpoints to be aired and argued.

Likewise, inconsistencies abound in the attitudes of many human rights activists towards multinational corporations (MNCs). These corporations have, time and again, been criticized for unethical practices, exploitation of labour, and interferences in the affairs of host governments. This is despite considerable evidence that they have improved, rather than worsened, the working conditions of employees in many poor countries, and created well-paid jobs where none existed before. It is true that MNCs do exercise enormous powers: the best way of safeguarding against the abuse of those powers is to put in place better accountability regimes rather than question the very existence of MNCs. Also, many domestic human rights community while expending considerable time and energy on criticizing the role of MNCs on labour standards and other human rights issues pay little attention to the functioning of domestic corporations and business enterprises which

---

[9] For example, it has been argued that the right to privacy, guaranteed under the Human Rights Act in the UK, justifies schools referring their female pupils to doctors for contraceptive advice—and even abortion—without their parents being informed, much less consulted.

[10] Frank Field, supra n. 8, at p. 78.

are equally culpable, if not more so, in violating human rights standards. Ironically, however, the activists also often accuse MNCs of *not meddling enough* in the domestic politics of the countries where they operate when it suits them. Jagdish Bhagwati, the well-known economist, offers a revealing example in his recent book on globalization, and his observations deserve to be quoted at length:

Royal Dutch/Shell was widely condemned by human rights and environmental NGOs [in 1999] for abuses by the [Nigerian] government. In Ogoniland, an oil-rich area in the Niger delta, the Nigerian government (a military dictatorship) was accused of siphoning oil revenues to uses outside of Ogoniland. The oil companies, when confronted with protests that involved seizures of property and their executives, were condemned for drawing on the often draconian enforcement resources of the Nigerian government. Moreover, the protesters complained that the oil companies were damaging the local environment.

But can the oil companies be blamed for the policies of the Nigerian government that redirect oil revenues to national priorities that, in the estimation of the Ogonis, reward the Ogonis inadequately? How export proceeds, revenue collections, oil royalties, and earnings are allocated among different claimants in the country is a decision of the Nigerian government and has nothing to do with human rights. If multinationals started interfering in decisions of this kind, it would be political intrusion that would be rejected by every government that values the independence that many nations fought for prior to their independence from colonial powers.[11]

Sometimes, self-interest rather than altruism guides the actions of some human rights activists.[12] As one writer observed not so long ago, human rights have 'become a war cry and blackmail weapon in the hands of aspiring "community leaders" wishing to pick up powers that the state has dropped'.[13] There is also often an element of narcissism which disguises itself as empathy on the part of professional human rights activists.[14]

[11] Jagdish Bhagwati, *In Defence of Globalization*, Oxford University Press, New York (2004), at p. 169.

[12] To cite but one example, in 2003 a Delhi-based public interest group, Common Cause, moved the Supreme Court of India raising apprehensions about large-scale misuse of funds by human rights NGOs operating in the country. The complaint recorded that, out of the millions of dollars that NGOs working in the field of HIV/AIDS had been receiving, only 30–40 per cent of the funds had been used to benefit AIDS patients. See, Binu S. Thomas, 'NGOs: Crisis of Credibility', at www.hvk.org/articles/0503/232.html (accessed on 6 June 2005).

[13] Zygmunt Bauman, *Postmodern Ethics*, Blackwell, Oxford (1993) at p. 64.

[14] See, for example, David Kennedy, 'The International Human Rights Movement: Part of the Problem?', *Harvard Human Rights Journal* 15 (2002), 101 at 121.

Sometimes, human rights activism serves as a mere cover for partisan activities, especially in contentious conflicts.[15]

A curious paradox about the modern human rights movement is that, whereas activists and NGOs constantly demand a very high degree of accountability from governments and other targets of their campaigns, they do not always show the same amount of eagerness to account for their own actions. Christian Tomuschat has rightly observed in relation to human rights NGOs that: 'No accountability exists towards the public at large, and sometimes even accountability towards the membership is poorly organized. Thus, the legitimacy of NGOs is not beyond doubt, depending on the circumstances of each case. This also means that it can hardly be said that the positions defended by a NGO are necessarily better in tune with the philosophy of human rights than the official position of a government'.[16]

Much the same point has been made by other writers. Don Habibi, who carried out an extensive study of the attitudes of the international human rights movement towards the Arab-Israeli conflict, came to the conclusion that NGOs 'have fumbled their special responsibility to function as watchdogs over nation states, defenders of human rights, or guardians of international humanitarian law'. He has suggested that 'there needs to be a watchdog for the unaccountable, politicised organizations masquerading as watchdogs and guardians'.[17]

Doubts have also been raised about the representative nature and democratic character of some NGOs. Peter Baehr, a veteran observer of the human rights scene from the Netherlands, has pondered the claims of certain NGOs that they represent 'the grassroots of society': 'Nobody can tell,' he says, 'precisely as to whether and how these grassroots find themselves represented by NGO lobbyists operating in

---

[15] Aryeh Neier highlighted this problem in a letter to the *New York Times* on 27 May 1989 when he referred to 'the proliferation of groups claiming to speak in the name of the human rights cause but actually engaged in efforts to promote one or another side in a civil conflict.'

[16] Christian Tomuschat, *Human Rights: Between Idealism and Realism*, Oxford University Press, New York (2003), at pp. 232–3.

[17] Don A. Habibi, 'The Politicization of the International Human Rights Movement', at http://people.uncw.edu.turrisip/par292/Sept04JHR%20draft.doc (accessed on 6 June 2005). Habibi's research indicates, for example, that Amnesty International issues far more documents criticizing Israel than it issues documents criticizing any Arab or Muslim country. Likewise, Human Rights Watch publishes many more reports naming and shaming Israel than it does in relation to human rights violations in other Middle Eastern countries (except Iraq).

the council chambers of New York, Brussels and Geneva. Some of them are membership organizations, but even among those the democratic nature of decision-making is sometimes questionable'.[18] Another scholar regards many NGOs as 'little more than self-appointed and self-created lobbies, despite their pervasive rhetoric of authenticity'.[19]

While there are a number of serious and genuine NGOs worldwide, clearly, the issue of transparency and accountability is a central matter that affects the credibility of this sector as a whole. While NGOs have become globalized and are increasingly accessing funds and other resources from different parts of the world, they have not opened up their activities sufficiently to serious public scrutiny. Such opening up is very important, given the fact that the wider society deposes trust in NGOs, and the actions of NGOs may have important consequences for protecting the moral integrity of the human rights movement.

The human rights movement should not assume that it alone is interested in ensuring transparency, accountability, and good governance and that other interest groups in society, including governments, operate only on behalf of vested interests. Governance is a complex process, which requires the concerted effort of a number of actors, including the government, non-governmental organizations, private sector actors, and the people. Good governance is about the actors exercising power and authority in a responsible manner. No particular individual or institution can assume the right to a higher moral ground in the governance process. The human rights constituency should be ready and willing to face criticism on some of the approaches adopted and the tactics followed by it to express dissent.

SELECTIVITY IN HUMAN RIGHTS ENFORCEMENT

Human rights activists also often display a curious selectivity and bias in their campaigns, which does little credit to their cause. Take, for example, the reaction of the global human rights lobby to the recent events in Zimbabwe, where the government of Robert Mugabe has been carrying out an organized campaign of brutal violence against that

[18] Peter Baehr, 'Human Rights NGOs and Globalization', in Karin Arts and Paschal Mihyo (eds), *Responding to the Human Rights Deficit*, Kluwer, The Hague (2003), at p. 40.

[19] Andrew Hurrell, 'Power, Principles and Prudence: Protecting Human Rights in a Deeply Divided World', in Tim Dunne and Nicholas J. Wheeler (ed.), *Human Rights in Global Politics*, Cambridge University Press, Cambridge (1999), at p. 289.

country's white farmers (and, it has to be added, large numbers of black people who are seen to belong to, or support, the country's Opposition parties). Although the international community and many governments have strongly condemned the actions of Mugabe, the protests against him from the global human rights movement have been not half as strident, despite the despicable nature of the atrocities committed by his government. It is the responsibility of the human rights NGOs to ensure consistency and moral coherence in their actions and not give the impression, as they do, that their response to, say, the human rights practices of the government of General Pinochet in Chile a few years ago deserves to be more robust than their response to the actions of Mugabe.

One increasingly common reason for such selectivity in the application of human rights standards by campaigners is the growing tide of political correctness, which decrees that there are certain favoured groups and communities in the contemporary world who are immune to criticism, no matter how misguided, wrong or harmful their actions might be. On the other hand, those representing traditional values are usually more vulnerable to criticism.

Political correctness has also resulted in the lack of sufficient recognition for the rights of victims, which are given second place to the rights of accused persons and criminals.[20] A particularly egregious example of political correctness arose in Scotland a few years ago: here, the parents of an infant who had smacked their child as a form of mild chastisement for improper behaviour were put behind bars and prosecuted for battery. In the face of such officially-sanctioned high-handedness, it will be a brave parent indeed who will dare administer even the mildest form of punishment to their children. These are serious issues involving parenting and the rights of children, areas where the global consensus is still weak, and any attempt by the human rights community to force the pace of change may not be the best approach to reach a greater understanding on how to deal with such issues.

Another example of political correctness gone mad is to be found in a recent judgment of the European Court of Human Rights, which decreed that prisoners serving jail terms should be allowed to receive

---

[20] In England, for example, a man who chased a gang of vandals with a rolling pin for his own protection because they had smashed his shop window was prosecuted, charged with carrying an offensive weapon, and bound over to keep the peace—see, 'Howard: Distorted Culture of Political Correctness', at www.conservatives.com/ tile.do?def=news.story.page&obj_id=115178&speeches=1 (accessed on 6 June 2005).

hardcore pornography. This, said the court, was implicit in their right to freedom of expression guaranteed by the European Convention on Human Rights. The judgment came after a sustained campaign by Dennis Nilsen, a serial killer jailed in 1983 for murdering six young men in England, who demanded explicit homosexual material while in jail. The ruling overturns the traditional policy of the British Prison Service under which those serving jail terms were only allowed access to such magazines as are being sold in high street shops. As a former police officer tartly observed, rulings such as these make a mockery of the justice system. 'It is not a human right to look at hardcore pornography. Soon, we will be apologising to prisoners for sending them to jail.'[21]

In India, the selectivity of some human rights activists can be seen in the alacrity with which they sometimes condemn particular groups or communities for misdemeanours and excuse others for similar conduct. This has led to complaints by the members of the Hindu community, for instance, that those combating communalism usually tend to be harsher on Hindu or pro-Hindu elements than on Muslim or other minority groups.[22] As Harsh Sethi, a journalist writing in a recent issue of *Janata* magazine pertinently noted, 'nothing damages the case for an unqualified respect for human rights than the demand by a section of the human rights fraternity that the state employ coercive force against those it describes as "fascist", for example Hindutva groups.'[23] By using terms such as 'fascist' loosely and indiscriminately, human rights groups are doing no favours to themselves or to their cause.

The challenges of commenting on human rights issues in conflict zones are significant. This is demonstrated by the general treatment of the events in Kashmir by the human rights movement. There has been at best, muted criticism of the large-scale and systematic harassment of Kashmir's Hindu population which has, in just the past couple of years, seen hundreds of its members ('the Kashmiri pandits') killed and thousands driven out of the state by Islamic militants.[24] Some sections of the

[21] 'Prisoners win claim that hardcore porn is a human right', The *Daily Telegraph* (London), 10 November 2002.

[22] See, for example, Nitin G. Raut, 'The Debauching of Secularism in India', at www.liberalsindia.com/freedomfirst/ff453-06.html; Balbir K. Punj, 'Godhra and Double Standards', at www.hvk.org/articles/0302/8.html (both accessed on 6 June 2005).

[23] Harsh Sethi, 'Rethinking rights', *Janata* (Bombay), 24 November 2002, at p. 5.

[24] See, for example, K.P.S. Gill, 'The Kashmiri Pandits: An Ethnic Cleansing the World Forgot', at www.satp.org/satporgtp/kpsgill/2003/chapter9.htm (accessed on 19 August 2004).

media have been equally complicit in this by not sufficiently bringing forward issues relating to plight of the pandits as fervently as they have covered the hardship suffered by the Muslims.[25] There is also, of course, a paucity of information on the human rights violations committed by the state apparatus more generally. The human rights movement's own research efforts in this area leave much to be desired.[26]

This also begs the question: how far should any society which believes in fairness go in pushing minority rights? Clearly, minorities are entitled to equal protection under the law, and they deserve to be made safe from harassment or oppression at the hands of the majority community (or from other minorities, for that matter); there may even be a case for incentives being offered—sometimes even at the expense of the public exchequer—for minority communities to set up institutions aimed at preserving their culture or traditions. But when it comes to conferring special rights or privileges, one needs to think very carefully indeed, for this may have profound practical consequences for societal harmony. The human rights movement has not fully accepted this principle.

EXAGGERATION AND FACTUAL ACCURACY

Human rights campaigners are sometimes prone to exaggeration, which also impacts adversely on their overall credibility. An example of such exaggeration happened during the 1990–1 Gulf crisis following the Iraqi occupation of Kuwait. Amnesty International published a report which stated, among other things, that the invading Iraqi soldiers had removed over 300 premature babies from their incubators in one of the Kuwaiti hospitals with a view to sending the incubators to Iraq, and furthermore that at least 72 corpses of such babies had been personally

[25] See, for example, Ashis Nandy, as quoted in 'A Dangerous Symbiosis', *Outlook*, 1 April 2002. An example of the double standards adopted by persons on the Kashmiri pandits issue is provided by the treatment of them by Teesta Setalvad, one of the leading anti-communalism crusaders, who argued that, unlike the Muslims of that State who had been the victims of 'home grown terror bands, terror bands who moreover speak of a narrow sense of Indian patriotism and nationhood', the pandits were the targets of 'foreign-bred mercenaries'—Teesta Setalvad, acceptance speech on the award of the Rajiv Gandhi Sadhbhavana Award, at www.sabrang.com/news/teesaward.htm (accessed on 6 June 2005). Interestingly, there was no reference in her speech to the victims of the Godhra carnage in which scores of Hindus were burnt to death in February 2002.

[26] See, for example, Arun Shourie, *Courts and their Judgments*, Rupa, New Delhi (2001), at p. 295.

buried by an unnamed Red Crescent doctor. The report added, for good measure, that an 'eyewitness' had seen several babies left to die on the cold hospital floor.[27]

This story caused quite a stir, not least in the United States, which had been at the forefront of military action to eject the Iraqi forces from Kuwait, but it was soon shown to be untrue. Alexander Cockburn, a journalist writing for the Los Angeles Times, characterized Amnesty as being 'remarkably off-hand' in putting it out, and asked: 'Is it likely that any hospital in Kuwait would have so many incubators? Columbia Presbyterian in New York, for example, has thirty-six'.[28] It turned out that the hospital in question had no more than 25 incubators, none of which had been stolen during the Iraqi occupation. Amnesty had to retract the story shortly afterwards, but its credibility had taken a battering by then. To the question, 'Does it matter that the Iraqis, amid their looting and their murders, did not kill scores, if not hundreds, of babies by stealing their incubators?', Cockburn answered: 'Of course it matters. Human rights organizations should have higher standards than the yellow press'.[29]

Another, more recent, example of exaggeration concerns a statement by Amnesty's Secretary-General, which equated the US military's detention camp for terrorists in Guantanamo Bay, Cuba, with the Soviet Gulag—a comparison which drew instant derision from a number of commentators. As the Wall Street Journal observed, 'A "human rights" group that can't distinguish between Stalin's death camps and detention centres for terrorists who kill civilians can't be taken seriously.'[30]

It needs to be stated, however, that not always is the exaggeration deliberate. More often than not, it is the result of time pressures, and the desire on the part of NGOs, like newspapers, to steal a march over their competitors. But that cannot excuse poor research. Human rights monitors should also be aware that oftentimes it may be necessary to step back from the 'here and now' of events, and look at developments from a slightly longer-term perspective in order to see the full picture. The risks of 'instant' reporting were highlighted by one analyst from the Brookings Institution who, writing about China, had this to say:

[27] Amnesty International, Iraq/Occupied Kuwait: Human Rights Violations since 2 August 1990, December 1990, at p. 57.

[28] 17 January 1991.

[29] Alexander Cockburn, 'Beat the Devil', Nation, 4 February 1991.

[30] See, for example, 'Amnesty's Gulag', at www.opinionjournal.com/editorial/feature. html?id=110006749 (accessed on 6 June 2005).

Human rights advocacy is inclined to take the pulse of societies under authoritarian rule on a daily basis. This may enable the international community to halt or prevent abuses when it has the leverage to do so. However, this approach skims the surface of political change, often missing significant developments, and leads to unwitting exaggeration of trends in either direction. Western observers are quick to declare a 'Beijing spring' when repression seems to ease on small groups of vocal individuals, or to decry a return to totalitarianism when the government tightens control on these same groups.[31]

These issues reflect a growing concern that the human rights movement should reflect on its inadequacies and how far it has been able to genuinely respond to the social expectations that it has generated.

OVER-AMBITIOUSNESS

The human rights movement is also, unfortunately, characterized by a degree of over-ambitiousness, which cannot but be counterproductive in the long run. Recent years have seen a huge proliferation of 'rights', some of which are actually antithetical to existing, time-tested civil liberties and to cherished social arrangements which command widespread support among the community at large. The 'right' to roam on private land, which has, for example, been asserted by campaigners in the United Kingdom, is clearly at odds with the landowner's right to hold and enjoy his property without let or hindrance. The 'right' to circulate pornographic material (which is often claimed as part of the right to freedom of expression) cannot but have serious adverse effects on the right of children and other vulnerable groups in society to be protected from undesirable influences. The 'right' to homosexual marriage would, likewise, be seen by many societies as an affront to the long-standing institution as a stable union between two persons of the opposite gender.

The last-mentioned issue is becoming the subject of a nascent, but growing, campaign in certain parts of urban India. A couple of years ago, for example, some of the national dailies carried hyped-up reports of an alleged homosexual 'marriage' between a minor Indian celebrity and his male French sexual partner in Goa—an event which was accompanied by complaints about the alleged unfairness of Indian laws on homosexuality. Such comments show a disregard for the views of those who

---

[31] Catherin E. Dalpino, 'Human Rights in China', Brookings Institution, Policy Brief 50, June 1999, at *www.brookings.edu/comm/PolicyBriefs/Pb050/pb50.htm* (accessed on 20 August 2004).

believe in the importance and relevance of stable and orderly family life, upon which the future of all societies depends at least in part. We need to remind ourselves that there are plenty of decent, fair-minded people throughout the world who accept homosexuals as equal citizens, but who may baulk at celebrating homosexuality for deeply-held moral or religious reasons. To accuse such people of bigotry, as many in the human rights movement instinctively do, would be grossly unfair.

Another example of over-ambitiousness of human rights campaigners is their advocacy of some so-called 'third generation' rights, i.e., group rights or collective rights which, they argue, should exist over and above individual civil and political rights (the traditional 'first generation' rights) and individual social, economic and cultural rights (the 'second generation' rights). This argument has profound practical consequences, such as the threat to the integrity of States and the dilution of existing guarantees for individual freedom, which many of the activists do not seem to recognize. It is ironic that such a campaign should be pursued at a time when there is, as noted earlier, no durable consensus on any of the first and second generation rights. In the long run, such proliferation of rights can only lead to the notion of human rights being diminished and to a large extent trivialized.[32] The sad truth is that 'rights-inflation' can be just as bad for public morality as monetary inflation. As the Italian philosopher, Amitai Etzioni, notes:

Once, rights were very solemn moral/legal claims, ensconced in the Constitution and treated with much reverence. We all lose if the publicity department of every special interest can claim that someone's rights are violated every time they don't get all they want.... Unless we want to generate a universal backlash against rights, we need to curb rights inflation and protect the currency of rights from being further devalued.[33]

Clearly, many of the special interest groups are unable to make a distinction between rights and mere goals or aspirations. Jeane Kirkpatrick, the former US Ambassador to the United Nations, brought out the effects of this confusion very well. 'Rights are,' she said, 'vested in persons or groups, but goals are achieved by human effort. The language of rights subtly vests the responsibility for achievement in some "other"— some other person, some other group, some other entity. If the people

[32] Rebecca Wallace, 'Human Rights: The Time for Reassessment', in Frances Butler (ed.), *Human Rights Protection: Methods and Effectiveness*, Kluwer, The Hague (2002), at p. 229.

[33] Amitai Etzioni, *The Spirit of Community*, Fontana Press, London (1995), at p. 5.

of the world do not enjoy their full economic rights, it must be because someone—the monopoly capitalists, say, or the Zionists or Communists or male chauvinists or someone—is depriving them of their rightful due.'[34]

OBLIVIOUSNESS TO CULTURAL DIVERSITY

Many in the contemporary human rights movement often show an insufficient appreciation of reality and of common sense in other respects too. There is insufficient appreciation of the fact that we live in a world in which differences and diversities of cultures abound—differences that cannot be wished away overnight, even with the best will in the world. As Lee Kuan Yew, the former Prime Minister of Singapore, put it in a speech delivered in Tokyo a few years ago:

One cannot ignore the history, culture and background of a society. Societies have developed separately for thousands of years at different speeds and in different ways. Their ideals and norms are different. American or European standards of the late 20th century cannot be universal.[35]

Even within the west, there are often sharp differences between nations in their approaches to human rights. The view which Switzerland takes on assisted suicide, or the Netherlands over 'soft' drugs, for example, is not the view that is taken in the United Kingdom, nor is there a congruence in the approach to sexually explicit material between, say, the Scandinavian countries and Ireland. Does this mean that any of those countries is less committed to human rights than the other? Sometimes there are differences even within countries on questions touching human rights: some of the States which form the United States of America favour capital punishment, while others are implacably opposed to it. Michael Ignatieff also points out pertinently, 'In the next 50 years, the moral consensus that sustained the [UDHR] will continue to splinter. For all the rhetoric about common values, the distance between the United States and Europe on issues such as abortion and capital punishment may also increase.'[36]

---

[34] Jeane Kirkpatrick, *The Reagan Phenomenon—and Other Speeches on Foreign Policy*, American Enterprise Institute, Washington (1983), at p. 42.

[35] 'Be prepared to intervene directly or don't force the pace of change, West told', the *Straits Times* (Singapore), 21 November 1992, p. 30.

[36] Michael Ignatieff, 'The Attack on Human Rights' in (2001) 80:6 *Foreign Affairs* 102 at 115.

There is clearly no escaping the wide chasms in values, practices, and morality that abound in the world of today. The 'clash of civilizations' to which Samuel Huntingdon has famously drawn our attention[37] is as real as it is troubling in its implications. To deny or ignore it would be naïve and not in the best interests of the human rights movement.

Of course, the argument on diversity should not be allowed to be used as a smokescreen by tyrants. Where, for example, there is clear evidence that the measures taken by a government have little or no popular support, or where the population in question is denied any opportunity to express an opinion on a contentious matter, or where the measures are so outrageous that they offend against basic norms of humanity, the human rights community would be quite justified in raising its voice against such measures. But otherwise, it would do well to show a measure of humility and tolerance, and not pretend that we live in a homogenous, morally pristine world.

As it happens, recent advances in communications technology have already begun chipping away at the elaborate edifices that tyrannical regimes have traditionally built to shield themselves and their abhorrent regimes from outside scrutiny. To quote Lee Kuan Yew again:

World-wide satellite television makes it increasingly difficult for any government to hide its cruelties to its own people...in the next 20 or 30 years, few societies will be isolated. All will be ever more open to outside contacts, through trade, tourism, investments, TV and radio. These contacts will influence their behaviour, because their values, perceptions and attitudes will change. There will be no convergence to [a] common world standard. But we can expect more acceptable standards where bizarre, cruel, oppressive practices will become shameful and unacceptable.[38]

There can, nonetheless, be genuine differences of opinion between nations and between societies on particular practices, and it is only healthy that such differences are made the subject of open, even vigorous, debate. Human rights activists are quite right in raising many uncomfortable human rights issues and in questioning their relevance in modern times. Often, by doing so, they provide an opportunity to those within societies which engage in seemingly harmful practices to women like female genital mutilation to give vent to their own opposition to those practices—opposition which otherwise may not find an outlet,

[37] Samuel Huntingdon, *The Clash of Civilizations and the Remaking of World Order*, Touchstone, New York (1996).
[38] Lee Kuan Yew, supra n. 35.

given the oppressive nature of some of those societies. What are to be avoided, however, are hectoring and the use of human rights as 'a vernacular of cultural prescription'.[39]

LACK OF RECOGNITION OF DUTIES

One of the unfortunate failings of the human rights movement is its reluctance to acknowledge that rights carry with them responsibilities and that unless those responsibilities are discharged, the stability and order that are necessary for the enjoyment of human rights would simply vanish. David Selbourne, a British writer who has written extensively on this subject, explains the imbalance thus:

It is…routine to find that, lip-service to duty once paid, generally at the outset of discussion, it is rights which are the dominating subject of discourse. Duties, never or rarely particularised, are soon forgotten, or alluded to in token or passing fashion as if their content and implications were taken for granted.[40]

An idea of the unrealistic position that the human rights lobby has taken on this issue can be had from its response to the attempt made a few years ago to introduce a draft 'Universal Declaration of Human Responsibilities' at the United Nations General Assembly. This draft, which was sponsored by, among others, the former German Chancellor Helmut Schmidt, merely attempted to set down certain norms of good behaviour, and expressly stated that it was intended to complement, rather than take away from, the Universal Declaration of Human Rights. And yet, the human rights lobby reacted to it with such hostility that one could be forgiven for thinking that what was being proposed was a totalitarians' charter.

A misguided emphasis on individualism often lies at the root of the rights lobby's unwillingness to countenance the idea of duties. Amitai Etzioni, a champion of communitarianism, draws attention to the absurd lengths to which such extreme individualism has sometimes been taken, citing the opposition of groups such as the American Civil Liberties Union even to measures of public health and safety. Such groups have, he says, blocked the introduction of seat belt and motorcycle helmet laws in many jurisdictions and ensured the repeal of such regulations in several localities where they had been in place, on the specious grounds

[39] Ignatieff, supra n. 36, at p. 113.
[40] David Selbourne, *The Principle of Duty*, Sinclair-Stevenson, London (1994), at p. 2.

that people have a right to do with their lives what they wish, including endangering them. But, as Etzioni notes, that argument is deeply flawed:

Reckless individuals, however, do not absorb many of the consequences of their acts. Drivers without seat belts…are also more likely to die and leave their children for society to attend to and pick up the pieces. And, of course, they draw on our community resources, from ambulance services to hospitals, when they are involved in accidents, for which they pay at best a fraction of the cost.[41]

The costs to society are indeed enormous, in both material and social terms. One result is the phenomenon of 'civic disaggregation'—a term coined by Selbourne, by which he means 'the gradual waning of knowledge of, and respect for, the civic bond and the principle of duty; the gradual transformation of the citizen-members of the civic order into a randomly associated mass of individuals or citizens-turned-strangers; the gradual dissolution, or disassociation, of a civil public possessed of civic consciousness, or civic sense, that is a sense of co-responsibility for the well-being of the civic order'.[42]

It is hardly a coincidence that societies which give undue prominence to rights are also societies that are highly conflict-ridden.[43] The climate of trust and understanding that is necessary for any real progress to be made in the matter of human rights cannot be created and maintained unless the human rights community realize that the evolution of human rights is a slow and gradual process and the objectives of human rights activism cannot be fulfilled if public opinion is not taken fully into confidence. The importance of maintaining a balance between rights and duties was neatly summed up in the following warning by the author of a recent study:

There has always existed in democratic societies a stable mutuality between individual rights and individual social duties. In the recent past, however, we have come to lose that mutuality. In our zeal to identify and elaborate upon human rights, norms, and standards since the end of World War II, we have sadly neglected the Aristotelian tradition of virtue ethics, public and community service and a sense of duty-consciousness which shaped western philosophies

[41] Etzioni, supra n. 33, at p. 8.

[42] Selbourne, supra n. 40, at pp. 17–18.

[43] Henry Rosemont Jr. has, for example, characterized American society, where the rights culture has dominated every aspect of life in recent years, as 'the world's most morally conflicted society'—Rosemont, 'Human Rights: A Bill of Worries', in W. Theodore De Bary and Tu Weiming (eds), *Confucianism and Human Rights*, Columbia University Press, New York (1998), at p. 56.

for so long. The west must reclaim that tradition if we are serious about shoring up the ailing health of our body politic.[44]

Those remarks apply just as well to eastern societies as they do to western ones. In the Indian context, there has been a progressive neglect, both by the country's political leaders and by the public at large, of the concept of *dharma*—a central tenet of Hinduism on which human rights have been grounded over the centuries. Even as far back as 1959, Jawaharlal Nehru bemoaned this neglect in ringing tones: 'All of us now', he said, 'talk of and demand rights and privileges, but the teaching of the old *dharma* was about duties and obligations. Rights followed duties discharged.'[45]

Much the same view was expressed, in simple but powerful language, by Mahatma Gandhi when he was approached for his views on the Universal Declaration of Human Rights by its drafters:

I learnt from my illiterate but wise mother that all rights to be deserved and preserved came from duty well done. Thus, the very right to live accrues to us only when we do the duty of citizenship of the world. From this one fundamental statement, perhaps it is easy enough to define the duties of Man and Woman and correlate every right to some corresponding duty to be first performed.[46]

For all the advances that have been made—and there is no denying that significant advances have indeed been made—the reality remains that human rights have yet to take deep root in many parts of the world. Barely a fifth of the 190 or so countries that comprise the United Nations enjoy a truly free press. Torture is still practised routinely in all but a handful of states. 'Disappearances' abound, as do other serious violations of fundamental freedoms. All this cannot be wished away by dogmatic posturing.

DIMENSIONS OF EQUALITY AND INEQUALITY

Yet another weakness of the contemporary human rights movement is the pursuit by many of its adherents of a form of equality that is

[44] Douglas Hodgson, *Individual Duty within a Human Rights Discourse*, Ashgate, Aldershot (2003), at pp. 258–9.

[45] Jawaharlal Nehru, 'India Today and Tomorrow', Azad Memorial Lectures, cited in Arvind Sharma, *Hinduism and Human Rights*, Oxford University Press, New Delhi (2003), at p. 18.

[46] Mahatma Gandhi, cited in Sharma, ibid., at p. 17.

destructive and self-defeating. This misguided approach stems from, among other things, a distorted reading of the oft-repeated cliché—which occupies pride of place in the US Constitution—that 'all men are created equal'. That statement cannot, of course, be literally true because, as is self-evident, people are born with different abilities, different intellectual qualities, different physical characteristics, different attitudes towards work, and different emotional attributes. What it is meant to signify is that all men are created equal before God and are entitled to expect equality before the law in the US context.[47]

Even the concept of equality of opportunity is not an unqualified one. It is premised on the laudable principle that the opportunities available to a person should be determined only by his abilities, and not by such factors as his colour, religion, sex, or ethnic origin, except where any of those factors can be shown to be relevant for the purposes of, say, a certain job or other activity. Equality of outcome, on the other hand, is counter-productive, because it goes against one of the most fundamental instincts of human beings, namely, the constant urge to better their lot, and that of their children and grandchildren. The pursuit of equality without fully recognizing its consequences can also lead to gross unfairness and resentment in society. As one writer noted, 'A society that puts equality—in the sense of equality of outcome—ahead of freedom will end up with neither equality nor freedom'[48]—a state of affairs which is antithetical to the *raison d'etre* of the human rights movement.

The results of this misguided thinking on equality (or egalitarianism, as it is sometimes described) are best summed up by Jim Kalb, a scholar whose reflections on the modern human rights movement are worthy of note:

To insist on radical equality with regard to traditional distinctions such as religion, ethnicity, class and sex deprives man of the particular qualities that give him a concrete place in the world, a specific viewpoint, and a set of alliances and interests that go beyond purely individual concerns. It abolishes the significance of traditional institutions like family and local community that give enduring moral substance to a man's life and thereby give meaning to whatever autonomy he has. It eliminates the stable network of personal connections needed for enduring

---

[47] Even the Founding Fathers of the US Constitution recognized this, because they continued: '...endowed by their Creator with certain inalienable rights: that among these are Life, Liberty, and the pursuit of Happiness'.

[48] Milton Friedman, *Free to Choose*, Avon Books, New York (1980), at p. 139.

loyalties and even culture to exist, and so leads to cynicism, self-centeredness and brutishness.[49]

Ironically, as Kalb points out, '[r]adical egalitarianism can only substitute one form of inequality for another, because he who defines and enforces equality is never equal to his fellows.'[50] Another result is that a whole category of people are given privileged status—the possessors of 'rights' become people to whom 'nothing can be denied and to whom no vice can be imputed and from whom no contribution can be demanded, and for whose benefit wholesale social uproar has to take place'.[51]

The need for common sense on questions of equality—and the treatment of minorities—becomes all the more pressing in the current global climate of fear and intimidation brought about by organized terrorism. Inevitably, the activities of terrorist groups such as Al-Qaeda pose serious challenges to liberal democracies which believe in the rule of law. These challenges have brought forth responses that involve significant restrictions on civil liberties—liberties which the inhabitants of freedom-loving countries world-wide have traditionally taken for granted and which they are, understandably, loath to surrender. While human rights campaigners have been quite right in raising their level of scrutiny in such circumstances, they have, not always acted with the sense of responsibility that the occasion demands. In many countries that are especially prone to large-scale terrorist attacks, some human rights activists have overreacted to governmental measures involving greater attention being paid by the law enforcement agencies to potentially suspect groups within the population than to others. Of course, the balance between protecting human rights and civil liberties on the one hand and ensuring national security and human security on the other is not an easy one to strike, and governments the world over are grappling with this problem.

Those working for change in the field of human rights would have to accept that, unless they are able to carry public opinion with them, all reforms run the risk of failure. The key here, as elsewhere, is education and persuasion rather than hectoring and compulsion. Human rights campaigners would do well to temper some of their zeal and enthusiasm with a dose of pragmatism and common sense.

[49] Jim Kalb, 'Human Rights as they are: An Introductory Discussion', at http://jkalb.org/human-rights/human_rights_as_they_are.php (accessed on 20 August 2004).
[50] Ibid.
[51] Jon Davies, 'Poverty These Days', *Salisbury Review*, Spring 2004, 4 at 5.

Common sense would dictate, for example, that human rights violations do not emanate from governments alone, and that violence by private groups is just as destructive of freedom and human security. No less important, human rights activists can be just as fallible as the governments they criticise. Jeane Kirkpatrick puts it well:

A serious commitment to human rights by this or any group... requires that one's judgment be fair and reasonable. Fair judgment of human rights practices would judge all by the same moral standards. A reasonable judgment requires that all nations be judged with reference to their specific character and situation. Thus it is not fair to judge one nation or group by the Sermon on the Mount and all other nations on the curve. It is not reasonable to expect weak governments in strife-torn societies to maintain order and administer justice as well as long-established governments in countries with stable institutions. And it is neither fair nor reasonable to single out for harsh criticism the human rights violations of some nations while ignoring entirely the gross abuse of others.[52]

Common sense would dictate, too, that human rights activists do not let their zeal undermine those basic notions of fair play and reasonableness which are the common currency of all civilized societies.

It is a fact, not sufficiently acknowledged, that in matters of human rights the whole world is still embarked on a voyage of discovery. Any claim of moral or legal certitude by the human rights movement would be premature. Makau Mutua, an American academic, has some wise words in this context. 'There needs to be a realization,' he says, 'that the movement is young and that its youth gives it an experimental status, not a final truth.... Like earlier Crusades, the human rights movement lacks the monopoly of virtue that its advocates claim.'[53]

The human rights movement would do well also to give up the Dworkinian notion of human rights as a 'trump card',[54] and instead begin, in the words of Ignatieff, 'thinking of them as part of a language that creates the basis for deliberation. In this argument, the ground we may share may actually be quite limited—not much more than the basic intuition that what is pain and humiliation for you is bound to be pain

[52] Kirkpatrick, supra n. 34, at pp. 47–8.
[53] Makau Mutua, 'The Complexity of Universalism in Human Rights', conference paper presented in Budapest, June 2002, at www.ceu.hu/legal/ind_vs_state/Mutua_paper_2002.htm (accessed on 6 June 2005).
[54] See, Ronald Dworkin, *Taking Rights Seriously*, Duckworth, London (1978), where human rights are presented as a 'trump card' which overrides the effects of the normal social decision-making process whenever the holder of the card believes that his entitlements have been trampled upon.

and humiliation for me. But this is already something. In such a future, shared among equals, rights are not the universal credo of a global society, not a secular religion, but something much more limited and yet just as valuable: the shared vocabulary from which our arguments can begin, and the bare human minimum from which differing ideas of human flourishing can take root.'[55]

Only then will human rights codes and declarations be accepted as setting the 'overriding moral benchmark'[56] for political, social, legal actions in our age, as many well-meaning people would like them to do.

[55] Ignatieff, supra n. 36, at p. 116.

[56] See, Jonathan Gorman, *Rights and Reason*, England: Acumen, Chesham (2003), at p. 135.

PART III

CRIMINAL JUSTICE, VICTIM JUSTICE, AND WOMEN'S EMPOWERMENT

14

Criminal Injustice

Impunity for Communal Violence in India

SMITA NARULA[*]

The melody of communal unity, the beauty of religious amity and the
secularity of Indian humanity—these glorious values are the mission and
message to the nation. Let us struggle to sustain this supreme value, lest
we, as a people, perish by divisive ideology. The Gujarat episode is an evil
event and disastrous portent. Let us battle for the success of our pluralist
culture, secular heritage and social-justice-illumined democracy.

—Justice V.R. Krishna Iyer, 24 October 2002[1]

The tragedy is that the people who ripped my daughter's child out of her
body and killed her are walking about freely. Why does it have to be this
way? ... The government should realize that on this earth, everyone is equal
because we are all Indians. So why these kinds of crimes against us? We just
want peace and quiet, that's all.... This is my request and this is my
testimony. Please make every effort that the criminals get punished. Even
if they don't get punished a lot, they should at least get punished a little.

—Gujarat massacre survivor Khalid Noor Mohammed Sheikh[2]

* The author acknowledges with deep gratitude the valuable research assistance of
Devyani Prabhat, Prabhat K. Prabhat, Jayne Huckerby, Angelina Fisher, and Jane Pek.
1 Concerned Citizens Tribunal, 'Crime Against Humanity: Incidents and
Evidence' (Vol. I) 6 (2002) p. 9–10 available at http://www.sabrang.com/tribunal/.
Justice Iyer was part of an eight-member tribunal comprising eminent members of
Indian society. Named the Concerned Citizens' Tribunal—Gujarat 2002, it collected
2,094 oral and written testimonies from victims, independent human rights groups,
women's groups, NGOs, and academics. The Tribunal also met with numerous
senior government officials and police officers.
2 Interview with Khalid Noor Mohammed Sheikh in Ahmedabad (5 January
2003). Sheikh is a former resident of Naroda Patia, Ahmedabad, site of one of the

Large-scale episodes of communal violence are neither inevitable[3] nor spontaneous. Often they are the end product of a systematic and deliberate strategy to exploit communal differences for political and economic ends.[4] The history of communal violence in India in the last two decades has indeed proven this hypothesis to be true. Following the assassination of Congress (I) Party president and Indian Prime Minister Indira Gandhi in 1984 by two of her bodyguards who belonged to the Sikh community, local political officials who were aligned with the Congress (I) party were widely reported to have orchestrated attacks against Sikhs in New Delhi and other Indian cities. At least 3,000 people were killed while countless Sikh homes and businesses were destroyed, leaving tens of thousands homeless.[5]

Eyewitnesses identified Congress party officials leading the mobs and inciting them to violence.[6] A fact-finding report by the People's Union for Civil Liberties, a leading Indian human rights organization, charged that 'attacks on members of the Sikh Community in Delhi and its suburbs...were the outcome of a well-organized plan marked by acts of both deliberate commissions and omissions by important politicians of the Congress (I) at the top and by authorities in the administration.'[7]

---

deadliest massacres in Gujarat on 28 February 2002. Sheikh lost nine family members in the Naroda Patia massacre, including his pregnant thirty-year-old daughter Kauser Bano. Her belly was cut open and the fetus was pulled out and hacked to pieces before she was killed. Though Sheikh was willing to testify to what he saw, he claims that the police refused to properly register his complaint and that other witnesses in the case were forced to recant their testimony.

[3] See Anthony Chase, 'Pakistan or the Cemetery!': Muslim Minority Rights in Contemporary India', 16 B.C. Third World L.J., 35, 38–9 (1996) (arguing that the notion that communal separation and violence are eternal and inevitable is ahistorical in that it ignores the fact that inter-communal interaction and syncretism has long been a facet of Indian life).

[4] See generally, Human Rights Watch, 'Playing the 'Communal' Card: Communal Violence and Human Rights' (1995) [hereinafter Playing the 'Communal' Card]. See further, Sara Ahmad, 'Judicial Complicity with Communal Violence in India', 17 Nw. J. Int'l L. & Bus. 320, 323–7 (1996) (outlining the history of communal violence in India, as corelated to development of movements to exploit communal differences for political ends).

[5] Human Rights Watch, 'Punjab in Crisis: Human Rights in India' 20 (1991).

[6] Ibid.

[7] People's Union for Democratic Rights (PUDR) and People's Union for Civil Liberties (PUCL), 'Who are the Guilty?', Report of a joint inquiry into the causes and impact of the riots in Delhi from 21 October to 10 November 1984, available at http://www.pucl.org/Topics/Religion-communalism/2003/who-are-guilty.htm

The Bharatiya Janata Party (BJP), a Hindu nationalist party that headed India's national coalition government until May 2004, is the political wing of the *sangh parivar*[8] and is Congress' main opposition party. It too is believed by many not to be free of blame. Although different from one another in many respects, sangh parivar-affiliated groups such as the Vishwa Hindu Parishad (VHP: 'World Hindu Council'), the Bajrang Dal (the militant youth wing of the VHP), and the Rashtriya Swayamsevak Sangh (RSS: 'National Volunteer Corps') have collectively promoted the argument that India should be a Hindu state because Hindus constitute the majority of Indians. Numerous commissions of inquiry officially appointed to investigate communal riots between Hindus and Muslims in India since the partition of India and Pakistan have indicted such groups for their role in violent crimes against India's minorities.[9]

Nationwide violence against India's Muslim community in 1992 and 1993 following the destruction of the Babri Masjid (mosque) in Ayodhya, and against India's Christian community since 1998, stemmed in large part from the violent activities and hate propaganda of sangh parivar-affiliated groups. The Srikrishna Commission, which presented its report to the government more than five years after the 1992–3 Bombay riots occurred, determined that the riots were the result of a systematic and deliberate effort to incite violence against Muslims.[10] Specifically, the report singled out Shiv Sena *Pramukh*[11] Bal Thackeray and Manohar

[8] 'Family' of Hindu nationalist groups.

[9] Concerned Citizens Tribunal 'Crime Against Humanity: Findings and Recommendations', (Vol. II) 73 (2002) available at http://www.sabrang.com/tribunal/tribunal2.pdf [hereinafter 'Crime Against Humanity Vol. II']. The tribunal compiled excerpts of reports by commissions of inquiry into communal disturbances from 1967 to 1982 which consistently found that 'provocative acts by Hindu communal organizations [are] responsible for injecting the poison of communalism into the atmosphere that manoeuvres Muslims into apparently throwing the first stone', Concerned Citizens Tribunal, 'Crime Against Humanity: List of Annexures' (Vol. III) 262–5 (2002), available at http://www.sabrang.com/tribunal/tribunal3.pdf. But see South Asia Human Rights Documentation Centre, 'Report of the Justice D.P. Wadhwa Commission of Inquiry: Judicial Commission or Injudicious Cover up?' (1999), available at http://www.hri.ca/partners/sahrdc/wadhwa/fulltext.shtml (critiquing the Wadhwa Commission report for its failure to acknowledge involvement of sangh parivar-affiliated groups in the killing of a Christian missionary in Orissa despite substantial evidence to the contrary).

[10] B.N. Srikrishna, Srikrishna Commission Report, in 'Damning Verdict—Report of the Srikrishna Commission' (Sabrang Communications 1998), available at http://www.sabrang.com/srikrish/sri%20main.htm [hereinafter 'Damning Verdict'].

[11] The highest leadership position in the Shiv Sena.

Joshi (who went on to become Chief Minister of Maharashtra)[12] for their role in inciting the violence.[13] The Shiv Sena-BJP-led state government refused to adopt the Commission's recommendations and labeled the report 'anti-Hindu'.[14]

Sangh parivar-affiliated groups were reported to be most responsible for the post-Godhra anti-Muslim violence in Gujarat in 2002.[15] Even according to some police reports, state officials of the BJP were also identified by survivors as being directly involved in the attacks.[16] In many cases, eyewitnesses have reported that the police led the charge, killing Muslims who tried to block the mobs' advance.[17] By many accounts the violence was unprecedented in its organization and unmatched in its brutality in the state of Gujarat.[18]

This essay addresses the longstanding impunity for large-scale episodes of communal violence in India: namely, the 1984 anti-Sikh violence in Delhi, the 1992–3 anti-Muslim violence in Bombay, and the 2002 anti-Muslim violence in Gujarat. The first part of the essay presents an overview of police and prosecutorial complicity in communal violence in India. A collapse of democratic structures in the world's largest democracy has resulted in longstanding impunity for these grave crimes. The second

[12] Joshi was chief minister from 1995–9.

[13] The doctrine of retaliation expounded by Thackeray and Joshi, which openly called for organized attacks against Muslims, whipped up communal frenzy and escalated the scale of rioting and violence by Hindus. Damning Verdict, supra note 10.

[14] See 'Srikrishna report indicts Thackeray, Joshi', The Indian Express, 7 August 1998; Human Rights Watch, 'World Report 1999: India', available at http://www.hrw.org/worldreport99/asia/india.html.

[15] Human Rights Watch, 'We Have No Orders to Save You': State Participation and Complicity in Communal Violence in Gujarat' 4 (2002) [hereinafter 'No Orders to Save You']. On 27 February 2002, in the town of Godhra, 58 Kar Sevaks, volunteers of BJP affiliated groups, were killed in a fire in two train cars. The attack was blamed on Muslims. In the days following the incident, Muslims were branded as terrorists by officials of the BJP and allied groups and the local media while armed gangs set out on a four-day retaliatory killing spree. Muslim homes, businesses, and places of worship were destroyed. Hundreds of women and girls were gang-raped and sexually mutilated before being burnt to death. In the weeks that followed the massacres, Muslims destroyed Hindu homes and businesses in continued retaliatory violence.

[16] 'We Have No Orders to Save You', pp. 47–8.

[17] Ibid. at 4–5.

[18] See, Human Rights Watch, 'Compounding Injustice: The Government's Failure to Redress Massacres in Gujarat' 4 (2003) [hereinafter 'Compounding Injustice'].

part of the essay looks at the dual role of the judiciary, and the supreme court in particular, as an alleged communalizing force and an arbiter of justice. Part three turns to the need for criminal justice system reforms. The information contained in this essay is current up to May 2005.

The information related to the 2002 massacres in Gujarat is based on investigations by the author when she was Senior Researcher for South Asia at Human Rights Watch. Her investigations were published in two Human Rights Watch reports. The investigations found that the anti-Muslim violence in Gujarat enjoyed considerable state support in both its planning and execution.[19] Soon after the attacks, the state began sabotaging police investigations and engineered a massive cover-up of its role in the violence, as well as the role of *sangh parivar* leaders.[20]

IMPUNITY IN DELHI, BOMBAY, AND GUJARAT

The involvement of political leaders and other state officials in episodes of communal violence in India has all but guaranteed impunity for the crimes outlined above. The role of the police, as both perpetrators of crime and saboteurs of investigations, is a significant part of this equation.

Police Complicity in Communal Violence

Since 1961, judicial commissions established by the government have indicted the police for their complicit role in communal riots.[21] The J. Ranganath Misra Commission's report on the 1984 riots in Delhi states: 'The riots occurred broadly on account of the total passivity, callousness, and indifference of the police in the matter of controlling the situation and protecting the people of the Sikh community.'[22]

[19] HRW report 'We Have No Orders to Save You', p. 5.

[20] Ibid., pp. 47–9; HRW, 'Compounding Injustice', pp. 15–25.

[21] See generally Colin Gonsalves, 'Institutionalized communalism in the police force: The breakdown in the criminal justice system', *Article 2*, 7 (June 2002) and Teesta Setalvad, 'How the bias shows', *Communalism Combat*, March 1998, at 37. See also Dr V. Kannu Pillai, 'Reforms now! To curb communal violence the nexus between politicians, criminals and the police has to be broken', *Communalism Combat*, September 2002, available at http://www.sabrang.com/cc/archive/2002/sep02/pillai.html.

[22] 'Damning Verdict', supra n. 10, at vii. See also PUDR & PUCL, 'Who are the Guilty?', Report of a joint inquiry into the causes and impact of the riots in Delhi from 21 October to 10 November 1984, available at http://www.pucl.org/Topics/Religion-communalism/2003/who-are-guilty.htm.

Police participation and encouragement of violence also occurred during the Bombay riots of 1992–3, as noted by the Srikrishna Commission report. The police remained indifferent to appeals by the victims and in some cases displayed harsh and brutal treatment toward Muslim riot victims.[23] Similarly, in many incidents documented in Gujarat during 2002 the police were directly implicated in the attacks.[24] At best they were passive observers, and at worst they participated in the burning and looting of Muslim shops and homes and the killing and mutilation of men, women, and children.[25]

Sabotaging Investigations

In addition to complicity or active participation in communal violence, the police have reportedly also undermined and sabotaged investigations to protect the accused.[26] Following the 2002 massacres in Gujarat, eyewitnesses filed numerous police First Information Reports (FIRs)[27] that named local leaders as instigators or participants in the attacks. The few that were arrested were released on bail shortly thereafter. The police reportedly faced continuous pressure from the state to avoid making arrests or to reduce the severity of the charges filed. In many instances,

[23] Damning Verdict, supra note 10, at vi (1998). See also Crime Against Humanity Vol. II, supra note 9, at http://www.sabrang.com/tribunal/vol2/distrends. html (summarizing the findings of various commissions on disturbing trends in the police system).

[24] To determine possible culpable police inaction or direct complicity during Godhra and its aftermath, the state of Gujarat appointed the Shah-Nanavati Commission of Inquiry, headed by two retired judges. When asked in May 2003 about the evidence collected to date, Justice Nanavati responded, 'the evidence recorded so far in other districts [does] not show any serious lapse on the part of police and the civil administration.': 'Godhra probe: No evidence of lapse against government', The Times of India, 19 May 2003. Statements made by Justice Nanavati on the purported lack of evidence of police and state government culpability during the violence led to a boycott of the Commission by several NGOs and numerous victims of the violence. The NGOs Shanti Abhiyan, PUCL, and several other organizations told the Commission that the people had lost confidence in the Commission's impartiality: Manas Dasgupta, 'NGOs boycott Nanavati panel proceedings', The Hindu, 17 June 2003, available at http://www.hinduonnet.com/ thehindu/2003/06/17/stories/2003061706381100.htm At this writing, the Commission had yet to release its report and inspired little hope for impartiality and justice.

[25] No Orders to Save You, supra note 15, at 5–6.

[26] 'We Have No Orders to Save You', pp. 47–9 and 'Compounding Injustice', pp. 15–25.

[27] The initial report of a crime recorded by the police.

the police refused to include in the FIRs, the names of perpetrators identified by victims. Instead, police registered what are known as 'omnibus FIRs', in which the accused is identified only as 'an unruly mob' or 'a mob of 10,000'. Police also filed false charges against Muslim youth arbitrarily detained during combing operations in largely destroyed neighbourhoods. Officers who tried to keep the peace or stop murderous mobs were reported to have been transferred or had to face the wrath of their superiors.

In numerous instances, in an effort to cover up their own participation in the violence, the police also instituted false cases against men and women injured in police shootings.[28] Some postmortems and medical certificates were manipulated to hide any incriminating evidence, falsely indicating that the victims were killed or injured by stabbing or sword injury during their participation in the riots, and not by gunfire. It was reported that if a case reached trial, Muslim victims faced biased or cowed prosecutors and judges. It has also been reported that lawyers representing Muslim victims or doctors providing medical relief also faced ongoing harassment and threats.

Vrinda Grover draws striking parallels in the sabotaging of criminal cases following the riots of 1984 and the Gujarat carnage of 2002.[29] The omission of critical information from FIRs, including the names of the accused, the lumping together of unrelated cases into single omnibus FIRs, and the scaling down of offenses, are but a few of the patterns described.[30] The report of the Srikrishna Commission investigating the 1992–3 Bombay riots also point to the police's 'lack of enthusiasm in registering offenses against Hindus even when the accused was clearly identified...'[31]

Lack of Prosecutions for Communal Crimes

The fumbling and sabotaging of investigations in Delhi, Bombay, and Gujarat has naturally led to a lack of prosecution at the trial level. Convictions, when achieved, have been few and far between. The justice

[28] 'Compounding Injustice', pp. 30–1.

[29] Vrinda Grover, 'The Elusive Quest for Justice: Delhi 1984 to Gujarat 2002', in *Gujarat: The Making of a Tragedy*, Siddarth Varadarajan (ed.) (2002) at 355. Grover has authored several independent research studies on the legal system's response to the anti-Sikh riots. She also deposed before the Nanavati Commission of Inquiry probing the riots.

[30] Ibid., at 357–67.

[31] Damning Verdict, supra note 10, at vi.

machinery also did little to investigate or prosecute cases of sexual violence. Problems included lack of medical examination for victims, the refusal to register rape cases in FIRs or include them in chargesheets, deficiencies in Indian rape laws, and the silencing of rape victims by members of their own families and community due to the stigma that often accompanies such crimes. In Gujarat, the widespread burning of victims' bodies also destroyed evidence of many rapes.

Deploring the lack of justice to victims of communal violence, Justice Hosbet Suresh[32] wrote in July 2003:

The majority of such victims [of communal riots] belong to the minority community, and they get no justice. It happened in Delhi in 1984. Officially the number of killings was placed at 2,733. It has been almost two decades and none of the assailants has been convicted…

It happened in Bombay after the riots in December 1992 and January 1993… Though cases had been registered against some of [the culprits], instead of prosecuting them, the government just decided to quietly close the cases. Nearly 3,000 cases were thus dropped.[33]

In the years that have passed since the anti-Sikh riots, very few individuals have been arrested, prosecuted, and punished for their involvement in the episode.[34] On 16 May 2005, a Delhi court sentenced five persons to life imprisonment for killing a man during the riots by setting him ablaze.[35] However, and not without some anguished justification, the survivors and next of kin, as well as human rights and social activist communities, may not regard this ruling as sufficient in light of prior acquittals, including the acquittal of a prominent politician.[36]

---

[32] Hosbet Suresh, 'And Justice for All', *The Little Magazine*, 25 July 2003, available at http://www.countercurrents.org/comm-suresh250703.htm. Justice Hosbet Suresh is a retired judge of the Bombay High Court and a leading human rights activist.

[33] Ibid.

[34] Human Rights Watch, 'India: Communal Violence and Denial of Justice' n. 4 (April 1996). See further, Human Rights Watch, 'World Report 1997: India', available at http://www.hrw.org/reports/1997/WR97/ASIA-05.htm.

[35] 'Five given life sentence in 1984 Sikh riot case', Press Trust of India, 16 May 2005, available at http://147.208.132.198/news/181_1364147,0006.htm; see also Indian—Muslim Council (USA), 'IMC-USA welcomes the sentencing of killers in 1984 Anti-Sikh pogrom—Urges UPA government to implement the recommendations of the Nanavati Commission', 17 May 2005, available at http://www.imc-usa.org/cgi-bin/cfm/PressRelease.cfm?PRID=107.

[36] For analysis of the acquittals, see generally Nirnimesh Kumar, 'Sajjan Kumar acquitted in anti-Sikh riots case', The *Hindu*, 24 December 2002, available at http://www.hinduonnet.com/2002/12/24/stories/2002122404870100.htm (recording

Grover found that only six out of 137 judgments delivered by trial courts in the Delhi riot cases ended in convictions.[37] All the cases against politicians had resulted in their acquittal.[38] Some reasons cited for the acquittals include the court's reliance on solitary witness accounts (due to the failure of the police to bring forward corroborating witnesses);[39] the delay in bringing proceedings (many cases came to trial over 18 years after the riots);[40] the filing of omnibus FIRs by the police (sometimes ten years after the riots had taken place);[41] and the absence of Test Parade Identifications which would enable the accused to be identified. And like Gujarat, the names of state officials allegedly involved in the riots were deliberately omitted in the FIRs.[42] The central government appointed the Justice Ranganath Mishra Commission, the Jain-Banerjee Commission and the Justice G.T. Nanavati Commission to look into the Delhi riots.[43] The appointment of such commissions is futile,

---

that Congress leader Sajjan Kumar and all other accused in a 1984 anti-Sikh riots case were acquitted by a Delhi court for lack of evidence); 'Sajjan Kumar acquitted in 1984 anti-Sikh riots case', 23 December 2003, available at http://www.rediff.com/news/2002/dec/23sikh.htm; Naunidhi Kaur, 'Acquittal of a politician', *Frontline*, January 2003, available at http://www.frontlineonnet.com/fl2001/stories/20030117004312000.htm (noting that acquittal is less than credible given that their involvement in the riots was documented by the PUCL, PUDR, and the Citizens' Justice Committee).

[37] Naunidhi Kaur, 'A life sentence', *Frontline*, Mar–Apr 2003, available at http://www.frontlineonnet.com/fl2007/stories/20030411002004500.htm.

[38] Ibid.

[39] Ibid. (citing Grover's statement that 'With the police not bringing forth neighbours who also witnessed the killings and relying on one witness, the prosecution's case falls apart in the trial court.').

[40] Ibid.

[41] Ibid.

[42] Ibid. See also Gonsalves, supra note 18, at 8.

[43] 'SC lambasts Centre for withdrawing anti-Sikh riot cases', The *Times of India*, 7 December 2003, available at http://timesofindia.indiatimes.com/articleshow/344546.cms. During May 2000, the BJP-ied government set up the Nanavati Commission to probe into the anti-Sikh riots. The government felt that the Misra Commission had played down the role of Congress leaders in the violence. 'Sikh riot victims seek U.S. intervention', Indo-Asian News Service, 31 October 2003, available at http://in.news.yahoo.com/031031/43/290jz.html. On 27 July 2004, the Central government extended by three months the term of the Justice Nanavati Commission probing the 1984 anti-Sikh riots in India. The Commission's term would have otherwise expired on 2 August 2004. 'Term of commission probing anti-Sikh riots extended', Newindpress.com. Justice Nanavati also heads the

however, without the adoption of other measures to fight impunity, further discussed below.[44]

In 2003, Amnesty International reported that '[t]en years after widespread communal riots in Bombay claimed 1,788 lives and five years after the Srikrishna Commission of Inquiry indicted several police officers for having actively sided with Hindu groups during the riots, no significant progress had been made to prosecute the alleged per- petrators.'[45] In their review of the Maharashtra government's Action Taken Report, advocates Shakil Ahmad and Jyoti Punwani found that all the officers were released on bail; the public prosecutor did not argue for their detention. In cases where departmental inquiries were completed, punishments were disturbingly minor and ranged from reduction in rank to compulsory retirements. Shockingly, many officers were promoted.[46]

After more than two years of repeated acquittals in Gujarat, the supreme court stepped in to transfer key cases outside the state and reopen over 2,000 cases prematurely closed by the police. In the seminal *Best Bakery* case (discussed further below) citing 'collusion between the government and prosecution' the supreme court ordered retrial of five cases, transferring them from the jurisdiction of Gujarat courts to the Bombay High Court.[47]

Commission of Inquiry into Godhra and its aftermath in Gujarat. In February 2005, both the report on the anti-Sikh riots and the report on Godhra violence were released by the respective commissions. However, the report on the anti-Sikh riots was never made public. Swati Maheshwari, 'Anti-Sikh riots—Justice delayed yet again', NDTV.com, 13 May 2005. During May 2005, despite assurances by both the Law Minister and the Home minister, the Indian Parliament, lend by the Congress party, ended its session without tabling the report of the Nanavati commission on the anti-Sikh riots of 1984. *Ibid.* For more on the Shah-Nanavati Commission of Inquiry into Gujarat see supra note 21.

[44] Echoing similar sentiments, the supreme court lambasted the central govern- ment in December 2003 for its decision to withdraw an anti-Sikh riot case, stating 'What is this—on one hand you go on appointing commission after commission to probe the riots and on the other you withdraw the case registered by the police.' 'SC lambasts Centre for withdrawing anti-Sikh riot cases', supra note 38.

[45] Amnesty International, 'Amnesty International Report 2003: India', available at http://web.amnesty.org/web/web.nsf/3cf824eb039d237c80256d2700483ac2/ 427e1b8d90f8c32180256d3a0046b8c1/$FILE/india.pdf.

[46] See Gonsalves, supra note 18, at 10.

[47] Rakesh Bhatnagar, 'Quit or act, SC tells Modi govt.', The *Times of India*, 12 September 2003, available at http://timesofindia.indiatimes.com/cms.dll/xml/ uncomp/articleshow?msid=179040.

ROLE OF THE JUDICIARY

The Indian judiciary, and the supreme court in particular, has been much extolled for its progressive stance on the implementation of constitutionally guaranteed rights. Indeed, in comparison with the executive and legislative institutions under the constitution, the judiciary represents the greatest prospect for continuing reform and increased commitment to the protection of civil liberties.[48] The call for judicial activism must, however, begin with closer scrutiny of the role of judicial decision-making in exacerbating communal tensions and divisions.[49] The next section examines whether communal thinking influences judicial decisions.

Influence of Identity Politics on Judicial Decisions

In 1996, Sara Ahmad examined a series of supreme court decisions that substantiate the influence of identity politics on supreme court decision-making.[50] Decisions analysed in her article include those that: (i) hold that certain religious practices (often Islamic ones) are un-Indian; (ii) undermine the constitutional rights to profess and practice religion in the name of promoting 'national integration'; and (iii) resolve communal violence cases 'on the basis of over-riding political considerations'.[51]

The first set of decisions involves determining certain religious practices of minorities to be 'un-Indian' and therefore unconstitutional.[52] In *Sarla Mudgal* v. *Union of India*,[53] the court considered the legal validity

[48] Hosbet Suresh, 'Your lordships, beware!', *Communalism Combat*, September 2002, at 13. See further Militant Hindu leader discharged, BBC News, July 25, 2000 available at http://news.bbc.co.uk/1/hi/world/south_asia/849923.stm.

[49] Ahmad, supra note 4, at 322 (noting that despite the active role of the judiciary in ending communal violence, several recent court decisions demonstrate the influence of communalism on judicial thinking).

[50] According to Ahmad, governments engage in identity politics when they '(1) claim the existence of a national monolithic identity; (2) use that identity as a rationale for judicial decisions against persons who do not share that identity; (3) excuse harassment of targeted communities; (4) fail to prosecute perpetrators of communal crimes; or (5) promote or direct violence against non-majority or non-member communities.': Ahmad, supra note 4, at 321. For more on the governmental exploitation of communal differences as a proximate cause of communal violence worldwide, see Playing the 'Communal' Card, supra note 4.

[51] Ahmad, supra note 4, at 329–47.

[52] Ibid., at 330-35.

[53] AIR 1995 SC 1531.

of second marriages by Hindu men after they had converted to Islam, and held that such marriages were void.[54] The court did not limit itself, however, to answering the specific legal question presented; instead, it called for a uniform personal law to supersede the Muslim marriage laws on the ground that the constitution mandated 'the establishment of a 'common civil code' for the whole of India.'[55] In so doing, the court implied that the Muslim practice of bigamous marriage ran counter not only to 'the cause of national unity and integration', but to the constitution itself.[56]

According to Ahmad, in cases such as *Sarla Mudgal*, the question of what it means to be 'un-Indian' is usually defined in opposition to a nationalist, monolithic, and static notion of what constitutes the 'true Indian' identity—which often coincides with the identity of the Hindu majority.[57] The court began its opinion in *Sarla Mudgal* by noting that '[w]hen more than 80 per cent of the citizens have already been brought under the codified [Hindu] personal law there is no justification whatsoever to keep in abeyance, any more, the introduction of 'uniform civil code' for all citizens', in effect seeming to assume that Hindu law, being the majority law, should apply to all.[58]

This type of judicial thinking is also evident in cases involving the prosecution of elected representatives of the Hindu nationalist Shiv Sena-Bharatiya Janata Party alliance government in the western state of Maharashtra for corrupt practices under the Representation of the People Act, 1951.[59] In *Prabhoo v. Prabhakar Kasinath Kunte*,[60] Shiv Sena-BJP candidate Ramesh Yeshwant Prabhoo appealed a Bombay High

[54] Ibid., at 1537.

[55] Ibid., at 1538.

[56] Ibid. ('The Hindus along with Sikhs, Buddhists, and Jains have forsaken their sentiments in the cause of national unity and integration, some other communities would not, though the constitution enjoins the establishment of a 'common civil code' for the whole of India.').

[57] Ahmad, supra note 4, at 330–5. See also Smita Narula, 'Overlooked Danger: The Security and Rights Implications of Hindu Nationalism in India', 16 Harv. Hum. Rts. J. 41, 56–7 (2003) (arguing that the Hindu right is succeeding in recasting the Indian identity as one exclusively reserved for its Hindu citizens).

[58] *Sarla Mudgal*, AIR 1995 SC at 1531.

[59] The Representation of the People Act, 1951, prohibits the use of religion or religious symbols to promote one's candidacy or to adversely affect the election of another candidate constituting a corrupt practice that debases the election and is an offense punishable under the law.

[60] 1995 SCALE 1.

Court judgment that pronounced Prabhoo and Shiv Sena leader Bal Thackeray (as Prabhoo's agent) guilty of violating the Act.[61] Prabhoo argued that the election campaign speeches made by Thackeray, which were the basis of the high court's decision, 'did not amount to appeal for votes on the ground of his religion [as] the substance and main thrust thereof was 'Hindutava' which means the Indian culture and not merely the Hindu religion.'[62] Although the supreme court upheld the conviction, it agreed with Prabhoo that Hindutva[63] 'is related more to the way of life of the people in the sub-continent [and] is not to be equated with, or understood as religious Hindu fundamentalism'.[64] Rather, the court found, the term 'is used and understood as a synonym of 'Indianization', i.e., development of uniform culture by obliterating the differences between all the cultures co-existing in the country.'[65]

The second type of judicial thinking emerges when courts are called upon to deal with the issue of secularism.[66] The Hindutva cases referred to above reflect a problematic engagement with secularism by the supreme court, whereby it erroneously accepted the secular nature of the speeches of the Hindu Right and failed to interrogate the 'anti-secular vision of secularism' that characterizes the Hindu Right.[67] Another example of the judiciary's failed engagement with questions of secularism emerges in cases concerning the relationship between secular law and

[61] Ibid., at 1.

[62] Ibid., at 7.

[63] A movement for 'Hindu awakening'.

[64] *Prabhoo*, 1995 SCALE at 22.

[65] In contrast to the Court's understanding of Hindutva, Cossman and Kapur point out that the term 'Hindutva' was developed by early leaders of the Hindu Right as a political conceptualization of the Hindu Nation that was centered around religion. See Brenda Cossman and Ratna Kapur, 'Secularism's Last Sigh: the Hindu Right, the Courts and India's Struggle for Democracy', 38 Harv. Int'l L.J. 113, 129–34 (1997) (arguing that 'the political category of Hindu has been constituted in opposition to religious minorities and premised on the very elimination of these minorities through assimilation or violence'). In the present-day political context, 'Hindutva aspires to the establishment of a Hindu Rashtra—a Hindu state based on a Hindu way of life'. Ibid., at 134.

[66] See Suresh, supra note 43, at 12; Ahmad, supra note 4, at 322.

[67] Cossman and Kapur, supra note 610, at 114–15. Gary Jacobsohn argues that the supreme court became 'wittingly or unwittingly, a medium for the achievement of antisecular aspirations' through the Hindutva cases. Gary J. Jacobsohn, 'The Wheel of Law: India's Secularism in Comparative Constitutional Context', 190 (2003).

religious law as associated with the rights under Articles 25 and 26 of the constitution to profess and practice religion and manage religious affairs.[68]

The landmark case of *Md. Ahmed Khan* v. *Shah Bano Begum*[69] addressed this relationship in the context of a possible conflict between the Muslim personal law and Section 125(1)(a) of the Code of Criminal Procedure[70] over the issue of whether a Muslim man was required to maintain his divorced wife beyond the period of *iddat*.[71] In a highly controversial ruling,[72] the supreme court first asserted the primacy of secular law over religious law in cases of conflict, holding that religion 'cannot have any repercussion on the applicability of such laws' as Section 125, which 'cut across the barriers of religion.'[73] The court went on to find no such conflict in the instant case, despite the accepted interpretation of the Muslim personal law as limiting a husband's liability to maintain his divorced wife to the period of *iddat*.[74] Instead, the 'true position' of the Muslim personal law distinguished between divorced wives able to maintain themselves, in which case the husband's liability would cease with the expiration of the iddat period, and divorced wives left destitute, who would be 'entitled to take recourse to section 125'.[75]

The court reached this conclusion based upon its own analysis of the Quran and other Islamic texts, which left 'no doubt that the Quran imposes an obligation on the Muslim husband to make provision for or to provide maintenance to the divorced wife'. Submissions by the All India Muslim Personal Board arguing otherwise were dismissed as 'facile' or as 'a shuffling plea'.[76] In the *Shah Bano* decision, as well as

[68] Ahmad, supra note 4, at 335.

[69] *Md. Ahmed Khan* v. *Shah Bano Begum*, AIR 1985 SC 945.

[70] The section allows a destitute wife to sue her divorced husband for monthly maintenance, provided that the husband has sufficient means and has neglected or refused to maintain his wife. Ibid., at 947–8.

[71] The obligatory three-month period following a divorce during which marriage is prohibited.

[72] See Ahmad, supra note 4, at 338–9 (describing how 'the *Shah Bano* decision provoked sharp reaction from Muslims throughout the country'). Jacobsohn has referred to *Shah Bano* as an example of the 'judicial excesses of theological exegesis'. Jacobsohn, supra note 62, at 113.

[73] Shah Bano, AIR 1985 SC at 948–9.

[74] Ibid., at 950–1.

[75] Ibid.

[76] Ibid., at 951–2, 954.

the unreported *Rahmat Ullah* decision,[77] the court evinced a clear preference for secular law on the grounds that 'a common civil code will help the cause of national integration by removing disparate loyalties in laws which have conflicting ideologies'.[78] While both cases served in part to advance Muslim women's rights, the language of 'national integration' and the disapproval of citizens' 'loyalties' to their personal laws were deeply troubling for India's minority groups.

The third set of cases reflect the influence of overriding political considerations on judicial decision-making.[79] For example, when a Especial Uttar Pradesh Court released seven leaders of the Hindu Right jailed over the demolition of the Babri Masjid, political sources characterized the outcome as a 'face-saving deal' between Prime Minister Rao's Congress party and the BJP.[80] Even when political considerations do not seem to be salient, the problem of communal bias on the part of the judiciary remains; this charge has been levied against judicial decisions viewed as extending impunity for violent police oppression of Sikhs in the state of Punjab.[81] Between 1984 and 1994, the decade-long police crackdown resulted in mass disappearances, extrajudicial executions, illegal cremations, and the deaths of at least 10,000 people.[82] However, habeas corpus petitions filed on behalf of the 'disappeared' with the Punjab and Haryana High Court

---

[77] Ahmad, supra note 4, at 341–2 (outlining the decision by which the court held that triple *talaq* divorce was illegal in India).

[78] *Shah Bano*, AIR 1985 SC at 954. According to Jacobsohn, however, 'for 'the Constitution…to have any meaning' does *not* require that the civil law apply in the same manner to all communities [given] the secular constitution's dual commitment to social reform and the integrity of group religious life'—indeed, while India's 'constitutive domain of religion is, by the terms of the Constitution, open to encroachment by forces of political and social transformation[,] the legitimacy of this undertaking is at least partially dependent on preserving political space for religious identity'. Jacobsohn, supra note 62, at 107–8.

[79] Ahmad, supra note 4, at 345.

[80] 'Indian court frees Hindu leaders in mosque case', Reuters News, 20 December 1993, available at LEXIS, World Library, ALLWLD File. See Ahmad, supra note 4, at 346–7 (arguing that the Uttar Pradesh court's decision was unfortunate in light of government inaction over Ayodhya riots as compared to its aggressive prosecution of Muslim militants over the 1992 Bombay bombings).

[81] See Jaskaran Kaur, 'A Judicial Blackout: Judicial Impunity for Disappearances in Punjab, India', 15 Harv. Hum. Rts. J. 269, 271–3 (2002) (describing developments that led to Sikh insurgency and government retaliation) [hereinafter 'A Judicial Blackout'].

[82] See generally Human Rights Watch, 'Dead Silence: The Legacy of Abuses in Punjab' (1994).

failed to obtain significant redress for, or even investigation into, police crimes.[83] Interviews with justices of the high court revealed that they tended to justify police action in Punjab along two lines—on one hand, they minimized human rights abuses committed by the police, describing them as inevitable accidents; on the other hand, they seemed to lay the responsibility for the insurgency upon the Sikh community as a whole, refusing to distinguish between Sikh civilians and Sikh militants.[84]

Among the writ petitions dismissed by the high court was a petition for a judicial inquiry into the disappearance of Kulwant Singh, a Sikh advocate at the Ropar District Courts, his wife, and their two-year-old son.[85] Their disappearance provoked an outcry from the Punjab and Haryana High Court Bar Association, which went on strike to protest the alleged abduction and murder of Singh and his family by the Ropar Police.[86] Despite strong evidence of police culpability,[87] the high court refused to order an investigation and dismissed the case.[88] On appeal, the supreme court was unequivocal in its censure of the high court. According to the court, '[t]he High Court was wholly unjustified in closing its eyes and ears to the controversy... [f]or the reasons best known to it, the High Court became wholly oblivious to the patent facts on the record and failed to perform the duty entrusted to it under the Constitution.'[89] The supreme court concluded that 'the least the High Court could have done in this case was to have directed an independent investigation/inquiry' into Singh's disappearance.[90]

The Promise of Public Interest Litigation

The detrimental impact of the decisions outlined above stand in sharp contrast to the self-fashioned powers of the supreme court to uphold

[83] Kaur's 2001 study of ninety habeas corpus petitions that had been filed from 1990 to 1997 revealed that forty-two cases had been dismissed by the high court and twenty-one cases were still pending; in only five cases had the court authorized the payment of compensation. 'A Judicial Blackout', supra note 786, at 286.

[84] Ibid., at 283–5.

[85] See Punjab & Haryana High Court Bar Assn. v. State of Punjab, [1994] SCC 616, 616–22 (recounting the background of the case and how it was dismissed by the high court).

[86] Ibid., at 616.

[87] See ibid., at 616–19 (reproducing the report of the Bar Association, which found 'glaring loopholes' in the police explanation for Singh's death).

[88] Id. at 622–3.

[89] Id. at 623.

[90] Id. at 623–4.

the rule of law through the mechanism of public interest litigation. Starting in the late 1970s[91] and led primarily by Justices Iyer and P.N. Bhagwati, the supreme court transformed itself from an institution of last resort for the privileged and moneyed classes to a place of 'easy reach'[92] that gave new hope to the disempowered and dispossessed. Alternatively referred to as 'public interest litigation' (PIL) or 'social action litigation',[93] the court invoked Article 32 of the constitution[94] and took radical steps to 'make basic human rights meaningful to the disadvantaged sections of the community and to assure them distributive justice'.[95] These steps included: abandoning the doctrine of standing;[96] waiving

[91] Burt Neuborne, 'The Supreme Court of India', Int'l J. Const'l L. 476, 500, n.111 (2003).

[92] P.N. Bhagwati, 'Social Action Litigation: The Indian Experience', in Neelan Tiruchelvam and Radhika Coomaraswamy, (eds) *The Role of the Judiciary in Plural Societies* 20 (1987).

[93] Ibid., at 22–3 (expressing agreement with Professor Upendra Baxi's preference for the term 'social action litigation' on the basis that the term 'public interest litigation' has a certain meaning in the United States and reflects a strategy that is peculiarly American).

[94] Article 32 empowers the court to 'issue directions or orders or writs... for the enforcement of any of the rights conferred' under the fundamental rights chapter of the constitution. It sets out the remedies for enforcement of rights in the following terms:

(1) The right to move the Supreme Court by appropriate proceedings for the enforcement of the rights conferred by this Part is guaranteed.

(2) The Supreme Court shall have power to issue directions or orders or writs, including writs in the nature of habeas corpus, mandamus, prohibition, quo warranto and certiorari, whichever may be appropriate, for the enforcement of any of the rights conferred by this Part.

(3) Without prejudice to the powers conferred on the Supreme Court by clauses (1) and (2), Parliament may by law empower any other court to exercise within the local limits of its jurisdiction all or any of the powers exercisable by the Supreme Court under clause (2).

(4) The right guaranteed by this article shall not be suspended except as otherwise provided for by this Constitution.

[95] Bhagwati, supra note 87, at 22.

[96] See S.P. Sathe, 'Judicial Experience: The Indian Experience', 6 Wash. U. J.L. & Pol'y 29, 71–2 (2001) (identifying reasons for liberalization of the locus standi rule as being to enable the court to reach the poor and disadvantaged; to enable individuals or groups of people to raise matters of concern related to governance and to increase public participation in constitutional adjudication processes). See generally Susan D. Susman, 'Distant Voices in the Courts of India: Transformation of Standing in Public Interest Litigation', 13 Wis. Int'l L.J. 57, 60–86 (1994)

formal pleading requirements;[97] abandoning adversarial fact-finding in favour of the appointment of socio-commissions;[98] and expanding the court's remedial powers.[99] Public interest litigation provided 'a model for courts struggling to balance the transformative aspect of law against the law's natural tendency to favour those rich enough to invoke it'.[100]

That the court was forced to transform itself into a mechanism responsible for enforcing existing laws[101] underscored the tragic reality that the police, the public prosecutors, and the lower courts had utterly failed in protecting the rights of the poor and upholding the country's laws. Though enthusiasm and support for PIL litigation inevitably waned with the emergence of more conservative judges following the retirement of Justices Iyer and Bhagwati in 1980 and 1986 respectively,[102] the

---

(outlining the transformation of standing and providing a brief overview of the Indian court and constitution); Jamie Cassels, 'Judicial Activism and Public Interest Litigation in India: Attempting the Impossible?', 37 Am. J. Comp. L. 495, 498–9 (1989).

[97] Ordinarily pursuant to Order 6 of the Code of Civil Procedure a litigant is required to file formal pleading before the court to seek appropriate remedy. The supreme court waived this formal pleading requirement in public interest litigation and considers letters written by people and newspaper reports as a sufficient means of petition under Article 32 of the constitution (see *Khatri* v. *State of Bihar*, AIR 1981 SC 928 (popularly known as *Bhagalpur blinding* case) in which a lawyer sent a newspaper article to the supreme court which was treated by Justice P.N. Bhagwati as a petition: see Susman, supra note 6591, at 58. See Bhagwati, supra note 87, at 24–5 (identifying how through this mechanism the court has evolved what has come to be known as epistolary jurisdiction and discussing how this shift enables greater access to justice by large masses of the people). See further Cassels, supra note 91, at 499.

[98] Generally the supreme court does not adjudicate matters involving detailed factual investigation. However in public interest litigations the supreme court has appointed advocates and experts to investigate the facts to assist the court in deciding the matter. See Bhagwati, supra note 87, at 27 (identifying these commissions as 'social-legal commissions of inquiry'). See further Susman, supra note 91, at 88–9 (discussing cases in which the investigative commission functioned).

[99] Cassels, supra note 91, at 505–7.

[100] Neuborne, supra note 86.

[101] The Court has, inter alia, enforced laws concerning undertrials [undertrials refers to people whose trials are in progress and in which the sentence has not yet been pronounced] (*R.D. Upadhyay* v. *State of AP*, AIR 1981 SC 939); police atrocities (*Dalit Singh Dalal* v. *UOI*, AIR 1997 SC 1203), the failure to release an accused despite court order (*Government of AP* v. *G. Laxmi Reddy*, 1997 (2) SCC 631); and custodial deaths (*Kalpana Bahera* v. *UOI*, 1997 (7) SCALE (Supp.) 24).

[102] Susman, supra note 91, at 82.

mechanisms they helped establish were firmly in place and continue to be invoked in times of grave communal violence.

Civil society groups successfully invoked public interest litigation in the aftermath of the 2002 massacres in Gujarat, ultimately changing the course of impunity in the state. One of the court's most notable decisions involved the infamous *Best Bakery* case[103] in which twenty-one people accused of burning fourteen people to death were acquitted by a Gujarat state court in 2003 after witnesses withdrew statements they had given the police identifying the attackers. Following information from the prime witness in the case that she was forced to change her testimony as a result of threats against her during the trial,[104] India's National Human Rights Commission (NHRC) filed a petition in the supreme court, asking the court to provide witness protection, ensure a retrial of the case in a court outside Gujarat state, and order the transfer of other key cases outside the state.[105] Treating the NHRC petition as PIL, the supreme court issued notice seeking the retrial of five cases, including *Best Bakery* and directed the Gujarat government to provide protection to victims and family members involved in the cases mentioned by the NHRC.[106]

Following the supreme court order, the Gujarat government reluctantly sought a retrial of the *Best Bakery* case on 29 September 2003.[107] The Gujarat High Court dismissed the government's appeal. After persistent pressure from the supreme court, the Gujarat government appealed the high court judgment to the supreme court.[108] On 12 April 2004, the

[103] On 1 March 2002, fourteen people were set on fire and killed in a bakery in Vadodara, Gujarat.

[104] Press Release, Human Rights Watch, 'India: Protect Gujarat Activists Now', (5 September 2003) available at http://www.hrw.org/press/2003/09/india090503.htm.

[105] Press release, Amnesty International, 'India: Gujarat—Denial of Justice for Victims', 26 February 2004, available at http://web.amnesty.org/library/index/ENGASA200032004.

[106] The NGO Citizens for Justice and Peace also filed a companion petition in the supreme court seeking protection of human rights activists involved in assisting the witnesses to the *Best Bakery* case. For a copy of the petition filed by the Citizens for Justice & Peace & Ors, see http://sabrang.com/news/scpetition.htm.

[107] 'Gujarat files appeal in Best Bakery case', The *Hindu*, 22 February 2004, available at http://www.hindu.com/2004/02/22/stories/2004022204321000.htm; 'SC reserves judgment in Best Bakery case', 24 March 2004, available at http://in.news.yahoo.com/040324/139/2c6oo.html.

[108] Amnesty International, 'India: Gujarat—Denial of Justice for Victims', supra note 100.

supreme court gave an unprecedented order[109] quashing the acquittal of all the twenty-one accused in the *Best Bakery* case and ordering a retrial and reinvestigation into the case (the latter to be overseen by the Director General of Police). In recognition of the subversion of the justice delivery system that had taken place, the supreme court directed that the re-trial, to be conducted on a day-to-day basis, take place in a court under the jurisdiction of the Bombay High Court.[110] In another unprecedented move, the court further directed the Gujarat government to appoint a new public prosecutor in consultation with victims and witnesses, and required the Gujarat and Maharashtra governments to provide adequate protection to victims and witnesses.[111] On 7 May 2004 the supreme court dismissed an application filed by the Gujarat government against the order.

Continuing its efforts to prevent impunity in the Gujarat violence, in August 2004 the supreme court moved the trial of what has been called the *Bilkis Bano* case[112] from Gujarat to neighbouring Maharashtra state in response to pleas that a fair trial was impossible in Gujarat.[113] At

[109] It was an unprecedented order as both the trial court and the high court had acquitted the accused in this case: see 'Best Bakery: SC orders fresh trial in Maharashtra', 12 April 2004, available at http://www.outlookindia.com/pti_news.asp?id=214341.

[110] At this writing, the re-trial was taking place in the Special Court in Mumbai set up to hear the case. The term of the court was extended to 31 May 2005. 'Court views videotape: Rescue operation by cops in Best Bakery case', *Central Chronicle*, 5 April 2005, available at http://www.centralchronicle.com/20050405/0504002.htm. The trial has, however, been plagued by controversies surrounding the primary witness. Ibid.

[111] 'Best Bakery: SC orders fresh trial in Maharashtra', 12 April 2004, available at http://www.outlookindia.com/pti_news.asp?id=214341.

[112] 'SC Transfers Bilkis Bano rape case to Mumbai', *Outlook India*, 8 August 2004, available at http://www.outlookindia.com/pti_news.asp?id=240584; 'Bilkis Yakub Rasool sees justice in case transfer', *Yahoo News*, 8 August 2004, available at http://in.news.yahoo.com/040808/137/2feka.html;-Bilkis Yakub Rasool was a pregnant Muslim woman who was gang-raped as she tried to flee a mob during the Gujarat massacres. Her relatives, including her three-year-old daughter, were burnt to death as they fled their village in Gujarat at the peak of the violence in early March 2002.

[113] At this writing, the *Bilkis Bano* case was being heard by a special court in Maharshtra. On 20 April 2005, the special court rejected the bail plea of six policemen who had been arrested on the charge of shielding the prime accused. 'Bail plea of six cops in Bilkis case rejected', Press Trust of India, 20 April 2005, available at http://www.hindustantimes.com/news/181_1329179,001301170000.htm.

this writing, other requests to move cases outside of Gujarat remained pending before the supreme court.[114]

On 17 August 2004, the supreme court took yet another momentous step, ordering investigations of over 2,000 Gujarat cases that had been dismissed by the police.[115] The court directed the Gujarat Government to set up a high-level police committee headed by the Director General of Police to reconsider the closure reports filed in these cases and to find out whether further investigation was required.[116] Following the court's directive, the Gujarat government set up a committee to reassess, evaluate, and decide on the reinvestigation and supervision of all summary cases—about 2,100—relating to the violence.[117] At this writing, no information about the work of the committee was available.

Just six days later, on 23 August, the supreme court directed the Advocate General of Gujarat to review the decision of the state's Law Department not to file appeals in over 200 cases where the accused had been acquitted by the trial court. In an unprecedented measure, a bench comprising Justices Ruma Pal, S.B. Sinha, and S.H. Kapadia told the

[114] Other cases pending before the supreme court include a petition seeking the court to, inter alia, issue directions to the Senior Inspector of Police, Azad Maidan Police Station, Mumbai, to (i) register petitioner's complaints under Sections 153A, 153B, and 505 of the Indian Penal Code (IPC) against Gujarat Chief Minister Narendra Modi and Vishwa Hindu Parishad president Ashok Singhal, (ii) conduct investigations if a prima facie case is made out, and (iii) obtain the necessary sanctions for prosecution in relation to a communal speech made by Singhal on 4 September 2002 (in which he expressed 'praise' for Gujarat as a 'successful experiment' of 'raising Hindu consciousness') and a speech made by Modi on 9 September 2003 (in which he enjoined others to 'teach a lesson' to Muslims whom he implied to be responsible for the 'alarming' increase in population). V. Venkatesan, 'A test case in Supreme Court', *Frontline*, Mar.15–28, 2003, available at http://www.flonnet.com/fl2006/stories/20030328002704100.htm. The supreme court also admitted a PIL by Mallika Sarabhai and two others seeking a direction to the Gujarat government to investigate all crimes committed since 27 February in the aftermath of the Godhra carnage. The three-judge bench issued notices on the petition to the central government, the Gujarat government, Chief Minister Narendra Modi, the Vishwa Hindu Parishad, the BJP and others. 'SC admits PIL on Gujarat, Notice to Centre and Modi government', *The Tribune*, 15 April 2003.

[115] 'India: Court Orders Review of Riot Cases', *New York Times, World Briefings*, 18 August 2004.

[116] 'Court orders Gujarat riot review', BBC News, 17 August 2004.

[117] 'On SC order, Gujarat sets up panel for review of riot cases', The *Indian Express*, 3 September 2004.

Attorney General to scrutinize all orders of acquittal made by the trial courts and to recommend whether appeals should be filed in these cases. The court added that in all future acquittals in riot cases, the Law Department will consult the Attorney General before deciding whether or not to appeal.[118] At this writing, the results of the review were not yet available.

For many in Gujarat, the supreme court presents a glimmer of hope amidst a landscape of acquittals that have undermined the citizenry's faith in the judicial process.[119] Such hope, however, remains elusive for victims in Delhi and Bombay. Despite its commendable resolve in bringing justice to the victims in Gujarat, the supreme court has been surprisingly inactive with respect to the Delhi and Bombay riots.[120] But the burden is not on the supreme court alone. As discussed below, both the court and the legislature must actively work to galvanize meaningful criminal justice system reforms to stamp out impunity at its roots.

REFORMING THE CRIMINAL JUSTICE SYSTEM

Time and again over the last three decades, every commission has recommended various measures to prevent communal violence, to de-communalize the police, to punish the guilty, and to ensure justice. All these have remained only on paper. No government, be it the Congress, or the Janata, or the BJP, has shown any interest or inclination in implementing any of the major recommendations.[121]

[118] 'SC asks Guj AG to review acquittals in riot cases', Press Trust of India, 23 August 2004.

[119] A survivor of the Gulbarg Society massacre, who lost ten family members in the violence, stated: 'We will get no justice in Gujarat... We believe in the supreme court.' Survivor's testimony at the World Social Forum, Mumbai, January 2004.

[120] Subsequent to the supreme court's order to reopen Gujarat cases, demands were made that all the cases related to the anti-Sikh riots of 1984 be re-opened as well. 'VHP demands re-opening of 1984 anti-Sikh riot cases', The Times of India, 18 August 2004, available at http://timesofindia.indiatimes.com/articleshow/818078.cms; 'Reopen 1984 riot cases against some politicians: Nanavati', WebIndia123.com, 20 April 2005 (Retired supreme court judge G.T. Nanavati, who probed the anti-Sikh riots of 1984, has asked the government to reopen cases against a 'few politicians' saying investigation against them was not 'properly carried out'.); Murali Krishnan, 'Reopen some cases: Nanavati', The Tribune, 27 April 2005.

[121] Suresh, supra note 27.

Malimath Committee Recommendations

Recognizing the need for reforms of the criminal justice system, in November 2000 the BJP-led government, through the Ministry of Home Affairs, constituted a Committee on Reforms of (the) Criminal Justice System (Malimath Committee). Headed by Justice V.S. Malimath, the Committee submitted its report (including 158 recommendations) to the Ministry of Home Affairs in April 2003.[122] Rather than promoting police accountability, the recommendations of the Malimath Committee centered largely around diluting checks and balances on police conduct.

Key recommendations for reform that have drawn criticism include those relating to the conduct of trial (such as allowing adverse inferences to be drawn from the silence of the accused; introducing defense statements; increased interrogation of the accused by the bench; substitution of the usual standard of proof of 'beyond a reasonable doubt' for a lower standard of proof of 'court's conviction that it is true'; and increased admissibility of bad character evidence and confessions); the role of the police, prosecution, and the judiciary (such as instituting investigative magistrates; diluting pre-trial safeguards against violence in police custody; and collapsing the distinction between the police and the prosecution) and the normalization of special legislation (such as the incorporation of provisions of the Prevention of Terrorism Act into the Evidence Act and the Criminal Procedure Code).[123]

[122] A full copy of the report prepared by the Committee on the Reform of Criminal Justice System is available at http://mha.nic.in/criminal_justice_system.pdf.

[123] For detailed overview of these changes and their human rights implications see Amnesty International, 'India Report of the Malimath Committee on the Reforms of the Criminal Justice System: Some observations', [hereinafter 'Amnesty International Report']. For further details on specific reforms relating to, inter alia, the right to silence, defense statements, lower standards of proof, investigative magistrates, bad character evidence, admissibility of confessions, and collapse of distinction between police and prosecution, see 'Malimath proposal on inquisitorial system—Mixing apples with oranges', 18 December 2003, available at http://www.hrdc.net/sahrdc/hrfeatures/HRF89.htm; 'Malimath panel finds reform vital but rights dispensable', 15 September 2003, available at http://www.hrdc.net/sahrdc/hrfeatures/HRF84.htm; Asian Legal Resource Center, 'The ramifications of the Report of the Committee on Reforms of the Criminal Justice System in India (Malimath Committee Report)', available at http://www.alrc.net/mainfile.php/60written/246/; Siddharth Narrain, 'Rights and criminal justice', Frontline, 30 Aug.—12 Sept. 2003, available at http://www.frontlineonnet.com/fl2018/stories/20030912001708300.htm.

The proposed reforms ignored issues of institutional discrimination and bias that have contributed to a crisis of impunity in Gujarat and elsewhere.[124] Indeed, the disproportionate focus on enhancing police powers stands in stark contrast to the '[d]eafening silence in the report on the criminalization of poverty; crisis in legal aid and the abject failures of the criminal justice system in protecting the human rights of the poor, Dalits, minorities, and other vulnerable sections of society.'[125] Tellingly, the proposed reforms also emphasized terrorism as the biggest threat facing India today while completely sidelining the issue of majoritarian fundamentalism.[126]

In April 2005, a meeting of chief ministers was called by Union Home Minister Shivraj Patil to initiate the process of amending the Criminal Procedure Code. It appears that the Malimath Committee recommendations were to be part of the discussion. Patil indicated, however, that there was no consensus on the Malimath Committee's report.[127] It is still hoped that the Indian government will take the initiative to reform the criminal justice system in a manner that is non-biased, includes appropriate checks and balances on the conduct of the police and prosecutors, and is otherwise consistent with the principles of democracy and human rights.

Initiating Meaningful Police Reform

The seriousness of the crisis lies not just in the fact that there has been a breakdown in the administration of justice. More importantly, there has been a breakdown in the constitutional machinery itself. The principal law enforcement agency has emerged as the single biggest threat to democracy.[128]

Any reform of the Indian criminal justice system must begin with meaningful reform of the police. Dissatisfaction with the police in India is a common refrain among citizens who have come into contact with the institution. Reasons for popular dissatisfaction include: the perception of the police as principal violators of the law; virtual impunity for crimes committed by the police; the nexus between the police and 'anti-social'

---

[124] Press Release, Amnesty International, 'India: Limited proposals to reform the criminal justice system', 19 September 2003, available at http://www.hrea.org/lists/hr-headlines/markup/msg01232.html attaching the Amnesty International Report at http://web.amnesty.org/library/index/engasa200252003.

[125] Ibid.

[126] Narrain, supra note 118.

[127] 'CMs' meet to review police system', *Business-Standard Online*, 14 April 2005.

[128] Gonsalves, supra note 18, at 11.

elements; the police's selective enforcement of the law; and police ignorance of, or disregard for, prevailing human rights norms that restrict
their behaviour in matters of arrest and interrogation.[129]

More than twenty-five years ago, the Indian government appointed
the National Police Commission (NPC) to examine the causes of police
negligence and abuse.[130] As part of its mandate, the NPC was required to
recommend measures to 'prevent misuse of powers by the police' and
'misuse of police by administrative or executive instructions, political or
other pressure, or oral orders of any type, which [were] contrary to law'.[131]

In 1980, the NPC released an eight-volume report, which followed
a series of similar reports by state-level commissions. The report was a
comprehensive account of the nature of police brutality and corruption
in India. In addition to documenting deficiencies in training, salaries,
and the de facto immunity that police continue to enjoy for their crimes,
the report also contained a multitude of recommendations designed to
address these problems.

For the last quarter century, activists and attorneys have argued that
implementation of the report's recommendations would go far in curbing
police abuse, improving overall police performance, and making the
police accountable to the citizenry. The importance of implementing
the NPC's recommendations has also been highlighted by the National
Human Rights Commission[132] and the supreme court, which in 1994
endorsed and reiterated the recommendations in *Joginder Kumar* v.

---

[129] See N.R. Madhava Menon, 'Police reform: The imperative for efficiency in
criminal justice', *Article 2*, 3, 3–4 (June 2002)

[130] The Commission was appointed on 15 November 1977 and held its first
meeting in December 1978: Commonwealth Human Rights Initiative, 'The National Police Commission (NPC)', available at http://www.humanrightsinitiative.org/
programs/aj/police/india/initiatives/npc.htm.

[131] Cited in Commonwealth Human Rights Initiative, 'The National Police
Commission (NPC)'.

[132]In its 'final proceedings' on the Gujarat 2002 massacres, the NHRC reiterated its call for the government 'to act decisively on the deeper question of Police
Reform, on which recommendations of the National Police Commission (NPC)
and of the National Human Rights Commission have been pending...' The Commission added that 'recent events in Gujarat and, indeed, in other states of the country,
underlined the need to proceed without delay to implement the reforms that have
already been recommended in order to preserve the integrity of the investigating
process and to insulate it from 'extraneous influences''. National Human Rights
Commission Proceedings, 31 May 2002, available at http://www.nhrc.nic.in/
guj_finalorder.htm.

State of Uttar Pradesh and others (1994 SCC (CRL) 1172).[133] Two years later, in *Prakash Singh* v. *Union of India* (writ petition 310 of 1996), a PIL was filed by the former Uttar Pradesh police chief, Prakash Singh, Shri N.K. Singh, and Common Cause (through Shri H.D. Shourie) calling for the implementation of the NPC recommendations and for the National Human Rights Commission to reform and reconstruct police organizations at the central and state levels. The supreme court responded by ordering the government of India to establish a sub-committee, headed by Julio Ribeiro, to examine the main themes of the NPC's recommendations.[134] The sub-committee issued its first report in October 1998, and its second in March 1999.[135] Both were submitted to the court for consideration.[136] Having completed its hearings on the petition, the court has, to date, reserved its judgment.[137]

The lack of police reform in India stems from a lack of political will to transform the police from a corrupt militia of the privileged classes and political elite, to a meaningful guardian of justice and the first line of defense against gross violations of human rights. Without such transformation, the patterns documented in Delhi, Bombay, and Gujarat will no doubt continue.

Role of the Public Prosecutor

While proper police conduct and a responsible judiciary are essential elements of the democratic justice system, attention must also be paid

[133] P. Venkateswar Rao, 'For better policing', Letters, *Frontline*, Sept. 29–Oct 12., 2002, available at http://www.flonnet.com/fl1820/18201030.htm

[134] Four specific issues were raised in the petition: (1) creation of a State Security Commission to ensure police compliance with the law; (2) adoption of a fixed tenure for the police chief; (3) separation of the law and order and investigative branches of the police force; and (4) introduction of a new Police Bill along the lines of the model Act drafted by the NPC. The terms of the Sub-Committee were detailed in MHA Memo No. 11018/1/98-PMA dated 25 May 1998: SAHRDC, 'Gujarat riots point to need for police reform' (13 Mar. 2002) available at http://www.hrdc.net/sahrdc/hrfeatures/HRF53.htm.

[135] Commonwealth Human Rights Initiative, 'Summary of Ribeiro Committee's Recommendations', available at http://www.humanrightsinitiative.org/publications/police/recommendations_ribeiro.pdf.

[136] Commonwealth Human Rights Initiative, 'Report of the Ribeiro Committee on Police Reforms: A Critical Analysis', available at http://www.humanrights initiative.org/programs/aj/police/india/initiatives/analysis_ribeiro.pdf.

[137] SAHRDC, 'Gujarat riots point to need for police reform', (13 Mar. 2002) available at http://www.hrdc.net/sahrdc/hrfeatures/HRF53.htm.

to the role of the public prosecutor. In India, poor performance of the prosecutor is one of the 'well-known causes for the failure of a large number of prosecutions'.[138] Often, prosecutors lack competence and, as was noted by the supreme court, 'it is common knowledge that appointments of Public Prosecutors are politicized'.[139] As a result the prosecution is often biased, lacks the required independence, and favours the accused.[140]

Given the crucial role assigned to the prosecutor in criminal proceedings in India[141] these deficiencies must be remedied. While the Malimath Committee has been criticized for many of its recommendations (see above), including those that undermine the independence of the prosecutor by blurring the distinction between the police and the prosecution,[142] it has made some constructive recommendations for the post of the Public Prosecutor. The Committee recommends that 'no person appointed as an Additional Public Prosecutor or promoted as a Public Prosecutor shall be posted in the Home District to which he belongs or where he was practicing'. In addition, 'sufficient representation shall be given to women' in appointing Public and Additional Public Prosecutors.[143] The Committee also recommended that intensive training, both theoretical and practical, be provided to the prosecutors on a regular basis.[144]

---

[138] 'Report of Committee on Reforms of Criminal Justice System', 125 (2003). See also Justice R. K. Abichandani, Judge, High Court of Gujarat, 'Obstacles to Justice and the Suffering Humanity', available at http://gujarathighcourt.nic.in/Articles/accesstojustice.htm.

[139] *P Ramachanra Rao v. State of Karnataka,* (2002) 2 LRI 337, para. 23.

[140] This is particularly apparent in the aftermath of the Gujarat carnage. See e.g. Compounding Injustice, supra note 17, at 25–6; 'See also SC throws the book, govt ducks behind Atre', 17 October 2003, available at http://www.ahmedabad.com/news/2k3/oct/17govt.htm (appointment of VHP members as public prosecutors).

[141] Among other powers the Public Prosecutor can withdraw a case. According to section 321 of the Code of Criminal Procedure, the Public Prosecutor or Additional Public Prosecutor in charge of the case may with the consent of the Court, at any time before the judgment is pronounced, withdraw prosecution of any person either generally or in respect of any one or more of the offences for which he is tried.

[142] See Amnesty International Report, supra note 12918 at 8, 24–6.

[143] Ibid. at Recommendation 56.

[144] *Ibid.*, at 57. For a more in-depth analysis on reforms to the public prosecutor mechanism, see Thomas Unger, 'The Role of the Public Prosecutor in India,' (2004) (on file with author).

The supreme court took a stand on the matter in a 1999 case, stating that a public prosecutor should be 'a person who possesses legal knowledge and necessary experience to appear on behalf of the State'.[145] While the role of India's Supreme Court—as both a forum for justice and a propelling force for reforms—cannot be overstated, the court cannot be the sole instigator of reforms in a democratic system, nor does it have the capacity to address every instance of corruption and abuse. In India, lawmaking powers are vested in the publicly-elected central and state legislatures that must step up to the challenge of overhauling India's criminal justice system. Until comprehensive reforms are instituted by the lawmakers, abuses against the country's disempowered and dispossessed will continue unabated.

In India, the tyranny of the majority is as, if not more, dangerous than the fundamentalism of the minority. It has the potential to seep into and communalize the executive, the legislature, and the judiciary. It can erode the very pillars of democratic governance and make a mockery of the rule of law. In the face of prolonged systemic injustice the calls for judicial activism and more specifically, for supreme court intervention, are getting louder. According to one scholar, 'Grave consequences would ensue if the court were to turn a blind eye to the government agencies' 'lawlessness' or to the abdication of their constitutional responsibilities. The state would then be left free to transgress the law and what would result is subversion of the rule of law.'[146] As the Gujarat cases demonstrate, the supreme court does have the power to step in and change the course of impunity. It should use those powers to deliver justice to victims beyond Gujarat.

[145] *Vijay Shankar Mishra v. State Of U.P. And Others*, 1999-(105)-CRLJ-0521-ALL, para. 88.

[146] Vijayashri Sripati, *Human Rights in India—Fifty Years after Independence*, 26 Denv. J. Int'l L. & Pol'y 93, 134 (1997).

15

Criminality of the Marginalized Sections or the *Lumpen-Proletariat* Criminality

Critical Perspectives

B.B. PANDE

The criminological thought still remains pre-occupied with the criminality of the members of the lower socio-economic strata or the marginalized sections of society. Such a pre-occupation is largely conditioned by the traditional criminological studies and researches, both of the kind that relate crime to isolated economic indices like the price of grain, unemployment, decline in real wages, and reversals in business cycle (in particular the researches of Sellin, Lafargue, Turati, etc.), or those that relate crime to the capitalist mode of production as a whole (in particular the researches of W.A. Bonger, Colagini, Thomas Moore, etc.). The reasons for associating criminality with the marginalized sections is ideological too. In the words of Hartjen (1978):

It can be argued that criminology's emphasis on studying criminals provides a kind of scholarly credence for political authorities. This is especially true since criminologists tend to concentrate on the criminality of the lower class (powerless) groups. This has led them largely to ignore the crime characteristics of more powerful classes...by concentrating on the criminality of lower class members, criminologists have not only helped to legitimize the power holders' evaluation of this group- but also provided the rulers with knowledge to solidify their power over the disadvantaged. (223–4)

Are the marginalized sections naturally more inclined to commit crimes? Or is their criminality a product of the externalities beyond their control? Or is their criminality merely a contraption for labelling them through differential application? The following discussion proposes to explore these and other leads, with a view to creating a better understanding of commonly known phenomenon, so well exemplified by the following real life interaction:

The released beggar had weakly and meekly walked to us and had expressed profound gratitude for the kindness we had shown by rendering legal services to him. His demeanour reflected that he had fully accepted the low, the sinner self-image imposed by the law. For once I told him the whole truth:

Why do you feel ashamed? It is we who should feel ashamed for putting you in this state of multiple disadvantages. First, by not providing you the means that will keep you away from begging and then by exposing you to this trouble of a formal stigmatization drama. Now, you have come to suffer a third disadvantage at my hands by accepting this myth that I have done you an obligation. Please do not.

He understood nothing'[1]

GENESIS OF THE MARGINALIZED SECTIONS OR THE LUMPEN-PROLETARIAT

The marginalized sections are primarily constituted by the fact of economic marginalization—that is, the product of multiple forms of resource-lessness like 'landlessness', 'homelessness', 'joblessness', etc. Economists and social scientists have commonly used the Below Poverty Line identi-fication as the root cause of all forms of economic marginalization. The below the poverty line or BPL status is measured in terms of a variety of indicators such as calorie intake deficiency,[2] scorable socio-economic household amenities availability,[3] earning below one American dollar per day as income poverty.[4] In India, during the British rule and even after independence, a substantial section of the population could be identified as marginalized because of their BPL status.[5] Though economic

[1] Pande B.B. 'The Administration of Beggary Prevention Laws in India: A Legal Aid Viewpoint', *International Journal of the Sociology of Law*, 1983, 11, 291–304 at p. 303.

[2] Dandekar and Rath worked out in 1971 a devise for identifying BPL population in terms of income required for buying 2250 calories per day, that is the minimum calorie requirement for a moderately hard-working person.

[3] The Government of India in its Poverty Line assessment in 2002, evolved a thirteen point socio-economic indicator scale for classifying households in 'poor' and 'non-poor' categories.

[4] The UN in its *Millennium Development Goals* 2000 has constructed a measure of 'extreme poverty' or 'deep poverty' as earning below one American dollar per day.

[5] The 2002 census indicates a clear decline in the BPL national population that has come down to 27 per cent, but even now BPL population in the state of Orissa is 47.15 per cent, followed by the State of Bihar that has 42.60 per cent.

marginalization is the root cause, marginalization can arise also on account of caste, tribe, religion, gender, regional factors, and geographical location as well. Generally those who suffer on account of caste and tribal disabilities are in most cases the ones who are the most marginalized as well. The social disabilities of caste, tribe, etc., are closely intertwined with the pre-feudal and feudal society disabilities that in a way created their own kind of marginalization and de-marginalization techniques. Such societies are characterized by their close-knit bonds, which to some extent took care of the disadvantages or disabilities whether of biological and physical nature (deformity or sickness) or social nature (resourcelessness or destitution). The society either through the immediate family or the larger village community was supposed to provide the necessary support and succour to offset the disadvantages. This collective spirit of early community existence might have crystallized into the religious practice of charity and almsgiving. These practices were given adequate social support by being extolled as virtue of self-negation or search for higher truth. The primary reason for such extollation of charity might have been to encourage people to part with their excessive acquisitions with a view to keeping down the discontent and rancour that might be the result of unequal distribution of wealth and resources. Even such public charity or charity by strangers would have come only as a second line of social security, after the family group or the immediate community had failed to give the required support. Furthermore, being in primitive stages of development, the ancient societies had no definite notions about work or industry, in the modern sense. The family or the community lived by hunting and other primitive modes of food gathering or simple agricultural operations that needed little division of labour. Therefore, the difference between an industrious and a non-industrious member was hardly perceived. There was no developed notion of the social consequences of indolent conduct.

However, with the advent of capitalist mode of production and the introduction of industrialized and urbanized way of living, the process of marginalization was subjected to revolutionary changes not only qualitatively but also quantitatively. Central to the modern day marginalization concept is the institution of wage labour, that became the driving force of the capitalist mode of production as well as the processes of urbanization and industrialization. Marxist thinkers have best conceptualized the steps by which the labouring class faces the threat of becoming marginalized almost constantly. According to David Greenberg (1981):

Marx identifies four different forms of relative surplus population. The 'floating' form consists of workers who are hired and fired according to the requirements of business.... The transformation of the agricultural population into an urban or manufacturing proletariat depends on the existence of a 'latent' surplus population in the countryside—'latent' because it may only move when the alternative employment opens up. The 'stagnant' form consists of very low-paid and irregularly employed workers, often in the decaying sectors of the economy.... This form is 'self re-producing and self perpetuating', in part because of an extremely high birth rate, but also because it recruits redundant workers from other sectors of the economy. Lastly, there are paupers. This form includes those who are unable to work (the elderly, the disabled, the sick, the orphaned), those who do not adapt to industrial labour discipline, and a 'dangerous class' of criminals. (p. 62)

The Marxist thinkers can also be credited for inventing the categorization better known as lumpen proletariat for subsuming every possible form of marginalized section in the capitalist society context. Lumpen proletariat is a descriptive label commonly deployed by the Marxist, in the course of class analysis of society, to identify that section of the working population that lives by indulging in diverse kinds of deviant activities. This section of the population resembles the proletariat or the working class in matters of their inferior position in the production process, lack of ownership of the means of production and subjection to the ruling class exploitation. But unlike the true proletariat, the lumpen proletariat encounters the exploitative social situation by indulging in dubious or shady activities, which are an anti-thesis of hard-work and industry. The opportunist and 'immoral' course of survival chosen by the lumpen elements justifies their description as 'false' or 'impure'—proletariat.[6]

Karl Marx (1968) described this assorted non-conformist population in these words:

Alongside decayed roues with dubious means of subsistence and dubious origins, alongside ruined and adventurous off-shoots of bourgeoisie, were vagabonds, discharged soldiers, discharged jail birds, escaped galley slaves, swindlers, montebanks, *lazzaroni* pick-pockets, tricksters, gamblers, *mague reaus*, brothel-keepers, porters, libereeti, organ-grinders, rag-pickers, knife-grinders, tinkers, beggars—in short, the whole indefinite disintegrated mass thrown higher and thither, which the French term *la boheme*. (p. 96)

Ultimately, the categorization or labelling of a section of the population as lumpen-proletariat must be understood in terms of the objective or

[6] Franz Fanon (1961, pp. 104, 109), preferred to describe thieves, prostitutes, shanty dwellers, exploited domestic servants, drunkards etc. as lumpen proletariat.

the purpose of such an exercise. The Marxist labelled a section of the proletariat as lumpen mainly with a view to appreciating its 'class struggle' potential. Describing the lumpen proletariat as totally unsuited for the revolutionary task, Engels (1968) observes:

The lumpen proletariat, this scum of the depraved elements of all classes, which establishes its headquarters in the big cities, is absolutely venal and absolutely brazen...every leader of the workers who uses these scoundrels as guards and relies on them for support proves himself by this action a traitor to the move-ment. (pp. 235–41)

In the same vein Marx (1950) at another place observes:

The dangerous class, the social scum, the passively rotting mass thrown by the lowest layers of the old society, may here and there, be swept into the move-ment by a proletarian revolution, its condition of life, however, prepare it far more for the part of a bribed tool for reactionary intrigue.

But unlike Engels, Karl Marx (1887, Vol. I) perceived lumpen prole-tariat also as the victims of capitalism when it came to critiquing the dominant class policy of their criminalization, thus:

The proletariat created by the breaking-up of the bands of feudal retainers and by forcible expropriation of the people from the soil, this 'free' proletariat could not possibly be absorbed by the nascent manufacturers as fast as it was thrown upon the world. On the other hand, these men, suddenly dragged from their wonted mode of life, could not as suddenly adapt themselves to the discipline of their new condition. They were turned *enmasse* into beggars, robbers, vagabonds. Hence at the end of the fifteenth and the whole of the sixteenth century, throughout Western Europe a bloody legislation against vegabondage. The fathers of the present working class were chastised for their enforced transformation into vegabonds and paupers.

Thus, the marginalized sections or the lumpen proletariat are not only generated by the socio-economic processes, but also socially constructed with a view to furthering the dominant section interests.

CRIMINALIZATION OF THE MARGINALIZED SECTIONS

Though all forms of criminalization are a product of the political and economic forces at work in a particular historical period, the social control and criminalization of the poor and marginalized sections assumes distant features that deserve special attention. Writing about the climate of opinion in England regarding the state of criminal law and its adminis-tration at the turn of the seventeenth century, Leon Radzinowicz

(Vol. 2, 1956) had identified prime motivation of criminal law reform as: 'strengthening the moral fibre of the nation', 'legislative intervention in support of public morality', and 'control of the unstable and dangerous, elements of society', which mainly relate to the poor and marginalized. In this context Radzinowicz has observed:

The recurrence of criminal behaviour in a comparatively narrow section of society, its cencentration within certain definable areas of the Metropolis, its prevalence among the very young, were all perceived with a new intensity. They helped to focus the public attention on the manners and habits of the poor. A pre-occupation with the immoral, loose or improvident behaviour of the lower order of society, became marked among all would-be reformers. The same ill-defined way, idleness, drunkenness or immorality came to be regarded as immediate causes of crime and therefore in themselves direct threats to social stability.[7] (pp. 2–3)

The poor were not only more readily criminalized but were also subjected to social control more easily. In the words of John A. Mayer (1983):

In the nineteenth century historical situation, the groups towards which controls were directed often were not deviants. They were sub-cultural ethnic groups. As such, they had great resources available with which to resist any attempts at control by the dominant culture. Their major resource, of course was simply their membership in an ethnic culture; they possessed a systematic set of values, ways of perceiving and group reinforcement of their beliefs, attitudes, norms and so on. (p. 23)

John A. Mayer, at another place in the same article, explains the rationale and the need for controlling the lower classes as follows:

The transitional stage of industrialism, with its breakdown of communal and differential authority patterns, its economic and residential separation of classes, its disjunction between people's actual behaviours and the new behaviours needed for a modern industrial society led to a sense of crisis among élites, generalized as a fear of the lower or dangerous classes. (p. 17)

Are the Marginalized Naturally more Prone to Criminality?

Wilful crimes involving violence to human body and property and other intended crimes may not be directly attributed to poverty and

---

[7] Radzinowicz was also quick in exposing the double standards of reformers in respect of the vices of the poor alone. 'As time went on, in the publications of the reforming societies there was an obvious tendency to thunder against the vices of the poor whilst saying nothing about similar failings amongst the rich.' (p. 15)

marginalization, but in all such cases, poverty does constitute a very significant condition for constraining, limiting or narrowing down the choices available for the exercise of the free will. Thus, a resourceless is much more likely to commit property crimes like theft and burglary than one whose needs are already met. Similarly, an unemployed youth is much more likely to join a band of robbers or terrorists than one who has a secure employment. Even in the ancient Hindu society's wisdom, conveyed in the famous snake (*Akhayaya bhadra*) and frog (*Gangadatt)* fable in *Panchatantra*, it is stated: *Khirnanarah nishkaruna bhavanti* (poor and weak are without kindness and mercy). A similar view was expressed in the context of a capitalist society by W. Bonger (1916), when he opined that by promoting 'egoism', capitalism not only brutalizes the poor, it also demoralizes all those caught up in the struggle and competition to survive or succeed.

The American criminologist David Gordon (1971) locates the causes of criminality in the competitive and basically inegalitarian nature of the capitalist societies, thus:

Driven by the fear of economic insecurity and by a competitive desire to gain source of the goods unequally distributed throughout society, many individuals will eventually become 'criminals'... nearly all crimes in capitalist societies represent perfectly rational responses to the structure of institutions upon which capitalist societies are based. Crimes of many different varieties constitute functionally similar responses to the organization of capitalist constitutions. For those crimes help provide means of survival in a society within which survival is never assured. (p. 58)

But all marginalized sections may not be making perfectly rational responses to adverse environment while committing crimes. Quite a few may be too alienated or psychologically maladjusted to make a rational choice. Criminal behaviour of such persons can be better explained in terms of strains, frustrations, and desperation faced by them in the ordinary course of their day-to-day existence. In order to appreciate the causal factors responsible for this kind of criminality, it may be useful to make a distinction between conventional criminality and unconventional criminality.

Marginalization and 'Conventional' Crimes

Conventional criminality can be best explained by a variety of causal theories such as the Behaviourist theories, the Psychoanalytic theories, and the Sociological theories. The Behaviourists opine that behaviour can be acquired by learning or by conditioning, susceptibility to which is related to the degree of extraversion displayed by an individual. Criminality occurs when there is lack of social conditioning as a result of which the individual has no means of restraining himself from the pursuits of primary activistic impulses. The people in lower socio-economic strata are generally not in a position to provide adequate and necessary socialization to their children, thus they become more susceptible to criminality and delinquency. Trasler (1962) attributes higher incidence of criminality to lower classes on the basis of different standards of child rearing practices followed by the lower or the working classes. Furthermore, poor socialization of the marginalized sections can also be attributed to greater possibilities of broken homes in their cases. Also absence of parental care or inconsistently administered parental care accounts for poor socialization too. Like the Behaviourists, the Psychoanalytic theorists also attribute delinquency and criminality to failure of 'domestication' of a naturally wild animal. But psychoanalysis's explanations of criminality are historically and biographically rooted, which makes the socio-economic background of the delinquent a decisive factor. A person born and brought up in an environment of deprivation and distrust, in which he neither had the benefit of a stable home-life nor adequate parental love and care is much more prone to delinquency and criminality according to psychoanalytic theorists.

The stock causal explanation for the criminality of the marginalized comes from the Sociological theorists. The early Chicagoans, who explained criminality in terms of ecology or physical environment, classified the urban neighbourhoods into 'healthy community' and 'pathological community'. Marginalized sections largely account for 'pathological community', which are characterized by social disorganization associated by factors like high rates of poverty, high rates of delinquency, and physical and moral deterioration. This kind of theorization explains the high rate of criminality in slums and other crowded areas which are inhabited by the poor and resourceless. Within the sociological tradition, Anomie theory of Merton (1957) is yet another causal explanation for the criminality of the marginalized. Since the material success goal is over-emphasized in most of the 'meritocratic' modern societies, the large section of resourceless and marginalized find it almost impossible to achieve success through legitimate means. Lea and Young (1984) have described the iniquitous competition in the context of the modern Anglo-American Society thus:

In reality some people seem to start half-way along the track (the rich) while others are forced to race with a millstone around their necks (for example, women with both domestic and non-domestic employment) while others are not even allowed onto the track at all (the unemployed, the members of the most deprived ethnic groups) (p. 95).

Perhaps the most elaborate treatment to the causal issues relevant for our purpose has been accorded by Steven Box in his book *Recession, Crime and Punishment,* which primarily relates to the phenomenon of crime and economic recession in the United Kingdom in the eighties.[8] Box explores the total causal theorization that mainly relates to some of the significant fall-outs of recession such as unemployment, decline in real wages that are associated with marginalization. According to Box, the poor and marginalized suffer more in this state: 'Thus a sense of injustice, discontent, and distrust generated by the apparent contradiction between proclaimed values and social experiences becomes, among certain groups too deeply irritating and too constantly whipped up by the media to be easily strugged-off'. (p. 39).

Crimes by the poor and marginalized have also been explained by the Social Disorganization and Cultural Conflict Theorists. The early social disorganization theorists explained the higher incidence of crimes by the lower strata in terms of the difference in their attitudes and values, which were resultant of strains and frustrations. They emphasized that the areas inhabited by the poor and marginal were not only characterized by physical deterioration but also by the attitudes and values shared by the inhabitants, which were at odds with the rest of the community. Cloward (1959) similarly attributes lower class male delinquency to the anticipation of failure in achieving goals as adults. Unlike most of the Social Disorganization theorists who perceive crimes by the poor in consensus of value frame, there are some social Disorganization theorists like Albert K. Cohen (1959) and W.B. Miller (1958) who see such crimes in counter-culture or culture of poverty frame. Poverty and marginalization of extreme nature generates its own values and culture that may be totally different, at times opposed, to the mainstream values.[9] Close to counter-culture, the Culture Conflict theorists locate the cause

[8] Box has also emphasized relative deprivation, control theory to strengthen his thesis that recession leads to rise in conventional crimes. See particularly pp. 28 to 106 which are devoted to inquiries such as: 'Why should Recession Cause Crime to Increase' and 'Does Recession Lead to More Crimes'.

[9] An interesting study of pavement dwellers in Kolkata reveals that the absolute destitutes lacked the consciousness of the larger society and were alien to the dominant values and culture: see Vijai N. Jagannathan and Animesh Haldhar, 'A Case Study of Pavement Dwellers in Calcutta', *Economic and Political Weekly*, 11 February 1989 at p. 315.

of criminality of the marginalized in the differences in the cultural backgrounds, particularly in cases of the migrant and ethnically and geographically differing groups. For these categories of marginalized sections, committing crimes may be culturally ordained and though a crime by the dominant viewpoint but merely a means of normal interaction according to the sub-group norms.[10]

THE EXPANDING NET OF CRIMINALIZATION

It may not be fashionable to talk of criminalization process being partisan and prejudicial to the poor and marginalized, but the fact is that the whole process of criminalization, particularly in the capitalist societies, has focused more on them (Douglas Hay *et al.*, 1975, E.P. Thompson 1975). This is done in two prominent ways: first, by including new forms of non-deviant behaviours within the ambit of conventional crimes and secondly, by the creation of new crimes or 'status offences' that mainly relate to many forms of innocuous behaviours of the poor and marginalized. The best example of expanding conventional crimes can be found in the wide range of property offences like theft and robbery in eighteenth century England and Europe.[11] The offence of theft was pressed into action for covering many new categories of behaviour patterns, relating to property, that had remained outside the conventional crimes ambit. Karl Marx in his five-article series, initiated an ideological debate about the law on the theft of wood in 1842.[12] In these articles, Marx critiqued the extension of the offence of theft to innocuous behaviours of the forest dwellers. The proposed law was considered to be unfair because it tended to over-criminalize the forest-dwellers, unduly favoured the interests of the forest owners, and supported the imposition of disproportionate punishments. Peter Linebaugh (1981) has summed up the articles of Karl Marx in these words:

[10] Some of the new forms of environmental crimes like destruction of fauna and flora, defecation in public places, property crimes like squatting on public land, etc., are examples of crimes generated by cultural-conflict.

[11] The Waltham Black Act, 1723, was a notorious piece of legislation for creating in one stroke a wide range of new crimes aimed at protecting the landed properties of the British aristocracy. For a detailed account, see, E.P. Thompson, *Wighs and Hunters—The Origin of Black Act,* Pantheon Books, New York, 1975.

[12] Proceedings of the Sixth Rhine Province Assembly: Third Article, Debates on the Law of the Theft of Wood, Karl Marx and Frederick Engels (1842); *Collected Works,* Volume 1, New York; International Publishers, 1975.

By applying the category of theft where it ought not to be applied you exonerate it? 'All the organs of the state become ears, eyes, arms, legs and means by which the interest of the forest owner hears, sees, appraises, protects, grasps and runs. The right of human beings gives way to the rights of trees'. As he stated this, Marx also had to ask, which human beings? For the first time he comes to the defence of the 'poor, politically and socially propertyless', when he demands for the poor a 'customary right'. (p. 80)

Similar problems of drawing the line between the 'customary rights' of local population and the crimes of property nuisance and theft arose in the coastal regions in England also in the eighteenth century. In the coastal regions where the ships ran aground, the local inhabitants indulged in the activity of 'wrecking', which involved salvaging the wrecked ships and cargo for their own use. Inspired by the petitions of ship merchants, the Government extended the legal measures relating to nuisance and theft with a view to effectively controlling the activity of 'wrecking' (Geoffrey Pearson, 1978).

Equally significant for expanding the net of criminalization is the creation of a whole lot of new crimes like vagrancy, beggary, and squatting in a public place, which can be subsumed under the blanket term 'status offences'. Status offenders are persons whose condition or behaviour is designated by the laws of a State, but not necessarily violative of the accepted customs or standards of that society or community. Such conditions or behaviours would not ordinarily fall within the accepted description of crimes, particularly in respect of their blameworthiness quality and social harm element. Crimes of this category mainly depend upon the value judgment of the dominant political group in the society, which is assumed to be acting in the larger interest of the society. Thus, in many societies, a woman is a status offender if she makes her living by receiving compensation for sexual favours to men. Likewise, under some systems, seeking employment and visiting areas not meant for a certain class of persons may turn a person into a status offender. Similarly, selling obscene literature or indulging in suspect trades and activities are status offences in most of the jurisdictions. In modern societies, vagrancy and beggary are the most commonly known instances of status offences. These status offences cover within their ambit a wide variety of conditions or patterns of behaviour that are not considered socially undesirable. This category of status offence present special difficulties at the policy formulation and enforcement stages. *Ledwith* v. *Robert*[13] amply highlights

[13] (1937) 1 KB 232.

these issues. The case concerned the petition of two window cleaners, who were arrested by the defendant, constables in the Liverpool Police Force, in terms of the Vagrancy Act, 1824, and the Municipal Corporation Act, 1582. The Acts in question gave wide powers to the police to arrest and apprehend any person loitering with intent to commit felony or being idle or disorderly. Thus a person committed an offence in terms of the provisions by: (1) failing to maintain his family when able to do so; (2) becoming chargeable on a parish from which he shall have been legally removed by order of justices; (3) if a pedlar, by wandering abroad and plying without licence; (4) if a prostitute, by wandering in the public street and behaving in a riotous and indecent manner; (5) by wandering abroad or taking up a position in a public place to beg, or causing children to do the same. Scott, L.J. aptly summarized the objectives of formulating such statutes and creating such offences in the following words:

In my view, these two expressions both refer to members of a class once prevalent in England to an extent which made it for four or five centuries a major political problem, a problem which taxed the forces of law and order to the uttermost and produced a long succession of repressive statutes. Those laws were framed exclusively in relation to that particular class of the community and had three purposes. The class consisted of the hordes of unemployed persons, many of them addicted to crime, then wandering over the face of the country; and the purposes were (a) settlement of able-bodied in their own parish and provision of work for them there; (b) relief for aged and infirm, that is, those who would not work; and (c) punishment of those able-bodied who could not work.[14]

As described by Ian Taylor *et al.* (1973, 221), 'much deviance is in itself a political act'. Thus, deviance is a creation of the ruling class judgment and ultimately dependent upon the demands of the dominant modes of production and ruling class interest. This process of criminalization is classically illustrated by the vagrancy and beggary type deviance in India. Till the 1930s, living through vagrancy and beggary was, by and large, condoned by society, and the mild social disapproval reflected in the Municipalities Acts and the preventive provisions under the Code of Criminal Procedure were attracted only in cases of persistent and habitual vagrancy and beggary. Vagrancy and beggary in general was never considered a serious kind of deviance mainly because, in the initial stages, the capitalist mode of production welcomed the presence of a surplus labour population that served as a reserve army for the ever growing capitalist work force. By the 1940s, substantially large sections of the working population had already migrated to the urban and industrial

[14] Ibid., at p. 270.

centres and had developed a total dependence on the urban job market.[15] The post war period was marked by economic recession and mass retrenchment of the work force. Thus, the surplus labour force not only lost its utility for the capitalist mode of production but also became a social menace and a drag on capitalist economy and was perceived as a source of a new form of urban deviance that needed to be repressed in the interest of beauty, decency, and the capitalist work morality. This kind of change in attitude led the states to come up with anti-beggary legislations that tended to turn, the once innocuous, destitution and alms seeking into a new form of deviance. The modern attitude towards this class of deviance is amply reflected in the following observation of Leon Radzinowicz (1968):

Seen as a threat to morality and industry, vagrancy could not but be especially infuriating. For in the eighteenth and early nineteenth century a strong moral indignation reinforced the feeling against vagrants. At a time when the disciplined industry of the poor seemed so essential to economic development, exhortations to hard work, condemnation of improvidence, criticism of indiscriminate relief combined to harden the attitude to professional beggars and imposters.... Their freedom and irresponsibility were bitterly resented. Idleness, 'a reluctancy of people to be employed in any kind of work', was regarded as the basis of both vagrancy, mendacity and a high offence against public economy as well as against good order.[16]

Apart from the vagrancy and beggary crimes, in India, like many other colonial states of Africa and Latin America, new forms of crimes were created to control the working classes in the plantations, industries, and even other forms of trade (Pande, 1981–2; Z.M.S. Siddique, 1983). The techniques used prominently against workers were:

(a) criminalizing breach of contract by workers;[17]
(b) criminalizing workers combinations and other collective ways of raising grievances.[18]

[15] The Royal Commission on Labour (1931) had identified lack of abundant supply of labour and temporary nature of labour migration as the main problem faced by the industrial and plantation capitalism in the 19th and the early 20th century. See *The Report of the Royal Commission on Labour,* Govt. of India Press (1931).

[16] Radzinowicz, Leon, *A History of English Criminal Law*, Vol. 4 (1968), p. 17.

[17] The Workman's Breach of Contract Act, 1859, The Employer's and Workmen's (Disputes) Act 1860, the Indian Emigration Act, 1901, and Ch. XIX (ss. 491–3) of the Indian Penal Code, 1860, made breach of contract of employment and services an offence.

[18] The Indian Criminal Law Amendments Act, 1913, that introduced the offence of conspiracy under sections 120A and 120B and the Criminal Law Amendment Act, 1932, criminalized picketing.

The rationale of criminalizing breach of contract by the workers in Ch. XIX of the Penal Code, 1860, has been provided by Whitley Stokes (1887) in the following words:

If, as sometimes happens the persons should, in a solitary place, set down the *palanquin* and run away it is difficult to conceive a more distressing situation than that in which their employer would be left. None but very high damages would be any reparation for such a wrong. But the class of people by whom alone such a wrong is at all likely to be committed can pay no damages. The whole property of the delinquents would probably not cover the expenses of prosecuting them civilly. It therefore, appears to us that breaches of contract of this description may with strict propriety be treated as crimes (p. 362).

The crime of breach of contract was a device in the hands of the employers to compel workers who had agreed to work for a period on payment of money advance, usually of small amounts.[19] Most of the cases of crime of breach of contract related to workers from the tea plantations of the east, where the working and living conditions were deplorable and sub-human.[20] Most of the criminals brought before the Magistrates Courts for crimes of breach of contract were the poor and resourceless villagers who had been duped into work-contract by the labour agents of the tea plantations under a promise of fair wages and good working and living conditions. Thus, under the fear of penal sanctions, a large number of the plantation and factory labour force was compelled to respect their work contract. Though by the second decade of the 1920s with the emergence of organized working class and trade unionism, the criminalization of breach of contract was more or less abolished, but other newer forms of crimes relating to unorganized and self-employed working classes like hawkers, rikshaw pullers, casual labour, etc., were created from time to time.[21]

[19] In *Govinda Chetty* v. *Munonoany Naik* 14 Cr. L. J. 400 (1913) (Mad.) the advance amount was rupees one hundred; In *Lucas, C.J.* v. *Ramai Singh* 15Cr. L.J. 233 (1914) (All.) the advance was barely rupees nineteen only.

[20] According to J.W. Badger's *Report on Tea Cultivation in Bengal*, 20 Parliamentary Papers, 1874, Vol. XLVIII, Comnd. 982: between 1863 and 1866 out of a total number of 84,915 workers recruited in plantations, 31,846 died. Just in one year from 1865 to 1866, out of 40,000 workers, 9147 died and 3187 deserted.

[21] The Municipal laws make it unlawful and criminal to vend on the streets without a valid *tehbazari*, which is a legal permit for stationary vending. Similarly, the Cycle Rikshaw Bye-laws framed under Section 481 of the Delhi Municipal Corporation Act, 1957, requires under Cl. 3(1) that no person shall ply a Cycle Rikshaw in Delhi unless he himself is the owner and has obtained a puller's licence. Thus, the law envisages two kind of licences; one for owning the rikshaw and the other for pulling it and any violation of licence requirement is likely to lead to confiscation and ultimately the destruction of the vehicle.

INSENSITIVE ENFORCEMENT OF STATUS OFFENCES

Achieving a real and critical insight into crimes by poor and marginalized is hardly possible without examining the enforcement aspects. This involves going into the diverse enforcement practices of the various formal agencies such as the police, the correctional officials, the court, and the custodial institutions. Since the formal enforcement practices are closely linked with the informal processes like rate of employment, migration pattern, the approaches to urbanization, the notions of beauty and decency, etc., it may be useful to refer to such processes in the course of present discussion as well.

Coercive Retention of Workers

In the initial period of plantation and industrial capitalism in India in the later part of the nineteenth and the first quarter of the twentieth century, the colonial rulers faced a paradoxical situation of growing need for workers on the one hand, and predominantly rural and migrant character of labour leading to perpetual problem of labour shortage, on the other. The Royal Commission on Labour (1931) has highlighted the problem of labour shortage in the following words:

Throughout the greater part of its history, organized industry in India has experienced a shortage of labour. A generation ago, this shortage was at times apt to become critical. Towards the end of the nineteenth century, after the plague epidemics, the difficulties of the workers were actuate, especially in Bombay; and in 1905 the complaints of employers in Bengal and United Provinces led to official enquiry into the causes of the shortage. (p. 12)

The problem of labour shortage was resolved at the level of employment by recruiting male, female, and even children as workers in the factories.[22] At the same time, the interest of the employer was secured by the coercive

[22] See particularly, the employment patterns statistics quoted in the Labour Investigation Committee Report (1943) as follows:

Year	Number of Factories	Men	Women	Children	Total
1892	656	2,54,336	43,592	18,888	3,16,816
1912	2710	6,85,82	1,30,025	53,796	8,69,643
1923	5985	11,13,508	2,21,045	74,6230	14,09,173
1933	8452	11,67,284	2,16,387	19,091	14,03,312
1939	10,466	14,98,218	2,43,516	9403	17,51,137
1943	13,209	22,58,319	2,65,509	12,484	24,36,312

technique of making breach of contract by workers a crime. The need for retaining workers in employment was much greater in the indigo, tea, and coffee plantations which had become notorious for escape of the workers. On the other hand, the planters were willing to do everything to prevent their escape, either by fraud or force. Watchmen were posted at every possible escape route and escaping workers were tied and flogged. Though most of the practices followed by the employer, to prevent escape were illegal, the administration rarely acted against the employers and their men. On the contrary, the Act IV of 1865 expressly empowered the employer to arrest the escaping worker without warrant and thus further strengthened the hands of the employer against the workers. Furthermore, the number of cases relating to crime of breach of contract that reached the various high courts in the country is an indication that this kind of technique was really being deployed as a potent means of control of the working people. A closer analysis of a few cases serves as an example of enforcement practices at the judicial level. In *C.A.A. Vernede v. Abdul Giri Chinna Swami*,[23] a workman who had received an advance was sentenced to 'imprisonment for breach of contract. On completion of his prison term, the employer sued the workman in the small causes court for the sum of advance. The workman pleaded that as he had already been in prison for the debt his liability was exhausted. The judge referred the matter to the high court saying that the workman must pay. Scotland C.J. and Frere J. of the high court observed:

The Act was passed for the purpose of punishing fraudulent breaches of contract and imprisonment... is the punishment provided for non-compliance with the Magistrate's order directing either re-payment of the money advanced, or performance of the contract. In the former case the Magistrate's order...remains unsatisfied... if the money has not been repaid at the end of the term of imprisonment.[24]

The import of such an interpretation by the high court is that the worker is not only legally coerced to fulfil his contract, but that his inability to repay the advance would turn him into a judgement-debtor with the possibility of the state auctioning all that the worker or his family possessed in execution of the court's decree, which gives to the employer a double security against the worker's escape. Similarly in *Queen Express v. Indrajit*,[25] the clever employer could use the handle of contract to get submission

---

[23] (1865) Mad. H.C. Report 427.
[24] Ibid., at pp. 427–8.
[25] XI, I.L.R. All. 262 (1889).

from an otherwise 'difficult' workman. In the instant case, the worker had entered into a three year work contract with Elgin Mills Company at Kanpur: under the terms of the contract the worker could get leave on emergent occasion after giving due notice. The company gave an advance of three rupees on entering the contract. After having served for a period of eight months the worker picked up quarrel with the management and after giving a twenty four hour notice desired quitting his job. On the management refusing to accept the notice, the workman applied for leave and on refusal to grant leave, he absented from duties indefinitely. The company filed a complaint before the Magistrate to compel the worker to perform his service contract. The Magistrate ordered the workman to return to his work or suffer imprisonment. The workman appealed before the sessions court on the ground that the summary trial by the Magistrate gave him no opportunity. The sessions court dismissed the appeal and on a revision before the Allahabad High Court the findings of the lower courts were upheld, both on procedural aspects and on merits. Straight J., who heard the revision had the following observation concerning the rationale of the statute:

I am of opinion that his conviction was a right one, because upon the facts found there was most undoubtedly a wilful, and without lawful and reasonable cause, neglect and refusal to perform the contract of service…I need not point out the importance of statutory provisions of this kind, and their being enforced in large commercial centres like Cawnpore, where by combined action on the part of persons employed in large commercial establishments there, the proprietors of those establishments might be placed not only at very grave risk and sudden inconvenience, but very serious pecuniary loss.[26]

Arbitrary Arrests and Whimsical Trials in Beggary Cases

The enforcement of the beggary and vagrancy laws brings to light some of the most glaring examples of arbitrary and even whimsical operation of the criminal justice processes. The various Beggary Prevention Acts[27] and the Bombay Prevention of Begging Act, 1959 (as extended to UT of Delhi in 1961) define begging fairly widely and include within its ambit behaviour patterns that involve not only receiving or taking alms but also other preparatory acts that are directed towards that end, like entering on

[26] Ibid., at 263.

[27] Presently in India, fifteen Beggary Prevention Acts are in operation in thirteen States and two Union Territories. These legislations were enacted, both in the pre-independence and the post-independence periods.

any private premises for the purposes of soliciting or receiving alms [Section 2(i)(c) of the BPB Act], or having no visible means of subsistence and wandering about or remaining in a public place [Section 2(i)(d)], or allowing oneselves to be used as an exhibit for soliciting alms [Section 2(i)(e)], etc. Such a wide ambit of the offence may be justified on the basis of the need to make the law more effective for dealing with the problem, but it does give unduly wide discretion to the police and the raiding party members to interfere with the lives of innocent citizens. The discretion of the arresting authorities is also widened by clause (a) of Section 2(1) which empowers them to treat 'singing', 'dancing', 'fortune telling', 'performing' or 'offering any article for sale' as a pretence for soliciting or receiving alms.

Such a wide definition enables the agency responsible for arrest to interfere with the life-styles of many self-employed groups by arriving at a conclusion that such activities are a mere pretence for begging. Furthermore, the law envisages 'begging in a public place' as an insignificant status offence,[28] but the Magistrate trying the offender can award sentence summarily in Poor House up to three years on first conviction Section 5(5), up to five years on second conviction Section 6(2), and up to ten years for more than two convictions Section 6(3). For poor and resourceless, who often indulge in begging, such wide powers of sentencing are just forbidding.

The Arrest
In the course of our legal services activities in the Beggars Courts (Pande, 1983),[29] we realized that the wide powers of arrest were being uninhibitedly exercised. Those arrested were a mixed lot—old and young, infirm and able-bodied, men and women, faithless and the ones who believed in God. Often the raiding party rounded up members of distinct professional groups such as *sepera* (snake charmers), *kirtania* (religious singers), *kanmelia* (ear cleaners), *jotishi* (palmists), *nat* (acrobats and trapeze performers), and *bazigar* (magicians), etc. The repercussions of such arrests were marked and wide-ranging. The closely-knit group existence of such petty professionals would lead crowds of other members to throng the Poor House compounds. Thus, the arrest of even one member could mean

[28] That is the reason for lack of analytical study of this offence as well as absence of social initiative for extending social or legal support, including legal aid, to this category of offenders.

[29] The author was the convenor of the Delhi University Students Legal Services Clinic during 1976 to 1978 when the Clinic extended the legal services to the Beggars court, situated in the Poor House Complex at Kingsway Camp, New Delhi.

loss of many days of earnings for a large number of others who felt morally bound to stand by the accused and his or her family in the hour of crisis.

We had seen Chottan Chaudhary in the court compound several times. On enquiry, Chottan and his two acquaintances revealed significant facts about the process of arrest. Chottan Choudhary, a man of frail health, had lost his right arm from just below the elbow in an accident during childhood. His problem was that this natural disability exposed him to a very high degree of risk of arrest. He had been arrested many times earlier also, and in the present arrest, he was picked up by the raiding party comprising of the police and the Social Welfare Directorate officials from the Sadar Bazar area. On verification, it was found that Chottan had a small grocery shop near the Inter-State Bus Terminus, thus his presence in the market area, for genuine reasons, was not improbable. Chottan's acquaintances had something more interesting to narrate. They told us how thousands of men like them, earning a living by pushing a *thela* cart or doing other manual jobs, spent nightmarish week-ends under the fear of beggary arrest.

We only get a Sunday for washing clothes, giving ourselves a shave and bath, that is why we keep clean for just two or three days in the beginning of the week. Since work involves sweating and soiling with dust and dirt, that makes things worst for us. Thus, with the whole week's dust and dirt in our clothes and bodies the last two days of the week are most dreaded, because once exposed to the gaze of the raiding party we have very little chance of establishing our innocence.

Perhaps to match the curious ways of arrest, one Magistrate relied on an equally curious method of testing the genuineness of arrests, by subjecting the hands and feet of the arrested people to a close physical examination. Rough, coarse, and blistered hands and cracked feet meant living through hard work and not beggary. The method was simple but effective. It led to a ready presumption which police found difficult to rebut.

The Trial
They were being produced before the magistrate one by one. The court room seemed too big and the proceedings too imposing for the dehumanized herd of men and women. Many of them trembled and broke down before their turn. Fortunately, the presentation before the magistrate was brief and the proceedings to the point. The magistrate asked questions which invariably proved too much:

'Would you fight the case?'
'No, Sir, how can I dare to fight!'

(Fighting in any form is considered a bad thing by a majority of these people.)
'Do you have a lawyer?'
'No, I have none'.

Daharu, a landless labourer from Madhya Pradesh, came to us with his uncle's release problem. The magistrate had sentenced the old man to '1 year C.I. Rs 1000.00 PBSB'. The personal bond or surety bond release required satisfying the magistrate about the financial soundness of the accused or the surety. The case was complex because Daharu had neither a ration-card nor any other document to satisfy the court. The bail bond and surety bond papers were filed, and we instructed Daharu to present them before the court personally. The magistrate was questioning Daharu, who had tattered clothes and mud soiled feet:

'What do you do?'
'I am a daily-wage labourer working for a construction contractor.'
'Do you have a ration-card?'
'No Sir, I have been in this town for less than a month only.'
'Do you know anyone who can speak for your financial standing?'
Daharu looked around the crowded court room and replied non-chalantly:
'No Sir, I do not know any one'.

Perhaps the outright truth of the answer satisfied the magistrate: PBSB release ordered.

One court day we learnt that the new magistrate had created a flutter by insisting on a visit to the Detention Centre and the Certified Institution for the purpose of having a first-hand experience of the living and training conditions. The magistrate also reminded the probation staff attached to the Poor House, in strong words, about their role under the Act. He pulled up the arresting agency for not complying with the formalities relating to date, place, time, alleged behaviour, witnesses, etc., in the arrest records. He acquitted many cases on technical grounds like insufficient evidence on record or the charge not being clear. This magistrate's fad for legalism had a good effect for it led a large number of irregularly arrested people to liberty.

Why was the magistrate transferred when he was doing so well in the beggars' court? We were told that there were representations against him. He was said to be upsetting the established practices and procedures. The magistrate who took over from him was trained in formal legal ways and was also known for his hard, anti-beggar attitude. In his view, beggars were like dirty scars that spoilt the beautiful image of the nation by parading their misery and want before foreigners; that is why he advocated stern and deterrent action against them.

'I do not like any sort of intervention, even in the name of legal aid.'

'But I am only trying to draw your attention to the wide range of punishments under the Act. When you have an alternative, why resort to this extreme sentence?

'You can go against my decision on appeal'.

This magistrate meant business. The number of daily disposals and the percentage of convictions went up considerably during his regime. The beggary law was acquiring a new image.

The Disadvantage of Facing Beggary Trial Alone

The relatives and friends would get information about the arrest of their near and dear ones either through informal neighbourhood sources or the formal communication coming from the Social Welfare office. For a majority of them, the Poor House experience proved excruciating. Many of them would wait outside the compound for hours before entering the main gate. Even the simple formalities like obtaining the 'meeting' permission and locating the appropriate office appeared too complex to an illiterate widow coming from some obscure corner of UP or Bihar State. However, the same system became much easier for people who were in a position to pay, because lawyers, operating through their touts, would be available just for the asking. As a matter of fact, that lawyer-tout had made it a point to reach the Poor House well before the court hours and 'capture' all the paying clients.

In the beginning, we were required to approach the clients for the cases that involved not only locating and identifying them, but also convincing them about our resolve to take up legal service formalities on their behalf without charge. It used to be, at times, difficult for them to accept the proposition that someone, particularly coming from the educated and well-off class, would render them services without any sort of reward. After their first meeting with us, in which they narrated the details of their specific cases, most of them regained confidence and seemed better disposed to get a solution to their beggary law encounters. They needed us for writing bail applications, trial stage representations (with the permission of the magistrate), filling bail bond and surety bond papers, and post acquittal property release applications. In addition, we were also needed by them for the presentation and other liaison formalities in connection with their cases.

It was a very cold winter afternoon; very few people could be seen outside the court premises; we were approached by a client whose case had been handled by us that morning; he came very near us and spoke almost in a whisper:

'Sir, I would like to have your address. I have not been able to pay anything for your services today, but I shall certainly pay you one day when I have a saving.'

'Forget about the payment part, our services were free. Furthermore, we hardly did anything for you, your release was mainly due to the Magistrate who detests irregularities.'

'Sir, but for your writing the application and your presence at the time of the trial I do not know how long I would remain inside.'

He was already in tears. I knew how little we had done in his case in terms of legal thinking and argumentation, yet how significant our small and non-legal efforts were from his point of view!

Collusive Regulation of Vendors, Hawkers, and Rikshaw-Pullers

A substantial proportion of India's workforce earns its livelihood through work in the informal sector. Street vendors, hawkers, and rikshaw-pullers are the most visible sections of the informal sector in urban areas. Most of the Metropolitan towns and cities abound with millions of street vendors, hawkers, and rikshaw-pullers, who migrate as economic refugees from the villages.[30] Since this form of self-employment requires small capital and little skills, it serves as an instant employment avenue for the destitute and needy migrants from rural areas. However, since street-vending, hawking, and rikshaw-pulling are likely to occupy public spaces and crowd the over-crowded streets, the administration has always strived to regulate them under the fear of penal sanctions in terms of the Municipal Corporations Acts and the Police Act. But the way these regulatory provisions are implemented leaves much to be desired (Madhu Kishwar, 2001 and 2003). For example, out of the estimated five lakh street vendor/hawker population of Delhi, only 4916 have been issued *tehbazari* (778 persons in NDMC areas and 4128 persons in MCD zones). This leaves lakhs of street vendors in the status of illegal encroachers. The illegal status of vendors leaves them at the mercy of the municipal authorities and the police, who regularly fleece them of their earnings and keep them frightened by conducting frequent raids and seizure of

---

[30] In the city of Delhi alone there are approximately five lakh street vendors and hawkers and approximately six lakh cycle rikshaw.

their goods and *rehdis* (push carts), which are confiscated and locked-up in municipal yards. For the release of seized goods and rehdis, the vendors (even legal ones) are required to pay a penalty of Rs 1450 plus Rs 300 as 'removal charges' and Rs100 per day as storage charges for the number of days their rehdis are kept in the yard. Such a raid, seizure, and release game goes on almost routinely and at times an entire market is demolished, to be re-built only after jacked-up rates fixed by the municipal officials, police and even the local corporators are to be paid by the 'illegal encroachers.' According to an unofficial survey conducted by *Manushi* in 2001: 'The current monthly extortion rates for pavement sellers range from Rs 500 to Rs 3000 a month for ordinary markets. In locations like Connaught Place, many are even paying Rs 10,000 and more per month. A majority of the small vendors pay between Rs 500 and 800 per month to the MCD, Police, and the local *goondas* as 'protection money'. Those with regular tehbazaris pay a little less, but are certainly not spared the humiliation of having to please the tyrannical deities of licence/permit *raj* through regular cash offerings. In addition, the police often take away their goods without payment, whenever they so desire...thus, if we calculate at a modest average of Rs 500 per person per month by way of cash bribes and Rs 300 per month for loss of income due to open robbery of their goods by government servants, the five lakh vendors of Delhi are being fleeced of Rs 40 crore a month, which comes to Rs 480 crore a year'.[31]

Like the street vendors/hawkers, the municipal authorities control the number of cycle-rikshaw trade and rikshaw-puller's destiny through a licence-quota system. Till 2002, out of an estimated number of six lakh rikshaws, municipal authorities had issued licences only to 73,000 cycle-rikshaws. Now the authorities have declared that only 90,00 rikshaws would be ultimately given licences in Delhi. Furthermore, the new MCD policy requires that the owner himself must be the puller of the rikshaw. Thus, plying rikshaws without a licence is an offence, as well as letting a licenced rikshaw on hire is an offence too. Such 'illegally plying' rikshaws can be confiscated and ultimately destroyed. The authorities claim that each year around 50,000 confiscated and unclaimed rikshaws are destroyed. Actually, the alleged 'destroyed' rikshaw are put back into the unlicenced rikshaw trade with the collusion of municipal officials, police, and illegal rikshaw owners, some of whom own upto

[31] Kishwar, Madhu, 'Blackmail, Bribes and Beatings', *Manushi*, No. 124, 2001, at p. 6.

500 rikshaws at a time. Thus, the enforcement of rikshaw licence law means many things to many persons, depending upon their primary interest: in the lowest rung of the ladder is the unprotected and the most exploited rikshaw-puller; in the middle of the ladder is the rikshaw owner and at the top again are municipal and police officials and local politicians and their agents who meddle with the livelihood of a vast section of the vulnerable urban population, mainly to augment their own interest.[32]

THE NEED TO CHANGE THE
POLICY OF CRIMINALIZATION

As discussed earlier, in Europe and particularly England throughout the sixteenth to eighteenth century period, the poor, the marginalized, and the migrants were indiscriminately criminalized and invariably treated as suspects.[33] The reasons underlying such an approach were diverse, such as: (a) poor were perceived as inferior or sub-human, (b) the way of life of poor was considered an antithesis to civilized way of life, (c) poor needed to be disciplined and educated in order to be converted into a resource for the larger society, and (d) the overwhelmingly large numbers of poor as against the well-off and elite sections, constituted a threat to the material interest, particularly the private property of the dominant classes. Things were no different in India either. With rampant deployment of coercive control techniques and creation of a plethora of status offences, coupled with differential application of criminal laws, the inherent bias of the criminal justice system against the poor became much too obvious. It is sad, but not surprising, that the policy of criminalization of the poor remains more or less uncontested even after five decades of independence.[34] Much worst is that factors like population explosion, accelerated rate of rural-urban migration, globalization, and increased faith in coercive regulation of society are all being used to

[32] Kishwar, Madhu, 'Denial of Constitutional Equality, Government's War on Cycle Rikshaw-Puller', *Manushi*, No. 134, 2003 at pp. 4–13.

[33] See particularly the incisive researches and writings of Leon Radzinowicz (1968), E.P. Thompson (1975), Peter Linebaugh (1991), etc.

[34] That is the reason why punitive approach taken against beggars and vagrants in the post second world war period that was associated with economic recession and massive retrenchment continues to hold sway even today, and many states have either enacted or extended these laws in the 1960s and 1970s to cope with the 'menace' of begging.

support the growing stance of insensitivity to the poor amongst the ruling elite, which in a way is contributing to the proliferation in the explicit and implicit ways of exploitation of the poor and marginalized.

However, there are some positive developments too, that raise hopes about the likely policy changes. The three notable developments in this regard are: *First,* conferment of, after the creation of Indian Republic in 1950, the constitutionally guaranteed rights to equality, liberty and dignity to all the citizens, including the poor and marginalized and the emergence of the conventional and statutory human rights regime that concerns them as well.[35] *Second,* increased emphasis on reform and rehabilitation ideal and inconsistency between over-criminalization and reform and rehabilitation. *Third,* focus shifting to processual determining line that identifies formal stigmatization itself as a major cause for the criminality of the poor. These developments may, it is hoped, trigger changes in the policy, both at the legislative as well as at the enforcement levels. The constitutional imperative of equality, liberty, and dignity is already reflected in the enactment of the laws meant to protect the weaker sections such as the Protection of Civil Rights Act 1955, the Bonded Labour System (Abolition) Act, 1976, the S.C. & S.T. (Prevention of Atrocities) Act, 1989 and some of the judicial decisions that envisage to compensate the poor victims against the abuse process.[36] But one can hardly say that the constitutional guarantees have already made a decisive impact on the criminalization policy, particularly relating to the poor.

In criminological theory, particularly in the line of consensus tradition, no distinction is made between crimes by the rich and the poor. The economic or social status of the law breaker is not to be taken into account at the time of either laying down the norms or its uniform enforcement, atleast as an ideal. This is because all crimes deserve punishment commensurate with their seriousness. But criminal policy is not concerned with retribution and deterrence alone. The ideal of reform demands understanding the offender—this is necessary because although people choose to act criminally, they hardly do so under conditions of their own

[35] It is significant that most of the modern textbooks on criminal law in England treat the constitutional principles and Human Right Conventions as the basis or source of their criminal policy, but it is curious that still criminologists in India pay little heed to the constitutional or Human Rights guarantees in the course of criminal justice policy discourses.

[36] See particularly *Khatri v. State of Bihar* (1983) 2 SCC 266; *Nilbati Behra v. State of Orissa* (1993) 2 SCC 746 *Shakila Abdul Gaffar Khan v. Vasant Raghunath Dhoble* (2003) 7 SCC 749.

choosing. They might be too compelled by the material conditions of poverty and alienation, and not remain fit subjects for faithful compliance with criminal law norms. An anecdote from Lord Buddha's life may be very pertinent here. Lord Buddha, after exposing his chosen three disciplines to advanced discourses on *nirvana* and renunciation, asked them:

> What would be the nature of your response if you happen to confront a sick, tired, haggard and emanciated person on the roadside, soon after you embark on your journey of spreading the message of Buddhism?

The response of all the learned disciples was more or less on the same lines:

> We will tell him about the futility of human existence and about the path of *nirvana* that lies ahead after true remunciation, etc.

Buddha was thoroughly disappointed and exclaimed:

> You have not understood my message at all. Because you must first nurse the person back to health by feeding him, resting him, treating him and then only subject him to the message of *nirvana*.

Is subjecting the poor and marginalized to criminalization indiscriminately not like 'feeding' the sick and hungry with the discourse on *nirvana*? The standards of right conduct, morality, decency, and hygiene conveyed through criminal law norms are likely to be better complied with by people who are in a position to enjoy minimum material conditions. Therefore, should the criminal law norm as well as its enforcement not be rationalized in the light of the material conditions of a substantial majority who are everyday arrested, prosecuted, tried, sentenced, and imprisoned more for their poverty rather than their 'deviations'.

Finally, most of the criminality of the poor and marginalized is merely an ascribed status since the self of the poor is socially located and his contact with the systems of social control can in fact have a negative effect on the rule breaker's self image. In a colonial society labelling those who breached service contract, who led a life of idleness and social parasitism, who indulged in trades that were designated as a pretence for begging may have been tolerated because the ruling class was merely interested in keeping the native population under control. But in a free and democratic society, if some people are labelled as criminals just because of their existential conditions, then the enforcement officials are getting a decisive say in creating and perpetuating criminality of the poor and the marginalized. Not only the beggar and the vagrant but also the vendor, the hawker, and the rikshaw-puller may constantly live under the perpetual fear of being labelled as criminal and be subjected to formal action. In a democratic order, such a disproportionate power in the hands of the enforcement officials is hardly tenable, much less defensible.

Thus, changing the policy of criminalization and enforcement practices would call for rationalization on some of the following lines:

Decriminalization of Status Crimes and Petty Offences

In Europe, decriminalization has been undertaken in right earnest. The European Decriminalization Committee Report[37] has suggested two major strategies for decriminalization, namely: (a) *De jure* decriminalization that involves reform by abolition or repeal of the laws, and (b) *De-facto* decriminalization that can be achieved by keeping the questionable laws in suspension or by deliberate non-enforcement in a selective manner. In the context of crimes by poor and marginalized both the strategies can be pressed into action, while as many status crimes can be de-jure decriminalized, while petty offences like theft under economic distress can be decriminalized by non-enforcement on a selective basis.

Recriminalization of Behaviours that Impairs the Poor Man

The various ways and means by which the poor are deprived of property right, right to fair wages, etc. would require to be criminalized and enforced effectively.

Measures to Enhance Access to Justice

Measures relating to right to legal aid need to be re-activated both by effective governmental and NGO intervention. Similarly, measures such as disposal of cases by Lok Adalat and compounding of criminal cases that aim at delivery of quick justice to poor and marginalized need to be activated.

De-constructing the Image of the Poor and Marginalized

Finally ,the biggest challenge faced by the criminal justice system is to dis-abuse its minds of the myths and prejudices against the poor and marginalized. We have suspected them for long enough without adequate evidence and proof; we have blamed them for being what they are without

[37] The Europe Council of Criminal Justice, Strasburg, 1981.

scientifically examining whether they could have really managed to be different. A substantial number of poor, beggars, child labour, and rikshaw-pullers are what they are, because of us—the dominant classes, who have wanted them to be that way. Therefore, it is high time for us to de-construct the image of poor and marginalized and re-construct it on more humane and scientific lines.

References

Box, Steven (1987), *Recession, Crime and Punishment*, Macmillan Education, London.

Cohen, A.K. (1959), 'The Study of Social Disorganization and Deviant Behaviour', in Merton (ed.), *Sociology Today*, Basic Books, New York.

Cloward, R.A. (1959), 'Illegitimate Means, Anomie and Deviant Behaviour', vol. XXIV, *American Sociological Review*.

Engels, F. (1968), 'Preface to the Peasant War in Germany', *Marx and Engels Selected Works in One Volume*, Lawrence and Wishert, London.

Gordon, David (1971), 'Class and the Economics of Crime', *Review of Radical Political Economy*, vol. 2.

Greenberg, David (1981), *Crime and Capitalism*, Mayfield Pub. Co., California.

Hartjen, Clayton A. (1978), *Crime and Criminalization*, Holt Rinehart and Winston Prager, New York.

Hay, Douglas *et al.* (1975), *Albion's Fatal Tree—Crime and Society in Eighteenth Century England*, Pantheon Books, New York.

Kishwar, Madhu (2001), *Manushi*, vols 124, 125, and 126.

———— (2003), *Manushi*, vol. 135.

Lea, Jock and Young, J. (1984), *Law and Order*, Harmondsworth, Penguin Books.

Linebaugh, Peter (1981), 'Karl Marx the Theft of Wood, and Working Class Composition', in David Greenbeg (ed.), *Crime and Capitalism*.

———— (1991), *The London Hanged—Crime and Civil Society in Eighteenth Century*, Allen Lane, England.

Marx, Karl (1887), *Das Kapital: A Critique of Political Economy*.

———— (1950), *Selected Works*, vol. 1.

———— (1968), 'Eighteen Brumaire of Loius Bonaparte', Marx and Engels, Selected Works in one volume.

Mayer, J.A. (1983), 'Notes Towards a Working Definition of Social Control in Historical Analysis', in Stanley Cohen *et al.* (eds), *Social Control and the State*, Basil Blackwell, England.

Merton, Robert (1957), *Social Theory and Social, Structure*, Free Press, New York.

Miller, W.B. (1958), 'Lower-Class Sub-culture as a Generating Meliue of Gang Delinquency', *Journal of Social Issues*, 14: 5 at p. 19.

Pande, B.B. (1981–2), 'Controlling the Working Class through Penal Measures in British India (1858–1947)', vols 10 and 11, *Delhi Law Review*.

Pande, B.B. (1983), ' The Administration of Beggary Prevention Laws in India—A Legal Aid View-Point', *International Journal of the Sociology of Law*, vol. 11, pp. 291–304.

Pearson, Goeffrey (1981), 'Goths and Vandals—Crime in History', in David Greenberg (ed.), *Crime and Capitalism*, pp. 98–117.

Radzinowicz, Leon (1956) and (1968), *A History of English Criminal Law*, Stevens and Sons Ltd., London.

Siddiqi, Z.M.S. (1983), 'Sanctions for Breach of Contract of Service (1843–1925)', *Journal of the Indian Law Institute*, vol. 25: 3.

Stokes, Witley *et al.* (1887), *Anglo Indian Codes*, p. 362.

Taylor, Ian *et al.* (1973), *New Criminalogy*, Routledge and Kagan Paul, London.

Thompson, E.P. (1975), *Whigs and Hunters—The Origin of the Black Act*, Pantheon Books, New York.

16

Towards Making Criminal Justice Human Rights-Friendly

Policy Choices and Institutional Strategies

N.R. MADHAVA MENON

Criminal justice involves use of coercive power of the state to compel obedience to laws through administration of sanctions. In the process, several decisions curtailing human rights have to be made which include arrest, detention, interrogation, search and seizure, punishment extending to death, and deprivation of civil liberties of persons suspected or convicted. Because of the possibility of abuses and the enormity of the consequences of mala fide action by police and other agencies of the state, every legal system from times immemorial has provided certain checks and balances, placing qualifications and limitations on state power. The object is to ensure that minimum interference is made with individual freedom and maximum scope is provided for a fair trial.

Ever since the adoption of the Universal Declaration of Human Rights and the ratification of the two covenants, there has been remarkable change towards making criminal justice more human rights-friendly, albeit to suspects generally and accused in particular. The rights were elevated from the status of being ordinary legal rights to constitutionally guaranteed fundamental rights. For countries governed by rule of law and an independent judiciary, this meant a tremendous qualitative difference in the administration of criminal justice though, in the process, such societies were open to the syndrome of more crimes, less convictions and delayed justice.

BALANCING RIGHTS WITH SECURITY

In India, the above syndrome wreaked havoc in many respects. There has been a spectacular increase in the incidence of crime and the violence with which they are perpetrated. The number of crimes awaiting investigation and prosecution, the number of undertrial prisoners in detention, and the number of pending cases in courts grew enormously, putting pressure on the system to contain public outcry against increasing violence and insecurity. The reaction of the state has been as expected. More police, more powers to the police, more jails, greater severity of punishment, and attempts to circumscribe the rights and guarantees provided to accused persons. The emergence of corruption and terrorism aggravated the situation threatening national security as well. Government responded with laws of greater severity like the Terrorists and Disruptive Activities Prevention Act (TADA), the Unlawful Activities Prevention Act, and the Prevention of Terrorism Act, all of which tended to enhance the powers of the police and curtail the freedom of citizens. At the same time, there has not been any discernible increase in the level of security nor decrease in the incidence of violent crimes.

While this was happening in the legislative and executive spheres, the judiciary was quietly going about expanding the scope of freedom and liberty, creating thereby a new criminal jurisprudence increasingly friendly to human rights. Norms and procedures for arrest were made strict and police was compelled to follow them strictly under threat of punishment and departmental action. Handcuffing was prohibited and bail provisions were liberalized. Right to legal aid was extended even at the investigation stage and stringent action was to be taken against policemen who indulged in custodial torture or third-degree methods. Right to speedy trial, right to privacy, and right to information were declared as part of personal liberty. Women and children were given special rights and privileges vis-à-vis police and custodial proceedings. Courts have gone to the extent of stopping police investigation by quashing FIRs when they found proceedings were initiated on the basis of insufficient material. Judicial supervision of pre-trial and post-trial proceedings with assistance of human right commissions, media and court-appointed commissions gave criminal justice administration a new face in conformity with human rights and civilized standards of behaviour.

National Human Rights Commission and Criminal Justice

Human Rights Commissions set up at the centre and in states under the Protection of Human Rights Act, 1993, is an important instrument to ensure observance of human rights standards in the entire administration, including criminal justice. One of the reasons that led to the establishment of the commission was the mounting criticism against repeated incidents of custodial violence, fake encounters, and atrocities against women, dalits, and children. The number of complaints that the National Human Rights Commission received increased exponentially with each passing year and in 2001–2 it crossed over 70,000.[1] In all, for an eight year period [1993–2002] NHRC had to process over 300,000 petitions on human rights violations and give relief to each one of them.[2]

The commission began its work when India faced terrorism and insurgency on a large scale in some parts of the country. The use of excessive force by police and paramilitary organizations constituted a major source of public criticism and NHRC had to investigate and intervene to arrest abuse of powers under special laws like TADA. It took the same position when parliament was considering enactment of a milder law (Prevention of Terrorism Act, 2001) to replace TADA.

Encounter deaths and complaints of custodial torture, which formed a substantial portion of petitions received by the commission, made it take a series of preventive steps, compelling prompt action by state agencies. NHRC directed Chief Secretaries to report such incidents within 24 hours of occurrence, under threat that the commission would draw adverse influence if they failed to do so. Postmortem examinations of deaths in custody were to be videographed to avoid foul play. A Model Autopsy Form was prepared and circulated by the commission. As interim relief, the commission passed orders directing state agencies to pay compensation in individual cases.

A significant intervention of NHRC in human rights-friendly criminal justice came after the violence that followed the Godhra train tragedy in Gujarat in February 2002. In a series of sittings, the commission found 'comprehensive failure of the state government in controlling violations of rights to life and liberty of the people of Gujarat' and decided to approach the supreme court to get the cases fully investigated and tried outside Gujarat.[3] The supreme court later conceded the request and transferred a few cases to courts in Maharashtra and reprimanded the Gujarat government for its acts and omissions in violation of constitutional obligations. The intervention of NHRC on behalf of the victims of communal riots strengthened the scheme of human rights surveillance

[1] Virendra Dayal, 'Evolution of NHRC: A Decennial Review', *Journal of NHRC*, Vol. 1 (2002) 41.

[2] Ibid., p. 51.

[3] See Commission's website at www.nhrc.nic.in.

and put a degree of fear on state governments inclined to distort the course of justice using pliable police and prosecuting agencies.

Police and prison reforms are two other important aspects of criminal justice which formed the core agenda of NHRC activities. In a pending public interest litigation[4] in the supreme court seeking implementation of the recommendations of the National Police Commission (1979), the NHRC intervened to submit how certain immediate requirements may be prioritized and implemented to free the police investigation processes from political interference. Similarly, the commission evolved a Model Prison Bill to replace the Indian Prisons Act, 1894, and canvassed for its adoption. The object was to avoid overcrowding in jails, improve living conditions of prisoners, standardize grant of remission and parole, and bring in human rights standards in prison administration.

With the government showing great reluctance to implement criminal justice reforms while enacting laws empowering the executive with more and more powers, it is important that courts and human rights commissions play a pro-active role in protection of human rights in criminal investigation, prosecution, and detention. In less than ten years of its existence, the NHRC made significant contributions in this regard.

STANDARDS OF HUMAN RIGHTS-FRIENDLY CRIMINAL JUSTICE

It is said that criminal justice is the true mirror of the degree of civilization of a society. Criminal justice in this regard includes the procedural guarantees to the accused in defending innocence, the extent to which law allows curbs on freedom, the nature and severity of punishment, the degree of victim support and witness protection, the sense of security enjoyed by the people, the nature of treatment given to inmates of jails and custodial institutions, and the scope for people convicted of crime to get back into normal social life.

If one were to assess the status of Indian criminal justice system in terms of the constitutional provisions and their impact on criminal law, criminal procedure, evidence law, and interpretations given by the high courts and supreme court, the system will easily be graded in the human rights-friendly category. Its foundations are democratic and are governed by rule of law. India has an open society based on a written constitution limiting the powers of the state with an independent judiciary to check

[4] *Prakash Singh v. Union of India* WP No. 310 of 1996 decided on 22 September 2006.

executive and legislative excess through judicial enforcement (which itself is a guaranteed fundamental right) the entire spectrum of civil liberties contained in major international human rights instruments.

Equality before the law and equal protection of laws to every person is a fundamental right (Art. 14). To achieve equal justice, the state is obligated to provide free legal aid to ensure that opportunity for securing justice are not denied to any citizen by reason of economic or other disabilities (Art. 39-A). No one can be convicted of any offence except for violation of the law in force at the time of commission of the act charged as an offence [Art. 20(i)]. Again, no person accused of an offence shall be compelled to be a witness against himself [Art. 20(3)], nor can a person be prosecuted and punished for the same offence more than once [Art. 20(21)]. The scope of protection of life and personal liberty guaranteed under Article 21 has been interpreted to mean the whole range of protection available under the 'due process' clause in the US constitution. It includes substantive and procedural due process and comprehends rights such as 'life with human dignity' (which changed prison practices drastically), right to speedy trial, right against custodial violence, right to free legal aid, right against handcuffing and humiliating treatment, right to privacy, etc.

Protection against unlawful arrest and detention is another guaranteed right most valuable in criminal proceedings. Article 22(1) prohibits the detention in custody of persons arrested without being informed early of the grounds of such arrest. He shall not be denied the right to consult, and be defended by a legal practitioner of his choice. Article 22(2) directs not to detain people without authority of the court and mandates the state to produce persons arrested and detained to be produced before the nearest magistrate within 24 hours of such arrest, excluding the time necessary for the journey. Of course, this clause does not apply to enemy aliens and those preventively detained under due authority of a preventive detention law.

Constitutional protections apart, the criminal law including criminal procedure incorporate the spirit of the bill of rights as elaborated in the constitution and international human rights law. Going by the rule book, the system of criminal justice prevailing in India today is a 'due process model' rather than 'crime control model' in the scheme described by Herbert Packer in his book, *The Limits of Criminal Sanctions*.

The substantive criminal law defines the offence in terms of the mental and physical characteristics and justifies dispensing *mens rea* only in rare and exceptional situations. '*Actus non facit reum nisi mens sit rea*' is the fundamental principle of criminal liability. General defences where *mens rea* can be presumed to be absent are excluded from liability. Private defence as a ground of exemption from criminal liability is given wide amplitude. So far as punishments are concerned, corporeal punishments are prohibited and death sentence is reserved for just five or six offences and that too in the rarest of rare cases where circumstances warrant the extreme penalty. Remission of sentence, probation, and parole are part of the system which gives a correctional thrust to imprisonment. There are separate custodial institutions for women and children. Children are not brought into the criminal justice system and are treated through a correctional-rehabilitative process under the Juvenile Justice (Care and Protection) Act.

Of course, the impact of criminal justice is felt more on how the legal provisions are implemented by the executive agencies of the state rather than the description of crimes and punishments in the substantive criminal law. In deciding what is a crime and what is not, the political-legal processes are so detailed, transparent, and participatory that it leaves little scope for interfering with human rights. And if such a thing happens, through judicial review its constitutionality can be challenged and tested in a court of law. As such, the threat to human rights from criminal justice arises mainly in the exercise of discretionary authority conferred on enforcement agencies under the laws of procedure. The way these agencies have been structured and administered through colonial period to a large extent determined the quality of their services. The adoption of democracy and human rights under a written constitution did not make concomitant changes in the attitudes and practices of criminal justice agencies, particularly of the police and prison officials. At the same time, the political class found tremendous power coming into their hands by letting the system continue in the colonial mould. The result has been large scale abuse of police powers with connivance of political masters, all of which could not be prevented through judicial interventions. Even to this day, the ruling parties are not prepared to give the police a chance to professionalize and be accountable to laws rather than to ministers and bureaucrats. The Police Act of 1861 is still the organizational legislation even though several committees and commissions appointed by governments of different political parties from time to time have uniformly recommended the repeal of the 1861 Act so as to create an independent agency (Security Commission) to oversee police operations in place of the existing bureaucratic-political mechanism.

Apart from the framework law establishing the control accountability structure, the other method for developing a human rights-friendly criminal justice system is to select and train people of integrity and character who will maintain acceptable standards of behaviour even in adverse circumstances. Unfortunately, it is here that the system has collapsed almost beyond repair. Training police is more oriented to muscle power than intellectual abilities. Training for prosecution and judiciary was almost non-existent till recent times. Even where it exists, it is more geared to information and analysis rather than to skills and attitudes. The service rules do not give much importance to training with the result that there is no motivation to be trained. There are no professional trainers either. Training is just a formality which is not taken seriously either by trainers or by trainees themselves.

The last strategy for a human rights-friendly criminal justice system is a reward and punishment scheme which encourages desirable conduct and puts down behaviour inimical to human rights standards. It is surprising how the system has evolved in such a way as to reward the dishonest and unscrupulous while the honest and efficient gets left out in the organization. Corruption is institionalized from top to bottom and has assumed a degree of legitimacy which is frustrating to any reformer of the system. Even if the laws are good and the institutions are suitably restructured, the system may not deliver in a manner respectful of human rights if the persons who occupy positions in it are corrupt and are uninspired by the values of the constitution.

There are people who explain the difficulties involved in terms of the prevailing social standards and justify the lawlessness making comparisons with more lawless situations prevailing elsewhere in the world. If such people are in politics and in leadership of organizations charged with law enforcement, nothing seems possible to reverse the process of degradation which has taken deep roots already. Nevertheless, the vast majority of people who are largely law abiding and are victims of lawlessness of enforcement officials deserve a better deal from the police, the prosecution, lawyers, the court, and the prison system. They cannot reconcile to their fate and give up, as that is the beginning of the end of democracy and rule of law.

What then are the possible options to redeem the criminal justice system to achieve the goal of social defence without compromising on minimum human rights standards which the Indian constitution guarantees to every citizen?

POLICY CHOICES AND STRATEGIES FOR REFORM

The objective of criminal justice is two-fold: to prevent commission of crimes and, when committed, to punish the guilty persons. In both these roles, protection of rights of liberty and property is the primary goal. Civil law also aims to protect right to life and property though the methods are different. In other words, the difference lies in methods used to protect life, liberty, and property. The problem of invasion of human rights is not a serious one in civil proceedings; whereas it is the central issue in criminal proceedings. When the state undertook the responsibility to protect right to life and property of all its citizens instead of private retribution, it had to assume police powers which constituted an invasion of human rights of persons proceeded against, though it was justified in terms of the larger social good of law and order, of peace and rule of law. So long as the state moderated exercise of this enormous power over the lives of citizens, criminal justice remained human rights-friendly. When the number of crimes increased and state authority was challenged, the system was used to do things illegally in the name of crime control and law and order. Today, criminal sanction is used to control a variety of acts and omissions, all of which do not receive popular support. In many western countries, there is a move to de-criminalize (in process, if not in substance) non-serious conduct even if it tends to disturb public peace and morality. They are treated like torts or misdemeanours for compensatory settlement without even police intervention. Avoiding police and criminal proceedings wherever possible is therefore an obvious strategy to reduce the workload of the system and divert minor offences for alternative systems of quicker and cheaper justice, eliminating scope for human rights violation in criminal proceedings.

RE-CLASSIFICATION OF CRIMES

My first submission for intelligent reform of criminal justice therefore is a plea for re-classification of crimes with a view to employ differential treatment depending on the gravity of the offence, the extent of harm, and the scope for prevention and reform. The principle is already there in Indian criminal law where it classifies offences into cognizable and non-cognizable offences and stipulates two or three types of trial. But the present proposal is different in quality and approach. According to statistics available, nearly 70 per cent of the total crimes reported are crimes under special and local laws (SLL). Even the 30 per cent Indian

Penal Code (IPC) crimes are not all serious cognizable offences punishable with long periods of imprisonment. We need to have a fresh look from the point of view of social harm and risk and identify the list of offences under IPC and SLL that deserve more than 7 years imprisonment. They may be declared hard crimes which alone be kept in the Penal Code. They are all to be cognizable offences to be tried and punished within a maximum period of three years by sessions courts according to the procedure prescribed for warrant trial. The revised Penal Code may have three parts—Part I dealing with serious conventional crimes already in IPC, Part II containing the new offences relating to terrorism, organized crime, narcotic offences, etc., and Part III dealing with serious economic offences like money laundering, bank and insurance frauds, serious stock market offences, major IPR offences, counterfeiting currency, etc. Legislature has to prescribe certain parameters to decide whether new offences created are to be considered for inclusion in the new proposed penal code. On a rough assessment, the number of hard core crimes which get into the proposed new penal code will not exceed 100. The major resources of the state available for criminal justice will have to be strengthened and directed for the prevention and prosecution of these crimes. They can be supervised and expedited by competent officials who may have to be drawn not only from police but also related professions depending on the nature and sophistication of the crimes concerned. No sanction should be required for investigation and prosecution of offenders involved. Appeal will be to the high court and in select cases a second appeal may be allowed to the supreme court because of the high stakes involved.

The less serious offences (punishable with less than 7 years and more than 2 years of imprisonment) should be grouped into a separate code to be called the Correctional Offences Code (COC). They are crimes where arrest can be made only with warrant and are open to settlement without trial through plea bargaining as proposed in the new Criminal Procedure Code (Amendment) Bill, 2003. There are offences triable as summons cases. Perhaps offences falling in this category may number three or four times the penal code offences. All courts below the sessions court should be capable of trying these offences against which one final appeal will be to the sessions court.

All offences presently spread in the Penal Code as well as in special and local laws punishable with fine only or with imprisonment of less than two years should be treated as civil offences to be settled through Lok Adalat or otherwise through Panchayat Courts at the earliest opportunity. No arrest is to be permitted in such cases and a specially trained 'Welfare Police' should investigate and prosecute such offences. The summary procedure is to be invoked for these offences and no stigma is to be attached except in repeat offences. Compensation, probation, and community service are to be used as punishment in these cases.

The rationale for this three-fold classification of crimes codified in three different legislations is the reduction of the power of police to arrest and detain people to the barest minimum cases and to promote early settlement of minor offences avoiding lengthy trials and imposition of imprisonment for short periods. This will release resources of the system to concentrate on hard crimes which constitute a real threat to society. Finally, opportunity for human rights violations will be substantially reduced and public participation will become a reality.

Naturally, the three-fold organization of substantive criminal law in terms of risk and severity of the harm, pre-supposes three different types of procedures as indicated above. In fact, it is the procedure designed to reduce scope for human rights violation which is the foundation of classification of crimes into hard crimes (India Penal Code), correctional offences (Indian Correctional Code) and welfare/civil offences (Indian Welfare Offences Code). By and large, the procedure recommended is warrant trial for hard crimes, summons trial for correctional offences, and summary trial for welfare offences. In the first case, police do have power of arrest on their own, while in the second, only with warrant, and in the third, not at all. In the third category, the suggestion is to avoid police intervention altogether unless serious violence is involved. They have to be dealt with by the enforcement officials of the relevant department administratively or by organizations like 'home guards'. The emphasis on the first category is a full-length trial with due safeguards as presented by law; while the emphasis on the second and third category offences is settlement without trial at the instance of the agencies involved including police, probation, legal aid, NGO, etc., or by parties themselves that is, victim and offender. Plea bargaining is the key mode in the correctional offences whereas mediation and conciliation are possible strategies for settlement of welfare offences. With decentralized adminis-tration under Panchayat Raj, it should be possible for local bodies with assistance of citizen groups to settle the third category offences on the spot without police intervention. Maintenance of detailed records are unnecessary and rules of evidence come into application very rarely. Trust, compromise, good neighbourliness, forgiveness, and re-socialization are key concepts in dealing with the misdemeanours included in the last category. In fact, these are offences which should not have been crimes at all in the first place.

RIGHTS OF VICTIMS IN CRIMINAL PROCEEDINGS

One of the serious drawback of the existing system is its total disregard of the victim and his claim for justice. When the offender is not apprehended and punished, the victim does not get any justice at all. He is alienated from the system and sometimes forced to take retributive action to satisfy his sense of revenge. A victim or his relative is the person who often initiate the proceedings. He is the prosecution's key witness whenever he is alive. He is the party most interested in the outcome of the case and his rights ought to be the primary concern of criminal proceedings. Instead, the whole system evolved around the rights of the accused to the total neglect of those of the victim. This is an obvious imbalance in criminal justice which needs to be corrected if the trial has to be fair to both the parties.

Victimologists have mostly bestowed their attention on the role of the victim in the commission of the crime (again to moderate the treatment to be given to the accused) and on schemes for compensating the victims of violent crimes. The rights of the victim in the conduct of the trial did not receive the attention it deserved either from the scholars or from policy planners. In the Malimath Committee Report on Criminal Justice Reforms (2003), some welcome recommendations on recognizing victims' rights statutorily have been made. Any human rights-friendly system of criminal justice necessarily has to accommodate victims' interest adequately in the entire criminal proceedings. Among the victims' rights Malimath Committee proposed are:

(a) Right of the victim, and if he is dead, his legal representative to implead as a party in every criminal proceeding where the offence charged is punishable with 7 years imprisonment or more (the IPC offences in the proposed scheme);

(b) Right to be represented by a lawyer and, if poor, to get free legal aid at state expense;

(c) Right to lead evidence and ask questions to witnesses with leave of the court;

(d) Right to be heard in respect of the grant or cancellation of bail and whenever prosecution seeks withdrawal of the case;

(e) Right to make arguments after the prosecutor has submitted his arguments;

(f) Right to participate in negotiations and plea bargaining;
(g) Right to prefer an appeal against any adverse order of the court acquitting the accused or imposing an inadequate sentence;
(h) Right to get legal services which in appropriate cases to include medical and psychiatric services as well as interim compensation and protection against secondary victimization;
(i) Right to get compensation whether the offender is apprehended/convicted or not.

Victims' active participation with his rights recognized in the proceedings will give a new dynamism to criminal justice and make it more human rights-friendly. Victim Compensation Fund can well be generated through fines, forfeited bail amounts, forfeited property seized, etc., and state should not delay the operation of victim support law any longer.

Use of Science and Technology in Investigation

One of the main sources for popular dissatisfaction with administration of criminal justice is the employment of 'third degree methods' by the police during investigation of crimes. Despite statutory controls on police powers and increased supervision by courts, the use of such extra-legal methods could not be completely stopped. Fortunately with the advances in science and technology there are today a variety of investigative tools which are less invasive, more reliable, highly cost-effective, and totally human rights-friendly. It is now empirically established that the more the use of scientific methods in investigation, the less the chances of human rights being violated. Of course, this calls for heavy investment in terms of infrastructure and training of personnel involved in scientific investigation. In the long run, it is cost effective and supportive of the goals of criminal justice. As such, a phased programme of the use of technology in crime control and investigation is the *sine qua non* for a human rights-friendly system of criminal justice administration. It is more so in the emerging areas like cyber crime, organized crime, and economic offences where the stakes are very high and any price for good investigation is never considered unwarranted.

There is, of course, one difficulty in respect of proof. Scientific evidence is still not admissible in all cases, and wherever admissible its probative value is not what it ought to be. It is treated as expert opinion only. The rules of evidence drafted 150 years ago need to be suitably modified if scientific evidence were to be acted upon by courts as substantive evidence to prove facts in issue or relevant facts. There are already some initiatives in legislating the relevance of DNA printing and cyber forensics. If legal and judicial education also take cognizance of the technological developments and prepare lawyers and judges to correctly appreciate scientific evidence, it is possible for the investigation machinery to switch over to scientific techniques thereby reducing scope for practices inimical to human rights.

TRAINING FOR PROFESSIONALISM AND EFFICIENCY

However, human rights-friendly the legal infrastructure be, and however efficient the institutional structures and procedures are, ultimately the quality of the services is dependent largely on the attitudes, behaviour, and disposition of the persons who man the institutions and exercise powers under the law. As professionals, lawyers, prosecutors, and judges are persons trained in law, committed to the cause of justice and human rights, and obliged to follow ethical norms and standards in discharge of their duties. Yet there are complaints of human rights violations, (though few against the legal community) particularly from women, dalits, minorities, tribals, and children, who need protection more than others. This would suggest that either their professionalization is inadequate or their training weak. Either way, there is need for more scientific training particularly focusing on attitudes and ethics vis-à-vis vulnerable sections of people caught up in the system. There are special laws for this purpose which need to be expressed in the action of lawyers and judges. Human rights in the final analysis is a matter of attitude towards fellow humans in distress.

The Malimath Committee on criminal justice has rightly stressed on the importance of training of prosecutors and judges not only at the time of initial recruitment but also on a continuing basis while in service. Unfortunately, training itself has not yet been organized on professional lines and whatever is being done in the name of training is series of lectures and some instruction on skills which does not serve anything more than cognitive learning. Training to influence attitudes and behaviour to remove biases and prejudices is a more complicated exercise which requires planning, assessment of individual needs, and interactive exercises in the context of tasks and challenges on the job. Training, therefore, is a process to make professionals conform to human rights standards and practices naturally in the ordinary course of nature.

The lack of proper training is more visible in police rather than in any other agency of criminal justice administration. The content of syllabus in police training institutions so far as law is concerned is about powers conferred rather than the limits and limitations of such powers. It is only recently that police curriculum started accommodating human rights modules. Even then, the instruction is so superficial that it is easily forgotten when back at police stations. There is no reward for human rights-friendly policing. In fact, some policemen seem to believe that the two are contradicting terms. The poor and vulnerable sections are the worst sufferers in police high-handedness. Complaint procedure against police is either non-existent in the organization or is too bureaucratic and unproductive to act as an effective remedy. Human rights commissions, the media, and the court are therefore constantly fighting a battle with police everywhere to keep them on the human rights path even in trying circumstances. Of course, policing in democratic societies is a difficult job and respect for human rights make it more challenging. There is no doubt some improvement in police behaviour at all levels which is a sign of respect to human rights.

One must admit, in all fairness to police, there is a heavy price being paid by policemen in defending rule of law and providing security. The advent of terrorism and militancy has taken a heavy toll of police forces who are unable to match the resources of these sections. In assessing human rights performance of the police, the human rights of policemen themselves and their families should not be ignored.

REFORM SENTENCING AND CORRECTIONS

For all practical purposes, the only two punishments now available under the law are imprisonment and fine. Death penalty is still available for half a dozen offences though its imposition is rare. The supreme court upheld that is not violative of human rights when administered in rarest of rare cases. Fine is token punishment as the amount statutorily fixed a century ago is relatively small. In the case of rich offenders, it serves no purpose and in the case of the poor, it results in imprisonment for non-payment. This leaves imprisonment as the only option to the courts. The result is overcrowding of jails, too many short-term prisoners posing problems of custodial care and correction, and imprisonment losing its value as a reformatory or deterrent penalty. Human rights abuses are rampant in prisons and custodial institutions. This is documented in the reports of the human rights commissions and a number of public interest litigation cases heard by the supreme court. In short, the sentencing alternatives and practices now in vogue not only do not serve a penal function but is a potential source for human rights violation and corruption. There is a clear need for new forms of punishments to advance the goals of criminal justice while fulfilling human rights demands. The Malimath Committee recommended alternative sentences such as community service, confiscation/forfeiture orders, disqualification from holding public offices, etc. From the human rights point of view, the committee wanted pregnant women or women with child below seven years to be kept under house arrest only and not sent to jail under any circumstance.

Wide variations in the exercise of sentencing discretion sometimes violate right to equality. As such, sentencing guidelines have to be evolved regulating discretion further. The Malimath Committee suggested a multi-disciplinary expert committee to formulate the guidelines for the consideration of government/parliament.

With settlement as a viable option for the vast majority of criminal cases, the necessity for depending on imprisonment will be considerably reduced. The scope for human rights violations in post-trial proceedings will substantially disappear in most cases. Compensation will replace fine and corrective measures like parole and probation will assume importance in negotiated settlements. Punishment will be reserved for serious crimes in which life imprisonment would mean imprisonment without remission and fine would be calculated on the basis of its deterrent impact on the offender. The sentencing regime can thus become more human rights-friendly and serve a social function as part of criminal justice administration.

An interesting suggestion of the Malimath Committee relates to popular education of rights as well as duties of informants/complainants, the victim, the accused, and the witnesses. Emphasis on rights alone will not serve the desired purpose of maintaining a system of criminal justice fair to all concerned. Duties of informants, accused, witnesses, the police, the prosecution, the defense counsel, and the judge are equally important for observance of rights. If duties are discharged properly, rights will be honoured naturally. Therefore, the committee desired that rights and duties be put in a consolidated and systematic form in separate schedules to the Criminal Procedure Code. It should not only give the list of rights and duties, but should stipulate the authority to be approached in case of violation. Such a document forming part of the statute should be translated in the respective regional languages and made available free of cost to the citizens as handouts, pamphlets through police stations, courts, and legal aid centres. When every decision is made on the balancing of rights and duties and is transparent, there will be lesser scope for corruption and human rights violation.

CORRUPTION—THE GREATEST THREAT TO HUMAN RIGHTS

The recent incident of an Ahmedabad Magistrate issuing warrant of arrest against the Chief Justice and President of India after accepting a bribe for the purpose reveals the extent to which corruption has invaded the judicial process as well. A former Chief Justice conceded the prevalence of judicial corruption though he found it confined to a small percentage of judges. The internal system of correction managed by superior judges seems to be not effective enough to arrest the malaise. The proposed National Judicial Commission is expected to be a more potent weapon to discipline erring members of the judiciary. In any case, some drastic action is necessary as the courts are the ultimate guardians of human rights and the providers of fair trial and even-handed justice without fear and favour.

It is said that lawyers are the primary source of corruption of court staff as well as of the judges. Even in the Ahmedabad case, lawyers were instrumental in bribing the judge. The Bar Council has failed miserably to do anything to curb this trend. The leaders of the bar seem to adopt an indifferent attitude when their colleagues do the mischief and get away with it. It is ironical that those who are advocates of human rights and rule of law are themselves becoming a threat to both. The dimensions of the problem are not yet fully studied and human rights commissions have to investigate it either in association with bar councils or independently to address possible solutions before it gets too late for correction.

On the question of police corruption, there is enough evidence available and is acknowledged by police themselves. The Telgi Scam and the Vohra Committee Report are illustrative of the magnitude of the problem. The nexus between the corrupt elements in police, politics, media, legal profession, civil services, and the underworld is a dangerous mix for rule of law and human rights. The higher judiciary, the media and enlightened sections of civil society have been resisting the spread of corruption but with little success. There is evidence to show that the corruption network is attempting to capture political parties and processes. If, and when that happens, criminal justice itself will be in their hands to give them immunity and protection and nothing but a revolution could save the system from total collapse.

Criminal justice reform is too important a task to be left to politicians and governments alone. It is the need of the hour and every right thinking person committed to rule of law and human rights has to organize, educate, and agitate, as Ambedkar would put it, till the state apparatus for criminal justice is cleansed of the scourge of corruption to which it is sinking day by day.

References

Annual Reports of the National Human Rights Commission, New Delhi.
Report of the Committee on Reforms of Criminal Justice System (Malimath Committee), Ministry of Home Affairs, Government of India, March 2003.

17

Victimology and Victim Justice

Human Rights Perspectives

K. CHOCKALINGAM

Crime has been found to be one of the major social problems in many societies and it has taken new dimensions in the last couple of decades. Crime, delinquency, violence, and the fear of crime diminish the quality of life and peaceful living of people in not only affluent and developed nations, but also poor and developing nations. Crime and delinquency have become great challenges for the organized governments for good governance and have become a political agenda in the elections of several democracies of the world. One of the yardsticks for good governance expected by the people as well as opposition parties in many countries is less crime and more security for the life and property of people. Crime has also increased the expenditure of governments in handling the problems of crime, detection, and prevention of crime and the incarceration and treatment of offenders in institutions. The private expenditure of people on employing preventive and protective measures such as security guards and utilizing modern gadgets of new technology have also increased to a substantial level, besides the increased expenditure incurred by governments on methods of crime prevention, police, courts, and other allied institutions.

A recent research of Clive Norris (2004) informs that more than four million surveillance cameras monitor people living in Britain, making it the most-watched nation in the world. The research further states that the number of closed circuit television cameras (CCTV) has increased four times in the past three years from one million in 2001; now there is one for every 14 people living in the UK. According to estimates, there are chances of residents of London being captured in

CCTV cameras up to 300 times a day during their daily routine wherever they visit. This is a consequence of not only the increase in crime but the increase in fear of crime victimization (The *Independent*, 12 January 2004). Violence and fear of violent crimes deprive people of the enjoyment of their freedoms and restrict their mobility in many cities around the globe.

The Universal Declaration of Human Rights, the basic document adopted by the United Nations Organization in 1948, envisages that every human being in this world should have the right to live as a free individual with all the essential freedoms required to lead a life with dignity. It is the moral and legal obligation of the state not only to refrain from interfering with these freedoms, but also its duty to facilitate the individual to realize such freedoms by all lawful means.

The legal framework for international human right includes the International Bill of Human Rights, encompassing (1) the Universal Declaration of Human Rights, (2) the International Covenant on Civil and Political Rights, (3) the International Covenant on Economic, Social, and Cultural Rights, and (4), the Optional Protocol to the International Covenant on Civil and Political Rights. Among these, the first three are general instruments of substantive international human rights law, and the last one deals with the procedure of implementation that is applicable to the parties to the treaty. All these instruments together recognize that the inherent dignity and the equal and inalienable rights of all members of the human family are the foundation of freedom, justice and peace in the world (Venkataramiah, 1989).

TRENDS IN CRIME, VIOLENCE AND FEAR OF CRIME

In many countries of the world, the incidence of crimes against persons or property is on the rise. Available data reveals that between 1975 and 1990, the number of offences reported worldwide every year rose from 350 to 500 million. According to the United Nations, violent crimes increased about 10 per cent during the last decade. Property offences such as theft, robbery, and fraud contribute for 70 per cent of reported crimes, and increased 30 per cent between 1980 and 1990. If all crimes are taken together, more than three quarters of them were found to have been committed in urban areas, with robbery and assault being the principal causes of victimization in industrialized countries. Another revealing finding was that in many countries, economic growth and urban development are associated with rates of crime two or three times higher than those reported 10 or 20 years ago (Chalom *et al.*, 2001). Van Dijk (1996) has reported that the incidence of crimes against property is mainly increased by urban characteristics of life such as high population density, anonymity, abundance of material goods, and urban development, all of which provide greater opportunity for commission of crime.

Criminal victimization involving violence has several dimensions and far-reaching consequences. Violence against women and children has multiplied alarmingly, although it is difficult to quantify it because of the private nature of the offence. While it mostly occurs within the four walls in many families rather than in a public place, the social and human costs of this widely prevailing form of violence are considerable (UNICEF, 1997). Violence against women and children has its impact not only on the individual victims, but also on the whole family and the web of relationship in the family and the future behaviour of the growing children.

Industrially and economically advanced nations are no exceptions in the behaviour of their men towards women and children, as United States and Japan also show high rates of women and child abuse, despite the absence of complete data in this area. Violence in the family contributes to social dysfunction, and learning, and assimilation of violent attitudes by children from the adults (Chalom *et al.*, 2001). According to Coomaraswamy (2005), South Asia continues to have the worst indicators on violence against women. The unique cultural and religious practices of this region also accelerate the problem of violence against women. For example, even before birth, women suffer much discrimination, starting from sex-selective abortion and female infanticide. As young children, they suffer due to incest and son preference; as adolescents, they are sexually abused or trafficked; as young women, they are subjected to rape, sexual harassment, acid attacks, dowry related violence and killings, marital rape, honour killings by forced self-immolations when their husbands die, and deprivation of property and dignity. The vulnerability to violence at every stage of their life makes a terrible South Asian legacy (http://www.usifem.org.in/pdf/Paper%20VAW%20in%205A% 20Radhika% 20CoomaraSwamy.pdf, visited on 5 December, 2005).

The Fourth UN Survey of Crime Trends and Operations of Criminal Justice Systems (United Nations, 1995) showed that the majority of the world's most populated cities have homicide rates which largely exceed the national rate, indicating the urban nature of this type of violent crime. The survey further revealed that countries with a lower index of human development, characterized by factors such as poverty, lack of housing, low education levels, and lack of community services, have the highest rate of homicides ranging from 22 to 64 per 100,000 inhabitants. A comparison shows that the 20 safest cities of Asia and Europe, with homicide rates lower than two per 100,000 inhabitants, have the highest development indices (Population Action International, 1990).

Despite the fact that crime rates and incidence of crime vary in different countries, there is an upward trend in crime and violence throughout the world and, with the exception of Japan, the risk of being a victim of crime doubled or even tripled over the past thirty years. The findings of International Criminal Victimization Surveys (ICVS) indicate that inhabitants of urban areas in Africa and Latin America are more likely to be victims, mainly of violent crimes (UNICRI, 1995). Crime is on the increase in many cities and neighbourhoods of Asian countries too. For example, in five districts of Beijing, an international victimization survey showed that, one person out of eight (13 per cent) was a victim of crime in 1993 and that over a five-year period (1989–94), the ratio became one out of every two people, proving the increase in violent crime. The World Conference of Mayors on Social Development, with the participation of Mayors of over 135 cities, showed that the question of crime, violence, and insecurity ranks on average as the fourth most serious urban problem, with first and second place going to unemployment and shortage of housing (UNDP, 1994).

IMPACT OF CRIMINAL VICTIMIZATION

Crime victimization results in several physical, physiological, and psychological consequences to the victims, affecting their body and mind. It is a stressful life event which produces many psychological reactions on the victim ranging from mild to severe, depending upon the nature and severity of crime, the type and quantum of loss. Mild reactions produce symptoms like sleep disturbances, irritability, worry, interpersonal strain, aggravation of already existing health problems. Severe reactions could result in Post-Traumatic Stress Disorder (PTSD) producing symptoms like persistent heightened arousal, psychic numbing, and recurring thoughts about the painful incident. Depending on the nature and seriousness of the crime, the caused effects in the psyche of the victims last for days, months, and sometimes years. Loss of dear ones like the children or the breadwinner of the family, the husband for example, due to homicide may cause permanent scars and psychological trauma besides pushing the family to a financial crisis beyond recovery (Markesteyn, 1992).

Since the evolution of Victimology as a discipline to study crime victimization in the late 1930s, beginning from Mendelsohn (1940) and Von Hentig (1948), (as quoted in Karmen, 2001), the focus of scholars on the study of victims has been progressively shifting from responsibility of victims to crime, victim precipitation, victim proneness, or attributes or characteristics of victims making them vulnerable to victimization, reporting behaviour of victims, fear of crime victimization, and costs of criminal victimization. Only during the last two decades or so, has there been more focussed attention on the psychological impact including Post Traumatic Stress Disorder, quantification of victimization rates through crime victimization surveys (ICVS), victims' rights, and victim services.

'Research conducted over the last decade has revealed that many individuals endure a wide range of psychological problems varying in intensity and duration as a direct result of criminal victimization. The current literature clearly indicates that the aspects commonly thought of as most unsettling (physical injury and/or the loss of property) may be less important than the psychological trauma experienced by crime victims. The consensus among researchers and service providers is that criminal victimization produces a variety of psychological and behavioural disruptions ranging from short-term relatively minor discomfort to serious long-term post-traumatic stress disorder' (APA,1985; Bard and Sangrey, 1986; Burgess and Holmstrom,1979; Kilpatrick et al.,1987; Maguire, 1980; Walker, 1985; Wirtz and Harrell, 1987, as quoted in Markesteyn (1992) in 'The Psychological Impact of Non-sexual criminal offences on victims': http://ww2.psepc-sppcc.gc.ca/publications/corrections/199221_e.asp).

The abuse of power and armed conflicts between nations has a more severe impact on the victims, mostly the civilian populations. The UN High Commissioner for Refugees estimates that in the beginning of 1996, there were 13.2 million refugees, 3.4 million returnees, 4.6 million internally displaced persons and 4.8 million victims of armed conflict worldwide. The UN Children's Fund has estimated that during the last decade, about 1.5 million children have been killed in armed conflicts, another four million children have been disabled, maimed, blinded or brain-damaged, and many others have been psychologically traumatized. Another 5 million children are being abused in exploitative forms of labour. Thus, wars and armed conflicts between nations cause much higher and more severe forms of victimization than conventional crimes (United Nations, 1999A). Besides the sufferings caused by the crime, many victims have been found to undergo secondary victimization due to the most unsympathetic and unhelpful behaviour exhibited by the criminal justice agencies, including the police, prosecution, judiciary, and medical personnel when the victims approach them in pursuit of justice. In sensational cases wherein the offenders are persons with power and money, the victims have been compelled by the courts to testify as witnesses without any protection absolutely for their life and property (Waller, 2003). Though figures on the cost of crime victimization in developing countries have not been analysed, an estimate reveals that in the US, the harm to the victims and cost to the public was about 425 billion dollars or the equivalent of $1600 per American per year, according to an article in a popular magazine (*Business Week*, 1993). Waller (1989) has stated that 'compared to more than $100 spent each year per Canadian to try to catch convict, and incarcerate offenders, we spent less than a dollar on all criminal injuries compensation and rape-crisis centres. If we add to this all expenditures on transition homes for battered wives and crime-victims support programmes, we still devote less than $2 per Canadian to specific services for victims'.

VICTIM'S POSITION IN THE CRIMINAL JUSTICE SYSTEM

Before the formal criminal justice systems developed in the world, victims of crime received better justice as the offenders were always asked to pay compensation to the victims in proportion to the amount of damage or injury caused. Later, in the course of the development of the state and its responsibility to preserve peace and protect the citizens from the onslaught of crime, the victim became a 'forgotten person' and justice was gradually meant to establish the guilt of the accused and punish the offender if the guilt was proved. In the whole process, the victims had no significant role except to serve as a primary witness during the trial of the case. Victims have to be content with the punishment of the offender, which depends, too, if at all the prosecution succeed in proving the offence.

During the middle of the twentieth century, the administration of justice, particularly after the formulation of the Universal Declaration of Human Rights, 1948, laid emphasis in protecting the human rights of the accused and the prisoners, perhaps due to the reason that law already punishes the offender by the curtailment of freedom. Hence, the offender should be protected from further encroachment on his human rights as he is in captivity and within the clutches of the state. The advanced scientific knowledge in social sciences on the etiology of crime also lent support to the reasoning that if the objectives of punishment demand a change in the behaviour of the offender for the good, the state machinery should treat him with human dignity by respecting his human rights, so to facilitate his reformation during the period of incarceration.

During the same period, the studies of Benjamin Mendelsohn and Hans von Hentig, the pioneers in Victimology, brought to the forefront a new perspective on the role of the victim in the criminal phenomenon, the problems faced by victims due to the crime, and also the problems caused by the criminal justice system itself. Since then, crime victims and their position in the criminal justice system have become a subject of intense research by scholars of different disciplines. Many researches have exposed the shabby treatment meted out to crime victims throughout the world (United Nations, 1999A).

A significant turning point occurred during the early 1970s because of the genesis of a victim movement in the United States, mainly due to the efforts of many volunteer groups, past victims who were survivors, and researchers who campaigned against the indifference of the criminal justice agencies towards victims and the enormous loss, sufferings, and the consequent psychological effects on the victims (Maguire, 1991). Though the US, Canada, and certain countries of the European Union have brought in many reforms in the treatment of victims by the justice system during the last couple of decades, crime victims continue to be in a state of complete neglect in a large number of the world's countries even today, without having any remedies to their loss and sufferings.

INTERNATIONAL DEVELOPMENTS IN VICTIMOLOGY AND VICTIM CONCERNS

Since the period when crime was considered as an act against the state and the state determined to initiate criminal proceedings against the accused and took up the entire responsibility for the investigation, prosecution, and trial of the accused, the role of the victim in the criminal justice system reduced to the status of a prosecution witness, mainly to prove the guilt of the accused. The interests of victims were never the concern of the police and prosecution, including the court, and their main goal was to prove the offence and punish the offender if the guilt was proved. This period, considered as the 'Era of the offender' by criminologists, however, witnessed new developments towards the protection of the human rights of the accused during investigation and custody and also the offenders during their incarceration after their conviction by the court of law. The United Nations also passed instruments like Standard Minimum Rules for the Treatment of Prisoners to protect the human rights of the prisoners. While this is a welcome development, as a civilized society should protect the dignity and human rights of the accused in custody, an equal if not more important duty of the criminal justice system towards the victims of crime was neglected until the Victimologists and victim advocates collectively voiced through the initiative of the World Society of Victimology in 1979 and spearheaded the cause of victims and their rights in the criminal justice system. Due to the persistent efforts of the World Society of Victimology, the Seventh UN Congress on the Prevention of Crime and the Treatment of Offenders, held in Milan in September 1985, approved the UN Declaration on the Basic Principles of Justice for Victims of Crime and Abuse of Power, which was adopted by the General Assembly on 29 November 1985 through its Resolution No. 40/34. Thus, it became a 'magna carta' for the victims, broadly emphasizing four important rights namely, access to justice, restitution, compensation, and assistance to victims of crime and abuse of power (Chockalingam, 1995).

VICTIMS' RIGHTS IN THE CRIMINAL PROCEEDINGS

Crime victims have attained the present position of certain recognition, at least in some developed nations, after passing through a long struggle and creating a victims movement (Galaway and Hudson, 1981; Elias, 1986; Mawby and Gill, 1987; Karmen 2001).

In the US and some of the developed countries, led originally by some good Samaritans and former victims and survivors, organizations providing essential services to victims of crime started to emerge. These organizations in course of time realized that the rights of the accused and the offenders were better protected by the criminal justice system than the rights of the victims and identified the gaps in the laws and started pointing out the need for reforms in laws to provide more rights for crime victims. Gradually, 'victim empowerment' became a keyword in these countries to improve the position of victims in the criminal justice system and also to provide services to victims to alleviate their problems and reconstruct their life.

Three countries that established the earliest comprehensive victim assistance programmes are the USA, England, and the Netherlands. England and the United States started providing services and assistance to victims simultaneously during 1973–4. Today, the United States has a record of more than a quarter century of experience in victim-assistance programmes. In England, Victim Support is a network of organizations that helps more than a million people who have suffered the effects of crime through a network of over 16,000 trained volunteers who provide emotional support, information, and practical help to all sections of the community. Similarly in the Netherlands, the Dutch National Victim Support Organization, started in 1984, has more than 75 victim support agencies and many walk-in locations throughout the country to assist victims. Everyday, 15,000 volunteers with adequate training provide emotional support, advice, and information, assisted by more than 200 professionals. More than 10,000 victims have availed the services of these organizations each year. Though victims are free to contact a victim support agency themselves, research and experience reveal that victims hesitate to seek help on their own even though they are in need of it. Hence, the National Victim Support Organization volunteers approach the victims who are referred to them by the police, and victims have appreciated this. Victim support organizations in Europe have been united and cooperating closely in the European Forum for Victim Services since 1989. The ties of cooperation among the countries in Europe have sparked a powerful political and social movement for the protection of victims' rights. The Statement of Victims' Rights laid down in Lisbon in 1995 and the Statement of Social Rights of Victims of Crime adopted in Budapest in 1997 are testimonies to their commitment to work together (Groenhuijsen, 1999).

The Statement of Victims' rights, Lisbon in May 1995 states:

'Victims must have the right to:

(a) respect and recognition at all stages of criminal justice proceedings;
(b) receive information about and an explanation of how their case is progressing;
(c) provide information to officials responsible for decisions relating to the offender;
(d) have access to legal advice, regardless of their ability to pay;
(e) protection of privacy and physical safety; and
(f) compensation from the offender and the state.

This is the victims' bill of rights as evolved from the international political and scholarly debate' (Groenhuijsen, 1999).

In the majority of the justice systems around the world, besides the sufferings caused by the offender as a consequence of the crime, many victims face indifference and insensitive treatment by the police, prosecutors and court officials, thus causing secondary victimization. Certain special categories of victims who are vulnerable, like minorities, migrants, women and children, face the brunt more. Even if the offender is apprehended and brought before the court, the experience of victims in many jurisdictions is that they have been marginalized and do not have the opportunity to express their views and concerns in the criminal justice process. Many criminal justice systems do not permit the victim to present his or her civil claim in conjunction with criminal proceedings. Even if the prosecution has succeeded in proving the guilt of the accused and the offender is convicted, sanctions like imposition of fines, probation, or imprisonment have little relevance to the victim, except to provide a little satisfaction of seeing the offender ultimately punished (United Nations, 1999a).

HUMAN RIGHTS OF VICTIMS

Robinson (1998), the former UN High Commissioner for Human Rights, views that 'human rights violations are frequently the root causes of conflict and humanitarian crises. Today's violations are tomorrow's conflicts'. Examining her statement in the context of the position of crime victims, it is true that in many human situations of interaction, the human rights violations of different sections of the human society, whether it is women, children, the elderly, minorities or prisoners, the human rights violations accepted, tolerated or condoned through generations have led to different forms of victimization. These include situations where people are victimized by conventional crimes or abuse of power through violations of human rights.

For example, in the operation of the criminal justice system, the single largest section or agency accused of violations of human rights all over the world is the police itself. Police torturing the accused for the extraction of truth is an open secret in many nations of the world, including India, despite the explicit prohibition of such practices by many international instruments and local laws. Despite this, the justification for indulging in third degree methods on the accused by the police have been heard during my interactions with even enlightened senior police officers in India mainly on the pretext that it is done in the interest of rendering justice to victims. In families with even educated parents, physical punishment of children is still justified on the pretext of disciplining the child in the process of socialization and to make the children conform to the expected standards of behaviour set by the parents. In all these situations, whether it is parents or the police, the claim made by them for their human rights violations on others; children by the parents and the accused by the police, is for a laudable goal and to fulfil their duty as parents or the police.

Police themselves have complained that even when petty thefts have happened in the houses of some VIPs who boast themselves as human rights advocates, if the police are not able to identify the culprit and recover their property, the persons who have lost the property have told the police to interrogate the suspects in the 'proper form' to get at the truth. So there is a double standard between the enforcement of even ordinary laws and the observance of human rights, which really creates a conflict in the minds of law enforcement personnel at the lower cadres. To safeguard the human rights of victims, what is required is to create a culture of zero tolerance of human rights violations in all situations, however justified it might appear because justifications vary on the basis of perceptions of each individual.

Despite the formulation of over sixty international human rights instruments, according to Robinson (1998), 'unfortunately, rights for too many remain little more than words on paper'. It is more than true in the case of victims, as many countries have not taken any serious steps to implement the Declaration on the Basic Principles of Justice for Victims of Crime and Abuse of Power. The only development after the adoption of the Declaration by the UN General Assembly in 1985 is to realize that many Governments have given least priority even to report to the UN about the measures, if any, taken by the member countries. This led the UN to bring out two important documents, Hand Book on Justice for Victims (United Nations, 1999a), an elaborate document for practitioners, and a brief document, Guide for Policy Makers (United Nations, 1999b). The World Society of Victimology has been vigorously pursuing the United Nations to adopt a rights-based approach for victims so that victims may benefit fully from the international instruments on human rights.

Victim Justice in India

Affirmative Action by the Higher Judiciary

Despite the absence of any special legislation to render justice to victims in India, the higher judiciary, particularly the supreme court, has adopted affirmative action to protect the rights of victims of crime and abuse of power. The court has, in several cases, used the concept of restorative justice to repair the consequences arising out of victimization by awarding suitable compensation or enhancing the amount of compensation to the victims. This is based upon the fact that after victimization, we cannot put the clock back and restore what has been actually lost by the victims. In such circumstances, creative restitution, making the offender participate in the rehabilitation of the victims, would improve the situation of the victims, if not total restoration to the original position.

As there is no specific law on compensation to victims of crime in India, the supreme court has used its inherent powers and started affording victim's justice beginning from the 1980s. Some of the important case laws would reveal that in different types of cases where either another citizen is a source of victimization or the governmental machinery such as the police agency is the offender indulging in human rights violations causing victimization, the supreme court and the high courts have come to the rescue of the victims.

There are many cases in which the higher judiciary in India has asked the offender to pay restitution to the victim, making the offender to participate in the rehabilitation of victims.

Victim Restitution

In *Sukhdev Singh* v. *State of Punjab* [1982 SCC (Cr) 467], the supreme court increased the fine amount of Rs 2000 imposed on the offender to Rs 10, 000 so that the widow and the children of the deceased victim may be compensated by payment of the amount of the fine to them without prejudice to their right to claim damages for the death of the victim.

The court, in its judgment in *Balraj* v. *State of UP* [1994 SCC (Cr) 823], while talking about compensation to the victim, held that the power to award compensation is not ancillary to other sentences but in addition thereto, and directed the accused to pay Rs 10,000 by way of compensation to the widow of the deceased.

In *Giani Ram* v. *State of Haryana* (AIR 1995 SC 2452), the court reduced the period of sentence already undergone by the offender but directed him to pay a fine of Rs 20,000 as compensation under Section 357, Criminal Procedure Code, to the widow of the deceased.

In *Baldev Singh* v. *State of Punjab* (AIR 1996 SC 372), the supreme court, after 'considering the nature of the crime, the fact that the accused and the victim are near relations, that it is a property issue which ended in the calamity, the fact that the accused are in a position to pay', ordered that the two appellant-accused shall pay by way of compensation a sum of Rs 35,000 each to the victim's wife and her children who have suffered irreparable loss due to the death of the victim, and restricted the sentence of imprisonment already undergone by them.

Justice to Rape Victims-Guidelines for Victim Assistance

In *Bodhisattwa Gautam* v. *Subhra Chakraborty* (AIR 1996 SC 922), the supreme court held that if the court trying an offence of rape has jurisdiction to award compensation at the final stage, the court also has the right to award interim compensation. The court, having satisfied itself on the prima facie culpability of the accused, ordered him to pay a sum of Rs.1000 every month to the victim as interim compensation along with arrears of compensation at the same rate starting from the date on which the complaint was filed. It is a landmark case in which the supreme court issued a set of guidelines for victim assistance in rape cases in consonance with the Principles of UN Declaration on Justice for Victims of Crime and Abuse of Power, 1985.

These guidelines of the supreme court will go a long way to help indigent rape victims who cannot afford to have the legal, medical, and psychological services:

(1) The complainants of sexual assault cases should be provided with legal representation that is well-acquainted with the criminal justice system. The role of the victim's advocate would not only be to explain to the victim the nature of the proceedings, to prepare her for the case and to assist her in the Police Station and in court but to provide her with guidance as to how she might obtain help of a different nature from other agencies, for example, mind counselling or medical assistance. It is important to secure continuity of assistance by ensuring that the same person who looked after the complainant's interests in the police station represents her till the end of the case. (2) Legal assistance will have to be provided at the Police Station since the victim of sexual assault might very well be in a distressed state upon arrival at the Police Station. The guidance and support of a lawyer at this stage and while she is being questioned would be of great assistance to her. (3) The police should be under a duty to inform the victim of her right to representation before any questions are asked of her and the police report should state that the victim was so informed. (4) A list of advocates willing to act in these cases should be kept at the Police Station for victims who do not have a particular lawyer in mind or whose own lawyer is unavailable. (5) The advocate shall be appointed by the court, upon application by the police at the earliest convenient moment, but in order to ensure that victims are questioned without undue delay, advocates would be authorized to act at the Police Station before leave of the court is sought or obtained (6) In all rape trials, anonymity of the victims must be maintained, as far as necessary. (7) It is necessary, having regard to the directive principles contained under Art. 38 (1) of the Constitution

of India, to set up Criminal Injuries Compensation Board. Rape victims frequently incur substantial financial loss. Some, for example, are too traumatized to continue in employment. (8) Compensation for victims shall be awarded by the court on conviction of the offender and by the Criminal Injuries Compensation Board whether or not a conviction has taken place. The Board will take into account pain, suffering and shock as well as loss of earnings due to pregnancy and the expenses of the child birth if this occurred as a result of the rape.

State Compensation for Abuse of Power

As early as 1983, the supreme court recognized the need for state compensation in cases of abuse of power by the state machinery. In the landmark case of *Rudul Sah v. State of Bihar* (AIR 1983 SC 1086), the supreme court ordered the government of Bihar to pay to Rudul Sah a further sum of Rs 30,000 as compensation, which according to the court was of a 'palliative nature' in addition to a sum of Rs 5000, in a case of illegal incarceration of the victim for long years. The supreme court ruled in this case that one of the telling ways in which the violation of the right can reasonably be prevented and due compliance of the mandatory provision of the Article secured is to mulct its violators in the payment of monetary compensation.

Similarly in *Saheli, a Women's Resources Centre through Mrs Nalini Bhanot v. Commissioner of Police, Delhi Police* (AIR 1990 SC 513), the court awarded a sum of Rs 75, 000 as state compensation, holding that as the victim died due to beating by the officer in-charge of the police station, the victim's mother was entitled to damages for the death of her son.

In the recent landmark case of *D.K. Basu v. State of West Bengal* (AIR 1997 SC 610), the supreme court held that state compensation is mandatory in cases of abuse of power and said that 'To repair the wrong done and give judicial redress for legal injury is a compulsion of judicial conscience'. The court continued further by stating

It is now a well accepted proposition in most of the jurisdictions that monetary or pecuniary compensation is an appropriate and indeed an effective and sometimes perhaps the only suitable remedy for redressal for the established infringement of the fundamental right to life of a citizen by the public servants and the state is vicariously liable for their acts. The claim of the citizen is based on the principle of strict liability to which the defence of sovereign immunity is not available and the citizen must receive the amount of compensation from the state, which shall have the right to be indemnified by the wrongdoer. In the assessment of compensation, the emphasis has to be on the compensatory and not on punitive element. The objective is to apply balm to the wounds and not to punish the transgressor or the offender, as awarding appropriate punishment for the offence (irrespective of compensation) must be left to the criminal courts in which the offender is prosecuted, which the state, in law, is duty bound to do. The award of compensation in the public law jurisdiction is also without prejudice to any other action like civil suit for damages which is lawfully available to the victim or the heirs of the deceased victim with respect to the same matter for the tortious act committed by the functionaries of the state. The quantum of compensation will, of course, depend upon the peculiar facts of each case and no strait-jacket formula can be evolved in that behalf. The relief to redress the wrong for the established invasion of the fundamental rights of the citizen, under the public law jurisdiction is, thus, in addition to the traditional remedies and not in derogation of them. The amount of compensation as awarded by the court and paid by the state to redress the wrong done, may in a given case, be adjusted against any amount which may be awarded to the claimant by way of damages in a civil suit.

In *Mohd.Zahid* v. *Govt of NCT of Delhi* (AIR 1998 SC 2023), the supreme court allowed the appeal and set aside the conviction and sentence of the appellant and acquitted him. Further, the court said that since the appellant has been made a victim of prolonged illegal incarceration by the police personnel, the court directed the Delhi Government to pay him a sum of Rs 50, 000 as compensation.

In cases relating to custodial deaths and those relating to medical negligence, the supreme court has awarded compensation under public law domain (*Nilabati Behera* v. *State of Orissa* (1993) 2 SCC 746: 2SCR 581:AIR 1993 SC 1960; *State of M.P.* v. *Shyam Sunder Trivedi* (1995) 4 SCC 262; *People's Union for Civil Liberties* v. *Union of India* (1997) 3 SCC 433: AIR 1997 SC 1203; *Kaushalya* v. *State of Punjab* (1996) 7 SCALE (SP) 13; *Supreme Court Legal Aid Committee* v. *State of Bihar* (1991) 3 SCC 482; *Jacob George* v. *State of Kerala* (1994) 3 SCC 430; *Paschim Banga Khet Mazdoor Samity* v. *State of West Bengal* (1995) 4 SCC 37:AIR 1996 SC 2426; and *Manju Bhatia* v. *NDMC* (1997) 6SCC 370: AIR 1998 SC 223).

In *S.S. Ahluwalia* v. *Union of India* (AIR 2001 SC 1309), the supreme court held that the state is liable to pay compensation to the family of the Sikhs killed during riots in the wake of the assassination of Mrs. Indira Gandhi on 31 October 1984, as his or her life has been extinguished in clear violation of Article 21 of the constitution.

Recommendations of Various Commissions and Committees

During the last decade, there have been significant changes in the thinking of the judiciary about the human rights of victims, and their violations.

The concern of the courts and the judicial commissions and committees about the plight of the victims and the need to have a law on victim compensation or a comprehensive law on victim justice has been reflected in their judgements, writings, and reports.

The Law Commission of India, 1996

The Law Commission, in its report in 1996, has stated that, 'The principles of Victimology have foundations in Indian constitutional jurisprudence. The provisions on fundamental rights (Part III) and directive principles of state policy (Part IV) of the Indian constitution form the bulwark for a new social order in which social and economic justice blossom in the national life of the country. Article 41 mandates, *inter alia*, that the state shall make effective provisions for securing the right to public assistance in cases of disablement and in other cases of undeserved want' (Law Commission of India Report, 1996).

The Report has said further that, 'the principles of compensation to crime victims need to be reviewed and expanded to cover all cases. The compensation should not only be limited to fines, penalties, and forfeiture realized. The state should accept the principle of providing assistance to victims out of its own funds (i) in cases of acquittals, or (ii) where the offender is not traceable, but the victim is identified, or (iii) and also in cases when the offence is proved'. In view of the lacunae in the existing provisions for compensation to crime victims under the criminal law, the Law Commission of India has stated that it is necessary to incorporate a new Section 357 A in the Code of Criminal Procedure to provide for a comprehensive scheme of payment of compensation for all victims fairly and adequately by the courts (Law Commission of India Report, 1996).

The Justice Malimath Committee

Despite the protest of the lawyer community on many aspects of the recommendations of Malimath Committee, this Committee has made recommendations of far reaching significance to improve the position of victims of crime in the criminal justice system and to provide justice to victims. The Committee has noted in its report that an important objective of the criminal justice system is to ensure justice to the victims, yet victims have not been given any substantial rights, not even to participate in the criminal proceedings. Therefore, the Committee focused on justice to victims and has made many recommendations, including the victim's right to participate in cases involving serious crimes and to adequate compensation. Some of the significant recommendations include:

- 'The victim, and if he is dead, his legal representative, shall have the right to be impleaded as a party in every criminal proceeding where the offence is punishable with 7 years imprisonment or more.
- In select cases notified by the appropriate government, with the permission of the court, an approved voluntary organization shall also have the right to implead in court proceedings.
- The victim has a right to be represented by an advocate of his choice; provided that an advocate shall be provided at the cost of the state if the victim is not in a position to afford a lawyer.
- The victim's right to participate in criminal trial shall, inter alia, include:

    a. To produce evidence, oral or documentary, with leave of the court and/or to seek directions for production of such evidence.
    b. To ask questions to the witnesses or to suggest to the court questions which may be put to witnesses.
    c. To know the status of investigation and to move the court to issue directions for further investigation on certain matters or to a supervisory officer to ensure effective and proper investigation to assist in the search for truth.
    d. To be heard in respect of the grant or cancellation of bail.
    e. To be heard whenever prosecution seeks to withdraw and to offer to continue the prosecution.
    f. To advance arguments after the prosecutor has submitted arguments.
    g. To participate in negotiations leading to settlement of compoundable offences.

- The victim shall have a right to prefer an appeal against any adverse order passed by the court acquitting the accused, convicting for a lesser offence, imposing inadequate sentence, or granting inadequate compensation. Such appeal shall lie to the court to which an appeal ordinarily lies against the order of conviction of such court.
- Legal services to victims in select crimes may be extended to include psychiatric and medical help, interim compensation, and protection against secondary victimization.
- Victim compensation is a state obligation in all serious crimes, whether the offender is apprehended or not, convicted or acquitted. This is to

be organized in a separate legislation by parliament. The draft bill on the subject submitted to Government in 1995 by the Indian Society of Victimology provides a tentative framework for consideration.

- The Victim Compensation Law will provide for the creation of a Victim Compensation Fund to be administered possibly by the Legal Services Authority. The law should provide for the scale of compensation in different offences for the guidance of the court. It may specify offences in which compensation may not be granted and conditions under which it may be awarded or withdrawn.'

The Report, while proposing ways to augment the state's resources for compensation fund, emphasized that dispensing justice to victims of crime cannot be ignored any longer on grounds of scarcity of resources (Government of India, 2003).

The National Commission to Review the Working of the Constitution

The Commission to review the working of the Constitution (Government of India, 2002) has advocated a victim-orientation to criminal justice administration. In the views of the Commission, 'victim orientation' includes greater respect and consideration towards victims and their rights in the investigative and prosecution processes, provision for greater choices to victims in trial and disposition of the accused, and a scheme of reparation/compensation particularly for victims of violent crimes. According to the Commission, the case for a viable, social justice-oriented and effective scheme for compensation to victims is now widely felt. The Commission recommended to the union and state governments that under the directive principles of state policy and under international human rights obligations, it should legislate on the subject with an effective scheme of compensation for victims of crime without further delay. The Commission felt that if the compensation scheme were to be introduced even in a modest scale, the criminal justice system might receive tremendous support from the people as it will ensure social justice; therefore, there is a strong justification for the state to find resources to float the scheme immediately.

NEED FOR CREATING AWARENESS ON JUSTICE TO VICTIMS

Criminal justice systems have a moral and legal responsibility to make all efforts to prevent crime victimization and also to provide relief and satisfaction to the victims. Generating awareness, mustering public opinion, and creating advocacy are important steps not only to draw the attention of the governments to enhance the legal status of the victim and improve victim services, but also to make the programme a people's movement. The success of any programme depends largely on its acceptance by the people and participation of the people. The United States of America, a leader in victim movement with many services to victims of crime, still devotes time and money for creating awareness in the general public to help crime victims. The Office for Victims of Crime (OVC: http//www.ojp.usdoj.gov/ovc/ncvrw/welcome.html), established by the Victims of Crime Act (VOCA), 1984, to oversee the various programmes evolved for the benefit of crime victims, has been sponsoring an annual event since 1981 every April to commemorate National Crime Victims Rights Week, and has been leading the communities across the country in the observance of Victims Rights Week with Presidential pro-clamations and other activities. Declarations are signed by many leading politicians such as state governors and mayors.

The week also provides opportunity for local communities to pay tribute to crime victims. The OVC has already released the 2006 Resource Guide for National Crime Victims' Rights Week to be held during 23–9 April 2006, with hundreds of ideas to increase public awareness of victim issues. They include runs, rallies, memorial walls, and sapling plantings; conducting forums, publishing editorials, and broadcasting public service announcements; displaying posters and distributing brochures and other information in court buildings, school, presentation of awards to victim advocates and service providers, etc.

In India, there is a basic and urgent need for creating awareness at all levels to send a message across the society that we recognize that being a victim of a crime is unfortunate and society condemns the acts of people who are responsible for causing such sufferings, and to motivate the entire society about the importance of providing care and services to crime victims.

Europe celebrates 'European Victims Day' with new initiatives annually. For example, in 2005, the Solicitor General published his statement in the website:

We have been making significant progress in our treatment of victims for some time now, reaching another milestone at the end of last year when we completed the nationwide rollout of our Victim Information and Advice Service. In publishing this statement today we are making a public commitment that all victims and witnesses coming into contact with the prosecution service can expect to be treated with courtesy and respect, and to receive relevant and timely information about their case. We want to continually improve our treatment of victims and witnesses, and it is important for people to have a public statement with which they can compare their own experiences of the system (European Victims Day: Solicitor General publishes Statement on Treatment of Victims: http://www.crownoffice.gov.uk/News/Releases/2005/02/01155611).

In the Netherlands, Victim Satisfaction Surveys (like customer satisfaction surveys) are regularly conducted by the office of the public prosecution. A peer review system in the police department has also been established in the Netherlands in which, after the victim has been questioned by a police detective, a second detective enquires of the victim regarding how he or she had been treated by the first detective. The responses are used to improve the training further. In Japan, a number of questionnaires regarding the treatment of citizens by the police are carried out both by the National Police Agency and prefectural police forces. These are used as a means of improving the police treatment of victims and civilians (United Nations, 1999a).

Many countries have created a section for victims in their home or interior or justice ministries like the OVC in the US. On similar lines, in the home ministry of the government of India and the home departments of all the state governments and union territories, a separate section to deal with issues of victims of crime should be created to recognize the problems of victims of crime and to chalk out programmes to alleviate them (Chockalingam, 2001).

NEED FOR A NATIONAL LEGISLATION FOR VICTIM JUSTICE

Though there is no legislation or scheme to provide compensation or assistance to victims of crime at the national level, due to the persistent efforts of the Indian Society of Victimology, founded in the year 1992 to spearhead the cause of victims, the government of Tamil Nadu one of the states in south India has constituted a Victim Assistance Fund. This fund, created in 1995, provides financial assistance to victims of some violent crimes such as legal heirs of victims of murder and victims of grievous hurt, and rape and dowry victims, particularly to help women and children in distress (Government of Tamil Nadu, 1995). Subsequently, some amendments in the scheme were brought in for more effective implementation of the scheme (Government of Tamil Nadu, 1997). As the fund is only a state scheme and is only an executive decision without any statutory or legal right for compensation or assistance to the victims, the Indian Society of Victimology (1996) prepared a Model Victim Assistance Bill with the support of the National Human Rights Commission and sent it to the government of India for consideration of adoption by the Indian Parliament. The Committee on Criminal Justice Reforms headed by V.S. Malimath has also recommended in its Report for a compensation law for victims in line with this Model Bill. In March 2004, in the thirteenth Lok Sabha, a member of Parliament gave notice for the introduction of this Bill for debate and adoption. Now, as the fourteenth Lok Sabha has been constituted in May 2004, efforts need to be taken to revive the task of introducing the Bill again for adoption.

At no period during the evolution of the modern criminal justice system has the plight and sufferings of victims of crime and abuse of power and the human rights of victims been a subject of international attention and debate as of present. Although, the victim, a forgotten element in the criminal justice system was reborn in the later half of the twentieth century, only a few developed countries have brought in some reforms in their domestic laws, providing rights and assistance to victims in recent decades. The United Nations has made a significant contribution by recognizing the rights of victims through its Declaration on the Basic Principles of Justice for Victims of Crime and Abuse of Power, adopted by the General Assembly in November 1985, and its subsequent efforts to disseminate the principles of victim justice through its two documents; Hand book on Justice for Victims and Guide for Policy Makers (United Nations 1999a, 1999b). India has a long way to go to recognize the rights of victims and to provide assistance/compensation to the victims of crime and abuse of power. Unprecedented in history, in recent years, there have been concerted efforts by the higher judiciary of India to recognize the rights of victims and to provide compensation for their sufferings through several precedents. The Law Commission of India, the Malimath Committee on Reforms of the Criminal Justice System and the Commission to review the working of the constitution, have all in one voice unanimously recommended the need to provide justice to victims during the different stages of criminal proceedings, including compensation and assistance as mandatory. It is the most appropriate time for us to enact a national legislation to render justice to victims, in line with the Model Bill submitted for consideration of adoption by the Indian Parliament. The recent observations of Chief Justice of India, Y.K. Sabharwal, while addressing the Chief Ministers and Chief Justices conference on 11 March 2006, are most relevant for victim justice in India as he stated that,

'Criminal justice system appears to be on the verge of collapse due to diverse reasons. The public outrage over the failure of the criminal justice system in some recent high profile cases must shake us all up into the realization that something needs to be urgently done to revamp the whole process, though steering clear of knee-jerk reactions, remembering that law is a serious business'. He further said, 'some of the responsibility will have to be shared by the executive branch of the state. Not much has been done for improvement of the investigative and prosecution machinery.... It is the investigation that is to be made stronger as courts can decide only on the basis of evidence on record' (The *Hindu*, 12 March 2006).

References

American Psychological Association (APA) (1985), 'Final Report of the APA Task Force on the Victims of Crime and Violence', *American Psychologist*, 40, 107–12, quoted in Trevor Markesteyn (1992), 'The Psychological Impact of Nonsexual Criminal Offences on Victims', http://ww2.psepc-sppcc.gc.ca/publications/corrections/199221_e.asp.

Bard, M. and D. Sangrey (1986), *The Crime Victims Book* (2nd edn), New Jersey: Citadel Press, quoted in Trevor Markesteyn (1992), 'The Psychological Impact of Nonsexual Criminal Offences on Victims', http://ww2.psepc-sppcc.gc.ca/publications/corrections/199221_e.asp.

Burgess, A.W. and L.L. Holmstrom (1979), 'Rape: Sexual Disruption and Recovery', *American Journal of Orthopsychiatry*, 49, 648–57, quoted in Trevor Markesteyn (1992), 'The Psychological Impact of Nonsexual Criminal Offences on Victims', http://ww2.psepc-sppcc.gc.ca/publications/corrections/199221_e.asp.

Business Week (1993), 'The Economics of Crime', *Business Week*, 13 December, pp. 72–81.

Chalom Maurice, Lucie Leonard, Franz Vanderschuren, and Claude Vezina (2001), 'Urban Safety and Good Governance: The Role of the Police', *International Crime Prevention Centre for the Prevention of Crime*, Montreal.

Chockalingam, K. (1995), 'A Review of Victimological Developments in India', *Japanese Journal of Victimology*, No. 5, pp. 78–95.

———— (2001), 'An Agenda for Victims of Crime during the 21st Century', in M.C. Gupta, K. Chockalingam, and Jaytilak Guha Roy (eds), *Child Victims of Crime: Problems and Perspectives*, Gyan Publishing House, New Delhi, pp. 31–44.

Elias, R. (1986), *The Politics of Victimization: Victims, Victimology and Human Rights*, Oxford University Press, New York.

Galaway, B. and J. Hudson (1981), *Perspectives on Crime Victims*, St. Louis (ed.), Mosby.

Groenhuijsen, S. Marc (1999), 'Victims' Rights in the Criminal Justice System: A Call for More Comprehensive Implementation Theory', in Van Dijk *et al.* (eds), *Caring for Crime Victims*, pp. 85–114.

Government of India (2002), 'Report of the National Commission to Review the Working of the Constitution', vol. I, Chapter 7.15, pp. 143–4.

———— (2003), 'Report of the Committee on Reforms of Criminal Justice System', http://www.mha.nic.in/criminal_justice_system.pdf.

Government of Tamil Nadu (1995), 'Creation of Victim Assistance Fund', G.O. M.S. 12 dated 21.08.1995, Home (Police-XII) Department.

———— (1997), 'Victim Assistance Fund—Working of the System Reviewed', G.O. M.S. No. 89 dated 24.01.1997 of Home (Police-XII) Department.

Indian Society of Victimology (1996), 'The Victims (Criminal Injuries) Right to Assistance Bill', Draft Bill prepared and adopted at the IInd Biennial Conference of the Indian Society of Victimology at the National Law School of India University, Bangalore, 5–7 October 1996.

Karmen, A. (2001), *Crime Victims: Needs, Services and the Voluntary Sector*, Tavistock, London.

Kilpatrick, D.G., B.E. Saunders, L.J. Veronen, C.L. Best, and J.M. Von (1987), 'Criminal Victimization: Lifetime Prevalence, Reporting to Police and Psychological Impact', *Crime and Delinquency*, 33, 479–89, quoted in Trevor Markesteyn (1992), 'The Psychological Impact of Nonsexual Criminal Offences on Victims', http://ww2.psepc-sppcc.gc.ca/publications/corrections/199221_e.asp.

Law Commission of India Report (1996), 'Victimology in 154th Report on the Code of Criminal Procedure', 1973 (Act No. 2 of 1974) Chapter XV, pp. 57–65.

Maguire, Mike (1980), 'The Impact of Burglary Upon Victims', *British Journal of Criminology*, 20, 261–75, quoted in Trevor Markesteyn (1992), 'The Psychological Impact of Nonsexual Criminal Offences on Victims', http://ww2.psepc-sppcc.gc.ca/publications/corrections/199221_e.asp.

———— (1991), 'The Needs and Rights of Victims of Crime: Developments in Research and Services in Britain and North America', in M. Tonry (ed.), *Crime & Justice*, vol. 14, University of Chicago Press.

Markesteyn, Trevor (1992), 'The Psychological Impact of Nonsexual Criminal Offences on Victims', no. 1992–21, http://ww2.psepc-sppcc.gc.ca/publications/corrections/199221_e.asp.

Mawby, R. and M. Gill (1987), *Crime Victims: Needs, Services and the Voluntary Sector*, Tavistock, London.

Maurice and Chalom (2001), 'Urban Safety and Good Governance: The Role of the Police', *International Centre for the Prevention of Crime*, Montreal.

Mendelsohn, B. (1940), 'Rape in Criminology', translated and cited in S. Schafer (1968), *The Victim and His Criminal*, Random House, New York, in Karmen, Andrew (2001), *Crime Victims: An Introduction to Victimology*, 4th edn, Wadsworth/Thomson learning, California.

Population Action International (1990), 'Cities: Life in the World's 100 Largest Metropolitan Areas', *Population Crisis Committee*, Washington DC.

Robinson, Mary (1998), 'Today's Violations, Tomorrow's Conflicts-Some Views of the High Commissioner', in *Human Rights Today*, United Nations Publication, pp. 36–7.

United Nations Development Programme (UNDP) (1994), 'International Colloquium of Mayors on Social Development', New York.

United Nations (1995), 'Fourth United Nations Survey of Crime Trends and the Operations of Criminal Justice Systems', Cairo.

————— (1999a), Hand Book on Justice for Victims—On the Use and Application of the United Nations Declaration on the Basic Principles of Justice for Victims of Crime and Abuse of Power.

————— (1999b), Guide for Policy Makers—On the Implementation of the UN Declaration on the Basic Principles of Justice for Victims of Crime and Abuse of Power.

United Nations International Crime and Justice Research Institute (UNICRI) (1995), Criminal Victimization of the Developing World, Rome.

UNICEF (1997), 'Children and Violence', *Innocenti Digest*, No. 2, UNICEF, International Child Development Centre, Florence.

Venkataramiah, E.S. (1989), 'Human Rights and their Enforcement', in Mahendra Pal Singh (ed.), *Comparative Constitutional Law*, Eastern Book Company, Lucknow, pp. 383–9.

Van Dijk, J. Jan (1996), Ministry of Justice, Strategic Planning Service, Pays-Bas, Excerpt from speech, 'Setting for Community Safety: Report on Progress towards World Change'. Final Report on the First International Conference for Crime Prevention Practitioners. Prepared by P. Pearcey, B.Welsh, I. Waller and S. French (16 July), 31 March and 1–4 April, Vancouver.

Von Hentig (1948), *The Criminal and His Victim*, Yale University Press, New Haven.

Walker, L.E. (1985), 'Psychological Impact of the Criminalization of Domestic Violence on Victims', *Victimology*, 10, 281–300, quoted in Trevor Markesteyn (1992), 'The Psychological Impact of Nonsexual Criminal Offences on Victims', http://ww2.psepc-sppcc.gc.ca/publications/corrections/199221_e.asp.

Waller, Irvin (1989), 'The Needs of Crime Victims', in E.A. Fattah (ed.), *The Plight of Crime Victims in Modern Society* (ch. 11). St. Martin's Press, New York.

Waller, Irvin (2003), 'Crime Victims: Doing Justice to their Support and Protection', Publication Series no. 39, European Institute for Crime Prevention and Control (HEUNI), Helsinki.

Wirtz, P.W. and A.V. Harrell (1987b), 'Victim and Crime Characteristics, Coping Responses and Short and Long-Term Recovery from Victimization', *Journal of Consulting and Clinical Psychology*, 55, 866–71, quoted in Trevor Markesteyn (1992), 'The Psychological Impact of Nonsexual Criminal Offences on Victims', http://ww2.psepc-sppcc.gc.ca/publications/corrections/199221_e. asp.

Case Law

S.S. Ahluwalia v. Union of India (AIR 2001 SC 1309)

Baldev Singh v. State of Punjab (AIR 1996 SC 372)

Balraj v. State of UP (1994 SCC (Cr) 823)

D.K. Basu v. State of West Bengal (AIR 1997 SC 610)

Bodhisattwa Gautam v. Subhra Chakraborty (AIR 1996 SC 922)

Mrs Nalini Bhanot v. Commissioner of Police, Delhi Police (AIR 1990 SC 513)

Giani Ram v. State of Haryana (AIR 1995 SC 2452)

Jacob George v. State of Kerala (1994) 3 SCC 430)

Kaushalya v. State of Punjab (1996) 7 SCALE (SP) 13

Manju Bhatia v. NDMC (1997) 6SCC 370: AIR 1998 SC 223

Mohd. Zahid v. Govt. of NCT of Delhi (AIR 1998 SC 2023)

Nilabati Behera v. State of Orissa (1993) 2 SCC 746: 2SCR 581: AIR 1993 SC 1960

Paschim Banga Khet Mazdoor Samity v. State of West Bengal (1995) 4 SCC 37: AIR 1996 SC 2426

People's Union for Civil Liberties v. Union of India (1997) 3 SCC 433: AIR 1997 SC 1203

Rudul Sah v. State of Bihar (AIR 1983 SC 1086)

State of M.P. v. Shyam Sunder Trivedi (1995) 4 SCC 262

Sukhdev Singh v. State of Punjab (1982) SCC (Cr) 467

Supreme Court Legal Aid Committee v. State of Bihar (1991) 3 SCC 482

18

India's International Obligations Towards Victims of Human Rights Violations

*Implementation in Domestic Law and Practice**

LUTZ OETTE

'In 1997, a pregnant dalit woman complained about inappropriate police behaviour. The local police proceeded to insult and beat her, and dragged her naked to the police station where she was further abused and held for several weeks, as a result of which she suffered a miscarriage. No action was ever taken against the police officers concerned and the woman did not receive any reparation'.[1] Leila Seth, who reported this case during a recent seminar on responses to human rights violations in India, raised the question that encapsulates the problem: *'If protectors become the perpetrators, where can we go? What compensation is there for loss of human dignity?'*[2]

---

* This article draws on research carried out by the author in his capacity as project co-ordinator at REDRESS, a human rights organization seeking justice and reparation for torture survivors worldwide. Its main focus is on serious violations of civil and political rights, in particular, torture. The opinions expressed in this article are those of the author alone.

[1] REDRESS, *Responses to Human Rights Violations, The Implementation of the Right to Reparation for Torture in India, Nepal and Sri Lanka*, Report issued February 2003 in collaboration with Commonwealth Human Rights Initiative, p. 94. All REDRESS publications referred to in this article are available at www.redress.org.

[2] Ibid., pp. 94–5.

The case is not an isolated one. As has been well-documented, a wide range of human rights have been and continue to be violated in India.[3] Many of these violations take place in the context of economic exploitation, social injustice, communal violence, as well as regional power struggle and conflicts.[4] The violations range from a denial of economic and social rights, such as the right to education, the right to work and healthy working conditions, to serious breaches of civil rights, including extra-judicial killings, enforced or involuntary disappearances, torture and arbitrary detention as well as violations of minority rights and the right to non-discrimination.[5] Human rights violations have not only been perpetrated by state officials, in particular the police and the army, but also by 'non-state actors', with or without the reported complicity of the state, such as in Bhopal,[6] Ayhodhya[7] and Gujarat.[8] This has resulted in a large number of victims whose plight and rights often remain unacknowledged. While the range of violations is diverse, it is noticeable that many, if not most victims belong to disadvantaged and marginalized groups, such as dalits as well as ethnic and religious minorities.[9]

These victims have a right, under international and domestic law, to obtain reparation for the wrongdoing.[10] The right to a remedy and reparation for a breach of rights has long been recognized, being an

[3] See, for example, National Human Rights Commission, Annual Report, 2001–2, at http://nhrc.nic.in; Usha Ramanathan, 'Human Rights in India, A Mapping', 2001, at www.ielrc.org/india/html; Supreme Court judgements on Article 21 of the Constitution, as well as reports by several UN human rights bodies and mechanisms, e.g., UN Docs. CCPR/C/79/Add.81, 4 August 1997, E/CN.4/2001/66, para.57 and E/CN.4/2002/83/Add.1, paras.27 et seq.

[4] Ibid.

[5] See Ramanathan, Human Rights in India, supra.

[6] See ibid., p. 44 et seq. and the International Campaign for Justice in Bhopal, at www.bhopal.net.

[7] See Amnesty International (AI), *India: Impunity 10 Years after Mumbai riots–Is this the lesson Gujarat should learn*, AI Index: ASA 20/023/2003, 6 December 2002.

[8] See Annual Report of the NHRC, 2001–2, pp. 20 et seq. and http://nhrc.nic.in/Gujarat.htm for the Gujarat orders. See also Human Rights Watch, 'We have no orders to save you, State Participation and Complicity in Communal Violence in Gujarat', 30 April 2002.

[9] See Ramanathan, Human Rights in India, supra, and 'Minorities in South Asia', Paper prepared by I.A. Rehman, Human Rights Commission Pakistan, UN Doc.E/CN.4/Sub.2/AC.5/2003/WP.13, 5 May 2003, p. 4 et seq.

[10] Infra, 2 and 4.

inherent concept of law.[11] While this holds true for individual civil rights in domestic legal systems, the individual had for a long time been excluded from the purview of international law. The increasing recognition of human rights in the wake of the Second World War initially focused on the content of individual rights and the corresponding primary obligations of states. Recent years have witnessed a strong momentum towards a comprehensive express right to reparation for victims of violations of human rights and humanitarian law, spurred on by the growing awareness of the importance of victims' rights.[12]

India has meanwhile steered its own course, marked by public interest litigation, which has attracted widespread attention.[13] The supreme court and high courts have developed a remarkable body of jurisprudence, giving constitutional rights a wide construction and granting relief for their violations.[14] The National Human Rights Commission (NHRC), set up in 1993, has provided an additional mechanism through which victims of human rights violations have obtained compensation. In spite of these developments, human rights violations continue, facilitated by a climate of impunity, and victims are often left with little, if any reparation.[15] As the case mentioned above illustrates, this is but a symptom of societal and political factors, namely the lack of empowerment of victims. In a vicious circle, the people who are most likely to suffer from human rights violations are therefore most often the ones who are least likely to obtain justice and reparation.

It is against this background that India's law and practice will be scrutinized with a view to determining to what degree it conforms to international standards on the right to reparation for victims of human rights violations, taking recent international developments into account. In so doing, international legal standards will be used as a benchmark, and that is not as an alien concept but as principles and rights that India has agreed to be bound by.

[11] See Dinah Shelton, *Remedies in International Human Rights Law*, Oxford University Press, 2000, p. 57 et seq.

[12] Infra, 2.

[13] See, for example, Justice A.S. Anand,' Access to Justice—Role of Courts—An Indian Experience', 2002, presented at the All India Seminar on 'Access to Justice', 26–7 April 2003, New Delhi.

[14] Infra, n. 4, 2 (ii).

[15] See, for example, South Asia Human Rights Documentation Centre (SAHRDC), 'Justice and Accountability in Kashmir—Chasing the Mirage', HRF/19/00, 24 February 2000 and 'Uttar Pradesh—Police Brutality Unchecked', HRF/82/03, 22 August 2003, available at www.hrdc.net/sahrdc/hrfeatures.

THE RIGHT TO REPARATION FOR HUMAN RIGHTS VIOLATIONS IN INTERNATIONAL LAW

International law has for a long time been concerned with the relationship between states only. Accordingly, the injury to an individual did not per se give rise to a claim for reparation based on that violation. Instead, it was only where an individual was injured by states other than his or her own that the state of his or her nationality had a claim against the offending state.[16] Such a claim was based on the law of state responsibility according to which a state violating the obligations it owned to another state was obligated to provide reparation for the injury caused.[17] The individual therefore only had a 'mediated right', depending on his or her state's willingness to espouse his or her claim and to pass on any reparation thus received.

This situation has changed significantly with the growing recognition of the individual as a subject of international law after 1945.[18] The international bill of rights and regional human rights treaties not only stipulate primary rights but also the right to an effective remedy in case of their violation.[19] Human right treaty bodies and courts have given substance to the right to an effective remedy and the right to reparation for human rights violations in a growing body of jurisprudence.[20] In 2005, after more than a decade of preparatory work, the UN General

[16] See 'Chorzow Factory' (Claim for Indemnity) (Merits), P.C.I.J., Series A, No. 17 (1928); Shelton, Remedies, supra, p. 92 et seq. and Ian Brownlie, *Principles of Public International Law*, 5th edn, Oxford University Press, 1998, p. 521 et seq.

[17] See on the law of state responsibility the work of the International Law Commission (ILC), in particular draft articles on the responsibility of states for internationally wrongful acts, adopted by the ILC at its fifty-third session (2001).

[18] See, for example, Albrecht Randelzhofer, 'The Legal Position of the Individual under Present International Law', in Albrecht Randelzhofer and Christian Tomuschat (eds), *State Responsibility and the Individual, Reparation in Instances of Grave Violations of Human Rights*, Kluwer Law International, 1999, pp. 1–25.

[19] See Article 8 of the Universal Declaration of Human Rights, Article 2 of the International Covenant on Civil and Political Rights, Article 6 of the International Convention on the Elimination of All Forms of Racial Discrimination, Articles 13 and 14 of the Convention against Torture and other Cruel Inhuman and Degrading Treatment, Article 13 of the European Convention on Human Rights, Articles 24 and 25 of the Inter-American Convention on Human Rights and Articles 3 and 7 of the African Charter of Human and People's Rights.

[20] See, for example, *Velásquez Rodriguez* v. *Honduraz* (Merits) (1988) 4 Inter-Am. Ct. H.R. (ser.C), para. 174 and *Papamichalopoulos* v. *Greece* (1996) 330-B Eur. Ct. H.R. (ser. A) (Article 50), p. 36.

Assembly adopted the Basic Principles and Guidelines on the right to a remedy and reparation for victims of gross violations of international human rights law and serious violations of international humanitarian law.[21] In another significant development, the Rome Statute of the International Criminal court (ICC) is the first international criminal tribunal providing for a reparation regime for victims of international crimes.[22] Victims' status and rights have also been increasingly recognized in international declarations, resolutions and treaties,[23] in parallel with a growing focus on victims in victimology[24] and in many domestic criminal justice systems.[25]

The right to reparation is based on state responsibility. Where the violation of an obligation, in this case a primary right, is attributed to a state,[26] the latter has the secondary obligation to provide reparation for the breach, either as a matter of treaty law or customary international law.[27] The right to reparation encompasses the procedural right to an effective access to a fair hearing[28] and a substantive right to one of the recognized forms of reparation, namely restitution,[29] compensation,[30]

[21] See UN Doc. A/RES/60/147, 16 December 2005.

[22] Articles 75 and 79 of the Rome Statute.

[23] See United Nations Declaration of Basic Principles of Justice for Victims of Crime and Abuse of Power, General Assembly Resolution 40/34, 29 November 1985; Principles on Reparation, supra, and Rule 85 of the Rules of Procedure and Evidence of the ICC.

[24] See the International Victimology Website, at www.victimology.nl.

[25] Both as participants in the criminal justice system and in the context of justice for gross human rights violations committed by a previous regime or during violent conflict. See on the latter Luc Huyse, 'Victims', in Reconciliation after Conflict, A Handbook, International Institute for Democracy and Electoral Assistance, Stockholm, 2003, p. 54 et seq., at www.idea.int/conflict/reconciliation/reconciliation_full.pdf.

[26] See Principles on Reparation, supra.

[27] See for an overview of victims' right to reparation and States' obligations, REDRESS, *Reparation, A Sourcebook for Victims of Torture and Other Violations of Human Rights and International Humanitarian Law*, March 2003, p. 11 et seq.

[28] See Principles on Reparation, supra.

[29] 'Restitution should, whenever possible, restore the victim to the original situation before the violations of international human rights or humanitarian law occurred. Restitution includes, as appropriate: restoration of liberty, enjoyment of human rights, identity, family life and citizenship; return to one's place of residence, restoration of employment and return of property.' Ibid.

[30] 'Compensation should be provided for any economically assessable damage, as appropriate and proportional to the gravity of the violation and the circumstances of each case, resulting from gross violations of international human rights law and

rehabilitation,[31] satisfaction[32] and guarantees of non-repetition.[33] The appropriate form of reparation depends on the nature of the violation. Reparation is often narrowly seen as being about monetary compensation only. However, it is a process meant to provide comprehensive justice to

serious violations of international humanitarian law, such as: (a) Physical or mental harm; (b) Lost opportunities, including employment, education and social benefits; (c) Material damages and loss of earnings, including loss of earning potential; (d) Moral damage; and (e) Costs required for legal or expert assistance, medicine and medical services, and psychological and social services.' Ibid.

[31] 'Rehabilitation should include medical and psychological care as well as legal and social services.' Ibid.

[32] 'Satisfaction should include, where applicable, any or all of the following: (a) Effective measures aimed at the cessation of continuing violations; (b) Verification of the facts and full and public disclosure of the truth to the extent that such disclosure does not cause further harm or threaten the safety and interests of the victim, the victim's relatives, witnesses. or persons who have intervened to assist the victim or prevent the occurrence of further violations; (c) The search for the whereabouts of the disappeared, for the identities of the children abducted, and for the bodies of those killed, and assistance in the recovery, identification and reburial of the bodies in accordance with the expressed or presumed wish of the victims, or the cultural practices of the families and communities; (d) An official declaration or a judicial decision restoring the dignity, the reputation and the rights of the victim and of persons closely connected with the victim; (e) Public apology, including acknowledgement of the facts and acceptance of responsibility; (f) Judicial and administrative sanctions against persons liable for the violations; (g) Commemorations and tributes to the victims; (h) Inclusion of an accurate account of the violations that occurred in international human rights and international humanitarian law training and in educational material at all levels.' Ibid.

[33] 'Guarantees of non-repetition should include, where applicable, any or all of the following measures, which will also contribute to prevention: (a) Ensuring effective civilian control of military and security forces; (b) Ensuring that all civilian and military proceedings abide by international standards of due process, fairness and impartiality; (c) Strengthening the independence of the judiciary; (d) Protecting persons in the legal, medical and health-care professions, the media and other related professions, and human rights defenders; (e) Providing, on a priority and continued basis, human rights and international humanitarian law education to all sectors of society and training for law enforcement officials as well as military and security forces; (f) Promoting the observance of codes of conduct and ethical norms, in particular international standards, by public servants, including law enforcement, correctional, media, medical, psychological, social service and military personnel, as well as by economic enterprises; (g) Promoting mechanisms for preventing and monitoring social conflicts and their resolution; (h) Reviewing and reforming laws contributing to or allowing gross violations of international human rights and serious violations of international humanitarian law.' Ibid.

victims, in which other forms of reparation are often of at least equal significance.[34] Of these, accountability of those responsible for the violations is increasingly perceived to be of crucial importance in combating impunity, one of the major causes of continuing human rights violations.[35] Criminal accountability is often a prerequisite for compensation.[36] More importantly, compensation without accountability fails to provide comprehensive reparation, excluding personal and official responsibility, and has led victims to reject compensation without such accountability as a tainted pay-off.[37]

The particulars of states' obligations to provide effective remedies and reparation have been elaborated upon by courts and human rights bodies. Yet, enforcement mechanisms remain weak.[38] This applies in particular to states, such as India, which have not recognized any international individual complaints mechanisms. Victims of human rights violations are therefore often left without legal recourse at the international level. In theory, third states can claim reparation for victims of human rights violations, both for their own nationals[39] and for nationals of other states in case of violations of *erga omnes* norms.[40] In practice, third states hardly do so, even where their own nationals are concerned, which is largely due to political considerations.[41]

[34] See REDRESS, 'Torture Survivors' Perceptions of Reparation', Preliminary survey, 2001.

[35] See report by Louis Joinet, 'Question of the Impunity of Perpetrators of Human Rights Violations (Civil and Political)', UN Doc. E/CN.4/Sub.2/1997/20/Rev.1, 2 October 1997 and 'Report of the independent expert to update the set of principles to combat impunity, Addendum: Updated set of principles for the protection and promotion of human rights through action to combat impunity', UN Doc. E/CN.4/2005/102/Add.1, 8 February 2005.

[36] See REDRESS, 'Reparation for Torture, A Survey of Law and Practice in Thirty Countries', April 2003, p. 48.

[37] See REDRESS, Perceptions, supra.

[38] See Obasi Ofakor-Obasi, 'The enforcement of state obligations to respect and ensure human rights in international law', SGM, 10, Menschenrechtszentrum Universität Potsdam, June 2003.

[39] See Brownlie, Principles, supra, pp. 406 and 521 et seq. See also first and second report on diplomatic protection by John Dugard, Special Rapporteur, UN Docs. A/CN.4/506, 7 March 2000; A/CN.4/506/Add.1, 20 April 2000; A/CN.4/506/Corr.1, 7 June 2000 and A/CN.4/514, 28 February 2001, respectively.

[40] See Article 48 of the ILC Draft articles on the responsibility of states for internationally wrongful acts, supra.

[41] See on the question of human rights in international relations, Rein Muellerson, *Human Rights Diplomacy*, Routledge, London: 1997.

The difficulty, if not impossibility, of obtaining reparation at the domestic level that still exists in a large number of countries, and the concomitant absence of international remedies, has prompted a growing momentum towards the exercise of universal jurisdiction.[42] Victims are increasingly taking their cases before courts in third countries. However, the exercise of universal jurisdiction is fraught with difficulties. Even where third states have adequate legislation in place, which is often not the case, the availability of sufficient evidence, immunity, both of individuals and of states, and effective enforcement are just some of the many obstacles that have to be overcome.[43] Against this background, the domestic level remains the main location at which victims have to seek and find justice and reparation.

INDIA'S OBLIGATIONS UNDER INTERNATIONAL LAW AND IMPLEMENTATION

India has become party to several international human rights treaties, incurring a range of obligations as a result.[44] However, India has not ratified all major human rights treaties, notably not the UN Convention against Torture.[45] Moreover, it has yet to become party to the ICC Rome Statute.[46] Perhaps the most striking feature is India's reluctance to consent to individual complaints mechanisms that would allow victims of human rights violations in India access to international treaty bodies. In the absence of regional human rights bodies, this leaves victims with recourse to more limited and weaker charter-based procedures before UN bodies only. It also lessens the scrutiny that treaty bodies might exercise, as they are confined to examining India's State Party reports to the respective bodies, a number of which have been overdue for several

---

[42] According to this principle, states may exercise jurisdiction, both in criminal and civil matters, irrespective of where the violation has been committed and of the nationality of the victim(s) and the perpetrator(s).

[43] See ibid., and REDRESS, Reparation for Torture, supra, pp. 49 and 50.

[44] In addition to both Covenants (ICCPR and International Covenant on Economic, Social and Cultural Rights (ICESCR)), India has ratified, inter alia, the International Convention on the Elimination of All Form of Racial Discrimination, the Convention on the Elimination of All Forms of Discrimination against Women and the Convention on the Rights of the Child.

[45] It has also not ratified the new Optional Protocol to the Convention. See SAHRDC, 'Optional Protocol to CAT, India cannot see the consensus', HRF/59/02, 21 June 2002.

[46] See for the current status www.iccnow.org/countryinfo/asia/india.html.

years.[47] Finally, India's reluctance to open its human rights performance to outside monitoring has manifested itself in its failure to offer an invitation to UN Special Rapporteurs.[48]

Irrespective of these factors, India is obliged to observe the relevant rights in its domestic law and practice. While there is no obligation to incorporate the treaty provisions wholesale, domestic law has to provide and protect the relevant rights granted under respective treaties. The Human Rights Committee has highlighted this obligation in relation to Article 2 of the International Covenant on Civil and Political Rights (ICCPR):

Article 2, paragraph 2, requires that States Parties take the necessary steps to give effect to the Covenant rights in the domestic order. It follows that, unless the Covenant's rights are already protected by their domestic laws or practices, States Parties are required on ratification to make such changes to domestic laws and practices as are necessary to ensure their conformity with the Covenant. Where there are inconsistencies between domestic law and the Covenant, Article 2 requires that the domestic law or practice be changed to meet the standards imposed by the Covenant's substantive guarantees. Article 2 allows a State Party to pursue this in accordance with its own domestic constitutional structure and accordingly does not require that the Covenant be directly applicable in the courts, by incorporation of the Covenant into national law. The Committee takes the view, however, that Covenant guarantees may receive enhanced protection in those States where the Covenant is automatically or through specific incorporation part of the domestic legal order. The Committee invites those States Parties in which the Covenant does not form part of the domestic legal order to consider incorporation of the Covenant to render it part of domestic law to facilitate full realization of Covenant rights as required by Article 2.[49]

The Constitution of India contains no explicit provisions governing the incorporation and status of international treaties.[50] The latter do not

[47] See on the latest status www.unhchr.ch/tbs/doc.nsf/newhvoverduebycountry? OpenView.

[48] See reports by the Special Rapporteur on Torture, UN Doc. E/CN.4/2003/68, 17 December 2002, para. 25 and by the Special Rapporteur on Extrajudicial, Summary or Arbitrary Execution, UN Doc. E/CN.4/2003/3, 13 January 2003, para. 24.

[49] General Comment No. 31 [80], 'Nature of the General Legal Obligation Imposed on States Parties to the Covenant', UN Doc. CCPR/C/21/Rev.1/Add.13, General Comment 31; 26 May 2004, para. 13. See also Comment No. 3 (which is replaced by this Comment), Committee for Human Rights, CCPR General Comment 3, Implementation at the national level (Article 2), Thirteenth session, 1981, 29 July 1981.

[50] However, Article 51 (c) provides that 'The State shall endeavour to foster respect for international law and treaty obligations in the dealings of organised people with one another...'

automatically become part of national law but have to be transformed into domestic law by a legislative act.[51] The exclusive power to do so rests with the Union.[52] To this end, parliament has adopted the Geneva Conventions Act, 1960, but has to date not adopted any law specifically incorporating the provisions of the ICCPR or the ICESCR. Customary international law is considered to be part of the law of the land.[53] A rule of customary international law is binding in India provided that it is not inconsistent with Indian law.[54]

As a general rule, national legislation has to be respected.[55] However, according to the jurisprudence of the supreme court, '[it is] now an accepted rule of judicial construction that regard must be had to international conventions and norms of construing domestic law when there is no inconsistency between them and there is a void in domestic law'.[56] The court has developed a doctrine of interpretation according to which rules of international law and municipal law should be construed harmoniously. It is only when there is an inevitable conflict between international and municipal law that the latter should prevail.[57] The

---

[51] *State of Madras* v. *G.G. Menon* AIR 1954 SC 517 and *People's Union for Civil Liberties* v. *Union of India* (1997) 3 SCC 433. See also Shah, J., Sep. Op., in *Maganbhai Ishwarbhai* v. *Union of India*, AIR 1969 SC 783, at 807 and S.K. Verma, 'International Law', in S.K. Verma and Kusum (eds), *Fifty Years of the Supreme Court of India, Its Grasp and Reach*, Oxford University Press, Indian Law Institute, 2000, pp. 621–49, in particular pp. 630 et seq.

[52] Article 253 of the Constitution and Entry 14 of the Union List of the Seventh Schedule.

[53] See Verma, *International Law*, supra, p. 623.

[54] *Gramophone Co. of India Ltd* v. *Birendra Bahadur Pandey* AIR 1984 SC 667, at 671.

[55] This applies even in those cases where it contravenes rules binding on India under international law (Ibid.) notwithstanding the rule of international law that contravening domestic legislation cannot be invoked to evade international obligations and state responsibility in case of a breach. See Article 27 of the Vienna Convention on the Law of Treaties, 1969, U.N.T.S., Vol. 1155, p. 331.

[56] *SC. Vosjala & Others* v. *State of Rajasthan & Others* 1997 (6) SCC 241. See also *Apparel Export Promotion* v. *A.K. Chopra* 1999 (1) SCC 759.

[57] See also Verma, CJ, in *Vishaka* v. *State of Rajasthan* (1997) 6 SCC 241, at 251 for cases not regulated by domestic law: '[a]ny international convention not inconsistent with the fundamental rights and in harmony with its spirit must be read into these provisions to enlarge the meaning and content thereof, to promote the object of the constitutional guarantee. This is implicit from Art. 51 (c) and the enabling power of parliament to enact laws for implementing the international conventions and norms by virtue of Art. 253 with Entry 14 of List 1 of the Schedule.'

supreme court has also repeatedly held, in interpreting the fundamental rights provisions of the constitution, that courts can rely on those provisions of the ICCPR that elucidate and go to effectuate the constitutional fundamental rights as facets of those rights and are, consequently, enforceable.[58] In a remarkable step, the supreme court has found Article 9 (5) ICCPR, which provides for a right to compensation for victims of unlawful arrest or detention, to be enforceable in India. It did so in spite of the absence of any legislation to this effect and the fact that India had entered a specific reservation to Article 9 (5) ICCPR when ratifying the convention in 1979, declaring that the Indian legal system does not recognize such a right to compensation.[59]

THE RIGHT TO REPARATION IN DOMESTIC LAW AND PRACTICE

Accountability for Serious Human Rights Violations

Accountability for serious human rights violations is a vital aspect of reparation.[60] International law has clarified state's obligations in respect of ensuring criminal accountability for serious human rights violations. This requires a system in which the relevant acts or omissions are made a criminal offence in domestic law, victims have the right to complain, alleged violations have to be investigated promptly, impartially and thoroughly, and the perpetrators, if found guilty, are to be punished in proportion to the seriousness of the crime.[61] This presupposes that alleged perpetrators are not shielded from prosecution by such means as immunities, amnesties or statutes of limitations.[62]

India's laws fall short of these requirements in several respects. Firstly, while India's Penal Code in principle allows for the prosecution of human

---

[58] *People's Union of Civil Liberties* v. *Union of India*, supra. See also *Prem Shanker Shukla* v. *Delhi Administration* AIR 1980 SC 1535 and *Visakha* v. *State of Rajasthan*, supra.

[59] See *Nilabati Behera* v. *State of Orissa* (1993) 2 SCC 746 (Ind SC) and *People's Union of Civil Liberties* v. *Union of India*, supra.

[60] Supra, II.

[61] See, for example, the Principles on Reparation and Articles 4, 12 and 13 of the UN Convention against Torture.

[62] See Human Rights Committee, HRI/GEN/1, Part 1, General Comment 20 (Art. 7) and, on the question of amnesties, 'Amicus on the legality of amnesties under international law', submitted by REDRESS, Lawyers Committee for Human Rights and International Commission of Jurists to the Special court for Sierra Leone in the Trial Chamber, *The Prosecutor against Michael Kallon*, 2002.

rights violations, it lacks specific offences to prosecute and punish a series of violations, such as extra-judicial killings, enforced or involuntary disappearances and torture.[63] As far as international crimes are concerned, the Geneva Convention Act, 1960, makes certain war crimes, that is, grave breaches of the Conventions, criminal offences.[64] However, genocide and crimes against humanity have not been recognized as specific offences in domestic law. While India has been quick to create new offences of terrorism,[65] it has not responded in a similar fashion to serious human rights violations whose particular nature and seriousness is consequently not reflected in India's criminal law.

Secondly, public officials, including the army, may not be prosecuted without the prior sanction of the government, thereby providing quasi-immunity.[66] Thirdly, there is no independent body tasked with fully investigating human rights violations constituting crimes. Criminal offences are largely investigated by the police, the very same institution held responsible for many human rights violations. There is no effective complaints procedure and a considerable number of victims have reportedly refrained from lodging complaints out of a well-founded fear of harassment.[67] In practice, most investigations against officials do not result in prosecutions, often being closed on the grounds of a lack of evidence.[68] Magistrates, while having some powers of investigation, have not come to play a prominent role in ensuring prompt and thorough investigations of human rights violations.[69] While the NHRC may investigate human rights violations,[70] it does not carry out a full criminal investigation and may only recommend what measures to be taken. In

---

[63] See REDRESS, Responses, supra, p. 13 et seq.

[64] See Section 3 of the Geneva Convention Act.

[65] Prevention of Terrorism Act, 2002, Act No. 15 of 2002.

[66] Section 197 of the Criminal Procedure Code (Cr. PC). See also Section 57 of the Prevention of Terrorism Act, 2002, which provides protection from 'suit, prosecution or other legal proceeding…for anything which is in good faith done or purported to be done in pursuance of this Act.'

[67] See AI, 'The battle against fear and discrimination—The impact of violence against women in Uttar Pradesh and Rajasthan', ASA 20/016/2001, 8 May 2001 and REDRESS, Responses, supra, p. 21.

[68] Ibid.

[69] Ibid., p. 22.

[70] However, the NHRC has, in spite of its recent demands to this effect, not been given the powers to investigate human rights violations committed by the armed forces (see on current powers of the NHRC in this respect Article 19 of The Protection of Human Rights Act, 1993).

practice, the NHRC has been criticized for not taking a tougher stance on combating impunity.[71] However, it has issued a list of important instructions and guidelines aimed at preventing future human rights violations, such as custodial deaths/rapes, cases of encounter deaths, visits to police lock-ups, polygraph tests and arrests and human rights in prisons.[72]

Fourthly, there have only been few prosecutions that have resulted in convictions and the imposition of appropriate sentences reflecting the gravity of the crime in question. Considerable evidentiary hurdles are to be overcome when proving crimes committed by officials, a problem that is not confined to India.[73] The burden of proof being on the prosecution, the latter commonly finds it difficult, if not impossible, to establish the guilt of the alleged perpetrator(s) in the absence of independent witnesses and compelling factual evidence.[74] In criminal trials, the Indian judiciary has not taken a rigorous stance against accused perpetrators of human rights violations that constitute crimes. While heavy sentences have been imposed in some instances, many cases ended in acquittals or the imposition of light sentences only.[75]

Fifthly, victims of crime have only a limited range of rights in Indian criminal procedural law and there is no express right to protection for victims and/or witnesses from harassment by the alleged perpetrator(s) and others. While courts may issue interim orders for protection in case of intimidation or threats, the system of protection falls short of institutionalized measures of protection.[76] Victims of crimes that constitute human rights violations therefore do not have the rights to participate in criminal proceedings and to protection that have been recognized in international law.[77] The Indian criminal justice system also lags behind

---

[71] See summary of presentation by Mr. Ravi Nair, REDRESS, Responses, supra, p. 93.

[72] NHRC, 'Important Instructions/Guidelines', New Delhi, 2000.

[73] See REDRESS, Reparation for torture, supra, p. 46.

[74] See on this point Law Commission of India, '185th Report on Review of the Indian Evidence Act 1872', by Judge M.J. Rao, Chairman, 2003, Annexure, The Indian Evidence (Amendment) Bill, 2003, Insertion of new Section 114B, para.65 and REDRESS, Responses, supra, p. 21.

[75] Ibid., p. 23.

[76] Such victim and witness programmes have been set up in several countries, such as in South Africa under the Witness Protection Act, 1998.

[77] See Principles on Reparation, supra, and on victims' rights in the ICC-Statute, Victims Rights Working Group, 'Victim Participation at the International Criminal Court, Summary of Issues and Recommendations', November 2003.

important developments in a considerable range of other countries where the recognition that criminal justice also has to serve victims' rights, needs, and wishes resulted in legal reforms strengthening victims position in the criminal process.[78] Consequently, victims are not empowered to play an active role in criminal proceedings and remain, by and large, passive bystanders whose interests appear to be seen as secondary, if not ignored altogether.[79]

Finally, perhaps the biggest factor impacting on the overall situation is the lack of sufficient political will to take necessary steps in combating impunity. Orders of the supreme court in fundamental rights cases to institute criminal proceedings against the alleged perpetrators have gone unheeded.[80] The NHRC has to date not succeeded in combating impunity effectively. Even where it has called for criminal accountability in such high-profile cases as the killings in Gujarat in 2002,[81] its calls have been largely ignored by politicians and competent authorities.[82] The police are widely held to be ill-equipped to combat crime by lawful means, often resorting to unlawful forms of violence instead.[83] Institutional self-control of police and army appears to be weak, and human rights education of officials has failed to translate into a better human rights performance on the ground.[84] This applies in particular to law-enforcement and military activities in areas of conflict.[85] Recent legislation has expanded the powers and immunity of armed forces rather than providing for greater accountability.[86] The emerging picture is one where impunity for human rights violations has become deeply ingrained and where the institutions that have spoken out against it have proved too weak in effecting substantial changes that would result in enhanced accountability.

[78] See, for example, the US Federal Victims of Crimes Act, 1984; the Victims' Bill of Rights, 1998, Manitoba-Province, Canada; and, in New Zealand, the Victims' Rights Act, 2002.

[79] See Justice A. Anand, 'Victims of Crime—the unseen side' (1998) 1 SCC (Jour) 3.

[80] See REDRESS, Responses, supra, p. 22.

[81] Supra, I.

[82] See AI, India: Impunity after 10 years, supra.

[83] See, for example, G.P. Joshi, 'Police Brutality in India', Commonwealth Human Rights Initiative (CHRI), November 2000.

[84] See the various publications emanating from the work done by the CHRI on police reform in India, available at www.humanrightsinitiative.org and SAHRDC, 'Gujarat riots point to need for police reform', HRF/53/02, 13 March 2002.

[85] See, for example, SAHRDC, Justice and Accountability in Kashmir, supra.

[86] See Prevention of Terrorism Act, 2002.

Judicial and Non-Judicial Remedies for Victims of Human Rights Violations

Remedies under Statutory and Common Law

Indian statutory law recognises no right to reparation in the form of state liability for official wrongdoing. Whereas other states have legislated specifically to provide for such liability, either for specific human rights violations or for all forms of official wrongdoing, reflecting a development towards state responsibility vis-à-vis its citizens, relevant Indian law largely remains the colonial one. Several attempts to put into place legislation expressly providing for reparation have come to nothing to date.[87]

Consequently, as a matter of statutory and common law, the only recourse left to victims of human rights violations is tort remedies. A victim of torture can claim reparation on the basis of tort law in civil courts.[88] Available remedies that may be utilized are the tort of public misfeasance or trespass to the person, namely assault and battery.[89] However, these remedies have not proved to be effective for several reasons. Any suits against the state are bound to fail on the grounds of sovereign immunity. The liability of the state is still defined by reference to the Government of India Act, 1858, according to which the liability of the government is the same as that of the East Indian Company.[90] The Government (Liability in Tort) Bill, 1967, envisaged liability of the state for unlawful acts committed by its public servants in the exercise of their duty. The proposed Act would have considerably strengthened victims' right to an effective remedy for human rights violations but has not been adopted subsequently. Instead, courts adjudicating civil cases have in their jurisprudence recognized sovereign immunity in relation to 'excesses' committed by police officials in the exercise of their duties.[91] In a recent development, the central government and state governments have been explicitly granted immunity from suit 'for anything which is done in good faith or purported to be done in pursuance of' the Prevention of Terrorism Act, No. 15 of 2002.[92]

[87] See overview in REDRESS, Responses, supra, pp. 32, 33.

[88] See *Common Cause* v. *Union of India*, 1999 SCC 667.

[89] See P.M. Bakshi, *Law of Torts*, in Verma/Kusum, Supreme Court, supra, pp. 590–620, at p. 608.

[90] Section 65 of the Government of India Act, 1858.

[91] The leading case is *Kasturi Lal Ralia Ram* v. *Union of India* AIR 1965 SC 1039. See for an overview of relevant cases and a critique of sovereign immunity Aman Hingorani, 'State Liability in Tort- Need for a Fresh Look' (1994) 2 SCC (Jour) 7.

[92] Section 57 of the Prevention of Terrorism Act, 2002.

Public officials who may in principle be subject to legal action by victims seeking damages in tort for wrongdoing may also be immune from suit, as provided by law.[93] In those cases where legal action against an individual responsible for human rights violations could possibly be taken, the lack of access to justice constitutes one of the biggest obstacles.[94] Even if these obstacles can be overcome, courts are overburdened with cases that are often drawn out for years, requiring considerable determination of the victims who face significant evidentiary hurdles, compounded by widespread impunity. Finally, compensation awards tend to be comparatively small and need to be enforced against individual debtors. Against this background, while victims may pursue such remedies, it comes as no surprise that common law remedies have played hardly any role in Indian human rights litigation vis-à-vis the state and its officials.

In contrast to other countries, in particular legal systems influenced by French law,[95] Indian law does not allow victims of a crime, including human rights violations that constitute crimes, to claim reparation in the course of criminal proceedings. However, a court has discretion, when imposing a sentence of fine to order the convicted person to pay compensation to the victim(s).[96] It may also do so in respect of sentences that do not include a fine.[97] In any subsequent civil suit relating to the same matter, the court, when awarding damages, will take into account any sum already paid or recovered by way of compensation in a preceding criminal case.[98]

In practice, criminal courts have rarely used their discretionary powers to compensate victims of crime.[99] The supreme court has pronounced

[93] Ibid., and Section 157 Cr.PC.

[94] See various contributions at the All India Seminar on 'Access to Justice', 2003, supra.

[95] See on the system of the '*partie civile*' Articles 1 et seq. and 85 et seq. of the French Code of Criminal Procedure.

[96] Section 357 (1) (b) and (c) Cr.PC.

[97] Section 357 (3) Cr.PC. Several Indian states, such as Andhra Pradesh, Bihar, Karnataka, Madhya Pradesh, Rajasthan, Uttar Pradesh, and West Bengal have adopted amendments to Section 357 (3) Cr.PC, providing that 'the court may' shall read 'the court shall' in those cases where the person against whom an offence is committed belongs to Schedules Castes or Schedules Tribes as defined in Clauses (24) and (25) of Article 366 of the constitution. This rule does not apply where both the accused person and the one against whom an offence is committed belong to either such castes or tribes.

[98] Section 357 (5) Cr.PC.

[99] See K.I. Vibhute, 'Victims of Rape and Their Right to Live with Human Dignity and to be Compensated: Legislative and Judicial Responses in India', *Journal of the Indian Law Institute*, Vol. 41 (1999), pp. 222–36, at 226, Fn. 15 for further references.

on Section 357 (3) Cr.PC. in several cases. In the *Hari Kishan*[100] and the *Chandraprakash* case,[101] it held, inter alia, that the requirement of social justice demanded the imposition of a heavy fine in lieu of a reduction of sentence to compensate the victims of crime. In *Jacob George* v. *State*,[102] the supreme court reduced a sentence but ordered the convicted person to pay an extra fine of 1 lakh. In *State of Punjab* v. *Ajab Singh*,[103] the supreme court directed the accused to pay compensation of Rs 5,00,000 to the families of the two deceased persons who had been killed even though it acquitted the accused on the grounds of a private defence.[104] While these cases have contributed to providing reparation to the victims concerned, they have remained too isolated to amount to anything resembling a consistent practice. In the light of widespread impunity, the prospect of obtaining reparation in criminal proceedings remains weak.

Constitutional Remedies

Triggered by public interest litigation brought in the light of the absence of effective remedies in statutory law, the supreme court has developed its jurisprudence on constitutional remedies for violations of fundamental rights over the last three decades. The constitution contains no express right to an effective remedy or reparation for human rights violations. However, the supreme court and the high courts recognized their

[100] In *Hari Kishan & State of Haryana v. Sukhbir Singh* AIR 1988 SC 2127, the supreme court awarded Rs 50,000 to the victims and directed the subordinate criminal courts to exercise the power of awarding compensation to victims of offences in such a liberal way that the victims may not have to rush to the civil courts for compensation. See also, at 2131: 'It is an important provision but Courts have seldom invoked it perhaps due to ignorance of the object of it. It empowers the court to award compensation to victims while passing judgement of conviction. In addiction to conviction, the court may order the accused to pay some amount by way of compensation to victim who has suffered by the action of the accused. It may be noted that this power of courts to award compensation is not ancillary to other sentences but it is in addition thereto. This power was intended to do something to reassure the victim that he or she is not forgotten in the criminal justice system. It is a measure of responding appropriately to crime as well as reconciling the victim with the offender. It is, to some extent, a constructive approach to crime.'

[101] In *State of Maharastra v. Chandraprakash Kewal Chand Jain* AIR 1990 SCC 486, the supreme court confirmed the sentence of 5 years imprisonment on the sub-inspector of police for raping a young girl and imposed a fine of Rs 1000.

[102] *Jacob George v. State* (1994) 3 SCC 430.

[103] (1995) 2 SCC 486.

[104] See also *Bodhisatwa Goutam v. Subha Chakraborty* (1996) 1 SCC 490 in which the court held that it can enforce compensation against private bodies or individuals who violate the fundamental rights of the citizen.

respective power to award compensation in writ proceedings brought under Article 32 of the constitution and under Article 226 respectively. The supreme court elaborated on the constitutional foundation and nature of compensation for violations of fundamental rights in *Nilabati Behera* v. *State of Orissa*.[105] In so doing, it referred to its duty to enforce fundamental rights under Articles 14, 21 and 32 of the constitution, the need to make the guaranteed remedies effective and its task to provide complete justice.[106] Such writ proceedings are a remedy based on strict vicarious liability[107] for a contravention of fundamental rights to which the principle of sovereign immunity does not apply.

The issue of compensation for breach of a fundamental right, namely Article 21 of the constitution, was first raised in 1981 in the supreme court in the case of *Khatri* v. *State of Bihar*, also known as the *Bhagalpur Blinding* case.[108] No compensation was awarded as the responsibility of the police officers concerned was still under investigation. The court did, however, order the medical treatment for the seven blinded prisoners to be paid by the State. *Rudul Shah* v. *State of Bihar,* a case concerning unlawful detention for a period of fourteen years, was the first one where the supreme court awarded compensation for a violation of Article 21.[109] In *Sebastian M. Hongray* v. *Union of India,*[110] a disappearance case, the supreme court issued a writ of habeas corpus for the production of the two missing persons, and, when the Army failed to do so, directed the state to pay exemplary costs of one lakh each to the dependants of the disappeared persons for contempt of court.

In the last decade, the supreme court and the high courts have awarded compensation under Article 21 for a considerable range of human rights violations. These violations include rape,[111] other forms

---

[105] The case concerned custodial death as a result of torture. *Nilabati Behera* v. *State of Orissa* (1993) 2 SCC 746 (Ind SC).

[106] Ibid.

[107] The State is vicariously liable for wrongful acts committed by its officials or employees. See *Uttarakhand Sangharsh Samiti, Mussoorie* v. *State of Uttar Pradesh* (1996) 1 UPLBEC 461.

[108] AIR 1981 SC 928.

[109] (1983) 4 SCC, 141, pp. 147–8. See also *Bhim Singh* v. *State of J & K* (1985) 4 SCC 677, which concerned compensation under Articles 21 and 22 (1) for unlawful arrest mala fide.

[110] AIR 1984 SC 571.

[111] *Uttarakhand Sangharsh Samiti, Mussoorie* v. *State of Uttar Pradesh,* Allahabad High Court, 9 February 1996. See for a critical review of the jurisprudence of the Indian Supreme Court and High Courts in rape cases, Vibhute, Victims, supra.

of torture,[112] death in custody,[113] enforced or involuntary disappearances,[114] a case of death resulting from army action[115] as well as other cases concerning infringements of fundamental rights.[116]

This includes compensation for culpable inaction on the part of the state that leads to a violation of fundamental rights.[117]

The supreme court and the high courts have discretionary power as to which relief to award. Both courts have in their respective jurisprudence awarded exemplary damages for the breach of fundamental rights.[118] Compensation may also be awarded as interim payment.[119] The supreme court appears to have been guided by compensatory factors as well as those of deterrence when assessing compensation.[120] The particular facts of each case, in particular the severity of the violation, will

[112] *Arvinder Singh Bagga* v. *State of UP* (1994) 6 SCC 565.

[113] *Ajab Singh* v. *State of UP* (2000) 3 SCC 521; *Amitadyuti Kumar* v. *State of West Bengal* (2000) 9 SCC 404.

[114] *Union of India* v. *Luithukla* (1999) 9 SCC 273 and *State of Punjab* v. *Vinod Kumar* (2000) 9 SCC 742.

[115] See *R.S. Sodhi* v. *State of UP* 1994 Supp (1) SCC 142 and 143.

[116] See overview in Dr. Paramjit S. Jaswal, 'Public Accountability for Violation of Human Rights and Judicial Activism in India: Some Observations' (2002) 3 SCC (Jour) 6, Fn. 48 and Usha Ramanathan, 'Tort Law in India (A Survey of Decisions of the High Court and the Supreme Court)', Annual Survey of Indian Law 2001, 615–28 (2002).

[117] Ibid.

[118] Justice Anand in *Nilabati Behera* v. *State of Orissa*, supra, para. 33 '...when the court moulds the relief by granting "compensation" in proceedings under Articles 32 and 226 of the Constitution seeking enforcement or protection of fundamental rights, it does so under the public law by way of penalising the wrongdoer and fixing the liability for the public wrong on the state which has failed in its public duty to protect the fundamental rights of the citizens. The payment of compensation in such cases is not to be understood in a civil action for damages under the private law but in the broader sense of providing relief by an order of making "monetary amends" under the public law for the wrong done due to breach of public duty of not protecting the fundamental rights of the citizen. The compensation is in the nature of "exemplary damages" awarded against the wrongdoer for the breach of its public law duty and is independent of the rights available to the aggrieved party to claim compensation under the private law in an action based on tort, through a suit instituted in a court of competent jurisdiction or/and prosecute the offender under the penal law.'

[119] *State of Punjab* v. *Vinod Kumar*, supra, and *Re Death of Sawinder Singh Grover* (1995) Supp (4) SCC, 450.

[120] *D.K. Basu* v. *State of West Bengal* (1997) 1 SCC 416, para. 54. See *also R.D. Upadhyay* v. *State of A.P.* (2001) 1 SCC 437, at 439.

determine the quantum of compensation awarded by the court. In 1987, the court stipulated a working principle on the amounts of compensation to be paid in case of death. However, it has subsequently not applied this principle and has awarded compensation on a case-by-case basis.[121] The court has also frequently held that the state, after having paid out compensation to the victim, can recover the money from the official found responsible for the human rights violation.[122]

The supreme court and the high courts have not confined themselves to awarding compensation but have on several occasions directed the state to suspend public officials alleged to be responsible for human rights violations or to impose other disciplinary sanctions. The authorities have also been ordered to institute criminal investigations and to sanction the prosecution of alleged perpetrators. [123]

In the case of *D.K. Basu* v. *State of West Bengal*,[124] which concerned death in custody resulting from torture, the supreme court not only awarded compensation but also directed the respondent state to take a wide range of specific measures aimed at preventing the recurrence of torture. Thus, with regard to custodial deaths, the supreme court pronounced the need for law reform to protect the interests of detainees. It also ordered the authorities to put safeguards into place, to undertake training and to provide medical care and other measures designed to assist victims of torture.

The brief review shows that the higher courts, especially the supreme court, have in their respective jurisprudence given effect to the right to reparation in the form of constitutional remedies. In so doing, the courts have elaborated upon and accorded various forms of reparation by way of a liberal construction of constitutional powers. The supreme court has also taken international standards into account and made use of them when developing the scope and content of specific rights.[125]

Acknowledging this impressive record, it is important to recognize the limitations. The award of reparation for a breach of fundamental remedies falls within the discretion of the supreme court and high courts

---

[121] See overview in Jaswal, Public Accountability, and Ramanathan, Tort Law, supra.

[122] See, for example, *Rudul Shah* v. *State of Bihar*, supra.

[123] See, for example, *Punjab & Haryana High Court Bar Association* v. *State of Punjab and Ors.* (1996) 4 SCC 742; *Sebastian M. Hongray* v. *Union of India*, supra, and *State of Punjab* v. *Vinod Kumar*, supra.

[124] (1997) 1 SCC 416.

[125] See Verma, International Law, supra.

rather than being a right of the victim(s). It is therefore subject to the policy of the court's judges, and the supreme court has indeed been criticized for its lack of consistency in awarding reparation.[126] Victims also face the problem of access to justice when seeking reparation before the supreme court. While the court has facilitated the bringing of writ petitions in fundamental rights cases, it has not followed a consistent practice and suffers from the length of proceedings, which undermines its effectiveness.[127] One, if not the greatest, limitation is the failure of state authorities to implement the decisions of the supreme court by way of holding alleged perpetrators of human rights violations accountable.[128]

Alternative Avenues: The National Human Rights Commission

The NHRC constitutes an alternative non-judicial channel through which victims of human rights violations can seek reparation. Thus, it may, after the completion of an inquiry, 'recommend to the concerned Government or authority for the grant of such immediate relief to the victim or the members of his family as the Commission may consider necessary'.[129] The Commission clarified that 'the 'immediate interim relief' envisaged under Section 18 (3) of the Act has to relate specifically to the injury/loss suffered as a result of the human rights violation, and that this will not absolve the state of its liability for compensation.'[130] It also stated that: '...for the purpose of award of compensation, substantiation on mere preponderance of probability, on the standard of civil evidence is sufficient. Even where a criminal charge may fail for want of evidence sufficient by standards requisite in criminal cases, yet a case of compensation can be sustained on a mere preponderance of probability'.[131] Notably, the NHRC's practice of recommending compensation has been influenced by international standards: 'This provision [18 (3) of the Protection of Human Rights Act, 1993] has been generously operated and the power conferred under it is widely exercised by the Commission in deserving cases. The Commission has in this connection kept itself alive to the spirit

[126] See SAHRDC, 'Sovereign Immunity and the Climate of Impunity, The Need for Change in India', HRF/29/00, 20 December 2000.

[127] See Pravin H. Parekh, 'Access to Justice', Paper presented at the All India Seminar, supra.

[128] See supra, n. 4, 1.

[129] Section 18, (3), The Protection of Human Rights Act, 1993.

[130] NHRC, Annual Report 1998–9, Rationale for Grant of Immediate Interim Relief/Compensatory Jurisprudence, Case No. 144/93–4/NHRC.

[131] Ibid., Case No. 294/13/98–9/CD.

of various United Nations instruments.'[132] In its practice, the Commission has recommended compensation in 528 cases, the total of which amounted to Rs 134,531, 934 for the period from 1993 to 2001.[133] The NHRC, in attributing ultimate responsibility, has repeatedly recommended that the concerned government, which was held responsible to pay compensation to the victim, recover the amount paid from the responsible public official.[134]

While the NHRC has no direct powers of enforcement, its recommendations have generally been followed in practice.[135] In case of non-compliance, the NHRC may use its power to seize the high court or supreme court for an order directing the responsible public body or person to pay the specified compensation.[136]

In practice, the NHRC has provided a valuable non-judicial channel through which victims of human rights violations can obtain compensation. It has also issued important guidelines aimed at preventing human rights violations, in particular in custody.[137] However, the NHRC has been criticized for its lack of effectiveness in combating impunity.[138]

[132] Ibid., Case No. 3177/96–7/NHRC, Comment: 'Article 9 of the International Covenant on Civil and Political Rights makes it explicit that everyone has the right to liberty and security of person and nobody shall be subjected to arbitrary arrest or detention. It further mandates that anyone who has been the victim of unlawful arrest or detention shall have an enforceable right to compensation. Article 14 of the Convention against Torture and Other Cruel, Inhuman or Degrading Treatment or Punishment, 1985 makes it an obligation of the state to ensure that in its legal system, the victim of an act of torture obtains redress and has an enforceable right to fair and adequate compensation, including the means for as full a rehabilitation as possible. In the event of the death of the victim as a result of an act of torture, his dependants shall be entitled to compensation. Principle 35 of the Body of Principles for the Protection of All Persons under Any Form of Detention or Imprisonment (1988), also prescribes for remedy of compensation, in case of any damage incurred because of acts of omission by public officials contrary to the rights contained in the Body of Principles.'

[133] See NHRC, Annual Report, 2000–1, p. 140.

[134] See overview of custodial death and torture cases in NHRC, Ibid., p. 140 et seq.

[135] Ibid. See for cases in which the state government initially failed to comply with recommendations by the Punjab HRC, AI, 'Breaking the cycle of impunity and torture in Punjab', AI-Index: ASA 20/002/2003, January 2003, pp. 44, 45.

[136] E.g., Writ Petition (Crl) No. 13/98, NHRC, Annual Report, 1998–9, II., 2.19. However, approaching the high court or supreme court for an order directing the responsible public body to implement the NHRC's recommendation(s) constitutes a rather exceptional course of action.

[137] Supra, n. 4, 1.

[138] Ibid.

The survey of the Indian system of relevant law and practice demonst-rates that it has, though providing for some reparation, failed to bring comprehensive justice. It is in particular the failure to ensure account-ability of perpetrators and to put into place effective safeguards, including a change in the mindset of the perpetrators that have contributed to one of the main defects of India's law and practice: not preventing or substantially reducing future violations. India's criminal law is riddled with features that facilitate impunity, often in the form of colonial legacies recently complemented by 'anti-terrorism' legislation providing broad powers and potentially far-reaching immunity. The law is weak in terms of ensuring accountability of officials, which also applies to the existing institutional arrangement of supervising official wrongdoing. Internal monitoring is also largely seen as ineffective. The existing system is therefore in need of a comprehensive review to be undertaken with a view to bringing it in line with international standards. The Istanbul protocol[139] or similar documents in respect of other human rights violations could be used as reference documents for future reforms of the investigation system.

The question of awarding reparation has been left almost entirely within the discretion of the supreme court and the high courts. Their jurisprudence in fundamental rights cases has in many ways been exem-plary. However, given the limited capacity of the supreme court and the discretionary nature of constitutional remedies, it would be benefi-cial to put the right to a remedy on a clear statutory footing. While there have been a number of proposals to fill the gap,[140] and some laws have indeed been adopted to cover specific aspects, such as Scheduled Castes and the Scheduled Tribes (Prevention of Atrocities) Act, 1989, these reforms appear to be piecemeal instead of being based on the recogni-tion of victims' right to reparation. Existing legislation should therefore be reviewed and new legislation introduced by utilizing international standards, such as the ones developed in the course of the work on the Principles on Reparation. This should take the form of a statutory law that provides for reparation in case of official wrongdoing and reparation that can be sought by the victim(s) through judicial and non-judicial remedies.

[139] Istanbul Protocol: 'A Manual on the Effective Investigation and Documenta-tion of Torture and other Cruel, Inhuman or Degrading Treatment', submitted to the UN High Commissioner for Human Rights, 9 August 1999.
[140] Supra, n. 4, 2 (i).

Considering the question of further measures that should be taken to strengthen victims, right to reparation in India, two areas appear critical. Firstly, the question of a general recognition of victims' right to reparation, whoever the victim, by society at large. This point raises broader issues, such as empowerment of marginalized victims, including awareness of rights and access to justice, as well as human rights education at all levels. While efforts by NGOs are already underway, the government, be it union or state, could take a lead role in developing and implementing human rights plans addressing these issues.

Secondly, the question that needs to be considered is what institutional set-up should and could be put in place that facilitates victims' access to justice and reparation. Taking comparative experiences into account, such bodies could take the form of criminal injuries compensation boards, an independent board for awarding reparation to the victims of human rights violations through a non-judicial procedure, rehabilitation services for victims and bodies that ensure protection of victims and witnesses from harassment, such as victims and witnesses protection units.[141] Such measures should be designed to provide additional protection and remedies, and not to replace existing judicial remedies or to preclude reforms towards enhanced judicial protection.

It remains an open question to what degree law can be a means to bring about social change, which includes tackling the causes of human rights violations. However, it can hardly be disputed that law granting rights and effective remedies to victims can be a tool of empowerment and, ultimately, justice.

---

[141] See C. Raj Kumar, 'State Torture in India: Strategies for Resistance and Reparation', *The Australian Journal of Asian Law*, Vol. 5, No. 2, September 2003, pp. 160–83.

19

Sexual Harassment and Violence against Women in India

Constitutional and Legal Perspectives

Sexual harassment is a violation of one's freedom and personal integrity. Although categorized by a judge as 'a personal proclivity, peculiarity or mannerism, raising a controversy underpinned by the subtleties of an inharmonious personal relationship',[1] sexual harassment can ruin the victim's life. Historically, sexual harassment is seen as being perpetrated by men in possession of power (physical, political, and economic) against women.[2] It is also seen as an outcome of male dominated society. Catherine MacKinnon says that women are sexually harassed as sex is a primary tool of oppression and that men show their power through harassment. She goes on to say that men see women workers as sexual beings.[3] While graver forms of sexual harassment such as rape, incest, and physical molestation were and are no doubt punishable as crimes, torts of assault, battery, nuisance, intentional infliction of nervous shock, breach of confidence, intimidation and defamation provide civil remedies in the form of damages.[4]

[*] The author gratefully acknowledges the assistance of Cheng Pui Yi Connie, LLB (Hons), City University of Hong Kong, in the preparation of this paper.

[1] *Corne v. Bausch & Lomb Inc D.C. Ariz* (1975) 10 FEP Cases 289.

[2] Jefferson N.C., *Power and Gender: Issues in Sexual Dominance and Harassment*, McFarland and Co, 1999, at p. 460.

[3] Catherine MacKinnon, *Sexual Harassment of Working Women*, Yale University Press, New Haven (1979), pp. 151 4.

[4] D.K. Srivastava, 'Recognizing Sexual Harassment as a Tort', *Hong Kong Lawyer* (September 1999), pp. 33–8.

After the Second World War and in the wake of giving effect to the United Nations Charter and the Universal Declaration of Human Rights, the prevalent idea was that there existed a set of universal human rights reinforcing the principles of gender justice, equality, and freedom.[5] Such principles were also enshrined in democratic constitutions of many countries, including that of India. Women began to be increasingly involved in every walk of life and the workforce. They began to mingle with men like never before. One of the ill effects of such developments has been the occurrence of sexual harassment of women in employment and educational fields. Sexual harassment in India, as well as elsewhere, is seen as a perpetration of inequality against women. In villages, how landlords have been treating their subjects and employees is well-known and documented. Several Indian movies advert to the fact that those who have political and economic power use it to exploit and molest others at their whim and caprice. Under-age girls are the most common target of sexual abuse. According to official statistics, there is one reported case of a woman being molested or sexually harassed in India every 26 minutes. If unreported cases were to be included, it would be a matter of seconds rather than minutes. According to another survey, 68 per cent of women suffer mental harassment out of which 26 per cent suffer physical molestation.[6]

Whereas in other jurisdictions, sexual harassment has been declared as a statutory tort, in India, the tort law does not play any significant role in dealing with this problem. Legislators largely see the problem from criminal law perspectives. However, the courts have been proactive, viewing the protection against sexual harassment as part of human rights and individual freedoms. Judges of the supreme court in *Vishaka & others v. State of Rajasthan*[7] used their ingenuity to declare the law relating to sexual harassment by relying on some of the constitutional provisions. The supreme court's decision epitomizes Indian women's movement for gender equality and the global discourse on women's rights.[8] The decision in *Vishaka*, however, has had a limited effect. Although codes of conduct to prevent and control sexual harassment in employment and

---

[5] See Tracy E. Higgins, 'Anti-Essentialism, Relativism, and Human Rights', 19 *Harv. Women's L.J.* 89.

[6] D.K. Srivastava, 'Recognizing Sexual Harassment as a Tort', *Hong Kong Lawyer* (September 1999), pp. 33–8.

[7] (1997) 6 SCC 241.

[8] Pratiksha Baxi, 'Sexual Harassment', at: http://hdrc.undp.org.in/resources/gnrl/ThmticResrce/gndr/Pratiksha%20Baxi-2001.htm.

educational fields have been drafted, no comprehensive legislation has been enacted so far.

This essay first discusses the meaning of sexual harassment. Secondly, it examines the constitutional and other legal backgrounds, including judicial response, to the problem of sexual harassment in India. Thirdly, it analyses sexual harassment issues in other jurisdictions.[9] Lastly, it addresses the inadequacies of sexual harassment law in India and makes suggestions for its improvement.

MEANING OF SEXUAL HARASSMENT

Before embarking upon the examination of the law relating to sexual harassment, it is important to understand what sexual harassment is. Sexual harassment refers to a conduct of sexual nature,[10] which has neither been solicited nor invited by the complainant.[11] The Supreme Court of India defined sexual harassment to include 'such unwelcome sexually determined behaviour as physical contacts and advance, sexually coloured remarks, showing pornography and sexual demands, whether by words or actions. Such conduct can be humiliating and may constitute a health and safety problem; it is discriminatory when the woman has reasonable grounds to believe that her objection would disadvantage her in connection with her employment, including recruiting or promotion, or when it creates a hostile working environment'.[12] This definition of sexual harassment is similar to that given in other jurisdictions.[13] Sexual harassment also includes what is called the *quid pro quo* sexual harassment. It occurs in employment establishments, where as a pre-condition to receiving employment or employment benefits, an employee agrees to confer sexual favours to meet the employer's demands.

Comprehensive illustrations of sexual harassment are also given by the National Commission of Women in India. It states that unwelcome

---

[9] (1997) 6 SCC 241.

[10] For a comprehensive discussion of this topic, see D.K. Srivastava and Charu Sharma, 'Corporate Liability for Sexual Harassment in the Workplace', *Journal of Corporate Law*, 11 (2000), pp. 170–91.

[11] *O'Callaghan* v. *Loder & the Commissioner for Main Roads* [1983] 3 NSWLR 89.

[12] *Vishaka & others* v. *State of Rajasthan* 1997 (6) SC 3011, at p. 3015. Followed in *Apparel Export Promotion Council* v. *A K Chopra* (1999) 1 SCC 759.

[13] For example, see Title VII of the Civil Rights Act 1964 (US), the EEOC Guidelines (US); the Sex Discrimination Act 1975 (UK); and the Sex Discrimination Act 1986 (UK); the Sex Discrimination Act 1984 (Australia); the Equal Opportunity Act 1984 (Western Australia); the Sex Discrimination Ordinance (Cap. 480) (HK).

sexual conduct includes eve teasing, unsavoury remarks, jokes that cause or are likely to cause awkwardness or embarrassment, innuendos and taunts, gender-based insults or sexist remarks, unwelcome sexual tone in any manner such as over telephone (obnoxious telephone calls) and the like, touching or brushing against any part of another's body and the like, displaying pornographic or other offensive or derogatory pictures, cartoons or pamphlets and forcible physical touch or molestation, physical confinement against one's will and any other act likely to affect one's privacy.[14]

Judicial decisions and published reports provide other illustrations of sexual harassment. These include uninvited and offensive touching,[15] especially the complainant's breasts and buttocks, grabbing her, staring at the complainant's breasts and other parts of her body in a sexual manner, commenting on the complainant with reference to nude pictures of women and on her clothes and under garments, making lewd and obscene remarks,[16] describing her as a bitch or a slut,[17] peeping under her skirts, unzipping trousers[18] and showing himself to the complainant,[19] videotaping the complainant while she is dressing or undressing,[20] and asking the complainant whether she is on the pill[21] or whether she has a boyfriend or an intimate girlfriend. Although the cases from which examples of sexual harassment have been derived are both Indian and others, it must be remembered that the emphasis of the Indian law is on protecting women. It should also be noted that there are cases in other jurisdictions where women have been accused of sexually

[14] Article 4 of the Malaysian Code of Practice on the Prevention and Eradication of Sexual Harassment in the Workplace introduced in 1999 provides that sexual harassment includes any unwanted conduct of sexual in nature having the effect of verbal, non-verbal, visual, psychological or physical harassment.

[15] *Faragher v. City of Boca Raton* USSC, 7th Cir 1998.

[16] *Porcelli v. Strathclyde Regional Council* [1986] ICR 564; [1986] IRLR 134.

[17] Ibid., see also *Burlington Industries Incorp v. Ellerth* US Ct of Appeal, 97–569.

[18] *Bloom v. Quadrant Stationery* Case no. 3201144/97, 9 April 1998.

[19] See N. Robertson, 'Sexual Harassment: Legal and Practical Aspects for Employers' (1999) ICCLR 118.

[20] *Yuen Sha Sha v. Tse Chi Pan* [1999] 1 HKC 731. A similar case also occurred in Malaysia. A top model and actress discovered that a small pinhole camera had been strategically placed in an air conditioner above a mirror, where she used to do her aerobic exercises. That camera took several nude pictures of the actress.

[21] *Bennett v. Everitt & Whyalla Fish Factory* [1988] HREOCA 7 (1 December 1988). See also *Hall v. A & A Sheiban Pty Ltd.* (1998) 20 FCR 217; 85 ALR 503 (HREOCA, No NG1185 of 1988, Fed No. 65, Sex Discrimination).

harassing men[22] and further, same sex harassment is also considered sexual harassment.[23]

THE LEGAL BACKGROUND

While there is no specific legislation dealing with sexual harassment in India, each incident of sexual harassment of a woman may result in the violation of constitutional provisions relating to fundamental rights of gender equality,[24] the right to life and liberty and the right to practise any profession, or to be involved in any occupation, trade, and business.[25]

Constitutional Provisions and International Conventions

Article 14 of the Constitution of India provides that the state shall not deny to any person equality before the law or the equal protection of the laws within the territory of India. Article 15 prohibits the state from discriminating against any citizen on grounds only of religion, race, caste, sex, and place of birth or any of them.[26] Article 19 declares, *inter alia*, that all citizens shall have the right to practise any profession or carry on any occupation, trade, and business.[27] Article 21 says that no person shall be deprived of his life or personal liberty except according to procedure established by law. The Constitution of India not only recognizes fundamental rights but also by Article 32, the right to move the supreme court by appropriate proceedings for the enforcement of those rights.[28] The right enshrined in Article 32 is itself a fundamental right. Article 32 provides, inter alia, that the 'Supreme Court shall have power to issue directions or orders or writs, including writs in the nature of *habeas corpus, mandamus,* prohibition, *quo warranto* and *certiorari*, whichever may be appropriate, for the enforcement of any of the rights conferred by this Part'. The supreme court held that it has inherent jurisdiction to pass

---

[22] *Ray Chen* v. *Taramus Rus and Another* [2002] 354 HKCU 1; D.K. Srivastava and A.D.P. Tennekone, The: Law of Tort in Hong Kong (Butterworths Asia 1995), p. 270.

[23] *Oncale* v. *Sundowner Offshore Services Inc* 523 US 75 (1998).

[24] Articles 14 & 15 of the Constitution of India.

[25] Articles 19 & 21, ibid.

[26] See Article 15 (1) ibid.

[27] See Article 19 (1) (f) ibid.

[28] Similar jurisdictions have also been conferred on High Courts in India under Article 226.

any order it considers fit and proper in the interest of justice or in order to do complete justice between the parties.[29] Article 42 imposes an obligation on the state to provide for securing just and humane conditions of work. Article 51A (e) enjoins every citizen of India to promote harmony and renounce practices derogatory to the dignity of women. The effect of Articles 51, 73 and 253 is to impose international obligations on the state to enact legislation to curb, among others, the evil of sexual harassment to uphold the fundamental right of gender equality of women.[30] Moreover, the courts in India have the power to enforce international conventions that are not inconsistent with the constitution. For this purpose, they can take into account international conventions and treaties when interpreting the provisions of the constitution.[31] The supreme court in *Vishaka* took into account these provisions and the Beijing Statement of Principles of the Independence of the Judiciary 1995 and the Convention on the Elimination of All Forms of Discrimination Against Women (CEDAW) to lay down the law of sexual harassment.

The views expressed by the supreme court in *Vishaka* have also been echoed in *Chairman Railway Board & Ors v. Chandrima Das & Ors*.[32] There, a foreign national (Bangladeshi) was gang-raped by several men, including employees of the railways at the railway premises in Calcutta. A petition was filed under Article 226 of the constitution against the railways and the government of West Bengal, claiming compensation for the victim. The high court awarded the sum of Rupees 1 million for the victim as it was of the opinion that the rape was committed in the building belonging to the railways. An appeal against the high court's decision was dismissed by the supreme court. The supreme court said that constitution guaranteed fundamental rights enshrined in the Universal Declaration of Human

[29] *Bodhisattwa Gautam* v. *Subhra Chakraborty* (1996) 1 SCC 490; AIR 1996 SC 922; (1995) 2 CHRLD 159.

[30] Article 51 states that the state shall endeavour to foster respect for international law and treaty obligations in the dealings of organized people with one another. Article 253 states that the parliament of India has power to make any law for implementing any international obligations. Article 73 provides that the executive power of the union extends to matters for which the parliament has power to make laws.

[31] *Prem Shankar Shukla* v. *Delhi Administration* AIR 1980 SC 1535; *Mackaninnon Mackenzie & Co.* v. *Audrey D' Costa* (1987) 2 SCC 469; *Sheela Barse* v. *Secretary, Children's Aid Society* (1987) 3 SCC 50; *People's Union for Civil Liberties* v. *Union of India JT* (1997) 2 SCC 311; *D.K. Basu* v. *West Bengal* (1997) 1 SCC 416.

[32] [2000] 2 LRI 273.

Rights, 1948,[33] and the principles set out therein could be read into domestic jurisprudence. It stated:

The International Covenants and Declarations as adopted by the United Nations have to be respected by all signatory states and the meaning given to the above words in those Declarations and Covenants have to be such as would help in effective implementations of those rights. The applicability of the Universal Declaration of Human Rights and principles thereof may have to be read, if need be, into the domestic jurisprudence... in construing any provision in domestic legislation which was ambiguous in the sense that it was capable of a meaning which either conforms to or conflicts with the international convention, the courts would presume that parliament intended to legislate in conformity with the convention and not in conflict with it.... It was later affirmed by the Colloquia [Judicial Colloquia (Judges and Lawyers) at Bangalore in 1988] that it was the vital duty of an independent judiciary to interpret and apply national constitutions in the light of those principles.

The supreme court said that the fundamental right to life under Article 21 of the constitution was therefore available not only to every citizen of India, it was also available to a person, who might not be a citizen of India.[34] So long as they were in the country, they also had the right to live with dignity and free from exploitation.[35] Being a national of another country, the victim could not be subjected to treatment that was below dignity, nor could she be subjected to physical violence at the hands of government employees who outraged her modesty. Therefore, the State was under a constitutional duty to pay compensation to her.[36] The

[33] See the Preamble, Articles 1, 2, 3, 5, 7, and 9 of the Universal Declaration of Human Rights 1948.

[34] Other fundamental rights guaranteed by the constitution discussed in this case included the right to equality (Article 14), right against discrimination (Article 15), right to equal opportunity (Article 16), basic freedoms (Article 19), right to protection in respect of conviction of offences (Article 20), judicial remedy (Articles 32 and 226).

[35] In *Kharak Singh* v. *State of UP* AIR 1963 SC 1295; [1964] 1 SCR 332, it was held that the term 'life' indicates something more than mere animal existence; *State of Maharashtra* v. *Chandrabhan Tale* AIR 1983 SC 803; [1983] 3 SCR 337; (1983) 3 SCC 387, it was held that the inhibitions contained in Article 21 against its deprivation extends even to those faculties by which life is enjoyed; *Bandhua Mukti Morcha* v. *UOI* AIR 19874 SC 802; [1984] 2 SCR 67; (1984) 3 SCC 161, it was held that the right to life under Article 21 means the right to live with dignity, free from exploitation; *Maneka Ganghi* v. *UOI* AIR 1978 SC 597; [1978] 2 SCR 621; (1978) 1 SCC 248, and *Board of Trustees of the Port of Bombay* v. *Dilip Kumar Raghavendranath Nadkarni* AIR 1983 SC 109; [1983] 1 SCR 828; (1983) 1 SCC 124.

[36] *State of Rajashthan* v. *Mst Vidhyawati* AIR 1962 SC 933.

supreme court went on to say that the running of railways was a commercial activity, as opposed to the exercise of sovereign power. If any of such employees committed a tort, the employer union government could, subject to other legal requirements being satisfied, be held vicariously liable in damages to the person wronged by those employees.

Legislative Provisions

There is no direct legislation dealing with sexual harassment as a crime or as a tort in India. However, there are laws relating to obscenity and acts that are considered as violating the modesty of a woman, which can be invoked against a person committing sexual harassment.

The Indian Penal Code (IPC) protects a woman against rape by imposing terms of imprisonment.[37] The IPC also punishes a person for having sexual intercourse with a woman 'against the order of the nature'.[38] Section 294 of the IPC also provides that whoever, to the annoyance of others, does any obscene act in any public place, or sings, recites or utters any obscene song, ballad or words, in or near any public place, shall be punished with imprisonment of either description for a term which may extend to three months, or with fine, or with both. Section 354 states that whoever assaults or uses criminal force against any woman, intending to outrage or knowing it to be likely that he will thereby outrage her modesty, shall be punished with imprisonment of either description for a term which may extend to two years, or with fine, or with both.[39] Section 509 also states that whoever, intending to outrage the modesty of any woman, utters any word, makes any sound or gesture, or exhibits any object, intending that such word or sound shall be heard, or that such gesture or object shall be seen, by such woman, or intrudes upon the privacy of such woman, shall be punished with simple imprisonment for a term which may extend to one year, or with fine, or with both.[40] 'Eve teasing' or sexual teasing of a woman can also be punished under this provision. 'Eve teasing' consists of making verbal remarks relating to sex. Under the Delhi Prohibition of Eve Teasing Act 1988, eve teasing is a non-bailable offence.

[37] Indian Penal Code, Section 375.
[38] Ibid., 377.
[39] See Girdhar Gopal (1953) Cr L J 964.
[40] *Rupan Deol Bajaj and Anr. v. K.P.S. Gill and another* 1995 (6) SCC 0194. Several women's groups have suggested that Sections 354 and 509 of the IPC be repealed, and the offences incorporated in a comprehensive Bill on sexual assault.

The Indecent Representation of Women (Prohibition) Act 1987 forbids harassment by the use of books, photographs, paintings, films, pamphlets, packages, containing 'indecent representation of women' and makes the offender liable for imprisonment for a minimum sentence of two years. Arguably, such activities on the part of the offenders could also amount to sexualized working environment.

Under the Industrial Disputes Act, 1947, it is an unfair labour practice to discharge a person by way of victimization.[41] Thus, where an employee is unfairly dismissed or denied employment benefits by her employer as a consequence of rejection of sexual advances, the employee can take up the matter against the employer. This provision, however, is confined to *quid pro quo* sexual harassment.[42]

Section 10 of the National Commission for Women Act, 1990, states that the commission shall investigate and examine all matters relating to safeguards provided for women under the constitution and other laws, make recommendations for the effective implementations of those safeguards for improving the conditions of women, including remedial legislative measures to meet the lacunae, inadequacies or shortcomings in such legislation and call for special studies or investigations into specific problems or situations arising out of discrimination and atrocities against women and identify the constraints so as to recommend strategies for their removal. Under this provision, the commission can investigate matters relating to sexual harassment and make appropriate recommendations for dealing with it.

The Human Rights Act, 1993, confers wide powers of investigation and recommendation of compensation for victims of serious crimes. The Human Rights Commission is also empowered to investigate and provide compensation for human rights violations when instructed to do so by the supreme court.[43] In other cases, it can make recommendations for the award of compensation to a person who is a victim of violence and sexual harassment.

Judicial Response

The law relating to sexual harassment in India was laid down by the supreme court in *Vishaka and others* v. *State of Rajasthan*,[44] which was the

---

[41] Industrial Disputes Act, 1947, Schedule 5 Rule 5 (a).

[42] *Shehnaz Mudbhatkal* v. *Saudi Arabian Airlines*, at http://www.indianexpress.com/ie/daily/19981126/33050884p.html.

[43] *Paramjit Kaur* v. *State of Punjab* (1999) 2 SCC 131.

[44] (1997) 6 SCC 241.

first attempt to comprehensively deal with the rights of working women against sexual harassment in the workplace. There, a social worker was brutally gang-raped for her crusade against child marriages.[45] A Public Interest Litigation was filed by several women organizations (one of which was called 'Vishaka') to enforce the fundamental rights and freedoms of working women under the constitution. According to the supreme court, the incident revealed the hazards to which a working woman might be exposed and the depravity to which sexual harassment could degenerate. The supreme court said that in the absence of legislative measures, the need was to find an effective alternative mechanism. Given the unusual nature of the case, the supreme court invoked constitutional provisions to prohibit sexual harassment of working women on the ground of violation of the rights to gender equality.[46]

The great contribution for which *Vishaka* is remembered is the willingness of the court to apply international conventions for giving a holistic interpretation of the provisions of the constitution to achieve gender equality and gender justice within the framework of the constitution.[47] The supreme court proceeded to deal with the case by deriving the principles of non-discrimination from the constitution and sustaining support from international obligations.[48] The thrust of the decision was that a woman had the right to gender equality, to dignity and honour, to work in an environment free from sexual harassment and abuse. The court was not deterred by the absence of legislation and was prepared to recognize that where legislation was non existent to enforce certain rights, international conventions can be profitably used so long as they were consistent with the spirit of the constitution. The supreme court said that international conventions and norms were to be read into the fundamental rights guaranteed in the constitution in the absence of domestic law when there was no inconsistency between them.[49]

---

[45] This incident was the subject matter of a criminal action against the culprits and no further mention of the criminal action is necessary here.

[46] Articles 14, 15, 19 (1), 21, 32, 42, 51, 51A, 73 & 253.

[47] Indira Jaising, 'Gender Justice and the Supreme Court', in B.N. Kirpal, Ashok H. Desai, Gopal Subramanium, Rajeev Dhavan and Raju Ramachandran (eds), *Supreme But Not Infalliable*, Oxford University Press, New Delhi (2000) 288–333, at p. 313.

[48] Sanjay Parikh and Manoj Kumar Sinha, 'Sexual Harassment: A Wrong Beyond Discrimination', *Journal of the Indian Law Institute*, Vol. 41, (1999), pp. 478–88.

[49] The court was strengthened in its view by the decision of the High Court of Australia in *Minister for Immigration and Ethnic Affairs* v. *Teoh* 128 ALR 353.

It is also important to note that the supreme court relied on a provision in the International Covenant on Civil and Political Rights (ICCPR) to support its view that 'an enforceable right to compensation is not alien to the concept of enforcement of a guaranteed right, as a public law remedy under Article 32, distinct from the private law remedy in torts. There is no reason why these international conventions and norms cannot, therefore, be used for construing the fundamental rights expressly guaranteed in the constitution which embody the basic concept of gender equality in all spheres of human activity'.

In the absence of specific enacted laws to provide for the effective enforcement of the basic human right of gender equality and guarantee against sexual harassment and sexual abuse, the supreme court also laid down guidelines and norms for observance until legislation on sexual harassment was enacted. This was done in the exercise of the supreme court's power under Article 32 of the constitution for the enforcement of the fundamental rights. These guidelines are of great significance because the supreme court exercised its power under Article 141 of the constitution to declare them as the law. First, a duty has been imposed on the employer and other responsible persons in workplaces or other institutions to prevent or deter the commission of acts of sexual harassment and provide procedures for the resolution, settlement, or prosecution of acts of sexual harassment by taking all steps required. Second, all employers or persons in charge of a workplace, whether in the public or private sector, are required to take appropriate steps to prevent sexual harassment. Third, where the conduct of sexual harassment amounts to a specific offence under the IPC or under any other laws, the employer shall initiate appropriate action in accordance with law by making a complaint to the appropriate authority. Fourth, when an act amounts to misconduct in employment as defined by the relevant service rules, appropriate disciplinary action is required to be initiated by the employer in accordance with those rules. Fifth, whether or not such conduct constitutes an offence under the law or a breach of the service rules, an appropriate complaint mechanism should be created in the employer's organization for redress of the complaint made by the victim. Such complaint mechanism should ensure time-bound treatment of complaints. Sixth, the complaints committee should be headed by a woman and not less than half of its members should be women. Seventh, employees should be allowed to raise issues of sexual harassment at workers' meetings and in other appropriate forums. Eighth, awareness of the rights of female employees in this regard should be created in particular by prominently notifying the guidelines (and appropriate legislation when enacted on the subject) in a suitable manner. Ninth, where sexual harassment occurs as a result of an act or omission by any third party or outsider, the employer and person in charge of the place of employment must take all steps necessary and reasonable to assist the affected person in terms of support and preventive action. Tenth, the central/state governments are to consider adopting suitable measures including legislation to ensure that the guidelines laid down by this order are also observed by the employers in the private sector. Eleventh, these guidelines are not intended to prejudice any rights available under the Protection of Human Rights Act, 1993.[50] Finally, the court observed that the above guidelines and norms should be strictly observed in all workplaces for the preservation and enforcement of the right to gender equality of working women.

In *Vishaka*, the supreme court defined sexual harassment, laid down broad guidelines creating an obligation on employers to ensure that there was no hostile environment in workplaces and set out the procedure for dealing with sexual harassment complaints. In *Apparel Export Promotion Council* v. *A.K. Chopra*[51] sexual harassment was committed by a superior ranking employee against a lower ranking employee. The high court found that the respondent's dismissal was unjustified on the ground that he was only trying to molest the employee and had not actually established physical contact with her. On appeal to the supreme court, Anand, CJ held that:

Any action or gesture, whether directly or by implication, aims at or has the tendency to outrage the modesty of a female employee, must fall under the general concept of the definition of sexual harassment...the respondent's behaviour did not cease to be outrageous for want of physical contact and the observations made by the high court to the effect that the respondent did not actually molest the victim because he did not establish such contact with her are

[50] The guidelines set out by the supreme court have been incorporated in the Sexual Harassment of Women at their Workplace (Prevention) Bill, 2003, drafted by National Commission for Women and in codes against sexual harassment introduced in workplaces and educational institution, for examples, The Code of Conduct For Workplace drafted by National Commission for Women; the University of Delhi: Guidelines for a Policy Against Sexual Harassment; Draft Policy To Prevent and Deal With Sexual Harassment in Universities drafted by the University Grants Commission (15 June 2001), at http://www.altindia.net/gender/harasment/draftguidelines.html.

[51] (1999) 1 SCC 759.

unacceptable. The courts should examine all evidence to determine the genuineness of the complaint and should rely on the evidence of a credible victim. The respondent's conduct offended against morality, decency and the victim's modesty. It constituted an act unbecoming the good conduct and behaviour expected from a superior employee and undoubtedly amounted to sexual harassment. It follows that the punishment imposed on the respondent was commensurate with the gravity of his objectionable behaviour and there was no justification for the high court to interfere with it. Any reduction in punishment is bound to have a demoralizing effect on women employees and is a retrograde step.

In *Shehnaz Mudbhatkal* v. *Saudi Arabian Airlines*,[52] a high court in India was for the first time confronted with a sexual harassment case. The victim, Shehnaz Mudbhatkal, was an employee of Saudi Arabian Airlines and the harasser was Station Manager (Airport) Abdul Allah Bahrani. The sexual advances started with offers of lunch and dinner and soon the station manager began to ask Mudbhatkal intimate questions. She objected to such sexual advances by him and made a complaint. However, she was forced to give an apology for her complaint and when she took the matter to higher authorities, her services were summarily terminated. The judge at the high court decided the case in favour of the victim. Justice Srikrishna held that:

Camaraderie between the boss and subordinates is welcome, (but) it should remain within bounds. And Bahrani often transgressed the limits of a healthy relationship with a subordinate of the opposite sex.

Rupan Deol Bajaj and another v. *K.P.S. Gill and another*[53] involved sexual harassment of a subordinate employee by her superior. The victim was in the Indian police service and the harasser, K.P.S. Gill, was the Director General of Police of Punjab. The victim was slapped on the bottom by Gill. She complained of indecent behaviour. Mr. Gill was convicted and was fined Rupees 2,50,000 in lieu of 3 months rigorous imprisonment.

There are many other instances of sexual harassment in India that have attracted media attention. These include writing graffiti on the walls of women's toilet, molestation of women in welfare institutions and sexual harassment of girls in buses and trains. A recent incident is that of the grandnephew of the former Prime Minister of India, who was savagely beaten by gangs of rascals when he tried to prevent sexual

---

[52] *Shehnaz Mudbhatkal* v. *Saudi Arabian Airlines,* at http://www.seasonsindia.com/education/woes_sea.htm.

[53] (1995) 6 SCC 0194.

harassment of some girls travelling in a train. However, it is beyond the scope of this paper to deal with such cases.

An important point that needs to be considered here is whether monetary compensation could be awarded to a victim of sexual harassment. In *Vishaka*, the supreme court did not specifically rule on this question, yet it seems clear from the decision that compensation could be provided to a victim of sexual harassment.[54] Arguably, the supreme court, the high courts and other courts in India have the power to award damages (ordinary, aggravated, and exemplary). In *Delhi Domestic Working Women Forum* v. *Union of India*,[55] six domestic servants were sexually assaulted and raped by seven army personnel. The Delhi Domestic Working Women's Forum filed a writ petition in the supreme court under Article 32 of the constitution. The supreme court while discussing at length the plight of hapless rape victims directed the National Commission for Women to evolve a compensation scheme under Section 10 of the National Commission for Women Act, 1990, for the rehabilitation of such victims. The court also said that it was necessary to set up the Criminal Injuries Compensation Scheme for rape victims as Article 38 (1) of the constitution provided that the state shall strive to promote the welfare of the people by securing and protecting as effectively as it may a social order in which justice, social, economic, and political shall inform all the intuitions of the national life.

In *Bodhisattwa Gautam* v. *Subhra Chakraborty*,[56] the complainant was the accused's student. The accused assured the complainant that he would marry her and began to have a sexual relationship with her. When the complainant became pregnant, the accused secretly married her but upon his insistence, the complainant aborted the child. The complainant filed a complaint against the accused alleging that the accused committed offences under Sections 312 (causing miscarriage), 420 (cheating), 493 (cohabitation by deceitfully inducing a belief of lawful marriage), 496 (marriage ceremony fraudulently gone through without a lawful marriage), and 498A (cruelty by husband and relatives of husband) of the IPC. The supreme court made an interim compensation order directing the accused to pay Rupees 1000 per month to the complainant pending the resolution of the criminal proceedings against the accused. It will be noted that the ruling by the supreme court went a step further than its earlier judgment in *Delhi Domestic Working Women Forum* v. *Union of India*,

[54] See S Parikh and MK Sinha, 'Sexual Harassment: A Wrong Beyond Discrimination', *Journal of the Indian Law Institute*, Vol. 41, Nos 3 and 4 (1999), p. 487.

[55] (1995) 1 SCC 14.

[56] (1996) 1 SCC 490 35.

in which it was held that compensation for victims would be awarded by the court on conviction of the offender, subject to finalization of a compensation scheme by the central government.[57] Apart from monetary compensation, the courts in India can also pass a variety of orders. In *Chairman Railway Board and others* v. *Chandrima Das and others*, discussed above, S. Saghir Ahmad J. held that where a woman was raped by employees of the government on government premises, her right under Article 21 was violated; consequently, the state was under the constitutional duty to pay her compensation. In fact in this case, as noted before, Rupees 1 million was awarded as compensation to the woman. In *Apparel Export Promotion Council* v. *AK Chopra*,[58] the supreme court affirmed the lower court's order to remove the guilty harasser from the workplace.[59]

Rewriting of the *Vishaka* Principles and Proposals for Change

Various attempts have been made to write a law on sexual harassment,[60] the most important being the Sexual Harassment of Women at their Workplace (Prevention) Bill, 2003, drafted by the National Commission for Women. The Bill provides for prevention of sexual harassment of women and women employees that is work-related or arises during the course of employment by anyone including their employers, superiors, and colleagues.[61] It defines sexual harassment in the same vein as the supreme court's decision in *Vishaka*.[62] It states that no person being an

[57] K.D. Gaur, *Criminal Law Cases and Materials*, Butterworths, 3rd edn, New Delhi (1999), p. 530. See also *People's Union for Civil Liberties* v. *Union of India and Another*, the supreme court awarded compensation in the petition it heard under Article 32. The compensation was paid to the families of the deceased who were killed by the police.

[58] (1999) 1 SCALE 57, AIR 1999 SC 625, [2000] 1 LRC 563, (1999) 2 CHRLD 455.

[59] See also *Shehnaz Mudbhatkal* v. *Saudi Arabian Airlines*, at http://www.seasonsindia. com/education/woes_sea.htm.

[60] See, for example, Draft Bill on Sexual Assault by the Ad-hoc Sub-committee of National Commission for Women, 1993.

[61] See also *The Code of Conduct for Workplace* drafted by National Commission for Women, at http://www.ncw-india.org/publications/code_of_conduct/page3. htm

[62] Clause 2 (c) states that sexual harassment includes any avoidable sexual advances either verbal or through gestures or through use of sexually suggestive or pornographic material, and includes amongst others; whistling, sexually slanting and obscene remarks or jokes; comments about physical appearance; demands for sexual favours; threats, innuendoes; avoidable physical contacts, touching, patting, pinching; physical assaults and molestation of and towards women workers by their male colleagues, or any one who for the time being is in a position to sexually harass the women.

employer or manager or supervisor in charge of an office or organization or factory or establishment or any other workplace or employee or any other person shall indulge or cause to be indulged in sexual harassment of women employees and provides for punishment of offenders with simple imprisonment for a term which may extend to five years or with fine which may extend to Rupees 20,000 or both. It treats sexual harassment in workplaces as misconduct.[63] The Bill makes an employer accountable for sexual harassment in the workplace whether or not it was done with the employer's knowledge or approval. Clause 4 states that notwithstanding anything contained in other law for the time being in force if an act of sexual harassment is committed at a workplace, the supervisor, manager, and managing director or the overall administrative head, shall also be jointly responsible for the commission of sexual harassment in the establishment. It will be noted that at common law, an employer will not be liable for the wrongs of his employees unless he has authorized the doing of the wrong or the employee does an authorized act in an unauthorized manner.[64] The problem with the case of sexual harassment is that it will be impossible to prove that an employer authorized the commission of the wrong by his employees or that sexual harassment committed by his employees was an unauthorized way of doing an authorized act.[65] The drafters of the Bill were apparently aware

[63] Clause 2 (e) defines workplace in a very broad term to mean a factory, a mine, a plantation, an agricultural field, place of sale of agricultural or other products, a brick kiln, a construction site, a shop or business establishment, any private office or house including a farm house, any government, semi-government establishment or department including telegraph office, post office, telephone exchange, a hospital or nursing home, court premises, police stations, remand homes or other judicial establishments, restaurants, clubs, hotels, resorts or any other hospitality establishments, school, college, university or like institution, a training institution, an establishment wherein persons are employed for exhibition of equestrian, acrobatic, athletic and other sports related performance, any other place, where a woman visits in connection with work.

[64] See D.K. Srivastava and A.D. Tennekone, *The Law of Tort in Hong Kong*, Butterworths, Singapore (1995), p. 252.

[65] D.K. Srivastava and Charu Sharma, 'Corporate Liability for sexual harassment in the Workplace', *Australian Journal of Corporate Law* 11 (2000), pp. 170–91, at pp. 184–5; see also *Post Office* v. *Irving* [1987] IRLR 289; *Jones* v. *Tower Boot Co Ltd.* [1997] 2 All ER 406 (CA), where the court of Appeal examined S. 32 (1) of the Race Relations Act which defines liability of employers in terms similar to those used in the Sex Discrimination Ordinance S. 46 (1). *Cf Lister* v. *Hesley Hau Ltd* [2002]1 AC 234, HL and *Ming An Insurance Co. Ltd. (HK)* v. *Ritz Carlton Ltd.* [2002] 3 HKLRD 844 CFA which have adopted a broader definition of course of employment.

of this limitation subject to which vicarious liability is imposed on an employer. Under the Bill, the employer's liability is strict. Another important provision is one that relates to the burden of proof. As a general rule, where a person alleges sexual harassment, he must prove that the wrong was committed by the defendant; however, proving the defendant's wrong is difficult.[66] Drafters of the Bill, therefore, by clause 7 of the Bill provided that notwithstanding anything contained in any other law for the time being in force the onus of proving the accused's innocence shall be on the accused and the complainant shall have the right to lead evidence in rebuttal. The Bill also imposes an obligation on employers to set up appropriate complaint mechanisms and provides that a complaint committee must be headed by a woman and that not less than half of its members must be women.[67]

The Policy to Prevent and Deal with Sexual Harassment in Universities was drafted by the Universities Grants Commission in pursuance to the guidelines laid down in *Vishaka*.[68] This applies to all students and employees and extends to all departments and faculties of universities, all the constituent colleges and all colleges and institutions affiliated to university, irrespective of whether sexual harassment is alleged to have taken place within or outside the college premises. The punishment for employees ranges from warning, reprimand or censure, withholding of an increment for a period not exceeding one year and reduction in rank to termination of service, whereas the punishment on students includes warning, reprimand or censure, suspension from the institution for a period up to one month, debarring them from appearing for final examination for a period up to three years and rustication from the institution. The Policy also provides that in the case of a third party sexually harassing the complainants, the university shall actively assist and provide all its resources to the complainant in pursuing the complaint and ensure her safety in the institution.

Another significant development is that the government is contemplating a special court to deal with cases of sexual harassment by women prosecutors and judges. The idea is that the victim will feel more comfortable before a woman prosecutor and a woman judge.

---

[66] D.K. Srivastava. 'Proving the Wrong of Sexual Harassment: The Futility of Applying the Objective Test', *Journal of Chinese and Comparative Law*, Vol. 5 No. 2, (2001–2), pp. 205–20.

[67] Clauses 12 and 13.

[68] Downloaded at http://www.altindia.net/gender/harasment/draftguidelines. html.

This will also prevent male point of view determining sexual harassment of women.[69]

Limitations of *Vishaka*

The supreme court's decision in *Vishaka* impresses upon the need to pass a comprehensive law to deal with the menace of sexual harassment. Yet, in the last ten years or so, no such legislation has been passed. Undoubtedly, the supreme court's decision in *Vishaka* is an excellent example of judicial law-making to fill the lacuna that existed in the law, but judicial law-making has its own limitations and the *Vishaka* decision is no exception. In this context, the author would like to make the following points.

First, sexual harassment is seen as an act perpetrated by men against women. The supreme court did not really consider the question of sexual harassment by persons of the same sex. Second, although indirect references have been made about compensation and other relief under public law that are available to the victim, *Vishaka*, as well as other cases relating to sexual harassment in India, seem to view sexual harassment as a crime. The idea that it is also a tort and damages, including exemplary damages, could be awarded is not ingrained in the minds of the judges. Apparently, the courts in India are not concerned with developing jurisprudence of compensation based on tort. The orders made against the harasser have ranged from fines and imprisonment to suspension and dismissal. In appropriate cases, the courts have also made orders for the reinstatement of the victim and payment of back pay and perks to her from the date of dismissal if that had happened. Third, *Vishaka's* case, other cases, and the Sexual Harassment of Women at their Workplace (Prevention) Bill are largely concerned with sexual harassment at work. The definition of sexual harassment talks about employment related disadvantages. There was no serious attempt to develop a general theory of liability for sexual harassment covering situations other than the fields of employment and education. Fourth, the supreme court in *Vishaka* did not extend the definition of vicarious liability for sexual harassment as proposed under the Bill, leaving this to be determined by complicated common law principles. Fifth, the supreme court also did not address the question of the victim's difficulties of proving a case of sexual harassment, thought this was dealt with in the Bill.

[69] The *Straits Times* (Singapore), 25 December 2003.

SEXUAL HARASSMENT ISSUES IN OTHER JURISDICTIONS

Salient Features of Sexual Harassment Legislation

In the last forty years, laws relating to sexual harassment have been enacted in several jurisdictions.[70] The United States Civil Rights Act, 1964, is the progenitor of modern laws relating to sexual harassment in the workplace in other jurisdictions, especially common law. The Act makes it illegal to discriminate on the grounds of colour, race, religion, age, national origin, and sex. Title VII of the Act specifically prohibits employers from discriminating on the basis of sex. Sexual harassment in employment has been defined as unwelcome sexual advances, requests for sexual favours, and other verbal or physical conduct that enters into employment decisions and/or conduct that unreasonably interferes with an individual's work performance or creates an intimidating, hostile, or offensive working environment.[71] In the United Kingdom, the Sex Discrimination Act, 1975, prohibits discrimination on the ground of sex.[72] Malaysia also comprehensively deals with the question of sexual harassment in a similar way as other common law jurisdictions.[73] The Sex Discrimination Ordinance (Cap 480) (SDO) of Hong Kong, although largely based upon the Australian Federal and State law, suffers from similar inadequacies as other legislation, but presents a better legislative model than others.[74] The salient features of the SDO are discussed here with a view to suggesting legislative reform in India. The SDO defines sexual harassment in broad terms.[75] It declares sexual harassment as a tort[76] and makes it unlawful

[70] For example, the Sex Discrimination Act 1984 (Australia); the Equal Opportunity Act 1984 (Western Australia); the Sex Discrimination Act 1975 (UK); and the Sex Discrimination Act 1986 (UK); the Sex Discrimination Ordinance (Cap 480) (Hong Kong).

[71] *Meritor Savings Bank FSB* v. *Mechelle Vinson* 447 US 57 (1986) clarified that sexual harassment occurred where it interfered with the plaintiff's performance in her work or significantly affected her psychological well being notwithstanding that it did not cause any financial disadvantages to the victim.

[72] The Act does not contemplate neutral or non-sex conduct as falling within its purview, see *Stratchlyde Regional Council* v. *Porcelli* (1986) IRLR 134.

[73] Code of Practice on the Prevention and Eradication of Sexual Harassment in the Workplace issued by the Malaysian Ministry of Human Resources in 1999.

[74] See, for example, the Sex Discrimination Act 1984 (Australia) and the Equal Opportunity Act (Western Australia).

[75] Section 2 (5) of the Sex Discrimination Ordinance (Cap. 480) of Hong Kong states that a person sexually harasses a woman if the person makes an unwelcome sexual advance, or an unwelcome request for sexual favours to her, or engages in

not only in employment and other related fields, but also in the field of education.[77] It allows the complainant to claim not only ordinary, aggravated, but also exemplary damages and equitable relief.[78] It has also extended the common law definition of 'course of employment'[79] and given jurisdiction to the Equal Opportunity Commission to mediate and try to settle sexual harassment complaints.[80]

Inadequacies of Sexual Harassment Legislations

There are basically two problems with the SDO and its equivalent legislation in other jurisdictions[81] on sexual harassment: one is the problem of proof by the complainant that she was sexually harassed and the other is the reluctance of the courts to award damages against the wrongdoers in deterrent amount.

Difficulties of Proving Sexual Harassment

Sexual harassment concerns a person's injury to feelings. The same act, which may be considered sexual harassment, could also be acts which would not be sexual harassment. There is a natural attraction between men and women. Where the conduct is one which would be accepted as normal human behaviour and where it will transcend that line is a question of interpretation. It is a question of presence or absence of the complainant's consent. The key is whether the harasser's conduct was welcome or unwelcome. The complainant is required to satisfy two tests: the subjective and the objective. The subjective test takes into account

---

other unwelcome conduct of a sexual nature in relation to her, in circumstances in which a reasonable person, having regard to all the circumstances, would have anticipated that she would be offended, humiliated or intimidated; or the person, alone or together with other persons, engages in conduct of a sexual nature which creates a sexually hostile or intimidating work environment for her. Section 2 (7) of the Sex Discrimination Ordinance also provides that 'conduct of a sexual nature' includes making a statement of a sexual nature to a woman, or in her presence, whether the statement is made orally or in writing. Section 2 (8) of the Sex Discrimination Ordinance (Cap. 480) provides that reference to sexual harassment of women is treated as applying equally to the treatment of men.

[76] Section 76 (1).
[77] Sections 16, 17, 23, and 24.
[78] Section 76 (3A) (e) (f).
[79] Section 46.
[80] Part VII.
[81] For example, the Sex Discrimination Act, 1984 (Australia).

that which is regarded as offensive by the complainant herself and is therefore easier to satisfy. The use of the objective test, however, may still pose problems as the objective test takes into account the behaviour of a 'reasonable complainant'. It is not concerned with the idiosyncrasies, character, nature or personality of the complainant.[82] Subjectively, a complainant may be offended, humiliated or intimidated by the defendant's conduct. Yet, the complainant may face insurmountable difficulties in establishing her case objectively. In most cases, the harasser is let off the hook because of the complainant's inability to prove that the harasser's conduct was unwelcome.[83]

In *Ratcliffe* v. *Secretary for Civil Service and Another*,[84] a female employee alleged sexual harassment by her superior, a Superintendent of the Police Force. The Investigating Committee found that the Superintendent touched the complainant's back, and talked in detail as to what sexual services, short of sexual intercourse, might be offered by a prostitute and whether or not a prostitute could be a virgin. It held that such conduct was unwelcome and of a sexual nature. The finding of the Investigating Committee was quashed on judicial review by Keith J as he was not satisfied that the Investigating Committee had applied the objective test of the standard of a reasonable person in the complainant's position. Nazareth VP remarked, 'I have to say that their view of the complainant's reaction to the touching as "close to hysterical" sits ill with any application of the objective standard'.

There is a problem with the application of the objective test. On the one hand, there is a possibility that the conservative element of society might consider women complaining of sexual harassment as having invited it by their conduct. On the other hand, there is also the possibility that certain groups of people are likely to hold different and perhaps ultramodern views. They may dismiss many complaints as being frivolous. Further, in most cases, the decisions are made by male judges which might primarily reinforce a male point of view.[85] Interestingly, in the one case in which the complainant succeeded in Hong Kong, the

[82] See *O'Callaghan* v. *Loder and Another* [1984] EOC 92–023.

[83] See D.K. Srivastava, 'Proving the Wrong of Sexual Harassment: The Futility of Applying the Objective Test', *Journal of Chinese and Comparative Law* 5 (2001–2) pp. 205–20.

[84] (1999) 4 HKC 237.

[85] D.K. Srivastava, 'Proving the Wrong of Sexual Harassment: The Fulitity of Applying The Objective Test', *Journal of Chinese and Comparative Law*, Vol. 5 No. 2 (2001–2), pp. 205–20, at p. 213.

decision was rendered by a female judge.[86] In *Vishaka* also, a woman judge was present on the bench.

In *Enoch Wong Kwok-mui* v. *Lee Yuen-tim*,[87] the plaintiff, a 27-year-old university graduate, was a pupil of the defendant, her former martial arts *sifu* (master-teacher). Eight incidents of sexual harassment were specifically pleaded, those being: the defendant deliberately touched and squeezed the plaintiff's waist; the defendant asked the plaintiff to be his woman; the defendant put his arm around the plaintiff's shoulders; the defendant repeatedly told the plaintiff about his sex life and boasted about his sexual prowess; the defendant telephoned the plaintiff, leaving messages on her pager and told her about his marital problems and asked her for dates. On all the above occasions, the plaintiff made known to the defendant that his acts were unwelcome. On the other hand, on a number of occasions, the plaintiff had gone out with the defendant to discuss matters relating to martial arts and performances, knowing well that the defendant might have other intentions. The plaintiff was neither shy nor weak or needing direction. The evidence also suggested that the plaintiff had a strong personal attachment to the defendant. Examining the plaintiff's case in this context, Judge Derek Pang Wai-cheong rejected her claim. He was not convinced that the plaintiff was able to objectively prove her case against the defendant. He said that she was highly sensitive to physical contact, and that most young ladies in Hong Kong would not give such incidents a thought or would have regarded them as trivial. The case suggests that the plaintiff's opposition to the defendant's sexual conduct must be loud and clear.[88]

Thus it is clear that where the plaintiff expressly and vehemently objects to sexual advances by the defendant, he or she will have a much stronger case against the defendant. The fact is strangers, seldom if ever, indulge in sexual harassment, yet decided cases reveal that if there is any

[86] *Yuen Sha Sha* v. *Tse Chi Pan* [1999] 3 HKC 731.

[87] (unreported), DCEO 9/99.

[88] Judge Derek Pang said that: 'the complainant's case is that she did resist. She had made it known every time that the defendant's conduct was unwelcome. The point is, it was undoubtedly within her power to put a stop to the whole thing, and she did not. Had she wanted, the things that she could have done were unlimited. Threatening publicity was one. Threatening to tell his wife was another. Making a scene... might also be a good deterrent. Incidentally, making threats or warnings was not something that would not occur to the complainant.... On a more passive note, the complainant could have left the IWTA [the institution] or at least followed another master.' Similar view appears to have been taken by the Employment Appeal Tribunal in the UK case of *Reed and Bull Information Systems Ltd.* v. *Stedman* [1991] IRLR 299.

evidence of prior relationship or sexual relationship between the plaintiff and the defendant, the odds are against the plaintiff.[89] In the case of *Ray Chen* v. *Taramus Rus & IBM (HK) Ltd.*[90] (the 'IBM case'), the plaintiff, a 31 year-old man, was employed by the second defendant, IBM Global Services Australia, and the first defendant, a 29 year-old woman, was his 'boss'. The complainant's allegations were that he was forced into a non-consensual sexual relationship, but his complaint was dismissed as the court found that he had some prior intimate relationship with the first defendant and he had never made any allegation of sexual harassment until he was dismissed.[91]

Furthermore, the defendant often works his way around the objective test by pleading the complainant's implied consent. The defendant may argue that he believed that the complainant had impliedly consented to the sexual act.[92] The IBM case also touches upon the difficulties that a complainant faces in establishing that the defendant's sexual conduct was unwelcome and without consent. The problem seems to be that a failure to protest is taken as acceptance of the defendant's behaviour. Even a reluctant acceptance of the defendant's behaviour is treated as a good consent in law.[93] The complainant's reluctance to report the defendant's sexual conduct promptly may be seen as acceptable by the complainant, as part of her relationship with the defendant. Delays in reporting may be caused because of the complainant's desire to seek advice from family or friends or because of other considerations. Yet, such delays could prove fatal to her claim.[94] This discussion suggests

---

[89] See *Aktieselskabet Dansk Skibsfinansiering* v. *Brothers and Others* [2000] 1 HKLRD 568. *See* also *Hornal* v. *Neuberger Products Ltd.* [1957] 1 QB 247; *Blyth* v. *Blyth* (No. 2) [1966] AC 643; *R.* v. *Home Secretary, exp Khawaja* [1984] AC 74; *Re H (Minors)* [1996] AC 563.

[90] DCEO 2/99. An appeal against Poon J's judgment was dismissed by the court of Appeal. See *Chan* v. *Taramus Rus and Another* [2001] 3 HKLRD 541. Leave to appeal to the court of Final Appeal was also dismissed. See *Yuen Sha Sha* v. *Tse Chi Pun* [1999] 3 HKC 731; *Chen Ray* v. *Taramus Rus and Another* [2002] 354 HKCU 1; D.K. Srivastava and Scarlet Tsao, *Remedies for Sexual Harassment* (2002), Asia Pacific Law Review Vol. 10, pp. 141–54.

[91] The author has referred to the statements of the complainant and the first defendant in order to highlight the difficulties of reconciling contradictory evidence in sexual harassment cases.

[92] See *O'Brien* v. *Cumard Steamship* C 28 NE 266 (Mas 1981).

[93] See *Latter* v. *Braddel* (1880) 44 LT 69.

[94] D.K. Srivastava, 'Proving the Wrong of Sexual Harassment: The Futility of Applying the Objective Test', *Journal of Chinese and Comparative Law* 5 (2001–2), pp. 205–20.

that India's attempt to reverse the burden of proof is a step in the right direction.[95]

The Problem of Awarding Appropriate Damages

Criminal sanctions against sexual harassment have proved inadequate. In the United States, courts have been awarding high sums as damages, especially against multinationals. The average amount awarded in sexual harassment cases was US$ 250,000.[96] Because of the fear of high compensatory and punitive damages, most of the multinational companies in the United States prefer to settle sexual harassment claims. In 1990, AT and T settled a sexual harassment claim by one of their personnel managers in the sum of US$ 2 million.[97] On 23 June 1998, Mitsubishi Motor Manufacturing of America reached the largest sexual harassment settlement in history with the United States Equal Opportunity Commission and agreed to pay US$ 34 million to the victims of sexual harassment at Mitsubishi's facility in Normal, Illionois. Each of the victims was entitled up to US$ 300,000 in gross monetary relief. The law firm Baker Mackenzie paid US$ 7.1 million for a sexual harassment claim brought by one of their secretaries in the United States. On 24 May 2001, the US Equal Employment Opportunity Commission announced a US$ 2.6 million settlement of a lawsuit alleging sexual harassment and retaliation against Trans World Airlines Inc. (TWA). Higher awards such as those made in the United States can pave the way for the elimination of sexual harassment in other jurisdictions. The SDO in Hong Kong allows the courts to award not only compensatory, but also exemplary and punitive damages. In this regard, the SDO represents a milestone in the effort to combat sexual harassment. It is rare for a statute to empower the courts to award punitive and exemplary damages.[98]

[95] See Clause 7 of the Sexual Harassment of Women at their Workplace (Prevention) Bill.

[96] See Roth and Jacoby, 'How to Get Insurance Coverage for Sexual Harassment Claims (Without Being President of the United States', www.phillipsnizer.com/artnew11.htm; and Elizabeth Larson, 'The Economic Costs of Sexual Harassment', www.libertyhaven.com/personalfreedomissues/consensualcrimesexualissues/ecosexual.html.

[97] *Bihun v. AT & T Information System*, see also *Larson* in note 73.

[98] The deterrent effect of the SDO has been taken away by the courts by awarding low level of damages. See *Chen Ray v. Taramus Rus and Another* [2002] 354 HKCU 1.

The preceding discussion clearly demonstrates the magnitude of the problem of sexual harassment. The signs are that India will face similar problems that have occurred elsewhere. India has not adopted a holistic approach to dealing with this social menace. There is an urgent need to legislate on the topic of sexual harassment and the following suggestions are offered.

First, the supreme court's decision in *Vishaka* was designed to protect only women against sexual harassment. However, given that both men and women are victims of sexual harassment and sexual harassment is often perpetrated by the wrongdoers against members of the same sex, the new law should apply not only to women but also to men and cover same sex sexual harassment.[99] Second, the definition of sexual harassment must specifically declare that it is unlawful for a person to create a sexually hostile or intimidating work environment.[100] Third, the guidelines in *Vishaka* and the Sexual Harassment of Women at their Workplace (Prevention) Bill only refer to sexual harassment in the field of employment, but sexual harassment is all-pervasive; it exists in educational institutions and other places. In educational institutions in particular, male teachers often abuse their position to get sexual favours from female students. Therefore, the new law on sexual harassment should not only cover sexual harassment at work, but also educational institutions and other employment and education-related fields. In fact, many universities have drafted policy on preventing and dealing with sexual harassment.[101] The new law should include those who work on the field, in villages, those who study and work in schools and those who render other services. Fourth, the existing burden of proof with respect to sexual harassment must be modified. Once the plaintiff has established a prima facie case, the burden should shift to the defendant to prove that the defendant was not responsible for the sexual harassment, that in no material respect did he contribute to the plaintiff's injury. The Sexual Harassment of Women at their Workplace (Prevention) Bill's approach is in the same

[99] In *Joseph Oncale v. Sundowner offshore services* the US Courts of Appeals Fifth Circuit, No. 95–305/0, it was held that same sex harassment was sexual harassment within the meaning of Title VII of the Civil Rights Act, 1964.

[100] Such provisions exist in other legislation, see, for example, Section 2 (5) the SDO, which, inter alia, provides that a person sexually harasses another if the person creates a sexually hostile environment for that person.

[101] See for example, the Draft Policy To Prevent and Deal With Sexual Harassment in Universities drafted by members of the Mumbai Campaign Against Sexual Harassment, at http://www.altindia.net/gender/harasment/draftguidelines.html.

direction. It states that notwithstanding anything contained in any other law for the time being in force, the onus of proving innocence shall be on the defendant and the plaintiff shall have the right to lead evidence in rebuttal. Fifth, sexual harassment should be declared a tort and the court should be empowered to award not only ordinary, but also exemplary, and punitive damages. This would allow the courts in India to award high sums of damages to deter not only the wrongdoer from repeating his conduct but also other like-minded persons. This would also make multinational corporations and companies in India take all possible measures to prevent sexual harassment at work. Sixth, the common law concept of vicarious liability must be duly extended so as to protect the harassees. As discussed earlier,[102] the common law approach to vicarious liability is not satisfactory as it would be difficult to make the employer liable for sexual harassment by its employees. 'The worse the sexual harassment was the less the likelihood of the employer being liable.'[103] Such difficulties have been overcome in other jurisdictions by making appropriate provisions in their legislation. For example, Section 46 of the SDO of Hong Kong provides that anything done by a person in the course of his employment shall be treated for the purposes of this Ordinance as done by his employer as well as by him, whether or not it was done with the employer's knowledge or approval. The only way the employer can protect himself is by proving that he had taken adequate steps to prevent the employees from committing acts of sexual harassment.[104] The National Consultation Discussion on the draft bill held in April 2003 also considered the issue of joint responsibility providing that where the offence of sexual harassment has been committed, the joint responsibility of the employer should be of a civil nature and should be the collective responsibility of the employer. The employer should be held responsible in case no action has been taken on the complaint of sexual harassment. A recent judgment of the supreme court in *Chairman Railway Board and others* v. *Chandrima Das and others*,[105] also makes it very clear that an employer could be sued for rape by its

[102] See supra.

[103] See Roberts and Vickers, 'Harassment at Work as Discrimination: the Current Debate in England and Wales', *International Journal of Discrimination and the Law* 3 (2) (1998) 89; D.K. Srivastava and Charu Sharma, 'Corporate Liability for Sexual Harassment in the Workplace', *Australian Journal of Corporate Law* 11 (2000), pp. 170–91.

[104] SDO Section 46 (3).

[105] (2000) 2 LRI 273.

employees committed at the employer's premises. Seventh, where the victim of sexual harassment is a female, the panel of judges hearing the case must include equal number of female and male judges so that a balance can be maintained between the male's and the female's points of view. Eighth, the Human Rights Commission should, like its counterparts elsewhere, be given jurisdiction to hear sexual harassment cases on its own.[106]

---

[106] In Australia, for example, the Equal Opportunities Commission has the power to decide sexual harassment cases and award damages.

Contributors

GRANVILLE AUSTIN graduated from Dartmouth College (New Hampshire) with a BA in American Literature and subsequently earned a DPhil degree in Indian History from Oxford University. He has worked in both the executive and legislative branches of the US Government. He has contributed articles to books, journals, and newspapers. He is author of *The Indian Constitution—Cornerstone of a Nation* and *Working a Democratic Constitution—the Indian Historical Experience* (Oxford University Press). Granville Austin lives in Washington, DC.

UPENDRA BAXI is Professor of Law in Development, University of Warwick. Formerly he was Professor of Law, University of Delhi (1973–96) and its Vice Chancellor (1990–4). He has taught various courses in law and science, comparative constitutionalism and social theory of human rights at the University of Sydney, Duke University, Washington College of Law, the American University, the New York University Law School Global Law Programme, and University of Toronto. His publications include: *The Indian Supreme Court and Politics* (1979); *The Crisis of the Indian Legal System* (1982); *Courage, Craft and Contention: The Indian Supreme Court in Mid-Eighties* (1985); *Towards a Sociology of Indian Law* (1986); *Liberty and Corruption: The Antulay Case and Beyond* (1990); *Marx, Law, and Justice: Indian Perspectives* (1993); *Inhuman Wrongs and Human Rights* (1994); *Mambrino's Helmet? Human Rights for a Changing World* (1994); and *The Future of Human Rights* (2006).

K. CHOCKALINGAM is Professor of Victimology and Criminology in the Tokiwa International Victimology Institute (TIVI) of Tokiwa University, Mito, Japan. Formerly, he was Vice Chancellor of Manonmaniam Sundaranar University, India, and Professor and Head, Department of Criminology, University of Madras, India. His areas of specialization include criminology, victimology, criminal justice, and human rights. He has more than sixty research publications in the fields of criminology, victimology, and criminal justice. He received the Distinguished International Scholar Award by the American Society of Criminology in 1996 and was thrice awarded the Max Planck Fellowship by the Max Planck Institute of International and Foreign Penal Law, Freiburg, Germany. He also worked as a UN expert for the UN Centre for International Crime Prevention, Vienna, and is the Founder President of the Indian Society of Victimology. He is a life member of the World Society of Victimology and at present an elected member of its Executive Committee. He served as its Vice President between 2000–3. He can be reached at profkcindia@yahoo.com

SURYA DEVA is Associate Professor at the School of Law of the City University of Hong Kong. Deva holds a PhD from the Sydney Law School, researching in the area of human rights violations by multinational corporations. His research interests include corporate social responsibility; foreign investment and development; the WTO and human rights; globalization; and constitutional law. Deva has published widely in journals such as the *Connecticut Journal of International Law*, *Melbourne Journal of International Law*, *Singapore Journal of Legal Studies*, *Georgetown International Environmental Law Review*, *ILSA Journal of International & Comparative Law*, and the *German Yearbook of Public Law*.

YASH P. GHAI is Head, Constitution Advisory Support Unit, UNDP, Kathmandu, Nepal and formerly holder of Sir Y.K. Pao Chair in Public Law. He was till recently chairperson of the Kenya Constitution Review Commission and previously Professor of Law at the University of Warwick, a Research Fellow at Uppsala University, and a Lecturer at Yale Law School. He is a constitutional advisor in Afghanistan and has been extensively consulted by governments of the Asia-Pacific region on constitution-making. He has published many articles and writings on public law, constitutional law, and human rights law and development. In 2001, Ghai was awarded the Distinguished Researcher Award by the University of Hong Kong.

VENKAT IYER is a barrister and Senior Lecturer in Law and a Research Fellow at the Transitional Justice Institute of the University of Ulster. He specializes in constitutional, media, and international human rights law. Between 1990–5, he was involved in establishing a global database on states of emergency at Queen's University of Belfast. In 2003, he was invited by the Royal Government of Bhutan to draft media laws for that kingdom. A former Nuffield Press Fellow at Wolfson College, Cambridge, Iyer edits *The Commonwealth Lawyer*. His books include: *Mass Media Laws and Regulations in India*; *States of Emergency: The Indian Experience*; *Democracy, Human Rights and the Rule of Law*; and *Constitutional Perspectives*.

SUDHIR KRISHNASWAMY is a Professor at National University of Juridicial Sciences in Calcutta. He was a Teaching Fellow in Law at Pembroke College, University of Oxford. He holds a Doctor in Philosophy degree at the Faculty of Law from the same university, on 'The Basic Structure Doctrine in Indian Constitutional Adjudication'. He pursues his interests in intellectual property law as an Independent Research Fellow at the SARAI Programme on Intellectual Property Law and the Knowledge-Culture Commons at the Centre for Study of Developing Societies, New Delhi, India. He is an editor of the Oxford University *Commonwealth Law Journal* and the *International Journal of Communications Law and Policy*. Krishnaswamy has taught at the National Law School of India University, Bangalore. His research interests include public law, property law, legal theory, and the reform of legal systems.

N.R. MADHAVA MENON was the first Director of the National Judicial Academy at Bhopal, India, where he was involved in the training of judges of the superior courts. He was the Founding Director of the National Law School of India University, Bangalore, and later became the Founding Vice Chancellor of the National University of Juridical Sciences in Kolkata, West Bengal, and worked there till September 2003. He has been member of the Law Commission, Government of India, and the Expert Committee on Legal Aid. He has been a consultant to the Asian Development Bank, First National Judicial Pay Commission appointed by the Government of India, and the Bangladesh Judicial Administration Training Institute. He also served as a member of the Civil Services Reform Committee and the Criminal Justice Reform Committee set up by the Government of India. The International Bar Association honoured Dr. Menon with 'Living Legend of Law Award' (1994). In the IX Annual Convocation of the National Law School of India University, Bangalore, Menon was conferred Doctor of Laws (LLD) (*Honoris Causa*) by the Chief Justice of India. The President of India conferred on him the national honour of Padma Shree on the occasion of Republic Day, 2003.

SMITA NARULA is the Executive Director of the Center for Human Rights and Global Justice at New York University School of Law. She also teaches at the law school's International Human Rights Clinic. Earlier, Narula headed the South Asia programme at Human Rights Watch (HRW). In this capacity, she oversaw HRW's work in India, Pakistan, Sri Lanka, Bangladesh, and Nepal, and helped coordinate the organization's work on the war in Afghanistan. Narula has investigated and authored several reports and articles on global caste discrimination and on the rise of religious nationalism in South Asia, including HRW's reports on the 2002 massacres in Gujarat. In 2000, she co-founded the International Dalit Solidarity Network, which brings international organizations, donor agencies, and non-governmental organizations together to build a world-wide movement against caste discrimination. Narula received the 1999 Human Rights Award from the Dalit Liberation Education Trust for researching and writing HRW's book-length report, *Broken People: Caste Violence Against India's 'Untouchables'*.

LUTZ OETTE worked as a consultant on several research projects before joining REDRESS, an international human rights organization seeking reparation for torture survivors, in 2001. He has carried out collaborative research on a wide range of issues, both thematic and country-specific, in particular, examining how states have implemented their international obligations relating to reparation for torture in their domestic law and practice. In 2002, he obtained his doctorate in law from the University of Cologne, Germany, for a thesis on the compatibility of UN Economic sanctions with international human rights and humanitarian law.

B.B. PANDE was a consultant to the National Human Rights Commission of India. He was a Professor of Law at the Faculty of Law, University of Delhi. His areas of specialization are criminal law, criminal procedure, law of evidence, criminology, juvenile justice, human rights and jurisprudence. He has published over 75 research papers and comments in both international and national journals and compilations. Before joining the University of Delhi, he taught at Lucknow University (1991–4), where he was also Dean and Head of the Department of Law from 1993–4. He was awarded the Max Planck Fellowship by the Max Planck Institute of International and Foreign Penal Law, Freiburg, Germany (1988, 1992, 1995, and 1997). He received the Senior Social Scientist Award (1995) and the Kumarappa-Reckless Award 2002, from the Indian Society of Criminology.

VIKRAM RAGHAVAN is Senior Counsel in the World Bank's Legal Vice-Presidency. Earlier he was an associate in the New York office of O'Melveny & Myers. At the World Bank, as a member of the Middle East, North Africa, and South Asia group, Vikram is country lawyer for Iraq, Iran and the West Bank and Gaza. In the Operations Policy practice group of the Bank his responsibilities include providing legal and policy advise on various post-conflict situations. In addition, he provides legal advice on development policy operations and loan conditionality. Vikram is a graduate of the National Law School of India University, Bangalore. He obtained his Masters degree in international law from New York University Law School in 1998, where he was a Hauser Scholar. He recently published his first book, *Communications Laws in India*.

BALAKRISHNAN RAJAGOPAL is the Ford Career Development Professor of Law and Development, and Director of the Programme on Human Rights and Justice at the Massachusetts Institute of Technology. He earned his first law degree (BL) from the University of Madras in India, a Master's degree in law (LLM) from Washington College of Law, the American University, and an interdisciplinary Doctorate in law (SJD) from Harvard Law School. He served for many years with the United Nations High Commissioner for Human Rights in Cambodia. He has published numerous scholarly articles in leading law journals and is most recently the author of *International Law from Below: Development, Social Movements and Third World Resistance* (2003). His current research focuses on the dialectic between social movements, human rights, and legal and institutional change in comparative and world politics and the role of law in globalization.

C. RAJ KUMAR is the Vice-Chancellor of O.P. Jindal Global University and Dean of Jindal Global Law School, Sonipat, Haryana, India. He is also a member of the National Legal Knowledge Council. He was a Rhodes Scholar at the University of Oxford, where he obtained his BCL; a Landon Gammon Fellow at Harvard Law School, where he secured his LLM; and a James Souverine Gallo Memorial Scholar at Harvard University. He obtained his LLB from the University of Delhi. His areas of specialization include international human rights law, law and development, law and governance, and comparative constitutional law. His work has been published in journals in Australia, Hong Kong, India, Japan, and the United States. He has co-edited *Human Rights and Development: Law, Policy and Governance* (2006) *Tsunami and Disaster*

Management: Law and Governance (2006). He is an honorary Consultant to the National Human Rights Commission in India. He can be reached at crajkumar4@yahoo.com

N. RAVI, Editor of the *Hindu*, was a Fellow at the Harvard Law School Human Rights Programme in 2000, and a Shorenstein Fellow at the Kennedy School of Government, Harvard University, in 2004. With a Master's degree in economics and a law degree from Madras University, he has written on issues of law and the constitution as well as economic policy and international relations. He is the recipient of several academic awards including the R.V. Raghavan Gold Medal for constitutional and international law and was awarded the degree of Doctor of Letters (*honoris causa*) by the Sri Venkateswara University in 1997. His research at the Harvard Law School Human Rights Programme focused on the place of the right of freedom of expression in the international human rights discourse and as Shorenstein Fellow in 2004, he produced a research paper on the coverage of the Iraq war in the American, British, and South Asian press.

ARJUN SENGUPTA is one of India's leading economists, who moved between economic research, teaching, and policy-making at the highest levels. He is currently the UN's independent expert on Human Rights and Extreme Poverty, Chairman, Centre for Development and Human Rights, New Delhi, and Adjunct Professor of Development and Human Rights at FXB Center of Harvard School of Public Health. A former Professor of the School of International Studies, Jawaharlal Nehru University, New Delhi, Sengupta has a PhD from Massachusetts Institute of Technology. He served as an Executive Director of the IMF and head of the technical team and administration of the Indian Planning Commission as its Member-Secretary.

CHARU SHARMA is Lecturer at the School of Law, City University of Hong Kong. Earlier, she was in legal practice in Delhi and also worked for the Center for Environmental Law, World Wide Fund for Nature-India as a Deputy Legal Officer. Her interests range from gender discrimination, sexual harassment, international and comparative environmental law, and commercial and banking law. She has authored and co-authored publications that have appeared in *Res Communes-Vermont Journal of the Environment, Journal of Chinese and Comparative Law*, and *Australian Journal of Corporate Law*. Her latest publication on wildlife laws in China is expected to appear in the forthcoming issue of the *Animal Law Review*.

MAHENDRA P. SINGH is the Vice Chancellor of the National University of Juridical Sciences (NUJS), Kolkata, and is former Professor of Law at the Faculty of Law, University of Delhi, and also Head and Dean, Faculty of Law. From 1981–2 and again in 1985, he was Alexander von Humboldt Fellow at Heidelberg. From1987–8, he was Visiting Professor and Head of the Law Division at the South Asia Institute, Heidelberg; and from 1991–2, he was Visiting Professor at the Faculty of Law, University of Heidelberg. From 1999–2000 and in 2001, he was a Fellow at the Max Planck Institute for Comparative Public Law and International Law, Heidelberg, Visiting Professor at the University of Hong Kong and the City University of Hong Kong from 1993–5, in 1998, and 2000, and at Kansai University, Osaka, in 2002. In 2002, he was awarded a Fellowship of the Institute for Advanced Study (Wissenschaftskolleg zu Berlin), in Berlin, Germany, where he spent ten months during 2002–3. Comparative public law and human rights are his major interests.

PARMANAND SINGH is former Professor of Law, Faculty of Law, University of Delhi. He has been the Dean and Head, Faculty of Law, University of Delhi (2001–3). Singh has been teaching law since 1964. He has written 70 research papers mainly on public interest litigation, equality and compensatory discrimination, and various issues of human rights relating to bonded labourers, untouchables, persons with disabilities, and the poor. He is the author of *Equality, Reservation and Discrimination in India* (1982). He was a visiting fellow at the Max Planck Institute, Heidelberg, in 2000, and has contributed papers at International Conferences held at the South Asia Institute, Heidelberg (1986), Waseda University, Tokyo (1999), Kansai University, Osaka (1999), and the Institute for Advanced Study, Berlin (2003).

SOLI J. SORABJEE started legal practice in 1953 and was designated Senior Advocate, supreme court of India, in 1971. He was the Attorney General of India from April 1998 to May 2004, which constitutional office he earlier held between 1989–90. Sorabjee mainly practises in the field of constitutional and administrative law. He has successfully argued for the Government of India in the International Court of Justice at The Hague in relation to the Pakistan complaint regarding aerial incidents. He was a member of the National Commission to Review the Working of the Constitution in India and is the President of the United Lawyers Association. He is also a council member of the Commonwealth Lawyers' Association. He has written many articles and books, including *The Law of Press Censorship in India*; *The Emergency, Censorship and the Press in India*; *Monographs on Equality in the United States and India*; and *Protection of Human Rights in Emergencies*.

D.K. SRIVASTAVA is the Pro Vice Chancellor of O.P. Jindal Global University and Vice Dean of Jindal Global Law School, Sonipat, Haryana, India. Earlier he was a Professor and Associate Dean at the School of Law, City University of Hong Kong. He has more than 35 years of teaching and research experience. He has held academic appointments at Monash, Canberra and Curtin Universities in Australia. He was the Head of the Department of Law at the University of Papua New Guinea. His areas of specialization include torts, contracts, and commercial law. He has authored, co-authored, or co-edited 15 books and published numerous journal articles and book chapters. He has held visiting appointments at the Australian National University, University of Victoria in Australia, and the University of South Pacific in Fiji. He is a leading authority on Tort Law and has authored *The Law of Tort in Hong Kong* (2005) and also co-authored *Halsbury's Laws of Hong Kong, Volume 25: Tort* (2000). Additionally, he is one of the editors of *Hong Kong Tort Law and Practice* (2005).

ARUN THIRUVENGADAM is currently Assistant Professor at the Faculty of Law, National University of Singapore and has a doctorate from New York University (NYU) School of Law. He graduated from the National Law School of India University, Bangalore, in 1995. Between October 1995 and March 1997, he served as a law clerk to Chief Justice A.M. Ahmadi of the Supreme Court of India. Thereafter, he practiced law for two years, principally before the High Court of Delhi and the Supreme Court of India. His research interests are in the areas of comparative constitutional law, comparative law, law and development, legal education, and legal biography. His two most recent publications, both of which are co-authored works, appeared in the *International Journal of Constitutional Law* and the *Chinese Journal of International Law*.